What's Divine about Divine Law?

What's Divine about Divine Law?

Early Perspectives

CHRISTINE HAYES

PRINCETON UNIVERSITY PRESS
Princeton and Oxford

Copyright © 2015 by Princeton University Press
Published by Princeton University Press, 41 William Street, Princeton, New Jersey 08540
In the United Kingdom: Princeton University Press, 6 Oxford Street, Woodstock,
    Oxfordshire OX20 1TR

press.princeton.edu

Cover art: Marc Chagall, *Moses Receives the Tablets of the Law*, 1960–1966. © 2014 Artists
    Rights Society (ARS), New York / ADAGP, Paris. Musée National Marc Chagall, Nice,
    France. Photo © RMN-Grand Palais / Art Resource, NY

First paperback printing, 2017

Paperback ISBN: 978-0-691-17625-3

The Library of Congress has cataloged the cloth edition as follows:

Hayes, Christine Elizabeth, author.
    What's divine about divine law? : early perspectives / Christine Hayes.
        pages cm
    Includes bibliographical references and index.
    ISBN 978-0-691-16519-6 (hardcover : alk. paper) 1. Jewish law—Philosophy. 2. Jewish law—
History. 3. Jewish law—Interpretation and construction. 4. Judaism—Doctrines. 5. Religion and law.
I. Title.
    BM520.6.H39 2015
    296.1'8—dc23
        2014033990

British Library Cataloging-in-Publication Data is available

This book has been composed in Arno Pro

Printed on acid-free paper. ∞

Printed in the United States of America

eighteen bright and curious freshmen who in the fall of 2010
enrolled in my seminar on divine law.

Your questions and insights
—beginning with that discussion in Starbucks after we saw *Antigone*—
helped me to formulate some of the central ideas in this book.

Figuring out what's so divine about divine law
has been a long journey,
but at that critical stage
I couldn't have wished for a
better band of fellow travelers.

I hope that what you learned
and what you may yet learn in this book
will repay you

and shine a light on your own continuing journeys.

CONTENTS

ACKNOWLEDGMENTS

For many years, I have thought about law and what people mean when they assert that some law is divine. My inchoate questions and ideas began to take firmer shape in 2005–6 when, thanks to the generous support of a New Directions Fellowship from the Mellon Foundation, I spent a year auditing classes at the Yale Law School and reading legal theory in a faculty-graduate workshop organized by Suzanne Stone. In the years to follow, I benefited enormously from opportunities to present my evolving ideas in a variety of settings. I would like to thank the faculty and students of the following universities, programs, and institutions for inviting me to share my research and for providing valuable feedback: the Benjamin N. Cardozo School of Law, Duke University, Princeton University, New York University Law School and Tikvah Center for Jewish Law and Civilization, the Ancient Societies Workshop at Yale University, the Program in Judaic Studies at Yale University, the Shalom Hartman Institute, the University of South Florida, Georgetown University, Harvard Divinity School, and the University of Illinois at Urbana-Champaign.

I owe a special debt of gratitude to Fred Appel, my editor at Princeton University Press. Fred attended a lecture I gave at Princeton University in 2011 in which I detailed the main argument of the book. Since that time his interest and support have been unflagging. Fred identified excellent anonymous reviewers whose detailed comments greatly improved the final product. He continued to shepherd the book through the various stages of production with an intelligence that is both deep and kind, and I am truly grateful.

This is a thick book, but not as thick or as rich as the relationships that have created the conditions for its successful completion: my friends who fill my life with song, my sons who fill my life with adventure, and my husband who simply fills my life. I can imagine the world without this book; I cannot imagine it without you.

Over the years, I have had occasion to present many of the ideas in this book to students in a variety of settings. Their unguarded excitement upon discovering that divine law has not always and everywhere been viewed as universal, rational, true, and immutable has fueled my own excitement. This book is dedicated to the students I have had the privilege of teaching for the past two decades, but especially to the eighteen students who in the fall of 2010 took a gamble on HUMS 092 in their freshman year at Yale College. Celebrating their graduation in the spring of 2014, I was proud to be able to show them the manuscript of this book. And although I know there is more I would like to say and say better in this book, I dedicate it to them, confident that they appreciate the importance of not allowing the perfect to be the enemy of the good.

ABBREVIATIONS

GENERAL

ANTIQ. = Josephus, *Antiquities of the Jews*

CPF = *Corpus dei Papyri Filosofici Greci e Latini*: Testi e lessico nei papiri di cultura greca e latina, Accademica Toscana di Scienze e Lettere "La Colombaria" (Florence, 1989–)

C. TH. = *Codex Theodosianus*

DK = Hermann Diels and Walthar Kranz, *Die Fragmente Der Vorsokratiker*, 6th ed., 2 vols. (Berlin, 1951–52)

LAC.POL. = Xenophon, *Constitution of the Lacedaimonians*

NICETH = Aristotle, *Nicomachean Ethics*

SVF = J. von Arnim, *Stoicorum veterum fragmenta* (Stuttgart, 1903–5)

QUMRAN TEXTS

1QS = Community Rule (*Serakh ha-Yaḥad*)

CD = Damascus Document

1QM = The War Scroll

1QH = The Thanksgiving Hymns (*Hodayot*)

1QpHAB = Habakkuk Commentary (*Pesher Habakkuk*)

4QBER^A = *Berakhot*

4QFLOR = Florilegium

4Q174 = Midrash on Eschatology

ABBREVIATIONS OF RABBINIC WORKS, WITH EDITIONS USED

For a general introduction to the major works of rabbinic literature see Strack and Stemberger 1996. Rabbinic sages active in the Land of Israel from the time of the destruction of the temple until approximately 220 CE are referred to as tannaim (sing., tanna). Their teachings are contained in tannaitic literature (Mishnah, Tosefta, and various works of midrash halakhah that comment on the legal portions of the Pentateuch: the Mekhiltas, Sifra, Sifre Numbers, Sifre Zuta Numbers, Sifre Deuteronomy, Midrash Tannaim), as well as baraitot preserved in the Talmuds. Rabbinic sages active after 220 CE for five generations in the Land of Israel and seven generations in Babylonia are referred to as amoraim (sing., amora). Their teachings are contained in amoraic literature (the

Palestinian Talmud (closed ca. 370 CE), the Babylonian Talmud (closed in the seventh century CE), Midrash Rabbah (exegetical works on biblical books such as Genesis Rabbah, Leviticus Rabbah, etc.), and other midrashic works. The Talmuds contain material that bears no attribution to a sage. These anonymous materials are stammaitic (stam = anonymous). In this book, the terms "stam" and "stammaitic" refer to the literary feature of anonymity. Much stam material is redactional in character, and stam that is highly discursive and developed is almost certainly of a late (i.e., postamoraic) date. However, while most of the stam in a given sugya (a sugya is a unit of extended discussion in the Talmuds) postdates the amoraic traditions in the same sugya, it is not the case that *every* stam source in the Talmud postdates *every* amoraic source anywhere in the Talmud and very brief stam glosses were likely produced in the time of the amoraim.

M. = Mishnah
T. = Tosefta
P. = Yerushalmi
B. = Bavli

MISHNAH: unsourced citations of the Mishnah follow Kaufman MS (Budapest Akademia, Kaufman, A 50) and numbering will follow Kaufman, with the numbering of the standard printed edition in parentheses where different. For example, m. Mak 3:18(15) means mishnah 18 in MS Kaufman but mishnah 15 in the standard printed edition.

TOSEFTA: unsourced citations of the Tosefta follow Lieberman's text (based on Vienna MS) where it exists, otherwise Zuckermandel (based on Erfurt MS).

PALESTINIAN TALMUD: unsourced citations of the Yerushalmi follow the Venice printed edition as found in *Synopse zum Talmud Yerushalmi*, ed. Peter Schäfer and Hans-Jürgen Becker (Tübingen: Mohr Siebeck, 1991–2001).

BABYLONIAN TALMUD: unsourced citations of the Bavli follow the printed edition as translated by the present author in consultation with all textual witnesses contained in the Lieberman database. Only significant variants are discussed.

Abbreviations of Tractates of Mishnah, Tosefta, and Talmud Referenced in This Volume

AVOT	Avot	NEG	Nega'im
AZ	Avodah Zarah	NED	Nedarim
BB	Baba Batra	NID	Niddah
BER	Berakhot	PAR	Parah
BETS	Betsah	PES	Pesaḥim
BIKK	Bikkurim	QIDD	Qiddushin

BQ	Bava Qamma	RH	Rosh ha-Shanah
BM	Bava Metzia	SAN	Sanhedrin
ERUV	Eruvin	SHAB	Shabbat
GIT	Gittin	SHEVI	Shevi'it
HAG	Hagigah	SHEVU	Shevu'ot
HOR	Horayot	SHEQ	Sheqalim
KEL	Kelim	SOT	Sotah
KER	Keritot	SUKK	Sukkah
KET	Ketubot	TEM	Temurah
KIL	Kilayim	TER	Terumot
MAK	Makkot	TEVY	Tevul Yom
MAKH	Makhshirin	YAD	Yadayim
MEG	Megillah	YEV	Yevamot
MEN	Menahot	YOMA	Yoma
MQ	Mo'ed Qatan	ZEV	Zevahim
NAZ	Nazir		

Midrash Halakhah (containing tannaitic era traditions)

MEKHRY = Mekhilta deRabbi Yishmael (Horowitz)
MEKHRSH = Mekhilta deRabbi Shimon (Epstein-Melamed)
SIFRA = (Weiss) (Note: for Ahare Mot 8:3 5, L. Finkelstein ed.)
SIFRE NUM = Sifre Numbers (Horowitz)
SIFRE ZUTTA NUM = Sifre Zutta Numbers (Horowitz)
SIFRE DEUT = Sifre Deuteronomy (L. Finkelstein)
MIDTAN TO DEUT = Midrash Tannaim to Dueteronomy (Hoffman)

Midrash Rabbah (containing amoraic and some tannaitic era traditions)

Note: Where no edition is listed, a standard text of Midrash Rabbah (1969) based on the 1887 Vilna Romm edition is consulted.

GEN RAB = Genesis Rabbah (Theodor-Albeck)
EX RAB = Exodus Rabbah (Shinaan through 14)
LEV RAB = Leviticus Rabbah (Margolies)
NUM RAB = Numbers Rabbah
DEUT RAB = Deuteronomy Rabbah (Lieberman)
LAM RAB = Lamentations Rabbah
RUTH RAB = Ruth Rabbah
SONG RAB = Song of Songs Rabbah

Other Late Midrashic Works

MIDTEH = Midrash on Psalms (Buber)
PESRAB = Pesiqta Rabbati—(Ish-Shalom)
ARN = Avot deRabbi Natan (Schechter)
PRK = Pesiqta deRav Kahana (Mandelbaum)
MIDTANH = Midrash Tanhuma (Buber)

What's Divine about Divine Law?

Introduction

This book explores the concept of divine law. To be more precise, this book labors to make sense of the explosive confrontation of radically diverse conceptions of divine law in the Mediterranean and Near Eastern world in the thousand-year period prior to the rise of Islam. This labor emerges from the firm conviction that the Western conversation about the nature of law and law's claims upon us has been unable or unwilling to escape the consequential paradigms generated by that confrontation—paradigms that remain as powerful today as they were two millennia ago.

The questions that animated so much of the premodern discussion of divine law—whether it is grounded in reason or in will, whether it expresses universal principles or the command of a sovereign, whether its claim to our fidelity lies in its inherent qualities or in its external mechanisms of enforcement, whether law addresses us as rational creatures with virtues to be cultivated or as defective creatures with impulses that must be constrained—are questions that eventually entered the realm of secular law, where they continue to animate discussions of the nature and purpose of law to this day.

These questions are not inevitable, and the specific forms they have taken over the centuries are historically contingent. But for those of us who live in the West, they are—for better or worse—our inheritance. Understanding the story of how and why these questions came to be our inheritance affords us a measure of control over the next chapter of the story. And it opens the possibility that we might better negotiate or overcome the dichotomous dead ends that lie at their base.

What's So Divine about Divine Law?

What does it mean to say that law is divine? Attributing divinity to a set of norms would appear to establish its authority and justify our fidelity to it, but *how* and *why* does it do so? What *constitutes* divine law's divinity? When we say that law is divine, what claims are we making on its behalf? What traits do we suppose a law possesses when we refer to it as divine, and why do we suppose that those traits will establish its authority and justify our fidelity? What is it about divine law that is so "divine"?

Divine law can be minimally defined as the idea that the norms that guide human actions are somehow rooted in the divine realm (Brague 2007, viii)—a concept common to Judaism, Christianity, and Islam. This is not an inevitable idea. Chinese civilization, for example, has never thought of law as being connected with the divine (ibid., 14). In ancient Near Eastern cultures, the gods are guardians of justice who authorize kings by establishing them and conferring upon them the principles of justice and the wisdom essential to their rule, but the *laws* of the land are produced by the kings themselves and are known by their names. A robust notion of divine law—in which divinity applies in some manner *to the law itself*—first appears in ancient Greece and in the Hebrew Bible (or Old Testament).

Here is where our story begins, and this is *why* it begins: the Greek and the biblical conceptions of the divine are radically different. To the extent that the two cultures conceived of the divine in radically different ways, their notions of divine law would also diverge dramatically, a fact with serious consequences for those who feel compelled to negotiate the claims of both traditions.

PART I—TWO CONCEPTIONS OF DIVINE LAW

In much Greek thought, divine law is divine "because it expresses the profound structures of a permanent natural order" (Brague 2007, 18).[1] On this view, divine law does not refer to a law of the gods. Divine law is an element operating within the physical world and our natures, rather than something imposed upon the world by a god from without. Many ancient Greeks would have answered the question "What's so divine about divine law?" by asserting that divine law is divine *by virtue of certain qualities inherent in it*, first and foremost its rationality, which entails its truth value, its universality, and its static unchanging character.

By contrast, according to biblical tradition, the law is divine not by virtue of an inherent quality but "because it emanates from a god who is master of history" (Brague 2007, 18). Divine law is not the expression of an impersonal natural reason, the rational order of the cosmos; rather, it is the expression of a personal divine being's *will*, which can take the form of detailed written instruction and legislation. Ancient adherents to biblical tradition would have answered the question "What's so divine about divine law?" by pointing to its origin in a divine will, a will expressed in history rather than nature. And while adherents to biblical tradition may have assumed that their god was good and his law was good, beyond establishing its point of origin the attribution of divinity did not in itself *necessarily and essentially* confer upon the law specific

---

[1] This somewhat reductive description will be complicated in due course.

qualities such as rationality and its various entailments. The specific character of the law is thus something to be discovered.

This book traces the distinctive discourses of divine law that emerged in these two ancient sources of Western civilization—discourses that collided head-on after Alexander's conquest of the eastern end of the Mediterranean, creating a cognitive dissonance that the West has been grappling with ever since. This book examines the way various ancient adherents to biblical tradition struggled to resolve the cognitive dissonance between biblical discourses of divine law and the very different discourses of their Greek (and, later, Roman and then Christian) neighbors. Their struggles gave rise to new and complicated synergies and spawned conceptual categories that continue to inform both the way we think and talk about law and the way we read Scripture to the present day.

Part I contains two chapters that inventory the various discourses of divine law that arose in antiquity. Chapter 1 describes biblical discourses of divine law. The dominant biblical discourse of the divine law revealed to Moses and the Israelites at Sinai grounds that Law and its authority in the will of a divine sovereign rather than a natural order. The divinely revealed Law is explicitly particular and at times arbitrary, subject to modification, and coercively enforced. The ideal human type to which the Law is addressed is the obedient servant. However, a secondary biblical discourse not only gestures toward the idea of a moral order in creation but also associates the Mosaic Law with wisdom and instruction. On this account, the ideal human type to which the Law is addressed is an educable being capable of moral reasoning. A third biblical discourse grounds this Law and its authority not in will or wisdom but in the shared narrative of a historical community. The inflection of a primary will-based discourse with discourses centered on reason and history creates a rich and multidimensional biblical conception of divine law that defies easy categorization according to contemporary theories of law. And yet, it is precisely the messy multidimensionality of biblical divine law discourse that will enable subsequent readers to claim a biblical pedigree for radically different constructions of divine law in response to the confrontation with Greco-Roman discourses of divine law.

Chapter 2 lays out ten different discourses and practices of law in ancient Greek and Roman sources (referred to as G-R 1, 2, etc. throughout the book). A critical feature of all of these discourses and practices is their presumption of a dichotomy between the unwritten natural or divine law on the one hand and positive human law on the other (a dichotomy not immediately apparent in biblical discourse where the Law of God *is* the written law of the community). Thus, all Greco-Roman constructions of divine law begin with a common premise: divine law and human law possess different and usually diametrically opposed traits. The divine or natural law—in addition to being unwritten—is generally portrayed as rational and universal, corresponding to truth, conducive to virtue, and static or unchanging. By contrast, human positive law takes the form of concrete rules and prohibitions that can be set in writing. It does not *of necessity* possess any of the characteristics that are inherent in the very concept of divine law: it will contain arbitrary elements that do not correspond with truth, and it must be enforced coercively; it is particular and subject to variation, and its ability to produce virtue is a matter of considerable debate.

It should be immediately apparent that there is a severe incongruity between the Greek and the biblical conceptions of divine law. The divine law of biblical tradition possesses many of the features that Greek thought attributes to *human* positive law and only a few of the features Greek thought attributes to *divine* law, and one may be forgiven for asking: to which category does it belong? This is not a modern question. The incongruity between Greek and biblical conceptions of divine law was as apparent in ancient times as it is today. Those espousing one view of divine law were well aware that others espoused a very different view of divine law, as indicated by the scornful and mocking remarks that each directed toward the other. Rémi Brague (2007, 22–23) writes:

> When Rome and Hellenism combined forces, they both considered (or would have considered) ridiculous the Jewish idea of the gods dictating a path of action to be followed and behavior to be observed—the *halakhah* of the Jews or the *sharia* of Islam—as a matter of principle and in all circumstances. In the third century Galen mocked, not the content of the laws of Moses, but the manner in which Moses gave them to the Jews, without offering the simplest proof, simply stating: "This is what the Lord has commanded" (Ex 35:4).

It is the claim of this book that this incongruity between the biblical and the Greco-Roman conception of divine law was obvious and troubling to ancient Jews to different degrees and prompted three general categories of response. Moreover, each of these responses relied on strategies for interpreting Scripture that would ensure the success of its approach by highlighting the dimensions of biblical divine law discourse most compatible with it.

Parts II and III—Three Responses

In very broad terms, the first response—an apologetic response found in Second Temple and Hellenistic Jewish writings—sought to emphasize the similarity or identity of biblical and Greek conceptions of divine law in order to bridge the gap between them. The second response—found in the letters of Paul—emphasized the differences between the two and created an unbridgeable gulf between them. These two responses are examined in chapters 3 and 4 of part II. A third response, that of classical rabbinic literature explored in part III of this volume, resisted the Greco-Roman dichotomy of divine and human law altogether. The somewhat scandalous portrait of divine law found in the literature of classical rabbinic Judaism has not been fully excavated by scholars of ancient Judaism. It is the goal of this book to give a full account of the rabbinic construction of divine law as a crucial, if often overlooked, partner in the Western conversation about law.

Part II—Mosaic Law in the Light of Greco-Roman Discourses of Law: Ancient Jewish Responses to the End of the First Century CE

The texts examined in part II bring us to the end of the first century CE. These texts show us how various adherents to biblical tradition—all of them ancient Jews—responded to the cognitive dissonance engendered by the encounter of biblical and classical conceptions of divine law. Chapter 3 focuses on Hellenistic Jewish writings and Second Temple period texts that to various degrees accept the Greek dichotomy between natural law and conventional law. We examine Hellenistic Jewish writings that try to bridge the gap between biblical and Greco-Roman conceptions of divine law by applying the latter's discourses of natural law to biblical divine law. This apologetic effort culminates in the writings of Philo, who identifies the Mosaic Law with the natural law and confers upon it the attributes of rationality, truth, universality, and fixity. We also examine Second Temple period writings that bridge the gap between biblical and classical conceptions of divine law by moving in the opposite direction: these writings transfer some of the attributes of biblical divine law to the laws that govern the natural world. In 1 Enoch and Jubilees, the laws of the cosmos are recast as the positivistic decrees of God that can be transgressed by "sinful" heavenly bodies. And finally, at Qumran, the correspondence of the Mosaic Law with the natural order finds expression in a realist approach to divine law.

Chapter 4 focuses on Paul, a first-century CE Jew. Like the authors of the texts examined in chapter 3, Paul accepts the basic Greco-Roman dichotomy between divine natural law on the one hand and human positive law on the other hand. However, his response to the incongruity between the biblical and classical conceptions of divine law is the opposite of Philo's. Philo bridged the divide by equating the Mosaic Law with the divine natural law and transferring to it the characteristic attributes of divine natural law. Paul made the opposite move, and applied to Mosaic Law various motifs from Greco-Roman discourses of human positive law. Paul represents the Mosaic Law as particular, temporary, nonrational, and not conducive to virtue. I argue that Paul's representation of the Mosaic Law in positive law terms was *a strategic accommodation to his audience.* His audience consisted of Gentiles for whom divine law must possess certain characteristics that the Mosaic Law does not clearly possess. Particularizing the Mosaic Law enables Paul to argue that it does not obligate Gentiles, whose entry into God's community—required if the end-time visions of the prophets are to be fulfilled—is effected through faith. Paul's strategic adoption of positive law discourse in connection with Mosaic Law would set the stage for a Christian discourse of denigration and delegitimation of the Mosaic Law; it would also allow Christianity's full embrace of natural law as an ontologically primary mode for God's communication of the norms that obligate universal humankind. How to situate positive human norms and their claim to our fidelity in light of the universal divine law revealed in nature is a problem that Christianity acquires for itself and, indeed, for the modern West. Since that is a story that has been told by others more expert than I, I turn in part III to a different story that has not yet been fully told.

Part III—The Rabbinic Construction of Divine Law

Part III addresses the distinctive rabbinic conception of divine law. While Philo and Paul arrive at radically different conclusions as to whether the biblical divine law (i.e., the Mosaic Law) possesses the characteristic features of the divine law of nature or of positive human law, they are at least united in this: both accept and employ the Greco-Roman dichotomy of divine law and human law as conceptually distinct and distinctive constructs, and seek to assimilate the Mosaic Law to one or the other pole of this dichotomy. In part III, I argue that the rabbis of the talmudic period take a different path, resisting the divine law–human law dichotomy as characterized by classical tradition and constructing a portrait of divine law in defiance of that dichotomy's constraints.

The first three chapters demonstrate that the rabbinic construction of biblical divine law (i.e., the Torah) challenges classical assumptions about divine law and its attributes, specifically the attributes of conformity to truth, universal rationality, and stasis. Each of these attributes is treated in a separate chapter. Chapter 5 considers the attribute of truth and argues that rabbinic texts do not represent Torah as necessarily conforming to or self-identical with truth according to three measures of "truth" invoked in rabbinic sources themselves; indeed, at times Torah confronts and defeats truth. Chapter 6 considers the attribute of universal rationality and argues that the Torah is not consistently represented in rabbinic texts as *intrinsically* rational or universally accessible by reason. Chapter 7 considers the attribute of stasis or inflexibility and shows that the rabbinic conception of Torah assumes its susceptibility to moral critique and modification as the very mark of its divinity.

The representation of Torah as susceptible to moral critique and modification raises a critical question: does moral critique of the law commit the rabbis to the existence of a standard of value *external* to the Torah? In other words, do the rabbis subscribe to a version of natural law *distinct from the Torah* and according to which there are moral goods embedded in nature, rationally accessible and universally obligating? Chapter 8 takes up this question by examining sources that discuss normativity prior to the revelation of Torah, including sources that deal with the so-called Noahide laws. I conclude that the sources are best utilized not as evidence for or against a rabbinic concept of natural law distinct from the Torah, but as evidence that the rabbis were aware of natural law conceptions and, for the most part, rejected them.

The chapters in part III demonstrate that the rabbis of the talmudic era did not shy away from attributing to the divine Torah features considered by others in antiquity to be unfailing indicators of human positive law. In that respect, they resembled Paul more than they did Philo. But the rabbis also insisted on the divinity of the Torah. In that respect, they resembled Philo more than they did Paul. In a third respect they resembled neither Philo nor Paul: insofar as they constructed a portrait of divine law whose very divinity was enhanced rather than impugned by its divorce from truth, its particular and arbitrary character, and its susceptibility to moral critique and modification, they were entirely unique.

They were also entirely scandalous. To those who accept the Greco-Roman conception of divine law, the idea that divine law is not self-identical with truth, is not rational, universal, and unchanging, is shocking, indeed laughable. An important thread that weaves its way through the argument in part III is that the rabbis knew this. The rabbis' construction of divine law was undertaken *in full awareness of what was at stake and how they appeared to others who did not share their view.* The rabbis understood that by constructing divine law in terms directly opposed or (to borrow a term from Shaye Cohen that will be explicated in part III) *antipodal* to the Greco-Roman conception of divine law, they exposed themselves to ridicule. Two primary pieces of evidence can be adduced for this claim.

First, the rabbis explicitly represent their conception of divine law as inspiring ridicule and mockery on the part of various external and internal "others." The rabbis' ability to articulate the alternative view of their opponents and to represent the latter's critique of their own view is strong evidence that their construction of divine law entailed both a familiarity with and a conscious rejection of the alternative view. Second, the rabbis employ dueling strategies of disclosure and concealment in their construction of Torah, indicative of a *conscious* effort to navigate the tension between these competing conceptions of divine law. Thus, alongside a rhetoric of disclosure that openly signals and embraces their unique conception of divine law in the face of mockery and ridicule, the rabbis sometimes adopt a rhetoric of concealment. This rhetoric masks and even modulates their unique conception of divine law in light of a critique that, at times, hits home. These two strategies—disclosure and concealment— are different but fully *self-aware* approaches to managing the tension between the rabbinic conception of divine law and its alternative conception.

In the medieval and modern periods, the rabbinic conception of divine law was overshadowed in the West. The Greco-Roman dichotomy of natural law and positive law became controlling paradigms in the conception of divine law in the West, and its attendant discourses were embraced by the three biblical religions, though in different ways and to widely varying degrees. But the rabbinic conception was far from extinguished. It is the goal of this book to bring its claims and contours into sharper focus in order to trouble the too-comfortable dichotomies that continue to shape the Western conversation about law, about the divine, and about what it means for law to be divine.

Writing this book forced me to confront a terminological challenge: what language should we adopt when referring to the divine? The undifferentiated term "God" obscures the great diversity in our sources' conception of the divine and, relatedly, their conception of divine law. My imperfect solution to this problem is as follows. In chapter 1, I adopt the various modes of reference for the divine being employed by the Hebrew Bible itself, usually El, Elohim, or Yahweh. I take this approach in the hope that it provides a relatively unmediated representation of the conception of the divine in ancient Israel. At the very least, I do not substitute the term "God" for any of these names. The translation "God" causes readers to confuse the deity of the Hebrew Bible with the deity constructed by the much later tradition of Western theology, a deity commonly referred to in English as "God" (with a capital "G"). The biblical character El, or Elohim, or Yahweh is not consistently represented by the biblical writers as possessing the attributes assigned to the deity referred to as "God" by the later tradition of Western theology (for example, in many narratives the biblical deity lacks the attributes of omniscience and immutability). Since our goal is to identify the characteristic features of divine law in biblical tradition, we would do well to avoid labels for the biblical deity that incline us to assume that this deity and this deity's Law possess certain traits (such as immutability) rather than others.

My translations also faithfully replicate the designations of the deity employed in rabbinic sources—usually "the holy one, blessed be he," but sometimes "Elohim" and sometimes "the creator." However, when summarizing and discussing the sources in my own voice, I employ the term God for the sake of convenience. I ask the reader to indulge this usage and to resist the temptation to attribute to this deity qualities and traits often associated with the term "God."

Finally, despite reservations about the term "law" as a translation for the Hebrew term *torah* and the Greek term *nomos*, I adopt this translation for lack of a better alternative and because it signals normativity, which is an important aspect of both *torah* and *nomos* and a central concern in this book. Where relevant, I adopt the convention of using a lowercase "l" to refer to law generally and a capital "L" to refer to the divine law of Israel (the Mosaic Law). This occurs mostly when I am discussing texts that themselves attest to a conceptual distinction between the two (for example, the letters of Paul)—a distinction that must be marked in some way. Thus, the phrase "divine law" refers to divine law of any description (Greco-Roman natural law as well as the Mosaic Law) while "divine Law" refers specifically to the Mosaic Law. In adopting this convention, I do not mean to invoke dated assumptions about the opposition of

Law and faith or of Law and grace. In part III, "Law" and "law" indicate the Torah of Moses and *halakhah* (both as an individual law and as Jewish law generally), respectively.

Translations of the Hebrew Bible are based on the Jewish Publication Society's translations as found in *The Jewish Study Bible*, but adjusted to more accurately reflect divine nomenclature and to illuminate the exegetical interventions of later sources. Translations of the New Testament are taken from the New Revised Standard Version unless otherwise indicated. The translations used for the Greco-Roman sources cited in chapter 2 and the Second Temple and Hellenistic Jewish sources cited in chapter 3 are listed in the bibliography or indicated as they arise. Translations of all rabbinic sources are my own after consultation with manuscript evidence. Significant variants are discussed in the notes.

PART I

Biblical and Greco-Roman
Discourses of Divine Law

Introduction

The chapters in part I explore the distinctive discourses of divine law that prevailed in the two sources of Western civilization—the Hebrew Bible on the one hand (chapter 1) and classical Greece and Rome on the other (chapter 2). Both the biblical tradition and the classical tradition feature *multiple* discourses of divine law. While one or two discourses may dominate within each tradition, alternative and even contesting discourses exert an important influence.

As noted in the introduction: Greco-Roman sources of all genres draw a distinction between divine law and human law, characterizing each in terms of, and in contrast with, the other. For this reason, a full account of Greco-Roman discourses of divine law will necessarily entail a full account of Greco-Roman discourses of human law. Indeed, the classical tradition of law exhibits a strong tendency toward dichotomies—the dichotomy between divine (or natural) law and human law is inflected by the dichotomies between reason and will, between universalism and particularism, between stasis and change, between truth and politics. The tensions between these dichotomies are often managed with the aid of mythic narratives about the emergence of human law and its relationship to divine law.

Biblical sources do not draw a clear distinction between divine and human law. The divine law and the laws of the state are one and the same—the Torah revealed through Moses to the Israelites at Sinai. The Bible does imagine two *modalities* of divine law. The primary modality, which dominates biblical conceptions of divine normativity, is the divinely revealed Torah, a set of concrete rules and instruction revealed at a specific moment in history. A second and much less explicitly attested modality of divine law is a universal moral order that obligates humankind more generally. The relationship between these two modalities is not dichotomous. As we shall see, biblical discourse is best understood as a complex entanglement of reason, will, and history; of wisdom, power, and myth. A full account of the biblical concept of divine law will necessarily underscore its multidimensional character.

The exposition of biblical and classical discourses provided in these chapters is purely descriptive. In chapter 1, I outline the rich array of biblical claims about divine law. My approach is not that of a biblical critic. I am not interested in identifying the actual historical provenance of the biblical materials or the manner in which they have been composed and combined. I am interested in identifying the conception and discourses of divine law *that would have been conveyed to the biblical text's earliest readers*. Thus, while I draw upon modern biblical scholarship insofar as it illuminates the *contents* of the biblical sources, I make minimal use of this scholarship insofar as it engages historical questions regarding the composition and development of these sources.

In chapter 2, it is not my intention to present, in successive systematic treatments, the totality of the thought of Plato or Aristotle or the Epicureans or the Stoics on divine and human law. My goal is to identify and describe the primary themes, motifs, and tropes associated with law across a wide array of sources of diverse provenance and genre in classical antiquity, and I have found it convenient to organize these themes, motifs, and tropes into seven distinct "discourses" and three legal or literary practices. If a given philosopher or philosophical school employs more than one discourse of law, that philosopher or school will be mentioned in connection with each of those discourses. In other words, the material in chapter 2 is organized around discourses, not around specific philosophers or philosophical schools.

CHAPTER 1

Biblical Discourses of Law

INTRODUCTION

> Moses went and repeated to the people all the commands
> of Yahweh and all the rules; and all the people answered
> with one voice, saying, "All the things that Yahweh has
> commanded we will do!" Moses then wrote down all the
> commands of Yahweh. (Ex 24:3–4a)

Biblical tradition portrays Yahweh as a divine sovereign commanding and enacting laws for his covenant partner, Israel. And yet, this portrayal is nuanced
and complicated by countervailing trends that emphasize the roles played by
wisdom on the one hand and history on the other in the articulation of norms
for Israel. Thus, to characterize the conception of divine law in the Hebrew
Bible as a law grounded solely in the will of a commanding sovereign is to provide only a partial account. Will, reason, and history interact in complex ways
to produce a rich and multidimensional conception of divine law in ancient
Israel. As we shall see, it is this multidimensionality that will enable later readers to claim a biblical pedigree for radically divergent notions of divine law.

We begin by examining those biblical texts that emphasize the emergence of
divine law from the divine will. These texts stand as resources for later readers
who seek to construe biblical divine law as positive law. We then turn to texts
that emphasize elements of divine wisdom in the Law. These texts stand as resources for later readers who seek to construe biblical divine law in terms of
natural law. Finally, we examine texts that narrate the historical circumstances
under which this multifaceted law came into being and its role in the divine
plan for Israel and humankind.

The varied contributions of will, reason, and history to the complex biblical
conception of divine law manifest themselves in different approaches to the
following topics: (1) the ontological status of divine law and the source of its
obligation (are divine norms grounded in and thus coincident with a natural
order or eternal "truth," or are divine norms grounded in authoritative decrees
that have no basis in nature?); (2) the nature of divine law as universal and
rational or particular and will-based; (3) the nature of divine law as static or

evolving; (4) the nature of divine law as instructive or coercive; (5) the ideal posture of humans addressed by divine law.

Discourses of the Law

Discourse 1: Divine Law as an Expression of Divine Will

Biblical passages that lend themselves to a positivistic account of divine law are generally silent on the question of the law's correlation to a natural order or eternal truth, and present the law as expressing the will of a divine sovereign, as particularistic, nonrational, evolving, coercive, and addressed to persons whose greatest virtue is unquestioning obedience.

(I) DIVINE LAW, DIVINE WILL

> The law [created by covenant or *berith* with Yahweh] was no eternal Tao or Dharma, but a positive enactment ... God's ordainments come from his hand and are *as such* changeable. He may bind himself to His enactments by *berith*, but that is the result of His free resolve. (Weber 1967, 132)

In this pithy formulation, Max Weber underscores the role of the deity's "free resolve" or will in the creation of the covenant. The law that comes, freely willed, from Yahweh's hand is a positive enactment. For Weber, it is the unique biblical conception of the deity that sets the stage for this positivistic understanding of divine law. Anthony Kronman (1983, 152) explains that according to Weber, the

> conception of God as a transcendent creator implies a view of religious authority that is essentially positivistic. The norms which the followers of such a God are required to observe are binding not because they are the expression of an eternal and uncreated natural order but because they are the commandments of god and have been deliberately enacted by Him. It is their origin in an act of divine legislation which gives these norms their obligatory force and hence their normative character. By contrast, the immanent and impersonal principles that in the Asian religions are believed to inform human conduct and determine the fate of individuals derive their ethical significance from the fact that they are considered part of an uncreated and eternally valid natural order.

There is certainly much in the biblical text to support this characterization of the Law. Exodus 24:3–4a (above) is only one of many passages that can be cited in support of the claim that "God is not merely the custodian of justice or the dispenser of 'truth' to man," as in Mesopotamian law, but rather "he is the fountainhead of the law, the law is a statement of his will" (Greenberg 1976, 22). In Exodus 21:1, Yahweh himself conveys the specific terms of the Law to the community through Moses: "These are the rules that you [Moses] shall set before them." Direct divine authorship of the Law is reinforced by the retention of first-person address in many individual provisions: "When a man schemes against another and kills him treacherously, you shall take him from My very altar to be put to death" (Ex 21:14); "If you lend money to My people, to the poor among you, do not act toward them as a creditor; exact no interest from them" (Ex 22:24); "You shall observe the Feast of Unleavened Bread—eating unleavened bread for seven days as I have commanded you" (Ex 23:15). Yahweh refers repeatedly to "my rules" (*mishpatay*) "my laws" (*ḥuqqotay*) and "my commandments" (*mitsvotay*) (Lev 18:4–5; 19:37; 26:3). In line with the notion that the laws are authored by, and express the direct will of, the deity rather than himself, Moses is portrayed as referring to the laws as rules that Yahweh has commanded him to impart to the Israelites (Deut 6:1), and warns the Israelites to do "as the Lord has commanded" (Deut 5:29). Likewise, the biblical narrator refers to the "commandments and regulations that Yahweh enjoined upon the Israelites" (Num 36:13; cf. Ex 31:18).

Consequently, to violate the Law is to defy the personal will of Yahweh. As Moshe Greenberg notes (1976, 22), "God is directly involved as legislator and sovereign; the offense does not flout a humanly authored safeguard of cosmic truth but an explicit utterance of the divine will."

In these and many other texts, divine law is characterized as the will of a divine sovereign rather than the expression of an ontologically primary natural order or abstract eternal truth. In line with this characterization, biblical divine law is not represented as possessing features typically attributed to an ontologically primary natural order or abstract eternal truth, but as possessing features typically attributed to positive law. Specifically, divine law is represented as particular rather than universal, arbitrary rather than rational, evolving rather than static, coercive rather than instructive, and as addressed to obedient servants.

(II) DIVINE LAW IS PARTICULAR AND NONRATIONAL

Certain biblical passages emphasize the particularity of the divine law of Yahweh. In contrast to the blood prohibition that is conferred upon all humanity through the covenant with Noah (Gen 9:1–17), the divine law delivered at Sinai is bestowed in covenant on a particular people—Israel—over whom Yahweh has established his sovereignty.

> For you are a people consecrated to Yahweh your god: of all the peoples on earth Yahweh your god chose you to be his treasured people. (Deut 7:6)

To be consecrated or sanctified (*q.d.sh*) to Yahweh is to be separated *to* Yahweh's service, through the observance of his rules and commandments, and *from* alien peoples and their practices. Here and elsewhere in Deuteronomy,

Israel's particular and unique relationship with Yahweh is expressed by the verb *baḥar* = to elect, or choose.

> Mark, the heavens to their uttermost reaches belong to Yahweh your god, the earth and all that is on it! Yet it was to your fathers that Yahweh was drawn in his love for them, so that he chose you, their lineal descendants, from among all peoples—as is now the case. (Deut 10:14–15)

Yahweh has given other nations over to other deities (Deut 4:19–20) but has taken (*l.q.ḥ*) Israel for himself to be his people living by his laws.

In these and other passages, biblical divine law is strikingly particularistic. It is designed to bring one nation among all the nations into a covenantal relationship with a sovereign ruler and enable it to live in a particular place—the land of Canaan (Deut 4:5). Indeed, according to some passages, the divine law's purpose is precisely *not* to promote universalism and sameness but to ensure the opposite—particularism and difference. The laws prohibiting abominable sexual practices are followed by this general admonition:

> You shall faithfully observe all my laws and all my regulations ... You shall not follow the practices of the nation that I am driving out before you ... I, Yahweh, am your god who has set you apart from other peoples. (Lev 20:22a, 23a, 24b)

The separatist purpose of the Law explains the presence of commandments and prohibitions for which a rational basis is not self-evident, laws whose very arbitrariness ensures that they will set Israel apart, in all her particularity. Unlike the prohibitions of murder and theft, which may be perceived as universal and rational in character, some of the divine law's regulations appear to be irrational (or at least nonrational). This is especially true of the dietary laws and purity laws, whose only explicit justification is that they set Israel apart, or "sanctify" (*leqaddesh*) Israel, as separate and particular. Thus, Deuteronomy 14 concludes its prohibitions of certain foods with the line "For you are a people consecrated [i.e., separated] to Yahweh your god," and Leviticus 20 underscores the separatist function of the purity laws:

> So you shall set apart the pure beast from the impure, the impure bird from the pure. You shall not draw abomination upon yourselves through beast or bird or anything with which the ground is alive, which I have set apart for you to treat as impure. You shall be holy to me, for I Yahweh am holy, and I have set you apart from other peoples to be mine. (Lev 20:25–26)

(III) DIVINE LAW EVOLVES

Insofar as the divine law is understood to stem not from a necessary natural order but from the will of a divine sovereign, it can be modified by subsequent acts of divine willing. New rules and ordinances can be issued as long as there is continued access to Yahweh's will through various oracular procedures. The Pentateuch reports four occasions in which a legal gap is filled through direct consultation of Yahweh.[1] In Leviticus 24, a man who pronounces the divine name in a blasphemous manner is brought before Moses and placed in custody "until the decision of Yahweh should be made clear to them" (v. 12). In Numbers 9, men who have contracted corpse impurity ask Moses and Aaron why they are debarred from offering the Passover sacrifice in its proper time. Moses answers, "Stand by, and let me hear what instructions Yahweh gives about you" (v. 8). Yahweh details an alternative sacrifice for persons defiled by corpse impurity or absent owing to a long journey. In Numbers 15:32–36 a man gathering wood on the Sabbath day is placed in custody "for it had not been specified what should be done to him." Yahweh rules that the man is to be stoned, and so it is done "as Yahweh had commanded Moses." Finally, in Numbers 27:1–11 the daughters of Zelophehad claim an inheritance from among their father's kinsmen. Moses brings their case before Yahweh (v. 5), who responds that the plea is just and the daughters must be provided with a hereditary holding. The deity goes on to formulate a general rule addressing such cases for the future. These passages depict divine law as subject to ongoing development in response to the shifting circumstances of human life.

Michael LeFebvre (2006, 40) has recently emphasized the role of divine oracle as the ultimate source of law in ancient Israel, based on Pentateuchal descriptions of Israel's court system (Ex 18:13–27; Num 11:16–25; Deut 1:9–17; 17:8–13). Widely recognized as monarchic-era retrojections to the time of Moses, these descriptions all retain a role for divine inquiry (*d.r.sh*) in the disposition of difficult cases. According to Exodus 18, minor cases will be handled by competent, trustworthy, and honest men appointed for the purpose (vv. 21–22), while difficult cases will be referred to Moses for inquiry before the deity (vv. 19–20, 22). Although some scholars deny an oracular element in this system and assert that Moses himself decides the cases that are brought to him, LeFebvre (ibid., 41) argues persuasively that cases brought to Moses (by definition, hard cases) are not decided by Moses but are presented to Israel's god— the ultimate source of the law (42–43). This is the meaning of Jethro's statement in verse 19: "You [Moses] represent the people before Elohim: you bring the disputes before Elohim." This text and the four Pentateuchal cases described above, in which Moses inquires of Yahweh concerning a legal gap, assume that change, growth, and development of the divinely given law are all integral to the process, because the law is not an eternal and static natural order but an expression of God's will for a particular people in ever-shifting historical time.

According to LeFebvre, Deuteronomy 17 describes the "continuation of this 'oracular judgeship' through the establishment of a central court in Jerusalem" (44) to handle difficult cases brought by lower magistrates.

---

[1] Either the substance of the law itself is unknown, or some aspect of its implementation and enforcement, such as the appropriate punishment. For a full discussion see Novick 2008.

> If a case is too baffling for you to decide ... you shall promptly repair to the place that Yahweh your god will have chosen, and appear before the levitical priests, or the magistrate in charge at the time, and you shall inquire (*d.r.sh*). When they have announced to you the verdict in the case you shall carry out the verdict that is announced to you from that place that Yahweh chose, observing scrupulously all their instructions to you. You shall act in accordance with the instructions given you and the ruling handed down to you; you must not deviate from the verdict that they announce to you either to the right or to the left. (Deut 17:8–10)

The verdict of the high court, which must be strictly observed, appears to derive its authority from the court's location in the place that Yahweh has chosen—that is, from its cultic position "before Yahweh" (LeFebvre 2006, 44). LeFebvre concludes that this text presupposes cultic inquiry—by means of which the divine will is ascertained—for difficult cases. Thus, the continued growth and evolution of the divine law in response to the dynamic conditions of human life are not only envisaged but institutionalized by this passage.[2]

Innovations point to the variability of the Law, as does the presence of self-contradiction, a striking feature of several of the commandments and prohibitions of the Pentateuch. To present just a few examples: the Pentateuch contains three different versions of the decalogue. The Exodus 20 decalogue is repeated in Deuteronomy 5 but with minor variations (cf. Deut 5:16 and Ex 20:12; Deut 5:16 and Ex 20:7; Deut 5:14 and Ex 20:10; Deut 5:17 and Ex 20:13). A more surprising variation occurs in Exodus 34. After smashing the first set of tablets inscribed with the decalogue of Exodus 20, Moses is given a second set of tablets. The biblical writer emphasizes that Yahweh wrote on the tablets the very words that were on the former tablets that had been broken (Ex 34:1). The reader expects, therefore, a verbatim repetition of Exodus 20. Yet the decalogue that follows has very little overlap with the earlier decalogue, and even where there is some overlap in substance, the wording is entirely different.[3]

In addition, the decalogue in Exodus 20 does not stand completely unchallenged. Exodus 20:5–6 enunciates a principle of intergenerational punishment that is explicitly rejected in Deuteronomy 7:9–10. Ezekiel and Jeremiah will also reject the idea of intergenerational punishment (Jer 31:27–30; Ezek 18:20),

[2] The representation of divine law as the positive enactment of a sovereign divine will is not significantly altered by the institution of charismatic judges and monarchs. As Yair Lorberbaum has argued (2011a, 1–26), many biblical texts assert that Yahweh alone is sovereign (direct theocracy); judges exercise temporary authority as an extension of the arm and power of the deity. As for kings, the royal theology that informs certain strands of biblical tradition identifies the king's political authority with the sovereignty of Yahweh such that the king is no mere executor of the Law but—insofar as he is imbued with the divine effluence—a source of law. Insofar as the king is the servant and representative of Yahweh, the king's will is effaced in favor of the divine will.

[3] Evidently different traditions regarding the contents of the Decalogue circulated in ancient Israel. The story of the Golden Calf and Moses's destruction of the first tablets is a brilliant narrative strategy for introducing and presenting one of these alternative Decalogue traditions.

declaring that although Yahweh used to punish intergenerationally, in the wake of the destruction he has renounced this modus operandi.[4] In short, the biblical god is depicted as a god who changes his mind in response to the activity of human beings, not only in these prophetic proclamations, but also in narrative texts (see, for example, Gen 6:6; Ex 32:14; 2 Sam 24:16; Jer 26:19). And as his mind can change, so can his Law.

In addition to gap filling, innovations, and self-contradictions, biblical divine law contains examples of revision and modification. Deuteronomy revises or updates earlier versions of the law found in Exodus, a phenomenon described with particular acuity by Bernard Levinson (2002). Levinson maintains that Deuteronomy deploys a variety of interpretative and rhetorical strategies designed to hide its revisionist activity—a "rhetoric of concealment" that camouflages the actual literary history of the laws.[5] Adopting "the garb of dependence to purchase profound hermeneutical independence" (2002,149), the Deuteronomic authors attempt to obscure their revision or annulment of older laws by retrojecting them to the time of Moses or conditioning them on changed circumstances.

For example, Deuteronomy's ban on sacrifice at local altars, with its accompanying centralization of sacrifice at a single site, is attributed to Moses and is justified as a response to a new historical situation—the transition to a settled existence in the land:

> You shall not act at all as we now act here, every man as he pleases, because you have not yet come to the allotted haven that Yahweh, your god is giving you. When you cross the Jordan and settle in the land that Yahweh your god is allotting to you, and he grants you safety from all your enemies around you and you live in security, then you must bring everything that I command you to the site where Yahweh your god will choose to establish his name. (Deut 12:8–11)

While Deuteronomy's retrojection of centralization to the time of the entry into the land may *conceal* the late date of the innovation, it nevertheless *discloses* the fact that divine law can and does change. In other words, although the strategy serves as a *rhetoric of concealment* insofar as it hides the hand of the Deuteronomic reviser, it serves as a *rhetoric of disclosure* insofar as it openly and explicitly asserts that Yahweh modifies his Law in response to changing historical circumstances.

On other occasions, no explicit justification for a change is provided. Deuteronomy's rules for tithing and for the seventh-year release of debts (15:1–

---

[4] For an excellent discussion of the modification of the principle of intergenerational punishment, see Levinson 1992.

[5] In his 1992 article he attributes this tactic to a belief in the inviolability of the canonical text. But in this connection, see LeFebvre 2006, 66–73, who argues that it is anachronistic to assume that canonicity entailed an intolerance for legal change.

11), for the release of slaves (15:12–19), and for the three pilgrimage festivals (16:1–17) simply revise and update laws in Exodus. Since many of the revisions exhibit a tendency toward increased humanitarianism, it is reasonable to suppose that they are ideologically motivated: the earlier law is critiqued and improved. The slave law is a case in point. Exodus 21:2–11 and Deuteronomy 15:12–18 deal with essentially the same law, moving from one topic to the next in a parallel sequence: the limitation of Hebrew slavery to six years, items given to the slave upon his release, the slave's option to remain a perpetual slave, and the treatment of the female slave. But despite the similarity in language and sequence, the differences between the two laws on these many points are stark. In Deuteronomy, the female is to be treated exactly as the male is (Deut 15:18); the master may not retain the slave's wife and children in the event that the slave chooses freedom; the master must give his freed slave gifts; the procedure to be followed in the event that a slave does renounce his freedom is secularized; and the law of slave release is incorporated into the seven-year calendrical cycle.

Thus, preserved side by side in the biblical text are two provisions of a divine law regarding slaves that contradict one another in several details. Deuteronomy 15's literary dependency on Exodus 21 suggests that it is a revision of the latter. In internal narrative terms, of course, Deuteronomy 15 is represented as Moses's recasting of a law delivered some forty years earlier, but unlike the centralization law this revision is not explained as necessitated by changed historical circumstances; on the contrary, it simply eliminates elements of the law that do not conform to the Deuteronomist's relatively more humanitarian viewpoint.

Such cases attest to the fact that in ancient Israel, the Law's divinity was not perceived as entailing its fixity or absolute nature. Terms of the divine law were modified, revised, updated, and interpreted in the course of their transmission. And while the identity of those introducing these changes is concealed by a strategy of retrojection to the time of Moses, the *fact* that divine law can and does change is not concealed but fully disclosed. The postbiblical claim that Yahweh's revealed divine law is fixed and immutable is not consistent with the Pentateuchal evidence. For the biblical writers and redactors, the flexibility, evolution, and even self-contradiction of divine law do not appear to have impinged upon its authoritative or divine status.

(IV) DIVINE LAW IS COERCIVE

Those who wish to characterize biblical divine law as a form of positive law— the command of a sovereign will backed by coercive force—will find further support in certain literary features of the biblical text. First, while many laws are casuistically formulated (employing if-then clauses), others are formulated in second-person apodictic form ("thou shalt/shalt not"). The rhetorical effect of this form is to create the impression of direct commands, unconditional and nonnegotiable, issued by a sovereign empowered to enforce his will.[6] Other literary features point to the coercive enforcement of the Law. The first is entirely direct and explicit: the Bible contains numerous passages (beginning with Ex 20:5–6 when the Law is introduced) which detail in no uncertain terms the severe punishments that await the disobedient and the rewards that attend the obedient. Deuteronomy threatens the disobedient with destruction (Deut 7:19–20) and promises long life, blessing, and prosperity to the obedient (vv. 12–15). The book ends with a colorful list of imprecations aimed at specific violations of Yahweh's Law (Deut 27:15–26; 28:15–19) as well as lengthy descriptions of the diseases, military defeats, poverty, and humiliation that will befall the nation if it defies Yahweh's will (Deut 28:20–68).

A second literary feature that underscores the coercive power behind the Law is prevalent in the Holiness Code (Lev 17–26) in connection with norms and behaviors that fall outside the power of the state to enforce, and that must be monitored by the individual conscience. In addition to being couched in the apodictic style, these ordinances are punctuated by the repeated assertion that Yahweh is Israel's god, a none-too-subtle reminder of the powerful authority behind the Law:

> "You shall not insult the deaf, or place a stumbling block before the blind. You shall revere your god: I am Yahweh."

> "You shall not hate your kinsfolk in your heart. Reprove your kinsman but incur no guilt because of him. You shall not take vengeance or bear a grudge against your countrymen. Love your fellow as yourself. I am Yahweh."

> "You shall rise before the aged and show deference to the old; you shall revere your god: I am Yahweh." (Lev 19:14, 17–18, 32)

The staccato repetition of the phrase "I am Yahweh" or the variant "I, Yahweh, am your god," in connection with these nonjusticiable norms of behavior, invokes Yahweh as the Divine Enforcer. Particularly when coupled with the phrase "you shall revere your god," these formulations remind the listener that Yahweh is monitoring the observance of his laws. If these norms are upheld, Yahweh—ever present, ever watchful, and ever to be revered—will bestow his reward; if they are violated, he will exact his punishment.

---

[6] Albrecht Alt (1934) identified two types of biblical law on the basis of form—casuistic law (employing if-then clauses) and apodictic law (employing concise commands). The distinction between the two forms is widely accepted (even though Alt's assertion of the Israelite uniqueness of apodictic law has proven to be exaggerated), but their significance continues to be debated. See Westbrook 2006, 16–17 and 28–32.

(V) DIVINE LAW ADDRESSES THE OBEDIENT SERVANT

When law is seen as stemming from the commanding will of a sovereign authority, the appropriate response of its addressees is obedience. To the extent, then, that the biblical text represents the divine law's claim to Israel's fidelity as grounded in its origin in the sovereign divine will, it is Israel's duty and obligation to *obey* by aligning her will with that of Yahweh. In line with this view are biblical passages in which the ideal human type is the servant (*'eved*) of unquestioning loyalty. Several biblical characters exemplify a trusting obedience (though none does so entirely consistently) that is explicitly praised or rewarded. Even before the giving of the Law at Sinai, Noah's obedience in fulfilling God's instructions is emphasized (Gen 6:22; 7:5, 9, 16), and Abraham is singled out for his trust (Gen 12:4; 15:6) and for his obedience to Yahweh's irrational command to sacrifice his son (Gen 22:16–18). In one remarkable passage that will play a key role in postbiblical constructions of divine law, Yahweh's fulfillment of his covenant promises is linked to Abraham's obedience to all of Yahweh's commandments:

> I will make your heirs as numerous as the stars of heaven, and assign to your heirs all these lands, so that all the nations of the earth shall bless themselves by your heirs—inasmuch as Abraham obeyed me and kept my charge; my commandments, my laws, and my teachings. (Gen 26:4–5)

The revelation of the divine law at Sinai is accompanied by the demand that Israel *obey* the commandments and laws that Yahweh enjoins upon them (Deut 4:40; 6:3; 7:11; 8:11; 10:13). The Israelites' acceptance of the covenant is signaled by a declaration of eager and unquestioning *obedience* ("we will do and we will obey" [Ex 24:7]; see also the covenant renewal declaration in Josh 24:24). The kings of Israel and Judah are condemned or praised by the biblical narrator in accordance with the degree of their obedience to Yahweh (e.g., 1 Kgs 15:11), and David is lionized as the servant of God (2 Sam 3:18; 1 Kgs 3:6; 8:66; Ps 18:1; 36:1; 78:70; 89:4, 21; 132:10; 144:10)—a term that seeks to emphasize his obedience (in the face of evidence to the contrary!) to Yahweh's commands.

(VI) RESOURCES FOR A CONSTRUCTION OF BIBLICAL DIVINE LAW AS POSITIVE COMMAND: A SUMMARY

The characterization of divine law as a set of commands issuing from a sovereign divine will wielding coercive power finds clear textual support in the biblical corpus. Many passages represent the detailed provisions of the Law not as an ontologically primary natural order or abstract eternal truth, but as an expression of the will of Yahweh for his covenant partner, Israel. In keeping with this basic conception, divine law is often depicted as decidedly particular and in some respects nonrational or arbitrary, rather than universal and rational.

Because the source of the Law is Yahweh's will, the Law is not static but can grow, change, and evolve with subsequent acts of divine willing. This fact necessitates oracular mechanisms for ascertaining Yahweh's evolving requirements (Ex 18) or institutional mechanisms for appropriating his authority (Deut 17). The frequent use of apodictic forms, the explicit detailing of reward and punishment, and an implied emphasis on the omnipresent vigilance of the Law's divine author underscore the extent to which the divine law may be conceived as a command backed by coercive force. Finally, because the divine sovereign esteems obedience to his commands, many texts depict the ideal human type as the obedient and unquestioning servant. In short, those who wish to cast biblical divine law in positivist terms will find a ready supply of textual support.

And yet, there are countervailing tendencies in the biblical text that emphasize the extent to which biblical law may possess features amenable to a less positivistic account. These passages emphasize the Law's grounding in, or association with, (divine) reason rather than (divine) will.

Discourse 2: Divine Law as an Expression of Divine Reason

The Hebrew Bible may be said to refer to divine law in two *modalities*. The primary and dominant modality is that of the divinely revealed Torah, a set of laws delivered through Moses at Sinai. A second and much less explicitly attested modality of divine law is that of a universal moral order that obligates humankind more generally. Discourse 1 focused on the first modality, presenting the divine law revealed through Moses at Sinai as grounded in *will*. Discourse 2, which explores divine law as an expression of reason, addresses *both* of the modalities of biblical divine law. On the one hand, it seeks to represent the divine law revealed at Sinai as a law grounded in *reason*. On the other hand, it assumes a universal moral order that appears to bear some relationship to divine wisdom. The relationship between these two modalities is a complex matter addressed below.

The question of whether the biblical tradition contains something akin to the Greek concept of unwritten law (a law higher than conventional law) or natural law (a rational order that governs the universe) has generated discussion from antiquity to the present, with diametrically opposed conclusions.[7] While the Greek term "unwritten law" has several referents, and the Stoic term "natural law" has a rather specific meaning, a precise definition can be delayed until the next chapter. Our primary concern in this chapter is to identify within the biblical text passages that will enable later readers of the Bible to construct from its pages a notion of divine law beyond the revealed Torah, a notion that might share (or be perceived as sharing) features with something like Greek unwrit-

---

[7] For a full survey of the subject and a summary of the natural law and ant–inatural law positions, see Novak 1998; for a recent appraisal of the question, see Statman forthcoming.

ten law or Stoic natural law. Such passages will tend to posit or assume the existence of a universal order of some kind.

After adducing passages that point toward a universal moral order (i), I consider biblical texts that may be said to ground the divinely revealed Torah (the primary modality of divine law in the Hebrew Bible) in reason. These texts present the divine law revealed through Moses at Sinai as (ii) rational rather than nonrational, (iii) static rather than evolving, (iv) instructive rather than coercive, and (v) addressed to rational moral agents as the ideal human type. In a final section we will be concerned with sorting out the relationship between these two distinct modalities.

(I) DIVINE LAW AS A UNIVERSAL ORDER

Although the Hebrew Bible takes pains to represent the laws of the Sinaitic covenant as positive laws issuing from Yahweh's sovereign will, narrative texts dealing with the pre-Sinai period occasionally assume the existence of a self-evident moral order of universal validity (Bockmuehl 2000, 91). Thus, the culpability of Cain rests on what has been described as the unexpressed assumption of the God-endowed sanctity of human life (Sarna 1966, 31). Despite the absence of an *explicit* positive law prohibiting murder, Cain is culpable because the sanctity of human life is an *implicit* universal moral law. It is not until Genesis 9:6 that the sanctity of human life is additionally expressed as a positive injunction of the divine will in the covenant with Noah, despite the principle's operation prior to that injunction.

The story of the Flood also presupposes a universal moral law, infractions of which are punished severely:

> The earth became corrupt before Elohim; the earth was filled with lawlessness. When Elohim saw how corrupt the earth was, for all flesh had corrupted its ways on earth, Elohim said to Noah, "I have decided to put an end to all flesh, for the earth is filled with lawlessness because of them." (Gen 6:11–13a)

The lawlessness (*ḥamas*) here decried by Yahweh refers not to the violation of positive laws divinely revealed (indeed no such revelation has yet occurred in the biblical narrative), but to the violation of the implicit and universal moral laws that make life in society possible.

In other Pentateuchal texts, expressions of outrage over a given behavior prior to the revelation of God's positive law at Sinai derive from the assumption of self-evident standards of morality (Bockmuehl 2000, 91). The outrage expressed by Jacob's sons over the rape of their sister Dinah ("a thing not to be done" [Gen 34:7]), and Abimelech's awareness of the culpability entailed in taking the wife of another man (Gen 20:3–4) are two examples.

The story of Sodom and Gomorrah likewise assumes a basic moral law that precludes murder and various forms of violence and oppression. Here again, no positive law has been revealed, and yet the inhabitants of Sodom and Gomorrah are culpable because they have violated an implicit moral law. They stand condemned not by a provision of positive law, but by the outcry of those they have harmed (Gen 18:21a). In the continuation of the story, Abraham challenges Yahweh's decision to destroy all of the people of Sodom, and in so doing he references what appears to be an implicit, universal, and rational moral principle—the principle of justice. Abraham says,

> Will you sweep away the innocent along with the guilty? . . . Far be it from you to do such a thing, to bring death upon the innocent as well as the guilty, so that innocent and guilty fare alike. Far be it from you! Shall not the judge of all the earth deal justly? (Gen 18:23, 25)

At first glance it seems that Abraham invokes a self-evident principle of justice independent of Yahweh, and that Yahweh is expected to conform his decrees and interactions with humanity to this self-operating principle. This text has been cited as "the most unambiguous example of a natural law type position in Scripture" (Novak 1998, 39). Daniel Statman writes (forthcoming):

> Abraham is best interpreted as referring to a notion of justice that is (a) universally valid and (b) independent of divine will. As the story unfolds, God seems to accept Abraham's moral-theological assumptions. He does not respond to Abraham by saying "Justice is defined by what *I* do, hence there can be no conflict between the destruction of Sodom and the demands of justice," nor by saying "In this culture, there is nothing unjust in slaying the righteous with the wicked." God neither assumes divine command morality, nor some form of moral relativism. He assumes that the requirements are universally valid.

Were this indeed the case—and it is possible to read the text this way—we might be able to speak of a robust principle of natural law in this section of the Hebrew Bible. However, the story falls short of affirming an *independent* and *universal* standard of justice in two ways. First, verse 19a (where God says he has singled Abraham out so that "he may instruct his children and his posterity to keep the way of Yahweh by doing what is just and right") refers to "doing what is just and right" as "the way of Yahweh." If so, then Abraham does not call upon Yahweh to observe an independent principle of justice that he has momentarily chosen to ignore. He calls upon Yahweh to be true to himself. "Shall not the judge of all the earth deal justly?" is a purely rhetorical question ("Of course!" is the appropriate answer), since both Yahweh and Abraham know that doing what is just and right *is* the way of Yahweh. Markus Bockmuehl describes this identification of "the way of Yahweh" with "what is just and right" as an important limitation on the biblical conception of what might be called "laws of nature":

In Old Testament and Jewish thought …, God and his creation never ultimately speak with two distinct voices. Although of course it is true that ancient Israel had no abstract concept of 'nature' or of the 'cosmos', God's voice is clearly heard both in creation and in the Torah, and the two are fundamentally related. And while there is thus, significantly, no 'law of nature' terminology as describing a reality distinct from the law of God, the Hebrew world view does operate on the assumption that all creation expresses God's law and moral purpose, and all of God's law is law according to nature.

… what might be called 'laws of nature' in the Psalms are not considered in either impersonal or Deistic fashion as in Stoicism … The laws of the universe are not the independent edicts of autonomous nature but the direct corollary of God's sending forth his word to the earth. (2000, 89, 90)

But even if we were to grant that the principle of justice invoked here is intended to point to an independent natural order, there is a second and more serious challenge to interpreting this passage as evidence of a robust and universal principle of natural law. Abraham's appeal to the rational principle of justice is simply the opening gambit in a longer argument that ultimately urges (and in fact convinces) Yahweh to *violate justice and adopt mercy instead.* Abraham does not seek to convince Yahweh to do justice; he *assumes* that Yahweh's ways are just. On the contrary, a close examination of his full speech reveals that Abraham's goal is to convince Yahweh to *dispense* with justice and forgive the guilty altogether.

> [23b]Will you sweep away the innocent along with the guilty? [24]*What if there should be fifty innocent within the city; will you then wipe out the place and not forgive it for the sake of the innocent fifty who are in it?* [25]Far be it from you to do such a thing, to bring death upon the innocent as well as the guilty, so that innocent and guilty fare alike. Far be it from you! Shall not the judge of all the earth deal justly? (Gen 18:23–25; emphasis added)

Abraham's argument is subtle and ultimately self-contradictory. In verses 23b and 25, he vigorously asserts his confidence that Yahweh would never destroy the innocent and would never act unjustly ("Far be it from you!"). He defines injustice as treating the innocent and guilty alike, rather than according to their deserts ("Far be it from you [to behave] so that innocent and guilty fare alike!"). Thus, it would be wrong for Yahweh to destroy the entire city as long as innocent individuals are present in it because innocent and guilty would "fare alike." But by the same token, would it not be equally unjust to let the wicked go unpunished? To do so would also be to treat the guilty and innocent alike. Doesn't justice require that the wicked be punished and only the innocent spared? And yet, slipped in amid his fist pounding about justice (vv. 23 and 25) is Abraham's startling request (v. 24): spare the wicked on account of the innocent. Forgo *justice*, O just judge of all the earth, and adopt *mercy*. Even more startling, the just judge of all the earth agrees. Yahweh says that he will spare the wicked if even ten innocent men are present in the city. If an independent principle of justice is invoked in this story, then it is neither universal nor absolute, since Yahweh dispenses with it in response to Abraham's impassioned plea for forgiveness of the *wicked*.

The narrator takes pains to point out that *all* the people of Sodom, to the last man, are wicked (Gen 19:4). Thus, Abraham's hypothetical conditions are not met, and Yahweh is able to destroy the city in perfect justice. Nevertheless, the lesson in mercy is not completely lost on Yahweh, who sets aside the demands of justice and spares Lot despite his wickedness, in consideration of his favored Abraham (Gen 19:29).

There is a delicious irony in Abraham's negotiations with Yahweh over the fate of Sodom. Early in the story, Yahweh is said to have decided to share his plans for Sodom and Gomorrah with Abraham for the following reason: "For I have singled him out, that he may instruct his children and his posterity to keep the way of Yahweh by doing what is just and right" (Gen 18:19a). Yahweh has shown favor to Abraham so that Abraham might instruct his children and the nation that will arise from him (v. 18) in the ways of justice. And yet Abraham's first pupil, a mere four verses later, is not his biological offspring but Yahweh himself, and he instructs Yahweh not in the ways of justice but in the ways of mercy that set aside justice.

According to Bockmuehl (2000, 91), a biblical conception of a law according to nature is best seen in a handful of prophetic passages whose moral instructions contain an appeal to universal nature rather than to the Mosaic Law. John Barton (1979, 4–5) points to the small number of texts that suggest that ethical principles may be drawn from observations of natural phenomena or consensus views of society. Thus, prophetic texts ridicule idolatry specifically and sin generally as unnatural nonsense (ibid., 5–7). Isaiah presents Israel's rebellion as unnatural, like the rebellion of children against parents or of an ox or donkey against its master (Isa 1:2–3). Amos and Isaiah are among those prophets who inveigh against foreign nations for war atrocities and crimes against humanity (Amos 1–2; Isa 13–23; cf. Jer 46–51), charges that assume universal and rationally perceivable standards of morality. While these few references do not amount to anything like Greco-Roman notions of natural law, they will be an important resource for those who wish to locate a theory of natural law in the biblical tradition.

(II) THE DIVINE LAW REVEALED AT SINAI IS UNIVERSAL AND RATIONAL

Turning to the biblical representation of the divine law as revealed to Moses at Sinai, we find frequent references to the divine law's wisdom.

See, I have imparted to you laws and rules, as Yahweh my god has commanded me, for you to abide by in the land that you are about to enter and occupy. Observe them faithfully, for that will be proof of your wisdom and discernment to other peoples, who on hearing of all these laws will say, "Surely, that great nation is a wise and discerning people." For what great nation is there that has a god so close at hand as is Yahweh our god whenever we call upon him? Or what great nation has laws and rules as perfect as all this Teaching that I set before you this day? (Deut 4:6)

The laws and rules given by Yahweh are said to be characterized by wisdom; this is their perfection and a basis for their claim to Israel's fidelity. Those who observe the laws make manifest their own wisdom, and foreign peoples who hear of them will be moved to declare Israel a wise and discerning people. In the same vein, Malachi 2:6–7 links true instruction with knowledge, and Ezra 7:25 seems to employ the term "wisdom" as a synonym for Yahweh's Torah (Schnabel 1985, 5). The so-called wisdom psalms declare that the perfect law of Yahweh makes wise the simple (e.g., Ps 19).

Joseph Blenkinsopp (1995, 118) has argued that the legal tradition and the sapiential-didactic (i.e., wisdom) tradition were two great streams of tradition with marked similarities in both form and content. The site of the greatest confluence of the legal and sapiential traditions is Deuteronomy, with its strongly scribal character, its interest in matters of state, its insistence that Yahweh's teaching be studied and taught, its characterization of that teaching as a path to wisdom for all who study and observe it, and its exhortative and admonitory style so reminiscent of the style of sapiential compositions, including Proverbs. Blenkinsopp describes the effect of Deuteronomy's "sapientializing" of the law.

One effect of the confluence of the two traditions, the legal and the sapiential-didactic, is to modify the sense of the law as a purely objective and extrinsic reality. The presentation of the legal compilations under the broader category of instruction mitigates the sense of law as bald, divine command hedging in the autonomy of the individual addressed. The 'sapientializing' of the law suggests that it is to be internalized by an activity which unites learning and piety in the pursuit of a goal freely chosen. (ibid.)

In Second Temple period writings, Wisdom was connected not only to the divine law revealed at Sinai but also to God's ordering of nature. In the book of Proverbs, for example, Wisdom, personified as a woman, relates her coming into existence at the beginning of Creation:

Yahweh created me at the beginning of his course
As the first of his works of old.
In the distant past I was fashioned,
At the beginning, at the origin of earth . . .

I was there when he set the heavens into place;
When he fixed the horizon upon the deep;
When he made the heavens above firm,
And the fountains of the deep gushed forth;
When he assigned the sea its limits,
So that its waters never transgress his command;
When he fixed the foundations of the earth,
I was with him as a confidant,
A source of delight every day ...
Now, sons, listen to me;
Happy are they who keep my ways.
Heed discipline and become wise;
Do not spurn it ...
For he who finds me finds life
And obtains favor from Yahweh.
But he who misses me destroys himself;
All who hate me love death.

(Prov 8:22–23, 27–30a, 32–33, 35–36)

The heavenly and preexistent nature of Wisdom is an established concept of the ancient Near Eastern sapiential tradition, according to which Wisdom is an uncreated and female divine being. Here, Yahweh "acquires" (q.n.y.) her at the beginning of creation, and she accompanies Yahweh throughout the rest of the process[8] so that creation may be said to be informed by Wisdom (cf. Prov 3:19–20: "The Lord founded the earth by wisdom; He established the heavens by understanding"). When humans keep the ways of wisdom, they are said to find life and obtain favor from Yahweh (Prov 8:35)—rewards that are also attendant upon the observance of Yahweh's Torah (Deut 5:29–30; 6:3; 6:24–25; 11:9; and many more). The Deuteronomic association of the revealed Torah with Wisdom, and the Second Temple association of Wisdom with the created order of nature, set the stage for an identification of the Torah with the natural order, an identification that would enable the transference of attributes between the two (see chapter 3).

(III) THE DIVINE LAW REVEALED AT SINAI IS STATIC

In Deuteronomy 4:2, Moses conveys to the Israelites Yahweh's prohibition against modifying the revealed Torah:

---

[8] A close parallel to this motif is the Egyptian myth of the birth of the goddess Ma'at. In the Hellenistic period, Ma'at was identified with Isis, whose cult was popular in the third-century Ptolemaic empire to which Judah belonged. The favorite child of the sun god Re, Isis appears at creation "as the embodiment of cosmic order and the preserver of law and justice" (Blenkinsopp 1995, 161).

You shall not add anything to what I command you or take anything away from it, but keep the commandments of Yahweh your god that I [Moses] enjoin upon you.

And again in Deuteronomy 13:1:

Be careful to observe only that which I enjoin upon you; neither add to it nor take away from it.

These passages refer to a prohibition against *human* modification of the law. While they do not preclude divine modification of the law, they nevertheless contribute to a sense of the law as something that does not change. This impression is bolstered by passages that assert that Yahweh does not change (Mal 3:6), or, more specifically, change his mind (Num 23:19; Isa 46:10–11), despite explicit statements in biblical narratives that he does (e.g., Gen 6:6; Ex 32:14, Jonah 3:10).

In Second Temple period writings, the identification of Torah with Wisdom entailed the transference of Wisdom's "biography" to Torah (relying on Prov 8, cited above). This further contributed to a perception of Torah, of Yahweh's Law, as eternal and unchanging: the divine law may have been revealed at Sinai, but it existed with Yahweh long before Sinai—indeed from the first moment of creation—and has continued unchanged ever since.

(IV) THE DIVINE LAW REVEALED AT SINAI IS INSTRUCTION

Torah, the biblical term for divine law, means "instruction," and many passages reinforce a conception of the divine law revealed at Sinai as wise teaching rather than bald commandment. In Deuteronomy 31, Moses instructs the priests and elders to ensure that the Teaching is read aloud to all Israel every seventh year "that they may hear that they may learn and revere Yahweh your god and observe faithfully every word of this Teaching" (v. 12).

Inasmuch as such passages place a high premium on the people's comprehension of the Law, they suggest a crucial link between knowledge and observance. According to this verse, those who hear will learn the Law and will be inspired to revere its author and observe his instruction faithfully. The passage envisions compliance and fidelity based on an appreciation of the content of the teaching and a cognitive assent thereto, rather than coerced obedience.

Several narrative texts represent priests in their role as teachers of Torah. In 2 Kings 17:24–28, the king of Assyria sends a priest from among the Israelite deportees to teach "the practices of the god of the land" to the foreigners newly settled in the towns of Samaria. In a retrojection of later practice, 2 Chronicles 17:7–9 describes King Jehoshaphat as utilizing Levites and priests as teachers to travel through Judah to instruct the people in Torah. Ezra, a priest and "scribe expert in the Teaching of Moses which Yahweh, the god of Israel, had given," is sent to Yehud by Artaxerxes (Ezra 7:6), in order to teach the laws of Moses to "those who do not know them" (7:25; cf. v. 10). Nehemiah 8:1–8 describes the instruction provided by Ezra and the Levites on the New Year Festival. Ezra read from the scroll of the Teaching of Elohim while the Levites translated and explained, so that the people understood the reading.

The conception of the divine law as wise instruction rather than bald commandment finds literary reinforcement in the casuistic formulations of the laws. Casuistic formulations consist of a hypothetical protasis ("when X happens …," or "if X occurs …,") and an apodosis that sets forth the legal consequence of the activity described in the protasis ("then legal consequence Y shall be applied"). These laws are stylistically and rhetorically distinct from laws formulated as apodictic commands (e.g., "You shall not murder") and often occur in series that have been described as academic exercises that create a habit of scientific judgment and correct reasoning (Bottéro 1992, 178–79). Elizabeth Alexander sums up the pedagogical character of casuistic formulations as follows:

> In sum, while it is certainly true that the casuistic form communicates a set of legal norms, it is equally true that the form does much more than that. It engages both those who construct or compose it and those who review it in certain kinds of analytic activities. One is led to 1) abstract general principles from particular cases, 2) compare similar cases in a series, 3) consider how diverse legal principles interact in the improbable case, and 4) evaluate the concerns of competing legal considerations in the borderline case. (2006, 127)

In the case of cuneiform law, the casuistic formulation has been interpreted as evidence that cuneiform law writings served primarily academic, pedagogical, or other nonlegislative functions (Bottéro 1992, 178; Westbrook 2006, 30). Indeed, for Michael LeFebvre (2006), cuneiform law exemplifies the *nonlegislative paradigm* for law writing in antiquity, while Athenian law exemplifies the *legislative*.

> In the society which views law writings non-legislatively, a conceptual separation exists between actual law and written law. That is, what is written may be a *description* of what law looks like, but what is written is not viewed as *being* "the law." When judges in a non-legislative society hear a case, they appeal to an abstract (generally religious) sense of righteousness to support their rulings; they do not look to texts to authorize their rulings … The idea of law, in these cultures, is abstract like the ideas of justice, truth, and righteousness. All of these ideas can be *discussed* in writings, but none of them are ever supposed to be *embodied* by a text … There is a distinction between actual law and law writings in the non-legislative society.
> Within the legislative society, actual law is identified with written law. A law writing is more than a portrait of law: it is law. Actual law and writ-

ten law are one and the same. Law is written down and becomes a *source* for legal practice ... The magistrate's task is no longer to discern justice, but to apply what the law writings prescribe for a certain kind of case. In such a system, law is by definition a text. Law is no longer an abstract reality like justice, righteousness, and truth, but is textual by nature. Legal practice in such a society appeals to texts as the source of rulings. (23–24)

LeFebvre's assertion that Mesopotamian law writings did not serve a regulatory or legislative function is not a new idea,[9] and scholars have cited two pieces of evidence for this idea in addition to the broad use of casuistic forms. The first is the incomplete nature of Mesopotamian law writings;[10] they omit large areas of legal practice that are attested in contemporaneous law-practice documents (records of commercial transactions, wills, contracts, judgments, and so on). Jean Bottéro (1982, 438–43) argues that law had no formal character but emerged from the actions of judges whose decisions reflected their understanding of society's basic principles of fairness and equity (*kittum u mišarum*). Further evidence that Mesopotamian law writings did not serve a regulatory or legislative function are the contradictions between the writings and law as practiced and attested in contemporaneous law-practice documents in our possession.

If legal practice was based not on the great cuneiform law collections[11] but on unwritten customs (LeFebvre 2006, 9) what purpose did the former serve? Some (e.g., Malul 1990) view these works as idyllic collections of hypothetical exercises produced by a scribal elite. For others (e.g., J. J. Finkelstein 1961) the prologues and epilogues suggest a monumental or apologetic/propagandistic purpose.[12] A third view, advanced by Raymond Westbrook (1985, 250–54), assimilates the collections to the "scientific list genre" used in professional circles (specifically medicine and divinity) in the ancient Near East.

We need not adjudicate this debate. Of significance for our inquiry is the emerging scholarly consensus that the cuneiform law collections were written

---

[9] F. R. Kraus (1960) described the Code of Hammurabi as an academic rather than a legislative document insofar as it appears to describe rather than prescribe the law. J. J. Finkelstein (1961) likewise questioned the assumed legislative character of Mesopotamian law writings. It should be noted that this view of Mesopotamian law is not universally accepted. Sophie Lafont (2006, esp. 96), for example, argues that the ancient Near Eastern legal writings are not academic texts but real legal codes containing actual legal rules set forth by the king in accordance with the prerogatives given him by the gods, valid for all subjects, and designed to remain in force permanently.

[10] The primary exemplars are the Code of Hammurabi, the Hittite Laws, the Laws of Lipit-Ishtar, the Laws of Eshnunna, and the Middle Assyrian Laws.

[11] As Westbrook notes (1989, 215), law-practice documents cite royal edicts but not the written collections, suggesting that the former served as sources of law.

[12] This view is favored by J. J. Finkelstein (1961) but criticized by Westbrook (1985, 250–51) as accounting for only some versions of some of the collections and therefore not constituting a primary reason for the creation of the collections.

down for purposes other than direct social regulation. LeFebvre notes that support for this claim comes from Aristotle, who observed in connection with the ancient Near East:

> [In those lands] laws enunciate only general principles but do not give directions for dealing with circumstances as they arise; so that in an art [*techne*] of any kind it is foolish to govern procedure by written rules (and indeed in Egypt physicians have the right to alter their prescription after four days, although if one of them alters it before, he does so at his own risk); it is clear therefore that [in those lands] government according to written rules, that is laws, is not [deemed] best, for the same reason. (Aristotle, *Pol.* 3.10.4; as cited in LeFebvre 2006, 13)

From the Greek perspective, there is something remarkable about a society in which written laws do not serve a regulatory function. This brings us to the second of the two basic paradigms for ancient law writing identified by LeFebvre and exemplified by Athenian law: the legislative paradigm. LeFebvre argues that Athens is "a known source for the concept of regulatory law writing in the ancient world" (ibid., 19). Reforms at the end of the fifth century led to a new use for law writings with the establishment of the principle of the sovereignty of written law (21). Ancestral legal traditions were harmonized, and a single consistent code was produced and written on the walls of the royal stoa (22). New laws, drafted by a board of legislators, were deemed superior to the laws of the assembly, and unwritten custom was stripped of legal force so that courts and magistrates had to follow and enforce only written laws (ibid.). To paraphrase LeFebvre, Athens established not merely the rule of law but the rule of *written* law—law writings as the source of law.

Where does biblical law stand in relation to the two basic paradigms of law writing in antiquity exemplified by the Mesopotamian collections on the one hand and Athenian written law on the other? LeFebvre argues that biblical law must be understood against the background of contemporaneous cuneiform law (31). Like the cuneiform law writings, biblical law is incomplete. There are discrepancies between the laws of the three primary legal corpora on the one hand and the norms that are depicted in biblical narratives on the other, as well as inconsistencies among the legal corpora themselves, suggesting that biblical law writings, like cuneiform law collections, were primarily idyllic and nonregulatory (33–36). These collections were not the *source* of law; law emerged from cases, from judgments. As Dale Patrick notes (1986, 191–93), the Bible exhorts judges not to consult legal writings or follow the letter of the law, but to pursue justice, to decide cases fairly, and to avoid bribes that blind them to discerning what is right (see Deut 16:18–20). Narrative descriptions of court proceedings (Num 27:1–11; 2 Sam 14:5–17; 1 Kgs 21:8–13; 2 Kgs 8:1–6; Jer 26:8–24) contain no appeals to or citations of written norms, relying instead on the judge's or king's ability to discern good and evil (2 Sam 14:5–17).

LeFebvre (2006, 88–90) does see a "heightened" concern for the law writings as "*a paradigm of righteousness even for kings*" in the Deuteronomic corpus. The king is instructed to read from the Torah each day of his life, making him not the chief law *teacher* but rather the first law *student*.

> When he is seated on his royal throne, he shall have a copy of this Teaching written for him on a scroll by the levitical priests. Let it remain with him and let him read in it all the days of his life, so that he may learn to revere Yahweh his god, to observe faithfully every word of this Teaching (Torah) as well as these laws. Thus he will not act haughtily toward his fellows or deviate from the Instruction to the right or to the left, to the end that he and his descendants may reign long in the midst of Israel. (Deut 17:14–15a, 18–20)

Deuteronomy 17 does not describe the king's ad hoc consultation of a code of legislation for the purpose of applying the relevant rule, but rather his deep internalization of the Teaching—its exhortations to justice and its paradigmatic cases—that will ensure the king's success and prosperity.[13]

Certainly the Israelite king is expected to execute justice. He was to accomplish this, however, not by consulting the Torah as prescriptive legislation but by relying on the wisdom and discernment granted by Yahweh. The case of Solomon illustrates this point. In 1 Kings 3, Solomon asks Yahweh for "an understanding mind to judge your people, to distinguish between good and bad for who can judge this vast people of yours," and Yahweh grants him the essential traits required of a leader: the wisdom and discernment needed to dispense justice. In the famous story that follows this passage, Solomon does not resolve the case by consulting a written prescriptive law but by correctly discerning the truth of the matter. "When all Israel heard the decision that the king had rendered, they stood in awe of the king for they saw that he possessed divine wisdom to execute justice" (v. 28). In this and similar stories, Yahweh may school the king in the ways of righteousness, but the law itself emerges from the king's wise and discerning judgment in actual cases.

Although there is considerable debate over the time at which and the process by which the transition from a descriptive to a prescriptive view of Israel's law writings occurred,[14] there is a general consensus that by the Hellenistic

---

[13] Similarly, Joshua is exhorted to study the teaching of Yahweh day and night (Josh 1:7–8), and the people agree to obey his commands and orders (Josh 1:16–18). LeFebvre argues that in this instance the law writings lend authority to the leader (2006, 91)—Joshua's immersion in God's teaching exalts him above his fellow Israelites (90).

[14] Most scholars locate the completion of this shift in the Persian era, though its roots may stretch back to the Deuteronomic reforms of Josiah in the seventh century. See the summary of the views of Westbrook, Patrick, Frei, and Jackson in LeFebvre 2006, 3–8. However, as LeFebvre argues persuasively, dating the beginning of the shift to the seventh century advances in time the rise of prescriptive law in both the Greek and the biblical sources and seems extremely unlikely. Although Israel's law writings

period the statutory view of biblical law was widespread. LeFebvre argues (2006, 143–45) that the most self-evident hypothesis is also the most likely: biblical law writings shifted from the ancient Near Eastern model of idyllic texts lacking regulatory force to the Greek model of legislation, during a period of intense Greek influence—the Hellenistic era (from the late fourth century BCE on).

(V) THE DIVINE LAW REVEALED AT SINAI ADDRESSES RATIONAL MORAL AGENTS

The didactic-sapiential view of divine law outlined above assumes that the law's addressee, and the ideal human type, is a rational moral agent. A literary feature of biblical law that reinforces the idea of the rational character of both the law and the individuals it addresses is the presence of motive clauses, or rationales for many of the laws. Rationales situate the law's foundation in reason rather than in arbitrary will, by appealing to standard tropes of moral reasoning: this good was done for you, so by virtue of a reciprocal logic you ought to do the same good for others; or, you have experienced a particular hardship as so distasteful that you can deduce that it should not be inflicted on others. For example, Exodus 22:20 reads, "You shall not wrong a stranger or oppress him, for you were strangers in the land of Egypt." The Israelites' experience of oppression as strangers in Egypt should lead them to conclude that oppression and mistreatment of strangers is wrong. The rational nature of the appeal to personal experience and empathy is made more explicit in the following passage:

> When you beat down the fruit of your olive trees, do not go over them again; that [which remains on the tree] shall go to the stranger, the fatherless, and the widow. Always remember that you were a slave in the land of Egypt; therefore do I enjoin you to observe this commandment. (Deut 24:20, 22)

---

may have enjoyed an enhanced and even exalted status at this time, they were not statutory legislation, as evidenced by the use of oracles and royal decrees as the source of law, and the many contradictions between these decrees and the terms of biblical law, e.g., Josiah's reforms regarding the Levites (59–63). However, there is even reason to doubt the rise of prescriptivism in Israel in the Persian era. As Anne Fitzpatrick-McKinley has observed (1999, 48, cited in LeFebvre, 5), Persian notions of law differed little from those of the ancient Near East. If Persia did not view law writings as legislative, why would it impose such a view on Yehud? LeFebvre tests the hypothesis of Persian-era prescriptivism by examining the evidence for the regulatory application of the Torah in Ezra-Nehemiah. He concludes that Ezra and Nehemiah do not employ the Torah prescriptively but referred to it as an authoritative ideal when formulating their own norms. Thus, although an official (i.e., Persian) endorsement of the Mosaic law collection may have heightened the Torah's importance, it didn't change its essential character or use. These writings remained idyllic, and there is no reason to think that Israel had yet adopted the idea that law itself could be embodied by words (LeFebvre, 142).

The word "therefore" ('al-ken) is an explicit indication that the law in question follows logically and rationally from Israel's own knowledge of the hardships faced by strangers.

In Deuteronomy 15, it is the experience of liberation from slavery that creates a moral obligation:

> If a fellow Hebrew, man or woman, is sold to you, he shall serve you six years and in the seventh year you shall set him free. When you set him free, do not let him go empty-handed. Furnish him out of the flock, threshing floor, and vat, with which Yahweh your god has blessed you. Bear in mind that you were slaves in the land of Egypt and Yahweh your god redeemed you; therefore I enjoin this commandment upon you today. (Deut 15:12–15)

The reference to the Israelites' redemption alludes to the fact that when Yahweh redeemed the Israelites from slavery in Egypt, they did not go out empty-handed. Yahweh saw to it that they were laden with supplies taken from the Egyptians (Ex 12:35–36; 13:18). It follows, then, that the Israelites should treat others as they themselves were treated. This motive clause moves beyond the empathic orientation of the previous verses (drawing on the Israelites' experience of oppression as strangers) to the ideal of *imitatio dei*.

Embedding moral arguments in the very formulation of the law comports with a conception of the Law as both accessible to reason and based on just principles transparent to common sense. That the Law is not mysterious, but entirely comprehensible, is the explicit claim of Deuteronomy 30:11–14:

> Surely this instruction [Torah] which I enjoin upon you this day is not too baffling for you, nor is it beyond reach. It is not in the heavens, that you should say, "Who among us can go up to the heavens and get it for us and impart it to us, that we may observe it?" Neither is it beyond the sea, that you should say, "Who among us can cross to the other side of the sea and get it for us and impart it to us, that we may observe it?" No the thing is very close to you, in your mouth and in your heart, to observe it.

When lawmakers seek to make the law intellectually and morally palatable, they imply that the law's claim to our fidelity turns, to some degree, on its rational and moral character, and that observance of the law is best assured by obtaining the subject's cognitive and moral assent. The presence of moral arguments implies that the individuals to whom the law is addressed are intelligent and empathic persons capable of moral reasoning, persons who can not only engage in and be persuaded by argument but also recognize and value principles of justice and morality. On such a view, the ideal human type is not the obedient servant but the sage—the rational moral agent whose study of the law leads to observance. Law deploys reason in order to *inspire* compliance rather than *coerce* it.

In line with this view of the ideal human type, several biblical heroes are represented as intelligent moral agents who challenge and argue with Yahweh in a manner that does not draw his condemnation. Indeed, on more than one occasion, Yahweh is persuaded by a good argument or a good piece of rhetoric, and accedes to a character's criticism and demands. These passages stand in stark contrast to passages in which the ideal human type is the servant of unquestioning loyalty. Ironically, the same biblical character may exemplify both ideals. Thus, Abraham, the obedient servant who made no objection when told by Yahweh to slaughter his own son in Genesis 22, rises to the defense of the wicked people of Sodom, arguing pointedly and successfully not only that the innocent should never be wantonly destroyed but that Yahweh should temper justice with mercy and spare the wicked for the sake of the innocent (Gen 18). In addition, despite affirmations of his trust in Yahweh's promises regarding an heir, Abraham voices his doubts (Gen 15:5), and even objections to Yahweh's plan (Gen 17:18), at times working to undermine it.[15] The patriarch Jacob is reluctant to rely on Yahweh's promises and bargains with him in Genesis 28:20. Indeed, Jacob's nighttime struggle with a mysterious divine figure at the river Yabboq stands as a metaphor for the divine-human relationship as a relationship of struggle.

Moses also exemplifies this ideal. Despite his designation as "the servant of Yahweh" (Gen 34:5), this remarkable figure enjoys an intimate relationship with Yahweh that features constant discussion, argument, and moral reasoning. The two work as partners to preserve and ready the Israelites for life in Yahweh's land as Yahweh's people. On more than one occasion (e.g., Ex 32; Num 14) Moses dissuades Yahweh from his plan of destruction. Elsewhere, Yahweh accedes to Moses's well-argued complaints about the burden that has been placed upon him (Num 11:10–17), and responds by creating mechanisms for the delegation of some of his duties.

In many ways Moses sets the paradigm for the classical prophet, performing the double duty of chastising and upbraiding the Israelites for their rebellion and failure, but at the same time presenting arguments in their defense before Yahweh and pleading for mercy even when the people deserve punishment. Such biblical figures—and I have named only two of many—challenge the model of the unquestioning obedient servant as the ideal human type.

(VI) RESOURCES FOR A NONPOSITIVISTIC CONSTRUCTION
OF BIBLICAL DIVINE LAW: A SUMMARY

The characterization of the Law revealed at Sinai as a body of divine *instruction* that cultivates *wisdom* finds textual support in the biblical corpus. The casuistic

---

[15] For a full discussion of Abraham's resistance to Yahweh's choice of Isaac over Ishmael and the steps he takes to reverse this decision (including the attempt to rid himself of Sarah in Gen 20 despite having been explicitly informed that she will bear the child of the promise in one year's time) see Hayes 2012, 79–83.

formulation of many laws, and the presence of rationales and exhortations to accept the Law, suggest not only that the law is fundamentally rational but also that it is addressed to rational moral agents. The idea that the Law might represent an eternal static rationality is assisted by assertions that the law cannot be amended (Deut 4 and 13) and that Yahweh does not change. Those determined to view the Torah revealed at Sinai as a law grounded in reason, rather than pure will, will find some textual support for their view.

To the extent that the Bible may be said to reference self-evident standards of universal morality or rational and stable principles of justice, it also contains resources for the development of a concept of a universal unwritten or even natural law. However, insofar as these self-evident standards and principles are understood to correspond to and express the will of a personal God, the biblical concept of a universal unwritten or natural law (to the extent that it may be said to exist) will differ markedly from the impersonal and autonomous Greek concept.

Discourse 2 has drawn attention to two modalities of divine law in the biblical corpus: the modality of a divinely revealed body of laws and instructions and the modality of a universal order that governs the universe. How are the two related?

(a) Bridging the Two Modalities of Biblical Divine Law

The biblical text represents Yahweh as both a creator god and a revealing god. As the revealing god, Yahweh is the ultimate source of the positive laws conveyed to Israel. As the creator god, Yahweh is the ultimate source of the natural order and presumably (as some later readers will infer) of any moral standards and principles that might be perceived in that created order.[16] What is the relationship between these two modalities of divine law?

As noted above, the Deuteronomic association of the Torah revealed at Sinai with Wisdom, and the Second Temple period association of Wisdom with the natural order at creation, set the stage for the identification of natural law and Mosaic Law in Hellenistic Jewish writings. As Bockmuehl notes:

> [I]t is precisely this easy juxtaposition of Torah and creation which prepares the way for the overwhelming assumption in Hellenistic Jewish writers that the Torah is self-evidently a law in full accordance with nature, indeed the most perfect expression of such a law ... [t]he mainstream view of natural law in Second Temple Judaism ... is neither that there is a law of nature given in addition to the law of the Torah, nor that there is nothing but the Torah. Instead, creation itself demands life in accordance with the will of the Creator, and the Torah, or at least the principles it embodies, are the most perfect expression of a law that is in accordance with creation rightly understood. (2000, 97)

[16] Horst (1961, 249) asserts that the impersonal natural law has been "Yahwicized" in the Hebrew Bible.

(b) The Trouble with Wisdom

However, while Deuteronomy in particular may have "sapientialized" the Law, this was not in all respects an "easy juxtaposition." To some extent, Deuteronomy's subsumption of wisdom to Law was an anxious one. "Gather the people—men, women, children, and the strangers in your communities—that they may hear and so learn to revere Yahweh your god and to observe faithfully every word of this Teaching" (Deut 31:12). Yahweh's Torah may be instruction that requires study and intellection, but study is tethered to reverence for Yahweh and fidelity to his instruction.[17] Certain kinds of inquiry, certain kinds of wisdom, are off limits.

> The secret [or: hidden] things belong to Yahweh our god while the things that are revealed belong to us and our children forever, that we may observe all the words of this Instruction [Torah] ... (Deut 29:28)
> Surely, this Instruction which I enjoin upon you this day is not too baffling for you, nor is it beyond reach. It is not in the heavens, that you should say, 'Who among us can go up to the heavens and get it for us and impart it to us, that we may observe it?' Neither is it beyond the sea, that you should say, "Who among us can cross to the other side of the sea and get it for us and impart it to us, that we may observe it?" No, the thing is very close to you, in your mouth and in your heart, to observe it. (Deut 30:11–14)[18]

The instruction revealed by Yahweh is public wisdom that requires no esoteric speculation (it is not in the heavens) or knowledge from other lands (neither is it beyond the sea). All that Israel needs has been provided and revealed. And yet the reference to "secret things" in Deuteronomy 29:28 suggests a hidden wisdom that has *not* been revealed and that belongs to Yahweh alone. Blenkinsopp observes:

> Deuteronomy is at the beginning of a certain distancing from secular learning, what will later be called 'Greek wisdom', a withdrawal into an intellectualism which has as its goal the perfecting of the moral life ... The true wisdom is a divine prerogative which is available to humankind only as God chooses to reveal it. As the author sees it, that part of divine wisdom which he has chosen to reveal is contained in the law. The law is therefore *the* expression of divine wisdom made available to Israel and, as such, can compete on more than equal terms with the vaunted wisdom of the nations. (1995, 152–53)

---

[17] Or as David Novak has observed (1998, 17), whatever wisdom may be perceived in the divine law of Israel, it is phenomenologically subsequent to the recipients' obedience.

[18] Most commentators believe that Deut 30:11–14 originally followed immediately upon 29:28. At the very least, it clearly resumes a line of thought that is interrupted by 30:1–10.

According to Blenkinsopp, tension between traditional Israelite religious ideas and practices on the one hand and the international wisdom tradition on the other was inevitable (ibid., 6). He finds ambivalence toward wisdom in the Court History of David as well as the Garden of Eden story. A dominant theme in the Court History is the disastrous and deadly consequences that follow the intervention of a "wise" individual such as Jonadab or Ahitofel (7). In the Garden of Eden, the serpent is another wise agent whose advice brings ruin (8). These stories attest to a fear that to follow wisdom is to risk alienation from Yahweh (ibid.).

The tension between traditional Israelite teaching and the Wisdom tradition became ever more apparent in the exilic and postexilic periods and reached a peak in biblical books dating to the Hellenistic period. Texts like Ezekiel 8:12, 9:9, Zephaniah 1:12, Malachi 2:17, and many later psalms voice skepticism about divine justice. Likewise, in Job, we find the idea that suffering is not always an expression of divine justice, while Ecclesiastes denies the idea of divine justice altogether.

Texts in which speculative wisdom introduces doubt about a moral order, and asserts the futility and meaninglessness of life, provoke defensive responses. Thus, a pious postscript appended to the book of Ecclesiastes reasserts the teachings of the book of Proverbs: wisdom should affirm Yahweh's faithful providence and justice, urge reverence and obedience to his teachings and a renunciation of the sort of speculation that inevitably undermines those teachings. Unless tethered to reverence for Yahweh and observance of his commandments, wisdom tends to ungodliness.

These dueling attitudes to wisdom (increasingly "Greek wisdom") attested in the biblical sources continue in nonbiblical Jewish writings of the Hellenistic period. As we shall see in chapter 3, writers like Philo assume an easy juxtaposition or even identification of wisdom and Torah, while other sources follow Deuteronomy's lead in subordinating Wisdom to Torah in an uneasy alliance.

Discourse 3: Divine Law and Historical Narrative

(I) NARRATIVIZING THE LAW AND LAW'S NARRATIVE

The integration of the Law of Moses and wisdom in certain biblical texts led to a "sapientializing" of the Law. By the same token, it may be argued that the integration of law and history led to a "narrativization" of the Law. Chaya Halberstam's work (2007) on the narrativized nature of biblical law reinforces a conception of biblical law as grounded less in divine will or reason than in the nation's story about itself—a story that encompasses past historical experience and future aspirations.[19]

---

[19] Halberstam's article also examines the reverse phenomenon of narratives that approximate the modalities of law. For other studies of the narrativity of biblical law, see the bibliography in Halberstam 2007 and Bartor (2007; 2010); Watts (1999).

Halberstam challenges the notion that there is a strict dichotomy between law and narrative in the Hebrew Bible. She demonstrates that the two genres share rhetorical techniques, with the result that narrative vision and legal praxis are often intertwined.[20] According to Halberstam, the historical and narrative elements of Israelite tradition penetrated the legal in both formal and substantive ways. The lost property commandment in Deuteronomy 22, for example, "exceeds the limits of the legal system and reaches towards narrative to affect the heart of the reader" (2007, 348). The law in question presents conflicting motivations and points of view, emotional reverberation, dramatic tension, and "a gesture towards resolution" (355). Employing the second-person "you," the law invites its addressees to identify with the unfolding minidrama in order to awaken their sympathy, remind them of who they are, and persuade them to do what Yahweh's people should do.[21]

The intertwining of law and narrative is achieved not only by the interpenetration of the rhetorical forms of these two genres. It is most dramatically achieved by the placement of biblical law within a larger narrative frame. The laws and commandments are preceded by a detailed historical account that stretches from creation through the patriarchal period, Israel's enslavement in and liberation from Egypt, and the encounter with Yahweh at Sinai. What is the purpose of this narrative presentation of the Law?

Although Israel's laws developed in a specific environment over an extended period of time, the biblical text imagines a different narrative and retrojects Israelite law to an approximately forty-year period beginning with the Israelites' escape from Egypt under Moses's leadership and ending with Moses's death on the plains of Moab. It is this imagined history, this narrative, that furnishes the Law with its specific meaning and purpose. Brague (2007, 62) argues that one immediate purpose of the history supplied for the Law may be seen in its emphasis on "a place within which the law pertained." Yahweh announces that he has brought the Israelites, quite literally, "to me"—to Yahweh himself and soon to his land, where they will be able to dwell with the divine presence by obeying his laws. According to the larger biblical narrative, Yahweh has been seeking suitable tenants for his land for some time. The Amorites were expelled because they did not honor the "house rules" (Gen 15:16; Lev 18:24–25, 27) and now Yahweh places his hopes on Israel (Lev 18:26, 28–30; Deut 8:7–20). Brague (2007, 58) likens the terms of the covenant to residency requirements set by the master of the land for those who wish to live in it with him. These

---

[20] Certainly, as Halberstam herself readily admits, some laws more closely approximate the modalities of narrative than do others. On the continuum between law and narrative, the laws of Deuteronomy, for example, lie closer to narrative than do some other biblical legal passages (2007, 361n10).

[21] See Watts (1999, 129), who claims that the Hebrew Bible presents a "dialectic of identification and alienation [that] intends to persuade readers of who they are and what they should do. The Pentateuch's rhetoric aims to convince its readers to be the true Israel" (cited in Halberstam 2007, 361).

requirements will have the effect of shaping the people, of molding their character as individuals and as a nation.

> The aim of the commandments is not to impose obedience but to provide an entry into the divine mores. Entering into the land of God is also, by that token, entering into the intimacy of the One who lives there.
>
> The overall framework, with its opening note of an experience of liberation, gives meaning to the commandments. Only men who have first been liberated can live according to them. Their aim is not to reduce men to slavery, to make them the slaves of God. To the contrary, it is to concretize their liberty in a conduct worthy of free men—people who, precisely because they are "gentlemen," and because *noblesse oblige*, will not permit themselves bad behavior.
>
> ... Thus the deepest meaning of the law is no less than life with the divinity.

On this view, Israel's Law is rooted in her particular historical experience and in the stories she tells about herself and her relationship with the deity, Yahweh. The Law draws upon the national myth of liberation and covenant in projecting a vision of what might be: the establishment of a holy community living on holy soil in the very presence of the divine.

Motive clauses that reference events of Israel's history appeal to the Law's addressees not only as rational creatures capable of moral reasoning (as argued in the previous section), but as members of a community whose story and shared experiences serve as the wellspring for moral behavior. Motive clauses are tied to the community's historical relationship with a deity whose behavior should be imitated (*imitatio dei*).

> For Yahweh your god is god [Elohim] supreme and lord supreme, the great, the mighty, and the awesome god [El] who shows no favor and takes no bribe, but upholds the cause of the fatherless and the widow, and befriends the stranger, providing him with food and clothing. You too must befriend the stranger, for you were strangers in the land of Egypt. (Deut 10:17–19)

The Israelites are urged to do as Yahweh their god does by befriending the stranger. The nation's historical experience has furnished the Israelites not only with an empathic understanding of the stranger's situation but also a knowledge of the divine mores. In this way, the narrative of Yahweh's selection of, and relationship with, Israel as a covenant partner contextualizes and nourishes the behaviors regulated and idealized by the Law.

Drawing on Robert Cover's notion of narratives that connect a community's social construction of reality to its visions of what the world might be, Steven Fraade (2005, 82–83) highlights the intersection and interdependency of the discursive modes of law and narrative in the Hebrew Bible:

[T]he divine commandments are themselves central events in the biblical soteriological narrative, while that narrative confers both historical and teleological meaning upon the commandments.

These features are evident in Exodus 19:3–7:

Yahweh called to him from the mountain, saying, "Thus shall you say to the house of Jacob and declare to the children of Israel: 'You have seen what I did to the Egyptians, how I bore you on eagles' wings and brought you to me. Now then, if you will obey me faithfully and keep my covenant, you shall be my treasured possession among all the peoples. Indeed, all the earth is mine, but you shall be to me a kingdom of priests and a holy nation.'" (Ex 19:3b–7)

Yahweh's self-introduction in this passage alludes to his *past* defeat of the Egyptians and protection of the Israelites on their journey from Egypt to Sinai. Yahweh offers Israel his covenant in the *present* and informs her that obedience to the covenant will seal her *future* as God's treasured possession and as a holy nation. While some ancient Near Eastern legal collections contain prologues, none provides a continuous historical context—past, present, and future—for its laws as Israel does (Blenkinsopp 1995, 97).

Jon Levenson (1985) is among those who have asserted that the purpose of this unique biblical presentation is to ground Israel's obligations to Yahweh *in the history of his acts on her behalf*.[22]

The leading theological implication of the historical prologue, then, is that it provides a grounding for the obligations Israel felt to God, a grounding that comes not from introspection or philosophical speculation, but from the recitation of a story ... In sum, the historical prologue provides the data from which the nature of YHWH the reliable suzerain can be known. (42)

[A]ll that history reveals about YHWH is that he has been faithful and gracious to Israel. The community comes into the fuller knowledge of God through a life of observance of the *mitsvot* [commandments]. History is the foreground of observance, but observance is the teleological end of history. (44)

According to Levenson (44), the commandments are not subservient to history. Rather, the telos of history is a continuing life under the Law for the purpose of creating a holy community.

History is recited so as to elicit a consciousness of obligation, a response to unmerited benevolence, and an awareness of the reliability of the

---

[22] See also Bartor 2010, 18.

would-be suzerain. History is prologue. What endures is the mutual relationship between unequals which is the substance of covenant. (45)

Similarly, as Assnat Bartor observes (2010, 20), the laws play a central role in advancing the main story of the Bible, as they constitute a necessary condition for the realization of the divine plan. So it behooves us to ask: What precisely is the Bible's narrative of the divine plan past, present, and future? Did that narrative shift over time? And how precisely does the Law figure in that narrative?

(II) THE LAW AT SINAI: A NARRATIVE CONTINUITY

The giving of the divine law is a watershed moment in the historical narrative of the Pentateuch. It is not uncommon to divide biblical history into the period prior to the giving of the Law (the pre-Sinai period) and the period initiated by the giving of the Law. In the pre-Sinai period, humanity in general turns its back on Yahweh, courting danger and destruction. Only a few individuals trust in the deity. But the covenant with Israel at Sinai ushers in an unprecedented era of divine-human interaction and even intimacy. Yahweh's redemption of the Israelites from slavery in Egypt was a redemption for a *purpose*, a purpose that becomes clear at Sinai where the people receive Yahweh's laws and bind themselves to the deity in covenant. Thus, the natural literary climax of the Pentateuch is the giving of the divine law at Sinai, and the climax of the Sinai episode comes with Yahweh's descent to dwell, finally, on earth with his covenant community (Ex 40:34–38).

The idea of divine law as the vehicle of an intimate divine-human relationship finds profound expression in the following text:

> You shall faithfully observe my commandments; I am Yahweh. You shall not profane my holy name, so that I may be sanctified in the midst of the Israelite people—I, Yahweh, who sanctify you, I who brought you out of the land of Egypt to be your god, I, Yahweh. (Lev 22:31–32)

This text expresses the idea that through Israel's observance of the divine law, Yahweh and Israel sanctify one another. First, Yahweh sanctifies Israel by redeeming her, making her a special possession from among the nations, and sealing the relationship with the giving of a covenant whose instructions would serve as the blueprint for Israel's holy vocation. In turn, Israel sanctifies Yahweh by living out that vocation, by faithfully observing the commandments and becoming a holy people. In the covenant relationship as embodied by the divine laws, Yahweh and Israel meet in a reciprocal sanctification.

In the biblical narrative, Sinai is both telos and ideal, and this double-barreled conception has two important corollaries. First, if the giving of the divine law is the telos of history, then the pre-Sinai period will likely be seen as preparing for that telos, rather than radically discontinuous with it. In keeping with this idea, the biblical narrative intimates that the pre-Sinai period was not entirely devoid of law. Yahweh is depicted as revealing his will to humans not all at once at Sinai, but in small increments, beginning in Eden with a commandment to the first couple to be fruitful and multiply. Admittedly, Yahweh's next attempt to set the conditions for human flourishing (establishing a prohibition that would guarantee continued human access to immortality through the tree of life) did not succeed, and humans exchanged eternal life for free will,[23] but Yahweh was not dissuaded from continued attempts to communicate instructions to benefit humankind and enable divine-human intimacy. These communications include the blood prohibition given to Noah, the commandment of circumcision given to Abraham, and laws regarding the Passover given to the Israelites while they were in Egypt, until finally the full terms of the divine law are revealed in the forty-year period initiated at Sinai. On this reading, there is no disjunction between Sinai and the period that preceded it, no "law-free" period that was suddenly succeeded by a period characterized by law. Instead, the narrative posits a gradual unfolding of Yahweh's instructions for humankind from the moment of creation until the full revelation at Sinai.

The second corollary of the narrative presentation of Sinai as both telos and ideal concerns not the pre-Sinai past but the messianic future. Because the giving of the divine law represents an ideal, some prophetic texts envisage the future messianic age as the time for the full and final establishment of the Law. According to this prophetic narrative, the three ages—pre-Sinai past, present Sinaitic dispensation, and messianic future—lie on a single narrative continuum whose telos is the full articulation and perfect implementation of Yahweh's divine law by his covenant partner living in his land in the sight of all the nations.

> In the days to come
> The Mount of Yahweh's House
> Shall stand firm above the mountains
> And tower above the hills;
> And all the nations
> Shall gaze on it with joy.
> And the many peoples shall go and say:
> "Come,
> Let us go up to the Mount of Yahweh,
> To the House of the god of Jacob;
> That he may instruct us in his ways,
> And that we may walk in his paths."
> For instruction [*torah*] shall come forth from Zion,
> The word of Yahweh from Jerusalem.
>
> (Isa 2:2–3)

---

[23] See Gen 3:9, 16–17, 22–24. For a fuller analysis of Gen 3, see Hayes 2012, 49–50.

When Yahweh rescues the crushed and scattered Israelites and reinstalls them in his land under his divine law, other nations will finally recognize the wisdom and virtue of Yahweh's Teaching and renounce their hostilities, ushering in an era of peace. Israel will be the instrument of a universal recognition of Yahweh, which will in turn enable Israel finally to dwell securely in her land. This prophetic narrative vision embodies the biblical understanding of *salvation*—an utterly this-worldly, political understanding: an end to the wars and exile that have plagued the nation from its inception, and the fulfillment of the ancient promise that Israel will dwell undisturbed in Yahweh's land, under Yahweh's divine law. Isaiah 11 waxes poetic in its description of the total absence of violence that will characterize this era—a time when the lion and lamb will lie peacefully together, and even the viper will pose no threat. This messianic vision doesn't merely envisage the full reign of Yahweh's Torah; *it is predicated upon it*—without worldwide admiration for Yahweh's divine law, Israel will never enjoy peace.

A distinctively new note is sounded by the two prophets of the destruction—Jeremiah and Ezekiel—in response to the tragic events of history. The destruction in 586 BCE brought Israel to the brink of a crisis, and many abandoned Yahweh in the conviction that Yahweh had abandoned them (Jer 44:15–19). Others accepted the prophetic judgment that the destruction was Yahweh's just punishment for sin, but even they were troubled by the future. Certainly, the people's observance of Yahweh's Torah was not perfect, but was total destruction really warranted? And if the nation is restored, won't the same thing happen again?

Jeremiah and Ezekiel addressed the doubts of the community in the depths of its despair. In an effort to comfort the nation and encourage continued fidelity to Yahweh, they promised a future that would be easier and more secure than the present. The day would come, they said, when Israel would follow Yahweh's house rules effortlessly. She would no longer struggle to obey the divine law; her obedience would be automatic. Yahweh would see to it.

> See, a time is coming—declares Yahweh—when I will make a new covenant with the House of Israel and the House of Judah. It will not be like the covenant I made with their fathers, when I took them by the hand to lead them out of the land of Egypt, a covenant which they broke, so that I rejected them—declares the Lord. But such is the covenant I will make with the House of Israel after these days—declares Yahweh: I will put my teaching into their inmost being and inscribe it upon their hearts. Then I will be their god and they shall be my people. No longer will they need to teach one another and say to one another, "Heed Yahweh;" for all of them, from the least of them to the greatest, shall heed me—declares Yahweh. (Jer 31:31–34)

Jeremiah prophesies an ingathering of the exiles of Israel and Judah and a new covenant etched on the heart, encoded as it were into human nature. We see a similar idea in Ezekiel:

> I will take you from among the nations and gather you from all the countries, and I will bring you back to your own land. I will sprinkle clean water upon you, and you shall be clean: I will cleanse you from all your uncleanness and from all your fetishes. And I will give you a new heart and put a new spirit into you: I will remove the heart of stone from your body and give you a heart of flesh; and I will put my spirit into you. Thus I will cause you to follow my laws and faithfully to observe my rules. Then you shall dwell in the land which I gave to your fathers, and you shall be my people and I will be your god. (36:24–25)

Significantly, for both of these prophets, it is not the law that will change in the messianic future. The same laws and rules will continue to function as residency requirements for those who would live in Yahweh's land. What will change is *human nature*. Israel will be hardwired to obey Yahweh's will without effort or struggle. The *elimination of human moral freedom* is nothing less than a utopian redesign of human nature, in which the difficulties associated with the exercise of moral freedom are obviated. With perfect knowledge of Yahweh's teaching, obedience to the divine law is automatic, a state we may refer to as "robo-righteousness."[24]

The prophets' utopian vision—comforting in a time of national defeat and despair—represents an extraordinary turn in the Bible's historical narrative, which is predicated upon the notion of moral freedom. It contests the givenness and the value of the moral freedom that underwrites the biblical notion of covenant, as well as the biblical understanding of divine law. The Garden of Eden story in Genesis 2–3 establishes the moral autonomy of humans gained at the cost of immortality. By eating from the tree of the knowledge of good and evil, humans learn that they are free moral agents able to choose actions in conformity with the divine will (good) or in defiance of it (evil). Indeed, the one clear limitation that the biblical text places on its divine being is the unpredictable element of human moral autonomy. On more than one occasion the deity must adjust his plans and respond to the unforeseen and surprising choices

---

[24] To be clear: These passages are not making a sophisticated philosophical claim about the elimination of free will in every respect. They express a simple longing for a time when God's teachings will be so completely internalized that people *will have neither the desire nor the ability to sin.* They will *know* what is right without study, and they will *do* what is right without struggle, as if the alternative doesn't even occur to them. The term "robo-righteousness" is intended to point to the condition in which sin is simply not an option, and doing the right thing flows automatically and effortlessly from one's knowledge of the divine instruction. It does not point to an erasure of all agency. Presumably, persons will still make choices of all kinds. But the choice to sin is off the table.

of humans.[25] Both Moses and Joshua present the covenant as a free choice: "I call heaven and earth to witness against you this day, that I have set before you life and death, blessing and curse; therefore choose life, that you may live, you and your offspring (Deut 30:19; cf. Josh 24:14–15). In addition, Yahweh accompanies his instructions and commandments with promises of reward and punishment, and exhortations to obedience that clearly assume Israel can choose to obey or disobey.

Thus, the destruction-era promise of a future robo-righteousness flies in the face of a general biblical narrative of divine law that assumes moral freedom and, while promoting aspirationalism, does not expect or postulate human perfection (as indicated by the inclusion of remedies for violations). Indeed, insofar as Jeremiah and Ezekiel assume that perfect Torah observance will require a future redesign of human nature and elimination of moral freedom that only God can effect, they reinforce the general biblical narrative—perfect Torah obedience is neither expected nor required of human beings as they are. It is only in the messianic age that the conditions for Israel's perfect fulfillment of the divine law—world peace arising from the universal recognition of Yahweh, the elimination of Israel's moral freedom, and the internalization of Yahweh's teaching—will finally prevail.

(III) THE LAW AT SINAI: A NARRATIVE OF RUPTURE AND RESTORATION

In some postbiblical writings, however, the linear narrative described above is eclipsed, and the relative values of the pre-Sinai period and the age ushered in by the giving of the divine law at Sinai are reversed. In these writings, the giving of the divine law represents a radical discontinuity and a falling away from an original ideal. The divine law is not the climactic telos of a linear historical continuum that will reach its full glory in a law-filled messianic era; it is a deviation from an original law-free state and must be overcome in order that a *law-free* messianic era may be (re)established. What biblical resources would support an interpretation of the biblical narrative along these lines?

To the extent that Eden represents an idyllic existence, the absence of the full Torah (as revealed at Sinai) may be interpreted as a sign that the "golden age" of the past, like the "golden age" of the future, is precisely law-free. Indeed, it is only after the introduction of a divine prohibition in Genesis 2:16–17, and the attendant discovery of human free will, that humans are expelled from the garden and access to eternal life. This will suggest to some readers that divine law is conducive not to divine-human intimacy but to divine-human estrangement. The revelation of the divine law at Sinai is accompanied by a litany of curses and punishments for its violation (Lev 18:24–30; Deut 27–28) that would seem to undermine an assessment of the Law as a divine gift and blessing.

[25] Gen 2:22–24; 6:5–7; 22:15–17; Ex 32:7–10; 33:2–3 are just a few examples of decisions and choices taken by Yahweh in response to unforeseen and freely willed human actions.

Israel's own experience of repeated invasion, destruction, and exile will be cited as evidence of the divine law's inability to secure the conditions of human flourishing. Moreover, promises of a "new covenant" (the Jeremiah and Ezekiel passages cited above) will be read out of context as an implicit condemnation of the Sinaitic divine law. And finally, a curious text in Ezekiel will be seen as a resource for those who view the divine law of Sinai as not only less than ideal but designedly corrupting. In Ezekiel 20 the people's rebellion in the wilderness causes Yahweh to swear

> ... to them in the wilderness that I would scatter them among the nations and disperse them through the lands, because they did not obey my rules, but rejected my laws, profaned my Sabbaths, and looked with longing to the fetishes of their fathers. Moreover, I gave them laws that were not good and rules by which they could not live: When they set aside every first issue of the womb, I defiled them by their very gifts—that I might render them desolate, that they might know that I am Yahweh. (Ezek 20:23–26)

Ezekiel represents Yahweh as saying that he gave Israel "laws that were not good" as punishment for various sins (v. 21). Given Ezekiel's generally positive view of the divine law, the passage likely seeks to brand some particular law(s) as an evil practice. Verse 26 suggests that the bad law in question has to do with firstling sacrifice. The exact meaning of the passage has exercised many scholars,[26] and the issue cannot be resolved here. For our purposes, the passage is significant for its assertion that Yahweh gave a bad law in order to punish Israel. Similarly, Ezekiel 14:9 states, "And if a prophet is seduced and speaks a word, it was I, Yahweh, who seduced that prophet." Here again Ezekiel represents Yahweh as causing harm to his own people through prophecy that, like law, is a standard tool of divine communication. These texts will be exploited by later readers whose conception of divine law is incompatible with the Sinaitic Law.

(IV) RESOURCES FOR THE CONSTRUCTION
OF THE LAW'S NARRATIVE: A SUMMARY

The predominant biblical narrative about divine law is a linear one in which the Law delivered at Sinai is represented as both the telos of the pre-Sinai period and the ideal for the messianic future. In many passages, particularly in the prophetic books, the messianic future will realize the ideal articulated at Sinai: Yahweh's people established securely and peacefully in Yahweh's land, abiding by his Law and admired by the nations who clamor to know the ways of Yahweh also. For Jeremiah and Ezekiel, this law-filled golden age will be made possible by a divine redesign of human nature that eliminates moral freedom and en-

---

[26] See, for example, Greenberg 1983, 368–70; Patton 1996; Maccoby 1999; Hahn and Bergsma 2004.

sures perfect observance of the Law in a kind of robo-righteousness. This is a narrative that affirms the divine law of Sinai in the present era, and envisions its perfect fulfillment in a messianic era. And it is a narrative that seeks to balance the universalist and particularist trends in the Bible: the particular divine law that nourishes and sustains Yahweh's covenant partner will shine forth from Zion in the messianic future, inspiring among the nations admiration and pacifism at least, recognition and worship of Yahweh at most.

A second and much less fully articulated narrative can be constructed, however, from textual elements that push in a different direction, particularly when decontextualized. This narrative is not linear but circular. It imagines a law-free golden age in Eden, followed by an alienation from Yahweh in some way attributable to or connected with the introduction of divine law, and an ultimate return to that law-free golden age in the messianic future. This is a narrative that diminishes the divine law of Sinai in the present era, and envisions its abolition in the messianic era. It is a narrative in which the biblical tension between universalism and particularism is resolved by imagining the former overcoming the latter: particularism, introduced with the Sinaitic divine law, represents a rupture of an original universalism. With the abolition of that Law in the messianic future, the cosmic universalism established at creation, and ruptured at Sinai, will be restored.

The Multidimensionality of Biblical Divine Law

Contemporary legal theory offers two primary models for understanding the nature and authority of law. According to legal positivism, law is a body of rules expressing the will and enforced by the power of lawmakers and their agents or institutional equivalents. The validity of any given law turns on social facts—its promulgation by structures or institutions of governance whose authority to produce law is socially accepted—rather than the merits of the law's content. By contrast, natural law theory, in all its variations, predicates the validity of any given law on its conformity to some criterion of character, quality, or content. These criteria are variously articulated, but classical natural law theory considers valid only such laws as conform to universal reason.[27]

Less influential than these two primary accounts of the nature and authority of law, the nineteenth-century school of historical jurisprudence located the sources of law in the history of individual nations. According to the historical school, the primary source of law is not reason or will but memory, not equity or legislation but precedent, not rational morality or politics but history.

In this chapter, I have argued that the Hebrew Bible's concept of divine law is complex. Biblical divine law has affinities with all three of the theories of law

---

[27] Some contemporary theories informed by natural law theory insist upon the law's conformity to moral principles, either external to the law or internal to it.

outlined above but no perfect correspondence to any one of them.[28] Indeed, the interweaving of the discourses of will, reason, and history—discourses that are often deemed mutually exclusive in contemporary legal theory—creates a rich and multidimensional conception of divine law that defies easy categorization.

Robert Cover's account of law (1983) captures this multidimensionality. Cover argued that all societies have narratives that situate and give meaning to legal norms. Communal narratives contextualize the behaviors regulated by law.

> No set of legal institutions or prescriptions exists apart from the narratives that locate it and give it meaning. For every constitution there is an epic, for each decalogue a scripture. Once understood in the context of the narratives that give it meaning, law becomes not merely a system of rules to be observed, but a world in which we live.
>
> In this normative world, law and narrative are inseparably related. Every prescription is insistent in its demand to be located in discourse— to be supplied with history and destiny, beginning and end, explanation and purpose. (4–5)
>
> A legal tradition is hence part and parcel of a complex normative world. The tradition includes not only a corpus juris, but also a language and a mythos—narratives in which the corpus juris is located by those whose wills act upon it. (9)

For Cover, the myths or narratives that endow law with meaning, that frame our interpretations of our actions, do not simply enshrine past custom. These narratives, rooted as they are in memory and tradition, also project a vision of what might be, an ideal in the light of which our actions are comprehended, critiqued, and even transformed. Law mediates between the reality in which we find ourselves and the ideals of our narratives, even as narrative explains the connection of our laws to both that which is and that which ought to be.

This brings us full circle to the concept of divine law found in the Hebrew Bible. In the Hebrew Bible, the divine law is provided with both history and destiny, explanation and purpose. Insofar as biblical law is grounded in the nation's story about itself—a story that encompasses past historical experience and future aspirations, and employs narrative techniques to mold and shape character—it may be described as teleological and aspirational. Law acts as the bridge between a present reality and an imagined future—a future in which a communal identity as Yahweh's people living in Yahweh's land in accordance with Yahweh's own mores is a goal to be realized. Moreover, insofar as biblical law is grounded in the nation's story about itself, its addressees and ideal human type are members of a covenant community whose *historical encounter* with a

---

[28] For the difficulties attending any attempt to classify biblical and Jewish law as a species of legal positivism or natural law, see Jackson 2011.

divine sovereign underwrites its continuing fidelity to his *will* for the formation and preservation of a holy, just, and *wise* community.

It is precisely the messy multidimensionality of biblical divine law discourse that enables postbiblical groups in strong disagreement with one another over the nature of divine law to claim a biblical pedigree for their diametrically opposed views. Each will point to and champion one or another dimension of biblical divine law discourse—be it will, reason, or history—and struggle to account for (and perhaps suppress or deny) those dimensions that support a competing conception of divine law.

What prompts postbiblical writers to do this is their encounter with a very different set of discourses of divine law, as set forth in chapter 2.

Greco-Roman Discourses of Law

The cultures of classical antiquity assume a basic dichotomy between divine law and human law. Divine law and human law are defined and characterized in terms of and in contrast to one another. In this chapter, we consider primary discourses associated with divine law (designated G-R 1 and 2) before turning to primary discourses of human law (G-R 3 through 7). In a final section, we examine literary and legal practices (G-R 8–10) in which divine law and human law are juxtaposed in some way. The material in this chapter is organized around these discourses and practices, and no attempt is made to provide a systematic or comprehensive account of individual philosophers or writers.

DISCOURSES OF NATURAL LAW

Discourse 1: Natural Law and Truth—*Logos* and Realism

The core idea of natural law theory is that there exists *in nature* a standard for right and wrong that is not mere convention, but an *independent* standard against which conventional human laws can be measured. Already in Sophocles's *Antigone*, we see the conflict between two norms—the king's *nomos* and "the gods' unwritten and unfailing laws (*nomima*)" (Brown 2009, 335, citing the translation in Lloyd-Jones and Wilson 1990). However, it is not clear that Antigone's unwritten divine law, though attributed to the gods, is grounded in nature (Brown 2009, 337);[1] for this idea we must turn to the philosophical tradition.

---

[1] The term "unwritten law" in Greek texts can refer to long-standing regulations transmitted orally, unwritten social customs and mores, or recognized standards of human conduct (universal moral laws). Although unwritten law cannot be equated with natural law (which refers to an unwritten rational natural order), insofar as it is divine, universally applicable, superior to written law, and on occasion connected to nature, it is very similar to natural law. A third term, "living law," refers to a king who is so just, virtuous, and wise that he embodies the higher law (see below). For these distinctions, see Martens 2003, 1–12.

(I) THE PRE-SOCRATICS

The pre-Socratics (sixth century BCE) introduced the idea of nonconventional standards embedded and discoverable in nature (Brown 2009, 338). Greek thinkers had discovered mathematical laws in music, astronomy, and physical sciences, and philosophers sought universal laws in the social order too. The pre-Socratics drew a connection between the rational order that governs the cosmos and the rational order that should govern human society. The terminology of law and justice came to be applied to both realms: the cosmos was described by Anaximander of Miletus (610–540 BCE) as a law-bound system in which all things exist in a dynamic balance that may be described as justice (Raaflaub 2000, 49).

Heraclitus of Ephesus (535–475 BCE) posited a universal reason or *logos* that governs the unified cosmos, and linked this *logos* to law: "For all human laws are fed by the one divine law" (Fragments, DK B114). This is not simply the idea that the gods support human laws, or that Zeus has given to humans a capacity for justice which is realized through the laws they create (an idea found already in Hesiod, eighth century BCE); rather, Heraclitus's radical claim is that human laws are grounded in the single rational order (*logos*) of nature and are thus neither conventional nor relativistic (Brown 2009, 340). Heraclitus followed Anaximander in postulating a correspondence between the order and balance (justice) in nature and the order and balance essential to human societies, attributing great importance to the middle or "right measure" (*metrion*) (Raaflaub 2000, 50). The rational principles in nature are not merely descriptive regularities but, because they are divine and governing, prescriptive norms for appropriate human behavior (Brown 2009, 341). This divine standard for human law is discoverable by human inquiry into the workings of both the cosmos and the human individual since humans can find within themselves the universal *logos* that orders the cosmos (ibid. 342–43).[2]

(II) THE STOICS

It was the Stoics who developed a full-blown theory of natural law.[3] The Stoics were the first to use the phrase "divine law" (*theios nomos*) to refer to natural law, because for the Stoics, God was not distinct from nature. God was nature; nature was divine. Therefore the rational order or eternal reason (*logos*) of nature is none other than the eternal reason of God. To say that law is divine is

---

[2] Not all are equipped for such an inquiry, however, and here Heraclitus expresses a pessimism that will reach full flower in later political philosophies that promote rule by experts (Socrates's political experts, Plato's philosopher-kings, Aristotle's aristocratic rulers, and the Stoic sage-king).

[3] However, the term "natural law" (*nomos phuseos*) occurs only six times in Greek literature before its appearance in Cicero's descriptions of the Stoics (in Latin, *lex naturae*) and in Philo; nevertheless, the Stoics had a clear concept of natural law (Martens 2003, 14).

to say that it is the eternal reason, rational order, of nature or the eternal mind of God.

The early Stoics adopted Heraclitus's notion of a natural standard for all civil laws and human behavior, tempered by a Platonic caution about universal exceptionless formulations (Brown 2009, 353; see Discourse 2 below). The right reason in nature cannot be codified in exceptionless rules, yet the Stoics continued to speak of it as law, because, like the Cynics, they were committed to locating normative authority in nature rather than convention (Brown 2009, 353). The Stoics emphasized the sharp distinction between *unwritten* divine law and *written* positive laws (human laws). Laws that are written are by definition human in the Stoic view because the divine law is not a code of written directives;[4] it is reason itself, the unchanging rational order of the cosmos that transcends the particulars of human existence and is therefore universal.

(III) DIVINE LAW'S ALLIANCE WITH TRUTH

The universal, rational, and unchanging character of the divine natural law underwrites its alliance with truth in classical thought. The alliance of natural law and truth is emphasized in the *Minos*, a dialogue attributed to Plato and included with his works in antiquity, but probably originating in the ambit of Plato's Academy. This dialogue asserts an intelligible natural standard for distinguishing genuine law from false law. In it, Socrates provides a realist definition of law as a true opinion and a discovery of "what is" (*Minos* 315a3, 315b1), as opposed to his interlocutor's more conventional understanding of law as the agreed communal opinion of a city's citizens. The definition of law as the discovery of "what is" (a mind-independent or objective reality) entails the further view that the law does not change, because "what really is" does not change. However, because human legislators do not always succeed in discovering the "unchanging truth," they make different laws at different times (315b2–5). Since genuine law itself never changes, the shifting legislation of human communities is not strictly speaking law. Thus, the word "law" is used in two senses: on the one hand the true law, and on the other human legislation.

(IV) CICERO'S FORMULATION OF STOIC DIVINE LAW THEORY

The first-century BCE Roman philosopher and political theorist Cicero, loyal to Plato's Academy but sympathetic to Stoicism and the Peripatetic tradition, described the Stoic doctrine of natural law. It is *his* Platonized formulation of Stoic natural law theory that spread throughout Western Europe via the church fathers. According to Cicero, there is only one true law: right reason, which is in accordance with nature. This universal rational law of nature (*logos*) is everywhere the same and unchangeably and eternally binding upon all peoples and

---

[4] To be sure, positive laws can also be unwritten customs or usages agreed upon by convention. The point is that while conventional laws are both written and unwritten, natural law is *never* written.

nations. To alter the natural law of right reason by human legislation is never morally right, and to abolish it is impossible.

(1) True law is right reason, in agreement with nature, diffused over everyone, consistent, everlasting, whose nature is to advocate duty by prescription and to deter wrongdoing by prohibition. (2) Its prescriptions and prohibitions are heeded by good men though they have no effect on the bad. (3) It is wrong to alter this law, nor is it permissible to repeal any part of it, and it is impossible to abolish it entirely. We cannot be absolved from this law by senate or people, nor need we look for any outside interpreter of it, or commentator. (4) There will not be a different law at Rome and at Athens, or a different law now and in the future, but one law, everlasting and immutable, will hold good for all peoples and all times. (5) And there will be one master and ruler for us all in common, god who is the founder of this law, its promulgator and its judge. (6) Whoever does not obey it is fleeing from himself and treating his human nature with contempt; by this very fact he will pay the heaviest penalty, even if he escapes all conventional punishments. (Cicero, *Republic* 3.33 [*SVF* 3.325])[5]

The authority of natural law is justified on internal rational grounds and not on the external coercive power of a sovereign will. Cicero distinguishes true (natural law) from conventional law:

[L]aw is the highest reason, rooted in nature, which commands things that must be done and prohibits the opposite. *When this same reason is secured and established in the human mind, it is law ... [L]aw is a power of nature, it is the mind and reason of the prudent man*, it distinguishes justice and injustice. But since all our speech is based on popular conceptions we must sometimes speak in popular terms and call that a law (in the language of the common people) which prescribes *in writing* what it wants by *ordering or forbidding*. But in establishing the nature of justice, let us begin from that highest law, which was born aeons before any law was written or indeed before any state was established. (Cicero, *De leg.* 1.18–19; emphasis added)[6]

The written rules and prohibitions of political states are not in a genuine sense law. They are positive legislation invented by humans and coercively enforced by a sovereign will to secure the basic conditions of a peaceful common life and to achieve certain social, political, and material ends. They do not necessarily deal with truth on the one hand, or the cultivation of a virtuous and rational character on the other, which is the true goal of the one true natural

---

[5] As found in Long and Sedley 1987, 1:432–33.
[6] Translations of *De legibus* are taken from Zetzel 1999.

law. Genuine law is known by its character (its correspondence to truth and justice) rather than its mode of promulgation by a legislating authority.

> The legislation that has been written down for nations in different ways and for particular occasions has the name of law more as a matter of courtesy than as a fact; for they teach that every law that deserves that name is praiseworthy, using arguments such as these: it is generally agreed that laws were invented for the well-being of citizens, the safety of states, and the calm and happy life of humans; and that those who first ordained legislation of this sort demonstrated to their peoples that they would write and carry such legislation the adoption of which would make their lives honorable and happy; and that what was so composed and ordained they would call laws. From this it should be understood that those who wrote decrees that were destructive and unjust to their peoples, since they did the opposite of what they had promised and claimed, produced something utterly different from laws; so that it should be clear that in the interpretation of the word "law" itself there is the significance and intention of choosing something just and right. (Cicero, *De leg.* 2.11)

Only the wise, or rationally perfect, grasp the natural law, and such persons have no need of positive law because the highest law resides in their minds:

> Therefore, just as that divine mind is the highest law, so too when in a human being it is brought to maturity, it resides in the mind of wise men. (Cicero, *De leg.* 2.11)

(V) THE STOIC REJECTION OF PLATONIC REALISM

Even as they asserted the existence of a *universal* natural law and a natural justice, which is the right reason that governs the world-city, the Stoics denied realism, that is, the mind-independent existence of *universals*.[7] Plato (like Socrates) was committed to the idea that parallel to the sensible world, there is a nonsensible world of unchanging intelligible existents or "Forms." These Forms arise from reason alone (they include, for example, abstract definitions, concepts, and universals) and are the only truly "real" things because they do not come into being or pass away. We grasp these Forms through sensible things when we perceive the intelligible in them; observing particular instances of the good or the just, we grasp the absolute Form of Goodness or Justice.

Plato's moral realism is evident in the *Euthyphro*, according to which piety, which is loved by the gods, is not piety because the gods love it; rather, the gods love it because it is piety—independent of the gods (10a–11b). In other

---

[7] See Plutarch's account of Chrysippus's views in *Stoic rep.* 1035c; see also Schofield 2000b, 451.

words, "piety is something *there* to be discovered, not something we, or the gods, create" (Penner 2000, 174). Universals, concepts, and abstract entities have an ontological reality outside of particular concrete things and minds.

By contrast, Stoics are not realists. They deny the existence of universals and abstractions *independent* of particular concrete things and particular minds.[8] To be sure, universals, concepts, and abstract entities have *existence*, but only in concrete things and minds:

> (Zeno's doctrine) They say that concepts are neither somethings nor qualified, but figments of the soul which are quasi-somethings and quasi-qualified. These, they say, are what the old philosophers called Ideas ... The Stoic philosophers say that there are no Ideas, and that what we 'participate in' is the concepts ... (Stobaeus 1.136,21–137,6 [*SVF* 1.65]; as found in Long and Sedley 1987, 1:179)

> The Stoics of Zeno's school said that the Ideas were our own concepts. (Aetius 1.10.5 [*SVF* 1.65]; as found in Long and Sedley 1987, 1:179)

For our purposes, it is important to note that the rejection of the mind-independent reality of universals is not incompatible with the idea of a universal right reason found in particular, individual minds. Moreover, insofar as it denies the mind-independent existence of ideas and universals, this Stoic conceptualism has a decidedly nominalist ring to it (a point that will be taken up in chapter 5).

(VI) SUMMARY

Discourse 1 features a clear dichotomy, particularly in its full Stoic formulation. On the one hand, natural or divine law is a rational order that is unwritten, universal, eternal, and unchanging; it is static in its perfection insofar as it is rational truth or *logos*; it is everywhere and always the same; it is internalized and followed by the wise man; and on some accounts (e.g., the *Minos*), the alliance of natural law with truth confers upon the law a mind-independent reality. On the other hand, separate and distinct from the natural law is positive law. Positive law consists of concrete rules and prohibitions that are posited by human beings and delivered in written form, in words and sentences, and enforced by coercive authority; it is particular to a given state; it is subject to change and evolution over time; it is conducive not to the inculcation of truth or virtue but simply to the good order of society; and the truly wise man doesn't need it because he follows the dictates of reason automatically. Thus, if one were to ask what is divine about divine law, the natural law answer would

---

[8] Realism holds that universals and abstract entities possess a mind-independent existence, while nominalism holds that abstractions exist, but not independent of a particular concrete object or mind. See further chapter 5.

be—its rational, and therefore universal, eternal, and unchanging character in accordance with "truth," and, on some accounts at least, with "what is."[9]

Discourse 2: Natural Law and Cosmopolitanism

The universalism of the natural law lies at the heart of Stoic cosmopolitanism: if there is a law, right reason, that governs the cosmos as law governs a city, then the cosmos may be likened to a city, or cosmopolis. The import of the metaphor is that one's community extends beyond one's native city (and may be understood less democratically to embrace an elite community of the wise, or more democratically to embrace all humanity as subjects of the natural law)—a view that on occasion encouraged a disengagement from civic affairs.

Stoic cosmopolitanism was influenced by the Cynics. When the Cynic philosopher Diogenes of Sinope was asked where he came from, he reputedly responded, "I am a citizen of the world [kosmopolitēs]" (Diogenes Laertius, bk. 6, chap. 63). Diogenes employed the term politēs, which indicates membership in a specific society, in order to connote membership in and allegiance to the cosmos. His cosmopolitanism was a rejection of the restrictions and exclusions inherent in civic affiliations; it freed him to live according to nature rather than the laws and conventions of the polis. According to John Moles (2000, 434),

> In asserting a 'cosmopolitanism' which rejected the city and transmuted the very notion of citizenship into a metaphor for the Cynic life according to universal nature, the Cynics provided the impetus for a crucial move in ancient political thought: that between theories based on the polis and those based on natural law.

Zeno of Citium (fourth–third centuries BCE), the founder of Stoicism, envisaged the ideal republic in cosmopolitan terms:

> The much admired Republic of Zeno ... is aimed at this one point, that our household arrangements should not be based on cities or parishes, each one marked out by its own legal system, but we should regard all men as our fellow-citizens and local residents, and there should be one way of life and order, like that of a herd grazing together and nurtured by a common law. (Plutarch, On the Fortune of Alexander 329A–B SVF 1.262 part, as cited in Long and Sedley, 1987, 1:429)

Zeno championed life lived according to nature, and since nature is governed by universal reason (logos), happiness is achieved only through a rational consistency that produces "a good flow of life." Zeno's rejection of certain con-

---

[9] Again, in contrast to the realist conception of the law articulated in the Minos, the Stoics denied the mind-independent reality of universals. For a fuller discussion of realist and nominalist approaches to the law, see chapter 5.

ventions, including existing educational curricula, the use of currency, and various sexual taboos, was muted by later Stoic thinkers. The latter developed Zeno's community of the good and wise into a doctrine of the cosmic city, and the definition of life in accordance with nature came to include marriage and child rearing, altruism, and involvement in the public life of the state.

Stoic cosmopolitanism made apolitical or metaphorical use of political terms such as "city," "citizen," "free," "slave," and "king." According to Cicero (*De leg.* 1.23), the Stoics held that the only true city is the community of gods and humans governed by the law of right reason (the natural law), which is to say persons of wisdom and virtue (Schofield 2000b, 452). Thus, the cosmopolitanism of the Stoics is not a democratic world community but a "state" composed of gods and sages. In this state,

> [The Stoics say]: Only he [the wise man] is free, but the inferior are slaves. For freedom is the power of autonomous action, but slavery is the lack of autonomous action ... Besides being free the wise are also kings, since kingship is rule that is answerable to no one; and this can occur only among the wise. (Diogenes Laertius 7.121–22; as found in Long and Sedley 1987, 1:431–32)

According to Musonius Rufus, a first-century CE Stoic, since kingship is a means for exercising the virtues of justice and self-control, only the wise person can be considered a true king, even if he is "king" only over himself and his household (Gill 2000, 603).

Stoic philosophers of the imperial period maintained the Stoic focus on the brotherhood of humankind, natural law, cosmopolitanism, and the shared city of gods and humans. For some, universal citizenship dwarfed local political allegiances and justified a withdrawal from the life of the polis, while others maintained that the Stoic goal of life according to virtue was best pursued within the context of a specific community. Marcus Aurelius (second century CE) bridges the two with the Stoic idea of dual citizenship:

> What benefits each thing is living in consistency with its own constitution and nature; my nature is rational and political. As Antoninus, my city and native land is Rome, as a human being it is the universe. The only thing that is good for me is what benefits both these cities. (*Meditations* 6.44; as cited in Rowe and Schofield 2000, 613)

The Stoic metaphor of the cosmopolis could be applied to Roman imperialism, and Cicero hints toward this in his construction of "an idealized version of the ancestral Roman laws to serve as a codification of natural law—exactly the law that is supposed to apply to all human beings" (Brown 2009, 359). In this way the cosmopolis governed by the natural law was connected with real-world imperialism.

DISCOURSES OF HUMAN POSITIVE LAW

Discourse 3: Law and Virtue—the Inadequacy of Positive Law

The primary Greco-Roman discourses of positive human law are marked by a deep ambivalence. Whether the norms of right and wrong that exist in nature can be codified into exceptionless human laws, conducive to virtue and justice, was a matter of considerable doubt (Brown 2009, 347).

(I) POSITIVE LAW AND THE MYTH OF A FALLEN WORLD

According to Plato, the only regime conducive to virtue is direct rule by the gods, as occurred in a past mythological age. Drawing on Hesiod's myth of the golden age of Cronos, Plato describes an original age in which the deity himself guided the world in its course (*Statesman* 269c–270c). Various lower deities or demigods were shepherds of various species, and there was no violence or predation, no war or quarrel. The life of humankind was blessed and spontaneous: the earth yielded its fruits in abundance; humans lived naked in the temperate climate; there were no forms of government or separate possession of women and children (271d–272b). But when the cycle was complete, "the pilot of the ship of the universe ... let go the handle of its rudder and retired to his conning tower in a place apart" (272e). Fate and innate desire reversed the motion of the world, the lesser gods also relinquished control over their dominions, and confusion reigned (272e–273a). In time, the universe righted itself and resumed its earlier course but less perfectly because of the bodily element in its constitution. Nature in its *fallen* (not its original) state was a place of danger and violence for unskilled humans, who had to acquire skills and resources to ensure their survival, including the ability to order their lives. While the political order is therefore a rescue from a state of chaos and disorder, it is clearly an imperfect substitute for direct guidance by divine beings, necessitated by a fall from an originary golden age of law-free abundance and divine care. This idea is explicit in Plato's *Laws*, where the golden age is described as the ideal regime, to which we can now only aspire:

> In that age of bliss, all life needs were provided in abundance and unsought, and the reason, we are told, was this: Cronus was of course aware that, as we have explained, no human being is competent to wield an irresponsible control over mankind without becoming swollen with pride and unrighteousness. Being alive to this he gave our communities as their kings and magistrates, not men but spirits, beings of diviner and superior kind ... he set over us this superior race of spirits who took charge of us ... providing us with peace and mercy, sound law and unscented justice, and endowing the families of mankind with internal concord and happiness. So the story teaches us today, and teaches us truly, that when a com-

munity is ruled not by God but by man, its members have no refuge from evil and misery. We should do our utmost—this is the moral—to reproduce the life of the age of Cronus, and therefore should order our private households and our public societies alike in obedience to the immortal element within us [reason], giving the name of law to the appointment of understanding. (*Laws* 713c–714a)[10]

The only true regime is rule by the gods. Thus, our current and nonideal condition—a condition in which human affairs are no longer managed directly by Cronos and the daimonic spirits—necessitates the emergence of political arts and persons possessing expertise in these arts and employing the faculty of reason, which is the immortal element within us. The only way to realize the ideal city—or a close approximation thereof—is to establish rule by persons who are passionately committed to, and educated toward the achievement of, a comprehensive and rational knowledge of eternal reality and truth. As Malcom Schofield (2000a, 227) notes, "Only philosophers can grasp the order and harmony they find in eternal reality, and only they can be guaranteed to reproduce them in their own lives and those of the citizens, both by the constitutional provisions they institute and by personal moral influence."

(II) HUMAN LAW AS A SECOND-BEST OPTION AND A FAILURE

Plato recommends rule by philosophers but is pessimistic about the dearth of experts possessing true knowledge. And so we are forced, as a second-best option, to make do with laws.

> I grant you readily that if ever, by God's mercy, a man were born with the capacity to attain to this perception, he would need no laws to govern him. No law or ordinance whatever has the right to sovereignty over true knowledge ... But, as things are, such insight is nowhere to be met with, except in faint vestiges, and so we have to choose the second best, ordinance and law. Now they can consider most cases and provide for them, but not all, and this is why I have said what I have said. (*Laws* 875c–d)

The alternative is chaos: "Mankind must either give themselves a law and regulate their lives by it, or live no better than the wildest of wild beasts, and that for the following reason" (*Laws* 875a).

The *Laws* imagines an expert statesman whose laws are an "imitation of the truth" so far as that is possible, and who adjusts the law according to circumstances; but when a ruler lacks knowledge or expertise, the written law reigns. Moreover, in the absence of the required expertise, the written law may not be changed (Rowe 2000, 249). Positive laws are a resented necessity (857e10–858c1; Laks 2000, 261) because they must remain fixed—imperfect though

---

[10] All translations of Plato's *Laws* are by A. E. Taylor, as found in Hamilton and Cairns 2005.

they be—as long as no alternative can be devised by reason (Rowe 2000, 257). Although born of necessity, they are nevertheless the result of failure. As André Laks writes (266):

> [T]his necessity is not—as with the agricultural laws—imposed by basic human needs. It signals rather a failure of education. This explains why this part of the legislative task takes place under the sign of 'shame'. (853b4)

Positive law represents a failure of education because the truly wise do not stand in need of laws themselves. Because of their proper education they are able to attain a knowledge of the order and harmony of eternal reality that govern the wise man. Thus, in Plato's *Republic*, Socrates argues that it is useless to legislate concerning business and contracts, the regulation of markets and harbors, as well as personal deportment, manners, and customs, because those who have been properly educated are in no need of such legislation, while those who have not been properly educated will pay no heed to them:

> [Adeimantus:] Nay, 'twould not be fitting, he said, to dictate to good and honorable men. For most of the enactments that are needed about these things they will easily, I presume, discover.

> [Socrates:] I, then, said I, should not have supposed that the true lawgiver ought to work out matters of that kind in the laws and the constitution of either an ill-governed or a well-governed state—in the one because they are useless and accomplish nothing, in the other because some of them anybody could discover and others will result spontaneously from the pursuits already described. (*The Republic*, bk. 4, 425e, 427a)[11]

Proper education eliminates the need for positive law altogether because proper behavior flows naturally from the fine and good man. Legislation is thus superfluous for the good man, while men of bad character will act wickedly no matter what, and legislation is powerless to stop them. It is for this reason that the legislator should not be content with merely producing laws but should seek to *educate* the citizens (*Laws* 857c4–5).

(III) HUMAN LAW AS INSTRUCTION VS. HUMAN LAW AS HABITUATION

According to Plato, the legislator educates citizens not through legal prescriptions, but through admonition, exhortation, praise, and blame such as may be found in legislative preambles that articulate reasoned explanations of the law. The best law must not speak bluntly and harshly but must seek to persuade its auditors (*Laws* 722e–723a). The good legislator may be compared to the "free" physician, who does not merely issue a brusque injunction (as an "unfree" or

---

[11] All translations of *The Republic* are by Paul Shorey, as found in Hamilton and Cairns 2005.

slave physician would) but investigates the patient's particular condition, confers with him and his family, and persuades the patient to compliance with the physician's prescription for a restoration of full health (*Laws* 720c–e). In a similar manner, law must speak in two voices (Lutz 2012, 94)—the voice of prescription, or unqualified law, and the voice of persuasive preamble that prepares the listener to receive the prescriptive laws.

To conceive of law as instruction is to assume that nonvirtuous acts stem from ignorance or erroneous ideas. This account of vice is found in Plato's early dialogues. In the *Protagoras*, Socrates holds that no one errs willingly, that mistakes in action are due to mistaken beliefs about the merits of desired ends (Penner 2000, 165), and that virtue is achieved by the acquisition of the relevant knowledge or science. On such an account, law provides needed instruction.

However, book 4 of the *Republic* attributes vice not to a lack of knowledge but to the irrational parts of the soul—appetite and spirit—that have not been properly subjugated to the rational part of the soul. For virtue to be achieved, the irrational parts of the soul must be trained to obey what reason commands, and such obedience is the result not of intellectual understanding but of habituation over time. This view is compatible with the idea of law as discipline (in the sense of training)—commands and prohibitions that inculcate obedience.

Both of these models of self-rule are discussed in book 3 of the *Laws*. The model of self-rule based on knowledge comes about when the prudent individual considers each passion and makes a rational judgment concerning the extent to which its counsel should be heeded in any given circumstance; "when [this] judgment takes the form of a public decision of a city, it has the name of *law*" (*Laws* 644d). The second model of self-rule is conveyed in the myth of the marionette. The myth describes humans as divine marionettes and our various passions as powerful strings that pull us in diverse and opposing directions. Our reason is a golden, noble, and divine cord (*Laws* 644e–645c), weaker than the others and requiring help. Thus, an individual must find support in the public law when pulling along the golden cord of judgment against the powerful strings of the passions (*Laws* 645a).

In the first model, there is no struggle or self-overcoming. One simply weighs the counsel of the passions and judges rationally which ones can be properly accommodated in a manner that is compatible with what is best. This judgment will take the form of a middle course between the excesses of too much pleasure and too much pain (*Laws* 792c–d), the course of those who would be like God. But according to the myth of the marionette, one is engaged in a constant struggle to defeat the passions and follow reason and the law. By encouraging citizens to defeat their passions, law promotes courage, moderation, and inflexibility, but these are antithetical to the development of a rational capacity to judge the relative merits of various pains and pleasures in every particular circumstance (the first model).

Both models are accommodated in Plato's constitution, according to which only the philosopher-rulers need to have knowledge of virtue and how to achieve it, while others need only the habituation, punishment, and reward conducive to obedience (Penner 2000, 172). Clearly, intellectual virtue is to be preferred; the virtue arising from habituation and fear of shame or punishment—mere obedience—is a second-best, or nonideal form of virtue.[12]

Discourse 4: The Flexible, Unwritten, "Living Law"
vs. the Inflexible, Written, "Dead Letter"

The inadequacy of positive law for the cultivation of virtue (Discourse 3 above) is often understood to be a function of its generality and its inflexibility, which impede its ability to ensure justice in the widely varying circumstances of human life. Discourse 4 focuses on the regrettable inflexibility of *written* human laws and considers the possibility of their correction or adjustment by means of wisdom or practical reasoning.

(I) WRITTEN LAW'S INFLEXIBILITY

In both the *Laws* and the *Statesman*, Plato expresses pessimism about the ability of written law to express the divine law's immutable standards of right and wrong, owing to the former's generality and lack of comprehensiveness:

> Law can never issue an injunction binding on all which really embodies what is best for each; it cannot prescribe with perfect accuracy what is good and right for each member of the community at any one time. The differences of human personality, the variety of men's activities, and the inevitable unsettlement attending all human experience make it impossible for any art whatsoever to issue unqualified rules holding good on all questions at all times. (*Statesman*, 294a10–b6, cf. 294e–295b)[13]

No positive human law can anticipate and issue rulings appropriate for all of the varied circumstances that require regulation and adjudication in human society. Positive law is thus inherently imperfect and perpetually in need of adjustment to the particulars of individual cases. *What is a positive trait in the case of the perfect divine law—immutability—is precisely a dangerous trait in the case of the imperfect human law.* Human law, owing to its imperfection, must be flexible. Because right and wrong depend on the particular circumstances of a case and no human law can capture all such circumstances, it would be better to be ruled not by fixed human laws but by sages—wise experts who employ reason in continually assessing particular circumstances (296e–297b). Such

---

[12] In the *Nicomachean Ethics*, Aristotle examines the role of nature, teaching, and habituation in the formation of virtuous character (10.9 1179b20–1180a24). Teaching is powerful, but the soul of the student must first be cultivated by means of habits. It is only through habituation induced by coercively enforced laws that one learns to withstand the passions and so prepare for the acquisition of virtue.

[13] All translations of *The Statesman* are by J. B. Skemp, as found in Hamilton and Cairns 2005.

experts would resemble a ship's captain who makes adjustments on the spot. The captain cannot operate wholly according to written rules but must supply "a law in action by practical application of his knowledge of seamanship to the needs of the voyage" (*Statesman* 297a). This is the only way to preserve the lives of all in his ship. Similarly, the legislator who cleaves to written law and precedent endangers the lives of his citizens.[14]

A similar idea is found in Plato's contemporary Xenophon, who praises the "living law" of kings as more flexible than the law of written codes (Gray 2000, 152).[15] The fourth-century BCE Pythagorean Archytas (*On Law and Justice*) denigrates written law as lifeless in comparison to the animate law (the law of nature) embodied in the king (*Stob.* 4.1.135; Walbank 1984, 80–81)[16] and maintains that the laws of political communities must be inscribed not "on houses and doors," but in the living souls of citizens (Centrone 2000, 573). The second-century CE Pythagorean Diotogenes stands within this tradition and provides the clearest statement that the king himself is living law (*nomos empsuchos*), which may be taken to mean he is so just, virtuous, and wise that he embodies the unwritten higher law (Walbank 1984, 80).[17] According to Diotogenes, the king is the people's benefactor and savior (*soter*), terms commonly applied to kings in the Hellenistic period. For Plutarch (a first/second-century CE Middle Platonist philosopher), the king is an incarnation of the divine *logos* and God's representative on earth, realizing the divine order in the world through the medium of law of which he is a living incarnation (Centrone 2000, 560). Plutarch draws an analogy between god and king, world and city: as God is to the world, so the king is to the city; the king who upholds justice has the *logos* of God. The ruler who imitates God is himself subject to a master—the law, written not on "wooden tablets" but in "living reason" (*To an Uneducated Ruler* 780c; Centrone 2000, 578). Imitating God's virtue, the ruler becomes a model for others who see the divine *logos* reflected in him as one sees the sun in a mirror.

Plutarch sets in opposition lifeless written law and the internalized living law (animate reason), and extends the reach of the latter beyond the king to all citizens. A properly educated citizenry can internalize the principles that lead to virtue, rendering recourse to inflexible written laws altogether unnecessary.

(II) ARISTOTLE ON VARIABILITY IN THE LAW:
EQUITY, *PHRONESIS*, AND RHETORIC

For Aristotle, the legislator who cleaves to written law and precedent, without making the necessary adjustments to achieve justice, is deficient. In the

[14] For the full spectrum of Platonic answers to the question of the relationship of writing and law (from negative to positive), see Lane 2013.

[15] For Plato, of course, this is true if the king is a philosopher.

[16] The authenticity of the attribution of this work to Archytas has been questioned.

[17] For a full discussion of the concept of the "living law," see Martens 2004, chap. 3, esp. 38–42.

Nicomachean Ethics, Aristotle discusses the moral virtue of equity (*epieikeia*). Equity, or correction of the written law, is needed because law (*nomos*) is both universal (i.e., formulated in general terms) and simple (i.e., without exceptions; Shiner 1994, 1252). The following passage is the locus classicus for the Aristotelian conception of equity and the variability of law.

> [T]he equitable is just, but not the legally just but a correction of legal justice. The reason is that all law is universal but *about some things it is not possible to make a universal statement which shall be correct.* In those cases, then, in which it is *necessary to speak universally, but not possible to do so correctly,* the law takes the usual case, though it is not ignorant of the possibility of error. And it is none the less correct; for the error is not in the law nor in the legislator but in *the nature of the thing, since the matter of practical affairs is of this kind from the start.* When the law speaks universally, then, and a case arises on it which is not covered by the universal statement, then it is right, where the legislator fails us and has erred by over-simplicity, to correct the omission—to say what the legislator himself would have said had he been present, and would have put into his law if he had known. Hence the equitable is just, and better than one kind of justice—not better than absolute justice but better than the error that arises from the absoluteness of the statement. And this is the nature of the equitable, a correction of law where it is defective owing to its universality. In fact this is the reason why all things are not determined by law, viz. *that about some things it is impossible to lay down a law,* so that a decree is needed. (*NicEth* 1137b10–28; emphasis added)[18]

What does Aristotle mean when he says that at times the law "is defective owing to its universality"? The term translated here as "defective" is a form of *elleipein,* which means "to fall short" (Shiner 1994, 1254). "Falling short" and "exceeding" are spatial metaphors (ibid., 1255) that convey the idea of a linear deviation from a line or mark, and draw upon Aristotle's famous theory of the golden mean. According to Aristotle's theory of the golden mean, virtue is

> a mean between two vices, that [vice] which depends on excess and that [vice] which depends on defect; and again it is a mean because the vices respectively fall short of or exceed what is right in both passions and actions, while virtue both finds and chooses that which is intermediate. (*NicEth* 1107a2–6)

Aristotle constructs justice as a fixed line or standard against which injustice—deviations of exceeding or falling short (*NicEth* 1134a6)—can be measured. Laws formulated universally will in certain particular cases fall short of the line of justice and create injustice. Equity rectifies this situation, provid-

---

[18] All translations of Aristotle's *Nicomachean Ethics* are by William David Ross.

ing an adjustment to the law that takes into account the particular circumstances not accommodated by the law's universal formulation.

But why should it be the case that the law's universality will render it defective in some cases? According to Aristotle, the defect does not lie in the law itself or the legislator—the law may be perfectly just and correct in the majority of cases, and legislators act well in formulating such rules for the majority of cases. At the same time, these legislators can envisage and endorse the later correction of the rule in order to ensure justice in specific cases.

Having established that the defect does not lie in the law itself, and that legislators formulate universal rules with full awareness of the necessity of equitable adjustment in particular cases, Aristotle attributes the cause of the defect to *the nature of the things that law seeks to order.* The realm of practical affairs is the realm of "truth-for-the-most-part" (Shiner 1994, 1257). Practical affairs (about which it is impossible to lay down universal and exceptionless laws) are indefinite and variable because they deal with material objects that are susceptible to change and accident. By contrast, the theoretical sciences that study immaterial objects can attain universal, exceptionless truth (*NicEth* 1140a14–1141a8). But such "truth" is unattainable in the realm of practical affairs regulated by law. Aristotle writes:

> [I]t is the mark of an educated man to look for precision in each class of things just so far as the nature of the subject admits; it is evidently equally foolish to accept probable reasoning from a mathematician and to demand from a rhetorician scientific proofs. (*NicEth* 1094b24–28)

Equity, which corrects laws that fall short of the just mean, requires tailor-made, particularized judgments (Shiner 1994, 1252), which result from the exercise of *phronesis* or practical wisdom. In any given instance, one must determine whether justice is better served by a mechanical application of the general, universal law or by the granting of an exception. Such deliberation is practical wisdom or *phronesis.*[19]

> [T]the man who is capable of deliberating has practical wisdom. Now no one deliberates about things that are invariable, nor about things that it is impossible for him to do. Therefore, since scientific knowledge involves demonstration, but there is no demonstration of things whose first principles are variable (for all such things might actually be otherwise), and

---

[19] Aristotle's use of the term *phronesis* differs from Plato's. Aristotle identifies three types of knowledge and three corresponding intellectual virtues. Theoretical knowledge is knowledge of scientific truths and axioms, and it is linked with the intellectual virtue of *sophia* (wisdom); productive knowledge is knowledge that brings things into being, and it is linked with the intellectual virtue of *techne* (craft); practical knowledge is knowledge concerning matters of conduct, and it is linked with the intellectual virtue of *phronesis*, or practical reasoning. *Phronesis* is the right reason (*orthos logos*) in respect to moral knowledge and matters of conduct; see Becker and Becker 1992, s.v. *phronesis.*

since it is impossible to deliberate about things that are of necessity, practical wisdom cannot be scientific knowledge nor art ... the remaining alternative, then, is that it [practical wisdom] is a true and reasoned state of capacity to act with regard to the things that are good or bad for man ...

Practical wisdom, then, must be a reasoned and true state of capacity to act with regard to human goods. (*NicEth* 1140a31–1140b1, 1140b3, 20–21)

Here, Aristotle asserts that while scientific knowledge provides demonstrations that can bring certain knowledge of universal truths, practical reason deliberates about what is good and expedient and employs rhetorical arts to persuade, effect agreement and cooperation, or spur to action.

Practical reasoning entails a mode of argumentation that is based on the tradition of classical rhetoric (Scallen 1995, 1733–34) because, like rhetoric, it is grounded in a philosophical perspective that rejects absolutist theories of reality, truth, and knowledge in practical affairs. Aristotle devoted an entire treatise to rhetoric, which he defined as "an ability in each [particular] case, to see the available means of persuasion" (ibid., 1725) rather than a demonstration of truth. He described both deliberative rhetoric (political discourse used in the evaluation of a proposed course of action) and judicial rhetoric (a forensic discourse used in the evaluation of a past action; ibid., 1726). A full description of various formal and informal arguments is found in Aristotle's *Organon*, a collection of treatises on logic. Two of these treatises—*Prior Analytics* and *Posterior Analytics*—adapt methods of deductive and inductive reasoning for argumentation about matters of law (Frost 1992, 108). A characteristic feature of classical rhetoric is its eclectic use of various kinds of arguments and "proofs." Aristotle identifies nonartistic proofs, such as testimony and documents, as well as artistic proofs based on the speaker himself and his methods, which include *logos* (appeals based on reason and logic), *pathos* (appeals based on emotions), and *ethos* (appeals based on the character and credibility of the speaker; Scallen 1995, 1755).

Greek writing on argumentation and rhetoric strongly influenced Roman legal culture, which likewise did not view positive law as a matter of "truth." Cicero (first century BCE) and Quintilian (first century CE) and the anonymous author of the *Rhetorica ad Herennium* built on the ideas of Isocrates, Plato, and especially Aristotle in the composition of handbooks advocating the persuasive use of analytical, logical, and rhetorical techniques in civic and legal contexts (Scallen 1995, 1729; Frost 1992, 108).

Discourse 5: The Opposition of *Phusis* and *Nomos*?

A fifth classical discourse of positive law—also marked by ambivalence—takes as its theme the opposition of law and nature. Certainly, the natural law is ipso facto in complete harmony with nature; however, in the fifth century BCE, some Greek thinkers argued that human law or convention (*nomos*) stands in opposition to nature (*phusis*). In this discourse, nature (*phusis*) refers sometimes to the state of nature prior to any norm, convention, or political ordering and sometimes to human nature.

Whether the state of nature or the law that opposes it is to be preferred depends on the characterization of each. If the state of nature is positively viewed as in Hesiod's golden age, the introduction of law is seen as a negative development: a burden or an enslavement. An explicit characterization of the idyllic golden age as law-free is found in the writings of the Latin writer Ovid (d. 17/18 CE), nearly eight centuries after Hesiod. Ovid's *Metamorphoses* is a history of the world that describes a succession of four ages, each worse than the previous one, and each corresponding to a particular metal.

> Golden was that first age, which, with no one to compel, without a law, of its own will, kept faith and did the right. There was no fear of punishment, no threatening words were to be read on brazen tablets; no suppliant throng gazed fearfully upon its judge's face; but without punisher lived secure. (1.89–93)

However, as Winton remarks (2000, 96), the fifth century generally "reverses Hesiod's analysis: mankind is rescued from the brutish condition in which it originally found itself by acquiring the various elements of civilization."

(I) EPICUREANISM—LAW'S UTILITY OVER THE STATE OF NATURE

Epicureanism does not treat nature and convention as entirely antagonistic alternatives. The relationship between nature and convention is best understood through the Epicurean concept of *utility*. The Epicurean account of the rise of law is one in which certain patterns of behavior were found to be *useful*, or advantageous, in countering the difficulties of life in the state of nature or, in more specifically Epicurean terms, in promoting pleasure and reducing pain. Thus, justice does not exist per se but is a historically conditioned phenomenon (Long and Sedley 1987, 134) grounded in a general recognition of the *utility* of social relationships.

> Justice was never anything *per se*, but a contract, regularly arising at some place or other in people's dealings with one another, over not harming or being harmed. Injustice is something bad not *per se* but in the fear that arises from the suspicion that one will not escape the notice of those who have the authority to punish such things. (Epicurus, *Key Doctrines* 33–34; as found in Long and Sedley 1987, 1:125)

Humans institutionalized advantageous behaviors by mutual agreement rather than coercion, but historical events and social conditions caused people to forget the utility of these behaviors. At that point coercion became necessary. However, were the rational calculation of utility to be restored and universalized, laws would be redundant (Long and Sedley 1987, 1:136). According to Epicurus's successor Hermarchus (as described by Porphyry):

> [I]f everyone were equally able to observe and be mindful of utility, they would have no need of laws in addition; of their own volition, they would steer clear of what is forbidden and do what is prescribed. For the observation of what is useful and harmful is sufficient to secure avoidance of some things and choice of others. The threat of punishment is addressed to those who fail to take note of utility. (Porphyry, *On Abstinence* 1.7.4; as found in Long and Sedley 1987, 1:129)

The recognition of utility brings spontaneous obedience. Positive laws, coercively enforced, are necessary only for those incapable of perceiving what is useful or beneficial and what is harmful, not for those able to engage in a rational calculation of what is useful and advantageous.

(II) LAW AS RESCUE FROM THE STATE OF NATURE

While some, in their own distinctive ways, spoke positively or in neutral terms about the state of nature, most classical writers described it disapprovingly as brutish and violent. In the state of nature, force rather than justice prevails. On such a view, the introduction of norms and laws is a positive good. In Protagoras's Great Speech in Plato's dialogue *Protagoras* (320c–324c), *nomos* is positively represented as a human institution that rescues humans from the state of nature. According to Protagoras, the earliest humans lived in scattered groups but were devoured by wild beasts. They sought to save themselves by coming together to live in cities but

> when they gathered in communities they injured one another for want of political skill ... Zeus, therefore, fearing the total destruction of our race, sent Hermes to impart to men the qualities of respect for others and a sense of justice, so as to bring order into our cities and create a bond of friendship and union. Hermes asked Zeus in what manner he was to bestow these gifts on men. "Shall I distribute them ... on the principle that one trained doctor suffices for many laymen ... or shall I distribute justice and respect for their fellows ... to all alike?"
>
> "To all," replied Zeus, "Let all have their share. There could never be cities if only a few shared in these virtues, as in the arts.[20]

Protagoras's view is optimistic and democratic. Law rescues humans from the state of nature. Moreover, the promulgation of laws and the establishment of justice does not require a particular expertise since all persons are endowed with the necessary sense of justice and respect.

---

[20] All translations of the *Protagoras* are by W.K.C. Guthrie, as found in Hamilton and Cairns 2005.

For the Epicurean Lucretius (first century BCE) early humans, worn out by violence, recognized the utility of submitting to laws and were thus voluntarily delivered from the ills of the state of nature:

> Then there were some who taught them to create magistrates, and established law, that they might be willing to obey statutes. For mankind, tired of living in violence, was fainting from its feuds, and so they were readier of their own free will to submit to statutes and strict rules of law. For because each man in his wrath would make ready to avenge himself more severely than is permitted now by just laws, for this reason men were utterly weary of living in violence. (*De rerum natura* 5.1146–1150)

(III) LAW AS INADEQUATE RESCUE FROM THE STATE OF NATURE

A more ambivalent view is found in an anonymous Athenian text known as the Sisyphus fragment, from roughly the same period (fifth century BCE). It provides a similar but not identical narrative of law's genesis.

> There was a time when human life had no order, but like that of animals was ruled by force; when there was no reward for the good, nor any punishment for the wicked. And then, I think, men enacted laws (*nomoi*) for punishment, so that justice (*diké*) would be ruler (*turannos*) ... and *hubris* its slave, and whoever did wrong would be punished. Next, since the laws prevented people only from resorting to violence openly, but they continued to do so in secret, then I think for the first time some shrewd and clever (*sophos*) individual invented fear of the gods for mortals, so that the wicked would have something to fear even if their deeds or words or thoughts were secret. In this way, therefore, he introduced the idea of the divine, saying that there is a divinity, strong with eternal life, who in his mind hears, sees, thinks and attends to everything with his divine nature (*phusis*). He will hear everything mortals say and can see everything they do; and if you silently plot evil, this is not hidden from the gods, for our thoughts are known to them. With such stories as these he introduced the most pleasant of lessons, concealing the truth with a false account. And he claimed that the gods dwelt in that place which would particularly terrify men ... Thus, I think, someone first persuaded mortals to believe (*nomizein*) there was a race of gods. (DK 88 B 25, trans. M. Davies; as cited in Winton 2000, 89)

According to this text, laws secure us from harm and introduce justice; yet insofar as they are powerless against secret wickedness, they provide only partial rescue from the wickedness that characterizes the state of nature (an idea explored in the legend of the ring of Gyges in Plato's *Republic*) and our own human nature. In order to motivate law observance in private, the idea of all-knowing, all-seeing gods capable of rooting out and punishing even secret wickedness was invented. Thus, while *nomos* is a critical advance over the state of nature (and positively viewed), without the fail-safe myth of divine enforcement it is in itself inadequate for the establishment of justice and personal virtue.[21]

A similar understanding of *nomos* is found in a fragment of Antiphon's *On Truth*.

> Justice (*dikaiosunē*) therefore, is not violating the rules (*nomina*) of the city in which one is a citizen. Thus a person would best observe justice to his own advantage if he paid heed to the laws (*nomoi*) when in the presence of witnesses, but to the demands of nature (*phusis*) when not in the presence of witnesses. For the demands of the law are adventitious, those of nature are inescapable ... Thus someone who violates the laws avoids shame and punishment if those who have joined in agreement do not observe him, but not if they do. But if someone tries to violate one of the inherent demands of nature, which is impossible, the harm he suffers is no less if he is seen by no one, and no greater if all see him. (*CPF* 1.1.192–94 = DK 87 B 44; as cited in Winton 2000, 97)

In Antiphon's view, conventional human law has no inherent claim on our fidelity; logically we should follow it only when we would be caught and punished for failing to do so. By contrast, the demands of nature (and Antiphon seems to have in mind *human* nature) are inherent and inescapable. If violation were possible, it would be *inherently* harmful, whether observed or not. Elsewhere in the fragment it is clear that *nomos* and *phusis* are antitheses. Convention is denigrated as repressive of human nature, which requires liberty.[22]

(IV) PREFERRING NATURE OVER LAW

A rejection of conventional law and a preference for the state of nature despite (or because of) its brutishness and violence are not absent in the classical sources even if their expression is somewhat tongue-in-cheek. Thus, Aristo-

---

[21] Winton (2000, 95) notes that fifth-century BCE Greece witnesses "a range of intellectual disciplines that marginalize or exclude supernatural factors in explaining the material they address, and ... expresses doubt and disbelief as to the gods' very existence."

[22] Criticisms of conventional law and morality that focus on the law's inability to motivate compliance in secret did not stand unanswered. One response is to deny the claim that self-interest is best served by avoiding conventional law and morality, and to assert that it is best served precisely by observing it (Taylor 2000, 125–27). This is the position of Democritus (d. 370 CE). According to Democritus, the antithesis between nature and law is incorrectly imagined as an antithesis between seeking one's self-interest (our natural inclination) and being inhibited from doing so (the behest of law contrary to nature). On the contrary, nature and convention point in the *same* direction, not different directions, because "the aim of law is to benefit the life of men" (B248, cited in Taylor, 127). Law frees people from the aggression of others and thus establishes the conditions under which humans can obtain the well-being that is nature's goal.

phanes's comedy *The Clouds* (fifth century BCE), depicts an argument between Right and Wrong in which Wrong rejects the *nomoi* of humans and endorses the unrestrained immorality, self-interest, and self-indulgence of *phusis* (nature). More seriously, in Plato's *Gorgias*, Callicles rejects some conventional norms as contrary to the state of nature. Specifically, he justifies the domination of the weak by the strong (objectionable by conventional moral standards) because such domination is commonly found in nature.[23]

The Cynics resisted convention and championed "life according to nature"— a life of reason, self-sufficiency, and freedom without the legal codes and political associations that compromise freedom. Diogenes of Sinope, the founder of Cynicism, rejected conventional norms (*nomos*) as opposed to nature and natural liberty. He is described by Diogenes Laertius as

> deferring in all things rather to the principles of nature than to those of law; saying that he was adopting the same fashion of life as Hercules had, preferring nothing in the world to liberty; and saying that everything belonged to the wise ... everything belongs to the Gods; and the Gods are friends to the wise; and all the property of friends is held in common; therefore everything belongs to the wise ... And he played in the same manner with the topics of noble birth, and reputation, and all things of that kind, saying that they were all veils, as it were, for wickedness; ... there was no impiety in tasting even human flesh, as is plain from the habits of foreign nations; and he said that this principle might be correctly extended to every case and every people. (Diogenes Laertius 7)

Diogenes was antinomian and cosmopolitan. He rejected the city and mocked its conventional social and political values as contrary to nature. He was not a relativist; he fervently believed that life is lived well only through nature, and that nature, not convention, is the standard for virtue and order. Convention imposes a pseudovirtue and order that are against nature.

This fifth discourse, which holds nature and positive law in antithesis, is a discourse of ambivalence. Cynics committed to the life of nature chafe against law's restrictions (a deprivation of freedom). Epicureans value law as securing certain advantages over life in the state of nature, but this value is compromised to the extent that the law's utility is forgotten and it must be coercively enforced. Even those who view law positively, as an important rescue that frees one from the brutish state of nature, point to law's inability to achieve the *full* realization of justice and human virtue.

---

[23] This text highlights the difficulties involved in determining nature's norms. Is something naturally normative because it is commonly found in nature (Brown 2009, 345)? In the face of this challenge, Socrates attempts to define how we might reliably identify the norms of nature, but he ultimately arrives at little more than a doctrine of coherence (ibid., 346).

Discourse 6: Positive Law in Need of a Savior

Our sixth discourse is found in the writings of Plato. According to Plato, the law's inability to bring humans to their highest virtue, its inflexibility in the absence of an expert statesman, and its failure to deliver justice tailored to specific circumstances undermine its authority, rendering it unstable and in need of rescue by a savior (*soter, soterion*). This rescue comes in the form of persons of discernment whose commitment to reason, the *logos*, and the idea of virtue qualifies them to interpret and guide the law toward its goal of virtue, thus securing its authority.

These ideas appear in the *Laws*. Near the end of the dialogue, the Athenian Stranger asserts that positive laws will always be unstable if there is no loyalty to the law in the soul. The laws are not established on a firm foundation and will not endure unless they have an *irreversible* quality. The laws are therefore in need of a "savior"—that which implants this irreversible quality in the laws is the "salvation" or "savior" of the law (*soterian ton nomon;* σωτηρίαν τῶν νόμων; 960d).

What ensures the law's stable and irreversible quality and thus serves as its savior? Persons possessing a suitable education, a belief in the soul's dateless anteriority to and sovereignty over the world of bodies, and a desire to discern the reason or *logos* that orders the heavens (*Laws* 964d–969c). Known as the "Nocturnal Council," these guardians keep ward over the state and, by securing the salvation of the law, secure the salvation of the state (968a).[24] Thus, even though the law is an imperfect medium for the establishment of justice and moral virtue, its authority is secured (the law is "saved") insofar as it is interpreted and guided by those who discern the *logos*. By the end of the dialogue, the Athenian Stranger has shown that through reason and expertise in the political art, he is able to establish a code of positive laws which, while imperfect, may be "saved" and recognized as "divine" insofar as it is grounded in the intellect that would guide a divine lawgiver (Lutz 2012, 178).

For our purposes, what is striking in Plato's discourse is its deep ambivalence regarding even a superior human law. Positive law is the best option open to us, and insofar as it is ordered by reason it approximates the divine law. However, in itself the law does not develop our full virtue because for most individuals it requires the subjugation of the passions to reason. Such indiscriminate self-overcoming depends upon the virtues of courage and moderation to the detriment of the greater virtue of rational judgment, and thus law ultimately

---

[24] The text describing the council as the state's custodian that preserves its salvation reads as follows: ὡς φυλακὴν ἐσόμενον κατὰ νόμον χάριν σωτηρίας τὸν τῶν ἀρχόντων νυκτερινὸν σύλλογον παιδείας ὁπόσης διεληλύθαμεν κοινωνὸν γενόμενον = that the nocturnal synod of magistrates shall be legally established, and shall participate in all the education we have described, to keep ward over the state, and to secure its salvation (968a–b).

fails to secure our highest virtue. *Logos* is the salvation of the law and makes possible the life of virtue.

Discourse 7: In Praise of Written Law— the Mark of the Free, Civilized Man

Despite its evident defects in the absence of rational guidance and adjustment, law would eventually become the mark of a civilized society in much Greek thought. The idea that barbarians lack law of any kind is already found in Homer's *Odyssey* (9.114–15), where the brutish, cave-dwelling Cyclopes are said to "have no shared laws (*themistes*), no meetings for counsels (*boulēphoroi agorai*) … each one sets the law for his own wives and children, and cares nothing about the others." The Cyclopes' failure to establish *communal* norms and counsels creates a situation of outrageous lawlessness and signals their hatred of the gods. In contrast to the barbarism, isolation, and lawlessness of the Cyclopes, the polis is represented as the site of civilization, community, and justice (Raaflaub 2000, 26). Shared laws in the communal context of the polis are the very mark of humanity for Homer.

By the mid-fifth century BCE, Greek identity was formulated in opposition to the "barbarian" other (Raaflaub 2000, 51). The civilized/barbarian dichotomy in which the sovereignty of written law was one of the marks of the civilized (LeFebvre 2006, 184) was featured in intercultural polemics. As the writings of Herodotus illustrate, this dichotomy was a political rather than a racial one (ibid., 186). Barbarians lived under a despotic tyranny and possessed no political liberty.[25] By contrast, the Greeks enjoyed the rule of law—*written* law in particular, which was understood to be an essential precondition for freedom. Freedom, the ability of male citizens to participate in the political and civic life of the polis, was highly prized by the Greeks. The association of written law with freedom may be understood against the backdrop of political changes in fifth-century Athens.

Following the restoration of democracy in late fifth-century Athens, the principle of popular sovereignty was subordinated to the principle of the rule of *written* law (LeFebvre 2006, 19–22). As noted in chapter 1, the ancestral legal traditions of the city were compiled and harmonized and recorded in writing on the walls of the royal stoa. A law was passed that deprived unwritten laws[26] of any legal force, and required the courts and magistrates to follow and

---

[25] Herodotus contrasts Greek "freedom" and Asian "servitude": the Greek polis consists of politically equal citizens living "free" under the rule of law, while the Persian empire is ruled by a single arbitrary and despotic king (Winton 2000, 103). Thus, Herodotus has the king of Sparta say to the Persian king Xerxes, "Though the Spartans are free men, they are not altogether free: law (*nomos*) is for them a master (*despotēs*) whom they fear far more than your subjects do you" (cited in ibid., 106). The law is king, but a king that ensures the freedom of its subjects.

[26] This refers not to the general category of unwritten law but to laws not recorded by, or officially enacted after, the time of the enactment in question; Gagarin 2008, 185.

enforce only written laws (ibid., 22; Gagarin 2008, 185). These reforms established not merely the rule of law, but the rule of *written* law.

By the Hellenistic period the idea of prescriptive written law as a necessary mark of civilization was deeply entrenched, and subjugated peoples who internalized Hellenistic conventions had to defend their native customs as prescriptive written law or be labeled "barbarian" (LeFebvre 2006, 183). "Many subjugated peoples learned … 'to beat their own drum'—even if they did so 'to the rhythm of the Greeks'" (ibid., 190)—and boasted that their native laws and traditions met the ideals of Greek culture.

While the enactment of large-scale codes of written legislation was an important step in enhancing the concepts of citizenship and community (Raaflaub 2000, 43) and in ensuring a single standard of justice for all (*isonomia*), some fifth- and fourth-century BCE sources express ambivalence about written legal texts in a democracy: written laws could become an instrument of inflexibility and ultimately tyranny (Scallen 1995, 1727, citing Steiner 1991). For this reason it is said that Lycurgus forbade the writing down of Spartan laws, and the written laws of Athens take the form of spoken discourses and refer to "the living voice of the lawmakers" (ibid.). Thus, in addition to the nomian understanding of freedom mentioned above, which emphasized political order, *isonomia*, and the benefits of civilization over barbarism, there arose an antinomian discourse of freedom. This antinomian discourse, which associated law with a loss of freedom, is often associated with schools of thought that understand law and nature (*nomos* and *phusis*) to be in opposition to one another.

It should be noted that in the Hellenistic period, moral philosophy increasingly emphasized the individual whose goals were understood to be achieved in the setting of the universe rather than the polis (Garnsey 2000, 403). Terms that originally bore a primarily political meaning (citizenship, freedom, slavery) took on a moral signification in the context of the individual's membership in a cosmic community. Thus, when the later Stoics say that the wise man is virtuous, free, and sovereign, they are making a moral rather than a political claim (see Discourse 2 above).

ADDITIONAL LITERARY AND LEGAL PRACTICES: THE JUXTAPOSITION OF DIVINE AND HUMAN LAW

(8) Divine Law as a Standard for the Evaluation of Human Law

Divine law and human law are juxtaposed in texts that directly or indirectly invoke the former as the standard of evaluation for the latter. Works of various genres participate in this literary tradition in which the constitutions of political states are examined to determine the extent to which they imitate an ideal, and even divine, standard.

The idealization of the laws of Sparta is a familiar trope in classical philosophical, historical, and political writings. Herodotus (1.65–66) describes Sparta's transformation into a well-governed state by means of the laws introduced by Lycurgus, who was subsequently worshipped by the Spartans.[27] The historian viewed Sparta as the archetypically well-ordered polis because of its inhabitants' reverence for the law (Winton 2000, 106), and attributed their military success to their constitution (Gray 2000, 151). Similarly, Xenophon (fifth–fourth centuries BCE) praises the laws of the Spartans in his work *Constitution of the Spartans*, attributing their military failures to abandonment of their laws (ibid.). His writings criticize the laws of Athens because they are less flexible than the "living law" of kings; by contrast, the laws established by Lycurgus in Sparta gave this flexibility to ephors (*Lac.Pol.* 8.4; Gray 2000, 152). The assessment of Xenophon's contemporary Isocrates was the reverse. Isocrates was critical of the laws of Sparta and touted the supremacy of the ancestral Athenian constitution, whose laws endured a thousand years and brought a military supremacy that benefited all of Greece (Gray 2000, 153). Diogenes the Cynic expressed admiration for the Spartans (Moles 2000, 421), as did various writers in subsequent centuries, such as Polybius (Hahm 2000, 470) and the Pseudo-Pythagoreans, who cited the Spartans' minimal use of written law (Centrone 2000, 573). When Josephus, a first-century CE Jewish historian, asserts that the Jews outdo the Spartans in the stability of their laws (*Against Apion* 232–35)[28] as well as their devotion to the laws (226–31), he exploits this

---

[27] Herodotus writes: "Before this they had been the worst-governed of nearly all the Hellenes and had had no dealings with strangers, but they changed to good government in this way: Lycurgus, a man of reputation among the Spartans, went to the oracle at Delphi. As soon as he entered the hall, the priestess said in hexameter:

... I am in doubt whether to pronounce you man or god,
But I think rather you are a god, Lycurgus.

Some say that the Pythia also declared to him the constitution that now exists at Sparta, but the Lacedaemonians themselves say that Lycurgus brought it from Crete when he was guardian of his nephew Leobetes, the Spartan king. Once he became guardian, he changed all the laws and took care that no one transgressed the new ones. Lycurgus afterwards established their affairs of war: the sworn divisions, the bands of thirty, the common meals; also the ephors and the council of elders. Thus they changed their bad laws to good ones, and when Lycurgus died they built him a temple and now worship him greatly" (trans. Godley 1920).

[28] Josephus writes: "[O]f the legislators, they most admire Lycurgus, and everyone sings the praises of Sparta, since she stuck to his laws for the longest time. So let this be granted, that obedience to the laws is proof of virtue. But let those who admire the Lacedaemonians compare their time-span with the more than two thousand years of our constitution, and let them consider, in addition, that for as long as they had their freedom the Lacedaemonians were of a mind to keep the laws scrupulously, but when changes of fortune came to affect them, they completely forgot almost all the laws! As for us, although we have undergone countless different fortunes, thanks to the changes among the kings who ruled Asia, we have not betrayed the laws even in the most extreme crises, fostering them not for the sake of idleness or luxury but, if anyone would care to examine, [he would find] imposed on us ordeals

long-standing trope of Spartan excellence (see Rajak 2000, 589–90) and participates in the literary tradition of evaluating the constitutions of political states against an ideal standard.

Special mention must be made of Plato. Plato also participates in this tradition, but his consideration of the excellence of the Spartan constitution is part of a larger inquiry into the nature and goals of divine law generally and the possibility of its realization in the positive law of states. In the *Laws*, an Athenian Stranger engages two interlocutors from Crete and from Sparta (Clinias and Megillus) who believe their constitutions to be divine law. In the course of the dialogue, the two interlocutors are led to articulate the criteria by which divine law may be recognized. Once they do, they are forced to concede that the laws of Crete and Sparta fail to meet these criteria. Specifically, they conclude that variability, or rational modification of the law, disqualifies the constitutions of Crete and Sparta from claiming the title of divine law. The Athenian Stranger is sensitive to the fact that for those who believe in the divinity of their laws, the idea of human rational adjustment of the law is threatening. It impinges upon, or indeed negates, the latter's divinity because of the popular notion that what is divine is unchanging. Such persons do not consider the possibility that the law's divinity might not entail an unchanging stability.

In the *Laws*, the constitutions of real states were evaluated for their degree of correspondence with the divine law and found wanting. But other writers were more sanguine about the ability of positive laws to mimic the divine natural law. Centuries later, Cicero would assert that Rome had, through the course of time and by dint of reason and long experience, developed a code of laws that measured up to the ideal standard of natural law (Griffin 2000, 534), with the result that the laws of Rome should apply universally and permanently without change (*De leg.* 2.23, 3.12). E. M. Atkins writes:

> Plato's ideal city was imaginary; Aristotle's collected constitutions were less than perfect. Cicero Romanizes the Platonic tradition from within by presenting republican Rome at her peak as an incarnation of the best possible constitution. Here was the city and statesmen that theory could describe, but only experience produce. Cicero's exaggerated patriotism encouraged him to a strikingly un-Platonic trust in historical and empirical evidence for the political enquiry. (2000, 515)

---

and labors far greater than the endurance supposedly required of the Lacedaemonians. They neither worked the land nor labored in a craft, but were released from all work and used to spend their time about the city looking sleek and exercising their bodies for the sake of beauty, using others as servants for all the business of daily life and getting their food from them, ready prepared, exercising endurance in doing and suffering anything purely for this one fine and benevolent task: to conquer everyone against whom they went to war. I pass over the fact that they did not succeed even in this; for not only singly, but many of them on many occasions and en masse ignored the commands of the law and surrendered, with their weapons, to the enemy" (*Against Apion* 2:225–31).

(9) In the Trenches—Juristic Theory vs. Juristic Practice

The juxtaposition of divine law (i.e., natural law) and human law occurs in yet another context: the writings of the Roman jurists. It has often been maintained that until Cicero's time, natural law doctrine exercised little practical influence on Roman law; subsequently, and under the influence of Stoic philosophy, the doctrine of natural law passed into Roman law and exerted a great influence on Roman jurisprudence. Thus, in 1936, Heinrich Rommen claimed that "[t]he great jurists of the golden age of Roman law were for the most part also philosophers" (23), and that "Stoic philosophy may with considerable justice be called the mother of Roman jurisprudence" (ibid.). Rommen asserted that according to the jurists the *ius naturae* was a norm and "must prevail in case of conflict: what the *ius naturae* forbids, the *ius civile* may not allow; nor may the *ius civile* repeal such prohibition" (25). However, recent scholarship provides a more nuanced assessment of the impact of (especially Stoic) natural law theory on the activity of the Roman jurists. Indeed, there is good reason to correct Rommen's primary claims, specifically the claims that (1) the jurists were for the most part also philosophers, such that Stoic philosophy nurtured Roman jurisprudence, and (2) the natural law prevailed in cases of conflict.

We turn first to the claim that the jurists were for the most part also philosophers influenced particularly by Stoic natural law thinking. A secular jurisprudence first emerged in third-century BCE Rome with jurists providing legal advice to magistrates (who issued edicts granting legal remedies) and judges (who decided cases). Over the next five centuries, these jurists produced a substantial legal literature, including commentaries on the civil law and the magistrate's edict, as well as books of collected legal opinions (Johnston 2000, 616). These writings indicate that the jurists were familiar with Greek philosophical and rhetorical traditions and various doctrines of law. Nevertheless, as David Johnston has observed (618), "there is little sign that such considerations impinged much on the jurists' practice of law: such theorizing as we do find appears only from the second century AD, and is typically to be found in textbooks rather than practical works."

Theoretical considerations of justice and law, including the relationship of positive law and natural law, are often placed in the introductory chapters (or titles) of juristic works, lending them a certain prominence that is misleading in light of the jurists' lack of engagement with these theories in their practical writings. Moreover, these theoretical statements are often more descriptive than prescriptive. So, for example, the opening passage of Gaius's second-century CE *Institutiones* (and the opening passage of Justinian's *Digest*, the sixth-century compilation of excerpts from the writings of the classical jurists) states:

> 1.1.9 All peoples who are governed under laws and customs observe in part their own special law and in part a law common to all men. Now that

law which each nation has set up as a law unto itself is special to that particular civitas and is called jus civile, civil law, as being that which is proper to the particular civil society (civitas). By contrast, that law which natural reason has established among all human beings is among all observed in equal measure and is called jus gentium, as being the law which all nations observe.

Gaius was likely simply describing what he observed—that Roman law consisted of the positive law governing Roman citizens only (*ius civile*) and laws that govern noncitizens too (*ius gentium*). He does not call the latter "natural law," though he does state that it is established by a natural reason (which presumably grounds its claim to authority). Johnston points out (2000, 619) that Gaius's conception of *ius gentium* differs from Cicero's. For Gaius, the *ius civile* and the *ius gentium* are two distinct, nonoverlapping types of law for two distinct classes of people (citizen and noncitizen); for Cicero the two are not mutually exclusive. The *ius gentium* is a higher law that binds all persons alike—citizens and noncitizens—in addition to their own *ius civile*.

The *Digest* contains an altogether different conception (possibly drawn from the third-century jurist Ulpian), which distinguishes among three primary entities: *ius civile*, *ius gentium*, and *ius naturale*.

1.1.1.3–4 Private law is tripartite, being derived from principles of *jus naturale*, *jus gentium*, or *jus civile*. *Jus naturale* is that which nature has taught to all animals; for it is not a law specific to mankind but is common to all animals—land animals, sea animals, and the birds as well. Out of this comes the union of man and woman which we call marriage, and the procreation of children, and their rearing. So we can see that the other animals, wild beasts included, are rightly understood to be acquainted with this law. *Jus gentium*, the law of nations, is that which all peoples observe. That it is not co-extensive with natural law can be grasped easily, since this latter is common to all animals whereas *jus gentium* is common only to human beings among themselves.

1.1.6 The *jus civile* is that which neither wholly diverges from the *jus naturale* and *jus gentium* nor follows the same in every particular. And so whenever to the common law we add anything or take anything away from it, we make a law special to ourselves, that is, *jus civile*, civil law. This law of ours, therefore, exists either in written or unwritten form; as the Greeks put it, "of laws some are written, others unwritten."

According to these passages, there are three types of law, two of which transcend the *ius civile*. The *ius naturale* is here understood as a law that nature teaches all animals—human and nonhuman—including behaviors that arise from our biological natures, such as procreation. The *ius gentium* is understood as a law that all humans have in common.

This is a fundamentally un-Stoic distinction. The Stoic natural law is by definition confined to and held in common by all rational beings only, that is, humans rather than animals. Yet here the natural law is said to apply to all beasts, while the *ius gentium* includes customs common to all humans. The *Institutes of Justinian* 2.11 provides a definition of *ius naturale* that is based not on the behavior of animals but on the divine:

> But the laws of nature, which are observed by all nations alike, are established, as it were, by divine providence, and remain ever fixed and immutable: but the municipal laws of each individual state are subject to frequent change, either by the tacit consent of the people, or by the subsequent enactment of another statute.

Finally, and in contrast, the *Institutes of Justinian* 2.1.11 virtually equates the *ius naturale* and the *ius gentium*:

> Things become the private property of individuals in many ways; for the titles by which we acquire ownership in them are some of them titles of natural law, which, as we said, is called the law of nations, while some of them are titles of civil law.

These diverse conceptions of *ius naturale*—it applies to all animals or to rational humans only; it is equated with the *ius gentium* or differentiated from it—attest to the unsystematic and eclectic nature of the ancient jurisprudential literature. The jurists are not systematic philosophers and do not adhere rigidly to a particular philosophical school, but invoke popular philosophical concepts and adopt compelling arguments as needed (Johnston 2000, 621). They are first and foremost jurists.

We turn now to the claim that the natural law prevailed in cases of conflict. The fact is that the jurists' remarks about natural law, like their remarks about justice generally, remain on a plane of abstraction (Johnston 2000, 622–23) and do not appear to determine practical questions of law. Thus, while the medieval jurist Gratian might assert that "whatever has been recognized by custom or set down in writing must be held null and void if it conflicts with natural law,"[29] the Roman jurists adopted a more pragmatic approach. In cases of conflict, the positive law sometimes prevailed over natural law, nowhere more clearly than in the case of slavery. According to natural law, all persons are equal but under the Roman *ius civile*, slaves are not persons (Johnston 2000, 621). E. Levy (1949, 15), as cited in Johnston, 621) writes:

> The Roman jurists to whom theory meant little and practical results meant everything cannot have looked upon natural law as an order of higher or even equal status. They did not deny its existence and credited

---

[29] *Decretum D.* 5.1; 8.2; as cited in Johnston 2000, 621–22.

it with the absence of slavery in prehistoric times. But within the framework of their actual system they must have thought of natural law as inferior rather than superior to the law in force.

In keeping with this assessment, Johnston (632–33) concludes that

[T]heir statements of general theory are often taken not only from works of an elementary or educational rather than practical nature (*Institutiones, Definitiones* or *Regulae*), but also from the first book of such a work. They may therefore be little more than flourishes of learning intended to provide a suitably stately proemium to those works. Second, they usually display little originality but can be connected with well-known philosophical positions, mostly of a Stoic orientation. What these two observations amount to is this: that so far as we do find any general theory in Roman juristic writings, it is mostly not integrated into any kind of reasoned philosophical position on law or political thought, and it plays no observable part in the approach taken by the jurists to questions of legal interpretation. In short, it appears to be little more than recital of educated commonplaces of the day.

(10) Magistrates and the Equitable Adjustment of Roman Civil Law

One reason for the lack of connection between natural law and the civil law in the writings of the jurists is the entirely secular nature of the Roman law. And yet despite its secular nature, the Roman legal system possessed institutional mechanisms for the rational modification of the civil law in line with what were perceived to be universal principles of justice and equity. To understand how the civil law could be adjusted according to rational moral principles and considerations requires a brief review of central aspects of the Roman legal system.

The Roman legal system consisted of several independent and equally primary secular sources of law. These are legislation (*leges*) (including the Twelve Tables[30] and subsequent enactments of the popular assemblies or *comitia*), *plebiscita* (resolutions of the plebian assembly), *senatus consulta* (resolutions of the senate, a consultative body with no lawmaking authority but whose resolutions eventually acquired the force of law), the edicts of the magistrates, and the interpretations of those learned in the law.[31] Magistrates were invested with

---

[30] The *Leges duodecim tabularum* (Laws of the Twelve Tables), probably produced around 450 BCE, was the first systematic treatment of Roman law in the form of conditional imperatives, and became the foundation of Roman civil law. It could not be simply replaced or abolished when its provisions proved inadequate or obsolete. There were modifications by *leges*, by the praetor's edict, and by juristic interpretation. See the detailed introduction to the Twelve Tables in Crawford (1996) and in Watson (1974, 111–22).

[31] According to Watson (1974, 3–5), there is no theory of sources in the *Republic*, and Romans never drew a distinction between *lex* as a formal authoritative creator of law and the sources of *senatus*

imperium (power of the Roman people), from which they derived the power to promulgate edicts (*ius edicendi*) within their sphere of competence, outlining how they would act and how they conceived their duties. For our purposes, the edicts of the magistracy of the praetor (established 367 BCE) are of greatest importance.[32] The praetor's edict, promulgated at the beginning of his tenure of office, set out the circumstances in which the magistrate would grant a legal action, presented the wording of a model action, and listed the legal remedy supplied by the civil law (Watson 1984, 20–22).[33] In addition, the edict could state that where the civil law granted an action, the praetor would refuse it; and conversely, where the civil law gave no action, he would give a remedy. In this way the praetor could introduce new legal remedies through the edict and so extend the old civil law. As Andrew Borkowski points out (1994, 30): "Edicts thus proved to be an ideal vehicle for law reform."

The edict of the praetor was in force during his one-year term of office (*edictum annuum*). It was customary, however, for a praetor to retain the edict of his predecessor, making changes where he saw fit. A fixed core (the *edictum tralaticium*) was therefore passed down, but the edict was fluid enough that any unsatisfactory clause could be modified or removed altogether and additions inserted by any subsequent praetor (Thomas 1976, 36–37).

Technically, praetors were not lawgivers—they could not alter the law by edict, but they had control of the courts (each within his own sphere) and in their edict determined the actions that would be granted, the remedies that could be sought (Jolowicz and Nicholas 1972, 98–100; Watson 1984, 21–22; Thomas 1976, 36). While the edict could not abolish clauses of the Twelve Tables, the new remedies provided would supplant them in practice. By 100 BCE individual edicts also granted totally new actions on substantive law, and the main period of the edict was in the following decades. Cicero said that in his day law came from the edict and not the Twelve Tables (Watson 1974, 61).

In short, the *ius praetorianum* arising from the urban praetor was a body of law distinct from the *ius civile* arising from statute and interpretation. It was a kind of gloss or supplement to the main body of civil law and was characterized by flexibility, good faith, and equity. Papinian (d. 213 CE) describes praetorian law as "that which in the public interest the praetors have introduced in aid or supplementation or correction of the ius civile" (D.1.1.7.1; as cited in Borkowski 1994, 31). The praetor could *aid* the civil law by granting more convenient

---

consulta, edicta, and juristic writings. *Leges* were authoritative in theory and practice; edicts were all-powerful in practice, though *in theory* they could not change the law.

[32] For details of the establishment of the praetorship, see Jolowicz and Nicholas 1972, 16, 48–49. The praetor's legal function was the administration of the civil process (*iurisdictio*) in Rome. Following the constitutional reforms of Sulla, a total of eight praetors served a year in Rome (in various capacities) before proceding to governorships of provinces abroad (ibid., 49).

[33] My discusssion of the praetor and the praetorian edict draws primarily upon the following works: Jolowicz and Nicholas 1972; Borkowski 1994; Thomas 1976; Watson 1974 and 1991.

and effective remedies for civil law claims. He could *supplement* it by granting a remedy in circumstances not covered by the civil law. *Correction* of the *ius civile* was infrequent and pursued cautiously. However, the praetor did have the power to act in the interests of the Roman people and thus at times acted in contradiction to the civil law.[34]

In 130 CE, Hadrian had all the edicts of past praetors consolidated into a code given the force of law. The resulting fixed edict was the Edictum Perpetuum, after which praetors were no longer innovative. However, the standard Edictum Perpetuum, containing about two hundred separate provisions, was still published regularly and so persisted as a functioning body of law alongside the old civil law, whose provisions it occasionally supplanted (Thomas 1976, 35; Watson 1984, 22). Thus, the Roman legal system comprised at least two complimentary bodies of law of independent authority that were never fully integrated. The lack of integration of these two coexisting and complimentary bodies of law is reflected in the writings of the Roman jurists of the second–fourth centuries CE. Gaius (second century CE) sets out the rules of the civil law and then explains that they have been rendered inoperative by the praetorian edict, while Paul and Ulpian (both early third century CE) compose separate commentaries on the civil law and the praetorian edict (Watson 1984, 22). Precisely because the edict enjoyed an independent legal authority, its rulings could correct and on occasion supplant provisions of the civil law.

The edict was important in Roman provincial administration. As Gaius states, the jurisdiction of the praetor in Rome corresponded in the provinces to that of the governors. Most provincial governors (including those of Judea after 70 CE) were promagistrates and so regularly issued edicts.[35]

CONCLUSION

Classical civilization produced a rich and variegated set of discourses and literary and legal practices around the themes of divine law and, relatedly, human law. I have grouped the discourses under seven general rubrics on the basis of common concepts, tropes, and motifs. These rubrics are entirely artificial, an attempt to impose order on an otherwise unwieldy mass of ideas. They are also purely descriptive. No attempt has been made to trace the systematic development of any given concept or to provide a complete account of a particular thinker or text. Indeed, since Plato, Aristotle, and other figures employ motifs and concepts of different discourses, they are cited in connection with every

---

[34] Introducing, for example, remedies for fraud and duress, better protection of proprietary interests, recognition of informal agreements, and an alternative form of succession to property upon death (Borkowski 1994, 31).

[35] For a summary of opposing views on these matters, see Katzoff 1980, 809–10, 823–25. For the historical link between provincial government and the praetorship, see Jolowicz and Nicholas 1972, 66–67.

discourse to which they contribute with no attempt to provide a comprehensive and systematic account of their individual views.

The seven major discourses of law identified in this chapter are as follows:

Natural Law Discourses

(G-R 1) Natural law and truth: this discourse defines divine law as natural law, a rational *logos* that is universal, immutable, and allied with truth. Some versions of this discourse assume an ontological realism, while others (e.g., the Stoic version) do not.

(G-R 2) Natural law and cosmopolitanism: this discourse regards right reason (the natural law) as the law of the world-city, or cosmopolis, and employs political terms metaphorically to describe the universal community of gods and persons of wisdom and virtue.

Positive Law Discourses

(G-R 3) Human law and virtue: this discourse concludes that unlike natural law, human positive law is inadequate for the attainment of virtue. The rule of law is deemed a second-best regime necessitated by a failure of education. Law that promotes self-rule through the acquisition of knowledge is preferred to law that promotes self-rule through discipline and habituation.

(G-R 4) The inflexible, written law vs. the flexible, unwritten law: this fourth discourse locates the deficiency of human positive law— particularly written law—in its generality and inflexibility. The written law is denigrated as lifeless in contrast to the animate unwritten law or the living law of kings. Some versions of this discourse propose the use of practical wisdom for the equitable adjustment of the law.

(G-R 5) The opposition of nature and conventional law: this discourse assumes the opposition of human positive law and nature. In some versions, positive law is said to achieve only a partial rescue from the brutish state of nature. In other versions, positive law is an infringement on natural liberty or human nature.

(G-R 6) Positive law in need of a savior: this discourse, found primarily in Plato, describes *logos* as the "savior" of the positive law, which in itself is incapable of leading to virtue.

(G-R 7) In praise of written law: this discourse views law, particularly written law, as the mark of civilization and freedom. Those without law are barbarians and slaves.

In addition, this chapter identified one literary and two legal practices in which divine natural law and human positive law are in some way juxtaposed.

(G-R 8) Divine law as a standard for the evaluation of human law: this literary tradition is found in works that evaluate the constitutions of political states to determine whether they possess the attributes of divine law—particularly constancy or immutability.

(G-R 9) Juristic theory vs. juristic practice: this refers to a literary-legal tradition found in the writings of Roman jurists who invoked an unsystematic and eclectic mix of natural law concepts (especially Stoic) in theoretical statements about the law but ignored the same in practical statements of the law.

(G-R 10) The rational adjustment of the civil law: this refers to the legal practice of magistrates, the praetor in particular, who drew upon rational principles of equity and good faith in promulgating an edict that modified, corrected, and set aside provisions of the civil law.

The discourses and literary and legal traditions enumerated in this chapter will be referenced in subsequent chapters as G-R 1, G-R 2, etc. Subsections of these discourses and traditions will also be indicated, for example, G-R 1(iii).

The basic conceptual dichotomy of natural law and positive law was held in common by Stoics, Aristotelians, and Platonists. As many scholars have shown,[36] the ideas of the philosophical schools—Stoicism in particular—migrated from their original settings in the imperial period and may be found in literary texts, inscriptions, and popular philosophical works (such as unsystematic epitomes) that were widely available throughout the Mediterranean region. As Edwyn Bevan (1923) argued nearly a century ago, in the Hellenistic period the various philosophical schools were in broad agreement on many topics, and their blended views were often generalized in popular representations of "what the philosophers think":

> [P]hilosophy ... became popular as it had never been before. Philosophers were to be seen everywhere—in the streets of the cities, at the banquets of kings—Platonic, Peripatetic, Stoic, Epicurean, Sceptic, Cynic ...
>
> Perhaps what most strikes one today in going over the remains of that voluminous ethical literature which they severally put forth, is the extent of that which all the schools had in common. The ideals of temper and conduct which governed that ancient world ... were embodied in a kind of popular philosophy, much of which might have come from any of the rival schools. (81–82)[37]

It should occasion no surprise, then, that the standard characterizations of divine and human law found in the several philosophical schools, but particu-

---

[36] See Strich 2007, chap. 2, summarizing the work of Bevan, Malherbe, Meeks, and Koester.

[37] This view is echoed in scholarship decades later. See for example, Koester 1995, 341.

larly in Stoicism, infused both elite and popular culture in a somewhat eclectic manner.

In the Hellenistic period, Jews, whose sacred writings contained a very different set of discourses about divine law, experienced a cognitive dissonance arising from the encounter with a conception of divine law so different from the representation of divine law in biblical tradition. Attempts by adherents of biblical tradition to make sense of biblical divine law in light of the very different classical discourses of divine law gave rise to processes of negotiation, accommodation, resistance, and revision that would forever change the way biblical cultures would read the biblical text. Those processes will be explored in detail in parts II and III.

Mosaic Law in the Light of Greco-Roman Discourses of Law to the End of the First Century CE

Introduction

In the Hellenistic period, popular and highly eclectic versions of the tenets of the central philosophical schools penetrated the eastern end of the Mediterranean, and Jews living in this area were exposed to the divine law discourses of the classical tradition. Hellenistic philosophical schools of all stripes commonly attributed certain traits to divine natural law. It was held to be universal, rational, unwritten, eternal, and unchanging, and to govern the sage without effort. By contrast, human positive law was held to be particular, grounded in a sovereign will, written, temporary, and flexible. Positive law is superfluous for the sage, who automatically pursues the virtue that he rationally perceives, and deficient for the fool, who rebels against its strictures.

The characteristic traits commonly assigned to divine law and human law are set out in the following chart:

Divine Natural Law	Human Positive Law
Universal	Particular*
Grounded in reason/rational*	Grounded in will*/arbitrary*[1]
Unwritten	Written*
Eternal*	Temporary
Unchanging	Flexible, capable of change*
Governs the sage*	Superfluous for sage; impotent for fool

An asterisk marks those traits that might be said to apply to the Bible's representation of the divine law revealed at Sinai (the Mosaic Law or Torah). Asterisks appear in both columns. This is because the Hebrew Bible portrays the Mosaic Law as possessing some qualities associated with natural law and some qualities associated with human positive law as defined by Hellenistic philosophical traditions. As we saw in chapter 1, the Mosaic Law is not represented as a rational world order, or *logos*, yet it does possess some rational features and is associated with wisdom; moreover, it is said to be eternal (although only

[1] While human positive law may possess rational features, it is not inherently rational and its authority does not derive from its rationality but from its origin in a sovereign will backed by coercive power.

derivatively, because the issuing authority and his covenant are said to be eternal), and it addresses people as wise and discerning. These qualities are characteristic of natural law. At the same time the Mosaic Law is not universal—it is addressed to a particular people precisely in order to set them off as distinct from other peoples and to enable them to live in a particular land in peace and justice; it is grounded in the coercive will of a sovereign authority; it is written, and it is flexible and evolving—all features associated with positive human law in classical tradition.

The Hellenistic dichotomy of divine law and human law is a poor fit for biblical divine law. Although the Mosaic Law is understood to be divine law, it possesses few of the features associated with divine law and many of the features of human positive law in the classical tradition. This incongruity was likely a cause of cognitive dissonance for many Jews. How were they to negotiate the differences between the biblical conception of divine law and the conceptions of divine law in the dominant culture?

Jewish responses to the cognitive dissonance engendered by the incongruity between biblical and classical notions of divine law can be grouped into three general categories. The first is an apologetic response that sought to elevate the status of biblical divine law by emphasizing its similarity to or identity with the Greek conceptions of divine law. Bridging the gap between the two may be accomplished by attributing to Mosaic Law the characteristic features of natural law (listed on the left side of the chart above) or conversely by attributing to the laws of the cosmos the characteristic features of positive law (listed on the right side of the chart above). Chapter 3 discusses the Hellenistic and Second Temple Jewish texts that exemplify this response.

In sharp contrast, a second response sought to highlight the Mosaic Law's similarity to positive law rather than the natural law, opening a path for its subordination to or supersession by the natural law inscribed on the heart. Chapter 4 discusses passages from the writings of Paul that exemplify this response.

A third response refused to accept uncritically the dichotomies of classical thought. Expanding upon the biblical text's representation of divine law as a multidimensional blend of will, reason, and history, this third response did not seek to re-create biblical divine law in the image of either classical natural law or positive law. This alternative characterization of divine law found in rabbinic literature of the talmudic era (first–seventh centuries CE) will be the subject of part III.

CHAPTER 3

Bridging the Gap: Divine Law in Hellenistic and Second Temple Jewish Sources

In the Second Temple period, Jews from Alexandria to Palestine inhabited a "sapiential milieu"[1] even as the divine law set forth in the Torah was becoming the rule and norm for practical life (Schnabel 1985, 6). The term "sapiential" has been applied to texts that stem from very different social groups and exhibit enormous variety, from Sirach and Baruch, to Enochic literature and the Letter of Aristeas, and to wisdom texts preserved among the Dead Sea Scrolls. Nevertheless, the question of the relationship between wisdom and law and the tension between universalism and particularism that this relationship embodied was a critical one for the authors of many of these texts. This chapter explores a representative sample of texts in which *some form* of reason emerges as a prominent category in the conceptualization of divine law, and energy is expended in clarifying its relationship to divine law. In their attempt to bridge the gap between classical and biblical notions of divine law, and to manage the tension between universalism and particularism, these texts generated new and diverse constructions of divine law.

BRIDGING THE GAP

The problem of the relationship between the universal divine law perceived in the natural order and the particular divine law received through the revelation at Sinai was solved by the assumption of some degree of indirect or direct correspondence between the two.[2] In many sources, the correspondence between the two was established on the assumption that both nature and revelation participate in the divine reason. Thus, it was widely held—despite appearances to the contrary—that God's voice in the positive laws given to Israel did not contradict his voice in the order of creation (Bockmuehl 2000, 111). God's reason is manifest in creation, *and* God's reason informs—indeed, on occasion is

---

[1] The phrase is used by many scholars, following Worrell 1968.
[2] So Nel 1982, 92–97, relying on Vriezen 1958 [= 1970], 25ff.

identified with—the laws of the Torah. Thus, writings from this period achieve the correlation of God's revealed law with the cosmic order of creation by correlating or identifying Torah with reason in some way.[3]

The texts examined in this chapter respond to the cognitive dissonance created by the confrontation of classical and biblical notions of divine law by seeking to minimize or bridge the difference between the universal law grounded in reason and the particular Mosaic Law grounded in will. They accomplish this by (1) drawing a strong correlation or even identification between Torah and either wisdom (*sophia*) or reason (*logos*),[4] which are understood to inform the cosmic order, and (2) transferring the properties of the one to the other. The degree of correlation and the direction of transfer varies from text to text. Some texts elaborate the sapiential and rational credentials of the revealed Torah, while others assert the positivistic and particular character of the laws that regulate creation. Still others adopt a dual strategy, both sapientializing the Law and positivizing the cosmic order.

The Correlation of Torah and Wisdom and the Mutual Transfer of Properties: Sirach, 1 Enoch, and Qumran

(1) SIRACH

Sirach (or Ecclesiasticus), a second-century BCE work by the scribe and teacher Jesus ben Sira in Palestine, connects wisdom with cosmic order on the one hand and God's revealed law on the other.[5] Thus, Sirach 16:24–17:14 opens with a

---

[3] The term "identification" is used here in the sense outlined by Schnabel, who explains that on an Aristotelian formulation of the law of identity, according to which every assertion of entity x is true of identical entity y, strict identity can subsist only between a term and itself. In regard to Sirach's identification of law and wisdom, Schnabel (1985, 91) notes, "It is obvious that if we tried to present Sirach's 'identification' of law and wisdom in the terms mentioned above, the 'identification' would disappear: it is certainly not possible to say that *every* assertion which is true of law is also true of wisdom, or that every constituent which makes up 'law' is always also a constituent of 'wisdom'. For this reason we use, instead of the term 'identification', also the term 'correlation' in the sense of a mutual relation of law and wisdom implying an intimate or, after Ben Sira, even a necessary connection." To say that a specific writer "identifies" law with wisdom is to say not that the writer has determined the strict logical identity of the two, but to say that the writer treats the two as the same or as inseparably associated (ibid., 90).

[4] Certainly there is a difference between *sophia* and *logos*. However, for our purposes these differences can be safely ignored; our interest is in the strategies employed by Second Temple period authors to lessen the perceived distance between biblical divine law and classical divine law, and both *sophia* and *logos* are mobilized to enhance the rational character of the Mosaic Law.

[5] This identification is not to be taken for granted, as indicated by the roughly contemporaneous Wisdom of Solomon, which emphasizes the identification of wisdom not with the Torah but with the divine *pneuma* and the divine *logos* through which God created the world (Gilbert 1984, 311). Thus, wisdom may be seen in the elemental forces of nature and the divine providence that governs history, but apart from a general statement to the effect that wisdom makes known what is pleasing to the Lord, the Torah is only obliquely addressed. Wisdom *knows* what is right in God's commandments and what pleases God, and by teaching humans what pleases God (9:18) wisdom reforms and *saves* them

declaration of God's wisdom and knowledge as manifested in the works of creation and continues with the instruction, law, covenant, judgment, justice, and commandment given to humans. Sirach follows Proverbs in personifying wisdom but goes further in explicitly identifying wisdom with the Law of Israel.[6] In chapter 24, Wisdom says of herself:

> 24:19 Come to me, you who desire me, and from my produce be filled.
>
> 24:20 For the memory of me is sweet beyond honey.
>
> 24:21 Those who eat me will hunger for more, and those who drink me will thirst for more.
>
> 24:22 He who obeys me will not be ashamed, and those who work with me will not sin.
>
> 24:23 All these things are the book of the covenant of the Most High God, a law that Moyses commanded us, an inheritance for the gatherings of Iakob . . .
>
> 24:25 It fills wisdom like Phison and like Tigris in days of new things.
>
> 24:26 It supplies understanding like Euphrates and like Jordan in days of harvest,
>
> 24:27 It shines forth education like light, like Geon in days of vintage.[7]

(9:18–19), but wisdom is not explicitly identified with the commandments. As Blenkinsopp notes (1995, 169), the work seldom alludes to the Law except in passing, omitting it even in its account of Moses's leadership of the Israelites in the wilderness. Wisdom is said to *save* the wicked from sin, by teaching them to do what is pleasing to God, and to bring immortality, claims that are not made on behalf of the Torah. The soteriological language is reminiscent of Plato (G-R 6). Reflecting on law's limited ability to ensure its own observance and to thus bring virtue, Plato asserted that the law is in need of a savior. In the Wisdom of Solomon, the clear implication is that without the instruction of wisdom, without knowledge of God's commandments and of what is pleasing to God, virtue is not possible, humans are not "delivered" from sin, and they do not gain immortality. Paul, of course, will move in the same direction.

[6] Bauckmann 1960, 49 as cited in Schnabel 1985, 10n10, has argued that Sirach's references to law and commandments do not refer to the Mosaic Law of Israel specifically, but Schnabel's recent extensive examination of Sirach's terminology supports the contrary view. Schnabel looks at all occurrences of the terms *torah, mitzvah, mishpat, hoq,* and *devar Yahweh* in Sirach, as well as the Greek terms *nomos, entole, krima,* and *logos Kyrion,* and concludes that there are between fifty-four and fifty-six unambiguous references to the Mosaic Law, demonstrating the importance of the *lex revelata* for Sirach (Schnabel, 39). He notes seventy-three occurrences of Greek *logos,* none of which refers to the Mosaic Law. On fifty-four occasions, *logos* is a sapiential concept connected with speech ethics. On five occasions, it denotes the word of God in creation or in prophets, and once it refers to a prophetic utterance. The contrast with Philo's usage will be evident below.

[7] All Sirach translations are those of Benjamin Wright, as found in *NETS.* The identification of Israel's Law and wisdom is suggested in some later additions to the text, specifically 1:5, "Wisdom's spring is God's word in the highest, and her journeys are everlasting commandments," and the prologue, which says in reference to the Law and the Prophets and other writings: "[F]or which reason it is necessary to commend Israel for education (*paideia*) and wisdom (*sophia*)." According to 1:16 and 18, the fear of the Lord (i.e., obedience to his Law) is the fullness and garland of wisdom, while 1:27 states more pointedly, "For wisdom and education are the fear of the Lord."

Although both the cosmic order and the Torah are separately identified with Wisdom (in the sense of correlation rather than strict logical identity), the two are not *directly* identified with one another. The realm of law is not *directly* identical with the realm of creation, and the law is not a comprehensive cosmic law but the particular Torah of Israel (Schnabel 1985, 62). The two are conjoined only insofar as each participates in, and is separately identified with, wisdom, but they are not identical with one another.

Nevertheless, because wisdom was identified with law on the one hand and creation on the other, it served as a bridge for the transference of properties between the two and in both directions. Sirach emphasizes the sapiential function of the Law, hints at its universalistic dimension through its association with Wisdom (ibid., 88), and enhances its status and dignity by retrojecting it to creation. However, Mosaic Law is not per se universalistic, and the apparent universalistic dimension of the Torah in Sirach should be regarded as the *result* rather than the cause of the identification of law and wisdom (ibid., 80). Moreover, the law does not give up its identity as God's Torah revealed to Israel through Moses (ibid., 72). For this reason, wisdom was also able to serve as a bridge for the reverse-direction transference of legal terms to the realm of creation. The terms *torah*, *devar Yahweh*, and especially *ḥoq* are used in reference to the order imposed by God upon creation (ibid., 43). Thus, Wisdom itself was affected and transformed by its identification with God's Torah. Schnabel (87) writes:

> Ben Sira's identification had consequences for the wisdom concept. The universalistic tendency of wisdom is limited and the possibility of profane wisdom is excluded. From now on, wisdom is the exclusive gift of Yahweh to Israel. Ben Sira is 'torahfying' and 'historifying' wisdom ... As a result, essentially sapiential instructions are now occasionally substantiated by references to law and revelation.

The reciprocal transfer of properties can be seen in the proliferation of motives for obedience to the divine law. Frequent references to the wisdom that attends observance of the commandments suggest that the Law's claim to human fidelity lies in its sapiential character. Studying and keeping the Law (i.e., "fear of the Lord") lead to wisdom: 1:26: "If you desire wisdom, keep the commandments, and the Lord will furnish her abundantly to you"; 6:37: "Exercise your thought in the Lord's ordinances, and on his commandments continually meditate. It is he who will make your heart firm, and the desire for wisdom will be given to you"; 15:1: "He who fears the Lord will do it, and he who has a hold on the law will lay hold of her" (i.e., wisdom)"; 19:20: "All wisdom is the fear of the Lord and in all wisdom there is doing of the law." Here, obedience to the Law appears to be motivated by the goal of acquiring wisdom (Schnabel 1985, 55).

However, Schnabel asserts that the wisdom teaching of Sirach is oriented by the sovereign will of God (46) so that observing the Law is motivated by the desire to comply with God's will (49). Sirach 35:1–7 states, in connection with keeping the Law and departing from injustice: "For all these things are for the sake of a commandment of God" (v. 7). At the same time, love is cited as a motive for observing the Law. Sirach 2:15–16 reads: "Those who fear the Lord will not disobey his words, and those who love him will preserve his ways. Those who fear the Lord will seek his favor, and those who love him will be filled with the law." Love and fear are both Deuteronomic terms that evoke the covenantal obligation of loyalty arising from Israel's historic encounter with her deity, an encounter that is renarrativized in Sirach's story of how Wisdom (Torah) came to dwell in Jerusalem (see below).

These diverse motives for obedience to the divine law attest to the multidimensionality of Sirach's conception of the Law. One keeps the commandments because it is God's will, because it leads to wisdom, and because it responds to God with the reverence and love due to him as Israel's partner in a covenantal history and as source of the gift of wisdom (i.e., law).

(II) 1 ENOCH

1 Enoch, a collection of writings composed in stages during the last three centuries BCE,[8] resembles Sirach in some respects but diverges dramatically from it in others. Like Sirach, 1 Enoch identifies wisdom with the laws or natural order of the universe; unlike Sirach it does not explicitly identify wisdom with the revealed Torah.[9] Yet 1 Enoch emphasizes the positivistic character of the laws that regulate creation, transferring some of the properties of the revealed law to the natural order. In 1 Enoch, the laws regulating the cosmos are represented not as the manifestation of a *logos* inherent in nature; rather, they are *commandments* issued by God to regulate the cosmos. The heavenly bodies are

---

[8] The most complete text of 1 Enoch (a composite work consisting of the *Book of Watchers* [chaps. 1–36], the *Book of Parables* [chaps. 37–71], the *Astronomical Book* [chaps. 72–82], the *Book of Dreams* [chaps. 83–90], and the *Epistle of Enoch* [chaps. 91–107]) is in Ethiopic. The Aramaic material from Qumran is unfortunately quite fragmentary but includes sections from the *Astronomical Book* (chaps. 72–82). According to Maxwell J. Davidson (1992, 20), the Ethiopic version of the *Astronomical Book* "is apparently more a summary than a translation of the longer Aramaic material corresponding to it." Moreover, according to Davidson and R. T. Beckwith (1981, 367), the *Astronomical Book*, along with *The Book of the Watchers* (1 Enoch 1–36), is the earliest of the books that constitute 1 Enoch, dating to a period around or before the end of the third century BCE. My discussion of the *Astronomical Book* refers to the most complete recension—the Ethiopic work—on the assumption that the longer Aramaic work at Qumran contained the same basic calendrical traditions. This approach is reasonable in light of the fact that similar calendric traditions appear in the work of Jubilees attested at Qumran as well as the Sabbath *Shirot* (see below).

[9] Although a few passages connect wisdom with righteousness (e.g., in 14:3 "words of wisdom" and "words of righteousness" are parallel terms; in 82:2–4 the righteous are those who learn wisdom; 99:10 states that those who understand words of wisdom "observe the paths of the Most High and walk in the path of his righteousness"), references to the revelation of the Mosaic Law, the covenant, or the Torah of Israel are minimal at best. In 1 En 5:4 the people are chastised for failing to do the commandments of the Lord, and 99:2 refers to sinners who transgress the eternal law.

understood to follow laws *laid down* by God. Specifically, the various natural elements and entities are moved by angels who are directly *commanded* by God (60:11–22; 66:1–2; 69:21–25). In obeying the commands of God, the natural elements and entities take an oath to fulfill the order, regulation, or law given to them.

> 41 (5) And I saw the storehouses of the sun and the moon … And they do not leave the course, and they neither extend nor diminish their course. And they keep faith with one another according to the oath that they have <sworn>. (6) And first the sun emerges and completes its path according to the command of the Lord of Spirits. (See also 1 Enoch 33:3–4; 73:1; 76:14)

1 Enoch's explicit characterization of the laws of nature as divine decrees facilitates an even more radical transference of legal attributes to the realm of the created order than is found in Sirach's "torah-fication" of wisdom. Specifically, 1 Enoch adopts the language of obedience and disobedience, sin and punishment: the laws imposed on the cosmos are binding, and if the forces of nature or the heavenly bodies *choose to disobey*—a distinct possibility—they are punished (21:1–6; 80:16; see Schnabel 1985, 106).

The possibility of cosmic disobedience that results from this "torah-fication" of nature is a remarkable departure from classical notions of natural law. In Stoic thought, for example, the universe operates in accordance with the *orthos logos* inherent in it; the idea of nature acting against its inherent reason would be nonsensical. But in 1 Enoch, the cosmic order by which the universe operates is not a fundamentally inherent reason or *logos* that governs naturally and inevitably. On the contrary, cosmic order is here recast as a divine command issued to "subjects"—the elements and entities of the natural world—that can choose to disobey and thereby incur punishment:

> 18 (15) The stars that are rolling over in the fire, these are they that transgressed the command of the Lord in the beginning of their rising, for they did not come out in their appointed times. (16) And he was angry with them and bound them until the time of the consummation of their sins—ten thousand years.

> 21 (1) I traveled to where it was chaotic … (3) And there I saw seven of the stars of heaven, bound and thrown in it together, like great mountains, and burning in fire. (4) Then I said, "For which reason have they been bound, and for what reason have they been thrown here?" (5) Then Uriel said to me, one of the holy angels … said to me … (6) "These are the stars of heaven that transgressed the command of the Lord; they have been bound here until ten thousand years are fulfilled—the time of their sins." (7) From there I traveled to another place … (10) … And he said, "This place is a prison for the angels. Here they will be confined forever."

Chapter 80 describes a future time of sin that will be accompanied by the rampant transgressions of nature:

80 (4) The moon will change its order [or law], and will not appear at its (normal) time. (5) At that time it [the sun][10] will appear in the sky and will arrive ... at the edge of the great chariot in the west and will shine very much more (brightly) than its normal light. (6) Many heads of the stars will stray from the command and will change their ways and actions and will not appear at the times prescribed for them. (7) The entire law of the stars will be closed to the sinners, and the thoughts of those on the earth will err regarding them. They will turn back from all their ways, will err, and will take them to be gods. (8) Evil will multiply against them and punishment will come upon them to destroy all.

Thus, in 1 Enoch, the notion of a cosmic order owes as much to will as to reason, insofar as the eternal laws by which the universe operates are the positivistic commands of a divine will, rather than an immanent, eternal, and unbreachable *logos*, and can therefore be disobeyed.

While 1 Enoch contains no developed characterization of the revealed Torah, wisdom does serve as a bridge that enables the regularities of the cosmic order to influence the norms guiding human behavior. In 1 Enoch 82:1–3, the term "Wisdom" refers to knowledge of the heavenly bodies and related calendric information (Schnabel 1985, 104), and the concept of law is primarily but not exclusively "understood as the universal and comprehensive order of the entire creation" (ibid., 106). In matters of the calendar, humans must conform their behavior to the regularities and patterns established in nature by the command of God. Moreover, 1 Enoch 80:7–8 (cited above) makes it clear that the transgression of God's commands by the heavenly bodies and forces of nature is correlated with error, transgression, and evil on earth. In short, there is a profound link or correspondence between God's commands for the universe and God's commands for humankind. This correspondence finds further expression in the idea that the (usually) faithful fulfillment of the law by nature should provide a model for human obedience (Schnabel 1985, 107), as in the following passages:

2 (1) Contemplate all (his) works, and observe the works of heaven, how they do not alter their paths; and the luminaries <of> heaven, that they all rise and set, each one ordered in its appointed time; and they appear on their feasts and do not transgress their own appointed order. (2) Observe the earth, and contemplate the works that take place on it from the beginning until the consummation, that nothing on earth changes, but all the works of God are manifest to you.

[10] Following the correction of Charles; see Charlesworth 1983, 59 note q.

5 (2) And his works take place from year to year, and they all carry out their works for him, and their works do not alter, but they all carry out his word … (4) But you have not stood firm nor acted according to his commandments; but you have turned aside, you have spoken proud and hard words with your unclean mouth against his majesty.

The (general) constancy of the natural elements serves as a rebuke to humans who are inconstant in observing the commandments of the Lord (identified here only as blasphemy or profanation of the divine name). Humans should model their fidelity to the commandments of God on that of the heavenly bodies and forces of nature.[11]

The idea that the regularities of the cosmic order should in some way shape or influence the norms guiding human behavior finds expression in the sectarian approach to Torah law attested at Qumran.

(III) QUMRAN

Some of the writings discovered in caves at Qumran, and widely believed to be the library of a community of Essenes living in the area, also correlate the cosmic order with the Law revealed through Moses in line with the sect's sapiential orientation.[12] J. E. Worrell (1968, 120–54 passim) describes the Q community as a wisdom community based on the diffusion of sapiential phraseology, concepts, and literary genres among Qumranic texts; the sapiential tendency of 1 QS and CD to regulate the life of the community; the community's claim to possess wisdom; the emphasis on teaching and right ethical conduct; the use of the term *etsah* for council/counsel; and the prestigious position of the *maskil*. The primary purpose of the *maskil*, the central teaching functionary (known also as the *mebaqqer* or *doresh hatorah*—interpreter of Torah) was to ensure that members of the community followed the commandments of Moses and the prophets, as well as the Community Rule (1QS). Certainly, by these measures, the Qumran community was a sapiential community.

---

[11] This idea appears also in the roughly contemporaneous Testament of Naftali (see Charlesworth 1983, 778, for a discussion of the provenance of this work). In chap. 3, Naphtali urges his children to hold fast to the will of God like the sun, moon, and stars. In this case, however, the will or law of God refers not to the Law revealed at Sinai but to the universal moral law implicit in the Genesis narrative (biblical discourse 2(i)). In chap. 3 the will of God (3:1) is said to be the law of God (3:2) and the universal order of nature (3:4–5). To change the law of God is to introduce disorder into one's actions—and thereby to sin. The nations changed the order of nature and engaged in idolatry. The people of Sodom changed the order of nature and sinned, as did the Watchers—the fallen angels who crossed ontological lines to engage in sexual activity with human women and brought about the destruction of the Flood (a favorite theme of 1 Enoch also). Such departures from the natural order, identified here as both the law of God and the will of God, lead to sin and punishment.

[12] Some of the texts appear to have been composed at Qumran by members of the sect and are thus a useful source for the ideas prevalent within the sect. In particular, 1QM, 1QH, 1QS, CD, and the *pesharim* are believed to be of Qumranic origin. These works will supply the main evidence for the ensuing discussion.

At the same time, the Mosaic Law was a supreme and organizing reality for the sect, which referred to itself as the "house of the law" (CD 20:10, 13) and the "community of the law" (1QS 5:2) and to its members as people who "observe the Torah" (1QpHab 8:1; 12:5; Schnabel 1985, 169). 1QS opens with an exhortation to "seek God with a whole heart and soul, and do what is good and right before him as he commanded by the hand of Moses and all his servants the Prophets" (1:1–3). Entrance into the community is described as a "return to the law of Moses" (CD 15:9, 12; 1QS 5:9), while the wicked are cursed for their eagerness to "alter (*lehamir*) the commandments of the Torah" (4QBer^a (286) frag 7, col II:12).

It is not surprising, then, that the "torah-fication" of Wisdom attested in Sirach and 1 Enoch is clearly evident in the writings of the sectarians, for whom devotion to the Mosaic Torah was paramount. While the term *torah* in Qumran texts refers to the Mosaic Law, Pentateuch, and/or Hebrew Scriptures as a whole, and *mitzvah* refers to commandments of the Torah, the terms *ḥoq* and *mishpat* can refer not only to the Torah but also to the cosmic order, the law of time, and the order of all created things (Schnabel 1985, 171, 178).[13]

> From the God of knowledge stems all there is and all there shall be. Before they existed he established their entire design. And when they have come into being, at their appointed time, they will execute all their works according to his glorious design, without altering anything. In his hand are the laws of all things (*mishpate kol*) and he supports them in all their affairs. (1 QS 3:15–17)[14]

As in 1 Enoch (fragments of which were found at Qumran), in the sectarian writings the world is governed not by an immanent or autonomous reason, but by a divine plan established and ordained even before creation (Schnabel 1985, 206). The cosmic order is among the "regulations" promulgated by the divine will in positivistic fashion. Indeed, 1 Enoch (like Jubilees, another work important to the sect) refers to ordinances written on heavenly tablets, applying a motif associated with positive law (writtenness) to the ordinances of nature.[15] Moreover, the use of the terms *ḥoq* and *mishpat* to apply both to God's commandments and to the created order blurs the distinction between the order regulating creation and the order regulating the life of the sect, and presents both as promulgations of the divine will. According to Schnabel, the double signification of *ḥoq* implies

> a concept of law according to which the cosmic order and Israel's law constitute but one reality ... The divine orders and stipulations inherent in

---

[13] Similarly, *tikkon* designates both the order established by God and the order given to the community (Schnabel 1985, 178).

[14] All translations of Dead Sea Scrolls are taken from García Martínez and Tigchelaar 1977.

[15] I am indebted to Anne Schiff for this insight.

creation and given to Israel were experienced as a unity. Thus it was natural for the Community to organize its life in a basic and scrupulous conformity and harmony with the laws of both the Torah and creation. (180)

As in Sirach and 1 Enoch, however, the "torah-fication" of Wisdom at Qumran was accompanied by the reverse-direction transfer of an important property of the cosmic order to human norms—in this case, the Torah's alliance with "truth." Organizing the life of the community in conformity with the laws of both the Torah and creation meant not only that legal terms were used in reference to the natural order but also that the details of the written commandments of the Torah were elaborated and developed in light of what the sect perceived to be *the objective realities of the natural order*. The result is a realist orientation to the Law according to which Law is expected to conform to "truth," understood as a mind-independent, objective reality—"the way things are" (reminiscent of the realist identification of divine law with truth found in G-R 1(iii)).[16]

In a 1992 article, Daniel Schwartz suggested that the Qumran sectarians (and the Sadducees) espoused a realist view of law in contrast to the manifestly nominalist approach of the later rabbis.[17] Chapter 5 takes up this claim in much greater depth. For now, I note only that sectarian determinations of law at times explicitly defer to, or anchor themselves in, what their own rhetoric asserts is the order of nature or an objective reality. It should be stressed that the point of this discussion is not to adjudicate or critique the sectarian assessment of what constitutes "objective reality" but simply to recognize that the sectarians believed that there *is* such a thing as a mind-independent, objective reality and truth; that we can gain certain knowledge of it in a variety of ways ranging from empirical observation to reliable calculation to divine revelation; and that God's revealed Torah must conform to this objective reality.

Schwartz's best evidence for a realist approach to law at Qumran is found in determinations of law that feature an explicit appeal to an objective reality as perceived by the sectarians. This may take any number of forms—an appeal to the natural order of creation as ascertained (1) through direct empirical observation; (2) through the record of creation preserved in the Scriptural account (which some ancient Jews believed provided utterly reliable factual data about the natural order); or (3) through special revelation of cosmic realities, regularities, and mathematical rhythms. An example of each follows.

(1) An appeal to nature (specifically, a law of creation) relying on simple empirical observation is found in CD 12:14–15 (see Schwartz 1992, 231). In this passage, the proper method of slaughtering locusts (by water or fire) is grounded in the fact that it is the rule/order of their creation (*ki hu mishpat*

---

[16] For an attestation of the phrase "what exists" or "things that are" in Jewish antiquity, see Wisd 7:17.

[17] In employing these terms, Schwartz relies on Silman 1984–85. For a full discussion of the debates initiated by this article, see chapter 5.

beri'atam), which may mean the natural characteristics with which they were created—possibly a reference to the fact that locusts possess no "blood" that can be spilled and covered.[18]

(2) An appeal to nature supported by the Scriptural record of creation occurs in CD 4: 21 (see Schwartz 1992, 231). Here, polygamy is rejected because it violates the principle of creation (*yesod habberi'ah*) as stated in Genesis 1:27 "male and female he created them" (*zakar uneqebah bara' 'otam*).

(3) An appeal to certain mathematical regularities of nature and the true created order, knowledge of which is said to have been vouchsafed to humanity by a special revelation, occurs in the case of the calendar. The calendar provides evidence of a highly realist orientation. The sectarians at Qumran took an oath to follow the sectarian calendar so as not to advance or delay (*lo leqadem ... velo lehitaher*) the dates of the festivals (1QS 1:14–15)[19]—a phrase that signals a belief in objectively *real* dates of the festivals as determined by the fifty-two-week pattern fixed by God at the time of the creation. Two important works in the Qumran library represent the fifty-two-week, 364-day calendar as divinely determined, eternal, and part of the inherited esoteric knowledge of the community. Those works are 1 Enoch (as we have seen) and Jubilees. According to Jubilees, the calendar was established at creation, when the Sabbath was appointed as a sign for all God's works (Jub 2:1). Since the beginning of time the highest angels have observed the Sabbath (Jub 2:17–18) and the Festival of Weeks (Jub 6:17–18). As the angels keep the Sabbath, and indeed all the festivals, in heaven, Israel is bound to keep them on earth (Jub 2:18–21; 6:30–32) as an eternal ordinance ordained and written on the heavenly tablets (Jub 6:29–30, 15:25–27; Van Ruiten 2007, 591–93). Failure to follow the true 364-day calendar results in asynchronous observance of the Sabbath and festivals in heaven and on earth—a major disruption (Jub 6:32–33). For the author of Jubilees, "God's intention is nothing less than perfect union, oneness, between heaven and earth as represented by the highest angels and Israel" (Hayward 1996, 63; see Jub 2:18, 21).

In their references to the calendar, the texts cited above employ a rhetoric of objective reality: the calendar reflects the objectively true created order (it is "written on the heavenly tablets"). It aligns with the divinely ordained, angeli-

---

[18] The first two examples discussed here access information about the natural order through the written record of creation and through direct observation. That we may not agree with the results of ancient Jewish empiricism or share its view of the nature of locusts, for example, is immaterial for the claim advanced here—that in these instances an attempt is made to work out the content of the law using the empirical methods and data of the time. Regarding the slaughter of locusts, see Schiffman, 2011, 69.

[19] The full passage from the 1QS reads, "They shall not stray from any one of all God's orders concerning their appointed times; they shall not advance their appointed times nor shall they retard any one of their feasts" (as translated in García Martínez and Tigchelaar 1977, 1:71). Whether the calendar was actually observed at Qumran or not is irrelevant—what is important for our purposes is the rhetoric of a festival date that is part of the divinely decreed natural order and cannot be changed.

cally monitored, and mathematically regular movement of the luminaries.[20] Human deviations are therefore false and sinful (Jub 6:34–38)—one must not advance or delay the (objectively real) times of the festivals.

In short, there is very suggestive evidence from Qumran of a realist approach to the revealed laws of the Torah, an approach that privileges appeals to nature and/or the created order when interpreting the content of the revealed Torah. This approach is predicated on the assumption of an alliance of divine law and truth in the sense of *conformity to the regularities of an objectively real natural order.*[21]

The Letter of Aristeas and the writings of Philo of Alexandria also assume that divine law is allied with truth and, therefore, that the revealed Torah is allied with truth. However, for Aristeas and Philo the truth that characterizes the Torah of Moses is first and foremost *rational truth.*

The Correlation of Torah and Reason and the Transfer of Properties: Aristeas, 4 Maccabees, and Philo

While Sirach and 1 Enoch focus on Wisdom (*sophia*) as a mechanism for correlating the universal divine law and the particular Mosaic Law, other works focus on reason (*logos*) as well as wisdom (*sophia*). This correlation allows the transfer of properties from the divine natural law to the Mosaic Law— specifically, the properties of rationality and alliance with "rational truth." The result is a refashioning of Mosaic Law that echoes the Hellenistic discourse of universal divine law in important respects.

(I) THE LETTER OF ARISTEAS

The Letter of Aristeas, a second-century BCE work by a Hellenistic Jew from Alexandria, is an apologetic defense of Jewish law and custom. The intention, it seems, is to demonstrate to Hellenized Jews and perhaps to Greeks that the divine law of Israel possesses the central attributes of the divine natural law of Hellenistic, particularly Stoic, tradition. The work asserts that every element of the Mosaic Law expresses the wisdom of its divine author. Verse 27 contains an explicit statement to this effect: Demetrius writes to King Ptolemy that the law of the Jews "in as much as it is of divine origin, is full of wisdom and free from all blemish." From this it follows that there is nothing irrational in the Law, no prohibition or obligation that lacks a *telos*, or rational end. It is to the demonstration of this claim that the work's discussion of the Law is dedicated.

---

[20] Again, the question of whether these claims are accurate, like the question of whether any community actually observed this calendar, is irrelevant. What matters is that these texts make bold claims of objective reality and expect the law to conform to it.

[21] For a detailed argument in support of the characterization of Qumran law as possessing the traits defined here and in chapter 5 as "realist," see Amichay 2013. Amichay employs the term "legal essentialism" rather than "realism" to refer to an approach in which unchangeable facts of nature are believed to bear implications for the law (p. 26).

The author begins his discussion of the Law by taking up precisely the two elements most likely to raise doubts about the Law's thoroughgoing rationality: the seemingly arbitrary dietary laws and the laws of ritual impurity.

> For I believe that most men feel some curiosity concerning passages in the law, dealing with food and drink and animals regarded as unclean. When we inquired, then, why it was that, creation being one, some things are regarded as unclean for food and some even to the touch (for the Law is scrupulous in most things, but in these doubly scrupulous), he [Eleazar, the high priest of the Jews] began his reply as follows: 'You observe what far-reaching effects are exercised by conversation and association; by associating with the evil, men become perverted and are miserable through all of life; but if they consort with the wise and prudent, then from a state of ignorance they acquire amendment for their lives.' (128–31)[22]

The author concedes that the dietary and ritual impurity laws engender curiosity—what possible reason could there be for treating some food, drinks, and animals as impure when they are all part of one creation? Is this not irrational?

In response to the envoys' curiosity about dietary and ritual impurity laws, Eleazar, the Jewish high priest, explains that human behavior is affected by daily habits and associations (139–43). The great wisdom of the Torah lies in the fact that it seeks to inculcate virtue not merely by setting forth principles and examples of virtuous behavior (and the rewards and punishments that attend virtue and vice) but also by establishing habits of life that will prevent harmful associations and so incline those who follow them toward piety and righteousness.[23] In addition to their functional significance in separating Israel from corrupting influences and habituating the nation to piety, these laws are *in their substance* deeply rational, conveying a direct knowledge of virtue. Here the Letter of Aristeas echoes G-R 3(iii), according to which the best positive law conduces to virtue in two ways: by instruction (conveying relevant knowledge to overcome ignorance) and by habituation over time (to overcome enslavement to the passions).

> In general all things are to the natural reason [*phusikon logou*] similarly constituted, being all administered by a single power, and yet in each and

[22] Translation of Hadas 2007.

[23] "When therefore our lawgiver, equipped by God for insight into all things, had surveyed each particular, he fenced us about with impregnable palisades and with walls of iron, to the end that we should mingle in no way with any of the other nations, remaining pure in body and in spirit, emancipated from vain opinions, revering the one and mighty God above the whole of creation ... therefore, so that we should be polluted by none nor be infected with perversions by associating with worthless persons, he has hedged us about on all sides with prescribed purifications in matters of food and drink and touch and hearing and sight" (139–40, 142).

every case there is a profound logic for our abstinence from the use of some things and our participation in the use of others. For the sake of illustration I will run over one or two details and provide an explanation. Do not accept the exploded idea that it was out of regard for 'mice' and the 'weasel' and other such creatures that Moses ordained these laws with such scrupulous care; not so, these laws have all been solemnly drawn up for the sake of justice, to promote holy contemplation and the perfecting of character. For of the winged creatures of which we make use all are gentle and distinguished by cleanliness and they feed on grain and pulse, such as pigeons, doves, 'locusts,' partridges, and also geese and all similar fowl. But of the winged creatures which are forbidden you will find that they are wild and carnivorous and with their strength oppress the rest and procure their food with injustice at the expense of the tame fowl mentioned above. Through these creatures then, by calling them 'unclean,' he set up a symbol that those for whom the legislation was drawn up must practice righteousness in spirit and oppress no one, trusting in their own strength, nor rob anyone of anything, but must guide their lives in accordance with justice, just as the gentle creatures among the birds above mentioned ... All of the regulations concerning what is permissible with reference to these and other creatures, then, he has set forth by way of allegory. (143–47, 150)

The author's argument is fascinating. By *nature*, foods and animals are all alike because they are all governed by one and the same power. To treat them as dissimilar is therefore to behave toward them in defiance of their natural constitutions, which would suggest that the rules establishing the categories of pure and impure are unnatural and presumably arbitrary or *willful*. But this is not so, Eleazar asserts. The categories of pure and impure (= clean and unclean), while admittedly unnatural, are not arbitrary, but deeply rational—as becomes plain when we understand them allegorically (as "symbols" [147] or "indications" [148]). The dietary and impurity laws are crafted in perfect wisdom to aid in the quest for virtue and the perfecting of character. Permitted animals possess certain traits of character that humans would do well to emulate, while prohibited animals possess traits that should be spurned. Thus, even these "unnatural" categories have been formulated with great wisdom to serve as signs, with the purpose of teaching a moral lesson. Although the author has put himself in the rather un-Stoic posture of asserting that something is at once unnatural and rational, he at least rescues the divine law from the unseemly charge of arbitrariness.[24]

After explaining the allegorical import of the prohibition of animals that do not chew their cud or possess a cloven hoof, Eleazar states outright that there

---

[24] In other texts, however, the identification of reason and law will find expression in the idea that Israel's Torah conforms perfectly to the facts of creation, and vice versa.

is nothing arbitrary or random about the dietary rules and laws of impurity. Allegorical interpretation reveals the deeper *truth* (*aletheia*), right reason (*orthos logos*), and righteousness at which each law, and the system as a whole, takes aim:

> The legislation was not laid down at random or by some caprice of the mind, but with a view to truth and as a token of right reason ... [and so he bids us] not, by misusing the power of reason, to resort to injustice ... The points I have briefly run over have shown you that all these norms have been regulated with a view to justice and that nothing has been set down through Scripture heedlessly or in the spirit of myth, but rather in order that throughout our life and in our actions we practice justice towards all men, being mindful of the sovereignty of God. All that is said of food, then, and of unclean creeping things and of animals is directed toward justice and just intercourse among men. (161, 163, 168–69)

Eleazar succeeds in demonstrating that even Jewish ritual law (which because "unnatural" might be thought to be arbitrary) is defensible, in its substance and not merely as a discipline, in rational terms that would appeal to a Greek or Hellenized Jewish audience, and our narrator remarks approvingly that Eleazar made a good defense on all points (170).

Some scholars see the allegorical defense of the Torah as an indication of the author's universal outlook and interest in promoting observance of the Mosaic Law among Gentiles as well as Jews.[25] G.W.E. Nickelsburg goes further and suggests that the Torah in the Letter of Aristeas is devoid of specific Jewish features, and that the allegorical interpretation "turns the Torah into a universal doctrine which may be accepted by every enlightened mind, especially by those who had Greek education."[26] Against this it should be noted that the author does not shy away from explicitly Jewish laws (e.g., the lengthy discussion of dietary laws and impurity laws, 83–100), Jewish customs (e.g., the discussion of banquet preparations in 182 and hand washing before prayer in 305–6), and Jewish concerns (see the discussion of the Temple and cult in loving, if erroneous, detail, 83–100). Certainly, the letter demonstrates that the Law's intent is "compatible with the finest in Gentile ethics and wisdom" (Schnabel 1985, 124); but it nevertheless has in view the specific commandments of the Mosaic Law binding on all Jews.

---

[25] See, for example, Schnabel 1985, 124: "The motivation of the author of EpArist implies also both the universalistic and the particularistic dimension: the law (as well as wisdom, embodied in the law) is the Mosaic Law of the Jews which is to be commended to the Gentiles. And the Mosaic Law with its wisdom has a universal significance and should be observed by all, whether they are Jews or Gentiles (note here the significance of the allegorical interpretation)."

[26] Nickelsburg 1981,168, as cited in Schnabel 1985, 124.

An instructive contrast may be found in Pseudo-Phocylides. Written by a Jew in Alexandria between 30 BCE and 40 CE[27] in the style of Hellenic gnomic poetry, this pseudepigraphic work purports to contain the counsels of "the most wise" Phocylides, a sixth-century poet from Miletus. Unlike the Letter of Aristeas, Pseudo-Phocylides manifests next to nothing of a particularly Jewish character, and the influence of Stoicism is undeniable (van der Horst 1978, 81–82). Although the work opens with what has been described as a summary of the Decalogue linked to commandments from Leviticus 19 (1:3–8), particularly Jewish and cultic elements have been eliminated. Thus, the Decalogue's commandments regarding idolatry and Sabbath observance are absent. Unlike both Sirach and the Letter of Aristeas, the work never mentions the name Israel, nor does it refer to specific cultic precepts, or to dietary, purity, or other ritual laws. The work bases its moral arguments on the order and harmony in creation: the moral imperative to seek harmony and avoid discord is based on the concord of the heavenly bodies that do not envy or contend with one another (75–79). Marriage is enjoined as part of the good order of creation ("Give nature her due, you also, beget in your turn as you were begotten" [175–76]) while homosexuality is rejected as transgressing "the limits set by nature" (190–92; Bockmuehl 2000, 102). Similarly, a work ethic may be derived from the ant and the bee (164–74).[28] The result is a universal ethic that eschews the particularism of Israel's Law.

This is not the path taken by the Letter of Aristeas, which seeks to hold together the universal and particular aspects of its identification of reason and Torah: the Mosaic Law that conforms entirely to the universal *logos* is to be observed by Jews, and cheerfully admired by wise Gentiles. This theme of ungrudging Gentile admiration occupies the latter half of the work. In the lengthy "table talk" section (172–300), the Jewish translators from Jerusalem answer the king's questions and prove themselves to be far superior to the Greek philosophers. Their superiority, the narrator declares, lies in their religious orientation.

Thus, notwithstanding the importation of natural law features, the particular character of Torah as the revealed law *of the Jews* is nowhere compromised in the Letter of Aristeas. Certainly, the rationalist defense of the Law is intended to show its fundamental compatibility with the teachings of Hellenistic ethical philosophy: the Law is grounded in a universal divine reason; it is utterly

[27] The conclusions of van der Horst (1978, 81–82), regarding the provenance of the work, have been widely accepted on linguistic and substantive grounds. There is general agreement that the author was a Jew who maintained a great openness to pagan culture, though the hypothesis that the work was written by a "God-fearer" accepting some Jewish precepts without becoming a Jew has not been dismissed (ibid., 76n21).

[28] Certainly, the work contains references to God that imply that ethical living is in accordance with the divine will (vv. 1, 8, 11, 17, 106, 111, 125–28). In this respect, the work differs from sophistic writings that understand wisdom and ethical living as emerging from education and rational reflection.

rational (G-R 1); and it is consonant with truth (echoing a Platonic realism). But from Gentiles convinced by the author's apologia, all that is expected is commendation, not conversion.

(II) 4 MACCABEES

Another apologetic defense of the Mosaic Law is found in 4 Maccabees, a first- or early second-century BCE work from Alexandria or Antioch. However, rather than a respectful debate, the narrative context of 4 Maccabees is inter-ethnic hostility and persecution. Against the charge that the divine law of the Judeans is not divine because it is neither rational nor true, 4 Maccabees seeks to identify the Mosaic legislation with "wisdom-loving reason" or *philosophos logos* (see 5:35). Like the Letter of Aristeas, 4 Maccabees betrays a concern to counter the charge of irrationality and to portray Jewish life under the Law as "philosophy" (5:11, 22; 7:9) and wisdom. Wisdom is defined as justice, courage, self-control, but most of all prudence (1:18), by which reason prevails over the passions. The restraint of the passions demonstrates the mastery of reason, the mark of the true philosopher. The passion of bodily pleasure is "expressed in indiscriminate eating" (1:16). Thus, the dietary laws are not disproof of the Law's rationality but the very mechanism by which it is instilled and exercised:

> [H]ow is it that when we are attracted to forbidden foods we turn our-selves away from the pleasure to be had from them? Is it not because reason is able to prevail over the appetites? I for one think so. Therefore when we crave seafood, fowl, quadrupeds and all sorts of foods that are forbidden to us by the law, we abstain because of the dominance of rea-son. For the passions of the appetites are restrained, checked by the temperate mind, and all the emotions of the body are bridled by reason. (1:33–35)[29]

The author of 4 Maccabees is well aware that others hold a different view of the dietary laws. The charge of irrationality is placed in the mouth of the tyrant Antiochus, who mockingly claims that Eleazar's adherence to the dietary laws is senseless, against nature, and untrue or vain—all evidence that the Law is *not* divine and that Eleazar is not a philosopher:

> Why should you abhor eating the very excellent meat of this animal when nature has provided it? For it is senseless not to enjoy delicious things that are not shameful and not right to decline the gifts of nature. But you seem to me to do what is even more senseless if, because you cherish a vain opinion concerning the truth, you continue to despite me at the cost of your own punishment. Will you not awaken from your silly philosophy, dispel the nonsense of your reasonings, and adopting a

---

[29] Translation of Stephen Westerholm in *NETS*.

mind worthy of your age, pursue a true philosophy of what is beneficial? (5:8–11)

Eleazar, who is described as a "philosopher of the divine life" living "in harmony with the law" (7:7), responds:

> Even if, as you suppose, our law were in truth not divine and we wrongly considered it to be divine, not even so would it be possible for us to invalidate our reputation for piety... You scoff at our philosophy (*philosophia*), as though our living by it were not sensible [*eulogistia*, rational]. But it teaches us self-control so that we overcome all pleasures and desires, and it also exercises us in courage so that we endure all pain willingly; it trains us in justice ... and it teaches us piety ...
>
> Therefore we do not eat defiling food, for believing that the law is divine, we know that the creator of the world shows us sympathy by imposing a law that is in accordance with nature. He has permitted us to eat what will prove suitable for our souls, but he has forbidden us to eat the flesh of what will prove contrary to us. (5:18, 22–26)

Eleazar and Antiochus agree on what it is for a law to be divine. A divine law is true, rational, and in harmony with nature. Their only dispute is whether the Law of the Judeans possesses those qualities so as to rightly be called "divine." Antiochus cites the dietary laws as evidence that the Law of the Judeans does *not* possess these qualities and therefore cannot be divine. For his part, Eleazar does not question the terms of the debate. He accepts the Greco-Roman conventions according to which divine law must be true, rational, and in harmony with nature, and sets about proving that the Law of Moses possesses these traits: the dietary laws conform to nature; they are rational not only in their purpose but *in their substance* and therefore true. Observance of the Law in general is not irrational since it entails mastery of the passions, which is the height of wisdom. Indeed, obedience to the Law under torture is the most perfect demonstration of the mastery of the passions by reason, the mark of the true philosopher (7:16–23).

(III) PHILO—REFASHIONING TORAH AS THE NATURAL LAW

It is Philo of Alexandria (fl. first century CE) who goes the furthest in resolving the cognitive dissonance between Greco-Roman and biblical conceptions of divine law. He asserts the identity of the two and then labors to demonstrate that the Torah of Moses possesses *all* of the properties and qualities of Greek natural law: it is self-identical with universal truth, which entails its rationality, its immutability, and its unwritten character.[30]

---

[30] For an excellent and detailed study of Philo's connection of the Mosaic Law with a unified version of all three forms of higher law in Greek thought (natural law, unwritten law, and living law), see Martens 2003, 103–30.

Philo's writings exhibit a deep familiarity with Hellenistic philosophy and the natural law tradition, particularly in its Stoic form.[31] Philo's presentation of the Mosaic Law stands in the Greco-Roman tradition of evaluating the constitutions of real states to determine the extent to which they imitate an ideal divine standard (G-R 7). It might be supposed that an evaluation of biblical law against the standard of natural law would lead Philo to conclude that his native constitution was not, after all, divine, just as Clinias and Megillus had concluded in assessing their native constitutions against an ideal divine standard in Plato's *Laws*. But Philo's response to the cognitive dissonance generated by the confrontation of biblical divine law and the Stoic conception of natural law was to assert, not unlike his near contemporary Cicero, that his native constitution *did* possess the attributes of divine natural law; indeed, that it was none other than the divine natural law. As Hindy Najman (1999, 76; 2003, 54–55, 62–63) has pointed out, the claim that a particular and written law is identical with the universal, unwritten law of nature would have been seen by any Stoic as utterly paradoxical, indeed impossible. Yet this was Philo's claim, and it was the basis for his creative attempt to attribute the features of classical divine law to biblical divine law.

Philo worked on three fronts to establish this extravagant claim. First, he applied prominent themes of Greco-Roman divine law discourses to the Mosaic Law, to demonstrate that (a) the Torah is the natural law, the universal *logos* of the cosmopolis or world-city; as a consequence (b) the Torah is truth; (c) the Torah is eternal and absolutely unchanging; (d) the Torah is not the arbitrary expression of a sovereign will consisting of commands and prohibitions enforced by rewards and punishments, but a rational teaching or instruction addressed to noncoerced, rational individuals and devoid of rewards or punishments; and (e) the Torah is unwritten. Second, he highlighted and elaborated those features of biblical tradition that are most compatible with the claim that the Torah is natural law. Third, he suppressed or allegorically reinterpreted those features of the biblical text that would contradict or undermine this claim.

(a) The Torah Is the Natural Law, the Universal *Logos* of the Cosmopolis

Philo's debt to Stoic discourse may be seen in his depiction of the universe as a vast polis (cosmopolis; see G-R 2) constituted ultimately by right reason (*orthos logos*; see G-R 1(ii)), also known as the law of nature (*nomos phuseos*; see G-R 1(iv); Bockmuehl 2000, 107–8), to which the Law of Moses is harmoniously attuned.

> [T]hus whoever will carefully examine the nature of the particular enactments [of the Mosaic Law] will find that they seek to attain to the har-

---

[31] On the influence of Stoicism on Philo, see n35 below.

mony of the universe and are in agreement with the principles of eternal nature. (*Life of Moses* 2:52)[32]

In this passage, Philo asserts the agreement of the Mosaic Law and the law of nature. But it should not be supposed that Philo is content with the weaker claims that the Law of Moses is merely *in harmony with* the universal law of nature, or *correlated* to the law of nature through their mutual origin in or identity with a third entity, such as divine Wisdom. Elsewhere, he clearly makes the stronger claim that the positive Law of Moses *is* the universal law of nature.

> Justice and every virtue are commanded by the law of our ancestors and by a statute established of old, and what else are laws and statutes but the sacred words of Nature ... ? (*Special Laws* 2.13)

Here Philo asserts that the law of his ancestors—presumably the laws delivered by Moses (see below)—are none other than the sacred words of nature. Elsewhere he asserts that to follow the law of Israel is to be a citizen not merely of the community of Israel but a citizen of the world polis, because to observe the Law is to regulate one's doings by the *orthos logos* or *nomos phuseos* that governs the world polis.

> The world is in harmony with the Law and the Law with the world, and the man who observes the Law is constituted thereby a loyal citizen of the world, regulating his doings by the purpose and will of Nature, in accordance with which the entire world itself also is administered. (*De opificio* 3)

Thus, while the positive law of Israel is currently the possession of one specific people, as the law of nature it is intended for all humankind (Reinhartz 1983, 344). Philo envisages a future in which the prosperity of Israel will lead each nation to "abandon its peculiar ways, and, throwing overboard their ancestral customs, turn to honoring our laws alone" (*Life of Moses* 2:44). Note Philo's ironic reversal of the charge of particularism commonly leveled at the Jews by their Gentile critics.[33] It is not Israel that clings to a particularist law against the rational and universal law of other societies. On the contrary, it is Israel that honors the universal law of nature while other nations follow particularistic and "peculiar" ways and customs. As Reinhartz (344) observes:

> Philo argues that the Law of Moses, given by God, is superior to other lawcodes because of its identity with the law of nature, and hence it is by following the Law of Moses that man can become a 'citizen of the world'

---

[32] Unless otherwise indicated, translations of Philo's writings are taken from the Loeb Classical Library editions.

[33] In a similar manner, Philo reversed the charge of misanthropy and xenophobia leveled at Jews by Gentile critics; see Schäfer 1998, 174–75.

... Philo has departed from the narrow definition of *nomos* and depicted the Pentateuch as a lawcode which not only provides specific injunctions but also points the way to the ideal life—life according to nature.

Philo's recasting of the particular law of a particular people as the law of nature intended for the world-polity is achieved by a radical re-vision of the narrative context within which that law is situated. As noted in chapter 1, the immediate narrative context of the Law in the Pentateuch is a *national* myth of liberation and exclusive covenant. The Law is grounded in the history of Yahweh's acts on Israel's behalf and constitutes Israel's—and only Israel's—exclusive obligations to Yahweh. For Philo, however, the narrative context that best illuminates the character, scope, and purpose of the Mosaic Law is not the immediately preceding national narrative that describes the events leading up to and surrounding its revelation (the story of the Exodus and the covenant with Israel) but the universal and patriarchal narratives in Genesis.

> [Moses] considered that to begin his writings with the foundation of a manmade city was below the dignity of the laws, and, surveying the greatness and beauty of the whole code with the accurate discernment of his mind's eye, and thinking it too good and godlike to be confined within any earthly walls, he inserted the story of the genesis of the "Great City," holding that the laws were the most faithful picture of the world-polity. (*Life of Moses* 2:49–52)

Here Philo argues that Moses deemed the Law too good and godlike to be confined to any one polis. He discerned that this great and beautiful code was intended for the entire world-polity, the *megalopolis* that is the entire universe. This is the reason that Moses prefaced the account of the giving of the Law to Israel at Sinai with the story of the creation: to signal that the Law is intended for all world-citizens, not Israel alone.

In the following passage, Philo describes the narrative context of the Law as consisting of two key elements—the creation account and the patriarchal history—omitting entirely the story of the Exodus from Egypt and the Law's bestowal in a special covenant with Israel. He then explains why the creation narrative and patriarchal history precede the presentation of the Law.

> We must now give the reason why he began his lawbook with the history, and put the commands and prohibitions in the second place. He did not, like any historian, make it his business to leave behind for posterity records of ancient deeds for the pleasant but unimproving entertainment which they give; but, in relating the history of early times, and going for its beginning right to the creation of the universe, he wished to shew two most essential things: first that the Father and Maker of the world was in the truest sense also its Lawgiver, secondly that he who would observe the laws will accept gladly the duty of following nature and live in accor-

dance with the ordering of the universe, so that his deeds are attuned to harmony with his words and his words with his deeds. (*Life of Moses* 2:45–48)

The purpose of the creation account is to show that the divine creator and the divine lawgiver are one and the same, which in turn suggests that by observing the Law one is following the natural order of the universe. The account of the lives of the patriarchs shows that those who observe the Law are simply conforming to the ordering of the universe, following the law of nature.

(b) The Torah Is Truth

For Philo, the identification of the Mosaic Law with the divine law of classical tradition entailed its rational and philosophical *truth* and therefore its verisimilitude,[34] its lack of genuine contradiction, and its immunity to historical development. This conception of the Law is explicit in Philo's *Exposition of the Laws*—a late work deeply indebted to contemporary Stoic conceptions of divine law.[35] It finds expression in Philo's harsh criticism of scholarly methods that resolve problems of biblical formulation, style, and content in a way that does not assume the Bible is rational and philosophical truth. As Maren Niehoff has demonstrated (2011, 3, 74, 92, 112, 129), some Alexandrian Jewish intellectuals applied Aristotelian text critical and literary methods to their study of the biblical text, on the assumption that the latter's divinity did *not* remove it from the realm of literature. These exegetes were content to explain the text's many imperfections, contradictions, and lack of verisimilitude (including its lack of correspondence to the truths expounded by various philosophical schools) in literary and historical terms, following contemporary interpreters of Homer.[36]

But for Philo this was the path of the impious.[37] Although Philo himself cautiously applied some literary techniques to the biblical text (Niehoff 2011, 186), he was critical of the scholarly methods of Alexandrian Bible exegetes influenced by the Homeric tradition. To attribute the text's various deviations

---

[34] I use the term "verisimilitude" as it is used by Maren Niehoff (2011, 46), who defines the term as the text's correspondence "to an external reality accessible by other disciplines, such as the natural sciences or history, which claim utmost objectivity and truth value." This is a highly realist stance.

[35] Niehoff (2011, 15) argues that Philo's *Exposition of the Laws* "indicates a significant transition from his early Aristotelian environment in Alexandria to a distinctly more Roman as well as Stoic context." Prior to this, she argues, Stoic influence on Philo's work is not clearly apparent.

[36] These interpreters were guided by the canons of literary interpretation set forth in Aristotle's *Poetics* (Niehoff 2011, passim).

[37] In reference to exegetes who pointed to comparisons between the biblical Tower of Babel story and Homeric motifs, Philo writes: "[T]hey feel annoyance at the ancestral constitution, always engaging in the censure and accusation of the laws, those impious ones" (AC, Conf. 2, as cited in Niehoff 2011, 78).

from perfection and truth[38] to textual error (that can be remedied through deletions and interpolations), to literary or rhetorical techniques (such as exaggeration for dramatic effect), to shifting historical conditions or authorial ignorance and the like, impeached the text's divine character. For Philo, the divinity of the text *did* remove it from the realm of literature and guaranteed its correspondence to truth: "in every respect the Holy Writings are true" (*QA on Gen* 1:12; as cited in Niehoff 2011, 154). Elsewhere he explicitly contrasts the Bible with works of (mere) literature on the question of truth: "In the poetic work of God you will not find anything mythical or fictional but the canons of truth all inscribed, which do not cause any harm" (*AC, Det.* 125; as cited in Niehoff 2011, 173). These truths are exposed through allegorical readings. For example, Philo prefaces his comments on the story of Cain with these words: "Perhaps then, as these things diverge from the truth, it is better to say allegorically ..." (*AC, Post.* 49–50; as cited in Niehoff 2011, 147).

As Niehoff points out (2011, 79), there was a profound conflict of views in Alexandria on this question of Scripture and truth. In the following passage from his *Allegorical Commentary* (cited in ibid.), Philo presents himself as the object of ridicule by opponents who dismiss his truth claims on behalf of the Bible.

> They say: now do you still speak solemnly about the ordinances as if they contain the canons of Truth herself? For behold, the books called holy by you contain also myths about which you regularly laugh whenever you hear others relating them. (*Conf.* 3)

Niehoff (2011, 79) writes:

> The issue at stake in this lively dispute between different exegetes in Alexandria is the overall conception of the Jewish scriptures. Philo and his followers are criticized for attributing too much holiness to the entire corpus and rejecting the notion of myth in Scripture. Following Aristeas, Philo indeed spoke of the Greek Bible as holy and true.

For Philo the divine status of the text entailed not only its perfection but its conformity to truth—which for Philo meant verisimilitude, noncontradiction, and rational/philosophical truth. For his opponents, the divine status of the texts did not entail conformity to such a conception of truth. They approached the Bible as many of their contemporaries approached the canonical works of Homer—as poetic texts that cannot be judged by scientific and philosophical canons of truth foreign to the very enterprise of literature.[39]

---

[38] Here I include the entire range of imperfections that disturbed ancient readers, from grammatical imperfections to the presence of contradiction, from evidence of historical development and the lack of verisimilitude to deviation from the rational truths as expounded by various philosophical systems.

[39] For the Aristotelian basis for this attitude, see Niehoff 2011, 84 and passim.

While Philo depicts himself here as the target of ridicule, there are many other passages in which he gives as good as he receives (if not better).[40] Indeed, those who rejected Philo's view that the Bible teaches rational, philosophical truth, and that apparent contradictions and lack of verisimilitude point to deeper truths, are subjected to abuse and mocking invective by Philo. He refers to them as "senseless," as "laughing at" and "making fun" of the biblical text, "unwilling to expose the inward usefulness of the things themselves [the allegorical meaning] and to follow the traces of truth" (*QA on Gen* 3:35; as cited in Niehoff 2011, 154). While several examples might be adduced, the following passage must suffice:

> I know that such things [redundant expressions] provoke laughter and mocking derision in uncultivated men and those lacking propriety of manners as well as those who do not see any form or manifestation of virtue and who attribute their own incorrigibility and stupidity as well as perversity and impudence to the Holy Scriptures, which are verified more than anything . . . the uneducated and the unskilled and those lacking study, their eyes of the soul having been blinded and become capricious, themselves dwell only on that which has been narrated in the story [i.e., the literal meaning], and come into contact and make connections only with names and words of the narration, while being unable to penetrate and look into the visions of meaning. (*QA on Gen* 4:168; as cited in Niehoff 2011, 117)

The identification of the Torah of Israel with the Stoic divine law entailed not only its truth but also its eternal and unchanging character.

(c) The Torah Is Eternal and Unchanging

In several works, Philo asserts the superiority of the Mosaic Law, which alone is divine in origin, over the positive laws of human societies. In part 2 of the *Life of Moses*, the Mosaic Law's superiority is connected with and expressed by its eternal and immutable character.

> (12) But that he himself is the most admirable of all the lawgivers who have ever lived in any country either among the Greeks or among the barbarians, and that his are the most admirable of all laws, and truly divine, omitting no one particular which they ought to comprehend, there

---

[40] To be very precise, the mockery attributed by Philo to certain opponents takes two forms. First, these individuals are depicted as mocking the biblical text itself for its grammatical infelicities, trivialities, exaggerations, contradictions, and lack of verisimilitude (at which Philo takes great umbrage). Second, they are depicted as mocking those who, in the face of these imperfections and deviations from truth, insist that the Bible nevertheless possesses perfection and truth (a description that resembles, and thus offends, Philo!). Both forms of mockery are paralleled in rabbinic literature, as will be argued in part III.

is the clearest proof possible in this fact, the laws of other lawgivers, (13) if any one examines them by his reason, he will find to be put in motion in an innumerable multitude of pretexts, either because of wars, or of tyrannies, or of some other unexpected events which come upon nations through the various alterations and innovations of fortune; and very often luxury, abounding in all kind of superfluity and unbounded extravagance, has overturned laws ... (14) *But the enactments of this lawgiver are firm, not shaken by commotions, not liable to alteration, but stamped as it were with the seal of nature herself, and they remain firm and lasting from the day on which they were first promulgated to the present one, and there may well be a hope that they will remain to all future time, as being immortal, as long as the sun and the moon, and the whole heaven and the whole world shall endure.* (15) At all events, though the nation of the Hebrews experienced so many changes both in the direction of prosperity and of the opposite destiny, no one, no not even the very smallest and most unimportant of all his commandments was changed, since every one, as it seems, honored their venerable and godlike character; (16) and what neither famine, nor pestilence, nor war, nor sovereign, nor tyrant, nor the rise of any passions or evil feelings against either soul or body, nor any other evil, whether inflicted by God or deriving its rise from men, ever dissolved, can surely never be looked upon by us in any other light than as objects of all admiration, and beyond all powers of description in respect of their excellence.

(17) ... it may fairly by itself be considered a thing of great intrinsic importance, that his laws were kept securely and immutably from all time. (emphasis added)

Ignoring biblical (and contemporaneous) evidence to the contrary, Philo describes the Mosaic Law as both eternal and immutable, characteristic of natural law theories that identify the law with *logos* or truth.

(d) The Torah Is Wise Instruction

Greco-Roman tradition contains accounts of the activities of lawmakers (e.g., Solon of Athens) as well as foundation stories in which an ancestral figure founds a city and establishes its laws (e.g., Lycurgus's founding of Sparta). In addition, philosophical writings discuss the best methods for formulating constitutions and laws (e.g., Plato's *Laws*, in which three interlocutors devise a system of laws for a proposed new city, Magnesia). Philo participates in these traditions when he describes Moses's process of reasoning when designing laws for Israel. To the extent that the Mosaic Law is designed as a system of positive law, like the laws of Athens or Sparta or Magnesia, it might be expected to possess the most basic feature of all systems of positive law: to be grounded in and enforced by an authoritative commanding will with the power to reward and punish. However, the Mosaic Law differs significantly from (and is superior to) other systems of positive law in its fundamental character, scope, and content. Contrasting Moses with other legislators and city founders, Philo explains:

> Moses, thinking that ... issuing orders without words of exhortation, as though to slaves instead of free men, savored of tyranny and despotism, as indeed it did ... took a different line in both departments. In his commands and prohibitions he suggests and admonishes rather than commands, and the very numerous and necessary instructions which he essays to give are accompanied by forewords and after-words, in order to exhort rather than to enforce. (*Life of Moses* 2:50–51)

Philo invokes the Greek tradition of lawmaking and foundation stories in order to demonstrate the superiority of the Mosaic Law. Unlike the founders/lawmakers of Greek tradition, Moses did not see fit simply to set forth bald commands and prohibitions with penalties for disobedience, like a tyrant addressing slaves. Moses adopted a tone of exhortation: his inclusion of rationales and sapiential admonitions (see biblical discourse 3(iii)) had a moderating effect, so that the commands and prohibitions in the Law assumed the character of "suggestions," "admonitions," and "instruction" addressed to free and rational individuals. Elsewhere Philo asserts that punishments are minimized in the Decalogue (ignoring biblical discourse 1(iv)) "that men might choose the best, not involuntarily, but of deliberate purpose, not taking senseless fear but the good sense of reason for their counselor" (*On the Decalogue* 177). Thus, in addition to its rational character and universal jurisdictional scope, the Mosaic Law's superiority over other systems of positive law may be seen in its instructional content.

Philo's distinction between commandments and prohibitions on the one hand and exhortations and instruction on the other bears a strong resemblance to Plato's distinction between law's two voices: the voice of prescription and the voice of persuasion (G-R 3(iii)). For Philo, the purpose of the Law is not merely to command what is right and prohibit what is wrong, but to instruct the people in matters of doctrine and philosophy (Reinhartz 1983, 340). Indeed, it is God's desire that humans should engage in the study of wisdom and contemplation of the truths of nature, as well as moral self-examination. To this end, God established the Sabbath at the time of creation, as a day for rest and philosophical and moral reflection, and provided the laws as guides and examiners.

> [W]e are told that the world was made in six days and that on the seventh God ceased from His works and began to contemplate what had been so well created, and therefore He bade those who should live as citizens under this world-order follow God in this as in other matters. So he commanded

> that they should apply themselves to work for six days but rest on the seventh and turn to the study of wisdom, and that while they thus had leisure for the contemplation of the truths of nature they should also consider whether any offence against purity had been committed in the preceding days, and exact from themselves in the council-chamber of the soul, with the laws as their fellow-assessors and fellow-examiners, a strict account of what they had said or done in order to correct what had been neglected and to take precaution against repetition of any sin. (*On the Decalogue* 97–98)

Just as God followed six days of activity with a day devoted to contemplation, each citizen of the world-polity should likewise set apart each seventh day to study wisdom and to meditate "on the lessons of nature and all that in thy own life makes for happiness" (ibid., 100). Moreover, Philo maintains that the laws themselves point to "the truths of nature." Like the author of the Letter of Aristeas he devotes energy to elucidating the philosophical content of specific laws through allegorical interpretation (see, for example, *Special Laws* 1.327, which also asserts the ontological realism of Ideas in Platonic fashion, against the Stoic denial of the same).[41]

The wisdom and rational character of the Law is further demonstrated by its principled structure. What might at first glance appear to be a chaotic mass of individual statutes and prohibitions yields, upon closer examination, to logical classification. The Law is presented in two major units: the Decalogue and the specific or special laws. Philo argues that the Decalogue is a summary of the special laws to follow, each of which is derived from and may be classified under one of the ten general principles of religious ethics set forth in the Decalogue: "[B]ut also we must not forget that the Ten Covenants [i.e., Commandments] are summaries of the special laws which are recorded in the Sacred Books and run through the whole of the legislation" (*On the Decalogue* 154). For example, the first commandment summarizes the laws on God's monarchical rule, the third subsumes all laws involving the taking of an oath, the fourth concerning the Sabbath gathers under one head all laws pertaining to feasts, the sixth includes enactments against sexual violations, and so on. In this way, Philo is able to present every detail of the Law as subserving a larger ethical principle and in no way arbitrary or "against nature." The laws of the Torah are never arbitrary or brute commands, but constitute rational instruction.

(e) The Torah Is Unwritten Law

One of the most obvious obstacles to identifying the Torah with the natural law is its written character. On the Stoic and Pythagorean view, written laws are by definition human positive law. But Philo draws on several tropes of Greco-

---

[41] "For some persons affirm that the incorporeal ideas are only an empty name, having no participation in any real fact, removing the most important of all essences from the list of existing things."

Roman discourses of law in support of the claim that the written text of the Mosaic Code is simply a copy of an original unwritten law of nature.

> [T]o carry out our examination of the law in regular sequence, let us postpone consideration of particular laws, which are, so to speak, copies (*eikonon*), and examine first those which are more general and may be called the originals (*archetupous*) of those copies. These are such men as lived good and blameless lives, whose virtues stand permanently recorded in the most holy scriptures, not merely to sound their praises but for the instruction of the reader and as an inducement to him to aspire to the same; for *in these men we have laws endowed with life and reason*, and Moses extolled them for two reasons. First, he wished to shew that the enacted ordinances are not inconsistent with nature; and secondly that those who wish to live in accordance with the laws as they stand have no difficult task, seeing that the first generations before any at all of the particular statutes was set in writing followed the unwritten law with perfect ease, so that one might properly say that the enacted laws are nothing else than memorials of the life of the ancients, preserving to a later generation their actual words and deeds. For they were not scholars or pupils of others, nor did they learn under teachers what was right to say or do: they listened to no voice or instruction but their own: they gladly accepted conformity with nature, holding that nature itself was, as indeed it is, the most venerable of statutes, and thus their whole life was one of happy obedience to law. (*On Abraham* 1:3–6; emphasis added)

Here Philo makes the following important claims: The Torah's written laws are "copies" of more general unwritten archetypes.[42] These archetypes are none other than the patriarchs who lived lives of virtue in accordance with the law of nature, later recorded in the narratives of the Torah. It must be emphasized that Philo's claim here goes beyond the claim that the patriarchs followed natural law. In connection with Genesis 26:5, which asserts that "Abraham hearkened to My voice, and kept My charge, My commandments, My statutes, and My Torah," Philo comments "that this man did the divine law and the divine commands," and further observes:

> He did them, not taught by written words, but unwritten nature gave him the zeal to follow where wholesome and untainted impulse led him. And when they have God's promises before them what should men do but trust in them most firmly? Such was the life of the first, the founder of the nation, one who obeyed the law, some will say, but rather, as our discourse has shown, *himself a law and an unwritten statute*. (*On Abraham*, 46:268)

---

[42] We see here the influence of the Platonic theory of exemplarism. See Laporte 1975, 126.

In other words, Abraham didn't merely obey the Law. He, like the other patriarchs, was an embodiment of the natural law.[43] Abraham *was* law "endowed with life and reason," flesh and blood; he is "himself a law and an unwritten statute." Philo's language recalls the Pythagorean concept of *nomos empsuchos*, of the sage or wise king who is a living law or law incarnate, superior to the law written on wooden tablets (G-R 4(i); see Paz 2009, 20; Martens 2003, 31–66 and 165–74). For Philo, the special laws of the Mosaic Code are written copies of the more original archetype—the unwritten law of nature and its embodiment in the patriarchs, whose words and deeds the written laws memorialize and preserve for a later generation. To be sure, Philo maintained that Abraham performed the Mosaic Law in a literal sense,[44] although not as one fulfilling a law that is external to him; Abraham had no need of an external law because his own impulses matched nature (Paz 2009, 34).

Philo's assertion that the patriarchs followed the law (the natural law and the Mosaic Law, which he holds are one and the same) is counterintuitive, given the biblical chronology and in light of the fact that the patriarchal narratives depict behaviors that blatantly contradict the terms of the later Mosaic Law. Jacob marries two sisters (strictly prohibited by Lev 18), Judah orders Tamar burned for adultery (which is the rule for a priest's daughter only), the patriarchs keep household idols, Jacob favors the children of his second, beloved, wife over the children of his first, "despised," wife in direct violation of a law in Deuteronomy, and so on. One must expend considerable exegetical energy to read the patriarchal narratives as studies in virtue, but such textual inconveniences can be overcome by the valuable technique of allegoresis.

Also counterintuitive is Philo's claim that the best and clearest iteration of biblical divine law is found not in the legal materials dispersed throughout Exodus, Leviticus, Numbers, and Deuteronomy, but in the narrative materials in Genesis. Indeed, the ordering of the biblical books is itself instructive. *On Abraham* 1:3–6 asserts that Moses had two reasons for preceding the story of the revelation of the written laws with the stories of the lives of the patriarchs: first, he wanted to show that the Mosaic Law is consistent with the law of nature, since the patriarchs in following the law of nature also performed the Law of Moses; and second, he wanted to demonstrate how easy it is to follow the Mosaic Law. After all, the patriarchs adhered to the divine law before any of the particular laws were set in writing and without the benefit of instruction in its details. Simply by conforming their behavior to nature, they may be said to have lived lives of happy obedience to the law. How much the more, then, shall those who know the law both from nature and from its revelation in writing be able to follow it with ease?

---

[43] See the discussion in Paz 2009, 33–35, and below, chapter 8.

[44] On this point, Paz (2009, 34) endorses the view of Martens (2003, 108) against Sandmel (1971, 209). According to Sandmel, Philo did not maintain that Abraham upheld the Mosaic Law in a literal sense.

Philo sought to identify the Mosaic Law with the law of nature in order to persuade his readers that observing the Law is both desirable and easy. After all, the untutored patriarchs were able to observe it. And yet, by declaring the Mosaic Law to be a copy of the law of nature that was observed intuitively by the patriarchs, Philo opens the door to the view that the life of virtue is accessible outside the specific written enactments of the Mosaic Law (Reinhartz 1983, 342).[45] Indeed, it would appear that God's law is more clearly manifested in nature than in the written or spoken word.

> Abraham, then, filled with zeal for piety, the highest and greatest of virtues, was eager to follow God and to be obedient to His commands; understanding by commands not only those conveyed in speech and writing but also those made manifest by nature *with clearer signs*, and apprehended by the sense which is the most truthful of all and superior to hearing, on which no certain reliance can be placed. For anyone who contemplates the order in nature and the constitution enjoyed by the world-city whose excellence no words can describe, needs no speaker to teach him to practice a law-abiding and peaceful life and to aim at assimilating himself to its beauties. (*On Abraham* 13:60–61; emphasis added)

Philo's assertion that divine law was fulfilled by the patriarchs prior to the giving of the Mosaic Law, along with his description of the Mosaic Law as a copy of the archetypal law of nature and the constitution of the world-city (echoing the Stoic *cosmopolis*), implies the inferiority of the enacted laws as a means to the life of virtue. The Mosaic Law reinforces laws that can and should be learned directly from nature, and are intended as a concession to those who, unlike the patriarchs, have difficulty discerning and living according to the law of nature (Reinhartz 1983, 343). Here Philo's argument resembles the Platonic description of written law as a second-best option (G-R 3(i–ii)), necessitated by the loss of direct divine rule and the scarcity of wise philosopher-kings. Rather than a divine gift bestowed upon God's elect covenant partners (biblical discourse 3(ii)), the Mosaic Law becomes a divine concession bestowed upon those whose failings or weakness prevent them from obeying the law of God as conveyed by nature.

One might suppose that those capable of accessing the law of nature directly need not trouble themselves with the details of the enacted laws. But Philo does not openly advocate dispensing with the literal requirements of the law once their rational import has been comprehended. In the following oft-cited passage, Philo confirms that grasping the deeper significance of circumcision does not justify ignoring the literal rite itself.

> It is true that receiving circumcision does indeed portray the excision of pleasure and all passions, and the putting away of the impious conceit,

---

[45] Martens (2003, 117) notes that an inevitable conclusion of Philo's thought is that any sage or "living law" must in the course of nature also obey the Law of Moses.

under which the mind supposed that it was capable of begetting by its own power: but let us not on this account repeal the law laid down for circumcising. Why, we shall be ignoring the sanctity of the Temple and a thousand other things, if we are going to pay heed to nothing except what is shown us by the inner meanings of things. Nay, we should look on all these outward observances as resembling the body, and their inner meanings as resembling the soul. It follows that, exactly as we have to take thought for the body, because it is the abode of the soul, so we must pay heed to the letter of the laws. If we keep and observe these, we shall gain a clearer conception of those things of which these are the symbols; and besides that we shall not incur the censure of the many and the charges they are sure to bring against us. (*Migr.* 92b–93; see also *Migr.* 89, 91)

Philo's argument for continued observance of the Mosaic Law seems somewhat halfhearted, offered almost in self-protection. Philo's response to the cognitive dissonance engendered by the confrontation between the two different conceptions of divine law prevalent in antiquity was to collapse the distinction by identifying biblical law and natural law. The paradox is that while this move may have been made in order to strengthen the Mosaic Law, it would *enable* precisely that which Philo here protests: the undermining of literal observance of the terms of the written Mosaic Law. Some of the Greco-Roman discourses mobilized by Philo (especially those with Platonic and Pythagorean pedigree) entailed a denigration of written law as a second-best option inferior to the "living law" of the sage (G-R 3 and 4). As a result, his identification of the Mosaic Law with the law of nature prepared a path for those who would drive a wedge between the two, championing the former and minimizing or even vilifying the latter.[46]

Strategies for Negotiating Universalism and Particularism

An inherent problem attends the identification of the Torah and universal wisdom (or reason). If the Torah is identified with wisdom—the same wisdom that expresses the *universal* order of creation—then how can it be the possession of one *particular* people? Most of the texts analyzed above adopt a dual strategy to ease the tension between universal wisdom and the particular Torah of Israel with which it is correlated or identified. First, most exploit the distinc-

---

[46] As Martens points out (2003, xvi), many have suggested "that in his attempt to relate the higher law to the written law, Philo, like the Greeks, pulled the foundations out from under the written law, in his case the law of Moses." However, Martens paints a more nuanced portrait and describes Philo as attempting to protect the Law of Moses from Hellenistic assaults by Jews and Gentiles. Aware of the dangers of his own allegorical methods and the possibility that the Law would be rendered superfluous, "Philo drew the line at observance of the law: it must be followed" (128–29).

tion between esoteric and exoteric wisdom in order to configure the relationship between the universal and the particular; second, they construct a mythic narrative in support and justification of this configuration.

Esoteric vs. Exoteric Wisdom: Law's Narrative
in Sirach, 1 Enoch, Qumran, and Philo

(1) SIRACH

For Sirach, the universal cosmic order and the particular Torah of Israel are represented as esoteric and exoteric wisdom, respectively. The distinction between esoteric and exoteric wisdom has a biblical basis in Deuteronomy 29:28: "The secret things belong to Yahweh our God; but the things that are revealed belong to us and our children forever, that we may observe all the words of this Law." The text implies that Wisdom belongs to the divine realm and is bestowed upon humankind. A biblical model for the bestowal of wisdom as a divine gift to those favored by God, particularly in response to prayer, may be found in Solomon (1 Kgs 3). This emphasis on wisdom as a gift of the divine realm rather than the accumulated teachings of sages may also be seen in Sirach 1:9–10: "And [he] poured her out upon all his works, among all flesh according to his giving, and he furnished her abundantly to those who love him." Nevertheless, despite these outpourings, some aspects of divine knowledge remain hidden.

> 42:18b For the Most High knew all knowledge, and he saw into the sign of the age,
> 42:19 relating the things that passed and the things that will be and revealing tracks of hidden things ...
> 42:22 How desirable are all his works, and they are like a spark to behold! ...
> 43:32 Many things are greater than these, for few of his works we have seen.

Humans are familiar with only a few of the works of God, for many of his great works—a reference to the mysteries of creation—have not yet been revealed. The wisdom that has been "poured out" or revealed is, first and foremost, the Torah. It is Israel's, but it is only the revealed part of a larger (presumably universal) wisdom that remains hidden. Thus, the hidden/revealed trope of Deuteronomy 29:28 is mobilized to ease the tension between wisdom as cosmic order and wisdom as Torah. Wisdom insofar as it is the cosmic order is to some extent still hidden from all, while Wisdom insofar as it is the Torah of Israel has been revealed and made known to a favored nation.

The biblical suspicion of wisdom (see biblical discourse 2 (vi) b) continues in Sirach but in connection with the wisdom that is hidden. Sirach warns its readers not to seek that which is too difficult and not to investigate that which is beyond their power but to reflect only on what God has commanded them, since what is hidden is of no concern (3:21–24).

> 3:21 Things too difficult for you do not seek, and things too strong for you do not scrutinize.
> 3:22 The things that have been prescribed for you, think about these, for you have no need of hidden matters.
> 3:23 With matters greater than your affairs do not meddle, for things beyond human understanding have been shown to you.
> 3:24 For their presumption has led many astray, and their evil fancy has diminished their understanding.

The Wisdom that is revealed is the divine Torah that is in the possession of Israel. But the great works of God's creation are beyond the understanding of humankind. Israel should occupy herself with and reflect upon the law and commandments—revealed wisdom—rather than pursuing wisdom's cosmic mysteries, which can deceive and distract the mind.[47]

Sirach eases the contradiction between universal Wisdom and the particular Torah of Israel by configuring the former as esoteric wisdom and the latter as exoteric wisdom, but this configuration requires some justification. How and why should wisdom exist in this dual form? Sirach answers this question through the medium of a myth modeled on Hellenistic myths about Isis.[48] Sirach 24 recounts Wisdom's journey through all of creation and all nations in search of a resting place until, in the course of time, universal Wisdom came to dwell in the particular Torah of Israel:

> 24:3 "I came forth from the mouth of the Most High, and like a mist I covered the earth ...
> 24:5 A circle of sky I encircled alone, and in the deep of abysses I walked
> 24:6 In the waves of the sea and in all the earth and in every people and nation I led.
> 24:7 With all these I sought repose, and in whose inheritance I would settle.
> 24:8 Then the creator of all commanded me, and he who created me put down my tent and said, 'Encamp in Iakob, and in Israel let your inheritance be.'

---

[47] As we shall see, the distinction between the hidden and revealed aspects of Wisdom is found in other Second Temple texts, though with very different assessments of the accessibility and the value of that which is hidden.

[48] Many scholars maintain, following Conzelmann (1971, 232), that the representation of personified Wisdom as the Law commanded by Moses is modeled on the syncretistic goddess Isis, popular throughout the Ptolemaic empire. The Hellenistic goddess Isis was identified with Ma'at, the principle of cosmic and social order, and was referred to as the lawgiver of both nature and humanity. She established the paths of the sun, moon, and stars, the works of the seas and rivers; and she promulgated laws for humanity, presided over the administration of justice, and sustained the social order (Blenkinsopp 1995, 165–66; see also Schussler Fiorenza 1975, 29).

24:9 Before the age, from the beginning, he created me, and until the age I will never fail.

24:10 In a holy tent I ministered before him, and thus in Sion I was firmly set.

24:11 In a beloved city as well he put me down, and in Ierousalem was my authority.

24:12 And I took root among a glorified people, in the portion of the Lord is my inheritance ..."

24:23 All these things are the book of the covenant of the Most High God, a law that Moyses commanded us, an heritage for the gatherings of Iakob.

Sirach's appropriation and revision of mythic materials generates a narrative about the law in which both universal wisdom and particular Torah, divine reason and divine will, are accommodated: Wisdom permeated the cosmos and enjoyed a possession within each nation, and yet in due time she was instructed by God to dwell permanently in Jacob and find her inheritance in Israel. The locus of Wisdom was determined to be the tabernacle and the temple in Zion; and this Wisdom that came to rest in the beloved city of Jerusalem amidst a glorified people—the portion of Yahweh—is said to be none other than "the book of the covenant of the Most High God, a law that Moyses commanded us, an heritage for the gatherings of Iakob" (v. 23).[49] The narrative of wisdom's cosmic emergence but eventual residence in Israel succeeds in reconciling logically incompatible elements of universalism and particularism as only a narrative can—by emplotting them as distinct moments in a chronological development. Even as it corresponds to the universal divine wisdom that infuses creation, the Mosaic Law has nevertheless become the gift of a particular nation.

The wisdom present before creation and encompassing the universe is now to be found in God's holy city, in God's holy temple, dwelling among an honorable people as its "law of life"—the Torah of Israel. As J. Marböck notes (1976, 94; as cited in Schnabel 1985, 86), Sirach's conception of the Law differs from, for example, the Stoic theory of a cosmic law in several ways: for Sirach, the Torah remains the expression of a deity's personal will, in contrast to the cosmic law of Stoicism; Sirach never translates the terms "Torah" or "mitzvah" with *logos* or *nous*, which are the rational terms that Stoics use for the divine law; and Sirach clearly conceives of the divine law as written—an impossibility for the Stoics.

(II) 1 ENOCH

The exoteric-esoteric distinction found in Sirach appears also in 1 Enoch, but the latter text departs sharply from Sirach. Sirach employs the distinction to manage the tension between universalism and particularism: God's universal

---

[49] Similarly, Baruch contains a narrative of wisdom descending to live among humanity in the guise of Torah. See Bar 4:1.

wisdom remains, in many respects, esoteric; to Israel he has given the (exoteric) Torah, and to seek esoteric wisdom beyond the Torah is to court disaster. By contrast, in 1 Enoch, esoteric wisdom is not the object of suspicion but a much-desired divine gift. 1 Enoch has little to say about the exoteric Torah and focuses almost exclusively on the esoteric wisdom that governs the universe and serves as a model and guide for a select few, both in the present and in the eschatological age.

As a guide for human conduct in the present, esoteric wisdom is given specific content in 1 Enoch. In the *Astronomical Book* or the *Book of the Luminaries* (1 Enoch 72–82), the fifty-two-week, 364-day calendar[50] is represented as esoteric knowledge and counted among the "heavenly secrets" disclosed from on high. During Enoch's ascent to heaven, Uriel, the angel in charge of all luminaries, guides him through the celestial sphere and reveals to him (1 En 72:1; 74:2, etc.) the laws governing the luminaries and the heavenly calendar unto eternity:

> 72:1 The book about the motion of the heavenly luminaries all as they are in their kinds, their jurisdiction, their time, their name, their origins, and their months which Uriel, the holy angel who was with me (and) who is their leader, showed me. The entire book about them, as it is, he showed me and how every year of the world will be forever, until a new creation lasting forever is made.
>
> 2 This is the first law of the luminaries: the luminary (called) the sun has its emergence through the heavenly gates in the east and its setting through the western gates of the sky ...

Uriel "explains the [luminaries'] courses and the laws they obey, thus providing information for the calendar" (Berner 2007, 400) that is to be followed on earth (see also 78:10; 79:6; 80:1; and 82:7).

The movements of the heavenly bodies, as commanded by God, determine the true and heavenly 364-day calendar (1 En 74:12; 75:3); consequently, noncompliance with the calendar is a sinful breach of God's commands to the cosmos (Davidson 1992, 310):

> (82:4) Blessed are all the righteous, all the blessed who will walk in the way of righteousness and have no sin like the sinners in numbering all the days the sun travels in the sky through the gates, entering and emerging for thirty days with the heads of thousands of the order of the stars, with the four additional ones that divide between the four parts of the year that lead them and enter with the four days. (5) People err regarding them and do not calculate them in the numbering of the entire year because they err regarding them and people do not understand them precisely. (6) For they belong in the reckoning of the year and are indeed

---

[50] This calendar is featured in the book of Jubilees and may have been used by the sectarian community at Qumran, for which see below.

recorded forever: one in the first gate, one in the third, one in the fourth, and one in the sixth. Thus a year of 364 days is completed. (7) The account about it is true and its calculation is precisely recorded because the luminaries and the months, the festivals, the years, and the days he showed me, and Uriel, to whom the Lord of the entire creation gave orders for me regarding the host of heaven, breathed on me. (8) He has power in heaven over night and day to make light appear over humanity: the sun, the moon, the stars, and all the heavenly powers which revolve in their circuits. (1 En 82:4–8)[51]

The calendar that should guide human observance of the Sabbaths and festivals is determined by the created order, knowledge of which has been vouchsafed to Enoch through a special revelation and to the small segment of humanity privileged to receive Enoch's esoteric teachings.

As a guide to life in the eschatological future, esoteric wisdom is given a *second* specific content in 1 Enoch. According to the *Book of Parables* (1 En 37–71), Enoch's vision of the secrets of the heavens includes not only the secrets of various natural phenomena and heavenly bodies (the orderly laws governing their activities and motion, 41:3–7) but also the palaces awaiting the holy and elect and the punishments awaiting the wicked (41:1–2). This knowledge is referred to as the "books of zeal and wrath" as well as the "books of haste and whirlwind" received by Enoch (39:2). In Enoch's vision of the final age (chap. 38), the Righteous One appears, and the wicked and righteous on earth receive their just deserts. Chapter 5 describes the transformation that will occur in that final age, when all those to whom God gives wisdom will attain to a state of moral virtue, never again returning to sin.

> 5 (6) Then you will leave your names as an eternal curse for all the righteous, and by you all who curse will curse, and all the sinners and wicked will swear by you ... (7) For the chosen there will be light and joy and peace, and they will inherit the earth. But for you wicked there will be a curse. (8) Then wisdom shall be given to all the chosen; and they will all live, and they will sin no more through godlessness or pride; In the enlightened man there will be light, and in the wise man, understanding.

---

[51] Davidson (1992, 297) observes that while the lunar calendar falls eleven days behind the solar calendar each year, the 364-day calendar was "itself beset with a serious problem," falling behind the true solar year by one and a quarter days each year. Because the calendar is the result of a positive command, it can be disobeyed by the heavenly bodies, a fact that explains certain irregularities. According to Davidson and Beckwith (1981; see also Beckwith 1969–71), 1 En 80:2–8 may be understood as an effort to attribute this problem to human and angelic sin. Nevertheless, while the failure of the true 364-day calendar to synchronize with the solar calendar (and thus the seasons) is caused by disobedient stars or angels (1 En 80:6; Davidson 1992, 305), the calendar itself is a basic function of the cosmos established by God.

And they will transgress no more, nor will they sin all the days of their life, nor will they die in the heat of God's wrath. (1 En 5:6–8)

This passage picks up the theme of "robo-righteousness" sounded in Jeremiah and Ezekiel (biblical discourse 3(ii)) though with a twist. The two prophetic books envisaged a future eradication of sin as the result of a redesign of human nature that would inscribe God's laws and commandments directly on the heart, eliminating the need for instruction. In that future time, the Israelites will simply know the Law, enabling them to fulfill it automatically and without struggle. For 1 Enoch, the eradication of sin also stems from a divine intervention but of a slightly different character: in a future time, God will give *wisdom* to his elect. Wisdom does not seem to denote an internalization of the commandments of the Mosaic Law. Wisdom likely retains the meaning it has throughout 1 Enoch—knowledge of the universal and comprehensive order of nature. Such knowledge is said to make the elect humble, with the result that they will never again return to sin. The link between wisdom as knowledge of the order of nature on the one hand and the acquisition of perfect virtue on the other resembles classical discourses that link rational perfection and the acquisition of true knowledge, rather than positive law, with virtue (see G-R 1(ii) and 3(ii)).

Esoteric wisdom thus has a dual content in 1 Enoch: it consists of the laws governing the natural elements and entities, to which human behavior in the form of calendrical observance must conform. It also consists of the events of the eschatological age in which wisdom will be given to the elect and sin will be eradicated.

Where Sirach expresses suspicion of esoteric cosmic wisdom and urges fidelity to the exoteric commandments of God's Law, 1 Enoch all but ignores the Mosaic Law, depicting the acquisition of esoteric cosmic wisdom—without which sin and error are inevitable—as an appropriate goal for the elect. Precisely how and why the benefits of universal wisdom should be reserved for a select few is addressed by a narrative. Like Sirach, 1 Enoch manages the tension between the universal and the particular with a narrative of Wisdom's search for an abode, but the morals of the two stories couldn't be more different. 1 Enoch's tale emphasizes the inaccessibility of Wisdom to all but the elect, a much more radical *particularization* of this cosmic entity than is found in Sirach. Sirach depicts the emergence of universal wisdom, her wandering throughout the earth, and her eventual residence on earth in the particular community of Israel. By contrast, 1 Enoch asserts that Wisdom—both the knowledge of the divinely ordained cosmic order and the knowledge of the eschaton—found *no* dwelling place among humans and was forced to retire to heaven, where she dwells among the angels and is available to the select few under very special circumstances.

(42:1) Wisdom did not find a place where she might dwell,
so her dwelling was in the heavens.

(2) Wisdom went forth to dwell among the sons of men,
But she did not find a dwelling.
Wisdom returned to her place,
and sat down in the midst of the angels.
(3) Iniquity went forth from her chambers:
those whom she did not seek she found,
and she dwelt with them,
like rain in a desert
and dew in a thirsty land.

Wisdom is here contrasted with iniquity, which, without even seeking one, finds a home in the earth as easily as rain soaks into the desert. Wisdom sought a home among humankind, but found none and so retreated to heaven where she is seated among the angels. Wisdom is relegated to heaven and unavailable to earthbound mortals, her treasures revealed only to those who ascend to heaven. Upon his ascent to heaven, Enoch was vouchsafed a vision of wisdom that was then recorded and transmitted to a select community of readers. For the most part, however, humankind remains locked in ignorance of esoteric cosmic wisdom and thus condemned to sin.

The sectarian writings from Qumran also invoke the esoteric-exoteric distinction in the service of a radically particularist ideology.

(III) QUMRAN

Like Sirach and 1 Enoch, Qumran sources distinguish between those things that are hidden (*nistar*) and those things that are revealed (*niglah*). However, the sectarians do not sever this dichotomy from its biblical basis: Deuteronomy 29:28's reference to hidden and revealed acts *in connection with God's teaching* or Torah. Thus, according to the sect's understanding, Deuteronomy 29 points not to an esoteric and universal wisdom, but to a hidden aspect of the *particular* Torah of Moses: God's Torah consists of commandments clearly revealed in the Written Torah imparted to Moses at Sinai and known to all Israel, and hidden precepts known only to the sect through progressive revelation or inspired interpretation (Schnabel 1985, 172). In sectarian writings, the one Torah contains within itself many precepts, some of which were revealed at Sinai and the remainder of which are the object of ongoing revelation to the sect. The Torah in its entirety—its exoteric and esoteric elements—is accessible only to members of the sect through continuing revelation in the form of interpretation and inspiration (ibid., 172–73). Each new entrant swears to follow *both* aspects—the exoteric and esoteric—of the single Law of Moses.

Whoever enters the council of the Community enters the covenant of God in the presence of all who freely volunteer. He shall swear with a binding oath to revert to the Law of Moses according to all that he commanded with whole heart and whole soul, *in compliance with all that has been revealed of it to the sons of Zadok,* the priests who keep the covenant and interpret his will and to the multitude of the men of their covenant who freely volunteer together for this truth and to walk according to his will. He should swear by the covenant to be segregated from all the men of injustice who walk along the path of wickedness. For they are not included in his covenant since they have neither sought nor examined his decrees (pl. *ḥoq*) in order to know the hidden matters (*hanistarot*) in which they err, by their own fault and because they treated revealed matters (*haniglot*) with disrespect. (1QS 5:7–12)[52]

According to this passage, the Law of Moses includes those things that have been revealed (the exoteric legislation in the Torah) but also those hidden matters that have been revealed to the sons of Zadok (the priestly members of the sect who correctly interpret God's will) and are followed by the members of the sect, persons who have devoted themselves to the truth and to following God's will. These hidden precepts include the order of creation, the true (364-day) calendar, observance of the Sabbath and festivals according to this calendar, as well as other regulations specific to the elaboration and observance of the exoteric commandments. However, these "hidden matters" are not a universal Wisdom alongside the Torah; they *are* Torah, and as Torah they are the possession of the sect. The Torah is still being revealed (the esoteric continues to be made exoteric), but only to the sect through the Teacher of Righteousness. The sect's regulations, derived from biblical exegesis, were believed to be divinely inspired continuations of the revelation of Torah that bore the Torah's authority (Metso 2006, 298). Certain rhetorical devices employed in sectarian writings—such as inserting Qumran traditions into rephrased biblical laws or formulating even nonbiblical traditions as first-person revelations of God—signal a tendency to "erase the distinction between biblical and non-biblical rules and to lend to all sectarian ordinances the aura of Mosaic authorship."[53]

Where Philo refashioned the Mosaic Law as classical natural law suited to the cosmopolis, Qumran is the clearest example of the refashioning of universal Wisdom and cosmic order as Torah, revealed (over time) to a *particular* human community.[54] The refashioning of Wisdom as Torah (rather than Torah as Wisdom) is supported by a narrative that places the sect at the center of world history. Drawing from CD 3:10–16, Aharon Shemesh (2013, 349) describes the sect's understanding of the history of the people of Israel as follows:

[52] Translation taken from García Martínez and Tigchelaar 1997.

[53] Baumgarten 1977, 17, as cited in Schnabel 1985, 184. See also Milgrom 1978, 109, as referenced in Schnabel 1985, 185, and Najman 1999, 1–19. Shemesh (2013, 347 and passim) also argues that the sectarians themselves did not distinguish between biblical and nonbiblical ordinances, such that every piece of law was understood to be of divine origin.

[54] The theme of gradual revelation appears also in the book of Jubilees, a work attested in multiple copies at Qumran. This theme is taken up in chapter 8, and a discussion of Jubilees appears in that context.

According to the sect's historical narrative, the Israelites, during the First Temple period, brazenly transgressed the revealed commandments, and were punished by exile and the destruction of the land of Israel. Only the group which remained loyal to the law was chosen by God for a covenantal relationship. God revealed the hitherto hidden commandments to it alone, in the context of the covenant.

As Shemesh notes (ibid.), this cycle of sin, punishment by exile, and redemption or return is forecast by Moses in his speech to Israel on the plains of Moab (Deut 29–30), the very speech punctuated by the reference to hidden and overt acts that was so important to the sect's conception of the dual nature of the Torah. The narrative is repeated by the prophets who warn of national punishment for sin and yet promise the redemption of a righteous remnant. The innovation of the sectarians is to place themselves at the center of this historical narrative. Shemesh (2013, 349–50) writes that the

> exposition, of a historical process involving sin, destruction, return to God, and redemption, is found in three places in the Damascus Document (1:3–11; 3:9–20; and 5:20–6:11). The circumstances of return and redemption are related to the sect alone, and not to Israel as a whole. It is in this context that the sect's self-perception as *"shavei Israel"* should be understood. The designation *"shavei Israel"* means both "penitents of Israel," their spiritual state, and "returnees of Israel," referring to the group's history. These two meanings are interrelated. Israel's misconduct corrupted halakhic traditions, and it is the sect's task to return to the Torah of Moses, the true meaning of which is now revealed to them.
>
> Both the Damascus Document and the Rule of the Community indicate this historical philosophy by the law stating that those who join the community should swear to return to the Torah of Moses.

Despite its belief that divine laws revealed in the Torah correspond to and are reflective of the facts of nature and the cosmic order, the sect—like all reclusive sects—did not adopt a universalizing discourse of the Law. Even as it invoked the cosmic order in its elaboration of the Mosaic Law, the sect maintained its radical particularism.[55] Writings from Qumran employ the esoteric-exoteric

---

[55] In 4 Ezra (late first-century Palestine), knowledge of a cosmic order does not lead inevitably to a universalism but is linked to a radical particularism. Esoteric knowledge consists of God's eschatological plan, a plan that will include some and not others, and is known to only a few. The Law is central to that eschatological narrative—it is the norm of judgment that determines the eschatological fate of each individual, and wisdom is the label for the esoteric-apocalyptic knowledge of that fact (Schnabel 1985, 151). Similarly in the Apocalypse of Baruch (early second-century Palestine), the centrality of the law is a paramount concept. Keeping the commandments is equated with storing up "treasures of wisdom," which in turn guarantees salvation in the eschaton. As in apocalyptic writings in general, the particularistic dimension of both the Law and wisdom are assumed—God possesses wisdom and gave his wise law to Israel as a path to eschatological salvation in the future (ibid., 161–62).

distinction not in order to accommodate universalism and particularism. Rather, the esoteric-exoteric distinction was used to *construct* the sect's separatist particularism *despite* its belief in a universal cosmic order, a particularism justified by the narrative of a returning righteous remnant.

(IV) PHILO

Philo's identification of the universal natural law with Mosaic Law created a new problem—the problem of redundancy. If the divine, universal, rational, moral order can be discerned in nature, why is a special revelation of positive laws to a particular nation necessary? This problem will plague all subsequent natural law thinkers who accept the special revelation of the divine will in the Mosaic Law. Like Philo, these thinkers will struggle to demonstrate that the divine law as made known in a special revelation was not in fact otiose but achieved some end that the divine law as intuited from nature was unable to achieve. Like Plato (G-R 3(i)), Philo explains the need for a law of commandments and prohibitions by means of a myth according to which the latter is an accommodation to the nonideal or fallen state of humankind. Although Philo does not make explicit reference to an esoteric and an exoteric wisdom, he does refer to a wisdom that is intuited (universal reason) and a wisdom that must be taught (the revealed commandments).

Philo's account of the fall that brought to an end our contemplation of the rational archetypes and necessitated the introduction of the positive law is found in his allegorical interpretation of the two creation narratives in Genesis 1–3. This allegory is deeply indebted to the broader Hellenistic culture in late antiquity, but two elements are of particular relevance to our study. First, Plato draws on the widespread Hellenistic myth of the "primal androgyne" (Boyarin 1995, 36). Second, his allegorical narrative is based on

> what might be broadly called a platonic conception of the human being, for which the soul is the self, and the body only its dwelling place or worse ... This was a commonly held conception through much of the Hellenistic cultural world. Philo speaks of the body as "wicked and a plotter against the soul," as "a cadaver and always dead," and claims that "the chief cause of ignorance is the flesh and our affinity for it ..." (ibid., 31–32)

As Daniel Boyarin has shown (1995, 37–40), Philo's interpretation of the biblical creation stories distinguishes two races of men. Exegetically, Philo's reading addresses the textual problem created by the existence of two creation stories that differ significantly in many details (Gen 1–2:3 and Gen 2:4–3). Philo exploits these differences to describe a first creation, a fall, a second creation, and a second fall.

> "And God created man, taking a lump of clay from the earth, and breathed into his face the breath of life: and man became a living soul." The races

of men are twofold; for one is the heavenly man, and the other the earthly man. Now the heavenly man, as being born in the image of God, has no participation in any corruptible or earthlike essence. But the earthly man is made of loose material, which he calls a lump of clay. On which account he says, not that the heavenly man was made, but that he was fashioned according to the image of God; but the earthly man he calls a thing made, and not begotten by the maker. (Philo, *Alleg. Interp* 1:31)

As Philo goes on to elaborate, the first Adam, created in Genesis 1, is entirely spiritual and incorruptible, an idea and object of thought perceptible only to the intelligence. Being noncorporeal, the first Adam is ungendered—which is the meaning of the text's claim that the first human is both male and female (Boyarin 1995, 38). It is this noncorporeal, ungendered human who is said to be "in the image of God." The second Adam, molded from the earth in Genesis 2, represents humanity as we know it—corporeal, mortal, an object of sense perception, consisting of body and soul, man and woman.

As Boyarin notes, "for Hellenistic Jews, the oneness of pure spirit is ontologically privileged in the constitution of humanity" (ibid., 38) so that the second, earthly human is already "fallen." Earthly humans can seek their fulfillment, perfection, and even immortality by turning away from the material world and participating in the life of the spirit and the divine intellect (Fraade 1986, 263–64). But the obstacles are many because the earthly human's soul is alienated from the very God it seeks, owing to its corporeality.

Philo reads the story of the second Adam's formation and disobedience as an allegorical tale describing this alienation: the human soul in its search for knowledge renounces the contemplation of rational archetypes and enslaves itself to sense perception (allegorically represented by Adam's connection with Eve) and the passions. Only a breath of the spirit of God remains in the human, manifested in a basic awareness of the distinction between good and evil. Humans must struggle against the passions and senses to return to God. In this corporeal state, humans have difficulty attaining to the rational perfection needed to perceive and follow the law of nature; they require the guidance of Law. This idea is reminiscent of Plato's marionette myth, in which the human pulls along the golden cord of reason aided by the public law, in a struggle against the passions (G-R 3(iii)).

In his comment to Genesis 2:16–17 (concerning God's commandment regarding the trees of the garden), Philo describes three human types who achieve virtue in three different ways:

A command indeed is given to man, but not to the man created according to the image and idea of God; for that being is possessed of virtue without any need of exhortation, by his own instinctive nature, but this other would not have wisdom if it had not been taught to him: (93) and these three things are different, command, prohibition, and recommendation.

For prohibition is conversant about errors, and is directed to bad men, but command is conversant about things rightly done; recommendation again is addressed to men of intermediate character, neither bad nor good. For such a one does not sin so that any one has any need to direct prohibition to him, nor does he do right in every case in accordance with the injunction of right reason. But he is in need of recommendation, which teaches him to abstain from what is evil, and exhorts him to aim at what is good. (94) Therefore there is no need of addressing either command, or prohibition, or recommendation to the man who is perfect, and made according to the image of God; For the perfect man requires none of these things; but there is a necessity of addressing both command and prohibition to the wicked man, and recommendation and instruction to the ignorant man ... (95) Very naturally, therefore, does God at present address commands and recommendations to the earthly mind, which is neither bad nor good, but of an intermediate character. (Philo, *Alleg. Interp* 1:92–95)

Philo's ideas in this passage can be correlated to Plato's ideas on the role of law in the acquisition of virtue (see G-R 3(ii) and (iii)). According to Plato, knowledge of virtue leads to virtuous behavior. The perfectly rational sage has no need of law. His comprehension of the Form of virtue leads him to virtue. Others, however, must be brought to virtue by the law. In the *Protagoras*, mistakes in action are said to be due to mistaken beliefs about virtue. Because they are caused by ignorance, these errors can be remedied by knowledge—a view compatible with the idea of law as instruction. In the *Republic*, however, errors in action arise from the irrational parts of the soul, which must be trained to obey reason's commands through habituation under the law—a view compatible with the idea of law as commands and prohibitions.

Philo presents the same tripartite structure in his reading of the creation myths of Genesis 1–3. The ideal and entirely spiritual human created in Genesis 1 corresponds to Plato's perfectly rational sage who comprehends the Form of virtue and is (automatically) virtuous. Like the rationally perfect sage, the first Adam had no need of law: having perfect knowledge, he required no instruction, and lacking all corporeality, he required no commands or prohibitions to discipline the body, the senses, and the passions. It is only the earthly man who requires law, and here we perceive two kinds of men. Bad men who struggle against the passions require commands and prohibitions, while ignorant men who fall into error owing only to a lack of knowledge require recommendations and instruction. Thus, God's Law contains commands and prohibitions (to bring the wicked to virtue) and recommendations and instruction (to bring the ignorant to virtue).[56] The Law at present is addressed to the

---

[56] Here Philo is sensitive to dueling biblical discourses according to which divine law is coercive command (biblical discourse 1(iv)) or instruction (biblical discourse 2(iv)).

"earthly mind" of intermediate character for which commands and recommendations are necessary.

In sum, Philo resolves the problem of apparent redundancy generated by the identification of the Mosaic Law and the law of nature by means of an allegorical reading of the creation story. This reading draws on Platonic ideas regarding the acquisition of virtue by distinct human types. The natural law is sufficient for the rational being (as it was sufficient for the first Adam and the occasional exceptional sage like Abraham). Such was the state of humankind as originally created—a spiritual and incorruptible intelligence, free from the disturbances of corporeality. Only the purely spiritual primal human created in the image of God possessed the rational perfection that brings perfect virtue and eliminates the need for command and prohibition, recommendation and instruction. But such is not the lot of humankind as we know it—a second race formed of both body and soul, distracted from its rational perfection by sense perceptions and passions, and requiring the teachings and commands of the Law because of the imperfections and limitations arising from and inherent in its corporeality. The Law is thus a second-best accommodation to the nature of humankind as twice-fallen: fallen first from a purely spiritual into a bodily or corporeal existence and fallen again into a life dominated by sense perception and the passions.

CONCLUSION

Convinced that God's voice in the particular and positive divine law given to Israel did not contradict his voice in the universal order of creation, many Jewish writers of the Second Temple and Hellenistic periods struggled to bridge the gap between the two. The idea of a correlation, extending in some cases to identification, between the cosmic order established by God at creation and the order that regulates human life runs like a scarlet thread through works of all genres, provenances, and languages—from paranetic works to philosophical apologetics to apocalyptic writings; works from Alexandria and from Palestine; works composed in Hebrew, Aramaic, and Greek (Schnabel 1985, 162).

The texts analyzed in this chapter correlate Torah with the wisdom or reason that governs the cosmos, a strategy that enables a transfer of properties that reduces the distinction between the universal divine law of creation and the particular divine law of the Torah. Reducing, and especially collapsing, the distinction between classical divine law and biblical divine law runs the risk of rendering the latter redundant. If there is a divine law in nature accessible to all, why is a particular revealed Law needed? Many of the texts examined in this chapter draw on the distinction between esoteric and exoteric wisdom to configure the relationship between the universal and particular divine law. These configurations are supported by mythic narratives that explain the circumstances of their formation.

For Sirach, the divine voice as perceived in the created order and the divine voice as revealed in the Law are correlated by their mutual participation in or identification with Wisdom. This correlation enables a reciprocal transfer of properties—a sapientializing of Torah and a "torah-fying" of wisdom. Sirach manages the relationship between the universal created order and the particular Torah by representing Torah as the revealed aspect of a larger, hidden Wisdom and constructing a narrative in which Wisdom roams the earth before coming to reside in Israel in the form of the Mosaic Law.

1 Enoch focuses on wisdom in the form of the universal laws that govern the cosmos and pays scant attention to the Torah of Moses. Nevertheless, Enoch goes further than Sirach in transferring to wisdom some of the characteristic features of the Law. The order of creation is cast in a positivistic mold, activating related concepts such as obedience, sin, and punishment. A reverse-direction transfer is hinted at in the idea that human behavior (particularly calendrical observance) should be guided or modeled on the regularities of the cosmic order. The failure of humans to be guided by the regularities of the cosmic order is due to the fact that knowledge both of the cosmic order and of the eschatological future is an esoteric wisdom unavailable on earth and vouchsafed to only the righteous view. Like Sirach, 1 Enoch employs a narrative to explain how this cosmic knowledge comes to be the possession of a particular group. In the case of 1 Enoch, the narrative of Wisdom's failed attempt to secure a residence on earth explains why the acquisition of wisdom requires a special revelation.

The "torah-fication" of wisdom continues in some sectarian writings at Qumran. However, a reverse-direction transfer of properties—from wisdom to Torah—may be seen in the assumption that the laws and commandments of the Torah are allied with "truth" and must conform to the realities of the natural order. The sect's realist approach to the determination of the law stands in stark contrast to the legal nominalism of later rabbinic halakhah (see chapter 5). Yet, for all its emphasis on the harmony of the Mosaic Torah and the created order, and despite its appeals to nature in determining concrete details of the law, the sect's writings are radically particular. The esoteric knowledge of the created order, the calendar, and other truths that enables the full elaboration and observance of the exoteric Torah is itself Torah and as such is not universally available. It is revealed exclusively to the sect. According to the narrative of the Qumran sectarians, the mass apostasy of the house of Israel left the sect in sole possession of the esoteric Torah, which they alone know and obey (Schnabel 1985, 223). The sectarian writings are an important reminder that correlating a divinely revealed legislation with the divinely established cosmic order does not inevitably produce a universalist discourse.

The Hellenistic Jewish author of the Letter of Aristeas connects Torah to reason by adopting the discourse of *logos* rather than *sophia*. On the model of the divine natural law of classical tradition, the divine Torah is refashioned as utterly rational. But it is Philo who goes the furthest in applying the discourses of the Greco-Roman natural law tradition to the Torah of Moses in an effort to identify the two. Resolving the cognitive dissonance generated by the encounter of biblical and Greco-Roman conceptions of divine law, Philo grasps the Law of Moses in terms of both wisdom (*sophia*) and universal reason (*logos*) and transfers to it the properties of the natural law: an alliance with truth, universal rationality, and immutability. In his attempt to explain the apparent redundancy of a law that is both the universal law of nature accessed by reason and the particular Law of Moses, Philo relates the fall of humankind from an original, spiritual, and rationally perfect state, in which virtue could be attained through universal reason, into a corporeal state, in which the search for virtue requires the assistance of the Law.

In Philo's myth of creation, the commands, prohibitions, and instructions revealed by God are an accommodation to the fallen state of humankind as a whole. The implication is that the Law's success will also be its defeat; insofar as the Law promotes a rational perfection transcending corporeality, it creates the conditions in which an external, written Law is no longer required. To escape the bonds of the flesh and attain virtue is none other than to escape the need for written Law altogether.

The sources examined here respond to the cognitive dissonance generated by the encounter between classical and biblical notions of divine law by attempting to bridge the gap and transfer the properties of one to the other, with the direction of the transfer varying from source to source. But not all Jews responded to the cognitive dissonance in this way. A second response denies the attempt to correlate God's voice in nature with God's voice in the Torah and instead emphasizes their differences. A key exemplar of this response is taken up in the next chapter.

CHAPTER 4

Minding the Gap: Paul

As noted in the introduction to part 2, Jewish responses to the cognitive dissonance engendered by the incongruity between biblical and classical notions of divine law can be grouped into three general categories. Chapter 3 examined the apologetic response of those who sought to affirm the status of biblical divine law by minimizing or bridging the difference between the universal law grounded in reason and the particular Mosaic Law grounded in will in one of two ways: by elaborating the sapiential and rational credentials of the latter (correlating or equating Torah with wisdom [*sophia*] or reason [*logos*]), or by elaborating the positivistic and particular features of the former (attributing to the cosmic order characteristic traits of positive law).

The current chapter explores a sharply contrasting response to the cognitive dissonance engendered by the incongruity between biblical and classical notions of divine law. This second response—in various ways and to various degrees—*distinguished* biblical divine law from classical divine law. Far from bridging the gap between the universal law grounded in reason and the particular Mosaic Law grounded in will, this response chose to emphasize it, attributing few or none of the features of classical divine law to biblical Law.

Versions of this response in the period of our study are found in the Gospels and other New Testament books, especially the letters of Paul, and in subsequent Christian writings. The literature on New Testament, Pauline, and early Christian views of the Law is vast, and its many controversies cannot be reviewed in their entirety or adjudicated here. The present chapter examines select passages touching on the Law in the writings of Paul as but one example of this second response. The goal of this chapter is simply to shed new light on the subject by showing how the passages in question were informed by, and participated in, Greco-Roman discourses of law, a topic insufficiently addressed in the general literature.[1]

---

[1] I am not suggesting that Greco-Roman law discourse is the only context within which to interpret Paul, but rather that it is one among many contexts and deserves more attention. This is not to deny the excellent work of scholars who have illuminated Paul's writings by identifying motifs and concepts from apocalyptic, Stoicism, mystery religions, and more.

PAUL AND THE LAW

Paul's statements concerning the Mosaic Law are notoriously inconsistent.[2] At times, his attitude toward the Law is mildly positive, at times neutral, and at times harshly critical and condemnatory. Scholars have struggled to agree on a single Pauline approach to the Law or, failing that, an explanation for his ambivalence.[3] I will argue that understanding Paul's statements concerning the Mosaic Law requires due consideration of his goals and his audience.

Paul may fairly be described as a rhetorician whose letters reflect the goal of persuading others to his particular messianic vision. In composing these letters, he had an acute sense of audience, exploiting Greco-Roman discourses of the law that would have resonated deeply with his Hellenized audience. Specifically, Paul was familiar with the basic Greco-Roman dichotomy of divine law and positive law that permeated the Hellenistic world in his day. In his references to the Mosaic Law he exploited those long-standing discourses of positive law that are marked by ambivalence: G-R3, in which positive law is a second-best or necessary evil; G-R 5(ii) and (iii), in which the positive law that rescues us from an undesirable state (a good thing) is inadequate for the inculcation of virtue (a bad thing); and G-R 6, according to which law is in need of a savior. In addition, Paul draws upon more explicitly negative discourses of law such as G-R 4(i), according to which law is lifeless, a dead letter.

Why does Paul adopt an eclectic mix of ambivalent and occasionally harshly negative discourses? To answer this question, we need to understand his particular messianic vision and the place of Gentiles in the divine economy. This, in turn, requires a digression into ancient Jewish views on the question of Gentile access to Israelite identity.

Genealogical Definition of Jewish Identity:
Circumcision and the Law

As I have argued at length (Hayes 2002), different definitions of Jewish group identity and of the access of non-Jews to that identity may be seen in biblical texts. Diverse views of the permeability of the boundary between Israelites/

---

[2] Heikki Räisänen (1987) details the many inconsistencies in Paul's statements about the Law (see esp. chap. 4). His work is critiqued by Van Spanje 1999. For a criticism of the standard scholarly attempt to explain these inconsistencies, see Sanders 1990; see further Sanders 2001, chap. 9.

[3] See, preliminarily, the works cited in the previous note and Dunn 1988, 141–52, and 1990, esp. chap. 8. Stowers (1994) focuses on rhetorical strategies (such as prosopopoeia), generic conventions, and the role of audience as the key to resolving some fundamental contradictions in Romans. Readers will detect the influence of Stowers's approach in the current chapter's focus on audience and rhetorical strategies. Another attempt to resolve the contradictions in Paul's statements of the Law may be found in Boyarin 1997, 69ff.

Jews and non-Israelites/non-Jews were expressed in widely divergent views on intermarriage and conversion, and played a central role in the formation of Jewish sects in the Second Temple period and in the separation of the early church from what would later become rabbinic Judaism.

The primary avenue of foreign access to Israelite identity in biblical times was assimilation, often effected through intermarriage, which required acceptance of the religio-moral norms of the community and, according to some texts at least, male circumcision (see Jacob's position in Gen 34). Biblical stories of the assimilation of foreign women through intermarriage (e.g., Moses's two non-Israelite wives; Ruth) and the uncontested Israelite identity of the offspring of foreign wives (witness the many kings of Israel born of foreign mothers) attest to the permeability of the boundary between Israelite and non-Israelite. At the same time, there are biblical texts that espouse a more separatist position (Simeon and Levi's position in Gen 34). Some of these texts represent the uncircumcision of non-Israelite males as an irremediable obstacle to their assimilation (1 Sam 18; Ezek 44:6–9).[4]

In the postexilic period Ezra articulated an unprecedented genealogical definition of Israelite identity and attempted to banish all foreign spouses—male and female—and their offspring from the community. Ezra's insistence on descent from two Israelite parents was an innovation because it extended to lay Israelites the genealogical purity and endogamy previously required only of priests (cf. Lev 21 and Ezek 44). Ezra rationalizes this innovation with the assertion that all Israelites, not only the priests, are a "holy seed" that must not be desacralized by intermingling with the profane seed of non-Israelites (Ezra 9:1–2). The designation of Israelites and non-Israelites as, respectively, holy and profane seed was intended to establish an impermeable boundary between the two. Intermarriage becomes impossible on the grounds that distinct genealogical seeds cannot be joined. Likewise, conversion is impossible because that which has been separated out and designated by Yahweh as nonholy seed cannot be "converted" into something it is not—holy seed.[5]

Ezra's innovation was by no means universally accepted. Indeed, in the Second Temple period the boundary between Jew and non-Jew was widely understood to be permeable, and the conversion of non-Jews was a broadly accepted phenomenon. But some Jews continued to prize genealogical filiation and contested the very possibility of "conversion" and assimilation of foreigners. For these groups, sympathetic Gentiles can be, at best, "resident aliens" (gerim).

---

[4] On the dueling visions of these and other passages pertaining to the rite of circumcision, see the excellent discussion in Thiessen 2011, 43–63.

[5] For a full discussion of Ezra's innovation and the holy seed ideology at its base, see Hayes 2002, 27–33.

These *gerim* constitute a distinct "fourth estate"[6] (after priests, Levites, and lay Israelites) and may not intermarry with native-born Jews.[7]

As I have argued (2002, 73–91), according to some of the more extreme articulations of this view the blemish of profane seed can never be overcome, and a non-Jew can never become a Jew. The permanent segregation of *gerim* is a prevalent idea at Qumran, consistent with its often realist approach to legal and ritual matters (see chapter 3, pp. 103–5). In 4QFl i. 3–4 *gerim* are forever and always excluded from entry into "the congregation of the Lord."[8] An Ezran "holy seed" ideology and concern for genealogical purity motivates 4QMMT's prohibition of not only interethnic unions but unions between genealogically distinct classes internal to Israel (priests and lay Israelites). Similarly, the book of Jubilees, many copies of which were found at Qumran, condemns interethnic unions as genealogically defiling the holy seed of lay Israelites and prohibits unions with all persons of foreign descent. The polemical target of 4QMMT and Jubilees is not the unconverted Gentile (unions with unconverted Gentiles were uncontroversially prohibited by all Jewish groups) but precisely the so-called converted Gentile. Because these texts, like Ezra, deny the very possibility of converting profane seed into holy seed, unions with these persons can never be anything but *zenut*—fornication. In these works, the divinely ordained status of seed as holy or profane is essential, intrinsic, and unalterable (Jub 16:17–18)—consistent with a realist legal orientation.

Matthew Thiessen builds on these claims in his pathbreaking book, *Contesting Conversion*. Thiessen argues (2011, 12) that for some ancient Jews the rite of circumcision could not efface the genealogical distinction between Jew and non-Jew. He traces this view to Genesis 17's establishment of the covenant of circumcision for every eight-day-old male. Thiessen argues convincingly that the priestly writer of Genesis 17

---

[6] I ask readers to indulge my use of this term to designate a social order less recognized and influential than the upper orders in a hierarchically conceived system. Although the term "fourth estate" has come to refer to the press, this was not its original meaning. In medieval and early modern Christian Europe, the clergy, nobility, and commoners constituted the first, second, and third estates of the realm. The peasants were sometimes referred to as a "fourth estate," powerless relative to the first three. The structural analogy to Paul's conception of the divine kingdom is clear: priests, Levites, and common Israelites constitute the three orders or estates of the realm, with varying degrees of privilege and influence, while righteous Gentiles form a fourth order or estate and possess the fewest privileges and the least influence.

[7] The term *ger* would acquire the meaning of proselyte or convert in rabbinic literature, but this is not its meaning in the biblical period or in sectarian texts that insist upon the nonassimilation of the *ger*. In these latter contexts, the term retains its biblical meaning of "resident alien."

[8] Presumably in both senses—access to the sanctuary and intermarriage into the community. See Hayes 2002, 61–67.

attempts to distinguish between Israelite circumcision (exemplified by Isaac) and non-Israelite circumcision (exemplified by Ishmael) through the timing of circumcision, in order to show that not all who are circumcised belong to the covenant. One is a member of God's covenant with Abraham via proper descent. Eighth-day circumcision, which only the descendants of Isaac practice, protects this genealogical boundary around Abraham's covenantal seed by linking ritual practice as closely as possible to birth. In other words, contrary to many interpretations of Genesis 17, including some early rabbinic ones, circumcision according to the priestly writer does not function as an initiatory or conversionistic rite.

That Genesis 17 should be the source of dueling understandings of the rite of circumcision is due to a basic ambiguity. Verse 12 propounds the requirement of eighth-day circumcision for every male "throughout your generations" and then specifies: "the home-born and he who is purchased from a foreigner who is not of your seed." The verse clearly indicates that circumcision seals membership in the covenant community for foreign-born slaves as well as native-born Israelites. Thus, for some Jews, Genesis 17 is a source for the view that the rite of circumcision brings non-Israelites into the covenant community. However, the same verse indicates that the circumcision that seals membership in the covenant community should occur on the eighth day. Thus, for other Jews, Genesis 17 is a source for the view that circumcision does not serve to bring into the covenant community non-Israelites circumcised after the eighth day of life. In short, two competing views find support in this verse: the view that circumcision serves as a rite of conversion even for adult males, and the view that it does not serve as a rite of conversion for any person "of foreign seed" older than eight days. On the latter view, "circumcision, properly observed, functions to buttress the wall between Jew and non-Jew."[9]

Thiessen focuses his attention on verse 14, which prescribes the punishment of *karet* (extirpation) for those lacking circumcision. Although the version preserved in the Masoretic Text (Hebrew) refers to the requirement of circumcision in general terms (timing unspecified),[10] the Septuagint (Greek) translation and other witnesses attest to a version of verse 14 that prescribes *karet* for the lack of specifically *eighth-day* circumcision.[11] This is the reading of the verse assumed by Jubilees, and, as Thiessen remarks, it underwrites Jubilees' rejection of the very possibility of adult conversion:

[9] Thiessen 2011, 13. Thiessen's discussion of these dueling views focuses more on the textual variants and versions of v. 14 than on the inherent ambiguities in v. 12, but his conclusions are essentially the same.

[10] "Any uncircumcised male who is not circumcised in the flesh of his foreskin shall be cut off from his people; he has broken my covenant."

[11] LXX: "And the uncircumcised male, who shall not be circumcised in the flesh of his foreskin *on the eighth day*, that soul shall be cut off from his people, for he has broken my covenant."

This law is (valid) for all history forever. There is no circumcision of days, nor omitting any day of the eight days because it is an eternal ordinance ordained and written on the heavenly tablets. Anyone who is born, the flesh of whose private parts has not been circumcised by the eighth day, does not belong to the people of the pact which the Lord made with Abraham but to the people (meant for) destruction. Moreover, there is no sign on him that he belongs to the Lord but (he is meant) for destruction, for being destroyed from the earth, and for being uprooted from the earth because he has violated the covenant of the lord our God (*Jub* 15:25–26).

By contrast, the absence of the eighth-day requirement in the Masoretic Text's version of verse 14 removes the link between the *karet* penalty and the timing of the rite on the eighth day, and opens up the possibility of circumcision at other times. This version of verse 14 (lacking the eighth-day requirement) is consistent not only with the later rabbinic willingness to delay the circumcision of an Israelite infant in order to avoid conflicts with the Sabbath or for medical reasons, but also with "the general openness to Gentile circumcision during the Second Temple and rabbinic periods" (Thiessen 2011, 27).

Thiessen's observations regarding the contested status of circumcision as a rite of conversion for non-Jewish males leads him to a radical revision of a central assumption of New Testament and Pauline scholarship. It is widely believed that those in the early Jesus movement who insisted on Gentile entrance into the covenant community via circumcision and adoption of the Law were motivated by an exclusivist ideology, while those who exempted non-Jews from the requirements of circumcision and the Law were inclusivists seeking to provide easy access to the covenant community and equalize the status of Jew and Gentile. But as Thiessen argues (ibid., 13) in connection with Luke-Acts, "this is neither the only, nor the most accurate, way one can understand early Christian perceptions of circumcision." He writes,

> Luke's view of circumcision belongs within the same trajectory as the views found in Genesis 17 and the book of *Jubilees*. Similar to the priestly writer and the author of *Jubilees*, Luke denies that circumcision functions as a rite of conversion; rather, he sees it as a custom only intended for and of value to Jews. Consequently, Luke believes that Jewish believers should still practice circumcision on their newborn males, while Gentile believers should not be circumcised. Contrary to the majority of interpreters who understand Luke to have broken from law-observant Judaism, this reading suggests that Luke's thinking had much in common with the most stringent forms of Judaism, which conceived of Jewishness in genealogical terms. (ibid.)

In the same way, Thiessen hints, Paul may be located within this more exclusivist stream:

Pauline interpreters ... often describe a Judaism that requires the conversion of Gentiles to Judaism as exclusivistic. Yet, in comparison with the definition of Jewishness that has been considered in the previous chapters [a definition that precludes conversion, or Gentile membership in the covenant community through the rite of circumcision], a Judaism that permits conversion is in many ways quite open and inclusive. In fact, Paul's opposition to Gentile Christians' adopting Jewish customs and identity may be better understood as a variation on the genealogical exclusivism of contemporaneous forms of Judaism. If so, to describe Paul as inclusive and his opponents as exclusive is to greatly simplify their positions. (ibid., 147)

Paula Fredriksen sees a natural connection between Paul's resistance to the circumcision/conversion of Gentiles and his conception of the place of Gentiles in Israel's redemption narrative, a narrative that drew heavily upon Jewish eschatology. Jewish apocalyptic eschatology contained various visions of the fate of non-Jews in the era of Israel's redemption—ranging from the utter destruction of all or some of the nations (see Isa 49:23; Mic 5:9, 15; 7:16–17; 10:7; Jub 15:25–26) to rehabilitation and inclusion (see Isa 2:2–4, 25:6; Zech 8:23; 1 En 91:14).[12] It is important to note that these narratives of Gentile inclusion are not speaking of Gentile conversion. The Gentiles prompted by Yahweh's end-time revelation to abandon their idols and worship the one god do not become Jews. They remain Gentiles, albeit Gentiles who have turned from idolatry in order to worship Yahweh alongside a reassembled Israel (see Fredriksen 1991, 547, and 2010, 241). Frederiksen (1991, 547) writes:

> When God establishes his Kingdom, then, these two groups will together constitute 'his people': Israel, redeemed from exile, and the Gentiles, redeemed from idolatry. Gentiles are saved as Gentiles: they do not, eschatologically, become Jews.

According to Fredriksen, Paul's eschatology followed the stream of Jewish apocalypticism according to which the nations will *join with* Israel to worship Yahweh, but will not *join* Israel (2010, 243). We might say that there is both *inclusion* and *exclusion* in this eschatological vision. Certainly, believing Gentiles are "Israel" in some sense (according to the *spirit*, according to the *promise*, through *faith*) but they must not (indeed, cannot) "convert" to become Jews (according to the *flesh*, according to the *Law*, through *circumcision*). Gentiles will join with Israel in the redemption, but only so far and no further.

> [T]his 'turning' to Israel's god is not the same as converting to Judaism, as Paul himself insists. His pagans are not to 'become' Jews. But they are to live as if they were eschatological pagans—which, by his lights, they

---

[12] See Fredriksen 1991, 544–48, for a review of inclusive and exclusive eschatologies.

are. During the brief wrinkle in time between the resurrection and the Parousia, Paul's pagans are to worship only Paul's god, the god of Israel, empowered to do so by that god's risen son.[13]

Fredriksen notes (2010, 250) that like other apocalyptically minded Jews of his era, Paul believed that the coming Kingdom's demography would reflect the present distinction between Jews and Gentiles, Israel and the nations. What was the apocalyptic vision? For apocalyptically minded Jews, Yahweh's eschatological kingdom maps neatly onto the concentric circles of the Temple precincts in Jerusalem (Fredriksen 2005, 205ff.). Specifically, the innermost and most holy area of the Temple accessed only by the high priest was ringed by zones of decreasing holiness that were accessible to ordinary priests, Levites, pure Israelite men, pure Israelite women, and finally Gentiles, respectively. Some believed that this distinction would continue in the final age (see 4QFlor, 4Q174 1 I, 3–4). As in the Temple, so in the end-time—Gentiles are included even as they are excluded.

There are elements of this delimited inclusion in Paul's writings,[14] and the mechanism for the believing Gentile's entry into the redemption narrative of Israel is the death of Jesus, or baptism into his death (Fredriksen 2005, 210).

> The Spirit, through baptism, has incorporated them (literally, somehow) into Christ's eschatological body, so that false gods, hostile cosmic forces, and sin itself no longer have power over them (I Cor. 12:12–13, 27; Gal. 3:28, 4:3–9; cf. Rom. 6:11). They have been set apart: this is the biblical sense of "made holy." (ibid., 212–33)

Gentiles who have been sanctified, or made holy, in Christ (1 Cor 1:2) and who abstain from morally polluting acts of idolatry and *porneia* are fit to approach holiness. As Fredriksen explains (ibid., 213), this is Paul's understanding of his role as apostle to the Gentiles: to be the servant of Jesus to the nations and to ensure that the offering of the Gentiles is made acceptable, that is, holy by the holy spirit (Rom 15:16).[15] While Israel is, by prior designation of its seed, already holy, Gentiles are sanctified or brought to a degree of holiness through the death and resurrection of Christ. These Gentiles together with

---

[13] Fredriksen 2010, 242. I would nuance Fredriksen's formulation by saying that Gentiles do not become Jews in the sense afforded by conversion—a kind of naturalization into the *ethnos*. Nevertheless, they certainly lay claim to the title of "Israel," though of a specific kind—Israel according to the spirit and not according to the flesh. Naturally, spiritual affiliation would be viewed, by those of a Platonizing tendency, much more positively than physical affiliation.

[14] Gal 3:28, however, suggests an ultimate erasure of difference. Nevertheless, Paul here refers to an erasure of difference *through faith or baptism in Christ, i.e., according to the Spirit.* Insofar as people have *bodies*, there is difference *according to the flesh.*

[15] For Paul's understanding of himself as the Apostle to the Gentiles in the messianic era, the agent by which the Gentiles would be brought as an offering to Jerusalem and would come to worship the god of Israel, see, preliminarily, Sanders 2001, 3.

Jews form a holy community worshipping Yahweh. And yet, they occupy distinct and separate stations within that community. Believing Gentiles may be the children of Abraham, and like him they will be justified by faith in a state of uncircumcision (Rom 4:9–12); but they are Abraham's sons or heirs according to the promise (Gal 3:29) and thus distinct from the Jews, who are his heirs according to the flesh as sealed by eighth-day circumcision and observance of the Law.[16] For Paul, the distinction of membership within the covenant remains. Thus, even as he opposed circumcision and Torah observance for Gentiles, Paul supported the continuing Torah observance of Jewish members of the Jesus movement and for the most part seems to have continued to observe the Torah himself.[17]

Mark Nanos (2009) has argued that the characterization of Paul as propounding a "Law-free gospel" is a misreading of Paul. That Paul was Torah observant is "consistent with his own self-witness and confirmed by his earliest biographer in the Acts of the Apostles" (21). This is a controversial point; less controversial is the assertion that if Torah observance was for anyone, then it was for the children of Abraham, Isaac, and Israel according to the flesh, and not the descendants of Abraham according to the spirit—the Gentiles.

> In this age, Christ-following non-Jews are obligated to bear witness to the righteousness expressed in Torah, that is, the love of God and neighbor, but as representatives of the *other* nations, and not as members of Israel and her Mosaic covenant. This age represents the fulfillment of God's covenant with Abraham, bringing blessing to all of the nations through his seed. But non-Jews becoming Jews by proselyte conversion, symbolized by circumcision for males ... would undermine the message that the awaited good for Israel *and* the nations had arrived *now* in Christ Jesus. (ibid., 8)

The traditional interpretive approach attributes Paul's rejection of Torah observance for Gentiles to his belief that the Torah was passé or inferior—a trap that would enslave the Gentile in a spiritually immature lifestyle of works-righteousness (ibid., 7). Nanos counters that given Paul's retention of Torah observance for himself and other Jews (at the very least, he probably *allowed* it), his rejection of Gentile conversion may be attributed instead to his belief

---

[16] Similarly, when Paul declares in Gal 3:28 that *in Christ* there is neither male nor female, he means to erase differences only *in Christ*, i.e., *according to the spirit* and not according to the flesh. As is well known, Paul advocated the continuing authority of embodied males over embodied females.

[17] Paul's Torah observance is a hotly debated issue. Passages that militate against the claim that he observed the Law are 1 Cor 9:20–21 and Gal 2:11–14. However, both passages are in the context of a discussion of how Jews should behave in their mission to Gentiles. Paul dispenses with Torah observance in the Gentile communities he addresses for the sake of church unity. We may add that Paul's effort to persuade Gentiles that Law observance is unnecessary and even undesirable would have been compromised were he to observe the Law when among them.

that in the awaited age the nations, qua nations, would recognize Yahweh as the one creator God (ibid.) in accordance with the words of the prophets. But on what basis, we may ask, would Paul allow continued Torah observance for Jews if it is faith in Jesus that brings righteousness? Here too the answer lies in the words of the prophets.

As I argued in chapter 3, Jeremiah 31 and Ezekiel 36 describe an ideal future in which the ingathered exiles will be able to observe the Law *without struggle or effort*.[18] This, Paul believes, is what justification through Christ Jesus offers to Jews—to Torah-observant Jews. Paul believes that Jews too are delivered from sin through faith in Christ Jesus and only through faith, not the Law (Rom 3:28–30). Having died to the body with Christ, Jews also are freed from the bodily passions and desires that prevented them from fulfilling the Torah perfectly. Thus, prior to Christ the Law aided Jews in their struggle against sin; but after Christ the Law no longer serves that function, for faith in Christ can abolish the struggle against sin and so void one of the purposes of the Law. Freed of sin (justified) through faith in Christ Jesus, Jews will be able to fulfill the Law effortlessly as intended and as envisaged by Jeremiah 31 and Ezekiel 36. Thus, Jews are not freed from the Law by the advent of Jesus; they are freed from the state of sin that prevents them from fulfilling the Law as intended.[19]

Nor, in Paul's view, should Jews desire to be free of Torah observance, for it is a privilege that marks their greater proximity to the divine. Paul's vision of the distinct demographic groups in the end-time kingdom may well be predicated on a system of concentric circles of proximity to the Holy One and *maintained by genealogical distinction*. The idea of concentric circles of proximity to holiness is a commonplace of biblical tradition, particularly the priestly source, and later Judaism. The innermost circle (that of priests) carries with it the greatest privileges (greatest access to and service of the holy) as well as the greatest ritual and legal obligations (purity requirements, marital rules, etc., in excess of the requirements and rules articulated in the covenant with the larger nation). Membership in this group is *genealogically* determined—only sons of Aaron may be priests and access the holiest parts of the sanctuary. The next ring out is that of Levites—slightly fewer privileges and ritual and legal obligations. Membership in this group is also *genealogically* determined, as only members of the tribe of Levi are accounted Levites. Encircling the Levites are the Israelites, possessing fewer privileges and ritual and legal obligations, and also

[18] In chapter 1, I coined the term "robo-righteousness" to describe this idealized effortless observance of the Torah, which will be achieved in the final age when the commandments are entirely internalized, the "curse" of moral freedom is eliminated, and humans are returned to the state of automatic obedience to God's will that they enjoyed in Eden, before trading immortality for moral agency.

[19] If it is only in that future messianic state of freedom from sin that the Law will be perfectly fulfilled, then it is little wonder that Paul does not emphasize its observance by Jews in the present. Nevertheless, while it may achieve little now, it has not been annulled, and indeed it will be fulfilled in the end.

genealogically determined—only the sons of Isaac are accounted members of the *nation* of Israel. Finally, Gentiles who recognize Yahweh as the one creator God have the fewest privileges and ritual and legal obligations (but not *no* privileges and obligations, as indicated by the prohibition of defiling sexual behaviors, blood, and meat offered to idols or from strangled animals; Acts 15:29). Membership in this group is also *genealogically* determined. As the seed of Abraham, Gentiles are members of God's kingdom and covenant of faith; but they are not the seed of Israel through Isaac according to the flesh, and, on the view of Paul and other "exclusivists" at least, they are not entitled to the privileges and obligations of the covenant of circumcision and the Mosaic Torah any more than an Israelite of the seed of Isaac is entitled to the privileges and obligations of the priestly seed of Aaron. It is hardly surprising that genealogical distinction should define and police the boundary between Jew and Gentile when it served to define and police the boundary between distinct groups even within Israel.[20] Indeed, it should perhaps occasion greater surprise that there were evidently large numbers of Jews (including James) who were willing to adopt a nominalist approach, trumping the claims of genealogy and allowing Gentile seed to be "converted" to the seed of Isaac through the rite of circumcision.

Paul's position on Gentiles must be seen as a paradoxical mix of exclusivistic and inclusivistic ideologies. Gentiles are included in the kingdom of God that is at hand—an inclusivistic ideology. Yet the seed of Abraham (Gentiles) can no more become the seed of Isaac (Jews) through a ritual of conversion than the seed of Isaac (lay Israelites) can become the seed of Aaron (priests) through a ritual of conversion—an exclusivistic ideology.[21] God's kingdom *includes* Gentiles as the seed of Abraham even as it *excludes* them from the rights and privileges of the Torah that is the sole patrimony of the seed of Israel through

---

[20] For a full consideration of the nuances of this claim, see Hayes 2002, 24–26, 34–37, 164–92. It should be noted that permeability of the boundary is often affected by gender as well as by factors such as moral purity. Thus, we see that women are able to move between groups a little more freely than men: according to biblical and rabbinic law, an Israelite woman can marry a priestly male, and her offspring will have full priestly status (though even this is contested by genealogical exclusivists such as the author of 4QMMT; see Hayes 2002, 82–89), but an Israelite male cannot perform any ritual or legal action that converts him into a priest. Similarly, non-Jewish women seem to have slightly greater access to Israelite identity than do non-Jewish males (already Pentateuchal law permits marriage with a captive woman from the otherwise entirely prohibited Canaanite nations). In short, while genealogy provides a first-order distinction among demographic groups, other factors occasionally determine mobility among the groups. Different factions within Jewish society tolerated different degrees of permeability—ranging from none to a little to a lot.

[21] Boyarin (1997, 8) focuses on the inclusive element of Paul's thought when he writes, "[T]he very impulse toward universalism, toward the One, is that which both enabled and motivated Paul's move toward a spiritual and allegorizing interpretation of Israel's Scripture and Law." But where Boyarin understands this universalist impulse as seeking to establish a "non-differentiated, non-hierarchical" humanity (ibid.), I would argue that it seeks to establish the fully differentiated and hierarchical (universal) kingdom of Yahweh as depicted in Israelite prophecy.

Isaac. Thus, it is not the Torah's *inferiority* that motivates Paul's rejection of the Torah for Gentiles, but precisely its *superiority*, its assignation as a privilege to the seed of Israel through Isaac only.[22] Paul may wish to include the Gentiles within the end-time kingdom of God, but as a genealogical exclusivist, he includes them only so far—and no further.[23]

Paul's Discourse of Ambivalence regarding the Mosaic Law

We are now in a position to understand Paul's mixed rhetoric of the Law. Paul's "exclusivistic view of Gentile inclusion"[24] likely led to feelings of marginalization and confusion among non-Jews (Nanos 2009, 8). Some Christ-believing non-Jews sought to escape this ambiguous identity of *"joining with* Israel while not *joining* Israel," by seeking to become proselytes (as in Galatia) or by claiming

[22] Thus, while I would agree with those who argue that Paul did not abolish the Law for Jews, I do not agree that it is because he thought the Law brought salvation for Jews. I think it is clear that according to Paul, Jews also are justified by faith, not Law. The mistake is in thinking that the Law is therefore dispensable for Jews. It is not, but until such time as Jews will be able to fulfill it properly (and Paul was hoping to hasten the day), the Law is not of central importance to Paul. It can't achieve anything in the current dispensation.

[23] It should be evident by now that I disagree with Dunn's characterization of Paul (1990, esp. chap. 7) as denying nationalism and attacking those who believe their standing before God depends on their physical descent from Abraham, on their national identity as Jews. Dunn argues that what Paul objects to is those portions of the Law that "had become the expression of a too narrowly nationalistic and racial conception of the covenant" (201–2), i.e., the racial rather than the ritual expressions of the faith (a distinction that Dunn believes is indicated by Paul's use of the term "works of the law" [conceived negatively] as opposed to "the law" [conceived positively]). I maintain that, on the contrary, Paul's view is in line with a well-attested minority ideology of genealogically based exclusivism.

Dunn seems to think that a nationalist understanding of the Law is an undesirable postclassical development. However, Dunn's assertion that certain laws *"had become"* the expression of a narrow nationalism is odd, in view of the fact that the biblical narrative that describes the giving of the Law states explicitly and repeatedly that the central purpose of the Law is to separate Israel from the nations, to mark Israel as a distinct *people.* Like all systems of positive law, certainly in antiquity but also in the modern era, biblical law is explicitly an expression of nationalism and governs only citizens of a particular community. What should occasion our surprise, therefore, is not that Jews understood the Law to both inscribe and police ethnic particularity but that any Jew could understand the Law to be the universal inheritance of humankind (i.e., Philo's view) or open to foreigners through the legal fiction of conversion (the rabbinic view).

For Paul, justification comes to all through faith in Christ, but this does not erase ethnic boundaries or the obligation of "Israel according to the flesh" to observe the Law. Boyarin (1997, 106–7), following Dunn, thinks it does. Boyarin argues that "the primary motivation, not only for [Paul's] mission but indeed for his 'conversion,' was a passionate desire that humanity be One under the sign of the One God—a universalism ... born of the union of Hebraic monotheism and Greek desire for unity and univocity," and that "the eradication of human difference and hierarchy" was a central theme of Paul's social gospel. While I agree that Paul was motivated by a desire to establish universal worship of the one god, I maintain that Paul's vision of the universal recognition of the one god was based on prophetic models that did not entail the erasure of differences and hierarchies, but retained them. Paul's views on his fellow Jews' continued observance of the Torah (its concrete and literal commandments, and not merely, as in Dunn's view, an abstract principle of neighborly love) will be addressed below.

[24] This is my description of Paul's position, not Nanos's.

to have replaced Jews (as in Rome; ibid.). Paul needed to develop a rhetorical strategy that would discourage these two options and persuade Gentiles to his vision of their place in the divine economy: recognition of the one creator God and abstention from idolatry and immorality were permitted to (indeed required of) Gentiles even as observance of the Torah was not permitted to (or required of) them.

To represent observance of the Mosaic Law as the "privilege" of a group whose ranks the Gentiles could never hope to join—while consistent with Paul's actual views—would not have been a welcome or popular message in Gentile ears. Paul had to inspire Gentiles to worship the god of Israel without creating in them a further desire to enter into the privileged ranks of the Torah-observant seed of Isaac. This was surely a difficult task, but it was one to which the classical discourse of ambivalence about law was beautifully suited.

Paul's rhetoric about the Law appears in letters written to primarily Gentile communities[25] whose very framework for thinking about law would have been grounded in the basic Hellenistic dichotomy between unwritten divine (natural) law that brings perfect virtue and written human law that does not. Seeing himself as the apostle to the Gentiles, Paul knew he had to address them on their own terms. If Paul states explicilty that he adapts his *behavior* to the behavior of those around him, behaving like a Gentile when with Gentiles (1 Cor 9:19–23), it is not difficult to imagine that he adapted his rhetoric to those around him as well.[26] How else could he be persuasive? After all, Paul was seeking to convince non-Jews to join with a community in possession of a divine law that, frankly, looked nothing like the classical understanding of divine law with which they were familiar, namely, a law of reason inscribed in nature and on the hearts of men. On the contrary, the Mosaic Law would have appeared to his Hellenized Gentile audience to possess the primary characteristics of positive law, namely, written rules for a particular community imposed and coercively enforced by a sovereign will. Confronted with that cognitive dissonance, acutely aware of the perspective of his audience, and wishing to *discourage* rather than encourage his audience's interest in the Law, Paul took advantage of the prima facie similarity of Mosaic Law and positive law to do precisely what Philo did not do.

Philo, in his desire to make the Mosaic Law *attractive* to persons immersed in Hellenistic culture, claimed that it was the natural law of Greco-Roman tradition; against a plain reading of the biblical text he asserted that the Mosaic Law is utterly rational, noncoercive instruction, is universal, never changes,

---

[25] Here I accept the argument of Stowers 1994, 29–30, that the explicitly encoded audience of Romans is Gentile. In Rom 9–11 Paul speaks *about* Jews, but he still addresses himself to Gentiles.

[26] We need not go as far as Nanos (2009, 17) and argue that this is the intended meaning of 1 Cor 9—that Paul argued like one outside the Law when with those outside the Law. Nevertheless, the adaptation of behavior to conform to context renders more plausible the suggestion that Paul adapted his rhetoric and conceptual framework to conform to his context.

and is actually unwritten. These are audacious claims, and one can hardly blame Paul for thinking that they might not convince a Gentile audience. Moreover, he did not *want* his Gentile audience to view the Mosaic Law as the universal divine law for all humankind lest they aspire to observe it—an unacceptable option for a genealogical exclusivist like Paul.

Thus, in the spirit of Clinias and Megillus, and in order to dissuade Gentiles from seeking to adopt the Torah, Paul conceded that his native constitution did *not* meet the criteria of divine law articulated by the natural law tradition.[27] Distancing the Mosaic Law from classical conceptions of divine natural law rendered it less appealing to Gentiles without entirely discrediting it. Paul was aided in his task by Greco-Roman discourses that emphasize not the harmony of *phusis* and *nomos*, but rather their opposition (G-R 5), as well as discourses that express ambivalence and even negativity about positive law (G-R 3 and 4).

In Romans 7, Paul speaks of the Mosaic Law as contrary to nature (G-R 5). He singles out the tenth commandment, against coveting, as a law that awakens awareness of natural impulses contrary to the Law.

> [I]f it had not been for the Law, I would not have known sin. I would not have known what it is to covet if the Law had not said, "You shall not covet." But sin seizing an opportunity in the commandment, produced in me all kinds of covetousness. Apart from the Law sin lies dead. I was once alive apart from the Law, but when the commandment came, sin revived and I died and the very commandment that promised life proved to be death to me. (Rom 7:7b–10)[28]

The opposition of nature and law (which here must refer to the Mosaic Law for which the tenth commandment functions as a synecdoche) would lead Paul's readers to conclude that the Mosaic Law is not natural but conventional—a temporary and particular positive law that coerces obedience, rather than rational instruction that cultivates virtue. Indeed, Paul points explicitly to the temporary nature of the Mosaic Law: like any conventional law it is not eternal; it was "added" at a specific point in history—430 years after the promise was made to Abraham, a promise that it does not supersede (Gal 3:19; see Lull 1986, 483).

> Now the promises were made to Abraham and to his offspring ... that is, to one person, who is Christ. My point is this: the Law which came four hundred thirty years later, does not annul a covenant previously ratified by God, so as to nullify the promise. For if the inheritance comes from

---

[27] And in this respect Paul, like Philo, stands in a long Greco-Roman tradition of evaluating a native constitution to determine the extent to which it may be said to possess the attributes of divine law (see G-R 8).

[28] All translations of the New Testament are taken from the New Revised Standard Version.

the Law, it no longer comes from the promise; but God granted it to Abraham through the promise. (Gal 3:16–18)

This categorization of the Mosaic Law as positive law enabled Paul to deploy several themes from classical discourses of positive law in his discussion of the Mosaic Law, discourses that underscore its limitations or flaws. For example, in his more hostile moments Paul draws on G-R 4, which associates written law with inflexibility and death in contrast to the animate law of nature inscribed in living souls or embodied in a king, as well as the antinomian discourse G-R 5 (iv) that associates law with a loss of freedom or with slavery. Paul mobilizes these negative discourses in a series of dichotomies that recur throughout his letter to the Romans: Law vs. grace through Christ Jesus; sin vs. justification; death vs. life; the Law of sin and death vs. the law of the Spirit in Christ Jesus; flesh vs. spirit; slavery vs. freedom; slavery vs. sonship. A clear example may be seen in Romans 8:2–4:

> For the *law of the Spirit of life in Christ Jesus* has set you *free* from the *Law of sin and of death*. For God has done what *the Law, weakened by the flesh*, could not do by sending *his own Son in the likeness of sinful flesh*, and to deal with sin, he condemned sin in the flesh, so that the just requirement of the law might be fulfilled in us, who walk not according to the *flesh* but according to the *Spirit*. (emphasis added)

In 2 Corinthians 3:2–6, the letter of the Law written on tablets of stone—a letter that kills—is contrasted with the letter of Christ written on the tablets of the heart—a letter that gives life. The close association of death and sin in biblical and Second Temple Jewish sources[29] may be seen in the interchangeability of the terms "Law of death" and "Law of sin" in Paul's writings, and in the equation of enslavement to death and enslavement to sin. In Romans 6 Paul says that those who are crucified with Christ are no longer enslaved to sin. By dying with Christ, they are freed from sin. Sin and death have no dominion over them since they are now under grace (= life), not Law (= sin and death; vv. 6–14). The written Law is also associated with the slavery of captivity in Romans 7:6: "But now we are discharged from the Law, dead to that which held us captive, so that we are slaves not under the old written code but in the new life of the Spirit." The verse assumes two kinds of servitude—the negative servitude of the written code, which is bondage or captivity, and the positive servitude of the spirit, which is actually life. The metaphor of slavery is elsewhere illuminated by a juxtaposition with sonship. In Galatians 4:4–7, Paul writes that Christ has

---

[29] Here we note the negative discourse of Ezek 20:25 (referring to "statutes that were not good and ordinances by which they could not have life") as a biblical support for Paul's radical association of the Law with sin. See Räisänen 1987, 156–58. As we noted in chapter 1, Ezekiel's statement refers to the law of firstlings. But as Räisänen points out (159), Paul likely exploits the verse to attribute an original negative purpose to the entire Law.

redeemed those under the Law that they might receive adoption to sonship: "So you are no longer a slave, but God's child; and since you are his child, God has made you also an heir" (v. 7).

Having linked the Law written on tablets of stone with slavery, sin, and death, Paul pauses to voice the incredulity he imagines his readers must be experiencing: is it possible that a divinely bestowed Law would be a law of slavery, sin, and death (7:7)?[30] Paul immediately pulls back from this implied characterization of Law as sin and makes two attempts to explain how a good Law can lead to sin. First, he argues that the Law is linked to sin in the sense that it provides sin with an opportunity to seize us (Rom 7:9–11):

> I was once alive apart from the Law, but when the commandment came, sin revived and I died and the very commandment that promised life proved to be death to me. For sin, seizing an opportunity in the commandment, deceived me and through it killed me.

Having asserted that it is not the commandment but sin working through the commandment that brings death, Paul can confidently state, "So the Law is holy, and the commandment is holy and just and good" (Rom 7:12).

And yet this doesn't satisfy. Can what is good bring death (v. 13)? Paul offers a second response, this time asserting that it is not the Law that is to blame but our fleshly nature:

> For we know that the Law is spiritual; but I am of the flesh, sold into slavery under sin ... For I know that nothing good dwells within me, that is, in my flesh ... For I delight in the Law of god in my inmost self, but I see in my members another law at war with the law of my mind, making me captive to the Law of sin that dwells in my members. Wretched man that I am! Who will rescue me from this body of death? (Rom 7:14, 18, 22–24)[31]

The Law per se is not the problem, and presumably neither is the lawgiver. The cause of the problem is the very corporeality of the Law's subjects,[32] and in this Paul's argument is reminiscent of Aristotle's explanation for why even just laws appear to be defective at times (see G-R 3(ii)). According to Aristotle, the defect does not lie in the law itself or in the legislator. The law may be perfectly just and correct in the majority of cases, and legislators act well in formulating

---

[30] For the idea that Paul presents an individual painted through speech-in-character in Rom. 7:7ff., see Stowers 1994, 39.

[31] Sanders (2001, 109–10) connects Paul's depiction of the first-person "I" that seeks to do good pitted against the "flesh" that desires sin with a widely known first-century anthropological dualism: the theory of a good mind or soul in an evil or weak physical body. For a full and nuanced discussion of Paul's dualism, see Boyarin 1994, 7, 59–86.

[32] See Stendahl 1963, 212: "This distinction [between the good law and bad sin] makes it possible for Paul to blame Sin and Flesh, and to rescue the Law as a good gift of God."

such rules for the majority of cases with equitable adjustments for particular cases. Aristotle identifies the cause of the defect as *the nature of the things that law seeks to order*: the realm of practical affairs. Practical affairs are by their very nature indefinite and variable because they deal with material objects that are susceptible to change and accident. Similarly, for Paul, the Law—holy and good in itself—does not bring virtue, because it seeks to order that which is ultimately incapable of being ordered: carnal bodies and their unruly passions and desires.

At the end of Romans 7, Paul despairs of his ability to achieve virtue under the Law because of his corporeality ("Wretched man that I am! Who will rescue me from this *body* of death?"). Hovering in the background of his despair is a question about the very purpose for which the Law was given. Why would a presumably good divine being—a being Paul hopes his Gentile listeners will be inspired to worship—bestow a Law that entangles persons in a losing struggle against their bodily passions?

This question is explicitly addressed in Paul's letter to the Galatians. In answering the question, Paul draws upon themes from yet another Greco-Roman discourse, but interweaves them with biblical themes to create a new narrative. As we have seen, narratives are a powerful strategy for negotiating the tension between logically incompatible commitments, such as universalism and particularism (see the narratives outlined in chapter 3) or positive and negative views of the law (see the classical narratives of successive human eras outlined in chapter 2). These narratives enable the retention of contradictory or even mutually exclusive principles by plotting them at different points on a chronological continuum.

Paul constructs a narrative that endows the Law with a clear, time-limited purpose. Specifically, he asserts that the Law was given in order to prepare the people for salvation through faith. In Paul's narrative of salvation, the Law functions as a pedagogue (Gal 3:24–25) for Israel but only until the arrival of Christ.

> Now the promises were made to Abraham and to his offspring ... that is, to one person, who is Christ ...
>
> Why then the Law? It was added because of/to increase transgressions,[33] until the offspring would come to whom the promise had been made ...
>
> Now before faith came, we were imprisoned and guarded under the Law until faith would be revealed. Therefore the Law was our pedagogue until Christ came, so that we might be justified by faith. But now that faith has come, we are no longer subject to a pedagogue, for in Christ Jesus you are all children of God through faith. (Gal 3:16, 19, 23–26)

[33] The Greek here is unclear and could mean either to control transgressions or to provoke and increase them. As I will argue below, there is every possibility that Paul intended to mobilize *both* meanings simultaneously.

The metaphor of the Law as pedagogue guarding Israel in the interim period between the promises to Abraham and the arrival of Christ echoes the Platonic depiction of human positive law as a substitute for the direct rule of the gods or of sages able to perceive eternal verities (G-R 3(i) and (ii)). Plato understood conventional law to be a second-best accommodation to our imperfect natures. It has the effect of curbing sinful behavior, but it is inadequate for the cultivation of human virtue, for which a savior (*soter, soterion*) is required, in the form of a person or persons of discernment whose commitment to the *logos* qualifies them to guide others to virtue (G-R 6).[34]

The giving of the Law did not supersede the promise of blessing for all who have faith as Abraham did. It was a stopgap measure, an interim arrangement designed to preserve the people in the sinful period between the original promise and the full realization of that promise through faith in Christ Jesus (Gal 3:13–14). The Law functioned like a pedagogue because it guarded the people until such time as all might be delivered from sin by faith.

Paul's narrative taps into both Greco-Roman and biblical narratives of the emergence of law in human history. In Greco-Roman tradition, discourses that assume an opposition between law and nature (G-R 5) vary in their assessment of the introduction of law as marking a deterioration from an original and idyllic law-free golden age or as providing rescue from the chaotic and violent state of nature. Even those that see law as a rescue lament law's inability to bring full virtue, opening the door to speculation about the best means to attain virtue apart from the law. Similarly in biblical tradition, despite a dominant narrative that views the revelation of the Law at Sinai as a climactic episode in a linear progression toward the fulfillment of God's purpose for humankind (biblical discourse 3(ii)), resources exist for the construction of a narrative of Law as rupture (biblical discourse 3(iii)). According to this second narrative more congenial to Paul, Law was introduced to govern the "fallen" period between two idyllic law-free ages (Eden and the messianic future). For Paul, as for Philo, the Law is a resented but temporary necessity introduced after humanity's fall from an idyllic, law-free past.

To appreciate fully the aptness of Paul's narrative choice of the pedagogue as a metaphor for the Law requires a closer examination of the ambivalent representations of this well-known figure in antiquity. The pedagogue was a household slave responsible for accompanying children from six to sixteen on their travels. They protected these children from moral and physical dangers, corrected them, and trained them (Lull 1986, 489–90).[35] Pedagogues were often

---

[34] Jesus, of course, is variously represented in the New Testament as savior/one who saves (John 4:42; Acts 4:12; 5:31; 13:23; 2 Tim 1:10; Titus 3:4–9; 1 John 4:14), as *logos* (John 1:14), and as the fulfillment of the Law (Matt 5:17; Rom 10:4)—extensions, it would seem, of the same discourse and a topic that deserves further study.

[35] I am grateful to my student Aviva Arad, whose unpublished paper, "Pedagogues in Rabbinic Parables," presented to the Yale Ancient Judaism Workshop series, 2009, drew my attention to Lull's article

ridiculed for being harsh disciplinarians who employed verbal reproach and physical punishment (ibid.). Philo defended the harsh discipline of the pedagogue because of the latter's good intentions: the pedagogue sought to improve the souls of his charges (Philo, *Migrations* 116, as cited in Lull, 490). As a moral disciplinarian, the pedagogue was associated with "teaching self-restraint" and belonged therefore to the institutions of "education toward virtue" (Lull, 491). Inculcating self-restraint conformed to Platonic notions of education according to which nurses, parents, and pedagogues should keep childish excesses in check (Plato's *Laws* 808d–e), while teaching children—with threats and beatings if necessary—to excel in doing what is just, noble, and holy, and to refrain from doing the opposite (Plato's *Protagoras* 324d–325d; *Laws* 653b–c; see Lull, 491). This notion of education considers children to be little different from slaves to the extent that they, like slaves, were believed to be governed by "unbridled passions" (Lull, 494). Children are depicted as resentful of their pedagogue's constraints and happy to exchange their pedagogues "for reason as the divine guide of their lives when they passed from immaturity to maturity" (ibid.).

Most important, however, is the fact that in antiquity the pedagogue as an institution of education was viewed with ambivalence at best. Plato himself raises serious doubts about the possibility of inculcating virtue in this manner. In the *Protagoras*, after detailing this method of education toward virtue, the title character asks Socrates: "Why then, you ask, do many sons of good men turn out worthless?" (327a). David Lull (492–93) describes a similar ambivalence about the pedagogue and his methods in Plutarch and Philo:

> Plutarch, for example, contrasts giving admonition in the manner of a friend (φιλιχῶς) to that of a pedagogue (παιδαγωγιχῶς): the latter consists of a relentless and ineffective stream of petty accusations, whereas the former is reserved for matters of greatest importance. And, after stating that "pedagogues, by their habits, shape the child's character and start the child on the path of virtue," he asks: "And yet, what do the pedagogues teach?" The answer is that they teach "petty and childish duties." However, Plutarch also attributes to pedagogues the more noble task of restraining a child's desires (ἐπιθυμίαι) and compares them as "rulers" (ἄρχοντες) to "reason" (λόγος), "the divine guide of life" (ὁ θεῖον ἡγεμών βίου) which was exchanged for the pedagogue after childhood. A similar ambivalence is displayed by Philo, who, on the one hand, includes pedagogues among the countless "teachers of sin" (διδάσχαλοι ἁμαρτημάτων) because they "foster" and "join in increasing" (ἀνατρέφω and συναυξάνω) the passions (τὰ πάθη). And yet, on the other hand, he defends the meth-

---

and to the need to explore the larger cultural and literary context of the pedagogue metaphor for a proper understanding of Paul's use of it.

ods of pedagogues as improving the souls of those under their discipline, so that those who are rebuked by their pedagogues are better than those who have no pedagogues ... Philo, therefore, admonishes "really foolish" children for hating their teachers and pedagogues "and every form of reason that would bring rebuke and chastisement." (Philo, *Sacr.* 51, as cited in Lull, 493)

For Paul, the pedagogue would have been an attractive metaphor for the Mosaic Law precisely because of the deep ambivalence with which the former was viewed, the same ambivalence with which Paul viewed the Law: like a pedagogue, the Law provides useful (albeit harsh, coercive, and resented) protection against sin, but does not ultimately deliver one from sinful desires and may even increase them.[36] In describing the Law as a pedagogue, Paul sought to convey the following points to his audience:[37] (1) the Law was given "because of/to increase transgressions" (Gal 3:19); the Greek can be understood to suggest that the Law either controls sin or provokes it, and it is entirely possible that Paul uses this formulation precisely to convey both meanings simultaneously. Pedagogues were ostensibly engaged to control their wards' passions and sinfulness, but, as classical writers indicate, their actual effect was often to increase the same. It may well be that Paul intends a double entendre that trades in the common trope of the pedagogue as a failed—indeed a perverse—institution: the very person engaged to restrain the child's wickedness only makes it worse; (2) it was because the people were under sin that they needed a pedagogue (the Law) to restrain their passions and fleshly desires (Gal 5:16–24); (3) to live under the Law is thus to live under sin and under a curse (Gal 3:19–22; 3:10; Rom 5:20); (4) to live under the Law is a kind of slavery because the Law/pedagogue is master (see Gal 4:1); and (5) the Law, like the guardianship of a pedagogue, is temporary; it was needed only until the offspring of Abraham (for Paul, that is Jesus) would come (Gal 3:19–25) to provide justification through faith. Paul says in Galatians 3:25, "[B]ut now that faith has come, we are no longer subject to a pedagogue" in our struggle against sin. Just as a child emerges from the custody of the pedagogue when he has gained self-control and is no longer subject to the passions and desires of the flesh, so too those under the Law emerge from its custody when freed from their passions and desires. The sacrificial death of Jesus brought deliverance from the desires of the flesh that previously required the restraint of the Law. Those whose flesh has been crucified with Jesus are liberated from its passions and no longer require the Law to help them battle sin, having the spirit as their divine guide.

---

[36] See Steinmetz 2005 for a brilliant analysis of Paul's exegesis of various Scriptural verses to support the very *impossibility* that Law observance could bring justification. Steinmetz ties Paul's views to a deterministic attitude to human nature, an argument that coheres with the view presented here.

[37] See Lull 1986, 494–95 for a fuller presentation, of which this is only a summary.

> Live by the Spirit, I say, and do not gratify the desires of the flesh ... if you are led by the Spirit, you are not subject to the Law ... the fruit of the Spirit is love, joy, peace, patience, kindness, generosity, faithfulness, gentleness, and self-control. There is no Law against such things. And those who belong to Christ Jesus have crucified the flesh with its passions and desires. If we live by the Spirit, let us also be guided by the Spirit. (Gal 5: 16, 18, 22–25)

It was never the Law's purpose to bring virtue—just as a pedagogue cannot truly bring virtue—but simply to guard the people in their period of vulnerability to sin, a situation akin to that of minors and slaves: "[H]eirs, as long as they are minors, are no better than slaves, though they are the owners of all the property; but they remain under guardians and trustees until the date set by the father" (Gal 4:1). Like a pedagogue, the Law was intended to restrain the passions during the period of the people's "childhood," until such time as deliverance from the desires of the flesh could be achieved, and righteousness and sanctification attained through faith. The Law provides some rescue from sin (a good thing) but it cannot deliver us to virtue (a bad thing); at best, it preserves us until such time as deliverance arrives, in the form of a savior. The resonances between Paul's ambivalent assessment of the Law and Plato's (see especially G-R 3 and 6) are clear.

And now we can understand why, for Paul, the continued Torah observance of Jews after the Christ event is not a matter of complete indifference but, under most circumstances, expected.[38] True, for Paul, it is faith, not Law, that brings salvation—to Jew and Gentile, circumcised and uncircumcised (Rom 3:28–30)—and the blessing of Abraham rests on all his descendants who have faith, Jew and Gentile (Rom 4:16). Abraham is

> the ancestor of all who believe without being circumcised and who thus have righteousness reckoned to them and likewise the ancestor of the circumcised who are not only circumcised but who also follow the example of the faith that our ancestor Abraham had before he was circumcised. (Rom 4:11–12)

The implication of the claim that faith brings salvation to circumcised and uncircumcised alike is that circumcision and Torah observance are matters of indifference, and that while Paul would not object to his fellow Jews' continuing to observe the Law, neither would he insist on it. But if we conclude that circumcision is a matter of complete indifference for Paul, we cannot satisfactorily

---

[38] See, for example Boyarin 1997, 9, 42, 111–12, for the view that observance of the Law is for Paul *adiaphora*—a matter of indifference. I wish to nuance this view by saying that it is not a matter of indifference *in itself.* Law observance is a desideratum, and it is expected of Israel according to the flesh, but until conditions are right for Jews to finally achieve the prophetic vision of effortless Torah observance (i.e., when the kingdom comes), insisting on it is not a good use of Paul's time.

explain his adamant resistance to Gentile circumcision and Law observance nor his own continued Torah observance. The most likely explanation for these two facts is that Paul adopts the prophetic vision of an ideal time in which ingathered Israel observes the Torah *effortlessly*, and Gentiles, recognizing the one true god, forgo idolatry and immorality, and finally leave Yahweh's people in peace.[39] Paul believes that the coming of Christ made this end-time ideal possible. How?

Faith in Christ Jesus brings justification for *all* of Abraham's descendants, a fact that has distinct ramifications for Gentiles and for Jews. We consider first the Gentile: through faith in Christ Jesus, Gentiles are justified/sanctified. Constituted as Abraham's heir "Isaac/Israel according to the spirit" (Rom 9:6–9), they will worship the one god and enjoy his blessing, avoid immorality, and leave Israel according to the flesh in peace as the prophets foretold. We consider now the Jews: when they die to the body with Christ Jesus, then "Israel according to the flesh" are also justified. Freed from the passions and sinfulness that have made it difficult for them to fulfill the Torah that is their exclusive privilege, they are finally able to realize the vision of Jeremiah and Ezekiel: effortless observance of the Torah, the longed-for robo-righteousness (see chapter 1). In a post-Christ world, Israel according to the flesh can finally fulfill the Law that distinguishes her from the other nations (even as all are united according to the spirit), and can do so with perfect ease as predicted by Jeremiah and Ezekiel.[40]

Paul does not want to describe Torah observance in a manner suggestive of privilege lest Gentiles aspire to the regimen of Torah observance that is not, on his view, open to them. This idea probably informs Paul's assertion in Romans 2:17–21, 23, that circumcision and Law observance are no grounds for boasting. (As noted in connection with G-R 7, a rhetoric of boasting about law as the mark of civilization and liberty was widespread in Greco-Roman literature.) Here, Paul addresses Gentiles, not Jews, so his words should be construed not as an admonition to boastful Jews but as an attempt to assure his Gentile audience that there is nothing desirable or enviable in Torah observance ("what those Jews do is nothing to write home about!"). He does this so that Gentiles

---

[39] This is, in a nutshell, the standard vision of the longed-for redemption/salvation found in the Hebrew Bible: the physical nation redeemed from exile and relieved of the assaults of neighbors who, recognizing and revering Israel's god, allow her to live peacefully under Yahweh's law in Yahweh's land.

[40] Thus, I agree with Boyarin (1997) that *as regards the question of justification* (deliverance from the struggle against sin) Paul believed that Torah observance is a matter of indifference; however, it does not follow that Paul believed Jews were exempt from observing the Law. Indeed, it is only when they are justified through faith in Jesus that Jews can finally achieve the goal of Torah observance—by which I mean observance of all of the legal and ritual and ethical rules and precepts of the Torah—without struggle.

will not be drawn to Torah observance. Indeed, it is the Jews, Paul says, turning the trope on its head, who will be envious of the Gentiles (Rom 11:11–14)![41]

CONCLUSION

Paul's answer to the cognitive dissonance between biblical and classical conceptions of divine law could not be Philo's answer, because Paul believed in the Ezran distinction between peoples. Paul hoped to discourage Gentiles from desiring that from which they were genealogically excluded—Torah observance. At the same time he strove to encourage them to adopt their proper place as a fourth estate in the divine kingdom, renouncing idolatry and immorality (Acts 15:29) and acknowledging the one creator god and his ministers, the seed of Israel through Isaac (i.e., Israel according to the flesh). He was surely aware that he had taken on a difficult task. Selling Gentiles on the idea of fourth-class status in the coming kingdom of God—a defective kind of inclusion—would strike some as a fool's errand. But Paul had to find a way to preserve the exclusive character of the Mosaic Law as a law for the genealogical seed of Isaac alone, and to do so without causing offense, because he believed that the inclusion of the Gentiles was a condition of the coming kingdom.[42]

The dichotomy between the unwritten natural law and the written law, a dichotomy fundamental to the worldview of his Hellenized Gentile audience, afforded Paul a golden opportunity to market his intrinsically unpalatable message. Adopting his audience's presuppositions and conceptual framework, Paul

---

[41] I take this as a rhetorical fillip. We may understand Paul's urgings for mutual tolerance between those who observe the dietary and purity laws and those who do not (Rom 14) as a more genuine expression of Paul's views and an attempt to moderate this rhetoric: no one should really be envious of anyone, and differences should be respected. Taking pride in one's native constitution, boasting about one's laws, valorizing law as the mark of a nation of free, civilized persons—these all have deep roots in Greco-Roman political and literary tradition (see G-R 7). Paul is again invoking a trope familiar to his Hellenized audience when he states that the Jews have no reason to boast about their law.

[42] In this connection I again mention Paul's distinction between "Israel according to the flesh" and "Israel according to the spirit." The latter term includes all who are justified by faith regardless of circumcision, i.e., Jew or Gentile. It is in *this* sense that Gentiles may understand themselves to be incorporated into the body of Israel and may lay claim to the designation "Israel," but they are not "Israel according to the flesh" with its obligations of circumcision and Torah observance. Paul is motivated by the need to create an *attractive* alternative for his target audience. Knowing that his Platonized audience would have valorized spiritual over physical realities (Platonic dualism was common currency in the Greco-Roman world), Paul argues that the "fourth-class" status available to Gentiles is a *desideratum* far superior to the status of those bound by the covenant precisely because it is based on spiritual rather than physical filiation: you Gentiles, he argues, can join the *spiritual* Israel, and as any good Platonizing thinker knows, it is the spirit that really matters. Boyarin (1997, 22–23, 106) is right to identify in Paul's language an erasure of human difference; I would contend, however, that this is less a genuine *erasure* of human difference than it is a deft distraction from it because of Paul's larger purpose: he seeks to *discourage* interest in what he believed was not an option for Gentiles—the Torah observance reserved for genealogical Israel—even as he seeks to *encourage* recognition of the god of Israel as the true god deserving worship by the entire seed of Abraham.

distanced the Mosaic Law from classical conceptions of divine natural law and applied to it classical discourses associated with human positive law. He asserted that like human positive law, the particular Mosaic Law is counter to nature; it is lifeless, bringing slavery, sin, and death; it doesn't guarantee virtue, and it is a second-best option restraining those subject to the passions and desires of the flesh until such time as they find deliverance from the flesh through a savior. The conclusion toward which his rhetoric points is that the Mosaic Law is the written law of a particular, genealogically defined people; it is not to be identified with the universal and unwritten law of nature inscribed upon the hearts of all persons.

After denigrating the Law in tropes familiar to his Gentile audience, Paul can ask them in astonishment why they would ever wish to adopt this Law as their own (see, for example, Gal 3:1–5; 4:21; 5:1). For the Gentile, it is nothing; indeed it is less than nothing. Its observance by a Gentile brings separation and alienation from the divine, enslaving him in the fallen and sinful state from which faith through Christ is intended to deliver him (Gal 5:2–5). To be sure, the Law was given by a good god to achieve an important end, and here Paul introduces a narrative that makes sense of his ambivalent assessment of the Law as good but not good enough: the Law was given to a fallen people in order to restrain and guard them until such time as faith—the true path to salvation—would be revealed (Gal 3:22–23), until in the fullness of time God would send his son for redemption (Gal 4:4), and until the Gentiles could be brought to a recognition of Yahweh (Rom 11:25). But the Gentile must not suppose that the basic positive function of the Law (restraining the passions) mitigates its inadequacy and flaws, for the Gentile, like his father Abraham, is rendered righteous and holy only through faith, not law (Gal 3:6–9). It is because Paul must both affirm and denigrate the Law to his Gentile audience, it is because he wants Gentiles to *join with* Israel without *joining* Israel, that he adopts, and is so well served by, a rhetoric informed by Greco-Roman discourses of ambivalence.

E. P. Sanders has stated that it wasn't easy for Paul to turn the Law into an agent of condemnation rather than atonement and grace (2001, 116), but this assertion can be contested. Given his goal—to ensure that Gentiles do not aspire to the observance of a law from which they are genealogically exempt, while simultaneously attempting to bring them to the worship of the God of Israel who gave that Law—and given the conceptual categories and law discourse of his target audience, it was perhaps not very difficult at all.

Indeed, Paul succeeded a little too well. In short order, Paul's rhetoric of denigration of the Law when speaking to Gentiles—a rhetoric intended to squelch any desire on the part of Gentiles to observe what was the exclusive prerogative of the literal seed of Israel through Isaac—would be distilled as Paul's definitive view of the Law *in all contexts*. Subsequent Christian writings engage in a campaign of vilification of particularism and the Law and the bodily practices that enshrine it, depicting Jews as stubborn, blind, or morally perverse for failing to see that the Christ event had brought an end to the Law of sin and death.

Daniel Boyarin (1997, 229) argues that the negative evaluation of genealogy as a ground for identity can be traced to Paul, but it would be more accurate to say that it can be traced to Paul's *rhetoric*, since Paul himself did not reject genealogical distinction within the kingdom of God. We may agree unreservedly, however, with the following statement by Boyarin (ibid.):

> In his authentic passion to find a place for the gentiles in the Torah's scheme of things ... Paul had (almost against his will) sown the seeds for a Christian discourse that would completely deprive Jewish ethnic, cultural specificity of any positive value and indeed turn it into a "curse" in the eyes of gentile Christians.

The Mosaic Law was, of course, emblematic of Jewish ethnic, cultural specificity. Paul's application of negative tropes drawn from various Greco-Roman discourses of human positive law—*a strategic accommodation to his audience*—would sow the seeds for a Christian discourse of total denigration of the Mosaic Law. This discourse rested on an absolute dichotomy according to which the old Mosaic Law was antithetical to the new divine covenant written on the heart. With the Mosaic Law abrogated or superseded,[43] Christianity would fully embrace natural law as the ontologically primary mode by which God communicates his will for universal humankind. As a result, the conceptual distinction between the universal law of nature and human conventional law has been a fixture of Western civilization ever since.

But that is a well-known story. In part III, we turn our attention to a very different and less familiar story.

---

[43] Christianity's posture toward the Law ranges from annulment to abrogation to supersession, and while there are specific doctrinal differences among these views, for our purposes they all assume a stark dichotomy according to which the Mosaic Law is not only not identified with the universal divine law but is entirely distinct from it, if not antithetical to it.

PART III

The Rabbinic Construction
of Divine Law

Introduction

In part II, we examined Jewish writings to the end of the first century CE that navigate the incongruity between Greco-Roman and biblical conceptions of divine law. For the most part, these writings accept and work within the framework set by the Greco-Roman dichotomy of divine law vs. human law. Philo and Paul are two of the clearest examples of writers who employ this dichotomy and seek to assimilate Mosaic Law to one or the other of its terms. They arrive at radically different conclusions as to whether the Mosaic Law can be classified as divine law or positive human law, and they rely on different elements of biblical divine law discourse to support their particular classification. Philo identified the Mosaic Law with the divine natural law of Greco-Roman (primarily Stoic) tradition. Paul differentiated Mosaic Law from the universal law written on the heart.

Part III is devoted to an examination of the conception of divine law attested in rabbinic literature of the classical talmudic period (the second to the seventh century CE). Do the rabbis resemble Philo in attempting to bridge the gap between these dueling conceptions of divine law and identifying the Mosaic Law with divine (natural) law? Or do they resemble Paul in "minding the gap"? Do they characterize the Mosaic Law as positive law and assert some kind of divine or natural order independent of the Mosaic Law (whether written on the heart or written in nature) in the light of which it may be evaluated? To pose the issue most succinctly: do the rabbis have a concept of natural law that is *either* identical to the Mosaic Law *or* distinct from it?

There is extensive scholarship on the question of natural law in *Judaism* (as distinct from the historically delimited talmudic period that is our concern), but opinions are sharply divided. Daniel Statman argues that one reason for the lack of a scholarly consensus is the lack of a clear definition of natural law. According to Statman (forthcoming), scholars fail to distinguish between natural law as a theory of law (a jurisprudential theory) and natural law as a theory of morality. The jurisprudential theory of natural law holds that law must meet specific criteria of content to be authentic law. In classical natural law theory the criterion of authenticity for the law is rationality. Because reason conforms to truth, is universal, and is unchanging, authentic natural law will be *universally true, rational, and unchanging.* This is why, having identified the Mosaic Law with the divine natural law, Philo set out to demonstrate that the Law is universally true, rational, and unchanging.

Do the rabbis do this? Do they subscribe to a jurisprudential theory of natural law according to which the Mosaic Law itself is deemed to be universally true, rational, and unchanging? Chapters 5 to 7 seek to answer this question. Chapter 5 employs three specific "measures" or standards of truth (formal logic, judicial correctness, and verisimilitude or realism) to demonstrate that the Mosaic Law is not portrayed in rabbinic texts as *necessarily* allied with truth. Chapter 6 argues that rabbinic texts do not represent the Mosaic Law as *intrinsically* rational or as deriving its authority from its rational character. Chapter 7 argues that the Mosaic Law is not consistently portrayed as static or insusceptible to modification. Insofar as they emphasize the Law's positivistic traits, the rabbis might be said to adopt Paul's perspective on the Law; however, their evaluation of Law is *antipodal* to Paul's—what Paul sees as a vice, the rabbis trumpet as a virtue. Nevertheless, the evidence in each of chapters 5 through 7 is rich and complex, and I take pains to highlight passages in which the rabbinic authors consciously consider alternative views and either defeat, disown, or accommodate them in a hybrid discourse.

In chapter 8 we turn to Statman's second theory of natural law—the moral theory of natural law. The moral theory of natural law holds that there are independent moral goods grounded in nature that are universally accessible by reason and that obligate us. Are we to conclude from chapter 7's discussion of the moral critique of the Law that the rabbis were committed to the existence of a standard of value external to the Law? Or, to phrase the question in terms of the moral theory of natural law: do rabbinic sources subscribe to the view that there are goods grounded not just in the commandments of the deity but in universal (human) nature, goods that obligate us, and that we can know and pursue? Chapter 8 seeks to answer this question by examining rabbinic constructions of normativity in the period prior to Sinai. Was humankind obligated by basic moral goods rationally accessed, prior to the giving of the Law? Do the so-called Noahide laws reflect a rabbinic version of a moral theory of natural law, that is, do they articulate a set of goods grounded in universal (human) nature that are accessible by reason and that obligate us?

It is clearly beyond the scope of this study to examine every rabbinic text relevant to the questions outlined above, and it is not my goal to declare that all rabbinic texts hold a particular view or to pronounce on "the" rabbinic view of a given matter. The rabbinic corpus is a vast and multicentury anthology, and one finds a great variety of views on many topics. While I pay attention to time and place, moving from early to late texts, from Palestine to Babylonia, my interest is in plotting rabbinic discourse(s) of divine law. If I were to identify a large and dominant set of texts in which the Mosaic Law, despite biblical evidence to the contrary, is depicted as possessing the characteristic features of the law of nature (as in the case of Philo), then it would be fair to conclude that natural law discourses served as the basis for the rabbinic construction of the Mosaic Law, even if there are some sources that do not fall into line with this view. Sources with a different view would not disprove my claim—but they would indicate that natural law discourses were not uncontested.

As it happens, we will see that there is a dominant tendency in rabbinic literature *not* to apply to Mosaic Law the themes and tropes of Greco-Roman natural law discourse. However, this does not mean that natural law discourses played no role in the rabbis' construction of divine law. Throughout these chapters, I will argue that the rabbis' unique construction of divine law is undertaken in *conscious defiance* of the Greco-Roman dichotomy between divine law and human law. Depicting themselves as ridiculed by those who claim that a divine law must be true, rational, and unchanging, the rabbis signal that they are aware of this alternative view and that they *consciously* reject it. Employing dueling rhetorics of disclosure and concealment, they simultaneously own and disown their somewhat scandalous construction of the *divine* Law of Israel.

CHAPTER 5

The "Truth" about Torah

In part III, we explore the rabbinic conception of biblical divine law in an attempt to discern the extent to which and the manner in which that conception may have been informed by Greco-Roman discourses of natural law and positive law. One major set of discourses of natural law in the Greco-Roman tradition identifies the natural law with truth, a mind-independent and objective measure of metaphysical or ontological reality (G-R 1). Some "law as truth" views identify natural law with an eternal and unchanging *logos* (G-R 1(ii) and (iv)); some adopt a realist definition of divine law as a discovery of "what is" (*Minos* 315a3, 315b1; G-R 1(iii)). As we saw in chapter 3, some late ancient Jews transferred the truth claims associated with divine natural law to biblical law. So, for example, for Philo the identification of the Mosaic Law with the divine or natural law of classical, particularly Stoic, tradition entailed its conformity to rational and philosophical truth and its verisimilitude (correspondence to a mind-independent reality accessible by other disciplines that claim objectivity and truth value).[1] Philo followed the author of the Letter of Aristeas in mocking (and being mocked by) those who denied that Scripture contains the "canons of truth all inscribed" (Niehoff 2011, 173). As another example, in sectarian writings at Qumran, the alignment of the law of the Torah with the laws of creation led to a tendency toward a legal realism according to which the Mosaic Law was believed to conform to and be confirmed by facts of the natural order.

In this chapter, we explore the rabbinic concept of divine law on the specific question of truth. We examine a wide range of rabbinic texts that shed light on a constellation of questions addressing the divine law's relationship to truth: Is truth in the form of a mind-independent, objective measure associated with the divine law in rabbinic texts, and if so, in what way? Is biblical divine law understood to be identical with or to conform to truth—whether an eternal, unchanging, and universal rational truth as for Philo, or empirically verifiable or divinely revealed ontological reality as for some Qumran writings, or some other standard or conception of truth? Alternatively, is divine law *divorced* from

---

[1] Following the definition of Niehoff 2011, 46.

truth, and if so, does the divorce of truth and divine law undermine the latter's claim to authority and divinity?

Finding the answers to these questions is complicated by certain structural dissimilarities between biblical divine law and Greco-Roman conceptions of divine law. As noted in chapter 2, all Greco-Roman natural law discourses assume a dichotomy between divine or natural law and human law. The divine law is a rational natural order that is by definition *self-identical with truth*. By contrast, human law derives from a sovereign human will rather than a rational natural order. Human law is not self-identical with truth. Natural law and human law derive from entirely distinct sources of authority; indeed, natural law serves as an independent standard or measure by which the legitimacy of positive human law may be assessed.

Such a clear dichotomy does not exist in biblical law. Even on the view that the Bible contains references to an "unwritten moral order," the Torah legislation revealed at Sinai is also considered to be divine, not human, law. Likewise, the later rabbinic distinction between the Written Torah (the Bible) and the Oral Torah (rabbinic oral elaboration of the biblical tradition, including rabbinic halakhah or "law") does not correspond to the Greco-Roman natural law/positive law distinction. The rabbinic Oral Torah is not human positive law on the Greco-Roman model. The Oral Torah that accompanies and elaborates the divinely revealed Written Torah, although transmitted and elaborated by sages, is not underwritten by an independent source of authority. It is subsumed under the divinely authorized system of revealed Torah.[2] Thus, the question that will occupy us in this chapter concerns the relationship between truth and the divinely revealed Torah *in both its written and its oral form*.[3]

---

[2] This is a necessarily generalized portrait that obscures a more complex reality, as articulated by Azzan Yadin 2006. For the school of R. Akiva, inherited legal traditions appear to enjoy an authority independent of Scripture, and midrash is a practice that serves not to generate halakhot from Scripture but merely to anchor existing halakhot within the Scriptural text. For the school of R. Yishmael, Scripture is central and midrash is the mode of exegesis that generates legal conclusions from it. According to Yadin, the Akivan method ultimately prevailed over the view of the school of R. Yishmael. For our purposes, however, the linking of existing rules to Scriptural verses is, in the end, a concession to the desire to connect laws to the source of ultimate authority, suggesting, in an odd way, a subtle victory for the Yishmaelian perspective. (For the irony that R. Akiva, the icon of Pharisaism, undermines the independent authority of *paradosis* by connecting halakhot to Scripture, see Shemesh 2011). Moreover, as Yadin himself recognizes, by amoraic times, scriptural authority had become the normative authorizing model, and sages are Torah scholars more than faithful tradents of extratextual traditions. Increasingly, extratextual traditions without a Scriptural base were understood to be reliably descendant from ancient Sinaitic traditions.

[3] Certainly there are important differences between the Written and the Oral Torah. A higher degree of severity attaches to the former, doubtful cases of biblical law are decided stringently while doubtful cases of rabbinic halakhah are decided leniently, and more. Nevertheless, rabbinic halakhic authority is underwritten by divine authority and is believed to express, in however attenuated a form, the divine will for Israel. For the rabbinic theory of the Oral Torah and continuity with the divinely revealed

Greco-Roman law understands divine law to be essentially self-identical with truth. Is this a view we find in rabbinic texts? Is divine law—which we will take in its broadest form to mean the Written and Oral Torah—self-identical with truth?

WHAT IS TRUTH?

Determining rabbinic views on these questions is not a simple matter. Just as rabbinic texts do not contain a linguistic equivalent of the Greco-Roman term "natural law," they also do not contain a linguistic equivalent for "truth" as broadly conceived by the Greco-Roman philosophical tradition.[4] If we wish to access rabbinic conceptions of the divine's law's relation to truth, we need to identify the criteria or measures employed by the rabbis when assessing the "truth" of the law. Legal theory can aid us in that task.

As Bernard Jackson notes (1987, 19–20), there are two general types of legitimacy criteria for any given law—two ways of saying that a given law is "true" or "correct." On the one hand, legal positivism maintains that legitimacy is a matter of *validity*, which is to say the production of a norm or decision according to authorized and recognized procedures of norm creation or decision making (e.g., an act of the legislature) regardless of the law's character, quality, or content.[5] By contrast, natural law theory maintains that legitimacy is a matter

---

Torah, see Schäfer 1978; Rosenthal, 1993; Jaffee 2001; Fraade 2004; Sussman 2005; and Sh. J. D. Cohen 2013. For a partial list of rabbinic sources that invoke Moses and the revelation at Sinai as the ultimate authority behind rabbinic law, see Sh. J. D. Cohen 2013, 14–15.

[4] In practical cases of judgment, *emet* generally refers to the procedural integrity by which a verdict was reached (its *validity*) and not the substantive truth of the verdict itself, even in phrases like *din emet* ("true judgment"), *dayyan emet* ("true judge"), and *din emet la-amitto* ("a judgment true to its [very] truth"). It is only when judicial procedures for settling disputes are contrasted with the process of arbitration that the form *emet* signals an objective standard of true or authentic justice. See Hayes 2008, 87–107, for a detailed argument demonstrating that in rabbinic literature the concept of a single authentic legal answer is not typically signaled by the word *emet* ("truth"). Likewise, *be'emet* (lit., "in truth"), which appears eleven times in tannaitic literature in connection with specific legal statements (m. BB 2:3, BM 4:11, Kil 2:2, Naz 7:3, Shab 1:3, Shab 10:4, Ter 2:1; t. BB 1:4, Ber 5:17, Kil 1:16; MdRY Nez 4) does not refer to the truth value of the ruling or law in question (i.e., its authenticity) but rather to its exceptional nature. For a thorough linguistic analysis, see Goldberg 2000 and Ginzberg 1941–61, 183–84. See further the brief discussion of *be-emet* cases in Hayes 2000, 80 and 93–94. A similar conclusion is reached by Landman 1974, 133, and by Goldberg 2000, 183–84, echoing the brief observations of Albeck 1952–58 in his comment to Kil 2:2; and Lieberman 2002, 2:605.

[5] This is the view of legal positivism (Patterson 1996, 60, 63). This view maintains that while a system *may* also choose to incorporate some additional criterion of authenticity (e.g., conformity to principles of morality, conformity to a mind-independent or ontological reality), the legitimacy of a norm or ruling turns only on its institutional validity. In the ensuing discussion, I will refer to a law or decision that possesses institutional or procedural legitimacy as "valid."

of *authenticity* (ibid., 20), which may be understood as conformity with some criterion of character, quality, or content.[6]

Greco-Roman sources that identify the divine natural law with truth are making a claim about *authenticity*. Divine natural law is true not because it has been *validated* by a recognized procedure of norm creation but because it conforms to substantive criteria of character. Or, more precisely, it is *itself* the criterion of authenticity for all other law. The question of whether a law is authentic or merely valid is a question that makes sense only in the context of *human* law. One may inspect human laws to determine whether they comport with the necessarily authentic natural law. If they do, they are true in the sense of authentic; if they do not, they are not true in the sense of authentic, even if they are valid because they have been promulgated according to a recognized procedure of norm creation. But in all circumstances—whether authentic or merely valid—they are assuredly not divine, and any authenticity they possess is not essential but *accidental*.

In this chapter, we examine texts in which divine law is compared with some *criterion* of authenticity (i.e., some measure of character, quality, or content). These texts will enable us to answer the following questions: Do the rabbis understand the legitimacy of divine law—in both its Written and its Oral form—to be a matter of validity (its promulgation by a divine being) or a matter of authenticity (its conformity to some criterion of character, quality, or content)? If the latter, does the Torah conform *necessarily* to substantive criteria of authenticity? Does that authenticity guarantee the law's legitimacy, or are even authentic divine laws occasionally "overruled" in favor of an "inauthentic" position? If the latter, how does the setting aside of an authentic divine law and validation of an inauthentic ruling comport with the law's divinity?

Measures of Authenticity

Rabbinic texts employ three criteria, or measures, of a stable, *authentic* truth: formal truth, judicial truth, and ontological truth. We consider each in turn.

The first measure of authenticity—formal truth—is captured by the term *din*, which signals a formally or logically correct law. Connected to the idea of a formal or logically correct legal truth is the question of monism: is there one right answer to legal questions?[7] In the first part of this chapter, we ask whether

---

[6] For a natural law theorist, an unjust law would not be a true or *authentic* law even if produced by authorized procedures, because the legitimacy of a norm or ruling turns not on its institutional validity but on its authenticity. In the ensuing discussion, I will refer to a law or decision that possesses substantive, content-based legitimacy as "authentic."

[7] The classic formulation of the "single right answer thesis" was advanced by Ronald Dworkin. In the preface to *Law's Empire* (1986), Dworkin argued against the positivist's claim that there is no single right answer to hard legal questions, only different answers. Dworkin held that even though ordinary judges may not be able to arrive at the right answer, and may have to choose among competing possible

rabbinic texts exhibit a commitment to legal monism, a single authentic answer (often labeled *din*), or to legal pluralism, the existence of multiple, equally authentic answers. Moreover, insofar as rabbinic sources may identify a single authentic answer or *din*, how controlling is that answer? In other words, do we find that divine law always conforms to or is self-identical with the authentic legal answer (i.e., the *din*)?

The second "measure" of a stable, authentic truth—judicial truth—moves from the realm of theoretical truth, that is, conceptual and formal correctness, into the realm of practical judgment: according to rabbinic texts, what is the role of "truth" (here the terms *din* and *emet* are employed) in rendering justice through judgment? Is it always required? Further, how does truth fare in contexts of divine judgment as opposed to human judgment?

The third and final "measure" of a stable truth is ontological truth and verisimilitude. Do rabbinic texts evince a realist understanding of biblical divine law according to which the law's categories and determinations accord with what the rabbis perceive to be an objective, mind-independent ontological reality? Or do the texts evince a more nominalist orientation according to which deviations between the divine law and objective ontological reality are tolerated?

The overarching question guiding our investigation in this chapter is this: do rabbinic authors represent the divine law of Israel as necessarily conforming to any of these three measures of a stable truth—formal truth, judicial truth, and ontological truth—or as deviating from truth? If the Law deviates from truth, what are the implications of this deviation for the Law's authority and the *nature* of its divinity?

Measure 1: Formal Truth

One approach to exploring the issue of truth in rabbinic conceptions of divine law is to determine whether rabbinic texts view divine law as advancing a single authentic answer to legal questions. According to the rabbis, is the divine law best understood in terms of legal monism or legal pluralism?

(I) THEORETICAL MONISM VS. THEORETICAL PLURALISM

We may define pluralism in general terms as the assertion of conflicting legal positions as simultaneously authentic, and monism as the assertion of a single authentic legal position. Within this broad definition there are nuanced variations, including the distinction between practical and theoretical forms of monism and pluralism. According to Richard Hidary (2009–10, 230–31), theoretical monism argues that there is in theory a single right answer in every

---

answers, there is—generally speaking—a right answer to hard cases that a superhuman judge would be able to discern. Despite the surface phenomenon of *practical* legal pluralism (disagreement over and diverse answers to hard cases), Dworkin maintained an underlying *theoretical* monism in most hard cases.

case (even if it cannot be found and an inauthentic answer must be legislated); theoretical pluralism argues that many authentic possibilities exist in theory as candidates for validation by the validation criteria of a legal system, even if only one can be chosen in practice; practical pluralism holds that within one jurisdiction there exist multiple legitimate options; and practical monism maintains that there can be only one legitimate option within a given jurisdiction, regardless of the existence of multiple theoretically authentic answers.

Practical monism and pluralism do not automatically entail a corresponding theoretical monism or pluralism. One may be a theoretical pluralist believing in several authentic legal answers but insist that the law must decide on a single practical rule (practical monism). Similarly, one may believe there is a single theoretically correct law, but because it cannot be determined or because of pragmatic considerations, one may allow a variety of practical rulings (practical pluralism). Thus, cases of practical pluralism cannot be adduced as definitive evidence for theoretical pluralism, and cases of practical monism cannot be adduced as definitive evidence for theoretical monism.

Rabbinic texts are famously full of controversy and multiple, conflicting opinions, which most scholars agree is indicative of a practical legal pluralism in some cases (for this view see Hidary 2009–10 and 2010a). But practical pluralism does not tell us whether the rabbis are *theoretical* pluralists or monists. Do the rabbis understand God's divine law—the Written and Oral Torah—as *essentially* pluralistic, or do they perceive it as providing in theory a single true or authentic answer to every legal question even if that answer cannot be ascertained at a practical level (resulting in practical pluralism)? Does the rabbinic notion of Torah approximate natural law in its monism? Or is it committed to a pluralism at the *theoretical* level that pulls against Greco-Roman discourses that describe divine law as a single stable truth?

A good deal of scholarly energy has been directed at the question of legal pluralism vs. legal monism (both halakhic and hermeneutic) in talmudic law.[8] Hidary (2010a, 1–36) adroitly summarizes the views of earlier scholars who, to

---

[8] See, for example, Lamm and Kirschenbaum 1979; Sh. J. D. Cohen 1984; Ben-Menahem 1987; Halbertal 1997, 53–72; Heger 2003; Boyarin 2004, 151–201; Ben-Menahem, Hecht, and Wosner 2005 (for a collection of relevant sources); Fraade 2007. Heger (2003, 17–19 and passim) argues for three stages in the move toward a fixed halakhah. In the pre-70 period Judaism was dominated by a pluralistic and tolerant halakhic environment; in the tannaitic period, Rabban Gamliel initiated a trend toward a fixed halakhah for political reasons, which finally triumphed only in the amoraic period. By contrast, Richard Hidary (2010a) analyzes the reactions of the rabbis to the reality of behavioral (practical) pluralism and argues that one finds a range of views in rabbinic literature: some statements reflect a universal monism that invalidates all but a single legal truth; some statements reflect a universal pluralism that accepts incompatible legal teachings as equal options; and some statements reflect moderate middle positions that tolerate alternative teachings with or without the assumption that they are authentic teachings. He also notes an increased tolerance for legal pluralism in the Babylonian Talmud (14). Hidary's work provides an important foundation for my own observations. See also Yadin-Israel 2014 and Fraade 2014.

varying degrees and with varying emphases, construe a small set of programmatic statements as indicating a rabbinic tolerance for diversity of practice and
different opinions on the one hand and a rabbinic principle of Scriptural polysemy and multiple interpretations on the other hand, both of which reach full
expression in the Babylonian Talmud.[9] Broad generalizations will necessarily
oversimplify a complex but well-rehearsed scholarly debate. Nevertheless, the
scholarly consensus holds that a very small number of programmatic statements in rabbinic literature (from the later, Babylonian period) espouse not
merely practical pluralism (which may be all that is indicated when conflicting
opinions are validated with the statement "these and these are the words of the
living God"[10]), but also a theoretical pluralism. The main source believed to
point to a theoretical pluralism is b. Ḥag 3b, which states that all contradictory
opinions were given by a single shepherd—God (see parallels in t. Sot 7:11–12;
PesRab 3; MidTanḥ Behaʿalotkha 15; Num Rab 15:22).[11] Other texts speak of
multiple ways to interpret the Torah. For example p. San 4:2, 22a states that
God did not tell Moses what the fixed halakhah is but instituted a majority rule
principle so that the Torah would be interpreted (*nidreshet*) forty-nine ways in
one direction and forty-nine ways in the other (cf. Lev Rab 26:2; and MidTeh
5:71 on Ps 119).[12] Similarly, Num Rab 13:15 speaks of "seventy facets" to the

[9] Suzanne Stone (1993, 849–50) summarizes the range of rabbinic views on the topic of the multivocality of the Sinaitic revelation. On the question of the multiplicity of interpretations and polysemy,
Hidary points to the work of J. Heinemann (1971, 146, 149–50), Kugel (1983, 146), Fraade (1991, 15–
17, 123–62; 2007, 7n21, 24–31), Stern (1985; 1996; 2004), Handelman (1982, 66–76; 1985; 1986),
Faur (1986), Boyarin (1990, 41–42; 2004, 189–92), Halbertal (1999,179–203), and Yadin (2004, 69–
70), among others. On the question of diversity of practice and opinions (pluralism), Hidary refers to
the work of Sh. J. D. Cohen (1984, 47), Naeh (2001, 851) (but see Fraade's and Hidary's cogent criticism of the same at Fraade 2007, 33n115, and Hidary 2010a, 21–22n78), and Boyarin (2004, 159).
Some scholars cite the rabbinic predilection for argumentation and dialectic as evidence of a general
pluralism. In this connection, Hidary cites the divergent views of Halivni (1986, 89–90), Kraemer
(1990, 126, 139), Elman (1994, 269, 275), Heszer (1997, 243), Rubenstein (2003a, 39–53; 2003b,
72), Fisch (1997, 43), and Boyarin (2004, 151–52).

[10] P. Yev 1:6(3b); b. Eruv 13b, and b. Git 6b. As regards the famous passage in b. Eruv 13b in which
the contradictory views of Bet Hillel and Bet Shammai are both declared by a heavenly voice to be "the
words of the living God," scholars have advanced conflicting interpretations. Jackson (1987, 33–34),
Boyarin (2004, 157–60; albeit assuming anachronism), and Naeh (2001, 862) see the passage as a rejection of legal monism. By contrast, Ben-Menahem (1987, 168) argues that the text seeks only to assert that the will of God will be done by following either of the two opinions because both are *valid*,
which is not to say that both are equally *authentic* solutions to the legal question/problem. See also
Kraemer (1990, 121–29, 139–48, esp. 145), who sees b. Eruv 13b and similar texts as asserting that
no opinion contains the truth fully, and that alternative views contain aspects of the whole truth. Certainly, in b. Git 6b, the context of the phrase "these and these are the words of the living God" makes
it quite clear that in that passage at least each of the two views mentioned is partially correct, and in
combination they give the full truth. Finally, see Elman (2005, 383–95), who interprets b. Eruv 13b as
indicating that disputes between rabbis appear as disputes only to the human mind.

[11] See Stone 1993, 838n138, and Hidary 2010a, 21.

[12] This text is discussed by Hidary 2010a, 28–29.

Torah. However, it is not clear that the assertion that the Torah can be interpreted in forty-nine or seventy different and even contradictory ways is tantamount to the claim that the Torah is *in its essence* multiform.

The evidence provided by programmatic statements is not only controverted; it is limited. Scholars examine and reexamine the same small sampling of core texts with disparate results. Moreover, we must be wary of basing our assessments of rabbinic concepts solely on self-consciously ideological texts, as there is often a gap in rabbinic literature between programmatic statements and actual praxis.[13] Recognizing the limitations of relying on programmatic statements alone, I propose to examine halakhic texts in which the law is determined in a manner that showcases the issue of monism vs. pluralism.[14] The following discussion is based on a survey of hundreds of cases in rabbinic literature that employ the term *din* to refer to a law or legal teaching that is authentic in the sense that it is formally or logically correct. Formal/logical correctness is a measure of authenticity rather than mere validity because it is a *substantive* quality inherent in the law. My survey of these sources reveals that despite programmatic assertions of legal pluralism in rabbinic literature, many texts employ the term *din* in order to signal the existence of a single "authentic" answer (a theoretical monism). However, in many instances these texts go on to accord that answer scandalously little deference, even setting it aside in favor of a different answer. If this is monism, it is a deeply compromised and non-Dworkinian monism.[15]

---

[13] One example must suffice: the Babylonian Talmud contains a number of aggadic traditions of a programmatic nature that praise the wildly creative midrashic techniques of early rabbinic authorities. It would be easy to conclude on the basis of these texts (and indeed, for generations it *was* concluded) that rabbis of the classical Talmudic period embraced and employed such techniques wholeheartedly, feeling none of the apologetic self-consciousness that would arise in the post-talmudic period. However, a close look at actual cases of Scriptural exegesis in the amoraic period reveals that midrashic pyrotechnics were all but abandoned, suggesting a negative view of such exegetical excesses despite a rhetoric of praise (Hayes 1998b). See also Fraade (2007), who draws a distinction between polysemy as a textual praxis and polysemy as ideology that is presented (or thematized) in often narrativized passages.

[14] Focusing on actual cases is the approach taken by Hanina Ben-Menahem in an important article on the question of legal pluralism in talmudic law (1987). As I have argued elsewhere (Hayes 2008), the five cases cited by Ben-Menahem are excellent examples of a *practical* legal pluralism that promises to uphold the legitimacy or legal validity of incompatible rulings *once they will have been declared*. However, practical pluralism does not automatically entail, prove, or even imply *theoretical* pluralism. Two views *can* be legitimated because both are deemed authentic (theoretical pluralism). However, two views can also be legitimated because even though one believes there is only one authentic answer (theoretical monism), one doesn't know which, *or even whether*, one of the available answers is the authentic answer, *or* because it might be pragmatic or otherwise desirable to legitimate an inauthentic view rather than a known authentic view (which the rabbis occasionally do, as will be argued below). See Hidary 2009–10 for a different view and Hayes 2010 for a response to Hidary's objections.

[15] See also Halberstam (2010, 6), who also argues that even though some rabbinic statements may have "rejected a singular, true divine will, seeing each one of their (often conflicting) interpretations of scripture as 'divinely authorized'" the rabbis "hold fast nonetheless to the notion of one correct deci-

(II) *DIN*—FORMAL TRUTH

As Tzvi Novick has demonstrated (2010), the term *shurat ha-din* is employed already in tannaitic texts to connote (1) a technically correct norm or governing rule or (2) a technically correct rule or norm that may actually or ideally be supplanted.[16] The term *din* standing alone can have the same meaning, especially in the form *badin* (ibid., 398).[17] In the Babylonian Talmud, the term *(shurat ha)-din* (lit., (the line of) the law), referring to the theoretically or technically correct ruling or norm, is sometimes juxtaposed with *lifnim mi-shurat ha-din*—a behavior within, or short of, the line of the law.[18] The metaphor of law's line (*shurah*) strongly implies a "correct" answer represented by the line. To cross over the line (*la'avor*) is to pervert justice or transgress—a negative deviation from the correct norm or proper behavior.[19] To stop short of the line of the law—renouncing the full rights and entitlements due under law and remaining within the area bounded by the line of the law—is to act piously and mercifully.[20] Such behavior comes to be associated with the pious, with the

sion that could be seen in the light of divine absolutes ... From this position, rabbinic judgment does not affirm polysemy and multivocality but rather the presence of a singular truth which limited human interpreters may approximate but perhaps never fully uncover." Significantly, Halberstam notes that "[i]n this sense, the rabbis sound less like the post-structuralists to whom they've been compared, and more like Plato, who laments the necessary human administration of the perfect, divine law." The question to be explored below, of course, is whether the rabbis do indeed lament this situation. I will argue that they construct an alternative and positive account of the Law's deviation from absolute truth.

[16] The tannaitic occurrences of *shurat ha-din* are m. Git 4:4, t. Pes 4:7, t. Ter 2:1–3, MekhRY Vayassa' 6 (Horowitz ed., 173) paralleled in MekhRSh Exod 17:2 (Epstein-Melamed ed., 117), all discussed in Novick 2010. More commonly *din*, connoting "logically and theoretically correct norm," stands alone.

[17] Pace S. Berman (1975 and 1977), who seeks to distinguish between *din* (the law), *shurat ha-din* (a limitation placed on the law that creates an exemption of some kind), and *lifnim mi-shurat ha-din* (an individual's choice to forgo the *shurat ha-din* and revert to the general undifferentiated *din*). *Shurat ha-din* and *din* do not occur together as dichotomous terms in any text and in fact appear to be interchangeable. See, for example, MekhRY Vayassa 6 (Horowitz ed., 173) and MekhRSh 17:2 (Epstein-Melamed ed., 117), where *shurat ha-din* and *din* are used interchangeably. See further, Novick 2010, 398–401, for the interchangeability of *din, shurah, derekh eretz,* and *derekh*.

[18] Following B. Cohen (1966, 1:52). The only instance of *lifnim mi-shurat ha-din* in tannaitic literature is in MekhRY Yitro 2 (Horowitz ed., 198) and its parallel in MekhRSh Exod 18:20 (Epstein-Melamed ed., 133). For the scholarly literature on the terms *shurat ha-din* and *lifnim mi-shurat ha-din*, see Novick 2010, nn 1 and 2; for a thorough analysis of the differences in early (tannaitic) and late uses of these terms, see ibid., 393–94.

[19] The phrase has this meaning already in tannaitic texts. See, for example, MekhRY Vayassa 6 (Horowitz ed., 173) and MekhRSh 17:2 (Epstein-Melamed ed., 117), where the phrase *avru al shurat ha-din* denotes the transgression of the Israelites in rebelling against Moses. In Ruth Rab 2 the phrase is used in connection with traveling on a festival day (a clear transgression).

[20] It is only in the medieval period that the phrase *lifnim mi-shurat ha-din* begins to be applied to supererogatory behavior that goes "beyond the law"; that meaning is not attested earlier (Novick 2010, 391). In the Bavli, the spatial metaphor of *lifnim mi-shurat ha-din* is not one of crossing beyond the line of the law but of acting within (*lifnim*) the law in a more limited manner than is strictly allowed (the line of the law marks an outer boundary of an area); see Novick 2010, 403. Saul Berman is right in

result that in b. BM 30b, standing squarely on the strict line of the law is viewed negatively in comparison: "Jerusalem was destroyed because everyone insisted on the formal (or strict) law of the Torah (*din ha-Torah*) rather than stopping short of the formal law (*lifnim mi-shurat ha-din*)." This text suggests that theoretically correct law can be destructive when applied in practice. The pious individual, who prioritizes religious values such as humility, compassion, modesty, peace, or charity, should at times forgo his right to the theoretically correct norm or ruling (stop short of the strict law), for in so doing he upholds these other values.[21] While not exercising the formally correct (and authentic) option, the pious individual who remains *lifnim mi-shurat ha-din* chooses what is in that particular situation a superior (even if less authentic) option.[22]

The term *din* carries the additional connotation of *rational* or *formal* correctness and thus signals a rule or teaching that is produced by a process of logical deduction.[23] Implied in such usage is a formalist view of the law. Formalism is the idea that law has an internally coherent structure and order. A contemporary proponent of legal formalism, Ernest Weinrib, argues that because of its internal conceptual structure, law is "immanently intelligible," capable of being understood on its own terms (cited in Patterson 1996, 22). A proposition of law is true or correct if it is consistent with, coheres with, the overall legal structure. When the rabbis assert that according to strict law (*badin/kadin*) the "correct" answer is X, they appear to be stating the law in a strictly formal and internally consistent sense, without factoring in specific circumstances that might arise in the real world. Formal logic may be understood as a stable measure of truth of a particular kind (logical truth). Thus, by examining rabbinic texts that describe the relationship between *din* (rulings that by formal logic are the technically correct norm) and divine law, we gain insight into rabbinic views on the relationship of divine law and logical or formal truth (authenticity).

It turns out that even in texts that identify a single formally or logically authentic ruling—generally referred to as the *din*—that ruling is not always iden-

---

noting that the five talmudic cases of *lifnim mi-shurat ha-din* (b. Ber 45b, BM 24b, 30b, BQ 99b, Ket 97a) involve a pious individual's waiving of a legal right, privilege, or exemption because he wishes to benefit another, but the exemption or right is correctly designated both *din* and *shurat ha-din*. Moreover, this meaning arises only in amoraic literature. See further the careful arguments in Novick 2010. Finally, *shurat ha-din* and *lifnim mi-shurat ha-din* do not connote a contrast between the letter of the law and the spirit of the law (here Berman [1975, 86, and 1977, 193] is correct). Both point to perfectly legal options.

[21] Many scholars have noted similarities between these rabbinic ideas and the ethic preached by Jesus in the Sermon on the Mount in Matt 5–7. See, preliminarily, Sigal 2008, 93ff., and Frymer-Kensky 2006, 130–31.

[22] For the later (and incorrect) medieval equation of the terms (*shurat*) *ha-din* and *lifnim mi-shurat ha-din* with *din emet* (a true judgment) and *din emet la-amitto* (a judgment true to its very truth), see Hayes 2008, 114–15.

[23] Indeed, *din* is a technical term that is used to introduce a variety of formal arguments including the *qal veḥomer* (a fortiori), the *binyan av* (an analogy), and the *gezerah shavah* (an analogy based on verbal equivalencies).

tical with or adopted as the operative ruling of the divine law. In rabbinic texts, early and late, Palestinian and Babylonian, there is a *conceptual* distinction between *din* in the sense of the rationally or formally authentic law and the operative ruling of the law. The formally authentic law and the operative ruling of divine law (Scriptural or rabbinic) may agree or disagree in substance—but they are always at least *conceptually distinct*.[24] We consider tannaitic texts first, before moving on to the Palestinian and Babylonian Talmuds.

The distinction between the formally correct law (*din*) and the operative ruling of divine law may be seen already in two cases from our earliest rabbinic text, the Mishnah. In this first example, m. Git 4:4, the rationally deduced law is distinguished from, and supplanted by, the operative ruling as declared by the rabbis:

> A slave whose master gave him to others as a security for a debt and then freed him, by strictly formal law (*be-shurat ha-din*) owes nothing. But for the better order of society, they force his master to free him and write a bond for his value.

In a second example, m. Men 8:5, the law produced by logical reasoning is distinguished from and supplanted by the operative ruling as declared directly by Scripture:

> Meal offerings might logically be thought to require the purest olive oil for if the menorah, which is not intended for consumption, requires the purest olive oil then the meal offerings, which are intended for consumption, is it not logical that they should require the purest olive oil? [But rather], Scripture says (Ex 27:20) *"Pure olive oil beaten for the light"* and not "pure olive oil for meal offerings."

There is nothing problematic about the view arrived at through rational deduction—the view that meal offerings require the purest olive oil—it just isn't identical with the governing norm of divine law. Scripture declares something else to be the law *against the dictates of formal logic*.

The same pattern is found in the Tosefta. In several cases, the law deduced by formal logic is not the operative divine law as declared by the rabbis or as stated directly in Scripture. An example of the first is found in t. Ket 5:1:

> If in the case of the Canaanite slave-girl, sex does not effect acquisition (for marriage) enabling her to eat *terumah* (heave offering), but a money-payment does, then in the case of an Israelite girl for whom sex does effect acquisition for *terumah*, it is logical that money should also effect acquisition for *terumah*. But what can I do—the sages have said an Israelite

---

[24] Compare Halberstam's use of absolute truth and legal truth (2010, 178). Halberstam's study focuses on judicial contexts and the problem of rendering judgment when access to absolute truth is lacking (10). In particular, she is interested in the conflict between law and what she calls "substantive reality" (11), for which see the discussion of Measure 3 below.

girl who is betrothed does not eat *terumah* until she enters the marriage canopy!

Here again, the law deduced by formal logic is not inherently problematic; indeed, the concluding line signals explicitly that the operative halakhah is actually counterintuitive ("what can I do?"). Similarly, in t. TevY 1:8–9 and t. Hor 2:10 the rabbis declare the law to be different from the law one would assume is true in formal logical terms.

The Tosefta also contains cases is which the logically deduced ruling is distinguished from and supplanted by a Scriptural statement. T. Tem 4:9 discusses the prohibition that attaches to the money paid to a prostitute (based on Deut 23:19):

> If one gave her animals that had been consecrated, these are permitted. Logic suggests that (*ha-din noten she-*) they should be prohibited for if fowl, which a blemish does not invalidate, is subject to the prohibition of the hire of a female prostitute and the price of a male prostitute, animals which have been consecrated, which a blemish does invalidate, is it not logical that they should be subject to the prohibition of the hire of a female prostitute and the price of a male prostitute? [But no, for] Scripture says—"*For any sort of vow*" (Deut 23:19)—excluding that which already is subject to a vow [having been consecrated].

Likewise, t. Zev 8:25–26 presents a series of laws in which formal logic would dictate a particular answer, but a Scriptural verse determines the law differently.

A different relationship between formally correct law and the governing divine norm as laid down by Scripture is indicated in t. Hag 3:18:

> Said R. Yosi: How do we know that that which is impure by a source of impurity in the fourth remove, is invalid in the case of sancta [*qodashim*]. It is logically deduced: If one who has not completed his atonement rites is not invalid as regards *terumah* but as regards sancta, that which is made impure by a source of impurity in the fourth remove[25] which is invalid in the case of *terumah*, is it not logical that it should invalidate [sancta]? We learn about the third remove from Scripture and we derive the fourth remove by an *a fortiori* argument.

In this passage, the law of Scripture is *supplemented* rather than supplanted by formal logic, highlighting again the conceptual distinction between the formal law and the teaching of Scripture.

These examples from the Mishnah and the Tosefta attest to (1) a conceptual distinction between the law deduced by formal logic and the governing norm of divine law (whether a direct Scriptural ruling or the rabbinic elaboration of

---

[25] The Erfurt manuscript and the parallels in Sifra Tzav 9:2, p. Hag 3:2, 79a, and p. Sot 5:2, 20b read "third remove"; see Lieberman 2002, 5:1324.

Scripture) and (2) at least two possible relationships between the formal law and the divine law. The formal law and the divine law may be opposed to one another (formal logic dictates that the law should be X, but Scripture/rabbinic halakhah supplants X with Y), or they may supplement one another (Scripture/rabbinic halakhah teaches X, and formal logic completes the picture by teaching a stage beyond X). Either way, divine law is not *necessarily* and *essentially* identical to the formal, logical truth.

In his study of the tannaitic midrash produced by the school of R. Yishmael (the MekhRY and Sifre Num), Azzan Yadin (2004) notes the varying relationships between law deduced by rational argumentation and law as established by Scripture. In some cases, *din* leads to a conclusion that is not aligned with the divine law (as we have seen in these examples from the Mishnah and the Tosefta) or to an aporia. When this happens, Scripture is needed to "set matters aright" (ibid., 126). A verse may be explicitly marked as responding to a failed logical argument.[26] But in some cases, the opposite obtains: *din* leads to a conclusion that is also established by Scripture as the divine law (see e.g., t. Ḥag 3:18). Finally, in the R. Yishmael midrashim, it is sometimes Scripture that fails to provide the requisite information, and the gap must be filled by a process of logical reasoning—one that Scripture anticipates and expects. This "partnership" between the Scriptural text and logical deduction leads Yadin to observe that "[t]he division between Scripture and human reason is not an antagonistic, zero-sum game; there can be a fruitful cooperation between the two" (130). The Yishmaelian midrashim understand Scripture to incorporate into itself the future responses of the reader (a trait that Yadin describes as "pre-sponsive"), thereby guiding the reader in a rational process of interpretive reasoning by means of which the law is articulated. Both *din* and Scripture have a vital role to play.

The conceptual distinction between the law arrived at through logical deduction and the divine law is apparent in the Akivan midrashim as well. In the Sifra, the two are occasionally aligned, but far more often they are juxtaposed in a manner that highlights their substantive differences—logic would dictate answer X, but Scripture determines that the law should be Y.[27] Often, there is nothing particularly objectionable about X—it simply is not the operative law.

The following text from Sifre Deut assumes the conceptual distinction between formal logic and Scripture even as it underscores the partnership between the two. Having identified a biblical commandment (Deut 14:6) that enjoins

---

[26] See, for example, the phrase "Thus since I could not succeed in proving it by logical inference, Scripture has to cite it" and the phrase "Why was this stated [in Scripture]?" which mark a verse as an anticipatory response (or "presponse") to a potential misinterpretation, logical error, or aporia (Yadin, 2004, 136–37).

[27] For a similar view of the Sifra's conceptual distinction between the dictates of logic and Scripture, see Neusner 1988.

the consumption of pure animals and, by inference, prohibits the consumption of impure animals, the text raises the following question:

> Whence do I learn that an impure animal is also prohibited by a negative commandment? From *"the camel, and the hare, and the rock-badger ... and the swine ... of their flesh you shall not eat"* (Deut 14:7–8).
>
> This tells me only about these particular animals—whence do I learn [that the negative commandment applies also to] all other impure animals?
>
> It is a matter of logic: if these particular animals are prohibited by a negative commandment even though they have some of the marks of pure animals, other unclean animals which do not have marks of purity, isn't it logical that they should be prohibited by the same negative commandment in connection with being eaten? Hence the camel, hare, rock-badger and swine are expressly prohibited by Scripture while other impure animals [are prohibited] by an *a fortiori* argument. Thus, the positive commandment regarding these animals is found in Scripture while the relevant negative commandment is derived by logical reasoning. (Sifre Deut 101, L. Finkelstein ed., 161)

In this passage, *din* and Scripture are not identical, nor are they opposed. Each contributes something unique toward the common project of articulating the divine law.

The partnership between *din* and Scripture takes other forms in Sifre Deut. In several passages, reason (*din*) leads to outcome X, but because a refutation of the reasoning that produced X is possible, it is necessary for Scripture to also teach X, in order to bolster the teaching of *din*. An example may be seen in Sifre Deut 76, where logic teaches that a limb torn from a living animal is prohibited to Israelites since it was prohibited to Noahides, and that which is prohibited to Noahides is logically prohibited to Israelites. However, since a counterexample can be found (the beautiful captive woman is prohibited to Noahides but *permitted* to Israelites), it was necessary for Scripture to teach explicitly that a limb torn from a living animal is prohibited to Israelites. The same structure is found in Sifre Deut 107 and 268. Similarly, Scripture is said to be necessary when logic leads to two alternative rulings (in order to adjudicate between them, e.g., Sifre Deut 249) or to aporia.

The conceptual distinction between the formal law (*din*) and divine law, as well as diverse representations of the relationship between the two, continues in the two Talmuds.[28] The Yerushalmi sometimes simply reports the gap be-

---

[28] Refining Lieberman's comment in his edition of the *Tosefta* (1992, 1:111), Novick (2010, 395, 406) argues that over time the term *shurat ha-din* begins to acquire a more consistent trumping implication, by which he means that to call a rule *shurat ha-din* is to say that it should be trumped by a different course of action. Similarly, rules designated with various forms of *din* are usually overruled in amoraic literature, but this is not always the case (see discussion below).

tween the law as it should be (in formal logical terms) and the operative hal-akhah as determined by the sages. Thus, p. Yev 7:1, 8a reports that "[a]s a mat-ter of strict logic (*badin*), he [a permanent slave] should not eat *terumah* and yet they [the sages] have said that he may"; p. Yev 13:1, 13b notes in regard to the marriage of a girl who has exercised the right of refusal that "*badin* the mar-riage is null, but the sages have said the marriage is valid"; and p. Sheq 7:3, 50d states in regard to the ashes of the red heifer that "*badin* the laws of sacrilege should apply to them, but they made a decree that the laws of sacrilege should not apply."

In about a dozen cases, the Yerushalmi employs a standard formula to high-light the gap between the formal law and the operative halakhah: "*badin* X; *lamah amru* Y = as a matter of strict logic, the law should be X; so why did they declare Y?" As for the relationship between logic and the divine law, p. Sheq 5:3, 49a follows tannaitic precedent in showing that Scripture establishes the law against the dictates of logic, while p. San 8:1, 26a makes the more ex-treme claim that the biblical law of the stubborn and rebellious son (Deut 21) is entirely illogical in several of its details (see the discussion of this text in chapter 6).

All of these patterns continue in the Bavli—the formal law and divine law are conceptually distinct and their relationship is variously represented. The two are often opposed. In a dispute over inheritance rights found in p. BB 8, 16a the position that is described as *badin* is attributed to Sadducees and is trumped by the Pharisaic view owing to an exegetical consideration. On other occasions the view described as *din* is in no way negatively marked. It is simply set aside or countered by a Scriptural verse (see, e.g., b. Pes 3a); at times, logic fails to lead to a single clear answer (*din*), and thus Scripture is required to de-termine the law (see e.g., b. Pes 41b or b. Yoma 45b); other texts highlight the partnership of *din* and Scripture (see e.g., b. Sot 29b which parallels t. Ḥag 3:18: "[W]e learned the rule of third degree defilement for sacrificial food from Scripture and fourth degree defilement from *a fortiori* reasoning"). Finally, b. Hor 13a shows that *din* and divine law can be aligned:

> If the bull of the anointed High Priest and the bull of the congregation are simultaneously presented, the bull of the anointed High Priest must take precedence over the bull of the congregation in every respect; since the anointed High Priest effects the atonement and the congregation re-ceives the atonement, it follows logically that he who effects atonement shall take precedence over the one who receives the atonement. And thus it is also stated [in Scripture, Lev 16:17]: "*And have made atonement for himself, and for his household, and for all the assembly of Israel*" [in that sequence].

Here the divine law coincides with the law as determined by formal logic. This phenomenon is noted explicitly in b. Qidd 4a: "Scripture sometimes goes to the trouble of writing something which could be inferred by an *a fortiori* argument."

In short, rabbinic literature of all periods, early and late, and east and west, maintains a conceptual distinction between formally correct law produced by logical reasoning (*din*) and the divine law as taught by Scripture or elaborated as rabbinic halakhah. The two may differ from one another in substance or they may coincide in substance, suggesting that in the rabbinic view divine law does not necessarily follow or coincide with the dictates of formal logic. To the extent that formal logic may be a measure of stable truth, the conceptual distinction between formal logic and divine law in the sources examined above suggests a disjunction between divine law and truth in the rabbinic conception. The difference between the rabbinic and the Greco-Roman discourses of law and truth could not be more stark. In Greco-Roman discourse, the disjunction between law and truth holds only in the case of human law, not divine law. Divine law is self-identical with truth. But for the rabbis, the disjunction between law and truth as measured by the standard of formal logic holds even in the case of *divine* law. While the divine law *may* align with the formally or logically correct law, this alignment is accidental, not *essential*.

The authority of divine law is not undermined by its lack of conformity to a formal or logical standard. For the rabbis, the formally or logically correct law does not obligate; God's divine law obligates and not because it is truth but because of its origin in the divine will. Thus, even when they identify a formally correct answer (a theoretical monism), rabbinic sources will not infrequently, and quite unapologetically, declare that the operative ruling of divine law deviates from it.[29]

Measure 2: Judicial Truth—Human Compromise and Divine Judgment

We have seen that the divine law is conceptually distinct from truth in the sense of formal logic. A second measure of truth in rabbinic texts is the standard of strict justice invoked in contexts of practical judgment (judicial truth). Of particular interest are texts that contrast judicial procedures that prioritize "truth" (determining actual liability or guilt) with a procedure that prioritizes "peace" (settling a dispute through a compromise that forgoes determining actual liability or guilt). After discussing rabbinic attitudes toward the resolution

---

[29] With their conscious and explicit identification of and deviation from what they determine to be the authentic or "right" answer, the rabbis diverge from Dworkin, for whom the best answer and the right answer are one and the same. Nor does their approach align with that of modern formalists, such as Weinrib, for whom a determination of the law that does not emerge from the formal structure of the system is a distortion (Patterson 1996, 25). Weinrib objects to what he would call a functionalist approach (viewing law as an instrument that must serve some end). For the classical rabbis, however, that which is—*formally* speaking—the law may be set aside, sometimes for no reason, and sometimes for pragmatic or moral reasons. Such functionalism is entirely untenable for a strict formalist like Weinrib.

of disputes in a manner that does not establish the truth, we turn to aggadic texts that examine the role of truth in divine judgment.

(I) TRUTH VS. PEACE IN HUMAN JUDGMENT

Zechariah 8:16, "*Execute the judgment of truth [emet] and peace [shalom] in your gates,*"[30] provides an occasion for rabbinic reflection on truth in the act of judging. Sifre Deut 17 (ed. L. Finkelstein, 28–29)[31] cites Zechariah 8:16 and then asks:

> What kind of peace includes a judgment of truth? Compromise (*bitsu'a*).
>
> R. Shimeon b. Gamliel, however, says: Compromise raises the humble to the place of the mighty and lowers the mighty to the place of the humble.
>
> Therefore the sages say: He who practices compromise [as opposed to judgment] is a sinner as it is said: "*The one who praises one who effects a compromise [botse'a] condemns the Lord*" (Ps 10:3).[32] The result [of compromise] is that one party praises the judge while the other condemns his creator.

Zechariah's reference to a judgment of *peace and truth* is interpreted in this rabbinic text as denoting a process of judicial compromise—a judgment in which truth is moderated by or combined with considerations of peace as opposed to a judgment of truth alone. The compromise referred to here is a judicial process[33] whereby parties agree to "divide" (*botse'a*) rather than to pursue a judicial ruling that would decide in favor of one party against the other according to the strict law. An initial and apparently positive assessment of compromise is immediately challenged by R. Shimeon b. Gamliel, who criticizes compromise as fundamentally unjust because it ignores the truth of the particular case. A further tradition attributed to the sages condemns those who prescribe compromise and draws support from a punning interpretation of Psalms 10:3 (reading *botse'a* [lit., "one greedy for gain"] as "one who effects a compromise").

T. San 1:2–3 develops these themes in an extended passage that has been insightfully and thoroughly analyzed by Haim Shapira (2010). Shapira notes (187) that while ancient legal systems, including Jewish law in the rabbinic period, recognized various methods of compromise, there was usually

> a clear separation between legal proceedings and extra-legal proceedings. According to Roman law, the judge was required to rule according to law and was not permitted to become involved in making a compromise.

[30] Literally, "judge truth and the judgment of peace in your gates."

[31] See L. Finkelstein 2001, 28n9, regarding the interpolated nature of this text.

[32] Literally, "the one greedy for gain (*botse'a*) curses (*b.r.kh* used euphemistically to connote cursing) and renounces the Lord."

[33] Correcting Hayes 2008, 109.

According to Shapira, while *nonjudicial* methods of compromise were accepted in tannaitic times, the permissibility of *bitsu'a*—a form of *judicial* compromise given by a judge without the agreement of the litigants—was the subject of a tannaitic dispute. *Bitsu'a* (lit., "dividing") is a ruling "that divides the rights between the parties and does not rule unilaterally on behalf of one side or the other" (201) because the judge is unable to decide according to the law.

In t. San 1:2–3 the judgment of *truth and peace* in Zechariah 8:16 is understood as a reference to *bitsu'a*, as opposed to a judgment of truth alone, which would declare the formal law in favor of one party. The passage presents three tannaitic views on the question of whether or not a judge is authorized to depart from the law (represented in this passage as truth) in order to rule in the form of a compromise (represented in this passage as peace). Shapira summarizes the three views and spells out the jurisprudential commitments that underwrite these views.

> According to the approach of R. Eliezer b. R. Yosi the Galilean, the purpose of the judicial process is to perform justice on the basis of objective standards. A judicial decision inconsistent with these criteria is a sin, as he thereby betrays his obligation. Hence, it is forbidden for the judge to perform *bitsu'a*. According to the two other approaches, the aim of the judicial process is to resolve disputes among human beings. In this respect, the law is merely a default option. Just as the parties involved are permitted to agree upon some other solution to their dispute, so too the judge is permitted to rule in a manner that departs from the law, if it serves some positive value. The question as to whether this is to be treated merely as an option open to the judge or as a duty that he must actively pursue (i.e., *mitsvah*) is subject to dispute. According to R. Joshua b. Korhah it is always preferable to make a compromise, as such a move is based upon agreement and brings about peace between the parties. As against that, R. Shimon Menasya does not automatically give preference to compromise. The decision as to what is the best approach in each case must be left to the judge. According to him, the only limitation that applies to the judge is in the procedural realm, so as to assure the equity of the procedure. (227–28)

This tannaitic dispute is taken up briefly in the Talmuds (p. San 1:1, 18b and b. San 6b–7a). Both endorse the moderate position according to which judicial compromise is an option. Thus, as regards the topic of judicial compromise, the relevant rabbinic sources give serious attention to the view that a strict adherence to law that is not contextualized or balanced by other considerations (charity, compassion, the promotion of peace) is less than ideal.[34] "Truth" in judgment is a fraught concept and the object of some ambivalence.

---

[34] Similarly, in t. Yev 1:10, Bet Hillel and Bet Shammai are praised because despite their many disagreements over the marital status of various kinds of women, they nevertheless overlooked these

(II) TRUTH IN DIVINE JUDGMENT

The ambivalence just described is captured in a passage from the Bavli (b. AZ 4b). The context of the passage is a discussion of God's judgment and, more particularly, the time of day that prayer is most likely to be accepted rather than rejected. R. Joseph holds that the first three hours of the day are inauspicious times to pray since God is engaged in judgment at that time and may scrutinize the person praying more than is desirable. An objection is raised: is there not an amoraic tradition that states that during the first three hours of the day God is engaged in Torah study, and during the second three hours God sits in judgment over the world? The stammaitic (anonymous) response to the contradiction between these amoraic traditions is revealing:

> [While engaged with] Torah study, which Scripture designates as "truth" (as it is written, '*Buy the truth and sell it not*' [Prov 23:23])[35] the holy one, blessed be he, will not hold back from the full extent of the strict (i.e., theoretically or logically correct) law[36] (*eyn oseh lifnim mi-shurat ha-din*); but [when engaged in] judging which is not designated by Scripture as truth, he will hold back from the full extent of the strict law (*oseh lifnim mi-shurat ha-din*).

The passage establishes a dichotomy between a judgment of truth on the one hand and a judgment to which the designation "truth" is not applied—which is not to say that it is false. The former is a judgment that is uncompromising in its application of the full extent of the law, while the latter does not insist on the full application of the law and operates *lifnim mi-shurat ha-din*. As applied to God here and in b. Ber 7a the phrase *lifnim mi-shurat ha-din* connotes merciful judgment.[37] The most propitious time to come before God in judgment is not

---

halakhic differences (i.e., truth) and intermarried (promoting peace). In short, they proved themselves to love both truth and peace in fulfillment of Zech 8:19: "*Therefore, love truth and peace.*"

[35] So Paris 1337 and Munich 95 MSS, but JTS 15 and the Pisaro printed edition cite Mal 2:6 ("*The Torah of truth was in their mouth*") as a proof text.

[36] I use the term "strict" to refer to a law that is logically and theoretically correct, with no suggestion of stringency (in contrast to leniency). S. Berman (1977, 182) assumes that strict law means substantively stringent rather than simply logically or theoretically correct. As a result, he objects to the characterization of *shurat ha-din* as the strict law, since on many occasions *shurat ha-din* is perfectly equitable and lenient. I have tried to ensure that this confusion does not arise by periodically glossing "strict" with terms like "logically/theoretically correct."

[37] Indeed, the five talmudic cases of *lifnim mi-shurat ha-din* involve a pious individual's waiving of a legal right, privilege, or exemption because he wishes to benefit another. The phrase is applied to God on two occasions: here and b. Ber 7a. In the latter case God "enters" (*niknas*) *lifnim mi-shurat ha-din*, and in the former he acts ('*asah*) *lifnim mi-shurat ha-din*. Novick (2010, 404–5) argues that '*asah* + *lifnim mi-shurat ha-din* signals the waiver of an exemption, while *niknas* + *lifnim mi-shurat ha-din* indicates something like mercy, though in b. AZ 4b, mercy also seems to be indicated. Novick (ibid., 405) points to "the classical Athenian commonplace, expressed by both Aristotle and Demosthenes, that the prosecuting party should seek less … than what it is by right entitled to lest it appear … 'fond of lawsuits' or … 'exact in suing.'"

when he is occupied with truth (understood, we may suppose, as strict or theoretically "correct" justice), but when he is occupied with judgment (an activity in which strict justice is balanced with other considerations). Thus, the text implicitly contrasts theoretical study of the divine law (study of Torah) and practical application of the divine law in the judging of particular cases. It is appropriate to speak of "truth" in connection with theoretical study, but in the judging of actual cases in all of their particularity, an uncompromising adherence to "truth"—the single correct answer that would emerge from abstract study or theorizing—is negatively viewed.[38] Indeed, we may go so far as to say that judgment proper should not be unduly obsessed with the theoretically true or correct answer.

The idea that truth is undesirable in the context of divine evaluations of humankind is featured in several aggadic traditions, perhaps none as well known as the following passage:

> R. Shimeon said: When the holy one, blessed be he, came to create Adam, the ministering angels formed themselves into groups and parties, some of them saying, "Let him be created," while others urged, "Let him not be created." Thus it is written, "*Loving-kindness and Truth met, Righteousness and Peace fought*" (Ps 85:11). Loving-kindness said, "Let him be created, because he will perform acts of loving-kindness;" Truth said, "Let him not be created, because he is nothing but falsehood;" Righteousness said, "Let him be created because he will perform righteous deeds;" Peace said, "Let him not be created because he is nothing but strife." What did the holy one, blessed be he, do? He took Truth and cast it to the ground. The ministering angels said to the holy one, blessed be he, "Sovereign of the Universe! Why do you despise your seal [i.e., Truth]? Let Truth arise from the earth!" Hence it is written, "*Truth, spring up from the earth*" (Ps 85:12).
>
> ... R. Huna the Elder of Sepphoris said: While the ministering angels were arguing with each other and disputing with each other, the holy one, blessed be he, created him. He said to them, "What are you arguing for? Adam has already been made!" (Gen Rab 8:5, Theodor-Albeck ed., 1:60)

In this aggadic passage, the value and merit of humans is weighed as God contemplates their creation. Truth's judgment of humans is harsh. Judged by the standards of truth, humans stand condemned of falsehood. Indeed, humans would never have been created had God followed the dictates of truth. The text implies that not only the creation of humans but even their ongoing existence at each moment depends upon God's willingness to suppress the truth when dealing with and judging them. God's assessment and valuation of humans is

---

[38] On the difference between legal scholarship and the judicial context in Jewish law, see, preliminarily, Jackson 1987, 34–35.

not grounded essentially and necessarily in truth and indeed stands in opposition to it.

The following aggadic text from the Babylonian Talmud (b. Yev 105a[39]) is one of the few sources to explicitly consider the truth value of God's judgments and decrees, and its conclusions are remarkable—divine judgments are not necessarily "true," and even the "true" ones can be overturned. The text opens with a question:

1.   [It is stated in Scripture]: *"However I will tell you what is recorded in the book (lit. writing) of Truth"* (Dan 10:21). Does this then imply that there exists a [divine] writing that is not of truth? He [Levi] was unable to answer.

2.   When he came and asked these questions at the academy, they answered him: ... [As to the question] *"However I will tell you what is recorded in the book (lit. writing) of Truth"*—does this then imply that there exists a [divine] writing that is not of truth?

3.   There is really no difficulty. For the former [writing of truth] refers to a [divine] decree that was accompanied by an oath while the latter refers to one that was not accompanied by an oath.

4.   [This is] in accordance with a statement of R. Shmuel b. Ammi. For R. Shmuel b. Ammi stated in the name of R. Yonatan: Whence is it deduced that a decree which is accompanied by an oath is never annulled? From the verse, *"Assuredly, I swear concerning the house of Eli that the iniquity of the house of Eli will never be expiated by sacrifice or offering"* (1 Sam 3:14).

5.   Rabbah said: It will not be expiated with sacrifice or offering, but it will be expiated with the words of the Torah. Abaye said: It will not be expiated with sacrifice or offering but it will be expiated with the practice of lovingkindness.

6.   Rabbah and Abaye were both descendants of the house of Eli. Rabbah who engaged in the study of the Torah lived forty years. Abaye, however, who engaged in the study of the Torah and the practice of lovingkindness, lived sixty years.

7.   Our Rabbis taught: There was a certain family in Jerusalem whose members used to die when they were about the age of eighteen. When they came and acquainted R. Yoḥanan b. Zakkai [with the fact,] he said to them, "Perhaps you are descendants of the family of Eli concerning whom it is written in Scripture, *'all the increase of your house shall die as [young] men'* (1 Sam 2:33). Go and engage in the study of the Torah, and you will live." They went and engaged in

---

[39] A parallel text in b. RH 18a contains essentially the same textual units but in a different order.

the study of the Torah and lived [longer lives]. They were consequently called "The family of Yoḥanan," after him.

8.   R. Shmuel b. Unia stated in the name of Rab: Whence is it deduced
     that a [divine] dispensation against a congregation is not sealed?

9.   Is not sealed! Surely it is written, *"Though you wash with natron, and
     use much lye, yet your guilt is ingrained before Me!"* (Jer 2:22).

10. But [this is the question]: Whence is it deduced that even if it has
     been sealed it is torn up?—From the Scriptural text, *"For what great
     nation is there, that has a god so close at hand as is the Lord our God
     whenever we call upon Him?"* (Deut 4:7).

11. But, surely, it is written, *"Seek the Lord while He can be found"* (Isa
     55:6) [implying that he is not always near]!

12. This is no contradiction. The latter applies to an individual, the
     former to a congregation.

13. And when may an individual [find him]?

14. R. Naḥman replied in the name of Rabbah b. Abbuha: In the ten
     days between the New Year and the Day of Atonement.

In Daniel 10:21, an angel or semidivine being tells Daniel that he will declare
to him what is inscribed in the "writing of truth" (*ketav emet*)—an apparent
reference to a divine decree. Our passage opens with a citation of this verse and
a question is posed: does the angel's reference to a "writing of truth" imply that
there is also a divine writing that is *not* truth? Although Levi is stymied by the
question, a response is provided in the anonymous voice: there are two types
of divine writing. That which is accompanied by an oath is a writing of truth,
while that which is not accompanied by an oath is not truth. But why does the
presence or absence of an oath make a divine communication true? The answer
is deduced from a teaching, attributed to R. Shmuel b. Ammi in the name of
R. Yonatan: a divine decree accompanied by an oath is true because it *cannot be
annulled.* The proof cited by R. Shmuel b. Ammi is God's judgment on the
house of Eli. According to this judgment, delivered with an oath, all descendants of the house of Eli will die young.

However, in the continuation of the passage, it becomes evident that there
is a way around the decree against the house of Eli. Where sacrifice and offerings are ineffective, human engagement in Torah study and acts of lovingkindness mitigate the decree. In response to these behaviors, God modifies the
decree and extends the life of the descendants of Eli. Thus, even sworn divine
statements are not as "true" as one might suppose. Indeed, R. Shmuel b. Unia
asserts in the name of Rav that a divine decree against the congregation, even
after it is sealed, may be torn up and utterly rescinded in response to human
petition. In the subsequent anonymous discussion of this tradition it emerges
that even the decree against an individual can be annulled if God is petitioned
between New Year's Day and the Day of Atonement. By the end of the sugya

(the term refers to a unit of talmudic discussion), the following claims have been made: (1) not all divine statements (here, judgments) are true in the sense of irrevocable; (2) even judgments that appear to be irrevocable (because accompanied by an oath) can be modified in response to virtuous human deeds; (3) even sealed divine decrees can be rescinded in response to entreaty.

Richard Hidary (forthcoming) illuminates these issues in an excellent study that contrasts the role of truth in human and divine judgment as indicated by the presence or absence of lawyers. Hidary notes the prominence of lawyers and advocates in rabbinic depictions of the heavenly court, a remarkable fact given the rabbis' negative attitude to lawyers and advocates in their own courts. Indeed, several texts indicate that advocates (*sanegorin*) were banned from rabbinic courts (Hidary forthcoming, 2–4). By contrast, Roman court procedure in tannaitic and amoraic times was highly adversarial and featured professional lawyers (ibid., 4). According to Hidary, the rabbis saw the Roman system as corrupt and capricious, as little more than a debating contest in which "the most persuasive orator will win regardless of truth or justice" (ibid.). Banning lawyers from their own courts was thus a logical resistance to a practice the rabbis disdained. Why then did they populate the heavenly court with advocates? The answer to this question, Hidary argues, reveals much about the rabbinic attitude to truth, law, and the nature of God.

After reviewing biblical and Second Temple Jewish precedent for the rabbinic materials, Hidary writes (ibid., 14):

> [T]he Rabbis not only inherit and transmit but also expand upon the rich heritage of Second Temple interpretations that conceived of advocates in the heavenly court. Some of these midrashim include curious and sometimes radical innovations ... As Meira Kensky notes, the Rabbis not only use technical terms from their surrounding Greco-Roman legal culture; the aggadic divine court also features the sense of trial as *agon* where advocates unscrupulously battle to produce any winning argument they can, regardless of truth or falsehood.[40]
>
> ... the Rabbis pictured the heavenly court in terms of Roman courts not despite the corruption of the latter but precisely because of it. They feared that a heavenly court that followed strict justice and judged human actions according to the truth would issue impossibly harsh, even if justifiable, verdicts.

Lawyers and advocates care nothing for truth—only for victory. The divine-human relationship cannot be sustained when truth is the ultimate goal, and the presence of lawyers and advocates in the heavenly court ensures that truth does not prevail. The midrashic texts surveyed by Hidary depict God as both more and less complicit in the defeat of truth. In some passages, "God would

[40] Hidary (forthcoming), citing Kensky 2010, 313–14.

prefer to be persuaded towards mercy by a good lawyer even at the expense of justice" (e.g., Gen Rab 49:2; see Hidary forthcoming, 16); in others, God is more reluctant, and extreme measures are needed to pacify his anger and motivate him to renounce his just punishment of Israel (e.g., Lam Rab 1:13; see Hidary forthcoming, 18–19). In these midrashim, the successful advocate, whose orations are modeled on those of Roman rhetors (Hidary forthcoming, 20), often utilize pathos rather than legal argument, even shaming God into acquiescing in the demand for mercy (Sifre Deut 343, Ex Rab 43:1; see Hidary forthcoming, 19–20). In some cases, the advocate—in particular, Moses—resorts to various ruses, tricks, and even bribery to avert a just verdict and win acquittal for Israel (Ex Rab 43:1, 3, 5; Hidary forthcoming, 20)—an effort that is depicted as heroic.

Hidary (forthcoming, 24–25) sums up the midrashic material this way. The rabbis

> transform the heavenly advocates into Roman lawyers and allow them to use all the sophistic tricks of the trade that one would find in a typical Roman court. The Patriarchs, Moses, Rachel, and even God Himself will do almost anything to obstruct the Attribute of Justice: flatter and bribe the judge, conceal evidence, take extra time, convince witnesses to withhold testimony, use grammatical loopholes to twist the law, and more. In their own earthly courts, the Rabbis recognize the corruption of the Roman adversarial system and the dishonesty promoted by the rhetoricians. They therefore made a concerted effort to exclude lawyers from their own courts as the best way to ensure truth and justice. When it comes to God's court, on the other hand, truth and justice become enemies for sinful humans who cannot survive their high standards. The injustices of the adversarial system are therefore introduced into the heavenly court, usually with God's implicit consent, so that Mercy may triumph.[41]

It is a short distance from the view that God consents to and is desirous of human assistance in defeating the strict justice of his own decrees to the view that he *needs* it. A dramatic illustration of God's *dependence* on human intervention to defeat him in the execution of his own decrees is found in Ex Rab 43:4, which refers to the Golden Calf story. The midrash describes God and Moses during the critical moment when Israel's fate hangs in the balance. Infuriated by the Israelites' disloyalty, God has declared his intention to wipe them out and begin anew with Moses (Ex 32:9–10). He orders Moses to stand aside, but Moses does not. Instead he implores (*vayyeḥal*) God not to destroy the people

---

[41] Compare Halberstam (2014) who analyzes tannaitic midrashic sources that represent the heavenly court as focused on pure procedural justice at the expense of a fair or just outcome, a slightly different manifestation of the idea that divine justice does not always adhere to "judicial truth."

(v. 11). The midrash punningly construes *vayyeḥal*, "implores," as the technical term for annulling a vow, as seen in Numbers 30:3: "*lo yaḥel devaro*" ("*[when a man makes a vow] he shall not annul his word*"). Moses, it seems, absolved God of his vow to destroy idolaters.

1. Another explanation of "*But Moses implored Yahweh his god.*" R. Ber-ekhiyah said in the name of R. Isaac that he [Moses] absolved his creator of his vow [a pun on *vayyeḥal*].
2. How? When Israel made the Calf, Moses began to implore Elohim to forgive them; but Elohim said, "Moses, I have already taken an oath that '*Whoever sacrifices to a god other than Yahweh alone shall be proscribed [destroyed]*' (Ex. 22:19) and I cannot retract an oath which has pro-ceeded from my mouth."
3. Moses said to him, "Lord of the Universe! Didn't you grant me the power of annulment of oaths by saying, '*If a man makes a vow ... he shall not break (yaḥel) his pledge*' (Num 30:3); that is, *he* himself cannot break *his own* pledge, but a scholar can absolve his vow if he consults him, and any sage who gives instruction, if he wants others to accept his decision, he should be the first to observe it. Since you have commanded me concerning the annulment of vows, it is only right that you should [seek to] annul your vow as you have commanded me to annul the vows of others."
4. Thereupon [Moses] wrapped himself in his cloak and seated himself like a Sage, and the holy one, blessed be he, stood before him like one petitioning [for the annulment of] his vow; ... What did he [Moses] say to him? A shocking thing ... "Do you now regret [your vow]?" He said to him, "I regret now the evil which I said I would do to my people" [based on Ex 32:14]. When Moses heard this, he said: "It is absolved for you, it is absolved for you. There is neither vow nor oath any longer"; for this reason it says: "*vayyeḥal Moshe*"—meaning that he absolved (*heḥal*) the vow of his creator.

God is trapped by the law pronounced in Exodus 22:19 proscribing those who sacrifice to idols. Although he wishes desperately to forgive Israel, how can he do so without breaking his earlier vow to destroy idolaters? The mid-rashic author places in God's mouth an assertion of the eternal and inflexible nature of his divine decree: "I cannot retract an oath which has proceeded from my mouth." But Moses has the answer. Even though God cannot retract his vow, a properly vested authority can be petitioned to absolve it for him based on the law in Numbers 30:3. Moreover, there is pedagogical merit in God's modeling his instructions for Israel by undergoing the procedure for the disso-lution of vows himself. Having persuaded God to this course of action, Moses wraps himself in a scholar's shawl and sits like a sage ready to interrogate one petitioning for the dissolution of a vow. Drawing on Exodus 32:14, in which the biblical narrator states that God repented of, or regretted, the evil that he said he would do to his people, the midrash has Moses ask God whether he regrets having taken the vow to destroy those who worship idols. God answers that he does indeed regret the vow and wishes to retract it. Immediately, Moses declares, "Your vow is released!" This is an astonishing portrait of God trapped by his own law of justice and true judgment, and dependent upon the ingenious intervention of a human partner in order to escape the execution of the divine law.

The divorce of truth and divine justice found in rabbinic texts stands in stark contrast to the conception of divine justice found in classical sources, as indicated by Hidary (forthcoming, 25–26). In Plato's *Laws*, the Athenian Stranger

> envisions a utopian city called Magnesia where the court system is inquisitorial and where lawyers are to receive the death penalty. In the *Gorgias*, Plato's Socrates similarly envisions a heavenly court where rhetoric has no place and where the judges can see things as they really are. Plato describes this post-mortem court in his myth of the naked souls ... [a court where Zeus] instituted a reform that the dead should judge the dead so that the disembodied soul of the judge could clearly perceive the soul of the judged and justice would be based on the naked truth, free from the trappings of rhetoric ... [42]
>
> The vast majority of rabbinic literature, however, describes a heavenly court teeming with advocates of all kinds: Patriarchs and Matriarchs, angels, the Logos, the Torah, the Holy Spirit, the Attribute of Mercy, and even God Himself. Many of these sources even model the heavenly court on Roman courts, with all their deceit, flattery, bribery, and corruption. The Rabbis agreed with Plato's assessment of lawyers and the rhetoric they use as a deterrent from achieving Truth. They also agree with Plato that there is no place in earthly courts for hired lawyers. However, taking inspiration from the great prophetic advocates in the Bible, they appreciate that God, in His mercy, allows and even requests advocates in His court who can persuade Him out of His rage.

We may add that God allows and even requests advocates in his court who can persuade him not to enact the truth, but to render judgment consistent with the goal of sustaining his people, Israel, despite their many sins.

Rabbinic references to *din* in discussions of the formally correct law, and to truth (*emet* and *din*) in discussions of judicial process and divine judgment, preserve a conceptual distinction between truth (whether formal or judicial) and divine law, in sharp contrast to Greco-Roman divine law discourses, which would view truth as a necessary feature of divine law. Because truth is under-

---

[42] Hidary cites Gorgias 523a–e and the work of Weinrib (1989).

stood to be conceptually distinct from divine law, the rabbis are free to imagine a variety of relationships between the two. At times truth and the divine law are aligned, but quite often they are not. Indeed, their relationship can be one of antagonistic opposition, and in the case of divine judgment in particular, God's defeat of truth in favor of mercy and compassion is extolled as a divine virtue.

We turn now to our final measure of a stable, authentic truth.

Measure 3: Ontological Truth—Realism vs. Nominalism

The third and final approach to exploring the issue of truth in rabbinic conceptions of divine law takes its cue from Greco-Roman discourses that identify divine law with truth in the sense of "what is"—that is, a *mind-independent* ontological reality, whether concrete or abstract. Do the rabbis understand God's divine law—the Torah—in realist terms? Do they understand its prohibitions and commandments, its categories and classifications, to conform to what they take to be an objective and mind-independent reality as is the case in some Greco-Roman discourses of divine law and in some Qumran writings? Or do they favor a more nominalist approach to the law instead?

As noted in chapter 3, Daniel Schwartz suggested in an article in 1992 that rabbinic literature is manifestly nominalist in its approach to law, in contrast to the realist view of law espoused by the Qumran sectarians. Schwartz's usage of the terms "realism" and "nominalism" was critiqued (Rubenstein 1999b) and further refined in subsequent literature (Hayes 2011). Because widely varying use and misunderstanding of these terms persist, I begin by clarifying their use and meaning in this study.[43]

[43] On the question of terminology, see the extremely clear and helpful discussion in Amichay 2013, chap. 1, where the terms "legal essentialism" and "legal formalism" are proposed as replacements for "realism" and "nominalism." See also Fisch 1997, 57–60, who refers to "realist" and "conventionalist" points of view, and Lorberbaum 2012, 3, who prefers "reality-based-*halakhot*" and "value-based *halakhot*." Whether the terms "realism" and "nominalism" are the most apt labels for the two approaches described here has become something of a red herring that distracts scholars from grappling with the substance of the arguments advanced by those who use the terms. More important than settling on a universally accepted terminology, however, is settling on a common characterization or definition of the two approaches so that scholars can stop talking past one another and address each other's evidence for the presence, absence, or interaction of these approaches in ancient Jewish literature. For that reason, I provide an extremely detailed characterization of the two approaches, and the criteria by which they can be identified. It is immaterial whether we call these approaches realism and nominalism, or A and B, or Fred and George. Rather than searching for a label to which no one will object (in academia, a virtually impossible task), it seems best to agree on a definition of the two approaches so that there can be a common conversation about the extent to which each may or may not be found in ancient Jewish texts of various kinds. As the subsequent discussion indicates, the term "realism" as it is employed here and by Schwartz has nothing to do with the school of American Legal Realism originating in the 1930s, which ironically enough possesses many of the characteristic features of a nonrealist nominalism. Nor should the term "realism" in its technical sense be confused with or reduced to the nontechnical notion of "real" or "realistic," which refers to existence *simpliciter* rather than *mind-independent* existence.

According to a basic philosophical definition (Rodriguez-Pereyra 2011), realism asserts not the existence but the *mind-independent* existence and reality of universals on the one hand and of abstract entities (like properties, numbers, propositions, etc.) on the other. By contrast, nominalism in its earliest version maintained that while universal Forms (like whiteness or squareness) and abstract entities (like numbers and mathematical relations) exist and are real, they do not exist outside particular things and minds. There are only particular things, and these particulars are not instantiations of universal Forms; a slightly later version of nominalism maintains that there are no abstract objects because everything is concrete (not material, but concrete).[44]

Nominalism is thus anti-Platonic inasmuch as Platonism is a realism that asserts the mind-independent existence and reality of abstract entities. Indeed, the more abstract, the more real because material things do not perdure. For nominalists, talk about abstract things or propositions is a useful fiction, a descriptive aid that enables us to talk about the world, but in fact these things have no ontological or *mind-independent* reality, a position held in antiquity by the Stoics, who consciously rejected Platonic realism. As William of Ockham argued, when we speak of someone as brave, we commit ourselves only to the existence of particular living beings who are brave, and particular braveries, but not to an ontologically real universal, "bravery." Similarly, the eleventh/twelfth-century nominalist Peter Abelard asserted that universals are mere words, or *nomina* (the origin of the term nominalism)—they are not an ontological fea-

---

[44] Realists about universals typically think that properties (e.g., whiteness), relations (e.g., betweenness), and kinds (e.g., gold) are universals that, generally speaking, exist outside their concrete instances and therefore outside space and time. So if something is white or square or prohibited, it is so because it instantiates an independently existent universal Form of whiteness, or squareness, or prohibitedness. Nominalism holds that there *are* such things as properties, numbers, propositions—they do *exist*; but it rejects the assertion that these things have an *independent* existence *outside* of concrete particulars and *outside* of minds. In other words, while such things are real, they are not *ontologically* real (real independent of minds). Only *particular* things have ontological reality; their properties (whiteness, impurity, prohibitedness) and the relations between them (similarity, causation) exist only in the mind and have no independent ontological reality. This is an important distinction. It is a common mistake to attribute to nominalists the view that ideas, abstract concepts, universals, etc., are not real and do not exist at all, and to imagine that if a particular text indicates that ideas and mental states are *real*, it cannot be nominalist. See, for example, Lorberbaum (2012, 54–55) who, curiously, views the ability of intentional states to create halakhic statuses as evidence of realism (!). This is an incoherent assertion. Realism *by definition* points to the *mind-independent* reality of abstract states and entities (like purity); thus it is a contradiction in terms to state that the creation of a halakhic status by a mental event is an instance of realism. It is, in fact, the exemplar par excellence of nominalism. Lorberbaum confuses "real" (i.e., existing) and "realist" (having a *mind-independent* existence). So to be clear: nominalists believe that ideas, mental states, abstract concepts, universals are all *real, existing entities*. However, these entities exist only in particular things and in minds. They do not have a *mind-independent* reality, and they do not exist in something like Plato's realm of Forms. Thus, to allow a mental state or intention to determine abstract (albeit *real*) qualities (like holiness or impurity) is unquestionably *nominalist* because even though the qualities are deemed to be real and existing, they do not exist *outside the mental event*.

ture of the world but a semantic feature of language. Because they apply to more than one thing, they are semantically general—in that sense only are they "universal"—but they are not metaphysically real, only semantically real.

The terms "realism" and "nominalism" are employed not only in the realm of metaphysics but also in the realm of ethics. Here, William of Ockham's view is instructive, for his is a will-based ethics in which intentions count for everything, and external behavior or actions count for nothing, in defining the prohibited and the permitted, the just and the unjust. In themselves, all actions are morally neutral (Spade and Panaccio 2011). According to Peter Abelard as well, morality is radically *intentionalist*: in themselves, deeds are morally indifferent and the agent's intention alone determines the moral worth of an action. Thus, for the nominalists Abelard and Ockham intention is of central importance and thoughts "create reality"–this is the technical definition of what it is to be a nominalist about ethics (King 2011).[45]

Contemporary legal analyses that deploy the terms "realism" and "nominalism" draw upon, but are not always precisely identical with, the long-standing use of these terms, particularly in ethics. Thus, I will spell out how these terms will be used here.

I will use the term "realism" to refer to a legal approach that tends to assume the *mind-independent* reality of legal categories, determinations, and judgments; I will use the term "nominalism" to refer to a legal approach that tends to assume the *mind-dependent* reality of the same.[46] The criteria employed in identifying a

[45] Some will object that medieval terminology cannot illuminate premedieval world views (see Amichay 2013, 22n16, and Lorberbaum 2012, 87n67, in the Hebrew text) but terms and concepts developed in later periods are regularly used to illuminate earlier periods (consider for example terms like "theism," "egoism," "racism"). Lorberbaum himself employs a slew of terms from contemporary legal theory to analyze rabbinic sources. My purpose in tracing the history of this terminology is simply to show that based on their original meanings, the terms are not inapt descriptors of phenomena apparent in earlier sources (including classical sources, for that matter, as indicated by the widespread application of the term "realism" to describe Plato's theory of forms). In short, when fully understood and clearly defined, the terms may be usefully employed as designations for the phenomena in question, whenever and wherever they might occur in history. It would be anachronistic to say that the rabbis wore wristwatches. It is not anachronistic to say that some rabbinic texts evince an approach to law bearing the characteristic traits of what would later be called (legal) nominalism.

[46] Again, on both views, these categories, determinations, and judgments are *real*—but for the realist that reality is mind-independent, while for the nominalist that reality is mind-dependent. Compare the definition of essentialism proposed by Amichay (2013, 25–26), which corresponds to the present definition of realism precisely because it assumes the element of mind-independence. Amichay follows Jane Wong, for whom the core concept of essentialism is "that the characteristics used to define a thing are thought to inhere in its very essence and, thus, to be unchangeable." Amichay continues, "The pork carries with it impurity, and the pentateuchal dietary laws thus only reveal a fact that is true regardless of whether the law was written. The holidays occur according to a celestial calendar that no human error can change, and if a certain holiday is not celebrated on the correct date, it does not change the fact that it was indeed the date of the holiday, since this is an essence of time that is instilled in nature, just as the sun rises and the moon sets. These unchangeable facts of nature, therefore, bear implications on the law, which is why I label this stance as 'legal essentialism,' rather than

realist vs. a nominalist approach to determining the content of the law are therefore as follows: a realist approach (1) will maximize appeals to what it perceives to be a mind-independent, objective reality. Concomitantly, a realist approach will be characterized by (2) a minimization of subjective, intentional states in the determination of legal status and (3) an aversion to legal fictions and contrary-to-fact presumptions and judgments, as well as a preference for constrained and contextual legal interpretation.[47] By contrast, a nominalist approach (1) often overrules appeals to objective reality. Concomitantly, a nominalist approach will be characterized by (2) a greater accommodation of subjective intentional states in the determination of legal status and (3) a greater readiness to deploy legal fictions and contrary-to-fact presumptions and judgments, as well as a greater tolerance for less constrained and contextual legal interpretation.

It is important to be clear on what is being claimed here. First, I make no claims regarding a rabbinic metaphysics (and I am not confident that anyone can). Even if we were to identify texts that point to a metaphysical realism, a commitment to such a view does not entail legal realism, that is, the belief that law must conform to objective reality. My claim is that whatever their metaphysical commitment, the rabbis exhibit a high degree of nominalism in their approach to law. Second, the question that concerns us is not whether the rabbinic legal approach is nominalist *or* realist (as if these constitute a binary of mutually exclusive terms). All legal systems appeal to nature and mind-independent reality in determining the law; what makes a system realist or nominalist is the *degree* to which such appeals are dispositive and uncontestable (more for the realist, less for the nominalist).[48] For the realist, "the way

simply 'essentialism.' It is an ontological premise that informs the attitude towards the law, its practice and interpretation. It bears consequences for the question of intention, since intent does not change reality."

[47] I have chosen my language very carefully. A realist approach is characterized by a *minimization but not total elimination* of intentional states, an *aversion to, but not absolute rejection of,* legal fictions and contrary-to-fact presumptions and judgments, and a *preference for but not absolute insistence upon* constrained and contextual legal interpretation. These are *tendencies,* not *absolute positions,* that are more typical of realism than nominalism. Thus, a few counterexamples against a wealth of supporting evidence would not disprove the claim that an approach is more realist than nominalist. The same holds mutatis mutandis for nominalism—a nominalist approach will *tend to* accommodate intentional states but not in every case; it will be *relatively* more willing to deploy legal fictions, contrary-to-fact presumptions, and judgments, and it will have a *greater* (but not absolute) tolerance for less constrained and contextual legal interpretation. These are tendencies rather than absolute positions, and a few counterexamples would not disprove the claim that an approach is more nominalist than realist. Indeed, I myself will argue below that rabbinic nominalism is conscious of and contested by realism.

[48] Again, lest I be accused of anachronism, the debate over the mind-independent existence of universals and abstract entities (including moral categories of good and bad) was a live one in antiquity. Platonists affirmed the mind-independent existence of universals; Stoics were not realists about universals. They had a material conception of the universal natural law. Philo was aware of this debate. In *Special Laws* 1.327 he scoffs at those who deny the mind-independent existence of universals.

things really are," in themselves and independent of mental perception, will tend to trump other considerations in determining the content of the law; for the nominalist, it is one consideration among many and may be set aside in light of other considerations, needs, or values. Thus, a central criterion for identifying a realist or nominalist approach to the law is the degree of deference accorded to "the way things really are" and the role played by appeals to this mind-independent reality. In a realist approach, appeals to "objective" reality (accessed in various ways) play a strong role in determining the content of the law; in a nominalist approach, such appeals play a relatively weaker role and are often overruled. My claim is that the rabbinic legal orientation is highly (but not exclusively) nominalist, and that rabbinic texts exhibit many of the characteristic features of a nominalist orientation to law. *This claim of a relatively strong nominalist approach is not refuted by the adducing of instances of realism*—and there certainly are some—within rabbinic texts.

(I) RABBINIC NOMINALISM AND ITS DISCONTENTS

In chapter 3, we briefly considered evidence from Qumran of a realist approach to law. Several Qumran texts appear to base a determination of law on an appeal to an objective (i.e., mind-independent) standard of truth. They employ a rhetoric of epistemological certainty about the law. Rabbinic texts, on the other hand, not infrequently ignore what are referred to as objective (mind-independent) standards of truth when making legal determinations. In so doing, they create a rhetoric of epistemological uncertainty about the law that is not resolved by appeals to an objective standard of some kind. Certainly, rabbinic texts are not *categorically* antirealist and antiempirical. Nevertheless, these texts do not consistently privilege "the way things really are" (however this might be determined) when deciding the law; indeed, at times appeals to "objective" measures of truth are openly and explicitly overruled in favor of other considerations. As a result, the rabbinic orientation may be said to tolerate a relatively high degree of nominalism. And yet, as we shall see, this nominalist orientation may be presented alongside a realist orientation or even as the target of realist opposition, creating a complex and hybrid discourse.

(a) Law's Deviation from Mind-Independent Reality

In one of the clearest examples of rabbinic nominalism, an appeal to astronomical reality is explicitly overruled in the determination of the law. Since this example has been widely discussed (Schwartz 1992; Rubenstein 1999b), particularly in relation to the contrasting realist approach of the members of the Qumran sect, our treatment can be brief.

As noted in chapter 3, Daniel Schwartz points to the calendar as evidence of a highly realist orientation among the sectarians at Qumran. The members of the sect took an oath to follow the 364-day calendar so as not to advance or delay (*lo leqadem ... velo lehitaher*) the dates of the festivals (1QS

1:14–15)[49]—that is, the objectively *real* dates of the festivals as determined by the fifty-two-week pattern fixed in nature by God at the time of the creation. (What the actual source of the calendar might be is irrelevant; what matters is that sectarian rhetoric marks it as a divinely ordained ontological reality.)

In direct contrast, rabbinic writings dealing with the calendar controversy thematize a nominalist disregard for determinations based *solely* on the actual movement of the luminaries. Certainly, the calendar adopted by rabbinic Judaism has a strong basis in astronomical reality, based as it is on empirical observation of the phases of the moon and adjusted to the seasons. Nevertheless, these facts can be overruled in the determination of the law. In their references to the calendar, several rabbinic texts employ an explicitly nominalist rhetoric—asserting the court's right to subordinate astronomical fact to other considerations. M. RH 2:9–12(8–9) is, perhaps, the best-known example.

> Once two witnesses came and said, "We saw it [the new moon] in the morning in the east and in the evening in the west." R. Yoḥanan b. Nuri said, "They are false witnesses." But when they came to Yavneh, Rabban Gamliel accepted them [i.e., their testimony]. Once two witnesses came and said, "We saw it at its proper time," but on the next night it was not seen, and Rabban Gamliel accepted their evidence. Rabbi Dosa b. Harqinas said, "They are false witnesses. How can men testify that a woman has given birth to a child when on the next day we see her abdomen still distended?" R. Joshua said to him: "I see your point." Thereupon Rabban Gamliel sent to him saying, "I order you to appear before me with your staff and your money on the day which according to your reckoning should be the Day of Atonement." R. Akiva went [to R. Joshua] and found him greatly distressed. He said to him, "I can cite [Scriptural] proof that whatever Rabban Gamliel has done is valid, for it says, '*These are the appointed seasons of the Lord, holy convocations, which you shall proclaim in their appointed seasons*' (Lev 23:4)—[meaning] whether they are proclaimed at their proper time or not at their proper time, I have no appointed seasons except these." He [R. Joshua] then went to R. Dosa b. Harqinas, who said to him, "If we call into question [the decisions of] the court of Rabban Gamliel, we must call into question the decisions of every court which has existed since the days of Moses up to the present time ..." Thereupon he [R. Joshua] took his staff and his money and went to Yavneh to Rabban Gamliel on the day on which the Day of Atonement fell according to his reckoning. Rabban Gamliel rose and kissed him on

---

[49] The full passage from the 1QS reads, "They shall not stray from any one of all God's orders concerning their appointed times; they shall not advance their appointed times nor shall they retard any one of their feasts" (as translated in García Martínez and Tigchelaar 19877, 1:71). Whether the calendar was actually observed at Qumran or not is irrelevant—what is important for our purposes is the rhetoric of an objectively *real* festival date that cannot be changed.

the head and said to him, "Come in peace, my teacher and my disciple—my teacher in wisdom and my disciple because you have accepted my decision."

In this text, we see *both* the realist view that the calendar should conform to the actual movements of the heavenly bodies, and the nominalist view that humans have a certain freedom in setting the calendar in defiance of the astronomical facts. The nominalist position (the position that prevails) is associated with classic rabbinic figures (R. Akiva and Rabban Gamliel), while the realist position is associated with at least one priestly figure (R. Dosa b. Hyrcanus, though the narrator has him ultimately concede the point),[50] further supporting Schwartz's claim that a realist approach is typical of groups with a priestly orientation (such as the Qumran covenanters and the Sadducees). In sum, this text rejects the idea that the actual movement of the heavenly bodies is the sole determinant in calendrical calculations. To be clear: the rabbinic position (as is true of nominalists generally) certainly takes objective reality into account (after all, the rabbinic calendar is established on the basis of eyewitness testimony regarding the moon!); nevertheless, in the final determination of status, other considerations (in this case, a desire to assert authority) are allowed at times to trump the facts of nature. Law does not have to conform to physical reality.

Rabbinic literature contains a few additional traditions that uphold the power and authority of rabbinic sages to make calendrical determinations that run counter to astronomical reality. T. RH 2:1 states that erroneous calendrical determinations are valid. In an elaboration of his statement to R. Joshua in b. RH 25a, R. Akiva is represented as finding Scriptural warrant for the right of rabbinic authorities to determine the calendar even if in so doing they are misled or otherwise err, whether inadvertently or deliberately.

> [R. Akiva] then said to [R. Joshua], "The text says, 'you', 'you', 'you', three times (Lev 22:32, 23:2, 23:4)[51] to indicate that 'you' [may fix the festivals] even if you err inadvertently, 'you', even if you err deliberately, 'you', even if you are misled." [R. Joshua] replied to him saying, "Akiva, you have comforted me, you have comforted me."

[50] This is not the only place that an empiricist or realist approach to the calendar is associated with a priest in rabbinic writings. In the mishnah immediately preceding m. RH 2:9–12(8–9), R. Eleazar b. Zadoq adopts a realist approach to the calendar, dismissing as unnecessary the court's declaration of the first of the month when the moon is not seen on the twenty-ninth day, because "they have already sanctified it in heaven." Rubenstein cites this passage as an objection to Schwartz's characterization of rabbinic calendrical law as nominalist (Rubenstein 1999b, 175–76). This objection overlooks two points. First, no legal system is either realist *or* nominalist, and evidence of some realist determinations in rabbinic literature should occasion no surprise. Second, R. Eleazar b. Zadok is a priest. The passage therefore supports Schwartz's claim that realist approaches to the law are more typical of priests and groups with a priestly orientation. For the phenomenon of sectarian views expressed in rabbinic texts, see Noam 2005 and 2006.

[51] Reading *otam* as *atem*.

In addition, the Babylonian Talmud's sugya (textual unit) on this mishnah contains a humorous story that again thematizes the disconnect between the halakhah and astrononmical reality (b. RH 25a):

R. Ḥiyya once saw the [old] moon in the heavens on the morning of the twenty-ninth day. He took a clod of earth and threw it at it, saying, "We want to sanctify you tonight, but you are still here! Go and hide yourself." Rabbi said to R. Ḥiyya, "Go to Eyn Tov and sanctify the month, and send me the password, 'David, king of Israel, is alive and vigorous.'"

In this tale, a late tanna who hoped to be able to declare the new moon (presumably for reasons of convenience) is annoyed to see the old moon lingering. Rabbi advises him to go to Eyn Tov (literally, "good eye"—a clear pun) to sanctify the new moon and to send a coded message when he has accomplished this task. Rabbi's furtiveness betrays the author's sensitivity to the fact that overruling astronomical facts—a nominalist move—is often met with opposition and is best done out of public view. I will have more to say about this kind of internal tension below.

A final and unapologetic defense of the nominalist position may be seen in the following late midrash:

R Hoshaya taught: When the lower court makes a decree and declares, "Today is the new year" then the holy one, blessed be he, says to the ministering angels, "Set up the tribunal, install the advocate, install the clerk of the court, for the lower court has decreed and declared that tomorrow is the new year!"

If the witnesses are delayed or the court reconsiders and puts it off to the next day, the holy one, blessed be he, says to the angels, "Take down the tribunal, and dismiss the advocate and the clerk of the court, for the lower court has decreed that the next morning should be the new year."

And what is the proof? "For a law in Israel is also an obligation for the God of Israel" (Ps 81:5)—what is not a law for Israel is also, if we may say so, no obligation for the God of Jacob.

R. Pinḥas and R. Hilkiah b. R. Simon say: When all the ministering angels assemble before God and ask, "Lord of the universe, when is the new year?" he answers them: "You're asking me? You and I should ask the lower court." And what is the proof? "For who is so near as the Lord our God, when we make known to him" (the festivals) (Deut 4:7). (PesRab 15)

(b) Intentional States in the Determination of Legal Status

In a recent article, Ishay Rosen-Zvi examined the Mishnah's assignment of various legal statuses on the basis of "mental events" of various kinds. He cites numerous passages from the Mishnah in which we see "the ability of thoughts to create reality, especially in the laws of purity and sacrifice." Although Rosen-

Zvi eschews the label "nominalism,"[52] the passages are excellent examples of nominalism precisely because thoughts or mental states are said to assign to acts, entities, and events the properties that they have. I review Rosen-Zvi's evidence before applying my own analysis.[53]

According to Rosen-Zvi (forthcoming, 2), the tannaim (rabbinic sages of the late first–third centuries featured in the Mishnah and the Tosefta) created new mental categories to determine the status of persons, objects, and actions.[54] These tannaitic innovations include "intention" (*kavvanah*) in the observance of commandments;[55] "thought" (*mahshavah*), which has an effect on the validity of a sacrifice; "will" (*ratzon*), which has an effect on susceptibility to impurity; and "contemplation" (*hirhur*), which can take the place of actual ritual recitations in certain circumstances (ibid.). As Rosen-Zvi notes, the term *kavvanah* (in the sense of having the proper intentionality when performing a deed) appears in relation to the twice-daily recitation of the Shema, the obligation to hear the reading of the Megillah (scroll of Esther) on Purim, and the obligation to hear the shofar on Rosh haShanah and Yom Kippur. In each case,

---

[52] Rosen-Zvi (forthcoming) seems to suppose that nominalism denies the reality of abstract entities altogether, and since thoughts and other intentional states are treated as "real" in the Mishnah, the Mishnah cannot be said to be nominalist (for this common confusion, see n41 above). For example, when dismissing the term "nominalism" as a label for the view that emphasizes mental aspects of negligence and faults, he writes, "[P]sychology is no less realistic than cosmology, and thus the mental aspect of the sin can in fact reflect a "real" and complex mental world" (4). This statement confuses the terms "real/realistic" and "realist." These terms are *not* synonymous. One can assert that something is real/realistic (that it has existence), but deny that it is realist (that it has an existence outside particular things and outside minds). Realists and nominalists *agree* that thoughts and psychology and virtue and vice are all real and realistic. The argument is over *where* these equally real entities exist—in particular things and minds (as a nominalist would argue) or outside and independent of particular things or minds in something like a Platonic realm of Forms (as a realist would argue). Nominalism does *not* deny the reality of abstract entities; it denies their *mind-independent* reality. For a nominalist thoughts are entirely real (i.e., they exist), but they are not realist (i.e., they do not exist outside of concrete particular minds). Thus, pace Rosen-Zvi, to hold that thoughts (which are *real mental states*) "create reality" is *precisely* what it is to be a nominalist. And when Rosen-Zvi states that thoughts create reality in the mishnaic laws of purity and sacrifice, he applies the classic definition of nominalism to these cases in the Mishnah. Lorberbaum (2012, 54–55) also confuses the terms "real" (i.e., existing) and "realist" (having a *mind-independent* existence) when he points to the ability of intentional states to create halakhic statuses as an example of halakhic realism. To say that the creation of a halakhic status by a mental event is an instance of realism (i.e., a mind-independent status) is simply a contradiction in terms.

[53] There are, of course, many other cases and many other areas of rabbinic law (beyond purity, sacrifice, and ritual) in which intention plays a determining role, but I focus on Rosen-Zvi's list because of his attempt to connect these data with the realism-nominalism debate. For the role of intention in rabbinic law more generally, see Higger 1927; Eilberg-Schwartz 1986; Bazak 2004, Strauch-Schick 2011; and Brodsky forthcoming. In two recent articles (2013, 2014), Yishai Kiel documents the increased emphasis on inward concentration, intention, and other mental events in the Babylonian Talmud, and points to parallel emphases in late antique monastic and Zoroastrian sources.

[54] These categories represent developments of, as well as innovations upon, the biblical categories of intentional and unintentional actions (*shogeg/mezid*).

[55] See Lorberbaum 2011b, 84–90, for various meanings of the term *kavvanah*.

the action in question is valid only if one has *kavvanah*—proper intention. Thus, m. Ber 2:1 states:

> One who was reading [the verses of the Shema recitation] in the Torah and the time for reciting [the Shema] arrived, if he directed his heart [*im kivven libbo*; i.e., had the proper intention] he has fulfilled his obligation and if not, he has not fulfilled his obligation.

Similarly, m. RH 3:(6)7 states:

> One who was passing behind a synagogue or whose house was near a synagogue and he heard the sound of the shofar or the sound of the Megillah being read, if he directed his heart [*im kivven libbo*; i.e., had the proper intention] he has fulfilled his obligation and if not, he has not fulfilled his obligation. Even though both heard, one directed his heart and the other did not direct [his heart.]

The presence or absence of the proper intention determines the character of the act as legally valid or invalid, a clear instance of classical legal nominalism as defined above. Note that these passages posit an objectively real act of reading or hearing; nevertheless, the act does not possess the abstract quality of "legal validity" or "legal invalidity" independent of a mental action.

Rosen-Zvi also points to the importance of thought (*mahshavah*) in the laws of purity and sacrifice. For example, susceptibility to impurity falls upon utensils, but whether an item is deemed a utensil and therefore susceptible to impurity depends upon human thought. If one has the thought (*mahshavah*) of making use of an item, it becomes susceptible to impurity because the abstract quality of "utensil-ness" has been attributed to it by a human mind. M. Kel 25:9 states explicitly: "All utensils become susceptible to impurity through thought." The role of thought in determining susceptibility to impurity may be seen in m. Kel 22:2, concerning a table from which the legs are removed (see Rosen-Zvi, forthcoming 4). According to the anonymous mishnah, a table loses the status of utensil and becomes insusceptible to impurity when one or two of its three legs are removed, presumably because the table will not stand and function as a table. However, if all three legs are removed, the anonymous mishnah declares that it is susceptible to impurity *if* someone has the thought (*mahshavah*) of using it as a utensil.

Thought also has the ability to effect the validity of a sacrifice, a topic that occupies the first four chapters of tractate Zevahim. A nominalist orientation toward sacrifice is seen in m. Zev 4:6, which lists the six categories of thought that must properly occupy the priest's mind in order for a sacrifice to fulfill the offerer's obligation. Other sections of tractate Zevahim detail the specific illegitimate thoughts that disqualify a sacrifice. Thus, thoughts about eating the sacrifice outside its time or outside its place disqualify the sacrifice (m. Zev 2:2).

One who slaughters a sacrifice [with the intention] to sprinkle its blood or a little of its blood outside, or to burn the entrails or some of its entrails outside, or to eat its meat or an olive's bulk of its meat outside or an olive's bulk of the skin of the fatty tail outside, the sacrifice is invalid though there is no punishment of extirpation.

[If he slaughtered it with the intention] to sprinkle the blood or some of the blood the next day, to burn the entrails or some of its entrails the next day, or to eat its meat or an olive's bulk of its meat the next day or an olive's bulk of the skin of the fatty tail the next day, the sacrifice is *piggul* [a term of abomination] and he is liable for the punishment of extirpation.

As Rosen-Zvi points out, in these cases intention is so powerful that even before the improper action is performed, the mere thought of engaging in the improper action has already disqualified the sacrifice. Thought (in the form of improper intention) trumps a mind-independent reality (i.e., the correctly executed ritual actions) in determining the status of the action.

Finally, Rosen-Zvi considers the mental category of "will" (*ratzon*). In the Mishnah, pure liquids make objects susceptible to impurity only if they reach their location at the will (*ratzon*) of the owner (see m. Makh 1:1). The rabbis locate this idea in Leviticus 11:38's use of a passive verb to describe water "being put on" an object (implying an intentional act by an agent) in contrast to verse 34's use of an active form to describe water "coming upon" an object (seemingly of itself).[56] The idea that water creates susceptibility to impurity only when it is intentionally introduced is extended rather remarkably to include cases of retroactive willing. Thus, m. Makh 3:5–8 lists various cases in which owners are pleased about the presence of water after the fact. This mental approbation of the situation after the fact is deemed to fulfill the legal requirement of

---

[56] Rosen-Zvi describes the concept of will as the boldest mental category to be introduced by the Mishnah based on a counterintuitive reading of Lev 11:38, but in fact the idea is not very bold and certainly not counterintuitive given rabbinic hermeneutic assumptions. Lev 11 uses two different expressions to indicate the presence of water as a "primer" for impurity. V. 34 employs an active verb with "water" as the subject: *asher yabo alav mayyim*, "when water comes upon it." V. 38 employs a passive verb (a rare *qal* passive): *veki yuttan mayim al*, "when water is placed on X"—implying an agent who places the water on the object. The rabbis appear to resolve the difference by assuming that v. 38 is the governing condition—the water must be placed on the object by an agent. It should be noted that 11QT 49:7 replaces the active verb of v. 34 with *yutsaq* ("is poured"), implying an agent who actively performs the pouring. This harmonization of v. 34 and v. 38 suggests that at Qumran, too, the passive form in v. 38 was taken as the governing condition, so that water creates susceptibility to impurity only when introduced by an agent. It is likely that the utter impracticality of the alternative—according to which any damp foodstuffs, for example, would be susceptible to impurity—led to both the Qumranic and the rabbinic interpretation of Lev 11 as referring to items that have been actively moistened by an agent. However, what *is* bold in the rabbinic treatment of this issue is the nominalist extension of the requirement of agency so as to include even *retroactive* intention that did not exist at the time the water was introduced.

the presence of will (*ratzon*), and thus the moistened item is deemed to be susceptible to impurity *as if* it had been moistened intentionally by the owner from the outset.

As this brief review of Rosen-Zvi's evidence shows (and as is widely accepted),[57] the Mishnah employs various mental states to determine legal status—a characteristic feature of legal nominalism. Indeed, this form of nominalism may be taken as a given in tannaitic texts. But there is more to be said. For while Rosen-Zvi notes in passing that "nominalism and realism are intertwined in the world of rabbinic halakhah," little work has been done to analyze the intertwining of nominalist and realist approaches and assess its significance. I turn now to a deeper analysis of several of the cases highlighted by Rosen-Zvi in order to demonstrate that they are part of a complex, hybrid, and contested discourse of legal nominalism and realism. I consider first cases of intention, then thought, and finally will.

Hybrid discourse reflects a kind of brokered compromise between realist and nominalist orientations toward the law: a nominalist approach is clearly present, but its exact reach—when mental events do and do not trump mind-independent realities in determining legal status—is negotiated. A hybrid discourse occurs in m. Ber 4:5 in connection with intention during prayer. According to this mishnah, under certain circumstances intention is a sufficient but not a necessary condition of valid prayer.

> One who was riding on an ass should dismount [to pray]. If he cannot dismount he should turn his face [toward the Temple in Jerusalem], and if he cannot turn his face he should direct his heart (*yekavven et libo*) toward the Holy of Holies.

There is nominalism in this passage: one can fulfill the obligation to pray facing the Temple in Jerusalem through a mental event rather than a physical turning of the body toward Jerusalem. However, the nominalism is not thoroughgoing because the option of fulfilling one's obligation of praying toward Jerusalem through a mental event is available *only when physical action is precluded.* Presumably, if one has the ability to physically orient the body toward Jerusalem, the nominalist remedy of "directing the heart" would not suffice to fulfill one's obligation. The availability of the nominalist remedy is thus qualified and regulated, creating a hybrid discourse.[58]

---

[57] See literature cited in n49 above.

[58] A similar qualification occurs in connection with the intention required for proper execution of the statutory prayer. "R. Eliezer said, A person must always evaluate himself: If he will be able to have the proper intention he should pray, and if not he should not pray" (b. Ber 30b); also, "One praying [the statutory prayer] needs to have proper intention in all [of the blessings], and if he cannot have intention for all of them, he should have inner intention for one (b. Ber 34b). But see also b. Ber 13a–b, for example, for the idea that intention is not necessary for all recitations and prayers—the physical act of prayer, even when it is not accompanied by the proper intentionality, suffices to fulfill one's obliga-

A hybrid discourse is also apparent in m. Kel 25:9, in connection with the power of thought to determine susceptibility to impurity. An initial nominalism is countered in subsequent clauses:

> All utensils become susceptible to impurity through thought but they do not become insusceptible to impurity except through an action that changes them. An action can cancel [an earlier] act or intention but an intention cannot cancel an earlier act or intention.

This mishnah both asserts and limits the power of thought to create reality. On the one hand, thought can establish the status of an item as a utensil, thereby creating a susceptibility to impurity. On the other hand, thought does not have the power to establish a different status for the item so as to render it insusceptible to impurity. The mishnah does not give a reason for this double standard, but we can be sure that it is not due to a simple desire to prevent further changes in status, because the text goes on to offer a strategy for effecting a further change in status: an action that causes a physical change in the object. Why changing the status of a utensil so as to create insusceptibility to impurity should require a mind-independent physical action is not indicated. What is important for our purposes is that even as rabbinic nominalism is asserted, its reach is qualified.

A similar hybridity may be seen in connection with the thoughts that render a sacrifice valid or invalid. In Mishnah tractate Zevaḥim, thought can establish some statuses but not others, which again suggests that the reach of mental states in determining the law is negotiated. M. Zev 1:1 states the general rule that animal sacrifices slaughtered under the name (*shem*) of another sacrifice are valid—suggesting that intention is nondeterminative of legal status. However, the mishnah goes on to say that the sacrifice, though valid, is *not* credited to the offerer as fulfilling his obligation. Thus, in the determination of whether a sacrifice counts as a valid sacrifice, proper action is sufficient and intention is not required (reliance on a realist calculation); by contrast, in the determination of whether the act fulfills the offerer's obligation, *both* proper action *and* intention are required (the insertion of a nominalist calculation). A different calibration of that reach appears in m. Zev 2:2, cited above, where an improper thought *does* invalidate the sacrifice, but not to such an extent as to incur the punishment of extirpation. Taken together, m. Zev 1:1 and 2:2 teach that a mental event can establish some statuses but not others—an improper intention regarding time and place has a greater (but not absolute) power to establish legal "facts" than does an improper name. Once again, an interweaving of realist and nominalist criteria results in a hybrid discourse in which nominalism is asserted even as it is delimited.

---

tion. In other words, a nominalist approach is clearly present, but its exact reach (when mental events do and do not trump mind-independent realities in determining legal status) is negotiated.

A different relationship between realist and nominalist approaches is found in other passages that juxtapose rather than blend the two. These passages reflect a relationship of contestation rather than hybridity, as may be seen in m. Kel 22:2. Rosen-Zvi notes that according to the anonymous mishnah, a table from which all three legs have been removed is susceptible to impurity if someone has the thought (*maḥshavah*) of using it as a utensil. What he does not note, however, is that the status of the legless table is subject to a dispute. R. Yosi disagrees that such a thought is required in order for the table to be deemed a utensil and thus susceptible to impurity. We may surmise that R. Yosi holds that a table that has lost all of its legs remains objectively (mind-independently) useful in a way that a table with only one or two legs does not, regardless of whether any particular individual has the thought to utilize it. Its "utensil-ness" exists independently of the intention formed in any mind to use it as a utensil. If this reconstruction of R. Yosi's position is correct, then m. Kel 22:2 presents both a majority nominalist approach and a minority realist approach, not as a hybrid, but as discrete and competing alternatives.

Similarly, as regards the role of thought in determining the status of a sacrifice, m. Zev 1:6(4) presents competing nominalist and realist alternatives side by side (rather than blended together as in the hybrid cases examined above). This mishnah details the stages in the sacrificial ritual during which an illegitimate intention can disqualify the sacrifice:

> For a sacrifice can be disqualified at any one of the four stages [of the ritual]: slaughtering, receiving [the blood], carrying [the blood to the altar] and sprinkling [the blood on the altar].
>
> R. Simeon declares it valid [if there is an illegitimate intention] in the carrying, because he argued: the sacrifice is impossible without slaughtering, without receiving and without sprinkling, but it is possible without carrying.
>
> How so? [If] one slaughters it at the side of the altar and sprinkles [forthwith then no carrying is necessary].
>
> R. Eliezer said: if one carries [the blood to the altar] when he *needs* to carry [because the animal was slaughtered at a distance from the altar], an illegitimate intention disqualifies; but when one does not need to carry [because the animal was slaughtered right next to the altar], an illegitimate intention does not disqualify it.

The mishnah features a dispute over the points in the sacrificial process at which an illegitimate intention can cause disqualification. All agree that an illegitimate intention formed at the time of (1) the slaughtering of the animal, (2) the receiving of the blood, and (3) the sprinkling of the blood disqualifies the sacrifice, but there is disagreement over an illegitimate intention at the time that (4) the blood is carried or conveyed by the priest to the altar. R. Simeon does not include carrying among the points in the sacrificial process at which disqualification can occur, because carriage is not an essential part of the sacrificial process. R. Simeon arrives at this conclusion because he conceives of carriage as the actual conveyance of an item over a physical distance, and such conveyance does not take place in every sacrifice;[59] sometimes the animal is slaughtered so close to the altar that the blood is sprinkled as soon as it is received, without an intervening act of carriage to the altar. Here again, competing rather than hybrid nominalist and realist discourses occur. Interestingly, R. Eliezer's position brokers a compromise by conceding to the realist impulse in R. Simeon's alternative view: when physical carriage occurs in a sacrifice, then it is an essential part of the ritual and an illegitimate intention disqualifies the sacrifice; when physical (mind-independent) carriage does not occur in a sacrifice, then it is not an essential part of the ritual and there can be no disqualifying illegitimate intention in connection with it.

In the preceding cases, hybridity and/or contestation occur within a single mishnah. Sometimes, however, realist and nominalist approaches are found not within a single mishnah but in widely separated teachings or in a parallel tannaitic source, attesting to broader controversy within the rabbinic estate. To illustrate this point, I compare two mishnaic passages with parallel material in the Sifra and the Tosefta. The first mishnaic passage, which in itself is a hybrid, we have already discussed briefly—m. Zev 2:2.

> One who slaughters a sacrifice [with the intention] to sprinkle its blood or a little of its blood outside, or to burn the entrails or some of its entrails outside, or to eat its meat or an olive's bulk of its meat outside or an olive's bulk of the skin of the fatty tail outside, the sacrifice is invalid though there is no punishment of extirpation.
>
> [If he slaughtered it with the intention] to sprinkle the blood or some of the blood the next day, to burn the entrails or some of its entrails the next day, or to eat its meat or an olive's bulk of its meat the next day or an olive's bulk of the skin of the fatty tail the next day, the sacrifice is *piggul* and he is liable for the punishment of extirpation.

In this hybrid text, some improper intention has the power to invalidate the sacrifice but not to create a liability for punishment. In m. Zev 3:6, other kinds of improper intention regarding various rites or regarding the person performing the sacrifice do not invalidate the sacrifice. The mishnah concludes that not all (improper) thoughts have the power to render a sacrifice invalid:

> The only [improper] thought that disqualifies a sacrifice concerns [an act] performed outside its proper time or place. In the case of the Passover

---

[59] The compromise position held by R. Eliezer is based precisely on this distinction—illegitimate intention can disqualify when there is actual conveyance over a distance, but it does not disqualify where there is no actual conveyance.

sacrifice or the purification offering, [slaughtering it] under the wrong name [also invalidates the sacrifice].

M. Zev 2:2 and 3:6 are hybrid texts and work together to both assert and delimit the power of thought to establish the validity of a sacrifice. Comparison with two other tannaitic sources points to contestation.

The Sifra discusses the case reflected in the second clause of m. Zev 2:2, regarding *piggul*. Paradoxically, the Sifra's endorsement of the nominalist approach to this case (according to which an improper intention regarding timing renders the sacrifice *piggul*) is motivated by a *realist impulse*. The Sifra appears to be bothered by the possibility of retroactive intention. Retroactivity is built into the very concept of the biblically prescribed status of *piggul*. Sacrificial meat that is not consumed within a certain defined period of time is declared *piggul* when the time elapses, and the sacrifice—which was otherwise properly performed—is retroactively invalid. The very nominalist idea of a retroactive invalidation of an otherwise valid sacrifice is thus biblical. In the Sifra, the rabbis object to this kind of nominalism in very realist terms.

> And it is impossible to say this [i.e., that if he ate from it on the third day it will be retroactively disqualified]! After it was accepted can it become disqualified?! (Sifra Tzav 8 [Weiss ed., 36a])[60]

What's done is done—the sacrifice was offered and valid, and a subsequent declaration to the contrary cannot change that fact. How can what is established and accepted as a sacrifice be subsequently reassigned to the category of a disqualified sacrifice? Such a reassignment is nominalist in the extreme. One might resolve this realist critique, paradoxically, by adopting a nominalist strategy. Since an accepted sacrifice cannot subsequently be disqualified, we must say that it was disqualified all along owing to an improper intention at the time of its offering. For this reason, the rabbis declare that if one intended from the outset to eat the sacrifice outside its proper time, it is disqualified. By adopting the nominalist strategy of allowing intention to determine status prior to the completion of the sacrifice, the rabbis eliminate the need for a more radical nominalist intervention: the retroactive declaration that an established status X is in fact not-X. The Sifra exposes the negotiation of realist and nominalist impulses at work in the construction of the law in m. Zev 2:2.

A different negotiation of nominalist and realist claims is explicitly marked in t. Men 5:6 and 8. The Tosefta passages parallel the mishnaic passages just cited (m. Zev 2:2 and 3:6) but contain introductory statements (boldfaced here) that reveal a conscious effort to negotiate the extent to which mental events prevail over mind-independent physical actions. Moreover, the text contains

---

[60] See also b. Zev 29a.

concluding statements (boldfaced and italics here) that confine the power of intention to the stages prior to the actual completion of the sacrifice.

t. Men 5:6 and 8.

5:6 Torah regards intention as stronger than action in cases of sacrifice and action as stronger than intention in cases of sacrifice. How is intention stronger than action in cases of sacrifice? One who slaughters a sacrifice [with the intention] to sprinkle its blood or a little of its blood outside, or to burn the entrails or an olive's bulk of its entrails outside, or to eat its meat or an olive's bulk of its meat outside, the sacrifice is invalid though there is no punishment of extirpation. *And if he actually did it, the sacrifice is not invalid.*

[If he slaughtered it with the intention] to sprinkle the blood or some of the blood the next day, to burn the entrails or an olive's bulk of its entrails the next day, or to eat its meat or an olive's bulk of its meat the next day, the sacrifice is *piggul* and he is liable for the punishment of extirpation. *And if he actually did it, the sacrifice is not piggul.*

5:8 How is action stronger than intention in cases of sacrifice? One who slaughters a sacrifice on condition that uncircumcised [priests] and unclean [priests] toss its blood, on condition that uncircumcised and unclean priests offer up its sacrificial parts, on condition that uncircumcised priests eat its flesh, it is valid. *But if he actually did it, it is invalid.*

[If he slaughtered it with the intention] to apply on the upper area blood that should be applied on the lower area, or vice versa, or to apply outside that which should be applied inside or vice versa, it is valid. *But if he actually did it, the sacrifice is invalid.*

T. Men 5:6 and 5:8 are introduced with a general rule which may be paraphrased as stating that according to Scripture sometimes intention and sometimes action determines the status of a sacrifice. T. Men 5:6, which parallels m. Zev 2:2, is an illustration of those cases in which intention determines the status. Like its mishnaic parallel, the baraita (a tannaitic teaching that does not appear in the Mishnah) holds that improper intentions regarding time and place have the power to invalidate the sacrifice.

And yet, the lines that conclude each paragraph in 5:6, lines that do not appear in the parallel mishnah, limit the power of intention in an important way. According to the concluding lines, intention determines the status of a sacrifice only *as long as the sacrifice has not been actually carried out*. Once the sacrifice has been carried out in a procedurally proper way, then despite any improper intention, it is valid. Like the Sifra, the Tosefta seeks to avoid a retroactive uprooting of a previously established validity. This is a strong realist limitation upon the law's nominalism—intention, it seems, is effective only when no fully valid mind-independent, physical action has already created a valid sacrifice.

The same structure appears in t. Men 5:8, which parallels m. Zev 3:6. This toseftan passage lists cases in which Scripture has declared that intention does not determine the status of a sacrifice. Like its mishnah parallel, the baraita holds that improper intentions regarding the priests performing the sacrifice and the application of blood do not render the sacrifice invalid. The lines that conclude each paragraph of 5:8, lines that do not appear in the parallel mishnah, provide further insight into the reason intention does not establish the status of the sacrifice in these cases. Once the sacrifice has been (improperly) carried out, it is invalid. The completed sacrifices in the ex post facto case in 5:8 are invalid because they were carried out in violation of Torah procedure. Their invalidity is based on a mind-independent violation of ritual procedure and would not be remedied even by proper intention. For that reason, action determines legal status in these cases, and intention has no effect.

T. Men 5:6 and 8 express a more strongly realist approach than is apparent in the parallel units in the Mishnah.[61] Improper thoughts cannot invalidate a sacrifice that has been actually carried out in accordance with ritual procedure. Nor can they validate a sacrifice that has been actually carried out in violation of ritual procedure. The Tosefta's negotiation of the reach of nominalism here affords less power to intention in the determination of legal status than do the parallel passages in the Mishnah.

The preceding analysis may be summarized as follows. There are cases of legal determinations in tannaitic literature that are nominalist in approach: they grant to mental activities (intentions, thoughts, etc.) the ability to determine the status of external acts and objects without recourse to mind-independent categories of pure, impure, permitted, prohibited. There are legal determinations in tannaitic literature that are realist in approach: they assume that the legal status of external acts and objects reflects mind-independent categories of pure, impure, permitted, prohibited that are not susceptible to modification as a result of human intentions. Sometimes these approaches are presented as alternatives that contest one another. Sometimes these approaches are blended in hybrid statements in which the nominalist approach is delimited and constrained by a realist approach.

(c) Legal Fictions and Contrary-to-Fact Presumptions

In a series of articles first published in the 1930s, and republished in 1967, Lon L. Fuller defined a legal fiction as "either (1) a statement propounded with a complete or partial consciousness of its falsity, or (2) a false statement recog-

---

[61] M. Zev 2:2 and 3:6 do not address the ex posto facto case, and it is possible that were they to do so, they would express the same halakhic position as the Tosefta. However, the absence of any reference to the ex post facto case results in a less clearly realist, more clearly hybrid position in the Mishnah.

nized as having utility" (9). A fiction is false, but it is not a lie, because the pretense or assumption involved in the fiction is not intended to deceive (7). Neither is the fiction an erroneous conclusion, because the author of the fiction is aware of its falsity. Thus, a fiction is an "expedient, but consciously false, assumption."[62] Legal fictions enable one to escape the consequences of an existing, specific rule of law or the implications of some unexpressed or vague principle of jurisprudence or morals (53). Fictions are also useful tools in the development and evolution of law, allowing one to assimilate and elaborate new legal phenomena within the linguistic and conceptual framework of existing law (61–62). Alterations in the law can be made while the appearance of traditionalism is preserved.[63]

Leib Moscovitz notes that legal fictions are barely attested (if at all) in any ancient legal system before the Roman period (2003, 111) and only first emerge and gain wide acceptance among the Romans and the rabbis.[64] The presence of legal fictions in all fields of talmudic law, civil and religious, is widely acknowledged and discussed by scholars of the Mishpat Ivri tradition.[65] Yitzhak Adler points to rules of comparison according to which two laws or actions, though different, are deemed by the legal authorities to be equivalent (1989, 86ff.). For example, the gemara claims that *shomea ke'oneh*—one who listens with intention to the words of another person (in a blessing or prayer) is deemed to be equivalent to one who recites the blessing or prayer himself. Samuel Atlas points out, however, that not all comparisons are legal fictions, since some are based on a shared common denominator between the entities compared (a legal analogy rather than a legal fiction). For a comparison to be a legal fiction, one entity must be regarded as if it were something else, *though in reality it is not* (Fuller's element of falsehood). For example, Hillel's prozbul (a legal stratagem explained below) involves a double legal fiction: one who makes a written declaration of having turned his debt documents over to the court is viewed as if he actually did turn them over, and if the declaration is merely oral, it is viewed as if it were written. Talmudic-rabbinic law is replete with such fictions (see the examples discussed in Atlas 1978, 228–36; but see also the caveats of Moscovitz 2003, 164n5, and 2003, 106–10). We consider but two examples of a fictive

[62] So Vaihinger as cited in Fuller 1967, 9.

[63] But see also Moscovitz (2003, 126), who points out that rabbinic fictions from the realm of ritual law are apparently not created for functionalist reasons (to make the law conform to certain desired goals or legal outcomes); rather, these fictions simply facilitate the theoretical analysis and explanation of the law.

[64] According to Moscovitz (2003, 119), typologically similar fictions in both systems "generally seem to stem from essentially the same period ... the development of similar types of fictions might be largely contemporaneous in Roman and rabbinic law."

[65] See, for example, Zuri 1939; Atlas 1978, 228–36; and Adler 1989, 86–93. Atlas takes Zuri to task for failing to differentiate between legal analogies and legal fictions, holding that the latter must contain an element of falsehood or contradiction, along the lines proposed by Fuller, whose work Atlas cites (228).

legal strategy in support of the claim that rabbinic halakhah exhibits features consistent with a nominalist legal approach.

Conversion

Conversion is by definition a legal fiction—a nominalist strategy that assigns Israelite identity to an individual who, prior to the moment of conversion, had no *naturally* grounded (no physically or biologically based) Israelite identity. This point may be seen more clearly when we contrast the nominalist rabbinic approach to the question of conversion with the realist sectarian approach.

Sectarian texts (e.g., 4QMMT, the Temple Scroll) as well as texts valued by the Qumran community (Jubilees) assert that Israelites and Gentiles are inherently and by their God-given natures distinct seeds—one holy and one profane—that cannot be intermingled. The status of seeds as holy or profane—as well as gradations of holiness within Israel so that even Israelite-priestly marriage is prohibited—is not subject to revision by humans; it is an immutable fact of a divinely determined and objective natural order, and it is the basis for the absolute ban on intermarriage across "seed-lines" and the view that conversion is simply impossible. This realist definition of Jewish identity and the attendant zeal for genealogical purity characteristic of some Second Temple and sectarian sources is based on the holy seed ideology found in the biblical book of Ezra.[66]

The approach to converts and conversion found in Ezra and related Second Temple and sectarian sources stands in sharp contrast to the rabbinic approach. For the rabbis, genealogy—actual biological filiation—is an important element in the determination of Jewish identity, but it is not the *sole* determinant and can be overruled. In other words, although the rabbis held that native descent guaranteed membership in the community of Israel, they did not view it as a sine qua non, because they recognized the power of halakhic (legal) conversion to trump biological fact. For the sectarians, an appeal to actual biological filiation trumps other considerations—a realist stance. For the rabbis, it is important but does not trump all other considerations—a highly nominalist approach.

One might object to this characterization of the difference between these two approaches as a difference between a realist and a nominalist orientation. Might it not rather reflect alternative definitions of Israelite identity? According to the Ezran/sectarian definition, an Israelite is one who meets certain immutable physical criteria of genealogical filiation; according to the rabbinic definition, an Israelite is one who meets certain minimum criteria of behavior and intention (observance of Torah norms and repudiation of idolatry). Each is realist because each makes determinations of Israelite status when the "objective facts" of the case line up with the criteria. They differ only in their ar-

---

[66] See Hayes 2002, 27–34, for details.

ticulation of the criteria—one genealogical and one behavioral. For the sectarians, no individual is an Israelite who does not *in fact* possess the objective trait of genealogical filiation. For the rabbis, no individual is an Israelite who does not *in fact* possess the objective trait of observing the Torah and repudiating idolatry.

This analysis falls short for the following reason: the rabbis did not propose an *alternative but equally realist* criterion of Israelite identity. They did not simply replace one realist criterion (the sectarian criterion of genealogical filiation that can never be achieved by a Gentile) with another realist criterion (the rabbinic criterion of Torah observance and faith in Israel's god that can be achieved by a Gentile). The rabbis, after all, *accept* the Ezran/sectarian definition of Israelite identity according to which a person born to fully Israelite parents is an Israelite, but they extend it fictively to persons who did not *in fact* meet that criterion. This is why rabbinic conversion must be understood as a legal fiction. It assimilates a new phenomenon (the Torah observant Gentile who worships the god of Israel) to an existing legal category (Israelite). It considers those who display a willingness to live as if they were born of Israelite parents as if they were genealogical Israelites though they are not.

That the rabbinic approach to conversion is best understood as a nominalist extension of a baseline realist definition of Israelite identity is evident in its hybrid character. Realist considerations are not absent from rabbinic discussions of the rights and privileges of the convert. Sometimes these realist considerations are overruled in determinations of status, but sometimes they serve to limit and constrain the nominalist impulse. Other scholars have noted that the foreign origin of the convert remains a relevant consideration in a handful of legal determinations: "The ambiguity of the convert's status is clear in rabbinic legislation. The rabbis declare that a proselyte is a Jew (Yisrael) in all respects, but this ideology cannot mask the fact that the proselyte remains in some matters at least, a non-Israelite" (Sh. J. D. Cohen 1983, 33). A few examples must suffice.

In some texts, converts are exempt from acts or obligations that are deemed to require or assume literal genealogical descent from Israel's biblical ancestors, such as liturgical declarations of the activity of one's ancestors. For example, m. Bikk 1:4–5 states that a convert born of two non-Israelites may not recite the prayer accompanying the presentation of first fruits because his foreign descent precludes him from saying truthfully, "[I have come into the land] which the Lord swore to *our fathers*, to give to us" (Deut 26:3); neither may he say, "God of our fathers" in public prayer (Sh. J. D. Cohen 1983, 33, and 1991). In this text, conversion does not render the convert equal to the native-born Jew in every respect, including genealogy. This would change, however, in post-tannaitic times. In p. Bikk 1:4, 64a we read that the recitation accompanying the offering of first fruits was opened to converts, in reliance on an alternative tannaitic teaching.

p. Bikk 1:4, 64a
It has been taught in the name of R. Yehudah: A convert himself both brings [first fruits] and recites [the required declaration from Deut 26:3].

What is the scriptural basis for this view? *"[No longer shall your name be Abram, but your name shall be Abraham;] for I have made you the father of a multitude of nations"* (Gen 17:5). In the past you were the father of Aram, but henceforward you are the father of all nations.

R. Joshua b. Levi said: The law accords with the view of R. Yehudah.

A case came before R. Abbahu and he decided it in accord with the view of R. Yehudah.

Ruling that a convert of entirely foreign origin may include himself in the promises to Israel's patriarchs and in prayers to the God of "our" fathers, R. Yehudah (a third-generation tanna) shows his notion of lineage to be statutory and nominalist, rather than realist. His view is subsequently said to be endorsed by a first-generation and a third-generation Palestinian amora. As Shaye Cohen points out (1991, 421–22), the debate between the Mishnah and the Yerushalmi is a debate over the nature of the claim to possess Jewish fathers. For the Mishnah, the claim is historical and factual, while for the Yerushalmi, the claim is metaphorical and mythic. In a similar vein, rabbinic law prohibits a convert from inheriting from his biological father because the convert is likened to a newborn child (b. Yev 62a). Thus, as regards the first fruits recitation and inheritance, conversion *is* a strong enough legal fiction to sever the convert's connection to his biological family and establish a new connection.

The negotiation of realist and nominalist approaches and the power of legal fiction to overcome genealogical fact is showcased in connection with the marriage rights of a convert. If conversion is a legal fiction according to which a Gentile is declared to be "of the seed of the house of Israel" (Ezek 44:22), one might suppose that the Gentile would be eligible for marriage into even the most genealogically restrictive echelon of Israelite society—the priesthood. The relevant texts indicate that this was a heavily negotiated question. We turn first to m. Qidd 4:1:

Ten genealogical classes came up from Babylonia: (1) priests, (2) Levites, (3) Israelites, (4) *ḥalalim* [= impaired or profaned priests], (5) converts (6) and freed slaves [= foreigners freed from servitude upon conversion],[67] (7) *mamzerim* [bastards], (8) *netinim* [foreign Temple servants] (9) hush-children, and (10) foundlings.

Priests and Levites and Israelites are permitted to intermarry.

---

[67] Hence just another class of convert. For the most part, throughout this discussion, the freed slave will be subsumed under the general term "convert."

Levites, Israelites, *halalim,* converts and freed slaves are permitted to marry among one another.

Converts, freed slaves, *mamzerim, netinim,* hush-children and found-lings are permitted to intermarry.

M. Qidd 4:1 mentions ten classes of persons with respect to marriage, comparable to Gaius's discussion in the *Institutes* of matrimony between various classes of persons (Romans, Latins, foreigners, slaves, freedmen, etc.) According to this mishnah, converts are a genealogical class distinct from priests, Levites, and lay Israelites.[68] However, while Ezra, Jubilees, and Qumran law prohibited intermarriage between Israelites and foreigners of any description (because conversion is impossible), rabbinic law permitted it in the case of a foreigner who converts (assimilates). Conversion eliminates the genealogical impediment to marriage with an Israelite.

Nevertheless, this mishnah indicates that in two respects the convert is not on a par with the lay Israelite as regards marriageability. First, although converts may intermarry with Levites and Israelites, they may not marry into the priesthood. Second, converts are permitted to intermarry with persons specifically prohibited to native-born Israelites (e.g., *mamzerim,* foreign temple slaves [*netinim*]). The retention of this Ezran disability in conjunction with the permission to intermarry with Israelites and Levites sets up a tension, if not an outright contradiction, in the marriage laws pertaining to a convert. On the one hand, rabbinic law ignores the fact of the convert's foreign origin in making its legal determination regarding marriageability to Israelites and Levites, and the legal fiction of conversion trumps the fact of foreign origin. On the other hand, the legal fiction of conversion does not take hold completely, for rabbinic law *is* cognizant of the convert's foreign origin in the cases of marriage to priests and marriage to persons prohibited to a native-born Jew. In these cases, the fiction of conversion does not trump the fact of foreign origin, with the result that marriage to a priest is prohibited and marriage to a *mamzer, natin,* and the like is permitted.

This internal legal tension, in combination with a desire fully to equate the convert with the native-born Jew,[69] may account for two later halakhic developments: the move to prohibit intermarriage between converts and persons

---

[68] As are freed slaves, but see previous note for the subsumption of the freed slave under the category of convert in this discussion. Note further that this mishnah makes no distinction on the basis of gender.

[69] Discomfort over the legal disadvantages suffered by a convert as compared to a native-born Israelite is voiced already in tannaitic texts. For example, in m. Sot 7:11(8) the people declare concerning Agrippa that despite his foreign descent he is accounted their brother and is entitled to the rights and privileges of a native-born Jew. The historicity of this incident is not important—what it tells us about its rabbinic author's attitude toward converts is. But note t. Sot 7:15, p. Sot 7:7, 22a, and b. Sot 41b, all of which dismiss the people's response as mere flattery! Clearly, there were widely divergent views on this question.

prohibited from marrying native-born Jews, and the move to permit intermarriage between converts (or their descendants) and priests (for details, see Hayes
2002, 168–84).

Post-tannaitic texts do much to overcome the claims of genealogy and the
blemish of foreign descent in various areas of law (for details, see Hayes 2002,
184–91), though steps in this nominalist direction were taken earlier in Palestine than in Babylonia.[70]

Presumptions of Menstrual Im/purity

Closely related to legal fiction is the legal presumption. A legal presumption
draws upon available facts and evidence to reach a conclusion regarding facts
for which there is no proof. Legal presumptions are held to be valid until rebutted
by contrary evidence. Both Roman law and rabbinic law employ presumptions
when a conclusion about facts is needed but proof of the facts is absent (Franklin 2001, 6–9). As an illustration we need look no further than rabbinic discussion of the laws of menstrual impurity, where cases of doubt are resolved through
the adoption of one or another legal presumption.

M. Nid 1:1 contains a dispute over the presumption that should apply when
a woman discovers a flow of menstrual blood. Should the woman's impurity be
reckoned from the moment the flow is discovered or should it be retroactive to
the time of the last self-examination in which no blood was found?

> Shammai ruled: for all women it is sufficient [to reckon] their [impure
> status from the] time [of the discovery of the flow].
>
> Hillel ruled: from [the last] examination [in which no blood was
> found] to the examination [in which the flow of blood was discovered]
> even [if the interval between them] was many days.
>
> But the sages ruled: the law does not agree with the view of the former
> or with that of the latter, but [a woman in this situation is presumed to be
> impure] for [the preceding] 24 hours when this is less than the interval
> from the [last] examination, and the interval from the [last] examination
> to the examination [in which the blood was discovered] when this is less
> than 24 hours. For any woman who has a regular period, it is sufficient
> [for her to reckon her impure status from the] time of the discovery of
> the flow.

Fuller notes that a legal presumption may be viewed as a special type of legal
fiction if it attributes to facts an artificial effect beyond their natural tendency
to produce belief. When a legal presumption knowingly gives an insufficient

---

[70] As Richard Kalmin (1999, 46–48) has shown, it is not until the mid-fourth century that Babylonian sages, perhaps increasingly aware of or susceptible to Palestinian teachings on the matter, voice
criticism of the preservation of hierarchical distinctions based solely on genealogy. For the reception
of Palestinian teachings in Babylonia, especially from the mid-fourth century CE, see Kalmin 1999,
90–94, and Dor 1971. The latter argues for a Palestinian influence on the "school" of Rava.

proof the value of a sufficient one, it is a fiction (1967, 40). M. Nid 1:1 uses precisely this language of "sufficiency": a clear signal that the legal presumptions proposed knowingly give an insufficient proof the value of a sufficient proof. Thus, Shammai holds that the observation of blood at time X is to be considered sufficient proof of no menstrual impurity prior to time X, even though the observation of a phenomenon at one time is actually insufficient proof of the absence of that phenomenon at an earlier time. Hillel's presumption is the inverse of Shammai's: Hillel holds that the observation of blood at time X is to be considered sufficient proof of menstrual impurity from the last known time of purity (the last examination), even though the observation of a phenomenon at one time is insufficient proof of the presence of that phenomenon at an earlier time. For their part, the sages effect a compromise, allowing the observation of blood at time X to be considered sufficient proof of menstrual impurity for a limited period of time that does not exceed twenty-four hours prior to the observation of the blood. This presumption also treats insufficient evidence as sufficient for determining a legal status, because the observation of a phenomenon at one time is insufficient proof of the presence of that phenomenon for even a limited period of time prior to the observation.

A legal presumption of pure status despite the possibility that a woman may in fact be menstruating is tolerated in m. Nid 2:4:

> All women are presumed to be ritually pure for [the purpose of sexual intercourse with] their husbands;
>   those that return home from a journey—their wives are presumed to be ritually pure for [the purpose of sexual intercourse with] them.

According to this mishnah, it is not necessary for a woman to examine herself to be certain of her status before having sexual intercourse with her husband. She may presume herself to continue in a previously established state of ritual purity, despite the fact that self-examination is not difficult and despite the fact that there will surely be a statistically significant number of cases in which the physiological indicators of menstruation will be present and the presumption incorrect. Related rabbinic texts suggest that the motivation for adopting lenient presumptions like this one in cases of menstrual impurity is connected with the value placed upon marital intimacy and the positive commandment of sexual reproduction (b. Yev 62b; b. BM 84b; b. Nid 31b). The rabbinic approach in these cases is typical of a nominalist orientation in which objective facts—especially when those facts are uncertain—are not consistently privileged in the determination of the law. Other considerations and values are allowed to trump objective facts, all the more so when these facts are only likely but not certain.

Presumptions are unavoidable in law because it is often the case that conclusions about facts must be reached in the absence of clear evidence, in order to resolve a dispute or determine a legal status. For this reason, *both legal realists and legal nominalists trade in legal presumptions.* However, a realist will tend to formulate and favor presumptions that have a reasonable chance of according with the (unknown) facts. A nominalist will be less constrained in this regard and will be relatively more willing to adopt presumptions that have little chance of according with the (unknown) facts. The rabbis' willingness to adopt presumptions that have little chance of according with physiological facts reflects a nominalistic orientation. We see this in the tannaitic laws of bloodstains. M. Nid 7:4 and 8:1 contain presumptions about bloodstains that are entirely reasonable—those found in rooms or places of impurity are presumed to be impure, while others are not; those found on the flesh near the genital area, on the heel, big toe, or inner side of the thigh or feet, are presumed to be impure, while those that are not near the genital area or are on the outer side of the thigh or feet, are presumed to be pure. However, m. Nid 8:2 presents a number of presumptions that are somewhat less reasonable, including some that strain credulity altogether.[71]

> [A woman] may attribute [a bloodstain] to any cause to which she can possibly attribute it.
>
> If [for example] she had slain a domestic or wild animal or a bird, if she was handling bloodstains or sat beside those who handled them, or if she killed a louse, she may attribute the bloodstain to them—
>
> how large a stain may be attributed to a louse? R. Hanina b. Antigonus replied: up to the size of a split bean—
>
> and [it may be attributed to a louse] even though she herself didn't kill it.
>
> She may also attribute it to her son or to her husband.
>
> If she herself had a wound that could open again and bleed, she may attribute it to that.

The opening line of this mishnah betrays a nominalistic disregard for mind-independent facts. A woman may presume about a bloodstain of unknown origin that it is not menstrual blood if she is able to attribute it to some other source, even if remote, such as a louse killed by another person. In an aside, however, this nominalistic strategy is subjected to some limitation—only a bloodstain of very small size may be attributed to a louse. The realist impulse behind this qualification is clear: to attribute a very large blood stain to a tiny louse is simply too great a fiction. The result is a hybrid discourse: on the one hand, a nominalist presumption that affords little deference to what is physically or objectively likely is accepted; on the other hand, the presumption's reach is limited in response to a realist deference to what is physically or objec-

---

[71] See the insightful and detailed discussion of m. Nid 8:2–3 in Halberstam 2010, 33–41. According to Halberstam, in these passages "[f]ormalism displaces the detection of objective reality, and the law's authority over truth triumphs" (11).

tively likely. The same hybrid discourse is apparent in t. Nid 6:17, which remarks in reference to the teaching that a woman may attribute a bloodstain to any cause to which she can possibly attribute it:

[If] she was handling red items, she cannot attribute [to them] a stain which is black;
[If] she was handling a small quantity of blood, she cannot attribute [to it a stain] which is of large quantity.

A realist discomfort over the designation of bloodstains as nonmenstrual in disregard of the most reasonable interpretation of the facts is thematized in the famous story that appears in the continuation of m. Nid 8:3(2).

A woman once came to R. Akiva and said to him, "I have observed a bloodstain."
He said to her, "Did you perhaps have a wound?"
She said, "Yes, but it has scabbed over."
He said to her, "Is it possible that it opened again and bled?"
She said, "Yes" and R. Akiva declared her pure.
When he saw that his disciples looked at one another in astonishment he said, "why do you find this difficult, since the sages did not lay down the rule in order to be stringent but in order to be lenient, for Scripture says, 'If a woman has a flow and her flow in her flesh be blood' (Lev 15:19)—only blood, but not a bloodstain."

The situation described is a situation of *doubt*. The status of the bloodstain as menstrual or nonmenstrual in origin cannot be determined as a matter of *fact*, and thus a legal presumption is required. R. Akiva adopts the presumption that the blood is nonmenstrual based on a far-fetched attribution that strains credulity. That the reader is to understand that R. Akiva's presumption is a rather far-fetched ruse is explicitly encoded in the mishnah: R. Akiva's own disciples are astonished by his presumption, and R. Akiva himself acknowledges that it is "difficult." In his defense, R. Akiva offers a Scriptural justification for the policy of adopting lenient presumptions in cases involving bloodstains, rather than fresh blood. According to Scripture, only fresh menstrual blood conveys impurity; the extension of impurity to bloodstains is a rabbinic innovation, and while doubtful cases of Scriptural law are decided stringently, doubtful cases of rabbinic law are to be decided leniently.

A couple of remarks are in order. As noted earlier, the distinction between Scriptural law and rabbinic law is not equivalent to a distinction between divine law and human positive law. R. Akiva has not "converted" the law of bloodstains into human positive law in order to eliminate an expectation that the law accord with "truth"—or, in this case, the most likely physiological facts. Scriptural and rabbinic law both fall under the umbrella of divine law, though they operate according to slightly different rules, rules that in this case allow R. Akiva to choose a lenient option on account of the doubt. But while this Scriptural justification assures us of R. Akiva's *authority* to endorse a far-fetched legal presumption, it in no way changes the *nature* of the presumption itself. It remains the case that R. Akiva's articulation of what is fundamentally an element within Israel's *divine law* shows a nominalist disregard for the most factually likely scenario. It is not simply that his presumption is factually unsupported; it is in all likelihood *contrary to fact*.

What is particularly remarkable about the passage in m. Nid 8:2 is its rhetoric of disclosure. The "amazed disciples" serve as a literary device by means of which the author of the text underscores and champions the highly fictive and (probably) counterfactual nature of R. Akiva's legal presumption. The ability and the desire to depict realist incredulity at nonrealist rabbinic strategies signals a high degree of self-awareness on the part of our rabbinic authors. Harnessing the gaze of the other, the rabbis communicate their awareness of a different perspective and underscore the fact that their nominalist strategies are chosen in conscious opposition to alternative strategies of a more realist bent. We turn now to a fuller treatment of evidence for the claim that rabbinic nominalism is highly self-conscious.

THE GAZE OF THE OTHER

Rabbinic nominalism is a self-aware choice. As evidence for this assertion we may adduce sources that explicitly present and grapple with a relatively more realist alternative to the nominalist position that is ultimately endorsed or adopted. These sources vary tremendously, however, in their *treatment* of the more realist view. In some cases, the realist position is delegitimized and the nominalist position is asserted. The delegitimation of the realist view is generally achieved by its displacement onto an "outsider"—usually a Sadducee or *min* (heretic)—whose attitude toward the more nominalist "insider" (Pharisaic-rabbinic) view is derisive and dismissive.[72] In such cases, little or no accommodation is made to the mocking outsider's perspective, and the nominalist position is affirmed despite the ridicule it inspires. In other cases, the realist position is not entirely delegitimized. This is generally achieved by a partial displacement onto a somewhat marginal insider—for example, anonymous "western rabbis" (who serve this function only in the Babylonian Talmud). The attitude of these anonymous "westerners" toward the normative nominalist position is also derisive and dismissive. However, because these mockers are not outside the Pharisaic-rabbinic estate but inside it, some accommodation may be made

---

[72] See Schwartz 2008, 138, for a similar claim: in rabbinic depictions of controversies between Pharisees and Sadducees (and other opponents), laws that are counterintuitive and illogical bother the Sadducees and other non-Pharisees, but not the Pharisees. Schwartz considers some of the texts to be discussed in section (i) (a) below.

to their perspective: the nominalist position to which they object may be modified or constrained in response to the ridicule it has inspired. Finally, in some cases the realist position is legitimized. Legitimation occurs when the text "owns" the realist position as a fully rabbinic alternative that expresses incredulity at the nominalist position. In such cases, the realist view will be fully accommodated; the nominalist position that inspired ridicule will be obviated, annulled, transformed, or interpreted away.

Sources in which a realist perspective is fully or partially delegitimized and rabbinic nominalism is fully or partially upheld may be said to engage in a *rhetoric of disclosure*. By juxtaposing the two perspectives and maintaining the nominalist approach even if only partially, these sources consciously disclose the extent to which the rabbinic conception of divine law tolerates a nominalist orientation. Sources in which the realist perspective is fully accommodated and rabbinic nominalism is dismantled engage in a *rhetoric of concealment*. By erasing the nominalist alternative, these sources attempt to conceal the extent to which the rabbinic conception of divine law tolerates a nominalist orientation. Both are evidence of a high degree of self-consciousness of the tension between realist and nominalist approaches to the divine law on the part of their rabbinic authors. And both are motivated by a rabbinic awareness that a nominalist legal orientation has a tendency to inspire resistance and even ridicule among its opponents when its results are patently counterfactual, unempirical, or absurd.

Rabbinic Self-Awareness: The Motif of Mockery

The literary motif of mockery provides a window onto the self-awareness of a text's author(s) precisely because the depiction of mockery requires authors to inhabit the mind-set of their opponents, to view themselves as they are viewed by others. The ability to identify within oneself the ideas and assumptions that others find objectionable or laughable requires an awareness of one's own ideas and assumptions, as well as a conscious consideration and rejection of alternative ideas and assumptions.

As noted in chapter 3, Maren Niehoff has traced the existence of competing views on the nature of Scripture by focusing on the literary motif of mockery in the writings of Philo. For Philo, the identification of the Mosaic Law with the divine law of classical, and particularly Stoic, tradition entailed its rational and philosophical *truth*, its verisimilitude, its noncontradiction, and its immunity to historical development. For others, the Bible did not convey rational and philosophical truth, was not marked by verisimilitude or noncontradiction, and was best understood in literary terms as possessing the traits of myth, drama, or history. Philo presents himself as the object of ridicule by opponents who dismiss his truth claims on behalf of the Bible, and in turn his writings contain abusive and mocking invective against these anonymous opponents. Philo's derisive characterization of his opponents' views provides Niehoff with an opportunity not only to reconstruct those views but also to gauge the extent to which Philo's own views were self-consciously adopted. Similarly, in 4 Maccabees, the mocking tyrant Antiochus gives voice to the view that the law of the Judeans lacks the standard attributes of divine law (see chapter 3). Most notably, it is not rational, true, or in harmony with nature. The author's ability to assign these views to Antiochus indicates his awareness of them.

Likewise, the literary motif of mockery in rabbinic sources can serve as an index of rabbinic awareness of different views on the nature of divine law and its relationship with "truth." By means of the "mocking other," rabbinic authors/redactors were able to voice and grapple with reservations about their nominalist tendencies. Thus, despite an overall nominalist orientation, rabbinic texts incorporate (self-)critiques of nominalism and its attendant legal strategies, especially the lack of verisimilitude, the elevation of intention over action, the use of legal fictions, and contrary-to-fact presumptions and rulings.

To be sure, the dynamic of the mockery depicted in rabbinic sources will be the mirror image of that depicted in Philo. Philo mocks those who *reject* his truth claims about the divine law; rabbinic sources tend to depict themselves as mocked by those who *assert* truth claims about the divine law. While I am not suggesting that Philo and the rabbis, separated in both time and space, were speaking to *one another*, I am suggesting that Philo and the rabbis imagined themselves to be speaking to *just such an other*: Philo asserted and his opponents rejected certain truth claims about the divine Mosaic Law; the rabbis rejected and their opponents asserted very similar truth claims about the Torah. The realist Philo mocks his nonrealist opponents; the nominalist rabbis are mocked by their realist opponents—a mirror image. Or, to borrow a term proposed in a recent essay by Shaye Cohen (2013) these texts are antipodal: "One is North to the other's South, Up to the other's Down, Yin to the other's Yang."[73]

We may conclude that the debate over the "truth" of divine law was a live debate in the Hellenistic east of antiquity as Scripture-based communities grappled with the dueling conceptions of divine law provided by biblical and Greco-Roman tradition. In Philo, we have a representative of the "truth" camp, and in rabbinic literature we find a healthy (but not exclusive) representation of the alternative position. The motif of mockery in both literatures indicates that each was aware of the existence of the other position.

(I) A RHETORIC OF DISCLOSURE

(a) Mocking Outsiders—Delegitimizing Realism by Attribution to Sadducees and Heretics

Sadducees are often depicted as objecting to rabbinic laws and teachings that lack verisimilitude or run counter to "objective" reality (by their standards). The reaction of these Sadducees ranges from incredulity to impatience to mockery,

---

[73] We return to this essay below.

and is represented as the primary reason for their rejection of the Pharisaic-rabbinic elaboration of the divine law in toto.

Elsewhere I have argued that in light of Schwartz's evidence for a realist orientation in sectarian circles in the late Second Temple period, the rabbinic depictions of mocking realists may be based on a historical memory of persons who objected to, ridiculed, and/or rejected halakhot or legal determinations that, in their view, lacked verisimilitude (Hayes 2011, 119 and passim). These internal others are often described as heretics or Sadducees.[74] This historically grounded portrait was subjected to further literary embellishment so that heretics and Sadducees became the ultimate scoffers.[75] In the rabbinic *imaginaire*, the sectarian's/heretic's repudiation of individual laws as absurd became a repudiation of the law in general, the authority of those who expound the law (the rabbis themselves), and ultimately the Scriptures from which they derived their authority.

The terms *tsadoqi* (Sadducee), *min*,[76] and to a lesser degree *apiqoros* (from "Epicurean") are not entirely interchangeable. Genuine occurrences of *tsadoqi* (i.e., correcting for censorial substitutions for *min*) tend to feature individuals who reject a Pharisaic (or rabbinic) practice or legal ruling, while genuine occurrences of *min* (i.e., prior to the deletions and substitutions of the censors) tend to feature individuals who additionally reject rabbinic exegesis and engage in heated theological and Scriptural debate.[77] Nevertheless, the *min* and the *tsadoqi* share an important characteristic with one another (and with the *apiqoros*) that has generally been overlooked. All three of these "internal others" consider and subsequently reject rabbinic teachings (both laws and exegeses) that, in the view of the "outsider," lack verisimilitude, are illogical, unempirical, or counterfactual.

M. Yad 4:14(6–8) features Sadduceean incredulity in the face of Pharisaic rulings that appear to be illogical or counterfactual. The text describes two disputes between Sadducees and Pharisees, including a dispute over the purity

---

[74] Not always. Below, we discuss realists within the rabbinic estate. But as we shall see, the realist claims of insiders generally gain more traction than do the realist claims of outsiders.

[75] The features I isolated in my previous study (2011)—skeptical or scoffing dismissal of rabbinic law, exegesis, and authority, leading to antinomianism of one degree or another—can be found in sources of diverse provenance. Preliminary study suggests only minor differences across time and space, and I hope to return to a more nuanced portrait at a later time.

[76] *Minim* are heretics of various sorts, not Christians. For an initial bibliography on heretics, see Kalmin 1994; Lachs 1970; Janowitz 1998; and Labendz 2003.

[77] The distinction is not a clean one. The legal disputes between Sadducees and Pharisees are often said to turn on competing interpretations of Scripture. Nevertheless, the primary tension between Sadducees and Pharisees lies in the former's articulation of an alternative halakhah. For a survey of scholarship on the Sadduceean-Pharisaic disputes, see Richardson, Westerholm, et al. 1991, chaps. 7 and 8. By contrast, *minim* are depicted as hostile to the entire project of Scriptural interpretation as conducted by the rabbis, and to Scripture itself.

status of Scriptures and a dispute over the *nitzoq* (the uninterrupted stream formed when one is pouring liquid from an upper vessel into a lower vessel).

> The Sadducees say: We complain against you, you Pharisees, because you say that the Holy Writings defile the hands, but the books of Homer do not defile the hands.
>
> R. Yohanan b. Zakkai retorted: Have we nothing against the Pharisees but this? Behold, they say that the bones of an ass are ritually pure yet the bones of Yohanan the high priest are impure!
>
> They said to him: Their impurity is proportional to their love for them so that nobody should make spoons out of the bones of his father or mother.
>
> He said to them: So also the Holy Writings. Their impurity is proportional to their love for them. The books of Homer which are not precious do not defile the hands.
>
> The Sadducees say: We complain against you, you Pharisees, that you declare an uninterrupted flow of a liquid to be pure.

The rabbinic elaboration of this dispute counterposes a realist approach (the Sadducean approach) that views impurity as a mind-independent quality of objects with a pragmatic nominalism that views impurity as a quality ascribed to objects for a utilitarian purpose. In the first case, the Sadducees are said to react negatively to the Pharisaic ascription of impurity to Scriptures, viewing it as an insult that the Holy Writ is deemed impure while pagan literature is not. R. Yohanan b. Zakkai, a Pharisee, pretends to go along with the Sadducceean objection so that the latter might be convicted out of their own mouths. He carries the Sadducean objection a step further: Not only, he asserts, do the Pharisees insult Scripture by saying that it defiles the hands, but they insult God's own high priest, Yohanan , by saying that his bones defile while those of an ass are pure. R. Yohanan ben Zakkai knows that the Sadducees accept the ascription of ritual impurity to human corpses and bones, and hopes to elicit from them a defense of the view. His ruse succeeds. The impurity of human bones, the Sadducees respond, is a pragmatic ruling to ensure that they are not handled disrespectfully. The ruling is thus not an insult, but an indicator of the preciousness of human remains. At this point R. Yohanan b. Zakkai removes his Sadduceean mask: by the same token, he retorts, the ascription of impurity to Scripture is an indicator of its preciousness, a pragmatic measure to ensure it is not much handled.

The rabbinic author of this staged dialogue depicts the Sadducees in a poor light (naturally enough). They rather obtusely object to the ascription of impurity to Scripture as insulting, suggesting that they take the ascription to be the designation of an actual or mind-independent status rather than the legal fiction it is. Their objection is that of a knee-jerk realist—if Scripture is not essentially and mind-independently impure, how can the Pharisees simply declare it to be so? The author of our text has the Pharisaic hero of the story teach his Sadduceean opponents a lesson in nominalism: don't pretend, he counters, that you are such hard-and-fast realists! You yourselves have engaged in the nominalist practice of ascribing a status to something for purely pragmatic purposes. Thus, the Sadducees are depicted not only as obtuse and literal-minded, but also hypocritical in their insistence on a realist standard.

The second case in our passage is not elaborated. The Sadducees object to the Pharisaic view that the uninterrupted stream of liquid (the *nitzoq*) connecting the bodies of water in an upper and lower vessel is ritually pure.[78] Presumably the situation imagined is one in which the liquid in the lower vessel is impure, as there would be no question of the impurity of the *nitzoq* were the liquid in the upper vessel impure. While an argument from silence is weak, we may suppose that the Sadducees object to the Pharisees' position because it ignores the very real physical connection between the two liquids, asserting instead that they are not deemed to form a single body of liquid with a single status of impurity. If so, then we have two instances in which Sadducees are depicted as adopting a realist stance and objecting to the nominalist view of the Pharisees because it is illogical (how can Scripture be both holy and impure when these are incompatible statuses?) or out of step with objective reality (anyone can see that the liquids join to form a single body!).[79]

Pharisaic practices of a (legal) fictive nature are said to expose the Pharisees to criticism, and even ridicule, by *minim* and Sadducees. Thus, a legal dodge that creates an appearance of propriety in preparing the ashes of the red heifer prompts R. Yosi to admonish his fellows this way: "Don't give the *minim*[80] occasion to find fault (*leraddot*)! Rather ... [do the act directly]" and do not rely on a dodge (m. Par 3:3).[81] A similar admonition is attributed to R. Akiva in t. Par 3:3 in reference to a ruse employed to draw the water for mixing the ashes. The rabbinic authors of these passages hint that stratagems that create an appearance but not a reality of propriety make the Pharisees vulnerable to the criticism and ridicule of their opponents.

The *eruv* provides another example. The *eruv* is a legal strategy by which the rabbis nominally declare objectively distinct domains to be a single domain, in

---

[78] Some see a parallel to the Sadduceean position in 4QMMT B57–58, which states that a liquid stream does not separate impure from pure liquids, because the liquids form a single stream. Schwartz (1992) understands 4QMMT to assert a realist position. For other hypotheses, see Elman 1996.

[79] To be sure, this reasoning is plausible but not explicit.

[80] MSS Kaufman, Parma, and a marginal insertion in Parma deRossi 138 read *minim*, as do the manuscripts of the parallel t. Par 3:3; compare b. Zev 21a, where "Sadducees" object to a purity issue related to the red heifer.

[81] The entire text reads: "A male from among the sheep was brought and a rope tied between its horns, and a stick or bushy twig was tied to the other end of the rope. This was thrown into the jar. The male sheep was then hit so that it started backwards, and he would take the ashes and mix as much of it as would be visible on the water. R. Yosi said: Don't give the *minim* an occasion to find fault (*leraddot*)! Rather he himself should take it and mix it."

order to dodge certain Sabbath restrictions. Thus, m. Eruv 6:2 and related texts (p. Eruv 1:1; 18c, p. Eruv 7:11, 24d; and b. Eruv 61b) discuss the fictive conversion of an alleyway into a single domain for the purposes of carrying on the Sabbath. Rabban Gamliel notes that a Sadducee lived in the same alleyway as his family in Jerusalem and refused to participate in the *eruv*, thus prohibiting the alleyway for the other residents. In the give-and-take of Talmudic argument, Sadducees are suspected of deliberately violating the law of carrying in the courtyard in p. Eruv 1:1, 18c. Here again, Sadducees are assumed to have little patience for Pharisaic-rabbinic determinations of legal status that do not reflect plain facts. As a consequence, it seems, the Sadducee simply does not observe the law.

These texts evince a high degree of self-awareness—the rabbinic authors of these passages are aware that the position they endorse (the Pharisaic position) is viewed as absurd by others, and they attribute that view to *minim* and Sadducees. No concession is made to the alternative position on its merits, even if steps are taken to try to avoid continued ridicule.

This analysis receives confirmation from a nonrabbinic source—the Gospel of Mark. In Mark 7:1–23, the Pharisees and scribes ask Jesus why he and his disciples do not follow tradition and wash their hands before eating. In his response, Jesus rebukes the Pharisees for *abandoning divine law in order to follow human law*. He summarizes Isaiah 29:13 as follows, "Abandoning the commandment of God, you keep the tradition of human beings,"[82] and then attacks: "How well you nullify the commandment of God, in order that you may preserve your tradition!" (7:8–9). He goes on to provide an example in illustration of this charge:

> For Moses said, '*Honor your father and your mother,*' and '*whoever reviles father or mother shall die.*' But you say 'if a man says to his father or mother: whatever of mine may benefit you is *korban,*' which means gift [to the sanctuary—CH]—you no longer allow him to do anything for his father or mother, making void the word of God by means of your tradition which you have handed on. And you do many similar such things. (7:10–13)

Jesus points to a legal ruse that exploits the rules regarding votive offerings to the sanctuary in order to avoid supporting parents without technically violating the fifth commandment to honor father and mother.[83]

This passage, which will be explored from other angles in chapters 6 and 7, is fascinating confirmation of several of the claims advanced here. First, the Greco-Roman dichotomy between divine law and human law is explicit in Mark 7, indicating that it was common currency in Jewish Palestine already in

---

[82] Following the translation of Collins 2007.

[83] The details of this procedure are explained in Collins 2007, 351–53, relying on the excellent study of Benovitz 1998.

the first century. Second, while the Pharisees believed that their legal traditions were elaborations of the revealed divine law, Jesus is represented as regarding their traditions as mere human law, and insofar as they are in opposition to divine law, they are *illegitimate*. Adela Yarbro Collins (2007) contrasts the view attributed to Jesus with that of rabbinic Judaism as found in Mishnah tractate Avot (The Fathers): "Whereas the mishnaic tractate 'The Fathers' assumes identity, or at least strong continuity, between the Law given on Sinai and the tradition of the elders, the Markan Jesus drives a wedge between the two by equating Isaiah's 'commandments of human beings' with 'the tradition of the elders.' "[84] Third, what marks this particular practice as illegitimate is its "fictive" character—it is a legal trick that creates an appearance of filial piety where in fact there is none. Jesus mocks and derides the Pharisees on two counts: the fictive nature of a practice that enables them to maintain an appearance of propriety while committing a grave misdeed, and their elevation of a purely human legal device over a divine commandment.

In a recent study, Shaye Cohen (2013) compares the rival truth claims of Mark 7 and a passage of the Talmud (b. Eruv 21–22) on the question of whether human authority ("tradition") can supplement or supplant the divine law. He concludes that the two texts are antipodal—"the truth claims of B. Eruvin 21–22 line up neatly with the truth claims of Mark 7:1–23 except that the one affirms and glorifies what the other denies and besmirches." We may extend the designation "antipodal" to the cases examined above: in these rabbinic texts, Pharisaic-rabbinic "heroes" resist the mockery of *minim* and Sadducees for upholding nominalist (i.e., mind-dependent and therefore human) strategies that rely on fictions and ruses; in Mark 7, Jesus (the hero of the Gospels) mocks and denigrates those who adopt these fictive "human" strategies over or against divine commandments. In each, there is mocker and mocked but he who is valorized in one text is denigrated in the other, and vice versa.

(b) Mocking Insiders and the Partial Accommodation of Realism: "In the west they laughed at it"

The incredulity and ridicule featured in rabbinic representations of Sadducees reappear in a small number of texts in the Babylonian Talmud, in which "western rabbis" are said to mock a teaching or a ruling. In these cases of only partial displacement (the mockers are rabbis, but distant and anonymous), a slight adjustment is made to the teaching or ruling as a result of the realist critique.

The Babylonian Talmud contains eleven occurrences of the phrase "In the west [i.e., in the Land of Israel], they laughed at him" (במערבא מחכו עלה).[85] The phrase does not appear in any other classical rabbinic source: not in the Mishnah,

---

[84] Collins cites Fraade 2004, which reviews other rabbinic texts that argue that the teaching of the elders is equivalent to the teaching of God. See, further, Sh. J. D. Cohen 2013, 14–15.

[85] Variant spelling: במערבא עליה מחכו. The passages are b. Bets 14a, b. BB 16b and 102b, b. San 17b and 109a, b. Shevu 26a and 34b, b. Yev 88a, b. Naz 42a, b. Zev 15a, b. Ker 4a.

the Tosefta, halakhic or aggadic midrash, or the Yerushalmi.[86] In eight of the eleven cases, the term is employed as part of the dialectical give-and-take of the sugya and introduces a criticism marked by ridicule or incredulity.[87] The criticism is generally realist in orientation and takes aim at a ruling or teaching that bears one of the characteristic features of a nominalist orientation toward the law. And in each case, a concession—usually slight—is made in response to the realist critique.[88]

Our first three examples take aim at a nominalist approach that relies on mental events or intention when determining legal culpability or legal status. According to the sugya in b. Ker 4a, the realist position advanced as a critique by the western mockers maintains that for a person to incur multiple counts of liability for the consumption of prohibited foods, the violations must be distinct from one another *in fact*, not just *in name*. Thus, although eating a single prohibited food on two separate occasions incurs two counts of liability, designating the food eaten in a single act of eating as two distinct pieces or kinds of forbidden food does not convert that single act into multiple transgressions. To assert multiple counts of liability requires actions objectively distinguished from one another in time or space and not merely in name (*shte shemot* or "two names" do not create two distinct liabilities). In response to this realist critique, a baraita that assigned two counts of liability for a single act in which two pieces of forbidden fat were consumed is reinterpreted by an early Palestinian amora:

> [The baraita] deals with one who ate two portions of forbidden fat in *two different dishes*, and is in accordance with R. Joshua, who holds that the [physical] separation of dishes effects a division with regard to offerings.

[86] The phrase occurs twice in Yalqut Shimoni, but these are parallels to two of the occurrences in the Bavli.

[87] The two aggadic occurrences of the phrase (b. BB 16b and b. San 109a) are not directly relevant to our discussion of realist vs. nominalist approaches to the law. The eleventh occurrence, found at b. San 17b, appears within a long list of rules for decoding the personal identities of impersonal subjects used in the Talmud. Two explanations are provided for the term "they" in the phrase "In the west, they laughed at him": R. Eleazar or R. Yosi son of R. Ḥanina. If we subtract this passage and the two aggadic passages, we are left with eight dialectical uses of the phrase. The eight cases of interest to us here are distinct from other references to laughter in the Babylonian Talmud, of which there are about two dozen. Most of these other references occur in narrative contexts and report the joyful or derisive laughter of a character in the course of a story; they are therefore irrelevant for this discussion of mockery in a dialectical context. A few are employed in a halakhic context but are associated with a specific motif—the great man who says something that seems at first blush to be trivial, ill-informed, or mistaken. Others laugh but are immediately rebuked: when a great man speaks, there is usually something to what he says, and one should not laugh. And indeed, the wisdom of the speaker is then revealed (see, for example, b. Ber 19b, b. Nid 50b).

[88] For a full discussion of all occurrences of this motif, see Hayes 2013. Here I provide only a very brief summary.

Nominal multiplicity (a multiplicity in name only) does not establish multiple liability. The baraita must therefore refer to a case of *actual* multiplicity, in which the forbidden foods were in *physically* distinct dishes.

Similarly, in b. Shevu 26a, a baraita distinguishes an oath in which one is unaware of the object of the oath and an oath in which one is unaware of the oath itself. This pseudodistinction evokes the ridicule of westerners ("In the west, they laughed at this"). Unawareness of an oath and unawareness of the object of an oath are not *in fact* two distinct things—only in name. If one is unaware of the object of one's oath, one is *automatically* unaware of the oath itself! In the final step, R. Eleazar is persuaded by the force of the realist attack and declares that the two are in fact one and the same thing.

A third example occurs in b. Zev 15a. We have already seen that Mishnah tractate Zevaḥim is a rich quarry for those seeking evidence of a nominalist approach in halakhah because of its focus on the role of intention in creating legal "facts." The first chapter of the tractate deals with the validity or invalidity of sacrifices offered under an incorrect designation or accompanied by an improper intention, and m. Zev 1:4 lists the points in the sacrificial process at which an illegitimate intention can cause disqualification, one of which is subject to a dispute: the time during which the blood is carried or conveyed by the priest to the altar. R. Simeon does not include carrying among the points in the sacrificial process at which disqualification can occur because carriage is not an essential part of the sacrificial process; sometimes the animal is slaughtered so close to the altar that the blood is sprinkled as soon as it is received, without an intervening act of carriage to the altar. In the gemara, an anonymous statement (memra) attributes the dispute between R. Shimon and the sages to different conceptions of "carriage." According to the memra, R. Simeon understands the term *holakhah* ("carriage") to involve actual movement of the feet, based upon the root *h/y.l.k* meaning "to walk"—a view that is consistent with a realist orientation. The rabbis, however, understand carrying (*holakhah*) as conveyance of the blood by whatever means, and, consistent with a nominalist approach, carrying may be deemed to have occurred even if no actual walking or conveyance has occurred. The memra's explanation of the dispute between R. Shimon and the sages provokes ridicule in the west ("In the west, they laughed at it"). The derision of the western mockers is explained by two late amoraim as follows:

> When R. Papa and R. Huna the son of R. Joshua[89] came from the academy they said: This was the point of their derision. Do they [R. Simeon and the rabbis] not differ about a long carrying [i.e., a carrying with actual movement of the feet]?[90] Surely, they differ over a long carrying, and

[89] Vatican 118: R. Huna the son of Rav.

[90] This distinction between a carrying in which there is actual movement of the feet and one in which there is not (= a long and a short carrying) is made explicit in an earlier step in the sugya.

as for a short carrying [in which no real walking occurred] everyone agrees that it does not invalidate.[91] They differ over a long carrying.

According to these two late Babylonian amoraim, no one could possibly apply the label "carrying" to an action in which no actual movement of the feet, no actually carrying, occurs. The original memra was mocked, therefore, because it assigned just such a nominalist understanding of carrying *to the rabbis*, and it is preposterous to suppose that anyone would consider conveyance (*holakhah*) in which no *real* walking occurs to constitute carrying.

The derision of the western mockers initiates a process that eliminates the rabbis' nominalist understanding of carrying. The irony is that this sugya occurs within a much larger nominalist discussion of the power of intentional states to determine the validity of a sacrifice, a discussion that is largely undisturbed. Thus, the realist reformulation of the rabbis' definition of carrying is a small victory establishing a tiny realist island in what is otherwise a sea of nominalism.

In three further examples, western mockers express realist objections to a legal fiction based on an imputed intention. A sugya on b. BQ 102b considers a tannaitic dispute. According to R. Yoḥanan, R. Judah holds that if an agent deviates from an entrepreneur's instructions when purchasing an item from a vendor, he is still deemed to be acting for the original owner because we may assume that the vendor believes he is giving ownership of the item to the entrepreneur and not to the agent. This is a highly nominalist position because the legal outcome is determined by an actor's intention, and that intention is itself a legal fiction! R. Yoḥanan's nominalist explanation of R. Judah's position is said to be ridiculed in the west.

> In the West, they laughed at the statement of R. Yoḥanan regarding the view of R. Judah for [they said]: who was it that informed the vendor of the wheat [that the purchaser is acting as an agent] so that he might transfer the ownership of the wheat to the [original] owner of the money?

R. Yoḥanan's explanation is mocked because it commits R. Judah to a counterfactual assumption, a legal fiction. It is not at all likely that the vendor *in fact* understands himself to be transferring ownership to some absent original owner of the money rather than to the man with whom he is dealing, and the

---

[91] So also the Venice printed edition, but Munich, Vatican 118, and Vatican 121 read: *it does invalidate*. The latter reading is not preferred, as it attributes to R. Shimeon the view that an illegitimate intention invalidates even in a case of short carrying, an attribution that was defeated in the passage immediately preceding this one. If this reading is correct, the sugya engages in less of a realist revision than is suggested here. Nevertheless, the force of the mockery in its immediate context remains the same: it draws a distinction between a realist and a nominalist understanding of carrying, and mocks the latter. Perhaps this alternative reading testifies to a continuing struggle to preserve the nominalism of the rabbinic position at the expense of a coherent *oqimta* (*limitation of the ruling to a specific circumstance*) on the part of R. Papa and R. Huna.

very idea inspires laughter. In the continuation, R. Eleazar offers an explanation of the tannaitic dispute that does not commit R. Judah to a counterfactual view, and this explanation, less offensive to realists, stands unchallenged.

In the parallel sugya in the Yerushalmi (p. BQ 9:5, 7a) the nominalist explanation of R. Judah's position is presented *without a hint of mockery*.[92] Only in the Bavli is R. Judah's reliance on a fictive construction of the vendor's intentions subjected to ridicule and revision.

In a fifth example, western mockers again disable the application of a legal fiction whereby "the majority is accounted as the whole (*rubbo kekulo*)" in certain cases of hair removal. On b. Naz 42a, R. Yosi bar R. Ḥanina derives from a Scriptural verse that it is only the defiled Nazirite who must be scrupulous about actually removing every single hair from his head when he shaves.[93] The pure Nazirite, like the leper and the Levite, may adopt a legal fiction: as long as a majority of the area being shaved is free of hair, we deem the entire area to be free of hair. R. Yosi bar R. Ḥanina's application of the lenient legal fiction to the pure Nazirite prompts the realist mockers to object. They work to halt the slippery slope toward nominalism, arguing that the pure Nazirite is analogous to the defiled Nazirite and must actually remove all of his hair. Once again, the mocking realists score a minor victory, halting an argument that would extend a legal fiction to yet another case, while losing the larger battle against antirealist approaches overall (after all, the legal fiction remains intact for the leper and the Levite).

In our last example,[94] a legal fiction is entirely eliminated in response to the mockery of westerners. M. Yev 10:1 concerns the case of a woman whose husband has gone abroad and is subsequently reported dead. She remarries, only to have her first husband return. If the woman's remarriage was formally authorized by the court, it stands as a valid ruling and marriage, despite the later emergence of facts to the contrary. However, law does not *entirely* trump the facts, because the first marriage is also said to retain legal validity. For this

[92] The MS Escorial contains an additional paragraph that is even more strongly nominalist than the version found in the Venice printed edition and MS Leiden. In MS Escorial's version, R. Yoḥanan explains that when the agent follows instructions, the vendor [is deemed to] intend to transfer the ownership to the original owner, but when the agent does not follow instructions, the vendor [is deemed to] intend to transfer the ownership to the agent. This is clearly a fictive manipulation of the vendor's intentions, and the sugya in the Yerushalmi takes this in stride and contains no mockery.

[93] The text reads: "[It follows that] from the fact that God revealed precisely in the case of the Nazirite that 'on the 7th day he shall shave it' [in addition to saying "he shall shave it"; Lev 6:9] we know that it is only here [in the case of the defiled Nazirite that he must shave] to the point that the *whole* [head is free of hair], but normally, [i.e., in all other cases of shaving, the principle of] 'the majority counts as the whole' [applies]."

[94] This case is discussed in Hayes 2004, 2006, and 2013. The current discussion is tailored to the topic at hand: the introduction of a realist critique by means of the rhetorical phrase "In the west, they laughed at him/it." My interpretation of this sugya is based on the thorough and compelling analysis of Friedman (1977).

reason, the woman whose husband returns is simultaneously married to two men and must therefore leave both. The mishnah makes a bold assertion of the power of legal determinations partially to *override* objective facts.

In both gemaras, the early Babylonian sage Rav radicalizes the nominalist tendency of this law by negating the first husband's claims entirely and allowing the woman to remain in the second marriage even upon her first husband's return. According to Rav as presented in the Yerushalmi, the court achieves this result by deploying a legal fiction and declaring, "You are not he," thereby fixing his legal status regardless of the actual facts of the matter. The fiction "You are not he" expresses the court's right to refuse the returning husband's claim by treating him *as if* he were not himself. This move by Rav is quite daring because through this patently counterfactual legal fiction, a legal determination stands even in the face of a clear and undeniable fact to the contrary, that is, that the first husband is alive and not dead as was declared by the court. The law trumps reality entirely.[95]

Rav's legal fiction found a mixed reception. His controversial teaching *is* accepted, although grudgingly, in later Palestine. By contrast, in the Bavli (b. Yev 88a), Rav's legal fiction is mocked, subjected to a realist critique, and ultimately disabled by being construed as fact.

> In the West, they laughed at him: "Her husband comes, and there he stands, and you say, 'She need not leave!'"
> *Rav's law applies only where she [really] does not know (recognize) him.*

According to the Bavli, anonymous Palestinian sages mock the absurdity of Rav's brazenly antirealist move. The mockers are incredulous: how can Rav say that the woman need not leave the second husband when her first husband is standing alive and well for all to see? Such a radically antirealist view is too absurd, too incredible. So what did Rav really mean? He must have been talking about a case in which the woman *really* does not recognize the man who claims to be her first husband.

Rav's legal fiction has been eviscerated. The phrase "You are not he," preserved in Rav's name in the Yerushalmi, is converted at the hands of the redactors of the Bavli from a fiction employed by the court *into a factual condition that limits the scope of Rav's leniency dramatically* to cases of actual, not fictive, nonrecognition by the wife.[96]

Here again, the phrase "In the west, they laughed at him/it" serves a specific rhetorical function: to introduce or facilitate a realist critique of a nominalist or antirealist position. In this case, the realist critique is fully *accepted* and Rav's

---

[95] The full context makes it clear that the rabbis themselves understand it to be bold, but they explicitly adopted this bold authority as a solution to the problem of women trapped in marriages to absentee husbands.

[96] And in a lengthy further discussion, Rav's lenient ruling is limited even more narrowly to a highly circumscribed and, one may say, virtually impossible circumstance.

legal fiction is fully *eliminated*. In a few short steps, b. Yev 88a moves from a rhetoric of disclosure ("In the west they laughed at it") to a rhetoric of concealment in which the realist critique is fully *owned* by its rabbinic author/redactor and the nominalist position is silenced.

The cases examined above appear in the Babylonian Talmud. The parallel passages in the Palestinian Talmud, when they exist, contain the same units of tradition and dialectic, but no element of mockery, suggesting a greater sensitivity to the realist critique in Babylonia. Below we consider cases—attested in both Talmuds—in which a nominalist teaching is entirely overwritten by a realist teaching. This is achieved through the conversion, or attempted conversion, of a contrary-to-fact ruling or presumption from fiction to fact.

(II) A RHETORIC OF CONCEALMENT—DISMANTLING FICTIVE ELEMENTS IN THE LAW

There are, according to Fuller, live and dead fictions. A fiction dies when the gap between the fiction and reality is somehow bridged (1967, 14). This can happen in one of two ways: rejection and redefinition. By rejection, Fuller means that statements perceived to be fictional may simply be discarded. By redefinition, Fuller refers to a change in the meaning of a word or words in the fiction that eliminates the element of pretense, with the result that the fiction now conforms to perceived reality. Fuller describes such redefinition as the result of a natural, unconscious process of linguistic evolution. What Fuller doesn't address is that a legal fiction's "death by redefinition" can occur as the result of a *conscious effort* to bridge the gap between law and reality. In other words, fictions may die of "unnatural" causes too. To drive the metaphor further, they can be murdered. In the cases examined below I will show how some early legal rulings that contain a fictive element are "unnaturally" (i.e., actively and intentionally) eliminated, or at least crippled, by later rabbinic authorities. As we shall see, it is not always the fictive element that is redefined to fit the facts, but the *facts* themselves that are "massaged" so as to conform to the terms of the fiction.

(a) Revising Astronomical Facts to Erase a Contrary-to-Fact Ruling

We return to the calendrical case in m. RH 2:9–12(8–9). As noted above, the mishnah upholds the power of halakhic authorities to make a legal determination even when that determination is contradicted by what the rabbis' own rhetoric marks as objective. To reverse earlier decisions simply because they are out of step with astronomical facts is explicitly rejected in this mishnah as posing a *threat* to rabbinic authority ("[I]if we question the court of Rabban Gamliel then we must question every court that has existed from the time of Moses until now!"). But in the Talmuds, the opposite intuition emerges. In the gemaras, it is the *legal declaration known to be astronomically false* (and *not* the reverse) that is perceived as posing a threat to rabbinic authority. This suggests a greater accommodation to the expectation that divine law will conform to objective, astronomical "truth." The legitimacy of the law depends not just on its validation by the relevant authority (the rabbinic court) but on its authenticity—its character as factually correct or true. Steps are therefore taken to bridge the gap between Rabban Gamliel's ruling and the "facts" of the matter.

The sugya in the Yerushalmi (p. RH 2:7, 58b) cites a memra and a baraita asserting the physical impossibility of the first witnesses' testimony. R. Ḥiyya bar Abba (PA 3) then poses a critically important question: how could Rabban Gamliel have seen fit to accept testimony that is palpably false? The answer: the testimony may not have been false, at least not by Rabban Gamliel's lights. "R. Ḥiyya bar Abba said: Why did Rabban Gamliel accept them? Because he had a tradition from his fathers, that sometimes it [the moon] travels by a short route, and sometimes by a long route."

This construction of the astronomical "reality" runs counter to the clear thrust of the mishnaic narrative. The theme of the mishnaic narrative is the conflict between law and astronomical facts. The two scenarios presented in the mishnah are carefully crafted to teach that law trumps the facts: in each case a demonstrably *false* legal determination is upheld in full cognizance of its falsehood. Without this element of legal fiction, the dialogues reported in the Mishnah involving R. Akiva, R. Joshua, and R. Dosa ben Hyrcanus make little sense. Yet, by attributing to Rabban Gamliel an old family tradition that the moon sometimes completes its circuit by a shorter path, R. Ḥiyya b. Abba undercuts the bold nature of Rabban Gamliel's behavior. Rabban Gamliel no longer consciously promulgates and upholds a legal determination based on objectively false evidence, and thus the mishnah no longer depicts a contest between law and fact. Rather, the mishnah is represented as depicting a contest between *competing versions of the facts* in at least the first case. According to R. Ḥiyya b. Abba, Rabban Gamliel and the other sages do not disagree over the power of rabbinic authorities to make calendrical determinations despite the patent falsehood of the evidence adduced for those determinations, for surely no one would support a legal determination based on false testimony. Rather, Rabban Gamliel and his colleagues disagree over the nature of the evidence in question as astronomically accurate or inaccurate. Rabban Gamliel believed the evidence to be astronomically accurate, and, if his family tradition is correct, it may indeed have been so.

The Yerushalmi has changed the terms of the mishnaic debate, and Rabban Gamliel's legal fiction turns out to be no fiction at all, but a wise decision based on little-known facts about the behavior of the moon. The impetus for this change is suggested by R. Ḥiyya bar Abba's realist objection: why would Rabban Gamliel accept, and make a legal ruling on the basis of, clearly false evidence? The assumption behind R. Ḥiyya bar Abba's question is that it would be improper for any court or legal authority to make a calendrical ruling that ignored astronomical facts.

The Bavli takes its domestication of Rabban Gamliel's bold behavior one step further than the Yerushalmi, by suggesting a reality-based explanation for his rulings in *both* instances of "false" testimony. The Bavli's treatment of the first incident (in which witnesses claim to have seen the old moon in the morning and the new moon in the evening) mirrors that of the Yerushalmi but goes on to cite a biblical support.

> It has been taught in a baraita: Rabban Gamliel said to the sages, "This formula has been handed down to me from the house of my father's father: Sometimes it [the moon] travels by a long route and sometimes by a short route."
>
> R. Yoḥanan said, "What is the reason of the house of Rabbi? Because it is written, '*Who appoints the moon for seasons, the sun knows his going down*' (Ps 104:19). It is the sun which knows its going down, but the moon does not know its going down." (b. RH 25a)

What appears as an amoraic tradition in the Yerushalmi—that the moon has both a short and a long route—appears in the Bavli as an explanation offered by Rabban Gamliel himself. Moreover, the credibility of this family tradition is enhanced by its connection to a biblical text (a connection offered by an important first/second-generation Palestinian amora, R. Yoḥanan). Thus, as in the Yerushalmi, Rabban Gamliel's ruling in the first of the two instances is said to be one based on his understanding of the facts (backed up by a biblical text) rather than a bold legal fiction or a bald assertion of rabbinic authority.

The Bavli goes on to suggest a reality-based explanation for Rabban Gamliel's acceptance of testimony in the second case—albeit indirectly. A tradition presented as a baraita claims that witnesses once saw "a likeness of the [new] moon" on a very cloudy twenty-ninth day of the month and were inclined to suppose that the new month should be declared. Even the court was so inclined. Rabban Gamliel, however, cited a(nother) family tradition, according to which the new moon never appears before approximately twenty-nine and a half days. Certain that the witnesses could not in fact have seen the new moon, Rabban Gamliel made a public display of the fact that the new moon had not been sanctified by the court.

This story may provide an interpretive key to the second case in our mishnah. It is analogous to our mishnah in important ways: witnesses provide evidence, Rabban Gamliel differs from the majority in accepting/rejecting this evidence, and Rabban Gamliel is willing to forcefully and publicly compel others to his view. But there are important differences between the cases in the baraita and the mishnah. First, in the baraita the witnesses, though mistaken, are sincere, having been misled by the prevailing weather conditions. Second, it is Rabban Gamliel who rejects (rather than accepts) the mistaken testimony. Third, he does so on the basis of a reliable family tradition concerning the precise time at which it is possible to see a new moon on the twenty-ninth day. The portrait of Rabban Gamliel that emerges from the baraita is of a man in possession of epistemologically certain astronomical knowledge who is not misled by evidence even when all others are. The implications of this baraita for interpreting the second case of the mishnah are clear: since (1) eyewitness testimony can be unreliable, and since (2) Rabban Gamliel's acceptance or rejection of testimony is based on mathematical calculations and reliable astronomical knowledge, it is possible that even in the second case, Rabban Gamliel's ruling was a ruling *based* on the facts rather than a ruling *in defiance of* the facts.

As noted above, the Bavli's sugya also contains more nominalist traditions that uphold the power and authority of rabbinic sages to make calendrical determinations that run counter to astronomical reality. The result is an ambivalent sugya. On the one hand, the halakhic prerogative of rabbinic authorities to determine the calendar, even if those determinations do not accord with astronomical reality, is asserted. On the other hand, a revisionist attempt to eliminate the element of falsehood from Rabban Gamliel's calendrical rulings is found in the Bavli as well as the Yerushalmi. This intriguing juxtaposition of opposing trends suggests an anxiety over (rather than a wholesale rejection of) the legal fictions elaborated in the mishnah and the gemaras as a whole.

(b) A *Mamzer* Does Not Live a Long Life

An attempt to ground the halakhic ruling of an earlier authority in mind-independent facts may be seen in a Yerushalmi passage dealing with the *mamzer*. The prohibition of marriage with a *mamzer* (a person of illegitimate descent), is based on Deuteronomy 23:3, "A *mamzer* shall not enter into the congregation of the Lord; even unto the tenth generation, he shall not enter into the congregation of the Lord." M. Qidd 4:1, which lists the ten castes that came from the Babylonian exile to the land of Israel (including priests, Levites, Israelites, and *mamzerim*) and precludes marriage between native-born Israelites and *mamzerim*, is the occasion for the amoraic discussion of various marriage prohibitions, including the prohibition of marriage with a *mamzer*.

In the Yerushalmi (p. Qidd 4:1, 65c) we read:

> They inquired of R. Elazar:[97] What is the law regarding the eleventh generation of descent from a *mamzer*?

[97] The Venice printed edition and MS Leiden read *'ly'zr*, which may be Eliezer (a second-generation tanna) or Elazar (ben Pedat, a third-generation Palestinian amora). I assume the latter here, given that the other sages in this sugya are amoraic, but this identification is not certain. In the parallel text of the Bavli the question is put to R. Eliezer, but given R. Eliezer's objection to the purification of a *mamzer* after three generations in m. Qidd 3:17(13), this is less likely.

He replied to them: Let someone bring me the third generation and
I shall purify him [i.e., declare him fit for marriage with Israelites]!

What is the basis of R. Elazar's position? It is because the *mamzer*
does not live a long life.

When asked about the status of the eleventh generation of descent from a
mamzer, R. Elazar states that he would declare even the third generation of
descent to be pure (i.e., fit for marriage with a genealogically unblemished
Israelite).

It is not clear by what authority and by what procedure R. Elazar proposes
to make this determination of status. We are told of at least one rabbinic
authority—the tanna R. Tarfon (a second-generation tanna)—who sought a
legal avenue for purifying *mamzerim*. The strategy for purification proposed by
R. Tarfon in m. Qidd 3:17(13) (and endorsed by some amoraim) was as follows: Since a *mamzer* who marries a slave girl produces female offspring of
slave status, the son of that female offspring and a male slave will be a full slave.
If that slave is then freed, he will be a fully free Israelite (rather than *mamzer*).
This strategy exploits the rules of the halakhic system so as to "relabel" the
grandson of a *mamzer* as a genealogically unblemished Israelite; thus, within
three generations, the taint of *mamzerut (illegitimate status)* is removed.[98]

Whether R. Elazar in the Yerushalmi proposes to purify the *mamzer* by
means of a legal process like that of R. Tarfon, or by means of a legal fiction—we
will never know. What is important for our purposes, however, is that in both
the Palestinian and Babylonian gemaras, later rabbinic authorities are concerned to represent the position attributed to R. Elazar as one that is grounded
in mind-independent facts. That is, later glossators insist that R. Elazar declares
pure the third generation of descent from a *mamzer* because in his view one
reputed to be the third generation of descent from a *mamzer* is *in fact* pure and
fit, and not because he relies on a legal ruse (a manipulation of halakhic categories) or a legal fiction, and it is a fact because *mamzerim* do not live long. This
somewhat surprising "fact" is supported by a tradition attributed to R. Ḥaninah
to the effect that *mamzerim* are wiped out every three generations (p. Qidd 4:1,
65c). Thus, a line that has survived to the third generation is presumably not,
in fact, a line of *mamzerim*.

The view that *mamzerim* are short-lived is not shared by everyone. For example, R. Zeira is said to point out that people may be heard employing the
labels *mamzer* and *mamzeret* quite regularly, suggesting that genuine *mamzerim*
exist. Nevertheless, and despite the fact that the claim that *mamzerim* are short-
lived is ultimately rejected, the claim signals an effort by the stam (anonymous
voice) of the Yerushalmi to ground R. Elazar's purification of a third-generation
mamzer in facts: according to R. Elazar as understood by this anonymous gloss,

---

[98] This view does not stand uncontested. See Zemer 1992, 100–101 and Fuss 1998, 127–29.

third-generation *mamzerim* simply do not exist. His statement must therefore be read as a rhetorical challenge: let whoever *can* bring me a third-generation *mamzer* bring him—and I'll declare him pure [since I am sure no such thing exists]! Thus, the disagreement between R. Elazar and those who do not accept his teaching is converted *from* a disagreement over the power of the halakhah to determine legal status contrary to the facts *to* a disagreement over competing versions of the facts (and in related passages the facts about the lifespan of *mamzerim* will be roundly disputed). Just as Rabban Gamliel in the previous case was said to have made his ruling not in violation of astronomical facts but in accordance with those facts *as understood by him*, so R. Elazar is deemed by the anonymous gloss in this passage to be acting not in violation of genealogical fact but in accordance with those facts *as understood by him*.

The Bavli's sugya (b. Yev 78b) follows the same basic structure, though the question put to R. Eliezer[99] concerns only a female (a *mamzeret*) of the eleventh generation. Once again there is a discussion of the claim that *mamzerim* do not survive. The stam of the Bavli does not clearly endorse one or the other view of the life span of *mamzerim*. It does not try to sort out whose version of the facts is correct (indeed it tries to make room for both views). But just as in the Yerushalmi, we are not to imagine that R. Eliezer's purification of *mamzerim* is based on a legal fiction or legal ruse; rather, it rests on what R. Eliezer believes is a "fact"—that *mamzerim* simply do not survive to the third (or in the case of the Bavli, the eleventh) generation—even if others reject this "fact." Once again, any suspicion that R. Eliezer engages in a nominalist exercise or legal ruse of some kind is put to rest—he is represented as a legal realist even if mistaken.[100]

(c) Presumptions of Ritual Status

Legal presumptions are also occasionally reinterpreted so as to remove the element of fiction and bring the law into line with objective facts or mind-independent reality. Indeed, Fuller notes (1967, 45) that if a legal presumption is to escape the charge of fiction, it must comply with at least three requirements: it must "(1) be based on an inference justified by common experience, (2) be freely rebuttable, (3) be phrased in realistic terms."[101] In the following case, amoraic authorities go a long way toward eliminating the fictive element in a tannaitic legal presumption in the manner described by Fuller.

M. Nid 2:4 states:

---

[99] All textual witnesses to the Bavli have the name Eliezer. There can be no doubt that this text parallels the Yerushalmi text that features the amora R. Elazar.

[100] For a full discussion of the tensions among the various sources that deploy (or reject) a legal fiction in connection with the *mamzer*, see Novick 2009.

[101] "Realistic" here is not to be confused with "realist." Fuller uses the term "realistic" in the nontechnical sense of not fanciful or imagined, but grounded in common sense or objective facts.

All women are presumed to be ritually pure for [the purpose of sexual intercourse with] their husbands;

those that return home from a journey—their wives are presumed to be ritually pure for [the purpose of sexual intercourse with] them.

The first clause of the mishnah makes the general claim that all women are presumed to be free of menstrual impurity and thus sexually permitted to their husbands. The second clause makes the same claim for a subcategory of women: those whose husbands have returned home from a trip. The apparent superfluity of this second clause will draw some attention in the gemaras. For our immediate purposes, however, it is important to note that the mishnah sets out a halakhic presumption with apparent indifference to the possibility that the actual menstrual status of a particular woman might render that presumption false.

The Yerushalmi's gemara (p. Nid 2:3, 50a) opens with a statement in the name of a first-generation amora (Shmuel) that immediately delimits the first clause of the Mishnah. According to Shmuel, the presumption of ritual purity applies only in the case of women who have a regular menstrual cycle (because, we may suppose, the couple has a good sense of whether or not this woman is likely to be actually menstruating when her husband returns from a trip). Women whose menstrual cycle is irregular must not have sexual intercourse without first examining themselves for signs of a menstrual flow. Thus, the first move in the sugya is to limit this halakhic presumption to cases in which there is a high probability that the presumption accords with the actual physiological status of the woman in question.

The stam of the gemara objects that the mishnah itself appears to preclude such a delimitation, emphasizing as it does that all women, and not some subset thereof, are presumed to be ritually pure for their husbands. The stam then suggests that Shmuel's statement was intended to refer to the second clause of the mishnah: in the case of wives whose husbands are returning from a trip, only those with regular menstrual cycles are presumed ritually pure. At the end of the dialectical exchange that follows, our mishnah is understood as follows: every woman is presumed ritually pure for her husband, even one whose husband returns after an absence, though in the latter case only if (1) she was in a state of ritual purity when he departed or (2) her menstrual cycle is regular. The Mishnah's halakhic presumption of ritual purity for the wives of returning husbands has therefore been confined to women regarding whom we may be more reasonably certain that the presumption of ritual purity accords with physiological reality.

After a brief discussion of the standard length of menstrual cycles to be used when calculating whether a woman known to be pure at a certain time is likely to be pure at a later time, the following teaching is presented: "R. Yoḥanan (PA2) said: I teach (= shoneh) that even after [an absence of] three years she is permitted, though only if she has a regular menstrual cycle." The basis for R. Yoḥanan's claim is not entirely clear. However, given the immediately preceding discussion about calculating menstrual cycles, the explanation provided by traditional commentators is quite possible: R. Yoḥanan assumes that the husband of a woman with a regular cycle can just do the math, and so determine even after an extended absence whether or not his wife is menstruating. If so, R. Yoḥanan is clearly concerned to take physiological reality into account (and that reality can be ascertained by calculation for a woman on her regular cycle). On the other hand, it may be that R. Yoḥanan is asserting a legal fiction. A woman who is regular, and who was last known to be ritually pure, remains in the presumption of ritual purity even for a period of three years. If so, R. Yoḥanan is indifferent to the fact that menstrual impurity will likely have befallen the women in those three years, seriously compromising, if not invalidating, the presumption of ritual purity.

That this indifference must have disturbed some authorities is suggested by the two amoraic traditions that follow, according to which women are presumed to purify themselves from menstrual impurity. Thus, even though a woman is likely to have become menstrually impure during the protracted absence of her husband, we assume that she has attended to the necessary purifications.

This assumption is immediately challenged, however, by R. Yosi (PA3), who explains that the presumption of purity does not hold if a woman is known certainly to have experienced a defiling genital flux in her husband's absence. R. Yoḥanan's statement applies, therefore, only in cases in which no certainly defiling event has occurred during the husband's absence. By the end of the Yerushalmi's discussion we see that the mishnah's presumption of ritual purity has been severely circumscribed. It does not apply to (1) wives (of returning husbands) who have irregular menstrual cycles, (2) wives who were in a state of ritual impurity when their husbands departed, or (3) wives who, though initially pure, are known to have incurred an impurity at some time during their husband's absence. The presumption of ritual purity does not apply because of the likelihood that such women have *in fact* experienced a menstrual event. Thus, while physiological considerations have not entirely overthrown the mishnah's legal presumption, they have limited its reach.

In the Bavli also, the discussion tends toward the delimitation of the halakhic presumption of ritual purity. The stam reworks the amoraic traditions in line with physiological facts, with the result that Resh Laqish and R. Yoḥanan end up in basic agreement on the following: m. Nid 2:4's presumption of cleanness applies to a woman with a regular menstrual cycle, whose husband can be mathematically certain of her nonmenstrual status even after an absence, either because he returns within her usual time of ritual purity (Resh Laqish) or because he can do the necessary calculations following a longer absence (R. Yoḥanan). Moreover, it is argued that even these women lose the presumption of purity under certain circumstances, specifically when there is certainty that a discharge occurred during the husband's absence but uncertainty that purificatory immersion occurred. All told, the Bavli's discussion limits the mishnah's halakhic presumption of ritual purity to cases in which there is either a certainty or a very high probability that the woman in question has not had an actual menstrual event or failed to perform the actions that would purify her from such an event.

In sum: the mishnah sets forth a halakhic presumption of menstrual purity status that is relatively indifferent to physiological facts—consistent with a nominalist orientation. Exhibiting a realist impulse, both Talmuds erode the "fictive" character of this presumption by limiting it to cases in which there is a strong chance that the presumption reflects physiological fact. It would seem that Fuller's three requirements for safeguarding a legal presumption from the charge of fiction have been met. The presumption of menstrual purity is shown (1) to apply only where it is justified by common experience concerning women's cycles, (2) to be freely rebuttable on the basis of events that have the power to cancel the presumption (intervening defiling fluxes), and (3) to be phrased in realistic terms.

Legal fictions are regularly tolerated in legal systems. A fiction that is so out of step with common experience or physical facts as to provoke incredulity and scorn will tend to undermine confidence in the law *if the law's authority is predicated on the expectation that it align with truth.* A nominalist orientation to divine law has a lower expectation of correspondence to truth and a higher tolerance for fictive elements. That the rabbis employed legal fictions and contrary-to-fact rulings and presumptions is evidence of a tendency toward nominalism. Nevertheless, alongside a rhetoric of disclosure that does not shy away from the fictive element in the law, one finds a rhetoric of concealment that seeks to eliminate or reduce legal determinations that deviate from what the rabbis' own rhetoric marks as objective fact and commonsense experience. This rhetoric of concealment emerges from a realist sensitivity that protests the divorce of divine law and truth.

CONCLUSION

We have examined rabbinic sources that thematize the connection between law and truth using three different "measures" of a stable, authentic truth. First, the conceptual distinction between *din* and halakhah shows that the operative divine law does not always align with formal, logical truth. Second, the high value placed on peace and mercy rather than truth in some cases of judicial compromise, and especially in divine judgment, shows that divine law need not always (and sometimes not ideally) promote judicial truth. Third, the deployment of a wide array of nominalist strategies shows that divine law does not always align with mind-independent ontological reality. The rabbis tolerated the deviation of divine law from "truth" according to the three measures identified here (formal truth, judicial truth, and ontological truth) because they did not embrace a broader conception of divine law that assumes the latter's verisimilitude and correspondence to some kind of objective truth.

I have argued that the rabbinic conception of divine law in which law and truth are divorced was a self-aware choice. In other words, the rabbis were aware of the truth claims about divine law that were advanced by other late ancient Jews[102] and non-Jews, and (for the most part) consciously resisted them. Evidence of this self-awareness may be found in texts that feature the motif of mockery. Mockery by external and internal others is part of a larger rhetoric of disclosure in which rabbinic authors/redactors signal their conscious use of strategies that deviate from the truth when determining the law, including deviations from formal logic and strict justice, counterfactual rulings, instances of intentionalism, legal fictions, and fictive presumptions. In both Palestinian and Babylonian sources, rabbinic authors reveal their awareness of the fact that these strategies expose them to the derision of individuals, *real or imagined*, of a more truth-oriented and realist bent.[103] In a corresponding rhetoric of concealment, rabbinic authors/redactors will occasionally internalize the realist critique and convert teachings that lack verisimilitude to fact.

The divorce of law and truth is not *in itself* remarkable as a theoretical orientation to law per se. No one imagines, for example, that, in Roman or American law, legal rules, determinations, and judgments are statements of an ontological or metaphysical truth. What *is* remarkable is that the rabbis divorce truth from *divine* law, not human law. Such a move strikes even contemporary students of rabbinic texts as scandalous—surely divine law is universally understood to be consonant or self-identical with truth!

The divorce of truth from divine law is scandalous only on certain descriptions of divine law—those informed by the classical natural law tradition (such as Philo's and, to be frank, much of Western thought to the present day). But this view of divine law is not inevitable, and it was not universally adopted in Jewish antiquity. Judging by the mocking invective of Philo, there were Jewish Bible exegetes in Alexandria shortly before the rabbinic period whose conception of the divine writings did not presume that the divinity of Scripture guaranteed its truth and verisimilitude. Likewise, as I have argued here, the view that divine law must conform to some criterion of truth does not prevail in rabbinic legal texts.

On this question, then, the rabbis did not take the path of either Philo or Paul. Unlike Philo, they did not depict biblical divine law as self-identical with truth, and to this extent their conception of divine law resembles Greco-Roman descriptions of *human* law more than it resembles Greco-Roman descriptions

---

[102] For such groups, see again Schwartz 1992 (also 2008) and Hayes 2011.

[103] I say "imagined" because in some cases the redactors may be employing the literary trope of mocking westerners as a displaced expression of their own anxiety about rabbinic nominalism.

of divine law. Paul also viewed the Mosaic Law in terms reminiscent of Greco-Roman discourses of human law, but unlike Paul, the rabbis continued to champion the Law's divinity and authority.

The rabbis' ability to represent the view of those who assert the identity of law and truth proves that they knew of and considered such views. For the most part, they divorced divine law from truth and openly adopted nominalist strategies in their elaboration of divine law, but the texts are not monolithic. At times, the realist critique gains traction and contests, curbs, or even erases, an earlier nominalism.

CHAPTER 6

The (Ir)rationality of Torah

In this chapter we continue to explore the rabbinic conception of Mosaic Law in an attempt to discern the extent to which and the manner in which that conception may have been informed by Greco-Roman discourses of natural law and positive law. Because the primary discourses of natural law in the Greco-Roman tradition underscore the rational character of the law, we take up the question of the rationality of the Mosaic Law as represented by the rabbis.

First we must understand what classical writers and philosophers mean when they state that the natural law is rational. The classical discourses described in chapter 2 understand the natural law to be rational in two ways. First and foremost, it is *intrinsically* and *essentially* rational in its substance, meaning that it is not arbitrary and contains no contradiction or absurdity, no illogical or paradoxical claims. Second, natural law is rational in the sense that it serves a rational purpose determined by its specific content; it has an intrinsic rationale and conduces to a specific rational good.

In chapter 3 we examined texts that made both of these claims on behalf of the Mosaic Law. The authors of the Letter of Aristeas and 4 Maccabees claimed that even the seemingly arbitrary dietary and purity laws have a clear rationale—their purpose is to inculcate ethical behavior or to subjugate the passions to reason. Moreover, they asserted (not entirely convincingly) that the laws are *in their substance* rational.[1] Philo went even further in identifying the Mosaic Law with the natural law and asserting that it is rational in both senses: it is rational *in its substance*, as revealed by allegorical interpretation, and its provisions serve rational ends. The laws have rationales that are *intrinsic*, or connected to their substance.

In classical thought there are two additional features that follow from the natural law's rational character. First, since natural law is constituted by or conforms to reason, it follows that it is rationally accessible. Second, its authority

[1] For Aristeas, the dietary laws may seem to contradict natural categories, but when understood allegorically, they are certainly rational, owing to their ethical content. 4 Maccabees on the other hand simply asserts that the dietary laws are in their substance in harmony with nature, which is itself informed by wisdom.

lies in its rational character rather than an external mechanism of enforcement. Philo relied on the principle of the Law's rational accessibility in explaining how the patriarchs were able to observe the Law before its revelation at Sinai, and there is good reason to suppose that for Philo, the Law's rational perfection is an inseparable element of its authority.

Is the rabbinic conception of the divine law of biblical tradition informed by these ideas? In this chapter, we examine rabbinic sources that shed light on a constellation of questions that address the matter of the Law's essential rationality: Is the Law depicted as rational in the sense that it is not arbitrary and contains no contradiction or absurdity, no illogical or paradoxical claim, or does it defy logic and natural reason? Is it depicted as possessing *intrinsic* rationales (purposes connected to its specific content) or only an extrinsic utility of some kind? Is the Mosaic Law represented as rationally accessible or inaccessible? And does it derive its authority from its rational character (consistent with an autonomous ethic) or from a coercive sovereign will (consistent with a heteronomous ethic)?

The following tannaitic text, commenting on Leviticus 18:4, "*[Y]ou shall observe my judgments (mishpatim) and keep my laws (ḥuqqim) to follow them; I am Yahweh your god*," can serve as an entrée into the subject of the rationality of the Mosaic Law:

> "*[Y]ou shall observe my judgments (mishpatim)*"—these are matters written in the Torah which—had they not been written—it would be logical (= *din*) to write, such as robbery, sexual violations, idolatry, blasphemy and bloodshed. If they had not been written [in the Torah] it would be logical (= *din*) to write them. And those [i.e., the *ḥuqqim*] are the ones which the evil impulse and the idolatrous nations of the world, object to, such as the prohibition against eating pork and against wearing mixed seeds, and the sandal-removal ritual [to annul a levirate bond], the purification rite for scale-disease, the scape-goat ritual. The evil impulse and the idolatrous nations of the world object to them. Scripture says, "*I am Yahweh*" meaning, you are not permitted to object to my statutes (*ḥuqqotai*). (Sifra Aḥare Mot 9:13, Weiss ed., 86a)[2]

The text distinguishes between *mishpatim* and *ḥuqqim*—the former are understood to be laws one would logically expect to be included in Scripture, and the latter are not.[3] The clear inference is that logic would *not* dictate the

---

[2] Translation based on the Weiss edition, p. 86a. The passage is from a longer unit, to be explored in greater depth below, known as the Mekhilta de-Arayot, which does not appear in all manuscripts. The unit is attributed to the school of R. Yishmael and inserted into the Sifra, which is traditionally ascribed to the school of R. Akiva. Details on the complex structure of the Sifra can be found in Naeh 1997 and 2000.

[3] This does not necessarily reflect the biblical usage of these terms. See, for example, Deut 4:6, which associates *ḥuqqim* with wisdom.

inclusion of the latter precisely because these laws are arbitrary or illogical. The text goes on to indicate that the arbitrary or illogical nature of these laws makes them objectionable in the eyes of some. But even as it asserts that arbitrary or illogical laws inspire objection and resistance, the text marginalizes that resistance by attributing it to idolaters and evil persons. The resulting text is oddly conflicted. On the one hand, the rabbinic author acknowledges that some divine laws are so arbitrary and illogical that no one would expect them to be a part of the divine Law. On the other hand, the rabbinic author takes pains to inform us that only an idolatrous or evil person—a person who does not accept the authority of the divine legislator—would actually *object* to these arbitrary and illogical laws. In short, the author recognizes the existence of irrational laws, but he distances himself from the critique of them—*that* is left to idolatrous and evil "others."[4]

In the previous chapter we noted that the strategy of displacement enabled rabbinic authors to voice and thus grapple with their own ambivalence and radical doubt about a nominalist understanding of divine law. Similarly, the strategy of displacement identified in this passage, and additional passages to be discussed below, will enable the rabbis to voice and grapple with the problematic assertion that divine law contains irrational elements.

Rabbinic literature contains four different responses to the assertion of irrationality in the law. The first response concedes the premise that there are irrational laws in the divine law and argues that this irrationality is not a liability but an asset, not a vice but a virtue. The second response disowns the premise by attributing it to rebellious heretics. The third response denies the premise—the Law is not irrational, though the reasons are not always accessible to us. The fourth response splits the difference—whether one describes the Law as rational or not depends on audience.

We begin by examining texts in which the arbitrary and irrational character of the divine law is asserted, before turning to the four rabbinic responses to this assertion.

MAKING THE CASE FOR THE LAW'S IRRATIONALITY

What does Sifra Aḥare Mot 9:13 have to say about the rationality or irrationality of the Law? David Novak (1998, 73) refers to this text as a "seminal text" and as an authentic source for the medieval distinction, developed first in the writings of Saadiah Gaon, between rational commandments and revealed commandments. According to Novak, the rational character of some of the

---

[4] Rosen-Zvi (2011, 89) also understands the ascription of these doubts to various internal and external "others" as a way to externalize them: "The *yetzer's* claims are rejected not because they are false, but, quite to the contrary, because they are convincing. The very act of identifying these seemingly good arguments with the *yetzer* is meant to discredit them, marking them as forbidden." See further Weinfeld 2000 and Havlin 1995.

Torah's commandments is so important that the point is repeated for emphasis. While Novak concedes that the text goes on to point out that not all of the commandments are rational, he believes that the ethical character of several of the *mishpatim* supports the idea that these *mishpatim* constitute a Jewish version of natural law (ibid., 74).

While the passage may have served as a resource for the development of a natural law view in post-talmudic Judaism, it hardly attests to such a view in its original context. First, nothing can be inferred from that fact that the logical nature of the *mishpatim* is repeated, given that the objectionable or illogical character of the *ḥuqqim* is also repeated in the immediately following lines. Second, the larger context of the text emphasizes the extent to which the Mosaic Law is unambiguously depicted as the arbitrary decree of a sovereign divine will. When viewed within that larger context, the notification that some laws are logical takes on a different cast and can hardly be construed as the source for a robust natural law view.

The passage as a whole is presented below. More salient sections are translated in full, while less salient sections are summarized in square brackets.

> A. "*Yahweh spoke to Moses saying, Speak to the Israelite people and say to them, 'I am Yahweh your god'*" (Lev 18:1) ...
>
> [This verse is understood as signaling Yahweh's exclusive relationship with Israel—by accepting Yahweh as their god the Israelites "accepted his sovereignty" and by extension they accepted his decrees (*gezerot*) and not those of any other god or people.]
>
> They accepted my decrees: "*You shall not copy the practices of the land of Egypt where you dwelt, or of the land of Canaan to which I am taking you; nor shall you follow their laws*" (Lev 18:3).
>
> B. Rabbi Yishmael says: The sexual prohibitions are grave since scripture prefaces and concludes these laws with the explicit name of Yahweh ...
>
> Rabbi says: It was manifest before the one who spoke and the world came into being that they [Israel] would object to the sexual prohibitions. Therefore they were imposed as a decree, with "*I am Yahweh your god*" meaning, 'Know who is making this decree over you.' And so we find that they objected to the sexual prohibitions as it is said, "*Moses heard the people weeping, every clan apart, each person at the entrance of his tent*" (Num 11:10) ...
>
> [The practices of the land of Egypt and the land of Canaan are said to be the most corrupt of all peoples and include idolatry, fornication, murder, pederasty, and bestiality.]
>
> C. "*nor shall you follow their laws*" (Lev 18:3).
>
> And what did Scripture leave unstated [since it already details many practices that should not be followed]? ...

It is that you should not follow their customs (*nimusot*) in matters that are established by law (*devarim haḥaquqin*) for them, for example, going to their theaters, circuses and game fields.

R. Meir says: These are forbidden as being among "the ways of the Amorites" which the sages have detailed.

R. Judah ben Betera says: it means that you should not dress extravagantly (?)[5] and not grow your (hair) fringe or cut the hair *kome*-style.

D. And lest you say, 'for them they are laws (*ḥuqqim*) but for us they are not laws' Scripture says, "*you shall observe my judgments (mishpatim) and keep my laws (ḥuqqim)*."

But still, the evil impulse can hope to quibble and say, 'Theirs are nicer than ours.' So Scripture says, "*You shall keep and do it, for it is your wisdom and your understanding*" (Deut 4:6).

E. "*you shall observe my judgments (mishpatim)*"—these are matters written in the Torah which—had they not been written—it would be logical to write, such as robbery, sexual violations, idolatry, blasphemy and bloodshed. If they had not been written [in the Torah] it would be logical to write them. And those [i.e., the *ḥuqqim*] are the ones which the evil impulse and the idolatrous nations of the world object to, such as the probation against eating pork and against wearing mixed seeds, and the sandal-removal ritual [to annul a levirate bond], the purification rite for scale-disease, the scape-goat ritual. The evil impulse and the idolatrous nations of the world object to them. Scripture says, "*I am Yahweh*" meaning, you are not permitted to object to my statutes (*ḥuqqotai*).

F. "*to follow them*" (Lev 18:4)—treat them as the principal thing and not as secondary.

"*to follow them*" (Lev 18:4)—you should deal only with them. You should never mix them with other matters in the world. Lest you say, 'I have learned the wisdom of Israel; I will learn the wisdom of the nations of the world' Scripture says, "to follow them"—you are not free to quit yourself of them ...

G. "[*you shall keep my laws and my judgments*] *by which, in doing them,* [*a man shall live.*]" R. Yirmiah used to say: you say 'how do we know that even a Gentile who does the Torah is considered like a high priest?' Scripture says, '*by which, in doing them,* [*a man shall live* ...]'"

The passage as a whole emphasizes God's sovereignty over Israel to the exclusion of all other sovereigns, divine or human (A). This sovereignty is manifest in the decrees that God imposes upon Israel alone and which Israel must

---

[5] For a full discussion of these somewhat obscure terms, see Berkowitz 2012, 89–106.

follow to the exclusion of all foreign laws (A), customs (C), and "wisdom" (F). And yet, simmering below this utter rejection of the ways of foreigners is an anxious awareness that God's decrees are not always appealing or easy to follow. Section B makes the remarkable claim that the sexual prohibitions revealed at Sinai caused Israel great distress. Knowing that the Israelites would object to these prohibitions, God formulated and imposed them as unequivocal decrees backed by coercive power. Section D gives voice to the perceived attractiveness of foreign ways that can undermine observance of God's laws, by asking: What is the harm in observing some of these customs if technically they are not *law* for us? And aren't these foreign ways *nicer* than so many of Israel's own laws? The first query is answered by the biblical insistence that Israel is to follow the judgments and laws of Yahweh *only*. The second is answered by the biblical insistence that the Mosaic Law is Israel's wisdom and understanding—in other words, it has attractions of its own.

The passage that is the focus of our discussion, section E (cited at the opening of this chapter), follows immediately upon the assertion that Israel's laws are wise, even though foreign laws may appear to be "nicer," and is followed immediately by section F's emphatic threefold demand: the Mosaic Law must be considered primary; the Law must not be mixed with other worldly matters; and one must be satisfied with the wisdom of Israel only, abstaining from the wisdom of other nations. This designation of wisdom as particular to various peoples (the wisdom of Israel vs. the wisdom of the nations) makes it crystal clear that we are not dealing here with a universal cosmopolitan wisdom or reason, but with the specific achievements of individual cultures. Sandwiched between these two sections, section E may be understood to say that God's decrees are not entirely bereft of wisdom, that is, *some* of them are logical and arouse no objection. On the other hand, some of them are *illogical* and likely to arouse protest. Since the Law *as a whole* is not essentially rational, it must be formulated and imposed as a coercive decree in order to signal that no objection will be tolerated.

In short, when the passage says that the inclusion of some commandments is logical, it simply means that those commandments *do not give rise to complaints and objections*. This, of course, would be true of many positive *human* laws also. The statement in its context does not point to a universal rationally derived human ethic. It does point to the tendency of human beings to object to requirements that do not strike them as logical! Despite this nod to the reasonable nature of some of the laws, the clear and overarching theme of the larger context is that much of the Mosaic Law is nonrational divine fiat that defies logic or runs contrary to human nature, a fact that inspires protest and necessitated the promulgation of the entire Law in the form of an absolute decree backed by a coercive and sovereign divine will.

Reversing the anxiety expressed in sections D and F, that an Israelite may be drawn to the "nicer "laws of other nations (D), may value other laws, or may desire to acquire the wisdom of other nations (F), section G imagines a

Gentile being drawn to the study of Torah, the wisdom of Israel. Such a person is praised by being compared to the high priest. This is the argument that has unfolded to this point: despite the difficult, coercive, and illogical nature of God's decrees, the utter distinctness of Israel's wisdom (which must not be mixed with the wisdom of the nations), and the evident appeal of foreign laws (D) and foreign wisdom (F), Israel's Torah is nevertheless capable of attracting Gentile observance. The author of this text is reassured of the value of his tradition by imagining its validation—in all its irrationality!—in the admiring gaze of an outsider or "other."

Far from articulating a universal rational ethic that connects Israel and the nations in a common humanity, this passage as a whole emphasizes the radical *discontinuity* between Israel's laws and the laws of the nations. The only time in which Israelite and Gentile find common ground is when the Gentile abandons his wisdom for the particular and at times irrational wisdom of Torah. Despite its final peroration representing the Torah as attractive to outsiders, the passage is rife with tensions so that doubts about "Israel's wisdom" surface repeatedly. Do Israel's laws inspire complaint and objection? Are Israel's laws truly "nice" (appealing), wise, logical? The rabbinic authors distance themselves from the doubts by attributing them to pre-Sinai Israelites, to idolaters, or to the evil impulse. The displacement of the rabbinic voice allows the rabbinic authors to express criticisms that they cannot safely claim as their own.[6]

The characterization of Mosaic Law as a coercively imposed divine decree, containing commandments that either run counter to the natural tendencies of humans or are so illogical as to inspire protest, is not confined to Sifra Aḥare Mot 9:13. The following tannaitic text equates Israel to a slave who must obey the orders of his master without question or complaint.

> "*I am Yahweh your god who brought you out of the land of Egypt to be your god*" (Num 15:41).
>
> Another interpretation: why mention the exodus from Egypt in connection with the detailing of each commandment?
>
> To what can the matter be compared? To a king whose friend's son was taken captive. When he redeemed him he redeemed him not as a free man but as a slave so that if the king should make a decree and he did not accept it, the king could say, "you are my slave!"
>
> When they came to a province, he said to him, "put my sandal on my foot, carry my garments and bring them to the bathhouse." The [friend's] son began to object. The king took out his redemption document and said to him, "you are my slave."

---

[6] In the parallel to this passage in b. Yoma 67b, the objection is attributed to Satan. Moreover the content of the objection is spelled out—these things appear to be empty or vain (*tohu*—a word indicating something chaotic and formless). For this reason they must be enforced as decrees that are to be obeyed without question.

Similarly, when the holy one, blessed be he, redeemed the seed of Abraham his friend he did not redeem them as free men but as slaves. If he should make a decree and they do not accept it, he will say to them, "you are my slaves." When they went out into the desert, he began to issue decrees for them—some light commandments and some heavier commandments, such as the Sabbath and the sexual prohibitions, fringes and *tefillin*. Israel began to object. He said to them, "you are my slaves. For this reason I redeemed you: so that I can make decrees for you and you will fulfill them." (Sifre Num Shelah 115, Horowitz ed., 127–28)

God's redemption of the Israelites from Egypt is analogized here to the "purchase" of a slave that confers upon the master full rights over the slave. It is by virtue of his acquisition of Israel as a slave, and precisely not a son, that God is entitled to issue decrees of any kind and Israel is not entitled to object or disobey. This text inverts the valence of the slave-free opposition in G-R 5(iv) and in Paul's letters (Rom 6:6–14, 7:16), as well as Paul's opposition of slave and son (Gal 4:4–7). While Paul valorizes the free son over the slave, Sifre Num Shelah 115, reflecting biblical discourses in which the ideal human type is the obedient servant (biblical discourse 1(v)), valorizes the slave over the son because of his unquestioning acceptance of his master's decrees.

The exemplary list of decrees in Sifre Num Shelah that must be obeyed without objection includes the sexual prohibitions, presumably because these run counter to natural impulses, as in the Sifra passage cited above. The list also includes ritual laws (wearing fringes on one's garments) and *tefillin* (prayer phylacteries), presumably because these appear arbitrary and illogical. Sabbath observance is also listed, suggesting that it too arouses protest, either because it is illogical or because it runs counter to the natural impulses of human beings. All of these laws are experienced as arbitrary decrees forcibly imposed against reason and nature, like the demands a master places upon a slave. And yet there is no indication in this tannaitic text that the characterization of the divine law as a decree imposed upon slaves is a denigration of the Law.

RESPONSE 1: CONCEDING AND TRANSVALUING THE PREMISE

The rabbinic passages cited above affirm the characterization of the divine law as containing illogical decrees that run counter to reason and human nature. In Sifra Aḥare Mot, this characterization of the Law is marginalized by being attributed to pre-Sinai Israelites, idolaters, and the evil impulse; nevertheless, the text as a whole *concedes* the premise of these marginal characters—the Law *is* divine fiat containing provisions that defy reason and human nature. Why does this rabbinic author accept this characterization of the Law? Why is it not viewed as inconsistent with the Law's claim to divinity—a criticism that must be deflected or corrected—as it would be in Greco-Roman divine law discourse?

The path toward an answer begins with a tannaitic text that comments on Leviticus 20:26:

> *"You shall be holy to me, for I Yahweh am holy"* (Lev 20:26)—just as I am holy, so you be holy; just as I am separate, so you be separate.
>
> *"and I have separated you from the peoples that you should be mine"* (Lev 20:26)—if you are separated from the nations you are mine, and if not then you belong to Nebuchadnezzar and his ilk.
>
> R. Elazar b. Azariah says: How do we know that a person should not say, "I do not want to wear mixed fibers, I do not want to eat pork, I do not want to commit an incestuous sexual act" but rather "I do want [these things] but what can I do? For my father in heaven has imposed his decree on me."
>
> Thus, Scripture says, *"and I have separated you from the peoples that you should be mine."* He will be separated from sin and will accept the kingdom of heaven upon himself. (Sifra Qedoshim 10:21–22)

The position outlined by R. Elazar—that there is virtue in suppressing one's natural desires in order to follow the divine law—stands at a great remove from Greco-Roman discourses of natural law. A primary discourse of Greco-Roman natural law (G-R 1) assumes the alliance of law and nature according to which the divine norms that govern human behavior are understood to be in line with human nature when that nature is uncorrupted and fully rational. Indeed, it is nonsensical to speak of the divine natural law as standing in opposition to human nature. But R. Elazar b. Azariah imagines an opposition—or, more precisely, a manufactured opposition—*between human nature and the divine law*: it is a virtue to desire the very things that the divine law prohibits because in this way one defines oneself as belonging to God rather than to the nations of the world. One should not state that one's desires run *with* the Law, but rather *against* it, so that the choice of the Law is a meaningful and conscious mark of identity.

Since natural law cannot stand in opposition to human nature, R. Elazar's statement about the divine Law would appear to have more in common with Greco-Roman discourses of human conventional law that *can* stand in opposition to human nature. However, there are important differences between the Greco-Roman discourses that view human law as antithetical to human nature (G-R 5) and R. Elazar's statement. For the Cynics (G-R 5(iv)), who idealized the untrammeled state of nature, positive law was oppressive in its opposition to human nature and should be overthrown. For the *Protagoras* (G-R 5(ii)) and other texts (G-R 5(iii)),[7] positive law provided a valued rescue from the violent and brutish state of nature, but on its own could not bring full virtue.

---

[7] The Sisyphus fragment, Antiphon's Truth, Plato's Ring of Gyges myth.

R. Elazar b. Azariah's position differs from both of these views, most obviously because the latter are speaking of human law while R. Elazar b. Azariah is speaking of divine law. More specifically, however, in contrast to the Cynics, R. Elazar b. Azariah deems the opposition between the Law and human nature to be a positive opportunity rather than an oppressive violation of liberty. The rabbinic view is closer to that of the *Protagoras* and other texts according to which the law "rescues" us from our negative natural desires, but here again, there are differences. Where Protagoras understands the state of nature to be essentially violent and brutish and requiring the remedy of law, R. Elazar b. Azariah's depiction of human nature is neutral. According to R. Elazar b. Azariah, it is entirely possible that a person's nature will align with the requirements of the Law (a person may by nature not wish to eat pork); but there is greater virtue in observing the Law when it goes against one's nature, and one should almost intentionally "create" the will to engage in the acts prohibited by the Law. This turns observance of the prohibition into a meaningful and conscious choice to "belong to" God.

The implicit moral of R. Elazar b. Azariah's teaching is that there is value in struggling to fulfill the Law, value in overcoming one's nature in order to obey the divine decrees of the god of Israel. In Greco-Roman discourse, it is only positive law that humans struggle against their nature to obey, not divine natural law, since natural law is by definition aligned with human nature. As we saw in the previous chapter, traits attributed to positive law in Greco-Roman discourse are transferred in rabbinic discourse to the divine law, with no indication that this impugns the divine law's reputation (contra Paul).

For R. Elazar, one becomes a member of God's people by observing the Law. The more difficult that choice is, the more meaningful it is. Explicit in the following mishnah is the idea that greater significance or virtue attaches to obedience to laws against which one chafes than to obedience to laws in line with one's natural impulses:

> R. Shimon b. Rabbi says:... If in the case of blood, for which a person's soul has a loathing, one who refrains from it receives a reward, how much the more so in regard to robbery and incest, for which a person's soul has a craving and a longing, shall one who refrains from it acquire merit for himself and for generations and generations to come, to the end of all generations! (m. Mak 3:18(15))

Commenting on Deuteronomy 12:23–28, which promises a reward for those who abstain from eating blood, R. Shimeon b. Rabbi makes an a fortiori argument: if God rewards us for what is easy (i.e., in line with our natural impulses), how much more will he reward us for what is difficult (i.e., contrary to our natural impulses and desires). The idea that the divine law could run counter to human nature, and that the tension between the Law and human nature is a spur to virtue, runs counter to Greco-Roman conceptions of natural law. And although the opposition of law and human nature echoes some aspects of Greco-Roman discourses of positive law, the latter do not see positive law as capable of conducing to *full* virtue. Paul adopts these positive law discourses in his condemnation of the Law. He depicts the opposition of the Law and the natural impulses of the flesh as a setup for inevitable failure and the reason for the Law's inability to bring virtue (Rom 7:14, 18, 22–24). By contrast, R. Shimon b. Rabbi depicts the *opposition of law and nature* as creating the conditions for the cultivation of a level of virtue that will bring the greatest possible reward—a portrait that defies both Greco-Roman discourses of natural and positive law and the Pauline application of those discourses to the Mosaic Law.

Given the tannaitic valorization of illogical laws or laws that run counter to human nature as opportunities to express unquestioning obedience to God, the designation of a handful of laws as "logical" in Sifra Aḥare Mot 9:13 cannot be construed as a compliment without further ado. These, it turns out, are the easy laws, the unremarkable laws, the laws that one would logically expect to find in any law code. They offer little to those who wish to demonstrate their obedience and loyalty to the divine sovereign, and they do not serve to mark the nation as distinctively wise or holy. Thus, the attention this passage has garnered from contemporary scholars seeking evidence of a rabbinic natural law theory or common human ethic bespeaks a failure to appreciate the constellation of ideas within which the passage is embedded. That larger context assigns little value to the rational laws and great value to the irrational laws—it is the latter that constitute the specific wisdom of Israel and distinguish her from the nations. Virtue attaches to and arises from the performance of commandments, *particularly* the commandments that are difficult to accept because they are illogical, arbitrary, and counter to one's natural desires.

The idea that the commandments provide opportunities to increase *virtue* may be seen as an inversion of Paul's condemnation of the Law as increasing *sin* (Rom 5:20). Indeed, Devorah Steinmetz (2008, 94–96) sees the following tannaitic text as a direct rejection of the Pauline association of law and sin:

> R. Ḥananiah b. Aqashia says: The holy one, blessed be he, wanted to make Israel righteous (*lezakkot et Yisrael*), therefore he gave them Torah and commandments, as it is said "*Yahweh was pleased for his righteousness's sake to make the Law great and glorious*" (Isa 42:21).[8]

As Steinmetz persuasively demonstrates, Paul argues that the Law given to Israel brings death and increases sin, while R. Ḥanania b. Aqashia makes the opposite claim: God multiplied Torah and mitzvot because he wanted to give

---

[8] *Ḥafetz lema'an tsidqo yagdil torah veya'adir*, which the rabbis seem to read literally as "he desired for his [i.e., Israel's] righteousness—he magnified and made glorious the law." Read this way, the verse attributes the magnification of the Law to God's desire to make Israel righteous.

merit to Israel by providing more opportunities for righteousness (justification). Paul insists that justification comes only through faith, and not law, because sinful urges prevent one from fulfilling the entire Law perfectly. By contrast, this mishnah and its larger context insist that sinful urges increase the value of obedience, and even partial (not perfect) obedience grants life. Because God wanted to justify Israel (move Israel toward righteousness), he gave a multitude of laws as opportunities for the obedience that brings life and justification. The sugya attached to this mishnah lists the number of commandments: 365 negative commandments, corresponding to the days of the year, and 248 positive commandments, corresponding to the limbs of the human body, for a total of 613. These correspondences to the days of the year and the limbs of the body suggest that the commandments permeate all of time and embodied experience. The invocation of the body's limbs may be contrasted to Paul's lament that there is "a different law in my members captivating me by the law of sin which is in my members" (Rom 7:23; Steinmetz 2008, 96). For the rabbis, it is not a different law but the very Law of God that permeates the body, captivates the obedient person, and provides endless opportunities—every day and with every action—for obedience and righteousness.

I noted above that classical sources understand the natural law to be rational in two ways. First, it is intrinsically and essentially rational in the sense that its substance is not arbitrary or illogical. Second, it has a rational purpose. The rabbinic texts examined thus far do not depict the Mosaic Law as *intrinsically* and *essentially* rational in the first sense. On the contrary, they openly admit that the Law has arbitrary and illogical elements. However, we have now seen that the rabbis identify a rationale for the promulgation of even these arbitrary and illogical laws: they provide opportunities to increase virtue. If so, then the Law may be rational in at least the second sense of having a rational purpose. Is that in fact the case?

Texts that identify the Law's rationale as the refinement of Israel shed light on this question. While some Greco-Roman discourses (G-R 3 and G-R 5(iii)) despair of the power of prescriptive law to bring virtue, and Paul (in his more charitable moments) credits the Mosaic Law with no more than holding or imprisoning Israel until righteousness is available through faith (Gal 3 and 4), some rabbinic sources depict the Law as a positive force that cultivates character. The Mosaic Law doesn't merely "hold" Israel until such time as she will be perfected and saved by faith; the Law itself, in all its minute detail, conduces to virtue:

> It is written, *"The way of Elohim is perfect; the word of Yahweh is pure* [= refined], *he is a shield to all who take refuge in him"* (2 Sam 22:31). If his way is perfect, how much the more is he himself perfect! Rav said: the commandments were given only that humans should be refined by them. For what difference does it make to the holy one, blessed be he, whether

one slaughters an animal by the throat or by the nape of the neck?! Hence, the commandments were given only that humans should be refined by them. (Gen Rab 44:1, Theodor-Albeck ed., 424–25)

According to the third-century amora Rav, the commandments were given to refine humanity; the Law has a rationale. It is significant, however, that the specific commandment singled out to illustrate this assertion is not one of the basic ethical commandments such as the prohibition of bloodshed or adultery, but a detail from the laws of *kashrut* stipulating the manner in which an animal is to be slaughtered.[9] The commandment is chosen precisely because of its arbitrary nature, as signaled by the phrase "what difference does it make to the divine being whether one slaughters an animal by the throat or by the nape of the neck?!" If the commandment itself is devoid of meaningful content, then it cannot be the *substance* of the commandment that refines the human. Rather, it is the very act of performing the commandment in obedience to God's will that refines the human actor. In other words, while the law is said to have a general rationale (refinement of Israel), that rationale is not instrinsic. It does not flow from the specific substance and content of the law; it is a purely extrinsic utility. This is quite different from the Greco-Roman conception of divine law's rationality (as well as that of Philo), according to which the Law's *intrinsic substance* promotes human rational perfection and, as a consequence, human virtue. But in Gen Rab 44:1 it is precisely the irrational laws that promote human perfection and virtue, not because of their substance (throat or nape of the neck—it is a matter of indifference!) but simply because of the opportunity they provide for obedience. Indeed, it is precisely *because* these prescriptive divine commands *lack* intrinsic reason and intrinsic utility that they generate an obedience that refines humans and conduces to virtue.

The difference between the two views turns on their very different notions of human virtue. The Greco-Roman discourse of law and virtue (G-R 3) understands true virtue to arise from rational perfection nourished by rational laws; the rabbinic text cited here understands virtue to arise from obedience best instilled by and manifested in the observance of irrational laws. This view is likely what animates R. Yasa, a Palestinian amora, when he goes *out of his way* to convert a nonarbitrary law into an arbitrary and illogical fiat. This occurs in p. San 8:1, 26a, in connection with the law of the stubborn and rebellious son (Deut 21:18–21).

R. Yasa said: All these rules are irrational (*la mistabrin*), for the opposite should be the case! It was taught: you can know that that is the case [i.e., that it is against reason] for by logic whom should be declared liable, a

---

[9] Rav's statement is found also in Lev Rab 13:3, where it refers to the dietary laws listed in Lev 11. Less explicit is Ex Rab 30:13, where God says that the law of the red heifer, elsewhere understood to be the paradigmatic "irrational" law (see below), was given to make Israel worthy of divine reward and serves no purpose for God.

son or a daughter? You would have to say the daughter, and yet Torah has declared the daughter to be exempt and the son to be liable.

By logic whom should be declared liable, the minor or the adult? You would have to say that is it is the adult, and yet the Torah has declared the adult to be exempt and the minor to be liable.

By logic whom should be declared liable, he who steals from others, or he who steals from his father and mother? You would have to say that it is he who steals from others, and yet the Torah has declared exempt the one who steals from others, and has declared liable the one who steals from his father and his mother.

This teaches you that all these rules derive solely from the decree of the King [and not from reason].[10]

While Deuteronomy 21:18–21 is arguably a harsh law, it is not on the face of it irrational in the sense of lacking a rational purpose. Indeed, the biblical text provides an explicit rationale—the rebellious child must be put to death in order to root out evil. R. Yasa rather gratuitously *constructs* the law's irrational character. It is, after all, the rabbis who *choose* to read the law as applying only to sons and not daughters,[11] to minors and not adults, to cases of theft from the parents rather than cases of theft from others. Yet R. Yasa points to the law's irrationality as if to suggest that it is an intrinsic fixture of the law. He then concludes that, irrational as it is, the law is to be obeyed because it is the decree of the divine king (and therefore precisely not rational). R. Yasa has moved in a more radical direction. No mention is made of any benefit to the person who obeys this law. Evidently, the *only* rationale for obeying the law is to affirm the sovereignty of its author, in which case the substance of the law is entirely immaterial.

This passage is the mirror image (or the antipodal partner) of the Letter of Aristeas, 4 Maccabees, and Philo. The latter were convinced of and asserted the rational character of biblical divine law, going so far as to argue that the most seemingly arbitrary Scriptural laws—the dietary laws and the ritual impurity laws—not only serve a rational purpose but are in their substance rationale (as revealed by allegorical interpretation). Rationality is a virtue and irrationality is a defect. This rabbinic text moves in the opposite direction. R. Yasa takes a law that is justified by an explicit rationale and expends tremendous effort in constructing it as an example of an *irrational* law. This text challenges the assumption that rationality is a virtue and irrationality is a defect. Irrationality

---

[10] See also t. San 11:6, Vienna MS, where R. Shimon b. Elazar observes that it ought to be (*badin hu*) the daughter and not the son, but "such is the decree of the king," and b. San 69a: "'a son, but not a daughter'—It has been taught: R. Simeon said: According to the law [*badin*], a daughter should come within the scope of the law of a 'stubborn and rebellious child,' since many frequent her in sin, but it is a divine decree: 'a son'—but not a daughter."

[11] This is not an inevitable reading. Elsewhere the rabbis read male nouns and pronouns as references to humanity as a whole. So the exclusion of the female here is an interpretative choice.

is positively viewed. Obedience to an irrational law, insofar as it has no utility, proclaims the sovereignty of the king.

An extreme affirmation of the law as arbitrary fiat may be seen in an amoraic tradition found in both the Palestinian and Babylonian Talmuds. The base mishnah underlying this tradition is m. Ber 5:3 (see also m. Meg 4:9):

> He who says [when leading the communal prayer] "May your mercies extend to the bird's nest," "May your name be mentioned for good," and "We give thanks, we give thanks"—is silenced.

The reference to the bird's nest recalls Deuteronomy 22:6–7, which states: "If, along the road, you chance upon a bird's nest, in any tree or on the ground, with fledglings or eggs and the mother sitting over the fledglings or on the eggs, do not take the mother with her young. Let the mother go, and take only the young, in order that you may fare well and have long life."

The mishnah does not explain why the reference to God's mercy is objectionable. Various explanations appear in the gemaras. According to R. Yosi b. R. Bun, a fifth-generation Palestinian amora, the statement that God's mercies extend to the bird's nest is objectionable because it represents God's ways (*middot*) as mercies. Likewise, it is wrong to represent the prohibition against killing a mother cow and her young, or a mother bird and her young, on the same day as a mercy, for these are decrees (*gezerot*; p. Meg 4:10, 75c). The same view appears in abbreviated form in the Babylonian Talmud.

> Two amoraim in the west, R. Yosi b. Abin and R. Yosi b. Zebida, give different answers [to the question of why these persons must be silenced]. One says it is because he creates jealousy among the works of creation [that God is merciful to the bird's nest but not to me!]; the other says it is because he represents the ways (*middot*) of the holy one, blessed be he, as mercies when they are decrees. (b. Ber 33b)

What is striking about this teaching is that it too denies a rationale to a biblical law that might otherwise be understood—quite easily and naturally—as arising from moral considerations. To ascribe a moral rationale or purpose to this law is portrayed not merely as misguided or unnecessary but wrong—divine law must be understood and affirmed first and foremost as pure fiat that attests to the sovereignty of its author.

Consistent with the idea that the divine law is pure fiat lacking in utility, and that virtue is best demonstrated by obedience to an irrational law that confers no benefit, are texts that insist on observing the law for its own sake. Thus, Sifre Deut 41 (L. Finkelstein ed., 87) reads:

> *"loving Yahweh your god"* (Deut 11:13).
> Lest one say: Behold I study Torah in order to get rich, or in order to be called "Rabbi" or in order to earn reward in the world to come,

Scripture says *"loving Yahweh your god"*—all that you do you should do only out of love.

The requirement of unquestioning obedience with no thought of reward or benefit appears also in a tradition attributed to Antigonus of Sokho in m. Avot 1:3: "Be not like servants who serve their master for the sake of reward; rather, be like servants who do not serve their master for the sake of reward, and let the awe of Heaven be upon you" (cited also in b. AZ 19a). Antigonus does not here deny that God rewards the righteous (that is a rabbinic assumption). He asserts rather that one must obey the Law not for the sake of the reward but in order to proclaim the sovereignty of the Law's author.

A more conflicted view is expressed in Sifre Deut 48 (L. Finkelstein ed., 113–14):

"loving..."
Lest one say: Behold I study Torah in order to be called a sage, in order to sit in the yeshivah, in order to enjoy long life in the world to come,
Scripture says *"loving"*—
Study in any event and in the end honor will come.
Thus it is said:
"She is a tree of life to those who grasp her" (Prov 3:18)
And *"they are life to him who finds them"* (Prov 4:22)
And *"she will adorn your head with a graceful wreath"* (Prov 4:9)—in this world, *"crown you with a glorious diadem"* (ibid.)—in the world to come.
"in her right hand is length of days" (Prov 3:16)—in the world to come.
"in her left [hand], riches and honor" (ibid.)—in this world.
R. Elazar b. R. Zadoq says: Do things for the sake of doing them, speak of them for their own sake. He used to say: If Belshazzar who used the Temple vessels when they were unconsecrated had his life uprooted in this world and the next, one who makes use of the vessel through which the world was created will all the more so find his life uprooted from this world and the world to come.

Those who study Torah without thought of reward will reap reward in this world and the next, while those who study Torah for the sake of reward will lose all reward in this world and the next. The paradox is clear—one should eschew reward, for only then is one guaranteed reward. This paradoxical premise is erased in the Babylonian Talmud's version of this passage (b. Ned 62b). After recounting a story forbidding the use of one's learning even when one's life is at stake, the gemara cites the baraita from Sifre Deut 48 but without the verses that promise material reward in this life and reward of any kind in the world to come. The modified baraita is consistent with the extreme position advanced by the Bavli sugya in which it is found: the commandments are to be obeyed unquestioningly as pure decrees without thought of benefit or reward. This idea lies behind exhortations to perform the commandments "for their own sake" (for example, b. Ber 17a, b. Pes 50b) and without deriving any benefit at all (b. RH 28a, b. Pes 8b, b. Naz 23a).

RESPONSE 2: DISOWNING THE PREMISE

A second response to the depiction of the divine law as illogical and arbitrary is to disown the view by marginalizing it. We saw an example of this kind of displacement in Sifra Aḥare Mot above. By placing protest and criticism in the mouths of various "mocking others," the rabbinic authors of these texts distance themselves from problematic views even as they raise and grapple with them. They discredit the objection to the Law's irrationality by presenting it as the barb of a rebellious figure or heretic and reasserting against it the Law's authority as the will of God.

An example may be found in p. San 10:1, 27d–28a, featuring Koraḥ—the rebellious biblical figure who challenged Moses's authority.

> Rav said: Koraḥ was an *apiqoros*.
>
> What did he do? He went and made a tallit that was entirely purple. He went to Moses and said, "Moses our rabbi: a tallit that is entirely purple, is it liable to the law concerning fringes?" He said to him, it is liable, for it is written, '*You shall make yourself tassels*'" (Deut 22:12).
>
> [Koraḥ said], "A house that is entirely filled with (holy) books, is it liable to the law concerning mezuzah?" He said to him, "It is liable for a mezuzah as it is written, '*And you shall write them on the doorposts of your house*'" (Deut 6:9).
>
> [Koraḥ] said to him, "A bright spot the size of a bean—what is the law [is it impure]?" He said to him, "It is a sign of impurity." "And if it spread over the entire body of the man?" He said to him, "It is a sign of purity."
>
> At that moment Koraḥ said, "The Torah does not come from Heaven, Moses is no prophet, and Aaron is not a high priest."

Koraḥ asks Moses "our rabbi" three halakhic questions. These are not questions on topics of ethical import. Each is a question of ritual law where logic would evidently dictate a certain answer, and yet Moses's responses deviate from the expected logical answer.[12] It seems that the unintuitive, illogical, or absurd nature of these responses motivates Koraḥ to declare that the Torah is not divine and Moses is no prophet. Absurd, illogical laws must be the work of men, not God. As such they need not be obeyed, and the authorities that seek to impose them may be flouted.

---

[12] This is clearest in the first and third questions—if the purpose of the purple thread in the fringe is to serve as a reminder, then surely the mnemonic effect is achieved when the entire garment is purple. Similarly if a small bright spot is impure, then surely a large spot should also be impure.

These themes appear in many rabbinic representations of nonrabbinic others and outsiders of various types: the *tsadoqi* (Sadducee), the *min* (heretic), and, to a lesser extent, the *apiqoros* (Epicurean).[13] Many of the rabbinic texts that feature these "mocking others" betray their authors' awareness of the widespread assumption that divine law—indeed divine Scripture generally—should be rational, containing no contradictions, paradoxes, illogical or arbitrary elements. Thus, in PRK 18 (Mandelbaum, 297–98) a *min* derides R. Yoḥanan's fantastic exegesis of Isaiah 54:12 as entirely illogical and absurd. Often the *min's* barbs are directed at Scripture itself, particularly when its form or content seems to violate linguistic conventions or logical norms, or to include grammatical or stylistic oddities. *Minim* point out problem verses that appear illogical or nonsensical (b. Shab 152b, reading "*minim*" with MSS) and that can be interpreted humorously (b. Sukk 48b) or to the detriment of Israel (b. Yev 102b, t. Meg 4(3):37, b. Ber 10a). That Scripture is vulnerable to such attacks is conceded by the rabbis in Gen Rab 8:8 (Theodor-Albeck ed., 1:61). Here Moses chastises God for writing, "Let us make man in our image" in Genesis 1:26, since the plural form fuels the heretical claim of multiple divine powers. "Sovereign of the Universe!" Moses exclaims, "Why do you give a justification to heretics?" "Write it," he replies, "whoever wishes to err may err." On the other hand, some rabbinic passages express the view that the apparently illogical or problematic content and form of Scripture were deliberately designed by God to include features that disable heretical claims and ridicule. A few examples will suffice.

According to m. San 4:5, a single man was created so that *minim* would not claim that there are many ruling powers in heaven. T. San 8:7 adds that man was created last so that *minim* would not assert that God had a partner in his work. According to another tradition, whenever Scripture seems to provide justification for a heretical view, the refutation is close at hand (Gen Rab 8:9 [Theodor-Albeck ed., 1:62–63] and b. San 38b–39a). Thus, the plural implication of "Let us make man in our image" (Gen 1:26) is refuted by the subsequent use of singular forms: "And Elohim created [sing.] man in his [sing.] own image." Likewise, we read in Deut Rab 2:13 (cf. Ex Rab 29:1):

> *Minim* asked R. Simlai, "How many powers created the world?"
>
> —He said to them, "Let's ask the [account of] the six days of creation."
>
> —They said to him, "Is it written '*a god* [*eloah*—singular] *created the earth*?' [No, rather] '*gods* (*elohim*—plural) *created the earth*' is written."
>
> —He said to them, "Is it written that '*elohim*—[they] created' (*bar'u*—plural form of the verb)? [No, rather] '[he] created' (*bara'*—singular form of the verb) is written.

---

[13] For more on these terms see chapter 5, and esp. n70.

Further examples are found in b. Ber 10a, b. Yoma 56b–57a, b, Ḥul 87a. In each case a *min*'s hostile or uncharitable construal of a verse is refuted by the continuation of the verse.

In all of these instances, *minim* ridicule—by poking holes in—the logic, language, and contents of divine revelation and law as if to say: is it reasonable to suppose that a divine revelation would contain material that is poorly written, misleading, illogical, and even hostile to the very people to whom it was given?

In the cases examined in chapter 5, the literary motif of the "mocking other" allowed rabbinic authors/redactors to voice and grapple with reservations about their nominalist tendencies. Thus, despite a general tolerance for a nominalist approach to divine law, rabbinic texts nevertheless incorporate occasional (self-)critiques of nominalism and its attendant legal strategies. In the cases examined in this chapter, the "mocking other" allows rabbinic authors/redactors to voice and grapple with reservations about the representation of divine law as divine fiat containing prescriptions that lack intrinsic rationality. In these texts, the idea that divine law might be illogical or irrational, or that it might lack a clear purpose, is ridiculed by outsiders as an indication that the Law is imperfect, a claim that impugns its divinity: if the Law has these features, it is not divine but human and can be rejected.

Once again, the motif of mockery serves as an index of the rabbis' self-awareness. In these texts, rabbinic authors ground the Law in the *will* of God and emphasize the value of unquestioning obedience, in full awareness of an alternative position that views the Law's irrationality as a liability rather than an asset. The view that is considered and rejected is displaced onto non-Pharisaic/rabbinic others so that it can be acknowledged but ultimately disowned. This assessment finds confirmation yet again in Mark 7:1–23. In chapter 5 we noted that the Markan Jesus mocks the Pharisees and scribes for adopting legal ruses that in his eyes annul the divine commandments. However, the passage also portrays Jesus as mocking the Pharisees and scribes for observing *precisely those laws widely identified as irrational*—the ritual impurity laws (7:1–4) and the dietary laws (7:18–19). Mark 7 is thus antipodal to the rabbinic texts examined in this chapter as well: while Jesus mocks the purity and dietary laws because they are incompatible with his view of divine law as rational, the rabbinic passages examined here assert and insist upon the irrationality of not only these but also other laws. The Law's irrationality is not incompatible with their view of divine law as divine fiat.

RESPONSE 3: DENYING THE PREMISE—RATIONALIST APOLOGETICS

The third response to the characterization of the divine law as arbitrary fiat is to deny the premise of the characterization in part or in whole by asserting the rationality of the law, despite appearances to the contrary. The rabbinic texts

that are most commonly adduced as evidence for a rabbinic belief in the rationality of divine law are texts that are believed to posit reasons (rationales) for
specific commandments (*ta'amei ha-mitzvot*).[14]

Ta'amei ha-Mitzvot/ Ta'amei Torah

While there is a generous scholarly literature on the search for reasons for the
commandments in Judaism generally, most of this literature focuses on the medieval period, when the question of the Law's rationality and the benefits and
dangers of identifying reasons for specific commandments occupied a central
place in the writings of philosophically inclined Jewish thinkers. In most of this
scholarly literature, the classical rabbinic materials are considered only to the
extent that they serve as the kernel or source for later post-talmudic developments; they are not analyzed on their own terms or in their ancient context.

Exceptions to this rule are Isaac Heinemann's *The Reasons for the Commandments in Jewish Thought: From the Bible to the Renaissance*[15] and E. E. Urbach's
The Sages: Their Concepts and Beliefs.[16] In their discussions of *ta'amei ha-mitzvot*
(reasons for the commandments) in rabbinic literature, these scholars assemble a wide variety of sources that appear to reflect on the rational purpose of
the Law as a whole, as well as the reasons for specific commandments. Both
compare the rabbinic materials to other ancient approaches to the same issues.
They contain important insights, but they also suffer from certain defects that
will become evident below.

I begin by noting that the term *ta'amei ha-mitzvot* does not appear in classical rabbinic literature at all—though scholars do not hesitate to use the term in
connection with this literature. The term is post-talmudic and reflects the later
philosophical enterprise of identifying reasons—usually ethical reasons—for
individual commandments so as to connect their performance with the achievement of a rational good. We do find the terms *ta'amei torah* and *ta'ama deqera*
(its Aramaic equivalent) in classical rabbinic sources, but they appear quite
infrequently—never in the Mishnah, only once in the Tosefta (t. Qidd 5:21),
and in eleven passages of the Babylonian Talmud.[17] Moreover the terms have a
specific meaning. Seven of the Bavli passages (including b. San 21a, examined
below) report that R. Shimeon, as opposed to R. Judah, would draw legal information from the rationales that accompany a biblical commandment (*ta'ama*

---

[14] See Urbach (1975, 365–99), I. Heinemann (2009, 25–33), and Novak (1998, 69–72), all of
whom will be discussed below in greater detail.

[15] First published in German in 1942; English ed. 2009.

[16] First published in Hebrew in 1969; 2nd English ed. 1979.

[17] B. San 21b, 102a, Pes 118–19a, BM 115a, Git 49b, Yev 23a, Yev 76b, Men 2b, San 16b, San 21a,
Qidd 68a. There is a twelfth occurrence in b. Ber 62a, but here *ta'amei torah* refers to the cantillation
marks on a Torah scroll (see also Derekh Eretz 5). There are about two dozen occurrences of *ta'amei
torah* in medieval midrashic works such as *Pesiqta Zutarta* (*Leqah Tov*), *Sekhel Tov*, and *Otzar ha-
Midrashim* combined, but these works fall outside the chronological purview of our study.

deqera). One passage (b. Yev 76b) points out that Scripture gives a rationale for the prohibition of Ammonites and Moabites in Deuteronomy 23:5. Thus, in eight of its eleven talmudic occurrences, the term *ta'ama deqera* simply connotes the explicit written verse that accompanies a biblical commandment as its rationale, as part of a discussion of the impact of that rationale on the proper application of the law in question.

The remaining three passages in the Babylonian Talmud make reference to *ta'amei torah*—reasons for biblical laws—as something that is hidden or revealed. In b. San 21b, R. Isaac states that the rationales of some commandments were not revealed because even a great person can err in a matter of law if he expounds the rationale incorrectly.[18] R. Isaac's statement addresses the fact that explicit rationales appear alongside some biblical laws but not others, but it is not at all clear that R. Isaac thinks there is a hidden rationale for every commandment. The idea that some rationales are hidden appears again in b. Pes 119a, which glosses the biblical phrase *mekasseh atiq* as a reference to God (*atiq*) who conceals (*mekasseh*) the rationales of the Torah. In the remaining passage, b. San 102a, the "hidden" rationales for the commandments are said to have been manifest to Jeroboam and the prophet Ahijah because of their scholarly superiority. We may compare this passage to the one tannaitic occurrence of the phrase *ta'amei torah* in t. Qidd 5:21. In the latter text, God rewards Abraham by revealing to him the rationales of the Torah.

To sum up, of the few appearances of the term *ta'amei torah* or its Aramaic equivalent in classical rabbinic sources, most connote an explicit biblical verse that provides a rationale for a biblical law, and are concerned solely with the question of the legal weight of these rationales in the application of the law. Four additional instances of the term suggest that (1) the biblical text does not provide a rationale for its laws if there is a danger one will make an erroneous deduction from it; (2) the rationales for commandments are concealed by God (b. Pes 119a), but (3) they can be revealed as a reward to those God loves (Abraham in t. Qidd 5:21), and (4) they are sometimes manifest before the exceptional scholar (b. San 102a).[19] From this small corpus of texts, it is clear that the phrase *ta'amei torah/ta'ama deqera* is not a significant term in rabbinic sources and sheds little light on rabbinic attitudes toward the rationality of the law.

If we are to gain a sense of the rabbinic attitude toward the rationality of the Law, we must look beyond terminology and ask: alongside passages that characterize the Law as a divine decree or that point to its irrational elements, do we also find passages in which the rabbis engage in rationalist apologetics of the

---

[18] This text is analyzed in more detail below.

[19] Post-talmudic and medieval aggadic texts (especially *Leqah Tov, Sekhel Tov,* and *Otzar ha-Midrashim*) will develop the theme of God's past revelation of the reasons for the Torah as a reward to those he loves (Moses in PesRab 14; Zerubavel ben She'altiel in Eliyahu Zuta 20) as well as the future revelation of these secrets to the righteous.

Law? The answer is a weak and very qualified yes. However, the rabbis' ratio-nalist apologetic (to the extent that it exists) differs from the rationalist apolo-getic of certain Hellenistic Jewish works, like the Letter of Aristeas and the writings of Philo, that attempt to prove that the divine law of biblical tradition is utterly rational. First, in their apologetics, the rabbis tend to be compara-tively more emphatic in maintaining that the basis of the Law's authority is its origin in the divine will rather than its rational character (Novak 1998, 90; I. Heinemann 2009, 36). Second, rabbinic sources do not in general assume the *intrinsic* rationality—that is, a rationality based on specific content and character—of the *entire* Law. Indeed, they are content to designate some parts of the Law as divine commands that serve no end beyond the extrinsic purpose of providing an opportunity for reward or the cultivation of virtue. Finally, even when the rabbis assert the Law's rationality, its rational character is not necessarily accessible to or discoverable by humans, an echo of the Second Temple trope of the hidden and the revealed aspects of divine revelation. I con-sider each of these claims before turning to the sustained analysis of a passage that captures the conflicted state of rabbinic discourse on the rationality of the Law (PRK 4).

(1) THE BASIS FOR THE LAW'S AUTHORITY: HETERONOMOUS VS. AUTONOMOUS ETHICS

Isaac Heinemann (2009, 1) describes various motivations for inquiring into the reasons for divine commandments. Even when observance of these com-mandments is grounded in belief in the authority of the divine legislator, the desire to understand and demonstrate—to oneself and to others—the wis-dom and justice of the divine legislator's laws is only natural. Sifra Aḥare Mot 9:13 makes it clear that the Law's wisdom and justice are not always self-evident, with the result that the Law is vulnerable to criticism by those who expect divine law to be wise and just. While logical laws engender no objection (their presence in divine Scripture is expected), the presence of illogical or arbitrary laws gives rise to criticism and rebellion. Seeking out reasons for the commandments is one strategy for silencing these objections, whatever their source.

However, Heinemann asserts that seeking out reasons for the command-ments can be a double-edged sword. While it may strengthen observance by elevating the status of the commandments in the eyes of those commanded, it also has the potential to weaken fidelity to the Law (ibid., 1–2). According to Heinemann, those who oppose the search for reasons for the commandments do so because identifying reasons "makes the observance of the Law dependent to some extent on the assent of the individual addressed by it" (2). In other words, it converts what is in principle a heteronomous system (in which law is imposed upon human beings from an external source) into an autonomous system (in which law emerges from the rational activity of humans).

The question of heteronomy vs. autonomy, according to Heinemann, is the fundamental difference between Hellenistic Jewish thinkers like Philo on the one hand and the rabbis on the other. Where Hellenistic Jewish thinkers stressed autonomous reasons for observing the commandments (36), the rabbis maintained a heteronomous position in regard to the Law (44–46). Heinemann finds heteronomy in the rabbinic use of slave imagery to describe Israel's obedience to the Law (16) and in traditions that value obedience to the Law even *against* one's natural impulses or autonomous validation (Sifre Num Shelah 115 and Sifra Qedoshim 10:22, above). Similarly, Urbach maintains that rabbinic texts adopt a heteronomous position (1975, 365).

Urbach's and Heineman's insistence on the heteronomous orientation of classical rabbinic sources (and Heinemann's denigration of the alleged autonomous orientation of Hellenistic Jewish writers) echoes twentieth-century debates over the nature of Judaism. Urbach writes:

> Since the publication of Moritz Lazarus' work on 'The Ethics of Judaism' there has been no halt to the attempts to point to various Rabbinic dicta as evidence of the correspondence between the fundamental principle of Kant's ethical system and the religious ethic of Judaism. However, Lazarus' hypothesis has been rejected in unambiguous terms by Hermann Cohen, who made it clear that an autonomous ethic means one that emanates from man and from him alone, that is to say, man is the source of the ethic and God is not its source but only its principle, whereas in all religions, and undoubtedly this is the case in the Jewish faith, God is the source of the ethical law. (317)

Urbach goes on to demonstrate that rabbinic sources adduced in support of Lazarus's thesis have been misread. In this respect Urbach continues the work of Heinemann (2009, 15–16, 25–26), whose review of a wide range of rabbinic sources had demonstrated that rabbinic reflections on the reasons for the commandments took place within a non-Kantian framework of theonomy. More recently, David Novak has argued that the identification of reasons for specific commandments does not take Jewish ethics out of a covenantal framework or ground it in anything other than divine command (1998, 90).

These statements reflect contemporaneous debates and a particularly modern fear that a Kantian esteem for autonomous ethics threatens fidelity to Jewish Law. Heinemann, Urbach, and Novak are correct that the basic rabbinic orientation to divine law was heteronomous, but there is little evidence that rabbinic heteronomy entailed the idea that the search for reasons for the commandments would undermine obedience to the Law. On the contrary, the sources examined above would suggest that the rabbis perceive the evident *irrationality* of parts of the Law as injurious to the fidelity of their coreligionists. Nevertheless, the following teaching attributed to a Palestinian amora is often cited as evidence of a rabbinic aversion to rationalizing the commandments, even though the teaching actually deals with a different issue:

> Ulla said: When an ordinance (*gezerah*) is made in Palestine, its reason is not revealed before a full year passes, lest there be some who might not agree with the reason and would treat the ordinance lightly. (b. AZ 35a)

Ulla's teaching refers specifically to *rabbinic* rulings, not biblical commandments. Publishing the reasons for *rabbinic* rulings opens one to criticism of those reasons, a criticism that could lead to a rejection of the ruling. But this danger is due to the fact that the rabbis' authority, while underwritten by divine authority, was nevertheless assessed by and therefore dependent upon their learning and on the evident wisdom and justice of their rulings. If one can find fault with the reasons behind a rabbinic ruling, one might be tempted to reject it altogether. By contrast, *biblical* commandments enjoy an authority independent of their qualities as rational or irrational. In the context of biblical commandments, the laws that *lack reasons*—not the laws that possess a clear reason—are the laws that undermine observance. Irrational commandments engender objections and are harder to fulfill (see the texts cited above); this is why the rabbis expend energy in asserting that the *irrational* commandments are authoritative divine decrees that must be obeyed no less than the rational commandments. By contrast, they do not expend energy urging the fulfillment of biblical laws for which a rationale is stated, because the attachment of rationales to biblical laws is not deemed to pose a particular threat. In short, b. AZ 35a cannot be read as evidence for a general aversion to legal rationales. It is only the rabbinic elaboration of divine law that is susceptible to criticism when reasons are provided.

Another text cited as evidence of an alleged rabbinic sensitivity to the dangers involved in identifying reasons for the commandments is b. San 21b.

> R. Isaac also said: Why were the reasons of [some] Biblical commandments not revealed?—Because in two verses reasons were revealed, and they caused one of the great ones of the world [Solomon] to err. Thus it is written, "*He shall not multiply wives to himself [that his heart not turn away]*" (Deut 17:17). Solomon said, 'I will multiply wives yet not let my heart be perverted.' Yet we read, "*When Solomon was old, his wives turned away his heart*" (1 Kgs 11:4). Again it is written: "*He shall not multiply to himself horses [or cause the people to return to Egypt to multiply horses]*" (Deut 17:16) concerning which Solomon said, 'I will multiply them, but will not cause [Israel] to return [to Egypt].' Yet we read, "*And a chariot came up and went out of Egypt for six [hundred shekels of silver]*." (1 Kgs 10:29)

R. Isaac's teaching responds to an exegetical problem—how could the great and wise King Solomon be guilty of such a clear violation of biblical law, multiplying both wives and horses for himself against the explicit teaching of Deuteronomy 17? His answer—that Solomon mistakenly interpreted the explicit rationales for these two biblical commandments as limiting the law's application to the circumstances stated in the rationale—is a local solution to the problem of mitigating Solomon's violation. R. Isaac phrases his teaching at a slightly higher level of generality—the reason some rationales are not revealed is that they create a potential for error in the application of the law. R. Isaac's teaching should not be raised to even higher levels of generalization. Contra Urbach (1975, 382–83) and Heinemann (2009, 2), this text does not suggest that identifying reasons for the commandments is dangerous because it leads to a rejection of divine authority and the establishment of an autonomous ethic. Knowing the rationale of the law did not cause Solomon to find fault with the Law, reject divine authority, or establish an autonomous ethic. On the contrary, Solomon sought to obey the law, but he misinterpreted it because he drew an erroneous legal deduction from the rationale verse.

That this is so is borne out by the tannaitic dispute on b. San 21a, preceding the passage about Solomon. The dispute centers on the interpretative practices of R. Judah and R. Shimon. When a biblical law is accompanied by a rationale, R. Shimon is guided in the application of that law by the information provided in the rationale, while R. Judah is not. Thus, R. Judah applies the law more broadly, while R. Shimon limits the application of the law to the circumstances covered by the explicit biblical rationale. The dispute is a simple disagreement over the legal weight of explicit biblical rationales and not disagreement over the virtues or demerits of identifying reasons for the commandments. R. Shimon's approach (which allows the application of a law to be guided by its rationale and is thus parallel to Solomon's) is not presented as a danger that threatens to undermine fidelity to the Law, or that substitutes an autonomous ethic for the authority of divine law. His is simply one of two different interpretative approaches that can be adopted in the determination of the appropriate scope of a given law. His opponent thinks that his approach is wrong and leads to error. Likewise, R. Isaac condemned Solomon's reliance on the rationale because it led to error.

As we have seen, there *are* rabbinic texts that insist that rational commandments be fulfilled not because of their rationality but because they are divine decrees, and Heinemann and Urbach correctly underscore this fact. This insistence can take the form of denying any utility or rationale to certain commandments (as we saw in the case of m. Ber 5:3 and related texts, concerning a commandment with a fairly clear moral purpose). However, the denial of a rationale for a commandment generally stems from a desire to ensure that the commandments are opportunities for refinement and virtue or for affirming God's sovereignty. In other words, rabbinic disinterest in reasons for the commandments has more to do with ensuring proper intention, and demonstrating selfless obedience to the Law, than it has to do with twentieth-century debates over autonomous vs. heteronomous ethics.

(II) EXTRINSIC VS. INTRINSIC REASONS

Prior scholarship investigating rabbinic attitudes toward reasons for the commandments does not distinguish between extrinsic and intrinsic reasons. Among the rabbinic sources dealing with *ta'amei ha-mitzvot*, Heinemann and Urbach include a number of passages that present *extrinsic* reasons for fidelity to the Law as a whole, connect a specific law with historical persons or events, or explain a specific law's symbolism. Thus, rabbinic sources assert the following extrinsic arguments for observing the Law: the Law (1) provides an opportunity for justification or refinement (m. Mak 3:18(15); Gen Rab 44:1; Ex Rab 30:13; Lev Rab 13:3), (2) confers holiness (MekhRY Shabbata 1, Horowitz ed., 341; MekhRY Kaspa 20, Horowitz ed., 320), and (3) provides divine protection or reward (Sifre Deut 114; Lev Rab 35:5–6; b. Yoma 39a; b. Qidd 39b; b. Men 43b; b. San 71a; and many others). However, such "reasons" would apply equally to any set of divine decrees regardless of content; they do not demonstrate an intrinsic connection between the content of a specific commandment and its obligatory character independent of its promulgation as a decree. Indeed, as we have seen, these "reasons" can accompany laws whose *irrationality* is acknowledged—often purity and dietary laws (e.g., Gen Rab 44:1; Ex Rab 30:13; Lev Rab 13:3). It is precisely because these laws are *irrational* that observance brings refinement, confers holiness, and provides protection and reward. Indeed, in the case of the law of the stubborn and rebellious son (b. San 71a), reward comes from *not* observing the law, but from expounding its details so that it can never be observed! In short, Heinemann and Urbach fail to show that the law itself is perceived to be rational when they cite texts in which the law is said to serve a religious goal or bring reward.

As evidence for the rabbinic conception of the Law's rationality, Heinemann and Urbach also adduce texts in which certain details of the Law are given a symbolic interpretation (the four species of plants bundled in the *lulav featured in the Festival of Sukkot* represent four patriarchs in Lev Rab 30:9; the placement of the *tefillin* (phylacteries) knot represents Israel's position in the world, b. Men 35b), or commandments are explained as measure-for-measure punishment or reward for actions by past figures (the three commandments given to women are measure-for-measure punishment for Eve's actions, Gen Rab 17:8; the commandments of fringes and shoe removal to cancel the levirate obligation are measure-for-measure reward for Abraham's abstention from "thread" and "shoelace" as spoils of war, Gen Rab 43:9; certain priestly perquisites are measure-for-measure reward for the zealous action of Pinḥas, b. Ḥul 134b). While these "reasons" explain a given law's origin in a historical event or point to its symbolic referent, they too fail to demonstrate the law's intrinsic rationality; they fail to demonstrate a connection between the content of a specific commandment and its obligatory character independent of its promulgation as a decree.

We might expect to gain insight into rabbinic attempts to identify the rational character of certain commandments from passages containing the phrase *mipney mah amrah torah* ("why did Torah state ...?"). Unfortunately, the phrase is rare, occurring just a few times in tannaitic literature and in only a dozen passages in the Babylonian Talmud.[20] In some cases, the inquiry concerns the reason for a particular *feature* of the law rather than the law itself (b. Sot 17a asks why dust is used in the ceremony for the suspected adulteress; b. Sot 46a asks why a heifer is chosen for the ritual employed to atone a certain kind of murder case; b. Nid 31b asks why the sacrifice for a boy is brought after seven days but for a girl after fourteen days, and why circumcision takes place on the eighth day; b Qidd 2b asks why a marriage law is phrased in a particular way). The responses are often symbolic (dust is used in the ceremony of the suspected adulteress because the outcome that awaits her is symbolically connected to dust; the heifer is used because it has not borne fruit and it is intended to atone for one who will not be able to bear fruit). Other responses employ the measure-for-measure principle (in b. San 112a, the property of even the righteous inhabitants of an idolatrous city is destroyed because the desire for property was what caused them to dwell there; in Nid 31b, the timing of the sacrifices brought to atone for the mother's curses during childbirth is tied to how long she remains angry over the pain of birth, and circumcision is on the eighth day because by then the parents of the newborn are rejoicing). Still other responses are based on customary or presumed behavior (b. BM 3a imposes an oath on a certain person because of presumptions about how such a person would behave; in b. Qidd 2b, the marriage law is phrased in terms of a man's taking a wife because normally men pursue women rather than the reverse). Thus, even in this small class of texts that explicitly inquire into the reasons for a commandment, the focus is on explaining *details* of the law rather than the law itself. Moreover, the answers do not establish an intrinsic connection between the content of a specific commandment and its obligatory character independent of its promulgation as a decree.

Urbach (1975, 388) notes that Philo sought ethical and social reasons for every commandment—reasons grounded in some good—because he couldn't accept the idea that the divine commandments were mere decrees. By contrast, argues Heinemann (2009, 30–31), the rabbis did not seek ethical reasons for every commandment:

---

[20] MekhRY Kaspa 20, Horowitz ed., 329; MidTan to Deut 13; b. BM 3a (paralleled in b. BQ 107a, b. Git 51b, b. Ket 18a, b. Shevu 42b), b. BQ 67b, b. Nid 31b, b. Sot 17a, b. Sot 46a, b. San 112a (paralleled in Num Rab 9:15), b. Qidd 2b, b. RH 116a.

When we survey the Sages' explanations of the mitzvoth, it is surprising that ethical reasons are relatively rare. It did not occur to them that circumcision and dietary laws are likely to restrain our carnal urges, as the philosophers would explain ... [H]ow can we explain that although the vast majority of the Sages believed in the religious-ethical purpose of our Torah, nevertheless they made hardly any attempt to find ethical reasons for the mitzvoth? ... the fact that the ethical explanations are so infrequent proves at least that they were not regarded as very important by the rabbis' audience or by the editors of the Talmud and the Midrash.

According to Heinemann, the rabbis' lack of moralistic interpretation highlights the profound difference between them and later rationalists (31):

The latter tried to find, insofar as possible, a sufficient reason not only for the mitzvoth themselves, but also for their observance. The proof that there could be a rational reason even for those mitzvoth that seemed to be arbitrary dictates of the Torah enabled them, if not to annul entirely the heteronomic aspect of our obedience, then at least to soften somewhat the harshness of that heteronomy. Such an intention never occurred to the rabbis. They were convinced that the mitzvoth had ethical reasons.

The rabbis were so convinced that the commandments had ethical reasons, says Heinemann, that they did not feel a need to work out those ethical reasons in a systematic way.

Thus the Sages did not try to find an ethical reason for all the commandments in the Torah, especially not for the majority of those that they called ḥukkim—positive laws in the narrow sense. Their purpose in explaining the mitzvot was twofold: (1) to demonstrate the value of the Torah to the people in order to endear it to them and (2) to reinforce its educational effect. (32)

Urbach and Heinemann are correct that the rabbis do not seem terribly interested in providing intrinsic ethical reasons for biblical laws. However, Heinemann's assertion that the rabbis did not propose ethical reasons for all the commandments because they simply assumed that they possessed them is an argument from silence and is unconvincing. It is far more likely that the rabbis do *not* engage in a vigorous effort to identify ethical reasons for the commandments (especially in the strong sense of an intrinsic justification for the commandments' authority) because they do not maintain that all of the laws, particularly ritual and purity laws, have reasons. Moreover, even the laws that are rational (including those that would by logic be included in any system of law) are authoritative because commanded. Thus, while identifying the reasons for commandments is edifying and can bolster observance, it is not essential to the Law's characterization as both divine and authoritative.

Heinemann's assessment that the rabbis were certain that the laws had reasons ignores explicit evidence to the contrary but is not entirely without support. There are a handful of texts that speak of "concealed" biblical rationales; Heinemann has simply given these few texts undue weight.

(III) HIDDEN REASONS

As noted above, four texts in classical rabbinic literature refer to *ta'amei torah* as something that can be concealed. At least one of these texts—b. San 21b—uses the term *ta'amei torah* to refer to the literary phenomenon in which an explicit rationale appears alongside a law in the biblical text, rather than to an abstract notion of (ethical) reasons for the laws generally. In this passage, R. Isaac seeks to explain why some biblical commandments are accompanied by a rationale verse and others are not. As for the other three passages, b. Pes 119a describes God as concealing the rationales of the Torah, while t. Qidd 5:21 depicts God as revealing them to Abraham as a reward. Finally, b. San 102a praises the scholarly excellence of Jeroboam and the prophet Ahijah, before whom the rationales of the Torah were manifest.

For our purposes, these texts indicate that the reasons for biblical laws are not accessible to or discoverable by humans without special revelation (t. Qidd 5:21) or prophetic ability (b. San 102a). Perhaps hovering just beneath the surface of these passages is an unrequited longing to know the reasons for the commandments; nevertheless, the expectation is that one must obey the Torah even in the absence of this knowledge.

These passages—few as they are—must be set against the larger discourse of the Law as divine fiat containing irrational elements. They offer an alternative perspective that emerges from a discomfort with the irrational nature of some of the laws on the one hand and a dissatisfaction with the prevailing rabbinic response that accepts the irrationality of some of the laws on the other. This small voice of protest asserts, in opposition to the dominant rabbinic discourse, that the commandments have reasons, but we cannot know them without divine dispensation. We see here an echo of the Second Temple trope of the hidden and the revealed aspects of divine revelation; however, here it is only the reasons that are hidden, and even these are not needed for virtuous observance (contrast G-R 3(iii)).

We turn now to an extended passage from a sixth-century CE text that captures the rabbis' conflicted discourse regarding the reasons for the commandments.

(IV) PESIQTA DERAV KAHANA 4

The fourth piska of Pesiqta deRav Kahana (PRK)[21] is a fascinating and complex composition that draws together many of the themes and tropes identified

---

[21] PRK is divided into textual units, each of which is referred to as a piska. The translation is based on the Mandelbaum edition, pp. 54–77.

in this chapter. Several sections of this lengthy piska appear independently in other sources, but their juxtaposition in a single sustained discussion in PRK creates a rich and conflicted portrait of rabbinic discourse on the rationality of the Law.

PRK 4 is the lesson for the Sabbath of the Heifer, the Sabbath on which Numbers 19 (concerning the ritual preparation of purification water from the ashes of the red heifer, used to remove corpse impurity) is read. The ritual of the red heifer is introduced in Numbers 19:2 as a statute (*ḥoq*) of the Torah. In rabbinic literature, *ḥoq* is generally construed as an irrational decree (see Sifra Aḥare Mot 9:13). Thus, according to the rabbis, *Scripture itself* proclaims the irrationality of the red heifer ritual. It is the presumed irrationality of this law that drives the discussion in the entire piska.

The first of the chapter's ten units opens with a citation of Job 14:4: "*Who can bring forth a clean thing out of an unclean thing? Not one*" (read by the midrashist as "is it not the One, i.e., God?").

> 4:1 "*Who can bring forth a clean thing out of an unclean thing? Is it not the One?*"
>
> Like Abraham out of Terah, Hezekiah out of Ahaz, Mordecai out of Shimei, Israel out of the nations, the world-to-come out of this world?
>
> Who did it? Who commanded it? Who decreed it?
>
> Is it not the One? Is it not the Unique One of the world?
>
> In a mishnah [see m. Neg 8:2] we learn: "If a man has on his body a bright spot no larger than a grain of bean grits, he is impure; but if the spot spreads over his entire body, he is pure."[22]
>
> Who did it? Who commanded it? Who decreed it?
>
> Is it not the One? Is it not the Unique One of the world?
>
> In a mishnah [see m. Ḥul 4:3] we learn: "If an embryo dies in its mother's womb, and the midwife puts in her hand and touches the infant, she becomes impure for seven days, but the mother is pure until the embryo emerges." While the dead embryo is in the house [in the womb] it is pure, but when it comes out it [the womb] is impure.
>
> Who did it? Who commanded it? Who decreed it?
>
> Is it not the One? Is it not the Unique One of the world?
>
> And in a mishnah [see m. Par 4:4] we learn: "All who are occupied with the Red Heifer from beginning to end their garments are defiled" but it [the Red Heifer] itself makes pure the impure.[23]

---

[22] See m. Neg 8:2 and p. San 10:1, 27d–28a, discussed above, in which Koraḥ challenges Moses with this irrational law.

[23] The parallel in b. Nid 9a cites Job and provides two examples of paradoxes involving ritual purity, including the red heifer. See Urbach 1975, 377–81. Urbach's assertion (380)—that the attempt to discover the reason of the precepts is "relinquished here, and instead there is a sense of joy at their observance as decrees of the Only One of the universe"—lacks clear evidence.

But the holy one, blessed be he, says, "I have set it down as a statute, I have decreed a decree and you are not permitted to transgress my decree." "*This is the statute [ḥuqqah] of the Torah which Yahweh has commanded*" (Num 19:2). (Mandelbaum ed., 54–55)

According to this midrash, the law of the red heifer is one of four divine actions or commandments that defy logic. In addition to the ritual of the red heifer, the midrash cites God's production or selection of "pure" (in the sense of positively valued) entities from "impure" (negatively valued) entities, as well as two further paradoxical purity laws. The first of these laws concerns the impurity of a bright spot that is paradoxically annulled if the spot spreads to cover the entire body. In p. San 10:1, 27d–28a, this ruling is said to be among the rulings that inspired Koraḥ's rebellion against divine and Mosaic authority (see above).

Thus far, the passage sounds a familiar rabbinic theme: irrational rulings have the potential to undermine fidelity to the Law. The response to the threat posed by such rulings is not to provide a rationale but to assert the ruling's origin in the coercive and sovereign divine will. This is the burden of the driving staccato refrain that follows each of the four paradoxical examples: Who other than the One can do, command, and decree such a thing? Only the unique god of the world can decree the irrational! In this way, the piska's opening volley establishes not only that some of God's decrees are irrational, but that this irrationality is the very mark and sign of their divinity.

PRK 4:2 opens with R. Tanḥum bar Ḥanila'i's citation of Psalms 12:7, which describes the words of Yahweh as pure, tested, and refined. Jeremiah 10:10, which describes God as a god of truth, is then cited and interpreted to mean that God's words are everlasting. The rest of the unit contrasts the pure (Ps 12:7) and everlasting (Jer 10:10) words of God with the finite and "foul" words of human beings and ends by identifying the laws regarding the red heifer as divine instruction that refines or purifies. This passage echoes another familiar rabbinic theme: irrational laws are a mechanism for the refinement or purification of human beings. Together these first two units of the piska reinforce a characterization of certain divine laws (especially those dealing with impurity) as everlasting irrational decrees that "refine" humans through a discipline of obedience.

PRK 4:3 waxes hyperbolic in asserting the impenetrable mystery of the law of the red heifer. The unit begins by citing Qohelet 7:23, "*All this I tested with wisdom. I thought I could fathom it, but it eludes me,*" and goes on to heap praise upon Solomon, the presumed speaker of the verse, as the wisest of all men. Solomon's wisdom exceeded the wisdom of those from the east; it exceeded the wisdom of Adam, of Abraham, Moses, and Joseph, of Darda and Mahol. Solomon spoke hundreds of verses and thousands of parables. He fathomed the reasons behind various laws (especially purity and dietary laws), explaining why the cedar and the hyssop are used in the purification of the leper, why ritual slaughter must be performed in a particular way, why culpability attaches to killing the eight creeping things on the Sabbath, and why fish do not require ritual slaughter. And yet, despite his storied wisdom,

> Solomon said: All the foregoing matters I understood but this passage concerning the Heifer, whenever I grapple with it, I search and investigate it and I say, *"I thought I could fathom it, but it eludes me"* (Qoh 7:23). (Mandelbaum ed., 65)

This passage complicates the claims of the preceding units. In the course of demonstrating the utter irrationality of the red heifer ritual, the text depicts Solomon as successfully discerning the (extrinsic) reasons for a variety of laws that appear to lack any rationale whatsoever. One ostensibly irrational law is explained in a symbolic fashion (cedar and hyssop are used in the purification of leprosy because they symbolize, respectively, the arrogance that induces scale-disease and the humility needed to cure it). The other three laws exemplifying Solomon's wisdom rationalize rules regarding the slaughter or killing of particular animals with arguments from nature (intrinsic reasons); there is something in the nature of the animals in question that justifies the rules regarding their slaughter or killing.[24] The reader is brought up short. Perhaps, despite the piska's opening insistence on the irrational nature of God's decrees, there *are* reasons for the irrational commandments after all. Discerning them may require the wisdom of Solomon, but in theory they are rational—with but one exception: the law of the red heifer. The number of truly irrational decrees has been reduced to just one. In a sharp reversal of the opening two units, this unit provides an almost completely successful rationalist apologetic.

The fourth unit, PRK 4:4, cites Qohelet 8:1: *"Who is like the wise man, and who knows the meaning of the adage: a man's wisdom lights up his face, so that his deep discontent is dissembled?"* Comments on this verse identify those whose wisdom enables them to know the meaning of something difficult—God himself, Adam, Israel, a sage, and finally Moses. The reference to Moses returns us to the red heifer law. Moses was unable to understand how a defiled priest might become pure again. But when God revealed to him the law of the red heifer, he had the answer to his question. After a digression on Moses and Aaron in PRK 4:5, the text returns in PRK 4:6 to the theme of the irrationality of certain laws, focusing specifically on laws that are contradicted by other provisions in Scripture.

> R. Joshua of Siknin said in the name of R. Levi: there are four things to which the evil impulse (*yetser hara*) objects and in connection with all of

---

[24] The closest parallel to this kind of nature-based reasoning to justify a legal prescription is found in CD 12:14–15, in which the proper method of slaughtering locusts is grounded in the natural characteristics with which they were created; see chapter 3, pp. 103–4.

them Scripture writes "*ḥuqqah*." And these are they: [a man marrying his] brother's wife; [the prohibition of] "diverse kinds";[25] the scapegoat; and the red heifer. (Mandelbaum ed., 71)

The passage goes on to explain that in each case the *yetser hara* can point to a contradictory verse or teaching:[26] the prohibition against marrying one's sister-in-law is contradicted by Deuteronomy 25:5, which requires a man to marry his widowed sister-in-law; the prohibition of wearing mixed kinds is contradicted by Numbers 15:38–39, which permits a linen cloak with wool fringes (*tsitsit*); the scapegoat paradoxically conveys impurity to the person who releases it while bringing purity to the larger community; and, as regards the red heifer,

> In a mishnah [Par 4:4] we learn: "All who are occupied with the Red Heifer from beginning to end their garments are defiled but it [the Red Heifer] itself makes pure the impure." And *ḥuqqah* is written in connection with it: "*This is the statute [ḥuqqah] of the Torah*" (Num 19:2). (Mandelbaum ed., 72)

This unit employs a trope found elsewhere in rabbinic discourse on the (ir)rationality of the Law: the trope of displacement in order to express and grapple with the problematic assertion that the divine Law contains arbitrary and irrational elements. The rabbinic authors of this text distance themselves from this critique of the Law's irrationality by attributing it to the evil impulse (*yetser hara*).

PRK 4:7 changes tack and introduces still another theme featured in a handful of rabbinic texts dealing with reasons for Torah laws (*ta'amei torah*)—the theme of concealed reasons that are revealed only to select individuals. The following tradition is attributed to R. Isaac:

> The holy one said to Moses, "Moses, I reveal to you the reasons for the red heifer, but to others it is a statute." For as R. Huna taught: [God said], "*When I take up my pledge of a world-to-come I shall give my reasons for the statutes I ordained*" (Ps 75:3).[27] ... [Zech 14:6 is then interpreted to yield the following:] things concealed from you in this world will in the time-to-come be as clear to you as crystal. That is what is meant by the verse "*I will bring the blind by a way they knew not. I will make darkness light before them ... These things have I done*" (Isa 42:16), "*These things I will do*" is not written but "*I have done*"—that is, I have already done them for

---

[25] Here, the prohibition of wearing cloth made out of mixed wool and linen.

[26] See Rosen-Zvi 2011, 190n2, regarding the paradoxical or self-contradictory nature of these commandments as the reason for the provocations of the *yetser*.

[27] The plain sense of the verse is "When I take the appointed time, I will judge equitably." R. Huna interprets the root *sh.p.t* (judge) in the sense of giving reasons, and *mesharim* (equitably) in the sense of statutes.

R. Akiva and his colleagues, for R. Aḥa says, things which were not revealed even to Moses at Sinai were revealed to R. Akiva and his colleagues
so the verse *"And his eye sees every precious thing"* (Job 28:10)—refers to
R. Akiva. (Mandelbaum ed., 72)

Where PRK 4:3 implied that the red heifer law is unique in being utterly
unfathomable, this unit suggests that even the red heifer law is explicable.
Reading 4:7 in the light of 4:3, we are left with the impression that there is no
law without a rational basis, a conclusion that sits uneasily with 4:1's bump-
tious correlation of divinity and irrationality. Moreover, PRK 4:7 brings the
rationality of this most irrational law within grasp not only with the promise
that its reason will be revealed in the world to come, but also with the declaration that the reason was revealed to a member of the rabbinic class—R. Akiva
(and his colleagues). Indeed, R. Akiva is elevated above Moses in terms of his
knowledge of divine secrets.[28]

After some words in praise of R. Eliezer's erudition in the laws of the red
heifer and the scrupulous concern of various priests when performing the ritual of the red heifer, the text in PRK 4:7 switches direction again.

A certain non-Jew (*goy*) questioned Rabban Yoḥanan ben Zakkai, say-
ing, "These things that you [Jews] do appear to be a kind of sorcery. You
bring a heifer, slaughter it, burn it, grind it, take its ashes; [when] one of
you is defiled by contact with a corpse, you sprinkle two or three drops
on him and tell him, 'you are pure!'"
Rabban Yoḥanan said, "Has the spirit of madness ever possessed you?"
He replied, "No."
"Have you ever seen a man whom the spirit of madness has possessed?"
He said, "Yes."
"And what do you do for such a man?"
"We bring roots and make smoke under it and we throw water on it
and it [the spirit] flees."
Rabban Yoḥanan then said, "Do your ears not hear what your mouth
is saying? So too that spirit is a spirit of impurity as it is written, '*And I will
also make the prophets and the unclean spirit vanish from the land*'" (Zech
13:2).
When he [the non-Jew] left, his [Rabban Yoḥanan's] disciples said:
"Our master, you put off that non-Jew with a reed, but what answer will
you give us?"
Rabban Yoḥanan answered: "By your lives! The corpse does not defile, and the water does not purify; rather it is a decree of the holy one,
blessed be he. The holy one, blessed be he, said, 'I have set it down as a
statute, I have decreed a decree and you are not permitted to transgress

---

[28] Cf. b. Men 29b, where Akiva is again compared favorably to Moses.

my decree.' *'This is the statute [ḥuqqah] of the Torah'* (Num 19:2)."[29] (Mandelbaum ed., 74)

This dialogue between Rabban Yoḥanan ben Zakkai and a non-Jew balances the dueling perspectives featured in this chapter, one apologetic and the other nonapologetic. When speaking to the non-Jew who seeks to know the *reason* for the seemingly irrational ritual, Rabban Yoḥanan ben Zakkai provides an apology for the law, explaining it in terms that are logical and acceptable to his interlocutor. Turning to his students, however, Rabban Yoḥanan ben Zakkai dispenses with the rationalist apologetics. The law is a decree, and like all of God's decrees it was given purely in order to be obeyed. We are left with the distinct impression that how one justifies fidelity to irrational laws is in the end a matter of *audience*.

PRK piska 4 is a rich and messy text in which the many and varied rabbinic responses to the question of the Law's rationality coexist and at times collide, replicating the collocation of dueling discourses within the biblical text (biblical discourses 1 and 2). Although it was made in a different context, the following observation by Heinemann comes close to capturing the shift from 4:1's aggressive declaration of the divine ability of the unique God to generate an irrational decree to 4:7's apologetic rationale for the same: the rabbis "responded to Jewish dissenters by reasserting authority while answering pagans with pro-forma replies" (2009, 32). While R. Yoḥanan's response in 4:7 is not pro forma so much as it is accommodating to the non-Jew's perspective, the point is clear: the imagined audience matters. It is only the imagined outsider who needs assurance of the rationality of the Law. The imagined insider—who may well feel the sting of the outsider's query—requires only the assurance that the Law is a divinely revealed decree. In the final section of this chapter we consider the role of imagined audience in shaping the rabbinic response to the problem of irrational laws.

RESPONSE 4: SPLITTING THE DIFFERENCE— AN ACUTE SENSE OF AUDIENCE

In her recent book *Socratic Torah* (2013), Jenny Labendz examines a small but important set of rabbinic texts in which rabbis and non-Jews discuss the reasons for certain practices and beliefs in a friendly and open exchange, one of which is PRK 4:7 (R. Yoḥanan discussing the red heifer ritual). These texts differ from texts that feature confrontational dialogues between rabbis and various nonrabbinic others discussed in chapter 5 and earlier in this chapter. The "others" who appear in the passages analyzed by Labendz are not Sadducees

---

[29] The piska's ruminations on the (ir)rational nature of the red heifer law end here. The final two units of the piska walk through the text of Num 19 and present symbolic interpretations of the various details of the red heifer ritual.

and heretics, nor are they hostile non-Jews (idolaters or enemies) bearing the classic markers of mockery or aggression. They are simply non-Jews posing a question.

Labendz discusses four dialogues relevant to our study. In each case, a non-Jew inquires about a Jewish law or practice that appears irrational, illogical, or inequitable. Specifically, the non-Jewish interlocutor questions the reasonableness of monotheism, the logic of a rabbinic ruling regarding a festival prohibition, the inequitable nature of a Torah law, and the logic of a strange purification ritual (the case involving R. Yoḥanan ben Zakkai in PRK 4:7).[30] The non-Jew poses his question to a rabbinic sage in front of the latter's students. The rabbinic sage provides an answer in terms that are logical and acceptable to the non-Jew. As Labendz notes (106), "the rabbi reaches *out* of the specifically rabbinic sphere of experience" and responds "based on standards ... that he assumes are accepted in the non-Jewish world that he and the non-Jew inhabit together." However, when addressing his students—who demand a different kind of answer—the rabbi speaks within the framework of Jewish tradition. In one case he employs standard rabbinic hermeneutical techniques (Lev Rab 4:5); in two cases he cites a biblical source for the law (p. Bets 2:5, 61c and p. San 1:2, 19b); and in the case of PRK 4:7 concerning the red heifer ritual he concedes the irrational nature of the ritual and grounds its authority in a divine decree.[31]

Why the students are dissatisfied with the rabbi's answer to the non-Jew is a matter of some debate. Labendz argues plausibly (118–19) that when the students complain that the rabbi "put off that non-Jew with a reed," they mean that the rabbi has given information too easily. This troubles the students either because, as initiates into the rabbinic world, they hold a proprietary view of Torah study (non-Jews should not be admitted to it) *or* because they think that Torah study should require more effort. The first option seems unlikely. Since the rabbi steps *out* of the rabbinic framework to answer the non-Jew on the non-Jew's own terms rather than initiating him into specifically rabbinic methods of argumentation, he cannot plausibly be accused of giving the non-Jew access to rabbinic learning. Labendz's second explanation of the student's objection—that the response was handed over too easily—is more likely.

Nevertheless, the question remains—what is it about the answers that causes the students to object that they are too easily transmitted? As Labendz

---

[30] The four cases are discussed in Labendz 2013, 101–20: (1) Lev Rab 4:5 (Marguiles ed., 92–93)—a non-Jew asks R. Joshua ben Korḥah why the Jews do not adopt polytheism if Scripture itself tells them to incline after the majority; (2) p. Bets 2:5, 61c//p. Shab 3:3, 6a—a philosopher asks Bar Kappara why it should be permitted to drink but not wash in hot water on a festival; (3) p. San 1:2, 19b—Agnatos hegemon asks R. Yoḥanan ben Zakkai why the owner of a goring ox should be put to death with the ox; (4) PRK 4:7—the red heifer case discussed here.

[31] The rabbi's citation of a biblical verse in p. San 1:2, 19b may also serve to remind students that the law is a decree.

points out, the answers are based on common sense, common experience, or simple logic. To understand them requires little effort and none of the specialized training and techniques of a rabbinic scholar. The students are satisfied only when the rabbi provides an answer that employs rabbinic parlance (e.g., rabbinic interpretive techniques), invokes Scripture, or asserts the character of the law as divine decree.

These dialogues may be seen as dramatizations of the scenario imagined in Sifra Aḥare Mot 9:13, the passage with which this chapter began. According to Sifra Aḥare Mot, Israel's divine Law contains provisions that one would logically expect to find in any society, as well as provisions that cause not only outsiders, but certain insiders (those given to an evil impulse!), to object. The four dialogues analyzed here dramatize the Sifra passage by presenting the puzzlement of both an outsider and an insider. First, the outsider raises a question about an irrational, inequitable, or otherwise problematic law and is answered on his own terms. By explaining the law, the rabbinic dialogue partner converts it from an irrational *ḥoq* to a rational *mishpat*, and the outsider is satisfied. But the insiders require an answer to the same question on their own terms. The insiders in these dramatizations of the Sifra's scenario are students who feel the sting of the non-Jew's question and as a result need a reminder and a reassurance that even irrational laws are grounded in the authoritative will of God. The rabbi's answer reflects the position outlined earlier in this chapter: the most highly valued laws are not the logical laws that one would expect to find in any legal system, but the irrational laws that inspire objection and complaint. These laws should *not* be explained away (and only an outsider would be satisfied by the attempt to do so) but accepted on the authority of Scripture as divine decrees, for these are the laws that challenge, refine, and purify those who labor to follow God's will.

In providing these two very different kinds of answer, Rabbi Yoḥanan ben Zakkai in PRK 4:7 employs "multiple discourses" for "multiple audiences" who ask the same question (Labendz 2103, 121, 132). He demonstrates a sensitivity to the values and expectations of his non-Jewish interlocutor as well as to the values and expectations of his students, answering each in a suitable manner.[32] Labendz (ibid., 121–45) argues that this attention to audience finds important parallels in the Gospel of Mark.[33] She focuses on two passages in Mark that portray a dialogue between Jesus and an outsider, followed by a reaction from insiders. The first is the passage referenced earlier: Mark 7:1–23. When the Pharisees and scribes ask Jesus why he and his disciples do not follow tradition and wash their hands before eating. Jesus gives three responses—

---

[32] The evident irritation with which the rabbi sometimes responds to his students suggests that he is disappointed in the students for feeling the force of the non-Jew's objection and for forgetting that fidelity to the Law does not depend on its rational character.

[33] Labendz notes that the similarity between these rabbinic texts and the two passages in Mark was already pointed out by David Daube (1956).

one to the Pharisees and scribes, another to the crowd, and finally, in private, a third to his students. In Mark 10:2–11, Pharisees ask Jesus whether divorce is lawful. Jesus provides two answers—one to the Pharisees and another to his disciples.

Labendz is interested in the formal similarities between the rabbinic and Markan examples. For our purposes, these formal similarities are enhanced by the antipodal substance of the passage, which can shed light on the confrontation between divine law discourses in first-century Palestine. As noted in chapter 5, Jesus's first answer in Mark 7 is a rebuke to the Pharisees for abandoning divine law in order to follow human law. As an example of Pharisaic neglect of divine law, Jesus points to a legal strategy employed by Pharisees to avoid supporting parents as prescribed in the fifth commandment. Jesus's charge is that the Pharisees ignore the divine commandment to honor father and mother (by exploiting a legal ruse) but insist on hand washing, a (mere) "tradition of the elders" (Mark 7:5). Jesus's language doesn't merely assume the Greco-Roman dichotomy between divine law and human law—it makes it entirely explicit. Moreover, the references to purity and dietary laws (vv. 2–5 and 18–19) map this dichotomy onto the difference between a rational moral law and an irrational ritual law.

Thus, in his second and third answers to the crowd and the disciples, Jesus critiques the Pharisaic understanding of purity itself and denies the power of foods to cause defilement. Impurity, he says, is what comes out of a person, not what goes in. What goes into the body seems to have two meanings here. When he addresses the crowd, it refers to food (and hence it is a denial of some aspect of ritual impurity associated with the consumption of food);[34] when he addresses the disciples, it is a reference to various moral misdeeds—fornication, theft, murder, adultery, and other heinous sins. Jesus is slippery here: the Pharisees have asked him about ritual impurity, but his answer shifts to the realm of moral impurity.[35] His somewhat dismissive rhetoric suggests that ritual impurity is not "real" and, therefore, not significant. The divine law concerns itself with issues of morality. This response reflects a Greco-Roman discourse that associates divine law with truth (realism; G-R 1(iii)) and virtue (G-R 3). According to the Markan Jesus, the divine law is not concerned with ritual purity (except, perhaps, insofar as it is conducive to moral virtue). It is simply a mistake to think that divine law concerns itself with, or attributes any reality to, purity of a strictly ritual nature.

In Mark 10, Jesus answers the Pharisees' question about divorce with an argument from *nature* as recorded in the creation account of Genesis: humans

---

[34] This is likely a reference to the fact that unwashed hands may bear a ritual impurity that can defile food. See the full and thorough discussion of the purity and dietary issues addressed in this passage in Collins's 2007 commentary, 348–62, and Klawans 2000, 146–50.

[35] On ritual vs. moral impurity, see Klawans 2000.

were created male and female; in marriage they become one flesh that, being joined by God, cannot be separated by any human. Moses's law permitting divorce was an unhappy concession to the hardness of the human heart. The clear implication is that the Deuteronomic law permitting divorce is a man-made law (an enactment by Moses) that cannot uproot an eternal divine law grounded in human nature from the time of divine creation. Jesus's response reflects Greco-Roman discourses according to which the divine law is grounded in nature and cannot be set aside by human laws (G-R 1).[36]

The combined evidence of these passages yields the following portrait: Jesus as presented by Mark accepts and assumes the binary distinction common in Greco-Roman discourses of law between divine law (which here promotes virtue and ethical goods like honoring one's parents and monogamy) and human law. The divine law is grounded in nature; it is realist, and its central concern is morality; it is superior to human law and cannot be contradicted by it. By contrast, human law is exemplified here by rules of *ritual* impurity (which are not "real" and do not conduce to moral virtue), nominalist legal ruses that subvert observance of a higher divine law, and a human (Mosaic) rule permitting divorce (which is against the dictates of nature). According to these Markan passages, Jesus inhabits a universe of discourse on the question of divine law that is inflected by the Greco-Roman characterization of divine law and human law, and assumes a dichotomy between them.

Labendz is correct that the Markan dialogues are usefully compared to rabbinic dialogues in which different answers are given to outsiders and insiders. And as we have seen, they are also usefully compared with the rabbinic dialogues considered earlier in this chapter. Because the Gospel dialogues are marked by hostility and confrontation, Jesus has much in common with the aggressive, mocking "other" featured in the confrontational encounters depicted in Sifra Aḥare Mot 9:13 and related texts. Those who mock and ridicule the rabbis object not only to the divorce of law and truth, as seen in chapter 5, but also irrational or unethical laws as unbefitting a Law that professes to be divine. In other words, they tend to mock those features of the biblical and rabbinic presentation of divine law that deviate from Greco-Roman notions of natural law. Jesus in Mark 7 and 10 matches this description: he does not view ritual impurity as "real," so the Pharisaic regulations of ritual impurity cannot be a command of divine law and can be set aside. Nominalist legal ruses that enable one to evade morally virtuous obligations (such as honoring one's parents) are also objectionable. Finally, he believes that human nature was created in such a way as to dictate the practice of monogamy, and that no statement by a man, even Moses, can override this truth. Finally, he implies that the primary concern of the Law is ethical, virtuous behavior. Thus, impurity is to be under-

---

[36] The realist legal approach of the Markan Jesus resembles CD 4:21, which rejects polygamy because it violates the principle of creation—"male and female he created them."

stood metaphorically as sin, and the obligation to honor one's parents cannot be circumvented.

Because Jesus is the hero of the Gospel story, his mockery is positively valued rather than condemned, and his Pharisaic opponents are silenced by his mocking critique. By contrast, in the rabbinic stories the hostile outsider (generally a *min*) is silenced by his rabbinic opponents. The two sets of stories are mirror images of each other. In the Gospel stories the mocking critic *triumphs* over those who do not conceive of divine law in natural law terms. In the rabbinic stories, the mocking critic is *defeated* by those who do not conceive of divine law in natural law terms.

These Markan dialogues are critically important evidence that the dueling conceptions of divine law traced in this volume were present and sparking controversy in first-century CE Palestine no less than in first-century Alexandria. There can be no doubt that first-century Palestinian Jews were familiar with Greco-Roman discourses of divine law as distinct from human law, and that they engaged in an evaluation and critique of biblical divine law in the light of those discourses. In Mark 7 and 10, Jesus makes the calculation—as Paul will also—that certain provisions of the Law as interpreted by the Pharisees are mere human provisions (stemming from Moses, from "the elders," or from the scribes themselves) and do not reflect the divine moral law grounded in nature. Jesus makes the further calculation in these dialogues—as Paul will also—that different audiences require different kinds of answers to questions about the Law. Of course, Paul is not the Markan Jesus; Paul's embrace of divine law discourse for Gentile audiences is more clearly opportunistic,[37] but both figures appear to have internalized Greco-Roman discourses of divine law, both evaluate biblical divine law in the light of those discourses, and both possess an acute awareness of audience when addressing the dissonance between the two.

CONCLUSION

Greco-Roman discourses of natural law and positive law informed the development and expression of rabbinic conceptions of Mosaic Law on the issue of the Law's rationality. A number of the texts analyzed in this chapter attest to a rabbinic consciousness of and sensitivity to the expectation that divine law should be rational (an expectation they likely internalized but displaced onto others), and an anxiety over the fact that parts of the Mosaic Law appear to lack an intrinsic rationality or even an extrinsic rational purpose or utility. It is no accident that the rabbinic authors of these texts, like the author of the Letter of Aristeas, 4 Maccabees, and Philo, are exercised by precisely those parts of the

---

[37] Which is not to say that Jesus is *not* also opportunistic in his deployment of various modes of discourse. It is simply to say that Jesus is, in these texts, a literary character, as opposed to an author like Paul, and his motivations as a character are obscured by the Gospel writer.

divine law that draw criticism for being arbitrary and irrational—the ritual laws and, especially, the laws of impurity and the dietary laws. While the author of the Letter of Aristeas and Philo responded apologetically to this criticism, asserting both the intrinsic rationality and the rational purpose of the Law, the rabbis tended to adopt a rationalist apologetic primarily when imagining themselves in dialogue with outsiders. The more common rabbinic response, and the response imagined as appropriate for "insiders," asserts that the divine law does indeed contain irrational decrees. This is not, however, a defect in the law but a virtue. Divine decrees—especially the irrational elements—cultivate obedience and provide opportunities for moral refinement and purification. This response is, of course, no less apologetic than Philo's rationalization of the Law. However, where Philo's apologetic is based on the premise that divine law's authority derives from its rational character, the rabbinic apologetic denies that premise. For the most part, the rabbis locate the Law's authority in the sovereign will of God and accept the existence of nonrational decrees. Rabbinic demonstrations of the rationality of the law tend to be found in contexts in which the rabbis imagine and represent the perspective of various external and internal others, ranging from the merely curious to the overtly hostile.

The attribution of rationality to divine law (an idea central to Stoic natural law theory) was widespread in late antique classical culture. The idea was known to Jews in Roman Palestine, and it is consciously rejected in many rabbinic texts. Rabbinic texts that represent the divine law as arbitrary fiat on occasion depict the rabbis as objects of ridicule and mockery. This representation finds confirmation in Mark 7:1–23, where Jesus is depicted as mocking the Pharisees for observing precisely those laws widely identified as irrational—the ritual impurity laws (7:1–4) and the dietary laws (7:18–19). The Markan Jesus, the author of the Letter of Aristeas, 4 Maccabees, Philo, and many rabbinic writings all agree on one point: the ritual impurity and dietary laws appear to be arbitrary and irrational. Those who accept philosophical and popular Greco-Roman claims of the inherent rationality of divine law and seek to "rescue" Mosaic Law from the charge of irrationality engage in apologetics to demonstrate the rationality of the dietary and impurity laws (Aristeas, 4 Macc, and Philo). Those who accept the inherent rationality of divine law but are not concerned to "rescue" Mosaic Law from the charge of irrationality dismiss these practices as unessential (the Markan Jesus in Mark 7; see also Paul in 1 Cor 8:8). The rabbis who do not accept Greco-Roman claims of the inherent rationality of divine law adopt a number of responses: they concede but transvalue the trait of irrationality such that the Law's irrationality is a sign of its divinity; they concede but disown the rationalist perspective partially or wholly by assigning it to hostile outsiders; they deny the premise but declare the Law's reasons inaccessible; or they adopt a mix of these responses depending on audience.

CHAPTER 7

The Flexibility of Torah

Greco-Roman discourses of natural law and positive law emphasize the stable or inflexible character of the former and the unstable or flexible character of the latter. Indeed, one of the key indicators of human law in classical discourse is its inconstancy in contrast to the eternal and unchanging natural law (G-R 1(ii)). In the *Laws*, Clinias and Megillus concede that variability, or rational modification of the law, disqualifies the constitutions of Crete and Sparta from claiming the title of divine law. The idea of human adjustment of the law is threatening to those who believe in the divinity of their laws, because of the popular notion that what is divine is perfect and therefore unchanging (G-R 8).

In this chapter we examine sources that shed light on a variety of issues bearing on the question of the flexibility of the divine law of Israel according to the talmudic rabbis. In many of these sources, the Law is seen to be susceptible to change through rational adjustments by humans. The rhetoric surrounding human adjustment of the Law varies. In some passages these adjustments are represented as a kind of natural evolution justified by values and commitments internal to the system. In some passages, however, they are represented as interventions based on values and commitments external to the system, raising important questions about the agency and authority of human beings in a system of divine law. On what grounds do humans modify the Law? How is it that rational modification of the Law and the implied fallibility of the divine lawgiver do not impinge upon the Law's divinity in the eyes of the rabbis?

Rabbinic literature is hardly univocal on this subject. Some texts celebrate the Law's flexibility and responsiveness to shifting circumstances and human moral critique, understanding these characteristics to be a *proof*, rather than a *negation*, of the Law's divinity. Other texts signal an unease with, and resistance to, the characterization of the Law as responsive to human intervention of any kind and attempt to soften the radical nature of this intervention by representing it as, at the very least, divinely authorized. For the most part, however, rabbinic sources maintain a view of divine law that is flexible and responsive to shifting circumstances, human rational argument, and even independent moral critique, in direct contradiction to classical discourses of divine law.

LEGISLATIVE MECHANISMS OF
CHANGE—A RHETORIC OF DISCLOSURE?

Aaron Panken's comprehensive study of the rhetoric of innovation in rabbinic literature provides important evidence of the rabbinic perception of divine law as susceptible to change. Panken (2005) examines sources that explicitly signal rabbinic self-consciousness of legal change by employing one of three semantic markers: *barishonah* ("at first"), *taqqanah* ("enactment" or "repair [of the law]"), and *gezerah* ("decree"). We begin with a review of the data assembled by Panken.

The first semantic marker of self-conscious legal change, *barishonah*, points to a reflective tendency inasmuch as it describes what was formerly the case ("at first, the law was X ...") and what will henceforth be the case ("but now in light of circumstance Y it will be Z ..."). Panken writes (xvii),

> [The term] claims that prior stages of Jewish law were considered carefully for their efficacy, and, when they did not meet appropriate standards of completeness, suitability for the current situation or fairness to members of the community, they were reshaped, rejected or renewed.

Of the 182 passages that employ *barishonah* as a marker of reflection on legal change, 86 percent provide an explicit rationale (ibid., 8). The most common rationales have to do with the inadequacy of the law. Unanticipated events may show a particular law to be dangerous or to lead to undesirable consequences or confusion. A law may be seen to be inadequate in light of changing social, agricultural, or economic conditions. Other motivating factors listed by Panken include changes in municipal and authority structures, changes in the behavior of the general populace, the desire to adopt the teachings of a revered sage, and the desire to prevent embarrassment. Only a handful of the changes signaled by the term *barishonah* are explained as a response to the destruction in 70 CE or "for the sake of the common welfare."[1]

The rabbinic *barishonah* cases participate in a long-standing ancient Near Eastern and Mediterranean tradition of *disclosed innovation* that draws a distinction between earlier and current norms. At one extreme, this tradition is found in the second-millennium BCE Hittite laws and, at the other, in the Sassanian legal collection *The Book of a Thousand Judgments* (Panken, 6–7). For a contemporaneous parallel, Panken points to the Sermon on the Mount (Matt 5:21–48) and Gaius's *Institutes*: in the former, Jesus introduces new norms that contradict existing norms; in the latter, Roman legal experts often reconsider earlier positions and formulate new laws to ensure equity. Indeed, the fact that all of the *barishonah* cases are reported by Palestinian tradents (tannaitic and amoraic sages) and occur in a Palestinian milieu (42) significantly increases

---

[1] Panken 2005, 8–76, details all of these rationales.

the likelihood that the phenomenon of reflective innovation was influenced or enhanced by the existence of comparable processes of revision in Roman law.[2]

The second semantic marker of legal change, *taqqanah*, is used to indicate a sheer innovation. Panken writes (xvii–xviii):

> The largest subcategory of legal changes introduced with this term shows the initiation of new practices that respond to an unmet need poorly served by the present state of the law ... Thus, *takkanot* generally represent innovations in law that layer entirely new practices, prayers or regulations never considered before onto the already accepted corpus of Jewish custom and law.

There are nearly two hundred texts (excluding parallels) that employ a form of the word *taqqanah* to denote halakhic change. The Talmuds are far more likely than tannaitic texts to refer to a measure as a *taqqanah*, by a ratio of 15 to 1. The authority to make *taqqanot* finds its biblical source in Deuteronomy 17:11 ("You shall act in accordance with the instructions given you and the ruling handed down to you; you must not deviate from the verdict that they announce either to the right or to the left").[3] More than 90 percent are accompanied by a rationale of some kind, with the vast majority proactively initiating a new practice, often to benefit the social welfare or encourage proper behavior. Many new practices are (anachronistically) attributed to biblical characters. Adam, the patriarchs, Moses, Joshua, various prophets and kings, Ezra, and the "men of the great assembly" are all credited with instituting various practices, such as prayer, festival observances, and customs ranging from the realm of commerce to the realm of ritual purity. Finally, while the Yerushalmi is very careful to distinguish *taqqanot* from Torah laws (Panken, 130), on at least nine occasions the stammaitic (anonymous and, in this case, probably late) layer of the Babylonian Talmud elevates the authority of *taqqanot* to something akin to biblical authority.

The third semantic marker of legal change, *gezerah*, is also innovative but in a different way. Panken writes (xviii):

> Instead of liberally expanding the purview of law as we so often find with *takkanot*, *gezerot* tend to employ an innovative legal approach to act conservatively—utilizing the radical device of creating new law to prevent the violation of older, accepted law. While the legal outcome is ultimately

---

[2] We will return to this point below.

[3] Another biblical source for the authority to promulgate *taqqanot* is Deut 32:7 ("Ask your father, he will inform you, your elders, they will tell you"). For the derivation of this authority from these verses, see MidTan to Deut 17:11 and b. Shab 23a. Panken properly notes (2005, 129) that these verses require significant hermeneutic intervention to be read as justifying the rabbinic power to legislate and alter law when necessary.

conservative in nature, it must be said at once that such a rhetorical choice is radically innovative at the same time.

The term *gezerah* in the sense of a "fence around the Torah" (a precautionary measure that extends the limits of a negative commandment in the Torah in order to prevent its violation; Panken, 253) comes into wide written use in amoraic texts and does not appear to have been current in the tannaitic period (309). Indeed, no tannaim refer to *gezerot* at all. Discussion of *gezerot* reaches a peak during the third and fourth generations of amoraim (late third–fourth centuries CE). The Babylonian Talmud contains four times as many occurrences of the term as all of the rest of rabbinic literature combined (310).

Panken's survey of the more than one thousand reported legal changes indicated by these three semantic markers reveals important geographical and chronological differences in the sources. Palestinian sources favor the terms *barishonah* and *taqqanah*, rarely using the term *gezerah*. These sources attribute the initiation of legal change to biblical and Second Temple figures, but not to rabbis or the rabbinic collective. In comparison to Palestinian sources, the Bavli's editors more frequently initiate new practices (*taqqanot*), retroject *taqqanot* onto earlier figures, and incorporate numerous *gezerot*. How are we to interpret these data?

Panken's interpretation of these data pulls in two different directions. On the one hand, he views the use of these three markers as signaling a steady and almost linear shift from an anxious biblical rhetoric of concealment, "due to an ideology of constancy and respect for a divinely transmitted core" (4), to a self-confident rabbinic rhetoric of disclosure:

> In biblical literature, the authors employed what Bernard Levinson has called a "rhetoric of concealment" with respect to legal change, which tended to conceal changes of law rather than highlight them. Rabbinic literature made a conscious choice to utilize new forms of rhetoric, some extending the trajectory of biblical rhetoric, while others were drawn from surrounding Greek and Roman societies. Rabbinic literature often tended to employ what we will now call a "rhetoric of disclosure." This rhetoric called for both a way of announcing legal change that acknowledged prior law and the revisions it had undergone, and additionally, a way of justifying it. (xxiii)[4]

Moreover, Panken views the expanded use of these three markers in the Babylonian Talmud as the expression of an even greater self-confidence regarding legal innovation and the assertion of rabbinic power than is found in Palestinian sources (198, 335). On this view, the Babylonian Talmud's retrojection of *taqqanot* onto earlier authorities and especially biblical characters, as well as its

---

[4] Panken refers here to Levinson 1992, 45

tendency to elevate the authority of *taqqanot* to something approximating biblical authority, are evidence of self-confidence and a lack of squeamishness regarding the power inherent in *taqqanot* (132). To root a *taqqanah* in a biblical source highlights the *importance* of the change it initiates (198).

However, the data are susceptible to a different interpretation, and Panken himself does not hide from this fact. Thus, he writes:

> The statements of the Amoraic tradents cited, and the apparent editorial acts of Stammaitic editors, especially, betray a tremendous angst about legal change ... While they utilized a rhetoric of disclosure, admitting that law was changing, they did not always admit that it was *their* decision to alter law. They often retrojected or demurred in other ways, bolstering and supplementing their own power with the weight of prior history and the authority of prior leadership. (334)

On this view, the Babylonian Talmud's retrojection of *taqqanot* onto earlier figures and its elevation of the authority of *taqqanot* to almost biblical heights are evidence of anxiety and a *lack* of self-confidence. To root a *taqqanah* in a biblical source highlights the need to "disown" the innovation.[5] To use Levinson's and Panken's terms, we might say that the attempt to justify and explain new law by inserting it into the inherited tradition is an attempt to conceal even as it discloses.[6]

The same tension exists in Panken's assessment of the blossoming of *gezerot* in the Babylonian Talmud. On the one hand, because it draws attention to a change in the law, it is a sign of self-confidence in the assertion of rabbinic power. On the other hand, and as Panken himself notes, *gezerot* represent an assertion of rabbinic power designed to ensure that biblical law is *preserved* and precisely not substantively modified (Panken, xvii, 219, 310, 314). In short, to construct a *gezerah* is to assert power, but it is an assertion of power in the service of the conservative goal of preventing the modification of biblical law (as Panken himself is aware). Given this tension, how are we to assess the proliferation of *gezerot* in the later Babylonian sources?

Gezerot certainly make additions to the law, and in that limited sense, they represent change. Nevertheless, pace Panken, additions that are designed to preserve the law and *disable* its further evolution must be distinguished from positive enactments and changes (those marked by the terms *taqqanah* and

[5] Panken (2005, 47) concludes as much in his analysis of b. Yev 39b. Here late amoraim distance themselves from a halakhic change by redescribing the "earlier" and "later" laws as equally valid alternative opinions preferred at different times.

[6] See chapter 1, where I suggested that Deuteronomy's rhetoric seeks to conceal the *authorship* of biblical innovation, not the *fact* of innovation. The rabbis are no different. They disclose the fact of innovation, but they seek to conceal its provenance by inserting it into the inherited tradition. Thus, the rhetoric of disclosure highlighted by Panken actually conceals (the identity of the innovators) even as it discloses (the innovations themselves).

barishonah) that are designed to modify the law and *enable* its further evolution. Viewed in this light, *gezerot* are more plausibly interpreted as participating not in a rhetoric of disclosure but in a *new* rabbinic rhetoric of concealment different from the biblical rhetoric of concealment noted by Levinson. This new rabbinic rhetoric of concealment is expressed not only in the proliferation of *gezerot* but also in the retrojection of legal change onto biblical and Second Temple authorities and the attribution of a nearly biblical level of authority to *taqqanot*. To the extent that these phenomena occur most frequently in Babylonian sources, we are forced to conclude that as we move from the Palestinian rabbinic milieu in terms of both chronology and geography, legal change is met with increasing unease and resistance. There is not here a uniform and linear move from a biblical rhetoric of concealment to a rabbinic rhetoric of disclosure. In the Babylonian Talmud, particularly its later layers, a new rhetoric of resistance to halakhic change surfaces in lockstep with, and in opposition to, expressions of rabbinic empowerment.[7]

This new rabbinic rhetoric of concealment or resistance appears even in the context of *taqqanot*. For Panken, the Babylonian Talmud's increased use of the language of *taqqanah* suggests that the Bavli is more inclined than the Yerushalmi to present rabbis as empowered in regard to rabbinic legislation (189). But here again, closer analysis reveals a more complex picture, since the treatment of *taqqanot* in later Babylonian sources sometimes works precisely to undercut rabbinic legislative power and to obscure the extent to which rabbinic legislation innovates. We may see this most vividly by comparing the two Talmuds' treatment of earlier *taqqanot* that directly overrule or uproot biblical law.[8]

Uprooting Torah Law[9]

Tannaitic materials[10] attribute to authorities and rabbis of the Second Temple and tannaitic periods (prior to the third century CE) 155 rulings that came to

---

[7] Fisch (1997) similarly identifies dueling rhetorics of disclosure and disguise in connection with the rational critique and revision of halakhah in the Bavli. Specifically, Fisch asserts (61–96) the simultaneous existence already in early rabbinic sources of two attitudes toward the halakhic tradition—a "traditionalist" attitude, which insists that the halakhic tradition is at all times absolutely and formally binding and expands only by accumulation rather than revision, and an antitraditionalist attitude, which holds the halakhic tradition in constant review and revises it as necessary (an attitude of "constructive skepticism"). According to Fisch, the Bavli's strategies of halakhic argumentation engage in antitraditionalist work (the rational revision of the halakhah) but under the guise of a traditionalist rhetoric (45, 119–33, 163–66).

[8] The following discussion draws upon and updates Hayes 1998a.

[9] For rabbinic sources that authorize not merely the reinterpretation but the outright rejection or uprooting of authoritative traditions deemed to be morally defective, see Shremer (2001). See, further, the discussion in chapter 7.

[10] I include here baraitot, though I recognize that some baraitot may not be genuinely tannaitic. However, since the vast majority of the material utilized in this study is from the Mishnah and the Tosefta, the chance inclusion of a few items that may not be genuinely tannaitic will make little statistical difference.

be identified by later tradition as *taqqanot*.[11] In nineteen cases (i.e., 12.5 percent), a *taqqanah* is described in such a way as to contradict and therefore modify biblical law.[12] While the Babylonian Talmud recognizes a limited rabbinic authority to overrule biblical law in the case of (1) acts of omission (*shev ve'al ta'aseh*, i.e., nonobservance of a positive commandment) and (2) acts of commission (*qum va'aseh*, i.e., performance of a prohibited act) as a temporary emergency measure in order to prevent a more serious violation of biblical law, it does not permit the abrogation of a prohibitive commandment for all time.[13] Tannaitic and amoraic sources that evince a vision of rabbinic authority modifying biblical law are neutralized in later strata of the Talmuds that deny the innovative or contradictory nature of these early *taqqanot*. The later neutralization or denial of rabbinic enactments that contradict biblical law is more pronounced in the Bavli than in the Yerushalmi. The Bavli adopts various strategies in order to redescribe all ten of the *taqqanot* that it identifies as ostensibly contradicting biblical law as not in fact contradicting biblical law. By contrast, the Yerushalmi is quite prepared to admit that at least some *taqqanot* are indeed innovations that contradict provisions of biblical law.

One of the strategies used to deny the contradictory nature of rabbinic *taqqanot* is legal revisionism in which a *taqqanah* is redescribed as emerging from biblical exegesis rather than rabbinic legislation. Revisionism of this sort—recasting an early law that is held to be rabbinic (a *taqqanah*) as biblical in origin because of a perceived contradiction between the *taqqanah* and biblical law—occurs five times in the Yerushalmi[14] and six times in the Bavli.[15] Four

---

[11] I rely upon the list compiled by Moshe Bloch in his *Sha'are Torat Ha-taqqanot* (with the addition of m. Ter 1:4, m. Ter 2:2, and m. Yev 7:3), which is a slightly smaller number of cases than the number surveyed in Panken's study of *taqqanot*. Volumes 3–5 list *taqqanot* attributed to halakhic authorities from Yoḥanan the High Priest to the last of the tannaim. For the most part these *taqqanot* appear in material of tannaitic provenance. While I cannot guarantee that Bloch's list is free of errors, it is unlikely that he has excluded or wrongly included so many cases as to alter significantly the claims I will make on the basis of the data.

[12] Nine *taqqanot* are so described by the Yerushalmi only (p. Bets 2:1, 61b–c; p. Sheq 7:3, 50d; m. Yev 7:3; p. Git 3:7, 46a; 4:2, 45c (regarding *terumah*); 4:4, 45d; 5:5, 47a; 5:7, 47b; p. BQ 10:3, 7c), three *taqqanot* by the Bavli only (m. Ter 2:2 [in b. Yev 89a–b]; b. Ket 52b; b. San 3a), and seven *taqqanot* by both the Yerushalmi and the Bavli (p. Shevi 10:2–3, 39c = b. Git 36a; p. RH 4:1, 59b = b. RH 29b; p. Sukk 3:13, 54a = b. RH 30a; p. Yev 10:1, 10c = b. Yev 89b; p. Git 4:2, 45c = b. Yev 90b [regarding an annulled get]; p. BM 4:2, 9d = b. BM 47b). Thus, while the Yerushalmi describes sixteen *taqqanot* as contradicting biblical law and the Bavli describes ten in this manner, the total number of *distinct taqqanot* said to contradict Torah law is nineteen or 12.5 percent.

[13] See Gilat 1970.

[14] The cases subject to revision in the Yerushalmi are (1) the *taqqanah* of Hillel regarding prozbul (p. Shevi 10:2–3, 39c); (2) the law of *eruv tavshilin* (p. Bets 2:1, 61a–b); (3) the law of sacrilege as applied to the ashes of the red heifer (p. Sheq 7:6, 50d); (4) the principle of acquisition by drawing (p. BM 4:2, 9d); and (5) the laws of *terumah* (p. Yev 7:2, 8a–b).

[15] The cases subject to revision in the Bavli are (1) the *taqqanah* of Hillel regarding the prozbul (b. Git 36a); (2) the *taqqanah* of R. Yoḥanan ben Zakkai regarding the sounding of the shofar when Rosh haShanah falls on the Sabbath (b. RH 29b); (3) the *taqqanah* of R. Yoḥanan ben Zakkai regarding the

additional cases of contradictory *taqqanot* are neutralized in the Bavli in other ways. A classic example of revisionism concerns the prozbul of Hillel.[16]

The Mishnah reports that in the early first century CE Hillel instituted the prozbul (m. Git 4:3; cf. m. Shevi 10:2–3). While there is some dispute over the way in which the prozbul actually worked, in essence it was a transaction with the court that enabled one to circumvent the release of debts commanded by the Torah to take place in the sabbatical year (Deut 15).[17] Hillel's prozbul is one of the most explicit examples of a rabbinic decree that uproots or over- turns a provision of the Torah, and of rabbinic deviation from a clear biblical norm.[18] Where the Bible prohibits the collection of debts in the seventh year, Hillel's prozbul makes it possible for debts to be preserved and ultimately collected.

Various strategies are employed to soften the innovative nature of the proz- bul by recasting it as the correct reading of Scripture rather than a new rabbinic *taqqanah*. The first of these strategies relies on a competing biblical text, and this appears already in the Mishnah, at m. Shevi 10:3.

> The prozbul ... is one of the matters instituted by Hillel the Elder. When he saw that people refrained from making loans and violated what is writ- ten in the Torah *"beware lest you harbor the base thought ['the seventh year, the year of release is approaching' so that you are mean to your needy kinsman and give him nothing]"* (Deut 15:9); [so] Hillel instituted the prozbul.

According to this mishnah, Hillel saw that people refrained from making loans to the needy late in the sabbatical cycle, thereby transgressing Deuteronomy 15:9's warning against the same. Realizing that people were incapable of fulfill- ing both commands—the command to release debts in the seventh year and the prohibition against withholding loans because of the approaching seventh year—Hillel made a decision. He decided that it was better that people obey the prohibition in Deuteronomy 15:9 against harboring a base thought and re- fusing to lend money than that they fulfill the obligation to release debts. Thus, while Hillel's enactment contradicts the letter of the Torah in one place, it may

---

lulav ritual outside the sanctuary (b RH 30a); (4) the appointment of lay judges for civil cases (b. San 2b–3a); (5) the assignment of a woman's ketubbah to her sons (b. Ket 52b); (6) the principle of acqui- sition by drawing (b. BM 47b).

[16] The interpretation of this case offered here differs markedly from the interpretation of David Kraemer (1991), which is the basis of the interpretation of Panken.

[17] Note that we are not here concerned with the details of the prozbul's operation or historical ques- tions of its rise, use, and application. For this information see, e.g., Zeitlin 1947 and Shiffman 1991. What concerns us here is the amoraic perception of this law and the source of its authority to set aside the biblical requirement of a sabbatical-year release of debts.

[18] This is also the assessment of Gordis (1991). This is not to say that the rabbis do not generate other laws that deviate radically from the norms of the biblical text. They certainly do, but through midrashic interpretation. Here we are concerned only with *taqqanot*—halakhic enactments that are not created by means of Scriptural interpretation.

be said to fulfill it in another. As an exposition of biblical law it enjoys full biblical authority.

David Kraemer does not believe that the tradition in m. Shevi seeks to provide the *taqqanah* with biblical justification. He states (1991, 66–67) that this
mishnah "leaves little doubt that the enactment is fundamentally rabbinic ...
[t]he Mishnah allows us to be sympathetic with Hillel's enactment. It does not,
however, ask us to ignore the essential nature of that enactment"—qua enactment. Pace Kraemer, I believe that m. Shevi's explanation of the situation does
significantly modify our understanding of what Hillel did. Although this mishnah does not explicitly deny that the prozbul was a *taqqanah*, or rabbinic ruling, by pointing out the existence of dueling biblical requirements it implies
strongly that Hillel's *taqqanah* did not innovate. Rather, Hillel saw that the
Bible contains two distinct requirements that have the potential to come into
direct conflict; he further saw that in his day they *had* come into conflict. In
instituting the prozbul, Hillel did not innovate so much as arbitrate between
competing biblical claims.[19] Thus, already in the Mishnah we find a rhetoric of
disclosure concerning Hillel's prozbul juxtaposed with a rhetoric of concealment that obscures the element of innovation by locating the cancellation of
the release of debts in Scripture.[20]

In both Talmuds, Hillel's prozbul is also subjected to a strategy of revision.
We begin with the Yerushalmi's sugya at p. Shevi 10:3, 39c.

> 1. R. Huna said: I posed a difficulty before R. Yaakov bar Aḥa. According
> to one who holds that tithing [since the exile] is observed on the author-
> ity of the Bible [and thus presumably the laws of the Sabbatical year too],
> *has Hillel created an ordinance that contradicts Torah law?*

R. Huna poses a difficult question. According to those who hold a particular
view on a related matter, has Hillel created an ordinance that contradicts biblical law (... *veHillel matqin al devar Torah?*).[21] In the second step, a third-century
CE Palestinian rabbi examines the Bible in an effort to decide the question.

---

[19] Regarding the parallel in Sifre Deut 113, Kraemer holds that identifying a biblical justification
for suspending the release of debts is an attempt to undercut the implications of language in m. Git that
refers to the prozbul as a rabbinic enactment (*hitqin ... mipney tiqqun ha'olam*) and to assert that the
prozbul is justified biblically (1991, 67). It seems, however, that if the midrash in Sifre Deut 113 claims
that "Hillel did nothing beyond what the Torah itself would permit" (ibid.), then the parallel text in
m. Shevi must make the same claim.

[20] In the same way, Levinson (1992, 2002) argues that the Deuteronomist conceals his innovations
by locating them in earlier authoritative sources.

[21] For *'al* in the sense of "contradicting/uprooting" (and not merely "in addition to" or "beyond"),
compare the phrase *hitnah 'al mah shekatuv batorah* in m. BB 8:5, which can only be translated as "he
made a condition contradicting/contrary to what is written in the Torah" (see Qorban ha-Edah to
p. Git 21b, who paraphrases R. Huna's question as follows: "It is a difficulty: How could Hillel make an
enactment not to release and so uproot [*'aqar*] biblical law?" and Pene Moshe to p. Git 21b, who paraphrases the question this way: "and if it is by Torah law that the seventh year releases then can Hillel

2. R. Yosi said: Is it not the case that when the Israelites were exiled to Babylonia they were exempted only from commandments dependent on the land? But the sabbatical cancellation of debts is biblical law both in the land of Israel and outside the land of Israel.

[The implication is that Hillel's prozbul therefore contradicts biblical law.]

R. Yosi's answer in step 2 contains the assertion that the sabbatical cancellation of debts is biblical law, both in the land of Israel and outside the land of Israel, with the implication that Hillel's prozbul contradicts biblical law. But in step 3 R. Yosi changes his mind.

3. R. Yosi reconsidered and said: [Deut 15:2 states] *"and this is the manner of the release: every creditor shall release."* This means that when the release of land is operative by biblical law then the release of debts is also operative by biblical law whether in the Land or abroad. When the release of land applies in the Land only by rabbinical law then the release of debts applies both in the Land and abroad only by rabbinical law.

On the basis of a midrashic reading of Deuteronomy 15:2, R. Yosi concludes that at times the cancellation of debts operates on the authority of the Bible and at other times only on the authority of the rabbis. This is because proper exegesis of the Bible reveals that the seventh-year release of debts and the fiftieth-year release of land operate in tandem or not at all. The requirement to release debts in the sabbatical year lapses during those periods (and Hillel lived during one of those periods) in which it is not possible also to observe the jubilee year's release of the land. Thus, R. Yosi argues, in Hillel's day the sabbatical-year cancellation of debts was not in force *according to biblical law properly understood.* Then why was Hillel's prozbul necessary? Because rabbis prior to Hillel had required its continued and supererogatory observance (= it "applies

---

make an enactment to transgress [*la'avor 'al*] Torah Law?"). That this is the proper understanding of *'al* in the phrase *lehatqin 'al devar Torah* is borne out by similar sugyot that utilize other, more explicit phrases for the same phenomenon. See b. Git 36a, in which the same legal question is phrased as follows: "is it possible that there be something [a debt] that according to Torah law is released in the seventh year but Hillel enacted is not released?" (*umi ikka midi demide'orayta meshameta shevi'it vehitqin Hillel dela meshameta?*), and b. Yev 89b where an identically phrased question ("is there something that by Torah law is X but … the rabbis declare it to be not-X?") is immediately rephrased in the following general terms: "can a court make an enactment that uproots (*la'aqor*) a law of the Torah?" B. Yev 89b is explicit: at issue are rabbinic rulings that uproot or contradict Torah law. Since b. Yev 89b, b. Git 36a, and the parallel sugya of the Yerushalmi all employ the same formula ("is there something that by Torah law is X but … the rabbis declare it to be not-X?"), we may conclude that the Yerushalmi's *lehatqin 'al devar Torah* means "to enact a *taqqanah* that contradicts or uproots biblical law." As we shall see, other sugyot of the Yerushalmi and the Bavli that struggle with the same phenomenon—a rabbinic enactment that contradicts biblical law—use even more explicit language (e.g., *vedivrehen 'oqrin divre torah?* = "can the rabbis uproot a rule of the Torah?"), leaving little doubt as to the meaning of the phrase (*hitqin 'al*) employed here.

only by rabbinical law"), an exercise of rabbinic power in the service of a conservative preservation of a biblical practice that was no longer technically obligatory. Hillel's institution of the prozbul merely set aside or repealed this *rabbinic* requirement to observe the release of debts and so restored the exemption envisaged by the biblical text. In the final step (step 4), a Babylonian tradition is cited to the effect that all agree that the cancellation of debts is not currently mandated by biblical law and is observed only on rabbinic authority.

> 4. There [in Babylonia] they say: Even one who holds that tithing is operative by biblical law agrees that the cancellation of debts is [currently] operative by rabbinic law [only]. For there is a tannaitic teaching [on this]: "*And this is the manner of the release: every creditor shall release*" (Deut 15:2). Rabbi says: There are two releases here. One refers to the jubilee release of land, the other to the sabbatical release of debts. When the jubilee is operative, the release of debts is operative according to biblical law. But when the jubilee is not operative, then the release of debts is only operative by rabbinical law.

It turns out that Hillel was no radical innovator. On the contrary, according to the Palestinian Talmud's revisionist account, he was a true conservative, returning the law to its original biblical condition after it had been modified by even more cautious rabbis before him. There is nothing unusual or daring in his action.

The fact is, however, the Bavli's discussion of Hillel's prozbul does not deviate from the path laid down by the Yerushalmi. It opens with the same question that opened the Yerushalmi's sugya on the prozbul: "[I]s it possible that there be something [a debt] that according to Torah law is released in the seventh year but Hillel enacted is not released ... (*umi 'ikka midi demide'orayta meshameta shevi'it vehitqin Hillel dela meshameta?*)" (b. Git 36a). Moreover, the strategies it adopts to address this anxiety are precisely those found in the Palestinian sources. First, m. Shevi'it's tradition, that Hillel was arbitrating between two competing biblical principles is cited. However, just as in the Yerushalmi, the question persists: "[I]s it possible that where the Torah requires a release, Hillel should say that it does not require a release of debts [i.e., can the rabbis enact a *taqqanah* that contradicts or overturns biblical law]?" The answer provided is the answer found in the Yerushalmi: *according to the Bible* itself the requirement to release debts in the sabbatical year had lapsed. However, rabbis prior to Hillel, exercising their authority in a conservative manner, required its continued and supererogatory observance; as a result Hillel's institution of the prozbul was merely a setting aside of the rabbinic stringency and a restoration of the exemption envisaged by the biblical text. This is the end of the sugya's analysis of Hillel's enactment of the prozbul.

What follows in the Bavli is a discussion seeking to justify *the action of the anonymous rabbis predating Hillel* who allegedly ruled that observance of the release of debts was to continue despite the fact that biblical law did not require its observance. It should be immediately apparent that it is much easier to justify the anonymous rabbis' authority to enact this hypothesized ruling—a conservative ruling that preserves and extends a lapsed biblical requirement—than it is to justify Hillel's authority to enact a *taqqanah* that seems to uproot or contradict a biblical requirement. It is an accepted principle that the rabbis are authorized to *impose* obligations where biblical law does not. The second half of the sugya shifts to a discussion of the authority by which this earlier group of rabbis imposed an obligation *protective* of biblical law.

Like the Yerushalmi before it, the Bavli has converted an innovative *taqqanah* that substantively uprooted biblical law (Hillel's enactment of the prozbul) into a conservative restoration of a biblical norm following a *conservative* rabbinic ruling that imposed an obligation *not* required by biblical law (a *gezerah* in the classic sense of a "fence around the Torah"). The prozbul restored the biblical status quo after a protective rabbinic *gezerah*. No one in this revisionist scenario has done anything remotely like overturning biblical law.

In discussing the case of the prozbul, Panken (2005, 196–98) follows Kraemer (1991, 67–69) in describing the Bavli in comparison to the Yerushalmi as far more willing to utilize the assertion of rabbinic power, and showing less need to ground its changes in Scripture. According to Kraemer (67): "when we come to the Bavli ... we discover a radically different approach." He claims, "In contrast with the earlier sources, the intent of the Bavli here has been to emphasize the innovative boldness behind the prozbul and to assert, in a broader way, rabbinic prerogative vis-à-vis Torah," and to require us "to recognize that the Torah yields to the rabbis, not the other way around" (69). The Bavli does not seek "to hide the assertion of rabbinic power behind the veil of scriptural justification," and thus we can conclude that "rabbinic Judaism grew immensely in strength and confidence as it established itself through the centuries" (70).

In fact, the radical and innovative nature of Hillel's ruling is explicitly denied in the Bavli precisely as in the Yerushalmi—Hillel's enactment did not overturn biblical law either because (1) it was based on a competing biblical principle or (2) it was setting aside an earlier rabbinic ruling only. The second half of the sugya turns to consider the action of the earlier rabbis who allegedly imposed the requirement to release debts in the seventh year even though the Bible grants an exemption, and seeks justification for their action. This justification is not difficult to find because *imposing* obligations where the Torah does not is an authorized conservative exercise of rabbinic power designed to disable any change in the divine law.

In short, the second half of the sugya does not, as Kraemer contends it does, contain bold and radical assertions of the rabbis' power to overturn biblical commandments (indeed, on the Bavli's revisionist account no one *has* overturned biblical law), nor does the Bavli maintain that in the case of the prozbul the Bible yields to the rabbis rather than the other way around. On the contrary, and in line with the Yerushalmi before it, the Bavli subjugates Hillel's enactment to the authority of the biblical text. After this act of damage control, as it were, the Bavli turns to a discussion of the legal principles undergirding the conservative exercise of rabbinic authority in making a *gezerah* (to continue the prohibition against collecting debts suspended by biblical law) that, on its revisionist account, preceded Hillel's enactment.

This is not the only site in which legal revisionism occurs. The Yerushalmi contains five cases of amoraic revisionism of contradictory *taqqanot*, while the Bavli contains six. In four of the Yerushalmi's cases and in two of the Bavli's cases a *taqqanah* is said to be a restoration of an original, biblically prescribed state of affairs that had been subsequently modified by anonymous rabbis in a manner consistent with the rabbinic authority to impose an obligation or prohibition. In the four remaining Bavli cases, revisionism is achieved by means of a corrective midrash, that is, by reinterpretation of the relevant biblical text so as to show its agreement with the law expressed by the *taqqanah* (b. BM 47b and b. San 2b–3a),[22] or by locating a competing biblical verse upon which the contradictory *taqqanah* is said to be based (b. Ket 52b and b. RH 30a).[23]

The two Talmuds do not always pursue the same strategy when confronted with a *taqqanah* that appears to contradict and modify biblical law. All ten of the *taqqanot* identified by the Bavli as contradicting biblical law are subject to revision or neutralization; by contrast, not all of the *taqqanot* identified by the Yerushalmi as contradicting or uprooting biblical law are subject to revision. The Yerushalmi is quite prepared to admit that at least some *taqqanot* constitute innovations that contradict provisions of biblical law.[24]

Our first example concerns a *taqqanah* by Rabban Gamliel to the effect that a husband cannot annul a writ of divorce (*get*) without his wife's knowledge. Employing the language of both *barishonah* and *taqqanah*, m. Gittin 4:2 states:

> [… Once the *get* has reached her hand, he cannot annul it.] At first (*barishonah*) [the husband] would convene a court wherever he was and annul [the get]. Rabban Gamliel enacted (*hitqin*) that this should not be done, to prevent abuses.

---

[22] In other words, the verse that the *taqqanah* is said to contradict is subjected to an alternative exegesis that removes the contradiction and so exposes the consonance between biblical law and the new *taqqanah*, reducing or eliminating its innovative character.

[23] Other cases of contradiction identified by the Bavli are subject to neutralization and will be discussed below.

[24] That the Bavli and the Yerushalmi do not identify exactly the same *taqqanot* as contradicting biblical law is of little consequence for the present discussion. Nor is it important that we agree or disagree with their identifications of conflict between Torah law and a *taqqanah*, since our purpose here is to understand how the amoraim reacted to the cases of contradiction that *they* identified as such.

In the Palestinian Talmud, the question is asked—what is the law if a husband transgressed and nullified the *get* in the manner described? Is the annulment recognized, since biblically speaking he has the right to annul a *get*, or not?

1. [If the husband] transgressed and nullified the *get* [in this way], what is the law?

2. Learn it from this.
    If they [the court convened by the husband] declared it null it is null—the words of Rabbi.
    R. Shimeon b. Gamliel says: He has not got the power to nullify it or to add to any term found in it.

3. R. Shimeon b. Gamliel ruled properly.

In step 2 we find a dispute. Rabbi dissents from the majority view—he maintains that the *get* should be considered null and void (in keeping with biblical law), and that Rabban Gamliel's *taqqanah* has no standing. R. Shimeon b. Gamliel supports the *taqqanah* of Rabban Gamliel modifying biblical law on this point, and his position is upheld by the gemara. The stam of the sugya inquires after Rabbi's reasoning:

4. But what is the reason behind the position of Rabbi? [This is his reasoning:] According to biblical law the husband may nullify the *get* but [the rabbis] ruled that he may not nullify it. *And do rabbinic rulings uproot a rule of the Torah?* (*vedivrehen 'oqrin divre torah?!*).

The question attributed to Rabbi is rhetorical. Is it possible that a rabbinic ruling can uproot, overturn, set aside, contradict a biblical law? In steps 5 and 6, the stam of the Talmud responds in the affirmative. The rabbis do indeed have the power to uproot a rule of biblical law, and a second case is then cited in demonstration of that assertion.

5. [Yes, as in the following case, m. Ter 1:4]: Olives [may be separated as *terumah*] for olive oil and grapes for wine.

6. Is it not biblical law that one may separate as *terumah* [the one for the other], but the sages ruled to the contrary, that one may not separate olives as *terumah* for olive oil or grapes as *terumah* for wine, in order to prevent the theft [of valuable goods—wine and oil] from the priests? And not only this but they also ruled that if one transgressed and separated [olives or grapes], that which he has designated as *terumah* is not *terumah*. (p. Git 4:2, 45c)

Although according to biblical law olives and grapes may be separated as *terumah* for oil and wine respectively, the sages ruled that they may not be so separated. In this case, as in the case of the nullified *get* itself, the rabbis overrule biblical law, prohibit that which the Bible permits ab initio and in the ex post facto case, declare invalid what Torah law declares valid.

The Yerushalmi's approach in these cases contrasts sharply with the neutralizing approach of the Bavli. B. Git 33a (//Yev 90b) deflects entirely the innovative nature of the taqqanah regarding the annulment of the get by introducing a principle that justifies the special authority of the sages in questions of marriage, enabling them retroactively to cancel the original betrothal (Gilat 1970, 119–20). The passage follows the general structure of the Yerushalmi's sugya, introducing the baraita that contains the dispute between Rabbi and R. Shimon ben Gamliel and then debating the authority of the rabbis to rule in contradiction to biblical law.

> Our rabbis taught: If they [the court convened by the husband] declared it null it is null—the words of Rabbi.
>
> R. Shimeon b. Gamliel says: He has not got the power to nullify it or to add to any term found in it since if so, what about the authority of the court?
>
> [But] is it possible that where a get is cancelled according to biblical law we should, in consideration of the authority of the court, allow a married woman to marry another man?
>
> Yes. When a man betroths a woman, he does so under the conditions laid down by the rabbis and in this case the rabbis annul his betrothal.

The question posed by the anonymous voice of the passage is scaled back significantly. The stam of the Yerushalmi phrased its question in bold general terms—can rabbinic rulings uproot Torah law? The stam of the Bavli phrases its question in limited terms specific to the case at hand—can the rabbis allow a married woman to marry another man? The answer is yes, because marital status laws are laid down by the rabbis, who therefore have the power to annul a betrothal. The question of a conflict between biblical law and rabbinic taqqanah is sidestepped by placing authority over marriage law squarely in rabbinic hands.

According to Panken (2005, 74), the Bavli

> points out that the rabbis are uprooting a law from the Torah for the sake of the welfare of this woman. BT makes its claim unabashedly, asserting that the power of defining the parameters of marriage rests entirely with the rabbis. This is in keeping with the prevalent rhetoric of disclosure active in BT.

Certainly, the Bavli clarifies the rationale for the taqqanah and to that extent engages in a rhetoric of disclosure. But the Bavli's discussion nowhere uses the language of "uprooting a law from the Torah"—that language occurs only in the Yerushalmi. The stam of the Bavli affirms not that the rabbis can uproot a law from the Torah; it affirms that the rabbis can allow a married woman to remarry because marriage contracts are made and dissolved by rabbinic, not biblical, authority. In this way, the Bavli eliminates any tension between biblical and rabbinic law, consistent with a rhetoric of concealment. The Yerushalmi does not.

As for the *terumah* case, the closest parallel to this case in the Bavli appears in the same sugya (b. Yev 89a–90b). Although the Bavli discusses m. Ter 2:2 regarding the separation of ritually impure produce for pure produce (rather than m. 1:4 regarding the separation of olives and grapes for oil and wine), the same theoretical question is raised—"[I]s it possible that there is something that by Torah law is [sanctified] *terumah* but the rabbis ... declare it to be *ḥullin* [unsanctified produce]? Can a court make an enactment that uproots a law of the Torah?" In an extended attempt to answer this question, an example of a rabbinic law that uproots Torah law is sought, but none is found. The cases adduced as potential examples of an uprooting of Torah law all involve emergency situations and acts of omission. Thus, where the Yerushalmi's sugya appears to allow unconditionally for the possibility that rabbinic law abrogates Torah law, the Bavli's sugya does not.[25]

In an important respect, the rabbinic ruling in p. Git 4:2, 45c uproots biblical law in a manner that is not bold: it prohibits something permitted by Torah law, which is a *conservative* use of rabbinic authority. A bolder move would be to permit something that the Torah prohibits or to declare valid something invalid according to Torah law. Do we find in rabbinic sources instances of self-conscious innovation of this truly bold type? There is, in fact, a small number of cases in the Yerushalmi in which such a bold exercise of rabbinic authority is tolerated.[26]

The first example involves a *taqqanah* by R. Yoḥanan ben Zakkai after the destruction of the Temple, to the effect that the *lulav* should be shaken in the outlying areas for seven days as a memorial to the sanctuary. The passage (m. RH 4:3) uses the language of both *barishonah* and *taqqanah*:

> At first, the *lulav* was shaken in the sanctuary for seven days and in the outlying areas for only one day. After the destruction of the Temple, R. Yoḥanan ben Zakkai enacted a decree that the *lulav* should be shaken in the outlying areas for seven days as a memorial to the sanctuary.

The stam of the Yerushalmi seeks to understand precisely what it is that R. Yoḥanan ben Zakkai did (p. RH 4:3, 59b//p. Sukk 3:13, 54a):

---

[25] In a further four cases in the Yerushalmi a rabbinic *taqqanah* is said to contradict Torah law, and no apology for or resolution of the contradiction is essayed: p. Git 4:4, 45d; p. Git 4:6, 46a; p. Git 5:5, 47a; and p. BQ 10:3, 7c. See Hayes 1998a, 657–58.

[26] The cases are found in p. Yev 10:1, 10c; p. Git 8:5, 49c; p. RH 4:1, 59b; p. RH 4:3, 59b; and possibly p. Git 5:7, 47b.

1. It is written, *"and you shall rejoice before Yahweh your god seven days"* (Lev 23:40).

2. There are some who teach that the verse refers to the *shelamim* sacrifices. There are some who teach that the verse refers to rejoicing with the *lulav*.

3. According to the one who says that the verse refers to the *shelamim* sacrifices, the first day [in the outlying areas] is biblically prescribed and the remaining days [in the Temple] are biblically prescribed and R. Yoḥanan b. Zakkai is enacting a decree that contradicts biblical law (*hitqin 'al devar torah*).

According to the one who says that the verse refers to the rejoicing of the *lulav*, the first day [in the outlying areas] is biblically prescribed and the remaining days [in the Temple] are rabbinically prescribed and R. Yoḥanan b. Zakkai is enacting a decree that contradicts rabbinic law (*hitqin 'al divrehen*).

4. And can there be a *taqqanah* after a *taqqanah*? [No, hence he enacted a decree contradicting biblical law.]

The Yerushalmi asks explicitly: did R. Yoḥanan ben Zakkai enact a decree contradicting biblical law or only rabbinic law? In other words, what was the status of the *lulav* ritual as practiced prior to R. Yoḥanan ben Zakkai's *taqqanah*? Was it a rabbinic institution, or was it biblically prescribed? The question is debated. Those who interpret Leviticus 23:40 as the biblical source for the practice displaced by R. Yoḥanan ben Zakkai's *taqqanah* will conclude that R. Yoḥanan ben Zakkai *hitqin 'al devar Torah*—enacted a decree contradicting biblical law. But if one holds that Leviticus 23:40 refers to the *shelamim* sacrifices, then shaking the *lulav* for seven days in the sanctuary was a rabbinic institution and R. Yoḥanan ben Zakkai's decree contradicts a rabbinic prohibition only (*hitqin al divrehen*). The sugya concludes with a rhetorical question: can there be a *taqqanah* after a *taqqanah*? No, there cannot, and thus R. Yoḥanan ben Zakkai's *taqqanah* is best understood as contradicting a biblical prohibition. No anxiety is expressed over the conclusion that a rabbinic enactment has permitted something prohibited by Torah law.

By contast, the Bavli neutralizes the innovative character of R. Yoḥanan ben Zakkai's *taqqanah*. The Bavli's consideration of the *taqqanah* is quite short and avoids entirely the question of whether or not there was a biblical prohibition against shaking the *lulav* for seven days in the outlying areas. Instead the Bavli focuses on the explanatory clause provided by the Mishnah—that the *taqqanah* instituted a seven-day *lulav* ritual in outlying areas *as a reminder of the sanctuary.* The Bavli demonstrates that the creation of such memorials to the sanctuary is itself biblically prescribed, the clear implication being that R. Yoḥanan ben Zakkai's *taqqanah* has full Scriptural warrant.

1. Where do we learn that we should do things in memorialization of the sanctuary?

2. From the verse *"For I will restore your health for you and heal your wound for you' says Yahweh, 'for they have called you an outcast: she is Zion and there is none who inquires after her."* (Jer 30:17)

3. From this we learn that inquiry after her is required.

The contradictory nature of R. Yoḥanan ben Zakkai's *taqqanah* is here neutralized by the assertion that the justification for—if not the substance of—the *taqqanah* has biblical warrant.[27]

A second example also involves R. Yoḥanan ben Zakkai and again employs the language of *barishonah* and *taqqanah*. According to m. RH 4:1, R. Yoḥanan ben Zakkai enacted a *taqqanah* after the destruction that when Rosh haShanah fell on the Sabbath, the *shofar* should be sounded in every place in which there is a court. Formerly (*barishonah*) the *shofar* was sounded in the sanctuary only and not in the outlying areas. In the Yerushalmi, three amoraim discuss the status of the law prior to the *taqqanah*. R. Kahana provides a series of three biblical verses which jointly prove that according to Torah law (1) the *shofar* is sounded everywhere when Rosh haShanah falls on a weekday, (2) the *shofar* is not sounded anywhere when Rosh haShanah falls on the Sabbath, except (3) in the sanctuary. This proof has important ramifications for the *taqqanah* of R. Yoḥanan ben Zakkai: the *taqqanah* permits that which the Bible prohibits— sounding the *shofar* outside of the sanctuary when Rosh haShanah falls on the Sabbath.

The Yerushalmi's relative equanimity on this matter is thrown into stark relief when compared to the parallel sugya of the Bavli—which is a classic example of amoraic revisionism. Rava, a fourth-generation Babylonian amora, goes against established tradition and argues that there is no biblical prohibition against sounding the *shofar* outside the sanctuary when Rosh haShanah falls on the Sabbath. Instead, he argues, biblical law permits the sounding of the *shofar* everywhere when Rosh haShanah falls on the Sabbath because it is not considered work. However, "rabbis" prior to R. Yoḥanan ben Zakkai decided to prohibit sounding the *shofar* outside the sanctuary when Rosh HaShanah falls on the Sabbath since it might lead to inadvertent violations of the Sabbath laws of carrying. According to Rava, R. Yoḥanan ben Zakkai's postdestruction decree was merely a revocation of this earlier rabbinic *gezerah* and a restoration of

---

[27] The Bavli employs a different strategy on b. Yev 90b. There R. Yoḥanan ben Zakkai's *taqqanot* regarding the *shofar* and *lulav* are described as involving acts of omission (*shev ve-'al ta'aseh*) rather than acts of commission (violations of prohibitive commandments). However, it is clear from the Yerushalmi's discussion that the *taqqanah* of *shofar* involves the violation of a biblical prohibition (commission). That the *taqqanah* regarding *lulav* involves a similar violation is less clear; nevertheless, it is certainly not a case of *shev va'al ta'aseh* (omission).

the original biblical law on this matter permitting the sounding of the *shofar* when Rosh haShanah falls on the Sabbath. This is a classic case of amoraic revisionism of the type we have already seen: a seemingly innovative *taqqanah* is said to restore rather than contradict biblical law. The only thing it contradicts and revokes is an intervening *gezerah* that was a conservative safeguard introduced to extend a biblical practice.

Two further examples occur in the area of personal status law. M. Yev 10:1 and m. Git 8:5 contain rabbinic decrees that declare a child to have the status of *mamzer* (an illegitimate Israelite), even though according to biblical law the child would not in fact be a *mamzer*. The consequence of such a ruling is not insignificant. Israelites are forbidden to marry *mamzerim*; *mamzerim* may marry only *mamzerim* by biblical law. Declaring an Israelite to be a *mamzer* when he is not will open the door to a marriage prohibited by biblical law, a marriage between that Israelite and a genuine *mamzer*. Thus, these rabbinic enactments not only overturn biblical determinations of personal status; they set the stage for violations of an important biblical prohibition. In both cases, the Yerushalmi accepts the rabbinic decree despite its broader implications regarding biblical law. By contrast, the Bavli neutralizes the innovative force of the *taqqanot* or the boldness of the exercise of rabbinic power. In the case of m. Yev 10:1, the Bavli states that the term *mamzer* is applied to the child in a nontechnical manner simply in order to signal that s/he is prohibited to Israelites, without the added implication that s/he is permitted to *mamzerim*. In the case of m. Git 8:5, the Bavli takes pains to ground the *taqqanah* in a broader power granted to rabbis regarding the validity of bills of divorce.

The Bavli's conservatism in connection with the subset of *taqqanot* that contradict and uproot biblical law is on display in a well-known passage in b. Yev 89a–90b. This text is often touted as the locus classicus for the Bavli's uniquely confident assertion of the halakhic prerogatives of the rabbis. That the entire passage is actually an exercise in neutralization and containment of the rabbis' halakhic prerogatives is a fact that often eludes scholars. The sugya searches for an example of a rabbinic law that contradicts or uproots Torah law and considers a series of rulings that *appear* to do so. No effort is spared in demonstrating that in every one of the cases adduced, the rabbis do not in fact uproot a prohibitive commandment for all time. Time and again in the sugya, legislative history is rewritten in order to conceal the extent to which the cases are innovative, and to support the contention that the rabbis' exercise of halakhic authority is within the bounds prescribed by biblical law.[28]

---

[28] My reading of the passage is consistent with that of Goldberg (1963) and Friedman (1977). In his study of the *gezerah*, Goldberg argues that the later Babylonian amoraim strove to connect every rabbinic prohibition to a Torah prohibition, to convert every *gezerah* into a *gezerah shema* designed to prevent the violation of a specific Torah prohibition. By contrast, the Palestinian amoraim view the same *gezerot* as additions to or expansions of Torah law.

To summarize: in tannaitic times, rabbinic authorities enacted rulings that, on occasion, overturned Torah law—even in matters of negative law (*qum va'aseh*) and even for the long term (Gilat 1970, 127). Amoraic attitudes toward these rabbinic enactments are varied. The Yerushalmi contains nearly a dozen cases in which a rabbinic *taqqanah* is said to contradict Torah law and this contradiction is accepted. It is not subject to the kind of revisionism we find in five other cases in the Yerushalmi and in six cases in the Bavli. Further, at least four of these contradictions are rather bold assertions of rabbinic authority in that they involve the overturning of a negative ruling or declaration in the Bible (i.e., they permit the prohibited or validate the invalid). By contrast, the Bavli contains no case in which a tannaitic *taqqanah* that uproots Torah law is not subject to some sort of revision (six cases) or neutralization (four cases).

How are we to explain the phenomenon described here, specifically, the tannaitic and early Palestinian acceptance of sometimes radical rabbinic modification of biblical law and the emergence in later Palestine and in Babylonia of a new rhetoric of "concealment" or resistance to innovations that directly overturn biblical law?

Yitzhak Gilat (1970, 128, 132) explains these developments on purely internal grounds. He sees the (primarily) tannaitic phenomenon of enactments that abrogate Torah law as part of an ancient tradition reflected in the books of the prophets, whose deeds and teachings sometimes deviated from Torah law. It was only later, when a clear distinction between biblical and rabbinic law developed, that the view that the rabbis could not uproot Torah law, except in very special and limited circumstances, was clearly formulated—for instance, as a temporary measure in an emergency situation. In other words, where Panken sees a shift from a biblical rhetoric of concealment to a rabbinic rhetoric of disclosure, Gilat sees the opposite. These very different assessments are possible because both rhetorics are present in biblical and rabbinic literature. The relative balance between the two—when and why one rhetoric is dominant and the other muted, or vice versa—may well be a function of external circumstances. Indeed, the shifts and tensions described here may be illuminated by reference to Roman legal culture and Greco-Roman discourses of the law.

Uprooting Torah Law in Light of the Praetorian Edict

Rabbinic sources indicate that the rabbis had more than a passing familiarity with Roman edicts that were so important in Roman provincial administration.[29] The many functional parallels between the praetorian edict (G-R 10)

---

[29] The Latin term *edictum* is translated in Greek as *diatagma* or *prostagma*, and both terms appear in various forms in rabbinic texts; see Lieberman 1944, 6–7; Krauss 1964, 196, 483; and Sperber 1984, 79–81. Josephus refers to decrees and edicts in, for example, *Antiq.* 19, 160; 19, 279; and 14, 321. Several Palestinian traditions suggest that Palestinian rabbis were familiar with the standard form, the manner of publication, and other specific features of the Roman edict (Sifre Deut 33, 59; Deut Rab 9,

and *taqqanot* issued by early rabbinic authorities living in Roman-controlled Palestine suggest that the rabbinic *taqqanah*, whatever its native roots, may have developed along lines informed by the praetorian edict. First, the praetor's edict provided legal remedies where none existed. The *taqqanah* of the rabbis was also in most cases geared toward providing a legal remedy where none existed, (Hebrew *taqqanah* can mean "[legal] remedy." Second, both the edict and the *taqqanah* were vehicles of law reform, and though in theory unable to erase clauses of the civil law and Torah, respectively, on occasion they did supplant them in practice. Third, the edict was in theory a temporary measure issued by a particular authority, but eventually a fixed core was passed down. Likewise, as Judah Goldin has shown (1965), *taqqanot* and *gezerot* were often ad hoc measures associated with a particular authority, which, once adopted, became a permanent part of the law. Fourth, the edict generally introduced considerations of good faith and equity in the technical sense (i.e., the ad hoc and limited adjustment of an existing and otherwise just law in order to relieve injustice to individuals resulting from the unfairness of that rule in a particular case). We have already seen Papinian's assertion that one of the functions of the praetor's edict was correction of the *ius civile*. On the Jewish side, the term *taqqanah*—which can mean "correction, repair, improvement"—reflects the same legal notion. The rabbinic *taqqanah* is clearly associated with considerations of equity and good faith, as evidenced by the phrases *mipney tiqqun olam, mipney darkhe shalom*, as well as many of the explicit rationales that appear as justifications for specific *taqqanot* (i.e., modifications to an existing law because in a particular circumstance that law will produce an unjust or undesirable result). Finally, the praetor's overriding power to act in contradiction to the civil law if in so doing he acts in the interests of the Roman people is paralleled by the rabbi's authority to issue *taqqanot* in the interests of restoring the people to observance of the law, or to safeguard the law (*lemigdar milta*), or because the situation requires such an action (*hasha'ah tserikhah lekhakh*; Elon 1994, 519–36).

It seems plausible that *taqqanot* that improved, repaired, and on occasion overturned Torah law were largely tolerated in Roman Palestine in the first three centuries of the Common Era, because of the highly visible and parallel phenomenon in the surrounding Roman legal culture, namely, edictal modifications of the civil law. Moreover, under such circumstances a rhetoric of concealment would have subsided in favor of a rhetoric of disclosure.

11, 178; Ex Rab 30:16; ARN II, 8, 24). For a complete list of the relevant rabbinic sources, see the Aruch, Krauss 1964, and Sperber 1984. On the phrase *paras diatagma* (= promulgated an edict), see Lieberman 1944, 6–7, and L. Finkelstein 1942, 387n1. The practical legal sphere was one area in which Jews and Gentiles of Palestine had regular interaction. Practical law was a mix of Roman provincial, Hellenistic, customary, and Jewish law; but even on the level of theoretical knowledge, the opportunity for rabbis to become familiar with basic concepts of Roman law certainly existed. Gulak (1933) has argued for direct influence of the Edictum de Alterutro on Jewish dowry law.

In previous chapters, we have seen the rabbis' application of Greco-Roman discourses of positive law to the divine law of Israel. In this chapter, we see that techniques of modification and correction, similar to those applied to the secular civil law in Roman legal culture, were applied to the Torah. Even corrections that set aside or "uproot" biblical law are disclosed with no indication that the nature of the law as divine and authoritative is thereby impugned. However, as time passed, resistance to enactments that went so far as to contradict provisions of Torah law increased, as indicated by new strategies of concealment (including some cases of legal revisionism) found in the Palestinian Talmud. This third- to fourth-century resistance to contradictory *taqqanot* coincides with a similar unease in the Roman world, culminating in Constantine's decree in 315 CE that rescripts contrary to the civil law were invalid (C. Th. 1.2.2).[30] Later layers of the Babylonian Talmud increasingly reflect the stance that rabbinic enactments have no authority independent of that ceded to them by the Written Torah. On this view, rabbinic enactments cannot abrogate provisions of the primary legislation, and innovative *taqqanot* are justified only in specified circumstances.[31]

It is possible that the emergence of new strategies of concealment (revisionism and neutralization) *alongside* the rhetoric of disclosure in later Palestinian and Babylonian sources reflects an increased sensitivity to Greco-Roman conceptions of divine law as immutable. Even if we allow for such a possibility, the effect of this discourse was likely complex. On the one hand, awareness of a view according to which divine law is immutable may have inspired a contrarian and nonapologetic insistence on the will-based mutability of the divinely revealed law of Israel and a strengthened commitment to a rhetoric of disclosure of change. On the other hand, the expectation that divine law is immutable may have fostered unease over rabbinic modification of biblical law, leading to apologetic strategies of concealment that attempted to reduce the appearance of innovation. Sometimes innovations were said to express or restore an older law of the Bible. Sometimes they were recast as innovations in rabbinic law rather than biblical law, exploiting a distinction that became sharper in the amoraic period (Gilat 1970, 128, 132).

However, rabbinic law is not in fact devoid of a divine dimension; even though different rules govern the operation and enforcement of rabbinic and biblical law, rabbinic law is *au fond* understood to be an articulation of the divine will[32] underwritten and authorized by Scripture. Categorizing a modified

[30] Constantine's decree is itself the result of internal constitutional developments in Rome that led to the consolidation of all lawmaking in the hands of the emperor and thus, for all practical purposes, a single source of law and legal authority.

[31] A study of institutional mechanisms for legal change in Sassanian legal culture is a desideratum but is beyond the scope of this volume.

[32] A claim internal to rabbinic texts themselves (see chapter 5, p. 170) and assumed in texts that thematize the audacity of the rabbis in defeating God in halakhic disputes.

law as rabbinic may explain how it is that the *rabbis* were the ones authorized to modify that law, but for those increasingly sensitive to the claim that divine law should be immutable, it does not deflect the basic "problem" of human innovation in a system of divine law.

Nevertheless, we may conclude that despite some instances of resistance, the rabbis did not in general hold that the divinity of law precludes the possibility of its modification. *For all their caveats and qualifications, their dueling willingness to disclose and desire to conceal, rabbinic sources early and late, east and west, do not deny that biblical law changed over time in response to the shifting circumstances of human life.* They applied to divine law techniques of modification characteristic of positive law in the Roman legal sphere. If the Greco-Roman discourse of divine law's immutability played a role in rabbinic culture, it was in contributing to the seesaw between tolerance and intolerance for legal innovation, between concealment and disclosure.

Nonlegislative Mechanisms of Change—a Rhetoric of Concealment?

Modification of the Law—Internal Values

The previous section examined rabbinic examples of *legislatively produced* changes to biblical law.[33] As legislation, these sources bear explicit semantic markers of self-conscious legal change or, to adopt Panken's terminology, they employ a prima facie rhetoric of disclosure. They describe changes from what was formerly the case (*barishonah*), and they announce innovations (*taqqanah* and *gezerah*) introduced by human authorities. However, on closer analysis some of these sources were seen to participate in a simultaneous rhetoric of concealment, employing a variety of strategies to obscure or entirely neutralize legal innovation, particularly in the later amoraic and postamoraic period, and particularly in Babylonia.

In this section, we examine rabbinic examples of *exegetically produced* changes to biblical law. As exegesis, these sources bear the semantic markers of legal *continuity* even as they effect changes—sometimes radical changes—in the law. Again, to adopt Panken's terminology, they employ a prima facie rhetoric of concealment, representing their conclusions as immanent within the biblical text. However, just as close analysis of rabbinic legislation discovered a rhetoric of concealment accompanying the explicit disclosures of legislatively produced changes, close analysis of rabbinic exegesis reveals a surprising rhetoric of *disclosure* accompanying the concealment considered characteristic of

---

[33] The term "legislatively produced change" does not assume a formal legislative process or legislative body. It is simply intended to designate a change *represented* as having been newly introduced by an individual or collective, as opposed to a change arising from "statutory interpretation."

exegetically produced changes. This rhetoric of disclosure coincides with an increased incidence of aggadic representations of humans confronting and critiquing divine morality, a phenomenon that seems to have reached a peak in sixth- to eighth-century Palestinian Tanḥuma-Yelammedenu literature (Weiss 2011).

Mark D. Rosen (2013) provides conceptual models for explaining changes that occur outside a legal system's formal mechanisms of amendment and legislation, changes that might otherwise be difficult to notice because they can create an appearance of fealty and continuity. He argues that meaningful change can arise when new applications are found for extant law or when a *value* is reinterpreted in such a way as to produce a new value. In addition, change in the law may also occur when there is a shift in the salience of certain values and the laws they support. A value's salience may be enhanced, with the result that laws driven by that value proliferate, or its salience may be reduced and limited to certain cases or subjects. When incommensurable values come into conflict, a society must decide which value will trump or override the other.

When change can be attributed to the application of a moral value that exists *within* the system, it is easily represented as faithful rather than innovative. Rabbinic literature contains examples of the modification of biblical law on the basis of a moral principle, and some of these principles are internal to Scripture. For example, rabbinic texts permit the violation of biblical Sabbath prohibitions in a case of danger to human life (m. Yoma 8:6; b. Yoma 85a–b). Sabbath observance and the preservation of life are both deemed to be obligations grounded in Scripture, but the rabbis determine that of these competing obligations the moral principle of the preservation of human life takes precedence over the commandment to observe Sabbath prohibitions.

When it draws upon moral principles inherent to the legal system, moral interpretation of the law enables modification of the law that does not appear to deviate from the law. Insofar as the values and commitments that prompt a change in the law are deemed to be internal to divine Scripture itself, the innovative nature of rabbinic modification of the law is obscured. Thus, moral interpretation of the law according to *internal* moral principles is by definition a rhetoric of concealment that obscures the extent of interaction.

Scholarly accounts of Jewish law often assume that moral interpretation of the law proceeds on the basis of *internal* moral principles only. According to Menahem Elon (1994, 142), there is a reciprocal relationship between law and morals in Jewish law. Because the Torah is the common source for both rules and morals ("You shall not murder" and "You shall love your neighbor as yourself" are both found in the biblical legal corpus), morals legitimately inform and shape the ongoing interpretation of the rules.[34] Thus, the legal system will,

---

[34] Students of legal theory will hear echoes of Ronald Dworkin (1986), who argues, against the positivists, that law systems incorporate both rules and morals, the latter legitimately being invoked to interpret and shape the former.

from time to time, invoke an (internal) moral imperative declaring what proper conduct is even if it is not strictly required by the rules (144).

Aaron Kirschenbaum also represents the moral interpretation of biblical law as an internal affair. He describes the interaction of law and morality in Jewish law in terms of equity, which is a method of negotiation "whereby law *modifies itself* in order to remain *faithful to itself*" (1991a, xxi; emphasis added). Kirschenbaum argues that although Jewish law lacks a specific term comparable to the Roman *aequitas, ius naturale,* or *naturalis aequitas,* it has a similar concept of equity. Following Aristotle, he defines equity as that which upholds and corrects the strict law in order to bring it closer to perfection, thereby fulfilling the true intention of the legislator (1991b, xxxv).[35] Just as equity is not so much a reform as a realization of the law's true essence, the interpretations and enactments of the rabbis that modify and develop the law are regarded as the fulfillment of the true intent of Scripture rather than an innovation or modification of it (ibid., xxxviii). According to Kirschenbaum, Jewish law also holds that when strict adherence to the law creates injury and injustice, a corrective is needed. In Jewish law, that corrective is the body of rabbinic interpretations and enactments that are made in the interest of justice.

Rosen (2013, 228–31), Elon (1994, 141–89), and Kirschenbaum (1991a, xliii–lxi) list the internal (i.e., Scriptural) moral principles that are invoked to modify and occasionally override biblical commandments: Leviticus 18:5 gives rise to the principle of *vehay bahem*—the value of preserving human life; Deuteronomy 6:18 is cited for the principle of *ve'asita hayashar ve-hatov*—the value of doing what is upright and good; Proverbs 3:17 is the source for the principle of *darkhe shalom/no'am*—the value of preserving pleasant and peaceful relations with others; Genesis 9:6 is the source of *betselem elohim*—the value of preserving the dignity of human beings; Psalms 119:126 is the source of *et la'asot,* which justifies temporarily setting aside biblical law in an emergency situation; Leviticus 19:5 and Deuteronomy 16:20 give rise to principles of *tsedeq*—the values of impartiality in judgment and of compromise. The principles of *qiddush ha-shem* and its counterpart *hillul ha-shem* (acting in a manner that sanctifies the name of God or that does not profane the name of God) are rooted in repeated biblical exhortations to sanctify God's name.

The simple fact is, however, that while talmudic literature contains numerous examples of the modification of biblical law on the basis of a moral principle, *these principles are rarely explicitly located in Scripture.* Because Elon and Kirschenbaum describe Jewish law as a whole rather than classical talmudic literature only, they base their accounts on medieval and early modern halakhic commentaries that devote considerable energy to identifying biblical bases for the principles guiding talmudic modifications of biblical law. These commentaries explain and justify changes in the law by linking them to moral principles

---

[35] Kirschenbaum (1991a, xxxvii) also maintains that Jewish law goes beyond equity by introducing into law the religious element of *hesed* (beneficence, compassion, or loving kindness).

encapsulated in Scriptural verses—but this is a post-talmudic rhetoric of concealment that is not widespread in the talmudic sources themselves. In fact, the moral principle *darkhe noam* appears only five times in the entire Bavli and four times in the Yerushalmi; *ve'asita hayashar ve-hatov* appears once in the Tosefta and four times in the Bavli; *betselem elohim* appears once in the Mishnah, once in the Tosefta, and three times in the Bavli.[36] We may conclude that at the rhetorical level at least, rabbinic moral interpretation of the Bible does not in general rely on moral principles *internal* to the biblical text. What, then, is the basis for rabbinic moral interpretation of biblical law, if the rabbis so infrequently point to moral principles internal to the biblical text? Do the rabbis recognize an ethic independent of Scripture, an external morality on the basis of which they critique and modify biblical law? If so, do they disclose this fact or conceal it?

Some scholars argue for an anemic version of the claim that Jewish tradition (not simply the talmudic sources) recognizes an ethic independent of halakhah. The claim is anemic because the rabbis are said to employ various techniques to incorporate the ethic into the halakhic system (so that it is no longer a truly *independent* ethic). These scholars assert that this ethic is a kind of natural morality (the idea that certain goods exist in nature) rather than natural law in the fullest sense. Thus, Aharon Lichtenstein (1975) cites quite meager talmudic evidence[37] for the recognition of a natural morality in Jewish tradition but argues

---

[36] In at least one passage (b. Git 59b) a principle is cited only to be rejected as the reason for a certain innovation.

[37] The evidence adduced is b. Eruv 100b, widely quoted as evidence of a natural morality, if not a principle of natural law, but when examined in its full context, it is nothing of the kind. The passage appears in a larger discussion of the view that a man may not compel his wife to sexual activity. The exegetical prompt for the specific passage that has drawn the attention of natural law enthusiasts is Job 35:11, which states that God teaches us more than the beasts and makes us more wise than the birds. R. Ḥiyya playfully reads the verse to say that God "teaches us from" beasts and birds (taking *mi-* as the partitive "from" rather than the comparative particle "more than"). R. Ḥiyya then identifies a behavior that is learned from a beast and a behavior that is learned from a bird: from mules women learn to urinate while kneeling; from a cock men learn to coax rather than coerce their sexual partners. Kneeling to urinate is hardly an example of a universal moral law, and it is clearly not the intent of this folkloristic exegesis to argue for the derivation of a natural morality from animal behavior. R. Ḥiyya's playful exegesis is followed by R. Yoḥanan's statement that there are four things that can be learned from animals:

> R. Yoḥanan observed: If the Torah had not been given we could have learnt modesty from the cat, honesty from the ant, chastity from the dove, and good manners from the cock who first coaxes and then mates. And how does he coax his mate? Rab Judah citing Rav replied, He tells her this: "I will buy you a cloak that will reach to your feet." After the event he tells her, "May the cat tear off my crest if I have any money and do not buy you one." (b. Eruv 100b)

Three of the four learned traits are explained in sexual terms—sexual modesty, avoidance of certain forbidden unions, and coaxing rather than coercing to the sexual act. Although R. Yoḥanan states that in the absence of the Torah, we can learn such behaviors by observing animals, it is not clear that this alignment of Torah with four animal behaviors is anything but coincidental, and his words should not be construed as a broader endorsement of nature as a source of knowledge of moral goods. Elsewhere,

that this natural morality is incorporated into the halakhic system through the concept of *lifnim mi-shurat ha-din*. *Lifnim mi-shurat ha-din* is a moral principle of supererogatory behavior that, according to Lichtenstein, is itself an aspect of halakhah and thus internal to it (70).[38]

Likewise Daniel Statman (forthcoming) points to the same limited talmudic evidence (b. Eruv 100b and b. Yoma 67b) for the claim that Jewish tradition recognizes the existence of goods grounded in nature, but he too understands the modification of law on the basis of these goods to be an *internal* (and somewhat marginal) instance of the "moral interpretation of halakhah."[39] Moreover, Statman believes that the moral interpretation of biblical law does not amount to a rabbinic recognition of a distinct natural law[40] because the rabbis never assume that the laws they interpret might be unjust and, on that basis, invalid. On the contrary, moral interpretation of the law is believed to reveal the assumed true reading of the biblical law in question.

Thus, according to Lichtenstein, the rabbis may recognize a limited natural morality (goods grounded in nature), but they adopt various strategies of *concealment* to subsume this morality within the halakhic system, and, according to Statman, despite some modifications arising from moral interpretation of the law, the rabbis never question the validity or underlying justice of biblical divine law. The rabbis adopt these strategies of concealment because the importation of external values into halakhah is illegitimate. On the rare occasion that the rabbis do not conceal the existence of an ethical value accessed independently of halakhah, they qualify and even denigrate it. For example, b. AZ 23b and b. Qidd 31a contain the story of Dama the son of Netinah, a non-Jew who exemplifies the principle of honoring one's father, for which he is richly rewarded. The oldest stratum of the story assumes the ability of a non-Jew to arrive at and to fulfill a moral obligation independent of revelation. However, in later texts, the story of Dama clearly generates some consternation, and in

---

learning from animals is the mark of a low character (Sifre Deut 306, L. Finkelstein ed., 329). The other text classically cited as evidence for a recognition of natural law, or at least a natural morality, is b. Yoma 67b, paralleled in Sifra Aḥarei Mot 9:13, which was considered at length in chapter 5. This text does little more than suggest that some of the Mosaic Laws are unobjectionable but many others are not.

[38] As Novick (2010) has argued, *lifnim mi-shurat ha-din* does not refer to supererogation until the post-talmudic period. For the literature on *lifnim mi-shurat ha-din*, see chapter 5, p. 177n20.

[39] Statman's discussion of natural law and Judaism (forthcoming) distinguishes between natural law as a theory of morality, i.e., the idea that there are certain basic human goods whose status as goods is grounded in human nature, and which provide reasons for action, and natural law as a theory of jurisprudence, i.e., the theory that law is backed by decisive reasons for action. In the previous chapter we considered whether rabbinic texts attest to a view of divine law as being backed by decisive reasons for action, and in this chapter we consider whether rabbinic texts attest to a recognition of goods grounded in human nature that provide reasons for action.

[40] Here, Statman means natural law in the jurisprudential sense, according to which the law would be invalid were it shown to be unjust.

b. Qidd 31a his achievement is diminished by the addition of the following comment:

> R. Ḥanina said, If one who is not commanded [to honor his parents] yet does so, is [rewarded] in this way, how much more will one who is commanded and does so, be [rewarded]! For R. Ḥanina said, One who is commanded and fulfills [the command] is greater than one who fulfills it though not commanded.

The counterintuitive assertion that heteronomy is more virtuous and praiseworthy than autonomy occasions surprise on the part of at least one rabbi in the passage immediately following, and may be contrasted with traditions that praise converts who have *chosen* to take on the yoke of the commandments and Gentiles who have *chosen* to study Torah (for example, b. BQ 38a, though this praise is also qualified). What the sugya grants with one hand—the accessibility of an ethical value independent of halakhah—it denigrates with the other.[41]

Modification of the Law—External Values

It must be said, however, that not every text that recognizes an ethical value independent of divine law seeks immediately to subsume it within the halakhic system or to devalue it. *Some texts openly acknowledge the existence of independently accessed ethical values and rely upon them for the modification of the law.* Thus, in addition to the anxious rhetoric that recognizes but *conceals* or denigrates an ethic independent of halakhah, there is a rhetoric that recognizes and *asserts* an ethical stance over and against halakhah. This rhetoric is found in texts in which the rabbis engage in an unapologetic moral critique of the law on the basis of an independently accessed ethical value. The classic example of this kind of independent moral critique of a biblical law is the case of the stubborn and rebellious son in Deuteronomy 21:18–21.[42] The biblical text reads:

> 18. If a man has a stubborn and rebellious son, who does not heed his father or mother and does not obey them even after they discipline him, 19. His father and mother shall take hold of him and bring him out to the elders of his town at the public place of his community. 20. They shall say to the elders of his town, "This son of ours is disloyal and stubborn (defiant); he does not heed us. He is a glutton and a drunkard." 21. Thereupon the men of his town shall stone him to death. Thus you shall sweep out evil from your midst. All Israel will hear and be afraid.

In some ancient societies the male head of household had extreme rights over the lives and well-being of the members of his household, and the discipline of

---

[41] See Urbach 1975, 324–25, and I. Heinemann 2009, 17–18, on this passage.

[42] This case has been widely discussed. See, for example, Halbertal 1999, chap. 2, and literature cited there. Statman views this law as an example of moral interpretation aimed at uncovering the true meaning of the law rather than an independent critique of the law aimed at disabling it.

children was not subject to civil scrutiny or control. This biblical law likely represents an attempt to curb the absolute authority of the father. Parents who wish to kill a disobedient child may not act independently but must bring their case to the larger community for judgment. The community acts together in executing the child. M. San 8 considers the case of the stubborn and rebellious son and asks:

> When can he be condemned as a stubborn and rebellious son? From the time that he can produce two hairs until he grows a full beard ... [referring to the pubic hair], for it is written, "*if a man has a* son" which means a son and not a daughter, a son [i.e., child] and not a man [i.e., adult]; yet a minor is exempt since he has not yet come within the scope of the commandments. (m. San 8:1)

In this passage the scope of the law is severely limited. The word "son" is taken in its most restricted semantic sense to refer to male offspring[43] who are neither sexually mature adults nor minors (i.e., younger than thirteen) as yet not responsible under the law. Consequently, the only son who can be prosecuted under this law is a thirteen-year-old who has not yet fully matured physically. The gemara commentary on this passage states that the appearance of two hairs occurs at age thirteen and one day, and the full growth of pubic hair occurs three months later, and this view becomes the accepted interpretation of this mishnah, limiting the period of liability to the first three months following a boy's thirteenth birthday. The Bavli's sugya contains the following exchange:

> R. Kruspedai said in R. Shabbethai's name: The extreme limit of a stubborn and rebellious son is only three months.
> But did we not learn: From the time that he can produce 2 hairs until he grows a full beard ... ?
> If he grew a beard, even if three months have elapsed [he is no longer liable], or if three months have elapsed, even if he did not grow a beard [he is no longer liable]. (b. San 69a)

Two criteria have been introduced—a time criterion and a maturity criterion—and the stam of the Talmud combines them to create the smallest possible period of liability: from the boy's thirteenth birthday until either sexual maturity is achieved or three months have elapsed, whichever occurs first. Further limitations of the law appear in the subsequent mishnahs:

> When is he culpable? After he has eaten a tritimor [about six ounces] of flesh and drunk a half-log [about a half cup] of Italian wine. R. Jose says: 1 mina [twenty ounces!] of flesh and 1 log [one cup] of wine. But if it was

---

[43] This is an exegetical choice. The rabbis do not consistently read masculine terms as excluding females.

the intercalation of the month, or if he consumed it as Second Tithe in Jerusalem, or if he ate carrion or flesh that was *terefah*, or forbidden beasts or creeping things [the latter four items being prohibited non-kosher foods], [in other words] if by consuming it he had fulfilled a command or had committed a transgression, if he ate any [general] foodstuffs but did not eat flesh, or drank any liquid but did not drink wine, he cannot be condemned as a stubborn and rebellious son; but only if he eats flesh and drinks wine for it is written, "*he is a glutton and a drunkard ...*" (m. San 8:2)

For the son to be prosecuted, he must be guilty of both gluttony and drunkenness. To qualify as a glutton and a drunkard he must eat specifically both wine and flesh, and only such flesh as is fit for consumption (ruling out non-kosher meats). He must consume these items of his own will and not in fulfillment of commandments to feast at certain times. The next mishnah articulates further limitations (the comestible must be the father's property that has been stolen and consumed outside of the father's domain). M. San 8:4–5 states:

If his father was willing [to accuse him] but his mother was not willing or if his father was not willing but his mother was willing, he cannot be condemned as a stubborn and rebellious son, but only if they were both willing ... If either of them was maimed in the hand, or lame or mute or blind or deaf he cannot be condemned as a stubborn and rebellious son, for it is written; "*his father and mother shall take hold of him*"—so they were not maimed in the hand; "*and bring him out*"—so they were not lame; "*They shall say*"—so they were not mute; "*This son of ours*"—so they were not blind [but could clearly see and identify him]; "*he will not obey our voice*"—so they were not deaf. (m. San 8:4–5)

In essence, then, the only person who could be prosecuted under the law of the stubborn and rebellious son was a male between the age of thirteen and one day and thirteen and three months (or less if sexually mature), who had consumed certain specified quantities of both meat and wine stolen from his father and eaten outside the father's premises, and who was accused by both father and mother, neither of whom suffered from certain physical defects, including an injured hand. The limitations are elaborated even further in the gemara—for example, the stolen food must be consumed in the company of wastrels.

How many cases fitting precisely these parameters could have been brought before the rabbis? No need to guess. The Talmud tells us.

With whom does the following Baraitha (= t. San 11:6) agree: There never has been a stubborn and rebellious son, and never will be.

Why then was the law written?

That you may study it and receive reward.—This agrees with R. Judah.

Alternatively, you may say it will agree with R. Simeon. For it has been taught: R. Simeon said: Because one eats a tartemar of meat and drinks half a log of Italian wine, shall his father and mother have him stoned?! But it never happened and never will happen! Why then was this law written?—That you may study it and receive reward.

R. Jonathan said: I saw him and sat on his grave. (b. San 71a)

This gemara reports that the death penalty for a stubborn and rebellious son has never been carried out and never will be. So, although the biblical text seems to grant to parents broad latitude in condemning to death a stubborn and rebellious child, this power is so drastically limited by the rabbis through various exegetical maneuvers as to become an empty letter. And despite the fact that the dismantling of the law is presented as exegesis—a prima facie rhetoric of concealment—it is accompanied by an explicit rhetoric of disclosure. The triumphant declaration that the law never has been and never will be fulfilled is designed to disclose the fact that the law has been disabled.[44]

The rationale for disabling the law is entirely explicit and is not grounded in an internal (i.e., Scriptural) principle: according to R. Simeon it simply offends moral logic for parents to put a son to death for overeating and overdrinking ("Because one eats a tartemar of meat and drinks half a log of Italian wine, shall his father and mother have him stoned?!"). That can't be what the text requires; it can't be what God intends—a god who demands such a punishment violates the rabbis' moral instincts. And so the rabbis modify the law—not by enacting a *taqqanah* but by subjecting the law to a painstaking and hyperliteral interpretation that renders it a dead letter. They employ what is commonly understood to be a rhetoric of continuity and concealment (interpretation), and yet they openly declare what they have done ("There never has been ...") so that ultimately there is nothing covert about this exegesis. The rabbis make a clear and explicit ethical calculation—the plain sense of the text is morally unacceptable, and we will be rewarded if we labor to disable this law. Indeed, this law was given to us precisely to challenge us to perform this task of moral critique and disabling.[45]

---

[44] R. Yonatan indicates that the law was fulfilled precisely *once*. Evidently, R. Yonatan can't accept the baraita's radical claim that God would give a law *solely* in order to hone moral reasoning or to teach the importance of critiquing and overruling God. There must have been one occasion, just *one*, in which this law—so seemingly outrageous—was in fact needed and put into practice.

[45] Roie Ravitzky has pointed out to me that it is possible to read R. Simeon's statement as a purely descriptive observation concerning the inclinations of parents—that no parent would ever put a child to death for overindulging, and that is why the law has never been and never will be carried out. If so, the rabbis are not engaging in a radical interpretation because they have a moral objection to the law but because the law is just a dead letter given the softhearted nature of parents. This interpretation strikes me as unlikely, particularly in light of the parallel case of the idolatrous city. T. San 14:1–3 states in connection with the biblical command to annihilate any city that has been persuaded to idolatry (Deut 13) that "there never has been a city annihilated for idolatry and there never will be. Why then

In his book *Interpretive Revolutions in the Making*, Moshe Halbertal examines the place of ethical values in rabbinic interpretation of the Bible, examining five cases in which ethical considerations play a clear role in the modification of biblical law, including the law of the stubborn and rebellious son (Halbertal 1999, chap. 2). In subsequent chapters, Halbertal argues that rabbinic restrictions of a father's authority over his daughter are based on an ethical objection to the harshness of the punishment prescribed for the loss of virginity; rabbinic modifications of the law of the suspected adulteress invoke explicit ethical calculations, such as a condemnation of jealousy and the rejection of a double standard for husband and wife; the delimitation and defanging of the biblical law prohibiting a woman from intervening in a fight between men is explicitly motivated by the ethical calculation that a woman should be permitted to rescue a man from an attacker; collective punishment is challenged by the objection that innocent children will suffer; and the laws of execution are modified in the direction of leniency in line with a variety of ethical considerations. There is no indication that these ethical values arise from the biblical text itself; no textual, philological, or formal proofs are provided. According to Halbertal, the weight given to morality in these cases varies, but in the case of the stubborn and rebellious son and the idolatrous city, external ethical considerations do not simply modify the law; they disable it altogether.

This latter point is significant. Independent ethical values are invoked not merely to decide between two equally legitimate alternative interpretations of an unclear or ambiguous law; they are invoked to promote a completely counterintuitive reading—indeed a wonderfully absurd reading—of a perfectly unambiguous law (such as the law of the stubborn and rebellious son) in order to create a new legal reality. This signals a high level of self-consciousness on the part of the rabbinic interpreters, and a key element in Halbertal's argument is that the rabbis' use of independent ethical values is *conscious*. Rabbinic authors represent themselves as *consciously* choosing to modify the law in keeping with their moral intuitions and do not conceal the moral outrage that is the impetus for their exegetical pyrotechnics. Returning to Panken's terminology, we may say that the rabbis employ a rhetoric of disclosure, openly announcing the fact that a more contextual or plain sense understanding of the law has been rejected on the basis of an independent moral critique. The evidence for this claim is

---

was the law written? That you may study it and receive reward." It is clear from the discussion of this law in Sifre Deut 94 and elsewhere that the rabbis were troubled by the fact that destroying an entire city for idolatry would entail the destruction of innocent children. Just as the reason for disabling the idolatrous city is moral, so the reason for disabling the law of the stubborn and rebellious son is likely to be moral, and R. Simeon's statement is thus most naturally read as expressing a moral critique of the law. Finally, even if Ravitzky's interpretation were correct, it would still be the case that (1) R. Simeon can imagine that *someone* would object to the cruelty of the law and refuse to implement it (even if it is only the parents) and (2) the rabbis see the law as less than perfect (because it is unactionable) and thus in need of reinterpretation if it is to have any positive effect.

found in the common rabbinic practice of (1) articulating an interpretive option that is marked as the "plain sense" or more intuitive reading, (2) exposing the moral inadequacy of that option, and (3) adopting a morally superior alternative that is generally not a plain sense reading. The plain sense reading may be marked by explicit terminology, for example, the terms *kishmu'o* or *kemashma'o* ("as it sounds").[46] Alternatively, the "plain sense" reading may be marked rhetorically, as in the case of R. Shimeon's statement: "Because one eats a tartemar of meat and drinks half a log of Italian wine, shall his father and mother have him stoned?!" Here, the plain sense of the text (that a child is to be stoned for gluttony and excess drinking) is both articulated and ridiculed (steps (1) and (2)) in a single rhetorical gesture.

Classical rabbinic sources contain many examples of exegetically produced modifications of the law in which an independent ethical value plays a central role and occasions neither protest nor apology. Although exegesis is typically perceived to be a rhetoric of concealment in which change is disguised as continuity, it will hardly function as such if the rabbis take pains to *disclose* the radical discontinuity of their interpretations. They do this by openly signaling that their interpretations deviate from the plain sense of the law, and that these deviations are conscious accommodations to an independent ethical value. In other words, they pair a surprising rhetoric of *disclosure* with the concealment characteristic of exegetically produced changes.

Halbertal wonders how the rabbis could justify modifications of divine Scripture—the presumed arbiter of good and bad—on the basis of external values (1997, 183). He rejects models of interpretation that posit a dichotomy between internal meaning and external considerations, and proposes a model that draws on Quine's principle of charity—an interpretive principle that would yield an optimally successful text—and its elaboration by Ronald Dworkin. According to Dworkin, the interpreter of law is actually *obligated* to introduce ethical considerations into his interpretation based on a charitable assessment of the law's author. Reading a holy text requires a maximal use of the principle of charity because it is inconceivable that a text written by God would be imperfect or contradictory (Halbertal 1999, 29). The rabbis did not understand themselves to be importing external values in their interpretation of the text; rather, they understood themselves to be drawing on their assumptions about the author of the text (as just, compassionate, and so on) in order to interpret the author's words.

Halbertal believes that Dworkin's model describes the rabbinic interpretation of biblical law because rabbinic interpretation completes the biblical text in the best way it can on the assumption that the author of the text is righteous

---

[46] See also Rosen-Zvi (2012), who argues that rabbinic interpretations that point to the literal or contextual meaning of a word (the word's meaning *kishmu'o*) are evidence of an ideologically self-aware hermeneutic, especially when that meaning is considered only in order to be set aside.

and just. The strength of this model is that it assumes that an ethical stance is *required* in interpretation and so dispenses with the internal-external distinction and with the problem of "external" ethical considerations overriding the "internal" meaning of divine Scripture.

Attractive as this model is, as an explanation of the rabbinic practice of ethical modification of the law it has one significant drawback: rabbinic texts sometimes represent the rabbis doing precisely what Halbertal assumes they would never do. Rabbinic texts sometimes criticize God for immoral or unjust behavior, and insist upon a genuinely *alternative* and morally superior position. In these texts, the rabbis engage in a less than maximally charitable reading of the law; they do *not* assume that the divine author is uniformly just and righteous; they assume and explicitly thematize the very internal-external dichotomy that Halbertal wishes to overcome; and they engage in a genuine moral critique that declares a divine behavior, decree, or law to be ethically inferior, even unjust, in order to replace it with a morally superior alternative.[47] In short, these texts do *not* assume a morally perfect God.

Rabbinic texts in which humans openly confront God for specific moral failures are analyzed in a recent study by Dov Weiss (2011). According to Weiss (58), the confrontational motif emerges in amoraic rabbinic writings (third–fifth centuries) and reaches a high point in the postamoraic Palestinian texts of Tanḥuma-Yelammedenu (sixth–seventh centuries), which include the Tanḥuma, and Tanḥuma-style materials in Ex Rab, Num Rab, Deut Rab, and Pes-Rab. There are 140 confrontational texts in this corpus, many of which modify and intensify third- to fifth-century texts that critique or challenge God.[48] Some feature a combative encounter between a biblical hero and God (13); some describe acts of protest (like drawing and refusing to step outside a circle (21); some represent the confrontation as a courtroom proceeding in which God is the defendant responding to the critiques of various litigants (42). In texts featuring parables, God is compared to a king whose abusive or unethical behavior is challenged by a member of his inner circle (32).

Sometimes an effort is made to blunt the sharp edge of the critique. Thus, parables that displace the critique onto a king rather than God obscure the radical nature of the confrontation (33). Confrontation is also softened by the rabbinic authors' drawing upon relational analogies. Thus, God and his human interlocutor are depicted as parent-child, judge-litigant, or even close friends—relationships in which confrontation is, if not entirely condoned, at least accepted (43). The rabbis often shift their responsibility for critiquing God by

---

[47] Pace Statman forthcoming.

[48] The later texts enhance the confrontational nature of earlier texts by transforming indirect critiques into direct critiques, intensifying the confrontational language, and increasing the number of protestors (Weiss 2011, 185). Weiss distinguishes a critique, which is an expression of frustration with God's past wrongful behavior but does not necessarily imply a desire to change the status quo, and a challenge, which is future oriented and aims to change the status quo (24). We do not require the same precision in this summary of Weiss's results, and I will use the terms more or less interchangeably.

imputing the critique to exemplary biblical characters (54). These displacements and analogies are familiar strategies of concealment. However, although they may soften the critique or deflect responsibility for it, they do not lessen its basic thrust—to expose the moral imperfection of God.

Sometimes God rejects or ignores the critique, but sometimes—significantly—he accepts it and even modifies his behavior, decree, or law in response (4). According to Weiss, a whole new lexicon of divine concession emerges in the Tanḥuma-Yelammedenu literature (27). Focusing on biblical narratives in which God acts unfairly or unethically, the rabbis "save God" by depicting him as courageously admitting his flaws and adopting the more ethical stance proposed by his human interlocutor (49). In this text from Num Rab 19:33[49] God concedes to Moses's criticism of the principle of vicarious punishment:

> When the holy one, blessed be he, said to him, "*visiting the guilt of the parents upon the children*" (Ex 34:7), Moses said, "Master of the World, how many evil people give birth to righteous people? Shall they take [punishment] from the sins of the parents? Terah worshipped idols, and Abraham his son was righteous. And also Hezekiah was righteous, and his father Ahaz was a wicked man. And also Josiah was righteous, and his father Amon was a wicked man. Is it appropriate that righteous people shall receive lashes for the sins of their parents?" The holy one, blessed be he, said to him, "You have taught me something. By your life, I will nullify my decree and establish your word."

Moses expresses moral outrage over the principle of vicarious punishment; God *learns* from him, annuls his decree, and establishes a new rule of individual punishment. This is said to be one of three instances in which Moses did or said something on his own initiative that subsequently won God's assent. The other two Mosaic initiatives to win God's approval are the breaking of the Tablets of the Law after the Golden Calf incident and the decision to seek peace before engaging in war with Sihon, a policy that God adopts in place of his earlier decree of war without an attempt at negotiations (see also Tanḥuma Shoftim 19 and textual notes in Weiss 2011, 121n126). Other passages contain human criticism and divine concession: in Tanḥuma Va-Yera' 5, Abraham gives voice to his moral doubts about the Flood, which moderates God's behavior in the case of Sodom and Gomorrah (ibid., 100); in Ex Rab 46:4, Israel confronts God for creating the evil inclination and blames him for human sin, prompting God to promise to remove the evil inclination; in Tanḥuma (Warsaw) Va-Yetse 8, God learns a lesson in compassion and altruism from Leah; in Tanḥuma Numbers 23,[50] Moses objects to the severity of the punishment of stoning for certain sins, and God revokes the punishment and institutes lashes instead. In

---

[49] According to the Paris 150 MS, as per Weiss 2011, 50.
[50] According to Cambridge 1212 MS, as per Weiss 2011, 212.

these cases, the rabbis present modifications of divine behavior or divine law as the direct result of human critique and divine revision.

In one subset of texts, God's concession is described as fulfilling the decree (*gezerah*) of the righteous, an inversion of the standard depiction of God issuing decrees that Israel must fulfill. Weiss cites PRK Ve-Zot ha-Berakha supp.1, commenting on Deuteronomy 33:1's "*the man of Elohim*" as an example (44):

> Resh Laqish said: were it not written in Scripture, it would be impossible to say such a thing: as a man makes decrees on his wife and she does them, so too Moses makes decrees on the holy one, blessed be he, and he does [them].

Weiss's comments in connection with God's revision of the principle of transgenerational punishment captures the significance of all of these traditions:

> By adopting the literary motif of confrontation, these TY midrashim openly admit their ethical outrage ... by imputing their own values and intuitive moral sensibilities onto the figure of Moses. They do not attempt to resolve the moral problematic by hiding behind formal exegetical reinterpretations, as found in the earlier strata of texts. Furthermore, these texts are also theologically striking, for in them is God taught the moral principle of individual responsibility; in these texts, God needs human assistance to reach the pinnacle of moral behavior. (125)

There are, as might be expected, pockets of resistance to these bold descriptions of divine concession to human moral critique. Weiss notes the emergence of a "minority rabbinic voice" that viewed confrontation with God as a sacrilegious act. A variety of literary strategies are used to denounce these confrontations. Once again, a rhetoric of disclosure is accompanied by a rhetoric of concealment or even denial—suggesting that the one is the shadow of the other.

The texts analyzed by Weiss afford a fascinating glimpse into what it was possible for rabbinic authors to think and say about God. Beginning in the amoraic period, and reaching a peak in sixth- to seventh-century Palestinian sources, some rabbinic texts depict a fallible God, capable of error and at times in need of moral instruction by humans. Despite the assertions of many scholars, rabbinic authors *could* conceive of God acting capriciously, unfairly, and unethically (98) and being corrected, subverted, or defeated by human interlocutors. Indeed, God is said to delight in such defeats (b. BM 59a; b. Pes 119a).[51] Weiss writes:

---

[51] B. BM 59a contains the famous case of the Oven of Akhnai, in which God is said to have smiled when his legal opinion was set aside on the basis of a majority ruling. Similarly in b. Pes 119a, God is said to be different from humans in that he rejoices when he is conquered, as when Moses prevented him from slaughtering the Israelites after the sin of the Golden Calf.

[T]hese findings challenge the accepted scholarly view that the sages imagined God to be morally perfect. In the first half of the 20th century, Arthur Marmorstein argued that the early sages were adamant about defending the existence of an ethically infallible God to counter the Marcionite "heresy" that deemed the God of the Hebrew Bible to be ruthless and unjust. Like Marmorstein, David Weiss Halivni asserts that the Rabbis never consciously chose their own sense of morality over a straightforward reading of a "difficult" biblical law, since this would imply that God's morality was in error—and the "Perfect Law Giver" could never err. Agreeing with Halivni's claim that the early sages would not overturn biblical legal texts based on their own moral conviction, Moshe Halbertal nonetheless maintains that the early sages did read biblical texts through a moral lens, with the fundamental assumption that a just God authored them. They thus reinterpreted apparently unethical biblical laws, confident in their knowledge of the divine author's complete righteousness. (128)

The idea of a morally flawed divine being, whose law should be subjected to moral critique and modified if necessary, stands at a great distance from Greco-Roman conceptions of divinity and divine law. Weiss writes:

Constructing a God who is not morally perfect, these radical images of the divine sharply contrast with the unchanging and morally perfect God championed by Greek philosophy, early Christian thought, and medieval Jewish philosophy. In these TY texts, although God is concerned with justice and morality, He also recognizes His moral limitations and fallibility. Significantly, also, God is willing to change His methods of governing the world when He receives human input. Unlike the image of God presented throughout most of the Bible, the TY's God does not appear as the unchanging and impassable ultimate moral sovereign. The rules of ethical and moral conduct now emerge through dialogues between God and various biblical heroes ... instead of defending God's problematic justice system by reinterpreting the biblical narratives or by questioning their own fallible ethical intuitions, these sages boldly depict God as the one who had adopted an unethical approach. Nevertheless, they still present God as open to moral revision. (130)

While I would take issue with Weiss's characterization of the biblical God as "the unchanging and impassable ultimate moral sovereign" (see chapter 1), his characterization of the divine being as presented in the texts that form the subject of his study is astute.

Moral Critique and *Phronesis*

We have established that the rabbis engaged in conscious ethical modification of divine law. An examination of their own rhetoric when describing ethical modification of divine law reveals that sometimes they understood themselves to be drawing upon values internal to the halakhic system (following Elon, Kirschenbaum, and Statman); and sometimes they appear to be "completing the law," making it the best it can be according to the just intentions of its divine author (following Halbertal). But other rabbinic sources appear to offer a moral critique of divine behavior and of specific divine laws based on an ethical stance that is independent of the halakhic system.[52] Further, some late Palestinian sources paint a confrontational portrait according to which humans oppose, critique, and challenge God, and God concedes to their arguments by modifying his morally flawed behavior, decree, or law. In these texts, two distinct positions are advanced. The position advanced by the human interlocutor is deemed morally superior, and the divine position is corrected against it or annulled. The dramatic juxtaposition of competing ethical perspectives championed in these texts does not fit the Dworkinian model that seeks to transcend the opposition of internal meaning and external values. How might we explain the rabbinic embrace of *all* of these many and varied forms of ethical modification of the law?

The activity of moral reasoning that leads to the modification of law in rabbinic sources bears a certain similarity to the Greco-Roman concepts of *phronesis* (practical wisdom) and equity (G-R 4(ii)). In the *Laws*, the Athenian Stranger emphasizes the importance of reason and true knowledge in developing positive laws that might best achieve the virtue that is the goal of divine law. This idea underlies the Platonic preference for rule by sages or wise experts who can employ reason in continually assessing particular circumstances, rather than rule by inflexible written rules (*Statesman* 296e–297b). In chapter 2, we traced this idea in Pythagorean philosophy as well (G-R 4(i)).

For Plato, *phronesis* refers to the highest form of reason that affords true knowledge. For Aristotle, *phronesis* refers to practical reason—the application of good judgment to human conduct—and is connected with the idea of equity. When a law falls short of the line of justice and creates injustice in particular cases, equity rectifies the situation by providing an adjustment to the law through the exercise of *phronesis* or practical wisdom. This process of determining whether justice is better served by a mechanical application of the general, universal law or by granting an exception is practical wisdom or *phronesis*. For Aristotle, an adverse law can be opposed on the grounds that it is inequitable, ineffective, outdated, or in conflict with itself or another law (Frost 1992, 119).

---

[52] For the idea that rabbinic sources authorize not merely the radical reinterpretation of morally defective halakhah but also its rejection, see Shremer 2001.

In its deliberations about what is good and expedient, practical reason employs rhetorical arts to persuade, effect agreement and cooperation, or spur to action (G-R 4(ii))—the kind of rhetorical arts on display in many of the texts examined in this chapter and in Weiss's study. As noted in chapter 2, Scallen (1995, 1733–34) describes practical reasoning as a mode of argumentation that is based on the tradition of classical rhetoric and is grounded in a philosophical perspective that rejects absolutist theories of reality, truth, and knowledge in practical affairs. A characteristic feature of classical rhetoric is its eclectic use of various kinds of arguments and "proofs," including artistic proofs based on the speaker himself and his methods, which include *logos* (appeals based on reason and logic), *pathos* (appeals based on emotions), and *ethos* (appeals based on the character and credibility of the speaker; ibid., 1755). All of these techniques are featured in rabbinic confrontations with God, which exploit the character and credibility of biblical heroes and appeal to reason, logic, and emotion in order to persuade God to modify his law.

Roman legal culture was strongly influenced by earlier Greek writing on argumentation and rhetoric, and, as we have seen (G-R 4(ii)), Cicero, Quintilian, and the author of the *Rhetorica ad Herennium* discuss and illustrate Aristotle's *topoi* (types of arguments). These writers suggest arguments to be adopted when the intention of the law's author appears to be at variance with the letter of the law (including demonstrating that obeying the letter of the law is impossible);[53] when language fails to express intent clearly; and when there is a conflict of laws, or ambiguity.

Greco-Roman discourses of the modification of law through *phronesis* and equity were widely known in late antiquity, as were the rhetorical handbooks that discussed and illustrated modes of legal argumentation employed in judicial settings. Rabbinic sources show familiarity with the terminology and practices of Roman legal institutions[54] consistent with the rabbis' status as elite members of a provincial minority. Certainly, the portrayal of biblical divine law as flexible rather than fixed has biblical roots, and the rabbis continue that portrayal. However, the modification of the law through practical reason, considerations of equity, and specific modes of argumentation may have been accelerated, especially in amoraic and postamoraic Palestine, by the example provided by the wider Roman legal culture.

There is, of course, a crucially important difference between Greco-Roman discourses of the law's flexibility and the rabbinic ethical modification of the law. Greco-Roman discourses of the law's flexibility apply to *human positive law* and are a function of its subject matter. On Aristotle's account, the law's subject

---

[53] This is, in effect, the strategy employed in disabling the law of the stubborn and rebellious son. The letter of the law, when expounded to an absurd degree, yields a law that cannot possibly be observed.

[54] See Hidary 2010b and literature cited there; also Lieberman 1944.

matter is practical affairs; it does not deal with universal truths and is not susceptible to rational demonstration. The realm of practical affairs is the realm of "truth-for-the-most-part" (Shiner 1994, 1257), so that although a legislator finds it "*necessary* to speak universally," in practical affairs it is "not possible to do so *correctly*" (*NicEth* 1137b15). *Phronesis* and equity have no place in the discourse of the *divine natural law*. The rational order that governs the universe and transcends the indefinite and variable realm of material objects susceptible to change and accident is by definition immutable.

The rabbinic portrait of a divine law that stands in need of moral critique and correction, and can be modified on the basis of practical reason, considerations of equity, and rhetorical argumentation, would have been nonsensical, if not scandalous, in a Greco-Roman context. This portrait attributes to *divine law* the characteristics that in Greco-Roman discourses are applied only to *human positive law*. And yet, the rational modification of the Law and the implied fallibility of the divine lawgiver did not impinge upon the Law's divinity in the eyes of the rabbis. This is because the rabbis follow biblical precedent in locating the deity not in static, uniform nature (or not only there) but in history—intimately involved in and responsive to human activity (biblical discourse 3). For this reason the divine law's perfection is not diminished but *constituted* by the fact that it is particular, flexible, responsive, and on occasion multiform rather than universal, static, and uniform. Resisting the Hellenistic ideal of a static and unchanging divine law, the rabbis felt less compunction about the ongoing adjustment of the divine law in response to changing historical circumstances and moral considerations. It would be wrong to say that they felt *no* compunction—dueling rhetorics of disclosure and concealment make it plain that the ethical modification of the divine law prompted some concern that also finds textual expression. Nevertheless, for the most part rabbinic sources represent divine law as responsive to the shifting conditions of human existence, and humans as active participants in its ongoing evolution.

The rabbinic theory of the dual Torah is one means whereby the divine law may be said to be both perfect and evolving. The divinely revealed Written Torah is understood to be static and eternal on the one hand, while the Oral Torah is understood to be a living, growing body of tradition that develops and revises the divine law over time. This is an ironic reversal of the classical model—in Stoic natural law theory, the perfect and immutable divine law is by definition *unwritten*, while the imperfect and changing laws of humans are *written*. For the rabbis, it is the perfect and eternal divine law that is the *Written* Law, and the ever-evolving law responsive to particular circumstances that is *unwritten*! Moreover, while God is understood to be the author of the eternal and perfect Written Law, humans play a crucial role in the articulation of the responsive and evolving Oral Law. The characteristics attributed by the rabbis to divine law—including mutability—*as a function* of its perfection and divinity are precisely those attributed by classical tradition to human law *as a function* of its imperfection and lack of divinity.

CONCLUSION

In the sources examined in this chapter, the divine law of Israel is not portrayed as invariable and immutable. Indeed, the very mark of its divine and perfect nature is its ability to *respond* to the shifting circumstances of human experience, and to *evolve* in response to moral criticism and rhetorical suasion. Greco-Roman natural law theory envisaged the critique and modification of human positive law in the light of the divine natural law. In a paradoxical reversal the sources surveyed in this chapter depict the critique and modification of the divine law in the light of human experience and moral intuition. It is the divine law that is adjusted on the basis of human moral reasoning, not human law on the basis of a divine rational standard.

We are left with one final question: does the rabbis' moral critique of the law commit them to what Statman has called a moral theory of natural law, which is the idea that there exist in nature independent moral goods on the basis of which the Mosaic Law can and should be critiqued? Certainly, they do not equate the Torah itself with the natural law of Greco-Roman tradition (indeed they seem to construct their divine law in defiance of that tradition). But does a moral theory of natural law underwrite their moral critique of Torah?

This is the question that will occupy us in the final chapter.

CHAPTER 8

Natural Law in Rabbinic Sources?

To paraphrase Statman (forthcoming), natural law is not just a theory of jurisprudence (our focus in chapters 5–7) but a theory of morality according to
which there are certain basic moral goods grounded in (human) nature that
can be known to all humans by reason, and that obligate us. Chapters 5–7
searched for evidence of a jurisprudential natural law theory in rabbinic texts. I
argued that the authority and legitimacy of the Mosaic Law is not a function of
inherent qualities, and that the dominant portrait of Mosaic Law in rabbinic
sources does not match classical, especially Stoic, descriptions of natural law *despite a general rabbinic awareness of the same.* Specifically, in the rabbinic sources
adduced, the Law does not conform necessarily and essentially to various forms
of "truth" (chapter 5); it is not *essentially* and uniformly rational in its substance
and in its purpose, and it is not discoverable through reason (chapter 6); and it
is not eternal and invariable (chapter 7). Nor does Mosaic Law conform fully
to classical descriptions of positive law. Certainly, it is depicted as possessing
many of the characteristic features of positive law. In addition to being written,
it is sometimes depicted as divorced from truth (chapter 5), as nonrational,
arbitrary fiat (chapter 6), and as flexible (chapter 7). However, while these
features occasionally give rise to some anxiety, the conclusion that they are
defects that impinge upon the Law's divinity is *not* drawn (as the Greco-Roman
conception of positive law would dictate). Unlike Philo and Paul, the rabbis do
not attempt to square Mosaic Law with either pole of the natural law–positive
law divide. Their approach to divine law was likely *informed,* directly or indirectly, by this dichotomy, as signaled by various rhetorics of disclosure that acknowledge alternative characterizations of divine law. But with some notable
exceptions, their response to competing characterizations of divine law as allied with truth, universal, rational, and invariable is a response of resistance.

The question remains: even though the rabbis do not depict the Mosaic Law
in natural law terms, is it possible that they posit the existence of moral goods
grounded in nature,[1] rationally accessible, and exerting an obligation, *distinct*

---

[1] In order to ensure that all possible candidates for something like an independent natural law are
considered, I construe the phrase "grounded in nature" to refer to being grounded either in a natural
order external to humans or in human nature itself.

from the Mosaic Law—what Statman calls a moral theory of natural law?[2] The present chapter searches for evidence of a moral theory of natural law, distinct from the Mosaic Law, in rabbinic texts.

Some scholars argue that a conception of natural law distinct from the Mosaic Law appears in rabbinic literature in sources that deal with norms that predate Sinai. In this chapter, we consider this claim by examining texts that deal with pre-Sinaitic normativity in general and the seven Noahide laws in particular. Our goal is to determine whether the rabbinic sources dealing with these topics provide evidence of a rabbinic natural law theory. There is no question that *post*-talmudic thinkers drew upon the notion of seven Noahide laws as a basis for the *construction* of a Jewish natural law theory, but is such a theory inherent in the talmudic conception of the Noahide laws, or of pre-Sinaitic norms in general?

By the Middle Ages, Jewish philosophers were explicitly engaged by the notion of natural law and its relation to the revealed law of Jewish tradition. The first Jewish thinker to apply the term "natural law" in a Jewish context was Joseph Albo (fifteenth century) who divided law into natural, conventional, and divine categories (Novak 1998, 124–25). Nevertheless, David Novak has argued that Albo was not the first Jewish thinker to conceive of natural law in the Jewish context (124) and that "natural law theory, using a variety of different terms for itself throughout the ages, has been a constant element in Jewish thought." In recent years, a number of scholars and constructive Jewish theologians have argued that a notion of natural law is compatible with Jewish tradition (as a supplement to the revealed Written Law and the Oral Law), while others have argued that the concept of natural law is incompatible with the doctrine of a divine revelation of law.[3] To be clear, it is not our purpose to determine whether *Judaism*—as a multimillenium religious culture—has developed or incorporated a conception of natural law as distinct from the Mosaic Law at any time in its long history, or whether it can draw upon the concept of Noahide law for the construction of such a view *today*.[4] Our question is rather more limited and distinctly historical: do the classical rabbinic sources of late antiquity (i.e., prior to the rise of medieval Jewish philosophy when Greek categories are more clearly adopted and adapted to Jewish tradition) evince a conception of natural law that matches and reflects natural law discourse in antiquity? This is not a philosophical or theological question about the compatibility of natural law theories and the abstract entity "Judaism." It is a historical question about the presence or absence of Greco-Roman natural law discourse and conceptions in the literature of rabbinic Jews from the second to the seventh century CE. Any candidate for the title of "rabbinic natural law theory" will

---

[2] For a review of divergent views on this question from the medieval Jewish philosophers and commentaries to modern scholars, see Halbertal 1999, 22–33.

[3] Most famously, perhaps, Marvin Fox (1990), who has argued that Judaism did not and could not have a natural law concept. See further Novak 1998, 185 and n23, for literature on the subject.

[4] These are the sorts of constructive questions that concern David Novak (1998).

therefore need to meet the criteria by which natural law was generally recognized in Greco-Roman antiquity—in addition to being grounded in nature, it must be universally true/obligating, rational (and rationally accessible), and immutable.

In the first part of this chapter we consider rabbinic sources against the backdrop of Second Temple Jewish and early Christian sources on the following question: was there a law before the Mosaic Law revealed at Sinai? If not, is the pre-Sinai period viewed positively or negatively? In other words, was the period before Sinai a *law-free* golden age that came to an end with the giving of the Law (reminiscent of G-R 3(i)), or was it a *lawless* dark age redeemed by the giving of the Law (reminiscent of G-R 5(ii))? Or is the pre-Sinai period best described in terms lying somewhere between these two extremes? If, on the other hand, there was a law before Sinai, what was its character, what were its contents, and how was it known? Did it possess the characteristic features of natural law as represented in various Greco-Roman natural law discourses? Was it a law embedded in nature entirely distinct from the revealed Mosaic Law and accessible to independent reason? Or was it in some way continuous with the Mosaic Law to which it was merely a precursor? In the second part of this chapter we consider the specific case of the Noahide laws, which have been touted by some scholars as a rabbinic version of natural law or, at least, as a resource for the construction of a natural law view. Does the rabbinic conception of Noahide law match classical definitions of natural law and function in the same manner as natural law as understood in antiquity?

As we have already seen, rabbinic texts are anthological in nature, incorporating thousands of traditions that passed through the hands of tradents and redactors, and thus it is rarely the case that a single "rabbinic position" can be identified on any topic. Yakir Paz (2009, 9, 58, 98–99) has rightly criticized the tendency of scholars to make sweeping generalizations when describing rabbinic attitudes toward law in the period before Sinai. Rather than seek to synthesize the sources into a single view, I will present the sources in such a way that the range of views on each topic is apparent. On occasion, one view may emerge as dominant, but rarely does a single view stand uncontested. And in such cases, the sites of contestation may be particularly revelatory.

Normativity before the Law

An important and comprehensive treatment of normativity before Sinai may be found in Steven Wilf's *The Law before the Law* (2008). On occasion, however, Wilf strives for a synthesis that ignores voices of dissent, a tendency that is corrected in Yakir Paz's recent and excellent work on the subject (2009).[5] I

---

[5] Paz does not refer to Wilf's volume, which was perhaps not available to him at the time of his research and writing.

will refer repeatedly to these two major studies even as I fine-tune their arguments and nuance their textual interpretations.

Law Precedes Sinai

According to a prominent strand of thought in rabbinic literature, the period prior to Sinai was *not* law-free. Many rabbinic sources, like Philo's writings, recognize a "law before the Law." However, in rabbinic texts the connection between this law and the Mosaic Law is not the connection sketched by Philo. For Philo, the law of the patriarchal period was the universal unwritten law of nature. Accessed through wisdom and embodied by the patriarchs (who were themselves a living law), it would take a written form later in the Law of Moses. By contrast, classical rabbinic texts that recognize a law before the Law often depict this law and the Mosaic Law *as members of a single set—discrete moments in a single, continuous act of divine lawgiving.*[6]

Rabbinic texts employ two distinct strategies in the effort to place law in the period prior to Sinai. According to the first strategy, the revelation of God's law is understood to be, in Wilf's terms, "a drama with many acts," so that prior to Sinai there are "multiple moments when norms are introduced" (2008, 7). In some rabbinic traditions the revelation of the law is said to occur not over a forty-day period at Mount Sinai, but over twenty-six generations (the number of generations from Adam to Moses, according to rabbinic chronology). God revealed his law in piecemeal fashion throughout history, beginning with the first command issued to the very first human, continuing through commandments given to Noah, to the patriarchs, to the Hebrews leaving Egypt and encamped at Marah, until reaching a climax in the delivery of 613 commandments at Sinai. The law before Sinai and the Law at Sinai are thus component parts of a single cumulative entity—God's normative demands for his people—the imparting of which began with the first human. According to the second strategy for placing law in the period before Sinai, pre-Sinai figures are anachronistically depicted as observing not merely isolated commandments but the entire Sinaitic Law—indeed, Sinaitic Law in all its rabbinic elaboration. We turn now to the first of these strategies.

(I) ONE LAW—ON THE INSTALLMENT PLAN

Some rabbinic texts locate law already in Eden. In his recent dissertation on rabbinic readings of Genesis 1–3, Ryan Dulkin discusses the rabbinic exegetical motif of commandments given to Adam in prelapsarian Eden (2011, 110–33). The passage that attracts this motif is Genesis 2:15–16:

> Yahweh Elohim took the human (ha-Adam) and brought him to repose in the garden to work/serve it and to keep it; and Yahweh Elohim

---

[6] For a critique of the very different view held by Wolfson, according to which the rabbinic conception of the law before the Law was the same as Philo's, see Paz 2009, 5 and 50–54.

commanded the human saying from every tree of the garden you shall surely eat; but of the Tree of the Knowledge of Good and Evil you shall not eat.

Rabbinic interpreters consider possible referents for the pronoun object "it" in the phrases "to work/serve it" and "keep it" in Genesis 2:15. A tannaitic work, Sifre Deut 41 (L. Finkelstein ed., 87), glosses these phrases as follows: "*'To work/serve it'*—this is Torah study; *'To keep it'*—these are the commandments." The idea that Adam (and the other patriarchs) engaged in Torah study will be taken up below. Our immediate concern here is with the idea that Adam kept the commandments. The commandments themselves are not specified, but according to R. Judah in another tannaitic source, the commandments given to Adam were supplemented in the time of Noah, and again when Israel was in Egypt, and at Marah and Sinai (Sifre Num Shelah 111, Horowitz ed., 116). This would suggest that Adam's commandments amounted to fewer than the seven that, according to rabbinic tradition, were given to the Noahides.

The contents of the commandments to Adam are the subject of several amoraic traditions. Gen Rab 16:5 decodes the terms "repose," "work," and "keep" in Genesis 2:15 as references to the commandment to observe the Sabbath: God made Adam *repose*, that is, he commanded him regarding the Sabbath by telling him to *work* for six days and then *keep* the seventh day as a Sabbath (Dulkin 2011, 119). A midrash in the Babylonian Talmud (b. San 38b; see parallels in Ex Rab 32:1 and PRK 23) assumes a single commandment—the prohibition of the tree of the Knowledge of Good and Evil itself—delivered to Adam in the ninth hour of his first day of life. In b. San 56b, diverse identifications of the commandments given to Adam are offered—the tanna R. Judah maintains that Adam was commanded only in regard to idolatry, while the tanna R. Judah ben Beterah adds blasphemy and others add the establishment of courts. However, an amoraic tradition in the same location expands the list to include six or even all seven of the Noahide laws.[7] The attribution of all seven Noahide laws to Eden occurs in b. San 56b (cf. Gen Rab 16:16),[8] which reads Genesis 2:15 atomistically in order to show that Adam was obligated by commandments against idolatry, blasphemy, murder, illicit sexual relations, theft, and the consumption of a limb torn from a living animal, and by the commandment to establish courts of justice:

R. Yoḥanan answered: Scripture says: "*And Yahweh Elohim commanded the man saying, of every tree of the garden you may freely eat.*"

"*And [He] commanded,*" refers to [the observance of] social laws [i.e., establishing courts of justice], and thus it is written, "*For I know him, that*

---

[7] Some lists exclude the prohibition of eating the limb torn from a living animal (see, e.g., the first derash in Gen Rab 16:6) on the view that this seventh commandment was superadded in the time of Noah. Others include it among the commandments given to Adam.

[8] While the Noahide laws are listed in t. AZ 8:4, they are not there dated to the time of Adam.

he will command his children and his household after him, and they shall keep the way of Yahweh, to do justice and judgment" (Gen 18:19).

"*Yahweh*"—is [a prohibition against] blasphemy, and thus it is written, "*and he that blasphemes the name of Yahweh, he shall surely be put to death*" (Lev 24:16).

"*Elohim*"—is [an injunction against] idolatry, and thus it is written, "*You shall have no other gods before me*" (Ex 20:3).

"*The man*"—refers to bloodshed [murder], and thus it is written, "*Whosoever sheds man's blood, in exchange for that man shall his blood be shed*" (Gen 9:6).

"*Saying*"—refers to illicit sexual relations, and thus it is written, "*They say, If a man put away his wife, and she go from him, and become another man's*" (Jer 3:1).

"*Of every tree of the garden*"—but not of robbery.

"*You may freely eat*"—but not flesh cut from a living animal. (b. San 56b)[9]

By retrojecting all or most of the Noahide laws to the time of the creation of humankind, these midrashim reject the idea of a law-free golden age (Wilf 2008, 39) that is valorized in some Hellenistic and later Christian thought (see G-R 3(i) and chapter 4). For the rabbis, law—not in the sense of abstract *logos*, or universal reason, but in the sense of concrete divine directives and commandments—began to be revealed as soon as there was a human subject to whom they might be revealed. The rabbinic idea of continuous divine law-giving collapses the difference between creation and revelation. By dating the inception of the revelation of concrete laws to creation, the rabbis brought creation under the umbrella of Sinai.[10]

According to various rabbinic traditions, subsequent installments of the law were bestowed upon individuals and upon the Israelites as a whole (consistent with the narrative of pre-Sinai/Sinai continuity in biblical discourse 3(iii)): the obligation of circumcision was given to Abraham and the prohibition of the sciatic nerve to Jacob;[11] commandments concerning the Passover sacrifice were issued to the entire community of Israel at the time of the Exodus, and further commandments were bestowed at Marah in the wilderness. The verse "*There [at Marah] he made for them a statute and an ordinance*" (Ex 15:25) prompts

[9] An alternative derivation of this last prohibition is provided in the same talmudic context by R. Isaac.

[10] Nor should we forget that the idea of the Law's introduction at a specific and rather later period in human history was used by Paul to argue for its secondary status relative to the promise made to Abraham. Since the Law was "added" 430 years after the promise was made to Abraham, it does not supersede that promise (Gal 3:19). The rabbis make it clear that lawfulness precedes the promise to Abraham.

[11] See m. Ḥul 7:6 and Ex Rab 30:9, to be discussed at greater length below.

rabbinic speculation about the normative significance of Marah, as may be seen in the following tannaitic dispute:

> "*There he made for them a statute and an ordinance*" (Ex 15:25).
>
> "*A statute*," that is the Sabbath law. "*And an ordinance*," that is the law about honoring father and mother—the words of R. Joshua.
>
> R. Eleazar of Modi'im says: "*A statute*," that is the laws against incestuous practices, as it is said: "*That you do not do any of these abominable practices*" (Lev 18.30). "*And an ordinance*," that is laws about robbery, laws about fines, and laws about injuries. (MekhRY Vayassaʿ 1, Horowitz ed., 156)[12]

The commandments at Marah were understood to be superadded to those already revealed to Noah—two in MekhRY but three in b. San 56b. Whether two or three, the resulting list—as Wilf points out—creates "almost an exact parallel to the Decalogue" (151), a further example of the rabbinic impulse to forge links interconnecting Sinai, the Noahide Commandments, and, ultimately, Adam (ibid.). Similarly, we read in Song Rab 5:2 that the Israelites were bound to God in Egypt by two precepts (the blood of the Passover and the blood of circumcision), received commandments and were distinguished by many precepts, virtues, and good deeds at Marah (citing Ex 15:25), and became fully devoted to God at Sinai.

The late midrashic work Exodus Rabbah expresses the cumulative revelation of the law of which the Decalogue is the "main event" by means of the image of a great lady (here the Decalogue revealed at Sinai) surrounded by her retinue (the laws that preceded and followed the Decalogue):

> [Here it says:] "*And let them judge the people at all seasons*" (Ex 18:22) and here it says "*Now these are the ordinances*" (Ex 21:1), with the Decalogue in between (Ex 20). Like a distinguished lady (*matrona*) walking in the center of armed guards, so the Torah has laws preceding it and laws following it, while it is in the center. Hence it says, "*I walk in the way of righteousness*" (Prov 8:20). The Torah says: In which path shall I walk? "*I will walk in the path of those who act righteously, in the midst of the paths of justice*" (ibid.)—with the Torah in the center and laws preceding it and following it; preceding it, as it says, "*There he made for them a statute and an ordinance*" and following it, as it says "*Now these are the ordinances.*" (Ex Rab 30:3)

This text singles out the Decalogue as more distinguished than the laws that both preceded and followed it. The distinction here is not between laws before and after Sinai, but between the Decalogue and all other laws: the Decalogue is more excellent than all other laws regardless of the time of their delivery.

[12] See also b. Shab 87b, which contains a dispute over the content of the laws given at Marah.

Other rabbinic traditions deploy the motif of continual revelation of the law to distinguish between Mosaic Law and pre-Sinaitic law and to emphasize the superiority of the entire Mosaic Law given at Sinai, not just the Decalogue, over the laws given in the period preceding Sinai (Paz 2009, 88). Paradoxically, the very motif used to assert continuity between the Mosaic Law and the laws that preceded it—the motif of continual lawgiving—is deployed to differentiate them, by stressing the superiority of the final installment of the law, the Mosaic Law given at Sinai. This differentiation can take on a polemical coloration. Thus, in the following tannaitic text, the description of Sinai as the grand culmination of the gradual revelation of commandments becomes a vehicle for the denigration of the nations owing to their inability to observe the laws given to them prior to Sinai. The fact that the Israelites undertook to observe both the seven Noahide commandments *and* the entire body of divine legislation, a total of 613 commandments—reflects badly on the other nations:

> It was not enough for them [the Edomites, Ammonites, Moabites and Ishmaelites] that they did not obey—they were not even able to observe the seven commandments that the children of Noah had accepted upon themselves, and they cast them off. When the holy one, blessed be he, saw that, He gave them to Israel. A parable: A man took his ass and his dog to the threshing floor and loaded the ass with a *letek* [of grain] and the dog with three *seah*. The ass went along [easily], but the dog began to pant, so the man took off a *seah* and put it on the ass, and so too with the second and the third *seah*. So also Israel accepted the Torah, with all of its explanations and details, as well as the seven commandments which the children of Noah had not been able to observe and had cast off. Therefore it is said (Deut 33:2) *"And he said: Yahweh came from Sinai, and rose from Seir unto them."* (Sifre Deut 343, L. Finkelstein ed., 396–97)

According to this well-known midrash (analysed in greater detail below), certain other nations were incapable of observing even the seven Noahide laws, much less the full provisions of the Sinai legislation. But Israel was willing and able to shoulder them all.

In a lengthy discussion of the theme of cumulative revelation, a late midrashic work takes the polemic in a slightly different direction, casting aspersions not on the other nations but on the law that was offered to them. In other words, relative to the revelation at Sinai, the pre-Sinai revelations are inferior.[13] The midrash is based on a verse that emphasizes God's bestowal of the law precisely on Israel and on no other nation, and thus lends itself to a polemical interpretation.

---

[13] Novak notes that in the view of the rabbis, "the general Noahide laws were clearly inferior to the specific laws of the Mosaic Torah" (2011, 27).

He issued his commands to Jacob, his statutes and rules to Israel. He did not do so for any other nation; of such rules they know nothing. (Ps 147:19–20)

The midrash understands the verse to say that the uniqueness of God's actions toward Israel lay in his giving a fully formed and perfect Law at Sinai; by contrast, what was given to the ancestors of the other nations before Sinai was unformed and deficient. This claim is communicated via a series of images that describe the cultivation or maturation of the law over time, such that Israel alone would receive the fully developed Law.

R. Abbahu, in the name of R. Yosi b. R. Ḥanina, said: It can be compared to a king who had an orchard in which he planted all kinds of trees and the only one to enter it was him because he was its keeper. When his children came of age, he said, "My children, I have been the keeper of this orchard and I have not allowed anyone to enter it. Now you will keep it as I kept it." This is what the holy one, blessed be he, said to Israel, "Prior to creating the world, I prepared the Torah," for it says, "*Then I was with Him, a nursling*" (Prov 8:30). What is the meaning of "nursling" (*amon*)?—a tutor (*omen*), as it says "*As a nurse (omen) carries an infant*" (Num 11:12).[14] "I did not give it to one of the idol worshipping nations, but to Israel for as soon as they stood and said—'*All that Yahweh has spoken we will faithfully do*' (Ex 24:7)—they were given the Torah." Hence, "*He issued His commands to Jacob, His statutes and rules to Israel. He did not do so for any other nation; of such rules they know nothing*" (Ps 147:19–20)—but to whom? To Jacob, whom He chose from all the idolatrous nations, giving to them only part [of the Commandments].

He gave Adam six commandments, and added one to Noah, Abraham had eight and Jacob nine, but to Israel He gave all.

R. Simon in the name of R. Ḥanina said: It can be compared to a king who had before him a set table with all kinds of dishes on it. A servant entered and he gave him a slice [of meat]; a second and he gave him an egg, a third and he gave him some vegetable, and likewise for each one. When his son came in, he gave him the entire table lying before him, saying to him, "To the others I gave only single portions, but to you I give everything." So also God gave to the idol worshippers only some of the commandments, but when Israel arose, He said to them, "Behold the whole Torah is yours," as it says, "*He hath not dealt so with any nation.*"

R. Eleazar said: It can be compared to a king who went out to war with his legions. He slaughtered an animal and distributed to each one a piece

[14] The apposition "as an *amon*" is read as applying to the deity rather than the speaker, Wisdom. In other words, the verse is understood to say that I, Wisdom, was with him and he was an *amon*—or as the midrash will claim, an *omen*—to me.

to toil over.[15] His son was watching and asked him, "What will you give me?" He replied, "[I will give you] from that which I have prepared for myself." So the holy one, blessed be he, gave to the heathen commandments in their raw state, for them to toil over, and he did not make any distinction among them between uncleanness and purity; but as soon as Israel came, He explained each precept separately to them, both its punishment [for nonfulfillment] and reward, as it says *"let him kiss me with the kisses of his mouth"* (Song 1:2). Hence *"His statutes and His ordinances unto Israel."* (Ex Rab 30:9)

The first image applied to the law in this midrash is that of an orchard planted by God and cultivated until such time as God's children—the people of Israel—can tend to the orchard. Proverbs 8:30 is cited. In this verse, the speaker, Wisdom—identified by the rabbis, as by so many others in antiquity, as the Torah—says that she was with God from the beginning and, with the help of a play on words, that God was her *omen*, meaning caretaker, or pedagogue. In other words, God created the Law but then, like a pedagogue, guarded and cared for it until the time was ripe for Israel to receive it.

God's reasons for keeping the Law for a period of time are explored in two parables that follow the pedagogue text. One parable attributes the period of caretaking to the need to wait for the appropriate and beloved recipient. In this parable, God is likened to a king who distributes portions of a meal to his servants before bestowing the entire feast upon his son (here we find echoes of the slave-son opposition of Gal 4). The other parable, however, attributes the period of caretaking to the unformed and deficient nature of the Law when first created (very like the opening parable comparing the Law to an orchard that must be cultivated). This final parable likens God to a king who provides his legions with raw food requiring work and preparation before it can be consumed, but who provides his son with his own fully prepared victuals. The parable suggests that the laws given before Sinai and intended for the nations were in some sense defective and difficult, and that it was only at Sinai that God took pains fully to prepare the Law, explaining it and spelling out the consequences of obedience and disobedience. Both parables suggest that Israel alone is the recipient of the fully formed and mature law at Sinai because of her special intimacy with God (likened in both parables to the intimacy of a son rather than that of a servant or soldier).

The idea that the Law is deficient and in need of a "custodian" to establish it on a firm foundation bears remarkable similarities to Plato's *Laws* (G-R 6), where it is said that the laws are deficient, unstable, and in need of a "savior" (*Laws* 960d) that can establish their irreversible quality. It is the Nocturnal Council that serves as a custodian or guardian of the laws (*Laws* 964d–969c)

[15] They had to prepare the food for eating, as it was given to them raw.

and, by securing the salvation of the Law, secures the salvation of the state (968a). In the midrash, God himself is custodian of the Law—preparing it and explaining it so that its recipients need not toil over it but can accept and observe it readily. God's preparation and explanation of the Law fosters loyalty to the Law in the souls of the Law's recipients.

As we have seen, Paul also employs the image of the guardian or pedagogue but to very different effect:

> Before the coming of this faith, we were held in custody under the Law, locked up until the faith that was to come would be revealed. So the Law was our guardian [= pedagogue] until Christ came that we might be justified by faith. Now that this faith has come, we are no longer under a guardian. (Gal 3:24–25)

Here, *the Law is a guardian of the people* until the arrival of justification through faith in Christ. In the midrash, however, the Law is not the guardian of the people. God is the guardian of the Law, tending and taking care of it until both the Law and Israel are ready for one another (evidently both require some kind of maturation). When that time arrives, Israel will become the guardian of the Law! For Paul, humans mature *out of the Law* that served as their pedagogue, but according to this rabbinic text, they mature *into the Law* and serve as its pedagogue.

The idea that pre-Sinai laws are deficient relative to the laws given at Sinai is found in a lengthy tradition in PRK 12:1 (Mandelbaum ed., 202–4) that also assumes the theme of a cumulative revelation of the law despite the qualitative difference between the earlier and later revelations. The passage ascribes six commandments to Adam (through a creative exegesis of Gen 2:16), supplemented by further commandments in the time of Noah (the prohibition of consuming a limb torn from a living animal), Abraham (circumcision), Jacob (the prohibition of the sciatic nerve), and Judah (obligation of levirate marriage), for a total of ten commandments. But to Israel, God made a full disclosure of his entire Law—613 laws whose virtue is said by the midrashist to exceed all that came before and to dim the vaunted grace of Noah and the beauty of Adam. These traditions, extolling the Mosaic Law over all other laws and particularly pre-Sinai law, are an inversion of Philo's elevation of the living law of the patriarchs over the "copy" written down at Sinai (see chapter 3), and of the Christian denigration of the Mosaic Law as a punishment or a curse (see chapter 4).[16]

The common element in these midrashic traditions, with all their diverse emphases, is the cumulative revelation of laws. Properly speaking, then, there is no law *before* the Law. There is only one law—one large set of detailed, divine

---

[16] This is a descriptive rather than a genetic statement.

commandments and prohibitions—issued by the deity in continuing installments. Or, to adopt the language of Steven Wilf, these classical rabbinic texts
construct "a narrative of multiple law-giving" (2008, 176). They understand
the first divine directive to have entered the world with the creation of the first
human, with more directives to follow in piecemeal fashion until the climactic
revelation of the vast bulk of divine law at Sinai.

According to these rabbinic traditions, why is it that the entire Torah was
not vouchsafed immediately to Adam? Wilf argues that for later readers of the
biblical text, the story that carries humankind from Eden to Sinai was seen as
a story about "how to devise a norm-bearing person, one capable of enduring
the tremendous burden of legal obligation not just for the extraordinary moment, but within everyday life ... In other words ... a kind of legalism *had to
predate revelation*" (8). In their meditations on the law before Sinai, the rabbinic traditions surveyed here betray a conception of law as critical to the cultivation of virtue and a mature ethical consciousness, in stark contrast to Greco-
Roman discourses that lament law's inadequacy for the cultivation of virtue
(G-R 3 and 5), and the Pauline characterization of law as detrimental to the
same. For the rabbis, since the very first commandment issued to Adam, the
piecemeal revelation of law has facilitated progress toward the emergence of
fully norm-bearing persons and prepared Israel for the Law that would be revealed at Sinai (reminiscent of biblical discourse 3(iii)). This idea is hinted at
in a tannaitic teaching (MekhRY Baḥodesh 3, Horowitz ed., 211), according
to which Moses prepared the Israelites for the acceptance of the full Torah by
reading to them the laws already delivered prior to Sinai, as if to remind them
that they were already norm-bearing individuals (Wilf, 24).

I have referred to the "installment plan" as one strategy by which the rabbis
sought to locate Sinai at creation and in some respects reduce the distinction
between the Law at Sinai and the law before Sinai (even as polemical uses of this
motif inscribed the inferiority of the latter). Philo also sought to integrate the
Law at Sinai and the law before Sinai, but with opposite (in the sense of antipodal) results: privileging natural law, Philo turned Sinai into the written copy
of the universal unwritten law established in nature at creation; privileging the
Written Torah, the rabbis turned creation into a precursor of Sinai by locating
the revelation of concrete divine norms and directives in Eden.[17]

A second strategy for retrojecting the revealed Torah to the period before Sinai involved the depiction of pre-Sinai figures as observant, or at least
knowledgeable, of Sinaitic norms—indeed, in some cases Mosaic Law in all its
rabbinic elaboration. We turn now to this second strategy, which in its most
developed form depicts the patriarchs not just as law-abiding but as fully rabbinic Jews.

---

[17] For a somewhat similar assessment, see Morgenstern 2011, 56.

(II) THE PATRIARCHS AS RABBINIC JEWS

While Paul relied on Genesis 15:6 ("Abram believed Yahweh, and he credited it to him as righteousness") for his prenomian presentation of Abraham as justified by faith alone without knowledge or observance of the Law, rabbinic sources highlighted a very different verse—Genesis 26:5—to characterize Abraham as thoroughly nomian. In Genesis 26:4, Yahweh promises that Abraham will be the father of numerous descendants, and Genesis 26:5 provides the reason: "Inasmuch as Abraham obeyed my voice and kept my charge, my commandments, my laws, and my teachings [torot]." The author of this verse employs Deuteronomic terms for divine norms revealed at Sinai and in so doing suggests, in the opinion of many biblical scholars, that Abraham fulfilled the Law of Moses (Paz 2009, 32). Some readers in antiquity understood the verse to signal as much, but Philo and the rabbis use Genesis 26:5 to link Abraham to the Mosaic Law in very different ways. For Philo, the verse proves the equation of the Mosaic Law and the law that can be read in nature; for some rabbis the verse proves the opposite: that the Torah of Moses was revealed to the patriarchs before it was revealed at Sinai.[18] Abraham may have been a man of faith—indeed, many midrashim celebrate his faithful endurance of repeated trials—but according to certain rabbinic traditions, he was no less a follower of God's commandments, statutes, and laws.

The depiction of Abraham as observing the Mosaic Torah prior to its revelation at Sinai appears already in tannaitic sources. M. Qidd 4:14 ends its discussion of the blessings bestowed by Torah study in youth and in old age with the assertion that blessings were bestowed upon Abraham because he

> kept all of the Torah in its entirety even before it was revealed, as it is said, *"Since Abraham obeyed my voice and kept my charge, my commandments, my laws, and my teachings [torot]"* (Gen 26:5).

Paz (42–48) makes the following important observations about this text and related traditions. The passage does not appear in all manuscripts and seems to be a late addition attested in different versions. The more original version (attested in the Kaufman and Parma manuscripts) states that Abraham was blessed both in his youth prior to his circumcision and in his old age after his circumcision, as does the parallel in the Yerushalmi. However, the parallel in the Tosefta and the Bavli are quite different. According to the Vienna MS of the Tosefta, and the Bavli, Abraham was *more* blessed in his old age than in his

---

[18] Paz notes (2009, 35–6) that compared to its significance in the thought of Philo and the rabbis, the verse is all but invisible in the voluminous writings of the church fathers, where it appears a mere three times (in Chrysostom, Origen, and Eusebius). It is not surprising that the church fathers would want to avoid a verse that so clearly connects Abraham to the Mosaic Law. See Paz, 37–42, for an excellent discussion of the strategies employed by Chrysostom, Origen, and Eusebius to neutralize the implications of Gen 26:5.

youth because in his old age he fulfilled the Law, as evidenced by Genesis 26:5. Paz argues that this version responds to the claim—problematic to some rabbinic minds—that Abraham was blessed prior to observing the Law as signaled by his uncircumcision (45). By emphasizing the greater blessing that came with full Torah observance (circumcision and all of the commandments, statutes, and teachings; Gen 26:5), these versions of the tradition (which Paz argues are later modifications) disable the Christian reliance on Abraham as proof that the Law is not needed to procure divine blessing.

What did Abraham observe according to Genesis 26:5? The precise content of Abraham's observance is not indicated in the Mishnah's version of this tradition. Nevertheless, the emphasis on quantity ("all of the Torah in its entirety/ kol ha-Torah kulah"), and the immediate context valorizing traditional Torah study, suggest that the Torah envisaged here is the Mosaic Torah known to the rabbis, rather than a Philonic natural law. This hypothesis is supported by the version that appears in the Tosefta, where the word torot—the plural form of the word torah—is read expansively:

> He did the Torah before it came, as it is said, "Since Abraham obeyed my voice and kept my charge, my commandments, my laws, and my teachings [torot]" (Gen 26:5); "my teaching [torah]" is not said, but rather "my teachings [torot]" which teaches that all of the reasons of the Torah [ta'amei torah] and its details [diqduqeha] were revealed to him. (t. Qidd 5:17; Vienna MS)

Since the reasons and details of the Torah are traditionally the purview of scribes and rabbis, Abraham is implicitly credited with knowledge of not only the Mosaic Law but its traditional interpretative elaboration. This idea is fully and explicitly expressed in the version that appears in the Erfurt MS of the Tosefta, which expounds the word torot as "the words of Torah and the words of the scribes." The idea that Abraham fulfilled both the Written and the Oral Torah is attributed to a fourth- or sixth-generation Babylonian amora, Rava or Rav Ashi, in the Babylonian Talmud. Rava/Rav Ashi's view is set against an earlier amoraic view, attributed to R. Shimi b. Ḥiyya, that understands Abraham's Torah observance in a minimalist manner (the seven Noahide laws plus circumcision):

> Rav said: Our father Abraham kept the whole Torah, as it is said, "Since Abraham obeyed my voice and kept my charge, my commandments, my laws, and my teachings [torot]."
>
> R. Shimi b. Ḥiyya said to Rav: Say, perhaps, that this refers to the seven laws?—Surely there was also that of circumcision! Then say that it refers to the seven laws and circumcision [and not to the whole Torah]?—If that were so, why does Scripture say: "My commandments and My laws?"

Rava or R. Ashi said: Abraham, our father, kept even the law concerning the *eruv* of dishes [a rabbinic legal device that allows cooking on days when cooking would otherwise be prohibited] as it is said, "*My Torot* [the plural form of Torah]": one being the Written Torah, the other the Oral Torah. (b. Yoma 28b)

Rava/Rav Ashi moves well beyond the "installment" model's attribution to Abraham of only eight laws (the seven Noahide laws plus circumcision, as maintained by R. Shimi b. Ḥiyya and in Ex Rab 30:9, above). In this sugya, the idea that Abraham observed *only* eight laws is explicitly rejected, and a maximally expansive understanding of Abraham's law observance is proposed. For Rava/Rav Ashi, the abundance of legal terms in Genesis 26:5 (*my charge, my commandments, my laws, my teachings*) implies not merely eight laws but a plethora of laws, suggesting that Abraham kept the Torah *in its entirety*.[19] Specifically, the plural form *Torot* is taken to indicate that Abraham observed not only the terms of the Written Torah but the entire Oral Torah of rabbinic Judaism, including such Scripturally remote and rabbinically generated legal fictions as the Sabbath *eruv*.[20] By including laws that emerge from rabbinic exposition of Scripture and dialectic engagement, Rava or Rav Ashi remakes Abraham in the image of a rabbinic Jew.[21]

How did the patriarchs come to know the laws of the Torah to observe them? Philo's answer rests on the assumption that the Mosaic Law is none other than the law of nature, and that the patriarchs, through the rational contemplation of nature, were able to conform their behavior to nature and so live lives of happy obedience to the divine law (of which the Mosaic Law is an iconic written representation). But do the rabbis hold such a view, and if so, does it attest to a natural law stream within rabbinic thought according to which the Law can be seen in nature? Paz (2009, 7, 50–51) describes the division of scholarly opinion on this question: Some (following Wolfson) point to rabbinic texts that appear to present Abraham discovering the Torah through his own reason, and argue that the rabbis had a notion of natural law similar to Philo's. Others (following Urbach) interpret the same sources differently, as-

---

[19] This trend continues in midrashic texts (see Seder Eliyahu Rabbah 7, where Adam, Noah, and the patriarchs are said to observe certain laws, while Abraham observes the Torah in its entirety). According to Margulies (1993, 1:46), the same tradition appears in Lev Rab 2:10 and is a late interpolation from Seder Eliyahu Rabbah 6.

[20] This tradition is paralleled, though attributed to Palestinian tradents, in Gen Rab 49:2 and 64:4. There, Abraham is also credited with knowledge of the various names that God will use to designate Jerusalem—quite distant from Philo's understanding of the laws and teachings known to Abraham.

[21] Other patriarchal figures are also said to have observed Sinaitic laws in the pre-Sinai period, e.g., Joseph observed all of the ten commandments as well as Lev 17's prohibitions of hatred, vengeance, and grudges (MekhRY Beshallaḥ 1, Horowitz ed., 79–80). See the parallels in t. Sot 4:7; b. Sot 13a–b; PRK 11:12. The parallel in p. Sot 2:3, 4c adds that Joseph kept the commandments of God, meaning perhaps all of the commandments and not merely the Decalogue.

serting that Abraham's knowledge of Torah derived from revelation or divine inspiration, and not independent rational effort. According to Urbach, the possibility of immanent knowledge of the Law occurs only in a few very late sources.[22]

Many sources describing patriarchal observance of commandments employ terms indicative of revelation (the patriarchs are "given" a commandment, or a commandment "is revealed" to them). Other sources refer to the patriarchs as studying Torah. Although revelation and study are distinct modes of acquiring Torah, they are nevertheless intimately connected in that revelation of the Torah is understood to be followed by a process of transmission that involves study and teaching. Thus, a leading rabbinic assumption is that, for the most part, the patriarchs learned Torah as the rabbis themselves learned Torah—through the study and interpretation of an initially revealed text under the guidance of a teacher (Wilf 2008, 120).

Thus, rabbinic texts contain numerous aggadic traditions that depict the patriarchs learning Torah from their fathers and often in a schoolhouse setting (*bet midrash*). However, there are minimalist and maximalist versions of the motif of the pre-Sinai study house. According to Paz (2009, 58), traditions concerning the study house(s) of Shem and Ever must be distinguished from traditions concerning the study house of Abraham and later patriarchs. The former traditions are less anachronistic and envisage the study of Torah as the study of the Noahide laws, rather than the Torah of Moses;[23] the latter tend to be ahistorical and depict Abraham as studying the Torah of Moses.

Ever is first mentioned in an educational context in Seder Olam Rabbah 2. The tradition that Jacob studies with Ever solves the chronological problem of fourteen years of Jacob's life unaccounted for by the biblical text (Paz, 60). All other references to Shem and Ever's study house(s) are found in amoraic texts (such as Gen Rab 63:9, 84:8, b. Meg 16b), and in at least one case the motif is again used to fill a gap in a patriarch's life story (Gen Rab 56:11, in connection with Isaac). But as Paz argues (62), while a few sources seem to posit the entire rabbinic curriculum as the object of study, most do not. For the most part, the Torah studied in the study house(s) of Shem and Ever consists of the Noahide laws, an indication that the anachronistic positing of an educational institution (*bet midrash*) does not necessarily translate into an anachronistic positing of its curriculum (the entire Torah).

By contrast, the Torah studied and transmitted by Abraham and the subsequent patriarchs is the Torah of Moses, judging from explicit references to the

---

[22] Underlying this debate may be deeper ideological commitments on the question of whether rabbinic ethics is autonomous or heteronomous. As Paz cautions (2009, 8), these prior commitments can lead scholars to dichotomous formulations and sweeping generalizations that distort the evidence. See the discussion of this issue in chapter 6.

[23] Likewise, it is likely that traditions regarding Adam's study of Torah, examined in the previous section, refer to the six or seven laws revealed to him.

biblical text as the object of study (see, for example, Gen Rab 95:3, where Joseph is said to recall that at the time of his descent into Egypt he was studying the chapter of the broken-necked heifer with his father); Lev Rab 25:6 (paralleled in Gen Rab 46:4) describes Abraham studying the biblical verses pertaining to the prohibition of *orlah* (fruit produced before the fourth year) and assumes therefore a Written Torah text.

The application to the patriarchs of the model of the rabbinic schoolhouse, in which learning from a revealed text is carried out by teacher and student, raises the following question: who was the teacher of the first Torah student, Abraham? Even if we assume that the patriarchs in general acquired Torah through study, how did Abraham acquire it if there was no one there to teach him? In the case of Abraham, did the rabbis allow for the possibility of an independent process of rational discovery of the Law similar to the process imagined by Philo? A tradition commonly adduced in answer to this question is Gen Rab 61:1 (see also Gen Rab 95:3). However, while the passage was read by Wolfson as evidence that Abraham discovered the Torah with his own reason, it was read by Urbach as evidence of revelation (Paz 2009, 51). The passage deserves a full explication.

In Gen Rab 61:1 (Theodor-Albeck ed., 2:657–58) two answers are given to the question "Whence did Abraham learn Torah?" The first answer is that wisdom gushed forth from Abraham's kidneys. This midrash is a meditation on Psalms 1:1 "Happy is the man who has not followed the counsel of the wicked or taken the path of sinners, or joined the company of the insolent; rather, the teaching of Yahweh is his delight, and he studies that teaching day and night." Abraham is identified as the subject of this verse, since he did not "follow the counsel of the wicked" generation of the Tower of Babel nor join "the company of the insolent" men of Sodom, but instead followed the way of Yahweh, as stated in Genesis 18:19. If Abraham is the subject of the psalm, then it is Abraham who studies day and night. Since every student needs a teacher, R. Shimon b. Yoḥai asks:

> His father did not teach him and he did not have a teacher—whence did he learn Torah? In fact, the holy one, blessed be he, appointed his two kidneys to serve as two teachers and they flowed forth and taught him wisdom[24] and that is what is meant by the verse, "*I bless Yahweh who has guided me; my conscience [lit., kidneys] admonishes me at night*" (Ps 16:7).

The exegetical artistry is clear: Psalms 16, which refers to admonitions in the *night* (Ps 16:7), is cited to elucidate the means by which Abraham, who has just been shown to have studied also in the *night*, learned Torah. The midrash-

---

[24] Reading *hokhmah* with MS London Add. 27169 and several other manuscripts, instead of the printed edition's "Torah and wisdom." Nevertheless, given the question "Whence did he learn Torah?" it is clear that the "wisdom" referred to in the answer may be understood as Torah.

ist exploits the verse's reference to kidneys that admonish (the verb translated here as "admonish" can refer to a kind of direction or instruction) to suggest that God appointed Abraham's own kidneys as teachers (this constitutes the divine guidance mentioned in the verse). The kidneys presumably set before Abraham the content of the Torah as any good teacher would do (they "flow forth [*hayu nov'ot*] and teach him"). This midrash does not depict Abraham deducing natural law via a rational contemplation of the universe; it depicts Abraham engaged day and night in the study of the rabbinic curriculum under the tutelage of miraculously appointed instructors, based on a verse that speaks of God providing guidance by means of admonishing "kidneys" at night.

The second answer to the question "Whence did Abraham learn Torah?" is attributed to R. Levi. R. Levi dismisses the suggestion that Abraham had a teacher, and states that he studied Torah on his own (*me'atsmo lamad*), in keeping with Proverbs 14:14, which may be read to say that a good man is satisfied from himself. Does the phrase "studied on his own" refer to a rational process of reflection by which the wise man deduces the natural law? Probably not. R. Levi likely refers to solitary study of the standard curriculum, as opposed to study under the tutelage of a teacher. This understanding of *me'atsmo lamad* may be seen in b. Ket 111a, where the two modalities of study are juxtaposed: "Even though you are a great man, studying by yourself (*lomed me'atsmo*) is not the same as studying under a teacher."

In short, for the rabbinic composers of this midrash, studying God's Torah refers to the traditional curriculum of Torah study by one of two modalities—under a teacher (the favored modality in rabbinic culture) or alone (the disfavored modality). The two answers to the question of how the first Torah-observant individual (Abraham) came to know Torah point to these two possible modalities—either he had unusual and divinely appointed teachers, or he studied the text on his own, a normally disfavored solution, but satisfactory in the case of a thoroughly good man. The rational contemplation of nature, along the lines of Philo's Abraham, does not appear in this midrash as an option, favoring Urbach's interpretation of the passage (1975, 318).[25]

Another text that emphasizes Abraham's reliance upon direct divine guidance rather than his own reasoning power in comprehending the Law is Lev

[25] Urbach objects to the use of these and other texts by scholars asserting a kind of Kantian ethical autonomy according to which the patriarchs arrived at a recognition of God and a knowledge of Torah on their own. Urbach concedes that there are a few traditions that credit Abraham and even some other patriarchs with recognizing God by their own efforts rather than through revelation, but these are decidedly later texts (never tannaitic or amoraic), and they are confined to the question of monotheism, not knowledge of the Torah. See Urbach 1975, 318–21 and notes there. Schultz (1975, 52) states that independent recognition of the one god and knowledge of his commandments may be found already in such works as The Apocalypse of Abraham (see esp. chaps. 3, 7, and 8), but in fact the latter work attests only to independent recognition of the one god and not knowledge of the commandments. See also Paz 2009, 8.

Rab 25:6 (//Gen Rab 46:4). In this passage, Abraham's ability to derive law by the rules of legal reasoning from the revealed text is itself said to be dependent on God's revelation of those very rules (specifically *gezerah shavah*, or analogy, and *qal vehomer*, or a fortiori argument)! Since God did not reveal these logical exegetical rules to Abraham, he was *unable* to deduce the law by means of them. This tradition strongly pushes against the idea of an innate rational capacity that can operate independently to discover the Law.

Paz (2009, 55) adduces MekhRY Beshallaḥ 1 (Horowitz ed., 79–80) as evidence for the immanent observance of the Law without direct revelation or traditional study. The text praises Joseph who, in the course of his life, managed to fulfill all ten commandments as well as Leviticus 17's prohibitions of hatred, vengeance, and grudges.[26] However, this fanciful postmortem correlation of the various commandments with events in Joseph's life neither implies nor assumes that Joseph had explicit knowledge of the commandments or acted *consciously* to obey them; any inference to this effect expects more of this text than it can yield. Similarly, traditions about the patriarchs separating tithes or establishing prayers (Gen Rab 64:6; b. Ber 6b) are not best read as evidence that the patriarchs could innovate commandments without direct revelation or tradition (Paz, 57). In these texts, the patriarchs' authority to institute certain practices may be compared to that of the rabbis themselves, who are empowered to institute rulings or directives for the community. This has little to do with autonomous knowledge of Torah norms or the Philonic characterization of Abraham as a living law. Given the paucity of these sources, the claim that such a view is well represented in rabbinic literature is difficult to support.

We have seen that various rabbinic texts contribute to a narrative of multiple lawgiving, of pre-Sinaitic revelations of the law, and of minimal or maximal Torah observance by the patriarchs prior to Sinai. This narrative of pre-Sinai encounters with, habituation to, and internalization of the law highlights the Israelites' readiness for the fuller revelation of God's commands at Sinai. It is a narrative, however, that creates tensions: the idea that Abraham and, according to some texts, the other patriarchs upheld the Torah is challenged by narrative details of the biblical text itself. Later commentators were often exercised by the need to explain the patriarchs' clear violations of Torah law.[27]

However, some rabbinic sources note the biblical record of the patriarchs' violations of Sinaitic Law without alarm.[28] These sources reject the ahistorical transfer of Sinaitic norms to the pre-Sinaitic period, a theme with variations to which we now turn.

[26] See the parallels in t. Sot 4:7; b. Sot 13a–b; PRK 11:12; and p. Sot 2:3, 4c.

[27] For a discussion of this phenomenon, see Wilf 2008, 85–86.

[28] See, for example, b. Pes 119b and Gen Rab 84:21 for the acknowledgment that Jacob married two sisters, "which Torah would later prohibit." This tradition is conflicted, however: on the one hand, Jacob's temporal priority to the Torah serves to excuse him; on the other hand, his action renders him unfit to offer a blessing in the time to come.

Sinaitic Law Begins at Sinai

Side by side with the depiction of the patriarchs as students and observers of the Mosaic Law is a strand of thought in rabbinic literature that evinces a more "historical" sensibility. Adhering more closely to the plotline of the biblical narrative, it rejects the idea of Torah observance before the giving of the Torah at Sinai.[29]

Significantly, the recognition that those living before Sinai were not subject to the laws revealed at Sinai is a halakhic principle assumed by and informing some halakhic discussions. M. Neg 7:1 states that bright spots that appeared on the skin before the giving of the Torah, like the bright spots that appear on a Gentile before conversion, are ritually pure. In other words, the mishnah clearly and understandably assumes that the laws of ritual impurity do not apply prior to their revelation at Sinai. This is but one example of a phenomenon attested in other halakhic contexts: the phenomenon of adducing pre-Sinai Israelites as the paradigmatic case of persons not familiar with or subject to the Mosaic Law and thus useful for determining the halakhic status and obligations of converts prior to their conversion (see Hayes 2002, 110–13).

The assumption that Israelites prior to Sinai were unfamiliar with and not subject to the Mosaic Law is in itself a plain reading of the biblical text unremarkable in itself. What *is* remarkable is the tendency in a few cases to deny the application to pre-Sinaitic Israelites (and by extension non-Jews) of laws that the biblical narrative takes pains to explicitly associate with the pre-Sinai era. It occasions some surprise, for example, that one of the earliest rabbinic expressions of the idea that the patriarchs did *not* observe the Mosaic Law occurs precisely in connection with the prohibition of the sciatic nerve—a law that the Bible connects explicitly to the patriarch Jacob:

> [The prohibition of the sciatic nerve] applies to a pure animal but not an impure one.
>
> R. Judah said: [it applies] also to an impure one. R. Judah said: And wasn't the sciatic nerve prohibited to the sons of Jacob while impure animals were yet permitted to them?
>
> They said to him: It was promulgated (lit. "prohibited") at Sinai but recorded (lit. "written") in its place. (m. Ḥul 7:6)

In this tannaitic text, R. Judah argues that the prohibition of the sciatic nerve dates to the time of Jacob, a reference to Genesis 32, when Jacob's hip socket was strained by the angel with whom he wrestled, and the biblical narrator observes: "That is why the children of Israel to this day do not eat the thigh muscle that is on the socket of the hip, since Jacob's hip socket was wrenched at the

---

[29] Paz (2009, 9) notes that most scholars ignore these sources in their effort to present a somewhat monolithic rabbinic view on the question of pre-Sinai law.

thigh muscle" (Gen 32:33). R. Judah reads this notification as indicating an immediate abstention from the sciatic nerve, beginning with Jacob's sons. His view is rejected, however, by anonymous authorities who hold that the law was promulgated only later at Sinai. Abstention from the sciatic nerve is recorded in Genesis 32 (the meaning of "in its place," i.e., its narrative context), rather than in the Sinai account in Exodus, in order to publicize the reason for the prohibition, a point made explicitly in the toseftan parallel, t. Ḥul 7:8–9. The toseftan passage goes on to contrast this prohibition with the prohibition of a limb torn from a living animal. The latter prohibition is "recorded" in Genesis 9 because that was the time it was actually given to Noah, and thus all humanity.[30]

These tannaitic teachings on the sciatic nerve are particularly telling because no apologetic motivation is apparent. If the biblical narrative were to contain a report of a patriarch eating the sciatic nerve, one might understand the rabbinic desire to "rescue" the patriarch's reputation by insisting that the prohibition was not yet in effect. This kind of apologetic move is found in the case of other patriarchal violations of Torah law. Texts resolve the problem of Jacob's marriage to two sisters by pointing out that such marriages had not yet been prohibited (Pes 119b and Gen Rab 84:21). But in this case, a biblical verse strongly implies that the patriarchs observed the prohibition of the sciatic nerve. It is one thing to reject the pre-Sinai applicability of a later law in order to rescue the reputations of those who have violated it; it is quite another to do so in the absence of such a motivation *and* when the biblical text itself seems to suggest that the prohibition in question was known and observed prior to Sinai!

Why do R. Judah's interlocutors discount textual evidence that could support the claim that a Sinaitic Law was observed in the pre-Sinai period when other rabbinic tradents attribute the observance of the entire Mosaic Law to the patriarchs? What was at stake for those who assert that the Torah was not observed at all until the revelation at Sinai? Paz (2009, 77) argues persuasively that the authority and status of the Mosaic Law are at stake in this dispute. This principle is articulated in connection with the sciatic nerve because this is the only law that is mentioned prior to Sinai and not repeated at Sinai. According to R. Judah's interlocutors, were this pre-Sinai law to retain its validity after Sinai, then Sinai would not be a uniquely authorizing event. If Sinai is to be seen as the unique source of normative authority, then *all* valid law must date to Sinai. Those who would "transfer" the prohibition of the sciatic nerve from its place in the story of Jacob and assert that it was delivered at Sinai do so because of the belief that only the revelation at Sinai has normative authority.

---

[30] The prohibition of a limb torn from a live animal is not, of course, explicit in Gen 9 but is located there by the rabbis via the blood prohibition. As a consequence, and unlike the prohibition of the sciatic nerve, the prohibition of a limb torn from a live animal is said to apply to both pure and impure animals, because its promulgation predated the distinction between pure and impure animals.

This view also informs an unusual teaching of R. Yosi b. R. Ḥanina discussed at length by Paz (90–94):

R. Yosi b. Ḥanina said: Every commandment which was given to the Noahides and repeated at Sinai applies to both [Noahides and Israelites]; [every commandment given] to the Noahides but not repeated at Sinai applies to the Israelites and not to the Noahides, and we have only the case of the sciatic nerve on the view of R. Judah. (b. San 59a)

This somewhat counterintuitive idea—that a law given to Noahides (including the patriarchs) in the pre-Sinai period and not repeated at Sinai applies to Israel and not to Noahides!—is based on the view that the Mosaic Law determines the validity of *all* law. The validity of pre-Sinai norms was merely conditional; their final status would be determined at Sinai. On this view, Sinai is imagined as the beginning of a new era, discontinuous with the past: if the Mosaic Law repeated a law given prior to Sinai, then that law was not only established for Israelites but reestablished for Noahides. If, however, the Mosaic Law did not repeat a law given previously to Noahides, that law lapsed for Noahides but continued valid for Israelites because Sinai does not release the Israelites from earlier law. Paradoxically, Sinai determines the law for both Israelites and Noahides.[31]

Paz (78–79) points out that a related idea is expressed by the phrase *nitnah Torah venithadshah halakhah* ("the Torah was given and the halakhah was renewed"). The phrase occurs in two passages from the Babylonian Talmud (b. Shab 135a–b and b. BB 110b) in connection with two laws that, according to explicit biblical evidence, were observed in the pre-Sinai period—eighth-day circumcision and inheritance by sons. In both cases, the phrase is introduced to indicate that even though the law in question was commanded and/or practiced prior to Sinai, its continuing validity was dependent on its restatement at Sinai. When the Torah was given, the validity of these two laws was reestablished (in both cases with some small difference). The effect is to disable the patriarchs as sources of legal validity (a position reflected in the twice-repeated claim that one does not learn halakhah from the actions of the patriarchs; see p. MQ 3:5, 82c and Gen Rab 100:7; see also b. Yoma 28a).[32]

---

[31] Paz 2009, 90–94. This is not to say that the Mosaic Law can't explicitly permit something to Israel that is prohibited to Noahides, a subject that will concern us below. It is merely to say that the non-repetition of a law at Sinai does not imply that the law has lapsed for Israel. On the contrary, the law continues valid for Israel even as it lapses for Noahides, on R. Yosi b. R. Ḥanina's view. It would require explicit permission for a Noahide prohibition to be overturned for Israel, and examples are given in Sifre Deut 76 and b. San 59a. See below.

[32] This is not, of course, a universally held view. There are several instances in which a law or practice is derived from the actions of the patriarchs. See below for a discussion of the patriarchs' institution of particular laws and practices in the book of Jubilees.

Thus, in three cases (concerning the sciatic nerve, eighth-day circumcision, and inheritance by sons), explicit biblical support for a claim of pre-Sinai observance is obviated by some rabbinic readers. This attempt to characterize the pre-Sinai era as relatively law-free or only conditionally normative, and therefore discontinuous with the post-Sinai era, stands in tension with the sources examined above that assert a continuity between the two eras.

Accounting for Diverse Rabbinic Views on Pre-Sinai Normativity

Rabbinic sources offer a wide range of views on the question of norms in the period prior to the revelation of the Mosaic Law at Sinai. While there is no text that suggests that the pre-Sinai period is entirely law-free, the extent and significance of pre-Sinai normativity and its relationship to the Mosaic Law introduced at Sinai are variously represented. While some rabbinic texts are ahistorical and anachronistic in their depiction of Abraham (and other patriarchs) fulfilling the full terms of the Written Torah and, in some cases, even the rabbinic Oral Torah, others portray the pre-Sinai period as law-free. They do not retroject the Mosaic Law to the period before Sinai, and they acknowledge explicit violations of later Mosaic Law (Paz 2009, 98). These views reflect different conceptions of the Mosaic Law. On the one hand, the Mosaic Law is depicted as continuous with, even if markedly superior to, pre-Sinai norms that are eternally valid in the case of Noahides and are superadded to in the case of Israelites. In these texts, the revelation at Sinai marks the culmination of a multistage process of revelation of continually valid divine law. On the other hand, the Mosaic Law is depicted in some texts as discontinuous with pre-Sinai norms whose ongoing validity even for non-Israelites in the new era ushered in by the Mosaic Law is conditioned on the reestablishment of those norms at Sinai. On this view, Sinai is a uniquely authorizing event.

How are we to account for these diverse views? It would be a mistake to suppose that there is a single explanation that encompasses them all. The complex range of views attested in these texts is likely the result of a number of simultaneous, intersecting, and even contradictory factors. In addition, an idea or motif generated under certain circumstances may over the course of time be embraced and restated—with or without modification—for reasons entirely different from those contributing to its original formulation. As noted above, Paz explains different rabbinic views of the continuity or discontinuity between pre-Sinai norms and the Mosaic Law as reflecting a principled dispute over the unique status of the Mosaic Law as the sole mechanism for authorizing divine norms for all humanity. This is an entirely persuasive hypothesis, but as Paz himself understands, it does not explain all of the nuances of the rabbinic views described here, nor does it exhaust the possibilities for understanding the view it does explain.

Joseph P. Schultz (1975) considers the historical and ideational roots of the two recurring images of the patriarchs: that the patriarchs observed little more than the Noahide laws on the one hand, or that they observed the entire Law, prior to its revelation at Sinai, on the other. Schultz notes that when the patriarchs are viewed as Noahides, then they are distinct from later Israelites and more easily identified with Gentiles; when they are viewed as pre-Sinai Israelites, then they are distinct from Gentiles and more easily identified with post-Sinai Israelites (a dichotomy that in his view underwrites the dispute over whether the patriarchs' actions can serve as legal precedents for Israel [53]). This observation leads Schultz to suggest that the portrait of the patriarchs as Noahides should be connected with the phenomenon of proselytism in the Second Temple and rabbinic periods (55). Depicting the patriarchs as Noahides offered a model for proselytes: beginning with Abraham, the patriarchs came to believe in God, and to accept circumcision and eventually the whole Torah at Sinai, charting a course to be followed by future proselytes (56).

Attributing the depiction of the patriarchs as Noahides to the phenomenon of proselytism finds support in the fact that other groups in antiquity—specifically Paul and early Christian thinkers—also pointed to the patriarchs as models for Gentiles who wished to join their communities. On the model of Abraham, Paul argued, Gentiles can be saved in an uncircumcised and law-free state by means of faith. Schultz sees the rabbinic portrayal of the patriarchs as Noahides as an attempt to encourage would-be proselytes to Judaism. However, while this hypothesis may shed light on some of the texts cited above, it does not account for those versions of the "patriarchs as Noahides" motif that bear a polemical coloration. Traditions that valorize Mosaic Law by actively denigrating Noahides and casting aspersions on their ability to fulfill even the most basic norms (Sifre Deut 343 [L. Finkelstein ed., 396–97]; Ex Rab 30:9; PRK 12:1) are more likely to reflect an intragroup discourse of self-encouragement, rather than an intergroup discourse intended to encourage and persuade proselytes.

As for the portrait of the patriarchs as pre-Sinai Israelites observing the entire Law, many scholars assume a rabbinic

> polemic directed against Paul's insistence that Abraham achieved salvation only through faith and later Christian antinomianism which claimed that the commandments of the Mosaic Law were a punishment inflicted by God upon Israel. (Schultz, 57)

An excellent recent example may be found in Wilf (2008, 19):

> [T]he rediscovery of a robust pre-Sinai legalism, then, is unconsciously or consciously a Jewish rebuttal to Christian antinomianism. Jewish commentators would find more law, not less ... dispensing with Paul's notion of a past untouched by law ... Abraham was transformed from Paul's antinomian figure into a [sic] exemplary legal scholar. Jewish tradition insisted Abraham knew all the law ... Indeed, the rabbis believed law

enveloped the narrative before Sinai. If Paul would cast law out of Eden, the Jewish response was to find it before and after revelation in the very marrow of the Biblical narrative.

Wilf's statement has merit, but it cannot be accepted as an assessment of *all* of the rabbinic data. Schultz (44) has already noted that texts that attribute law observance to the patriarchs cannot be wholly explained as a response to the Christian representation of Abraham as prenomian, because similar views can be found in Second Temple literature, such as the book of Jubilees, prior to the rise of Christianity.[33] Schultz believes it is more likely that the "Paulinian view and its later Christian exposition is a polemic against the Jewish outlook, not vice versa" (ibid.). However, caution on this point is required. A closer look at Jubilees' characterization of the patriarchs as norm-bearing individuals reveals important differences between that text and later rabbinic traditions.

Schultz (44) provides an inventory of the Sinaitic laws observed by the patriarchs in Jubilees, beginning with Adam and Eve, who observed ritual impurity laws relating to childbirth (Jub 3:9ff.). In Jubilees 7:20, Noah prescribes

> for his grandsons the ordinances and the commandments—every statute which he knew. He testified to his sons that they should do what is right, cover the shame of their bodies, bless the one who had created them, honor father and mother, love one another, and keep themselves from fornication, uncleanness, and from all injustice.[34]

Noah additionally commands his sons regarding the agricultural laws (7:36), and he, like the later patriarchs, is said to celebrate the festival of Shavuot (6:18–19; 15:1; 22:1; 44:4). Similarly, Abraham summons his sons and commands them to observe the way of God, which includes loving one's neighbor, doing justice and righteousness, practicing circumcision, and refraining from fornication and uncleanness (20:2–3). More specific injunctions regarding the punishment for fornication, intermarriage, idolatry, and images follow:

> If any woman or girl among you commits a sexual offence, burn her in fire; they are not to commit sexual offences (by) following their eyes and their hearts so that they take wives for themselves from the Canaanite women, because the descendants of Canaan will be uprooted from the earth . . . love the God of heaven and hold fast to all his commandments. Do not follow their idols and their uncleanness. Do not make for yourselves gods that are molten images or statues . . . do not worship them or bow to them. (20:4, 7–8)

---

[33] Of course it is possible that the idea of pre-Sinai legalism was a rebuttal to antinomian tendencies that might have predated Paul.

[34] Bockmuehl (2000, 156) notes that this is the earliest extant Jewish text that explicitly links Gen 9 with a universal ethic for the children of Noah.

In addition, Abraham, Isaac, and Jacob celebrate Sukkot and Passover (Jub 16:20) and observe sacrificial laws (21:6ff.).

On the basis of these texts, Schultz (1975, 45) argues that even though Jubilees stresses certain commandments above others, especially those that would later be identified as "Noahide" commandments (e.g., theft, murder, adultery/fornication), for Jubilees the patriarchs were full Israelites observing the Mosaic Law.[35] Against this, Paz argues (2009, 32–33) that according to Jubilees, the patriarchs did not follow the entire Mosaic Law—only the laws included or implied in the biblical narratives that feature them (the Noahide laws, circumcision, some sacrificial laws, and so on). Indeed, Jubilees recognizes patriarchal deviations from later Mosaic Law and accounts for these lapses with a theory of partial revelation: the Mosaic Law was not revealed to the patriarchs in its entirety (an idea that has affinities with other Second Temple texts; see chapter 3). So, for example, Reuben was not fully punished for violating the laws of incest by having intercourse with his father's concubine because the law had not been completely revealed in his day:

> They are not to say: Reuben was allowed to live and (have) forgiveness after he had lain with the concubine-wife of his father while she had a husband and her husband—his father Jacob—was alive. For the statute, the punishment, and the law had not been completely revealed to all but (only) in your time as a law of its particular time and as an eternal law for the history of eternity. (Jub 33:15–16)

So while Schultz is correct in the observation that Second Temple sources depict the patriarchs as norm-bearing, he overstates his case when he asserts that the rabbis drew on an older, pre-Christian tradition in representing the patriarchs as pre-Sinaitic Israelites observant of Mosaic Law. Jubilees and related sources do not depict the patriarchs as pre-Sinai Israelites fulfilling the entire Mosaic Law; rabbinic sources that do so must be seen as a significant shift from Second Temple representations of the patriarchs as Noahides. Thus, a full account of the various factors that coalesce and collide in the formation of the rabbinic data might run as follows: (1) the view of the patriarchs as to some degree following norms revealed prior to Sinai is a view that predates the Christian era. This view most likely arose as a response to the tension between dueling conceptions of divine law as, on the one hand, universal and eternal (thus operative in some way prior to Sinai) and, on the other, particular and promulgated in time (thus not fully revealed prior to Sinai);[36] (2) The view of the patriarchs as law-observant was likely "stressed with renewed vigor in the

---

[35] He points to similar assertions in the later Testaments of the Patriarchs and the Syriac Apocalypse of Baruch; he claims that these works also refer to the patriarchs as observing post-Sinaitic commandments, with emphasis on the so-called Noahide commandments.

[36] See n33 for an additional possibility.

face of the Christian challenge" (Schultz 1975, 57) and expanded to encompass the entire Mosaic Law that was the subject of Christian polemic; (3) The expansion of patriarchal law observance to include even the rabbinic Oral Torah was likely a response to an internal sectarian rejection of the Pharisaic-rabbinic "traditions of the fathers" or Oral Torah (Paz 2009, 47).

This survey of rabbinic depictions of normativity before Sinai has revealed that the period is seen neither as a *law-free* golden age that came to an end with the giving of the Mosaic Law at Sinai, nor as a *lawless* dark age redeemed by the giving of the Mosaic Law at Sinai. The Greco-Roman dichotomy of law-free or lawless is sidestepped in the rabbinic materials, which envisage instead some form of law observance by humans—including the first human pair—living in the period before the revelation of the Mosaic Law. Although the content of the norms observed by the patriarchs and their relationship to the revelation at Sinai vary widely, none of the rabbinic traditions about the law observed by the patriarchs represents this law as embedded in nature, distinct from the revealed Mosaic Law, and accessible to independent reason. In the next section we survey a wider set of texts on the Noahide laws in order to determine whether they might be understood as a rabbinic version of, or response to, the claims of a natural law tradition.

THE NOAHIDE LAWS

We turn now to the specific case of the Noahide laws, which have been touted as a rabbinic version of natural law or, at least, as a resource for the construction of a natural law view.[37] Does the rabbinic conception of Noahide law match classical definitions of natural law and function in the same manner as natural law *as understood in antiquity?*

The Bible, of course, depicts God delivering not seven commandments to Noah but only one—the blood prohibition of Genesis 9:6 (Morgenstern 2011, 49). The claim that seven commandments were delivered to Noah and his progeny is found in full form only in postbiblical rabbinic sources. Some scholars maintain that the rabbinically articulated concept of the Noahide laws encapsulates a Jewish natural law theory (Novak 1998, 149) because the Noahide laws represent norms binding on all humankind. Others demur and assert that the seven Noahide commandments are nothing more than a Jewish version of

---

[37] See Bockmuehl 2000, 162: "There is thus an overlap in content between the Noachide and natural law traditions ... this doctrine upheld the biblical notion of an international morality that makes ethical communication possible. It did so against the background of the widespread Graeco-Roman ideas like the *ius gentium*, natural law and unwritten law, which applied to all humanity equally." Falk (1980, 65) asserts that talmudic law was influenced by natural law. Novak (1998, 2011) has been a leading voice in the effort to utilize the Noahide commandments in the construction of a Jewish natural law theory compatible with modern humanistic principles. For a review of the literature on this subject, see Stone 1991.

the Roman *ius gentium* (laws applicable to noncitizens).[38] Novak (ibid., 150; 2011, 35) dismisses the latter characterization. Unlike the *ius gentium*, the Noahide commandments, he argues, were never a vehicle of actual Jewish political power over Gentiles in the way the *ius gentium* was the means by which Rome exercised power over foreigners. Nor were the Noahide laws genuinely derived from authoritative texts;[39] they function more like principles than actual prescriptive rules, and they were always entirely speculative, which is precisely "how natural law thinking operates" (1998, 151).

Novak's assertion—that the general (nonprescriptive) and speculative nature of the Noahide laws supports the claim that they are a kind of Jewish natural law—is not convincing. First, much of rabbinic law in the same period was speculative and inoperable owing to the lack of Jewish autonomy and changed historical circumstances (e.g., the loss of the sacrificial cult), but Novak would certainly not characterize it as natural law on those grounds. Second, the derivation of these laws from Scriptural texts, sometimes against the dictates of reason (see below), cannot be dismissed out of hand as purely allusive rather than genuinely generative—it says *something* about the rabbinic conception of these laws that they are linked to an authoritative text even on the view that these links are not genuinely exegetical. Third, the Noahide laws as articulated by the rabbis are in fact prescriptive rules. The prohibition against theft, even though somewhat general in character, is not a mere statement of principle regarding natural rights to property but a concrete prescriptive rule, no less than the prohibition against eating a limb torn from a living animal, which is also among the seven Noahide commandments.

In order to assess the extent to which the rabbinic conception of Noahide law reflects Greco-Roman conceptions of natural law, we must determine whether the Noahide laws possess the essential characteristic features of natural law.[40] As we have seen, Cicero's classic definition of natural law states that "true law is right reason in agreement with nature; it is of universal application, unchanging and everlasting … We cannot be freed from its obligations by senate or people, and we need not look outside ourselves for an expounder or interpreter of it. And there will not be different laws at Rome and at Athens, or different laws now and in the future, but one eternal and unchangeable law will be valid for all nations and all times" (*Republic*, 22.211, as cited in Wilf 2008, 54). Cicero's definition reflects key elements that dominated the discourse of natural law in the Hellenistic east of the rabbis: natural law is invariable and universal, rational, and embedded in nature. If the Noahide laws possess these features,

---

[38] Novak (1998, 149, and 2011, 19) points to B. Cohen 1966, 26–27, as an example. See also Bockmuehl 2000, 150: "Briefly put, the *topos* of Noahide Law in rabbinic thought governs relations between Jews and non-Jews, and is thus a kind of functional equivalent to the Roman *ius gentium.*"

[39] According to Novak, when rabbinic texts link the Noahide laws to biblical verses, the verses are allusions to rather than sources of the law.

[40] It is not an essential characteristic of natural law that it is speculative or that it is generalized.

then a good case can be made for a version of natural law, distinct from the Mosaic Law, in rabbinic literature.

Are the Noahide Laws Invariable, Universal, Rational, and Embedded in Nature?

(1) EARLY SOURCES

In the earliest rabbinic sources, the Noahide laws are not depicted as invariable or universal. Rabbinic sources record (1) significant dispute over the actual content of the Noahide commandments and (2) differences between Gentiles and Israelites in their application. These features may be seen in what is arguably the earliest rabbinic enumeration of the Noahide laws—t. AZ 8(9):4–9. For ease of presentation, I have divided the passage into sections and provided explanatory headings (in boldface) for each section:

(a) **Introductory statement**
Concerning seven mitzvot (commandments) were the children of
Noah commanded:

(b) **List of commandments**
Setting up courts of justice,
idolatry,
blasphemy,[41]
fornication,
bloodshed,
and robbery
and a limb from a living animal[42]

(c) **Glosses on each item in the previous list**
"Setting up courts of justice"—How so? Just as Israel is commanded
to establish courts in their towns so also the Noahides are
commanded to establish courts in their towns.
"idolatry and blasphemy"—how so? A non-Jew who worships idols
and a blasphemer, the only death penalty a Noahide receives is
execution by sword.
"fornication"—how so? Any illicit sexual relation for which an Israelite
court inflicts the death penalty, Noahides are warned against and
for every illicit sexual relation against which an Israelite court
warns, Noahides are executed—the words of R. Meir, but the

---

[41] Following the Vienna and Erfurt MSS here and throughout the passage against the printed edition. The order of the first three items is different in Seder Olam Rabbah and the baraita cited in b. San 56a–b (where blasphemy precedes idolatry) and in several midrashim. See Novak 2011, 11–12 and 243n5.

[42] The Erfurt MS omits this item.

sages say there are many illicit sexual relations for which it is not the case that the court inflicts the death penalty and the Noahides are warned. One who violates a sexual prohibition according to Israel is judged by the laws of Israel and one who violates a sexual prohibition according to the Noahides is judged by the laws of the Noahides and the only [difference] is the case of [sexual relations with] a betrothed young woman.

"bloodshed"—how so? A non-Jew who [kills] a non-Jew or a non-Jew who kills a Jew is liable; but a Jew who kills a non-Jew is exempt.

"robbery"—how so? Theft, robbery, the captive woman and similar cases—a non-Jew against a non-Jew or a non-Jew against a Jew, it is prohibited; but a Jew against a non-Jew, it is permitted.

"a limb from a living animal"—how so? A dangling limb on an animal that can't be healed or dangling flesh on an animal that can't be healed is prohibited to Noahides and all the more so to Israelites. If it can be healed it is permitted to Israelites and all the more so to Noahides.

If one took a bird that is less than an olive's bulk and ate it, Rabbi declares exempt but R. Elazar beR. Shimeon declares liable, for if one is liable on account of a limb from an animal should one not be liable for the entire animal?

If he strangled it and ate it he is exempt.

(d) Additional commandments

R. Ḥananiah ben Gamliel says:
also concerning blood from a living animal.

Rabbi Ḥidqa says:
also concerning castration.

R. Shimeon says:
also concerning witchcraft.

R. Yosi says:
all that is said in the [biblical] section of the Noahides they [the Noahides] are warned against as it is said (Deut 18:10–11) *"There shall not be found among you one who passes his son or daughter through the fire, one who practices divination, a soothsayer, an augur, a sorcerer, a charmer, a medium, a wizard or a necromancer for they are an abomination to Yahweh."* Is it possible that Scripture would inflict punishment without first giving a warning? [No], rather Scripture warns and afterwards punishes to teach that it warned and afterwards punished.

R. Eliezer (= Erfurt MS) says:
concerning mixed seeds, it is permitted for Noahides to sow them and to wear mixed fibers but it is prohibited for them to cross-breed animals or graft trees.

The baraita contains the following elements: (a) an introductory statement announcing that seven commandments were given to the Noahides; (b) a list of the commandments; (c) glosses on each item in the list; (d) attributed teachings that add additional items to the list of Noahide commandments.[43]

Problems beset this text from the outset. The introductory statement (a) refers to seven commandments, and the subsequent list (b) and its glosses (c) identify seven commandments, but not in all witnesses, some of which lack one or more of the following due to scribal errors: courts, blasphemy, and the limb torn from a living animal. Section (d), which features a number of additional commandments offered by various tannaitic sages, further destabilizes this number.[44] In this section, R. Ḥananiah b. Gamliel suggests that the blood of a living animal was among the Noahide laws, R. Ḥidqa adds the prohibition of castration, and R. Shimon, the prohibition of witchcraft. R. Yosi includes a prohibition against all sorts of magical and occult practices, and R. Elazar adds a prohibition against certain mixtures.[45] Thus, the list of Noahide commandments is unstable—the number ranges from seven to a dozen if the prohibitions in section (d) are cumulative.

The lack of fixity—in terms of both number and content of the Noahide commandments—is treated as any other halakhic dispute is treated: different traditions reflect the teachings of different schools and require no further adjudication. There is no attempt to argue the merits of the respective lists. There is no attempt to advance rational arguments for or against the claims of each to represent basic universal norms common to all humanity, which we might expect were the list the result of philosophical reflection about basic universal norms. But it is not. According to t. AZ 8(9):4–8, the Noahide commandments are specific prescriptive rules, not ethical first principles; they are revealed by God, not arrived at through rational speculation; their specific contents can be derived from Scriptural exegesis and received traditional teachings, modalities that are (in this as in all areas of rabbinic deliberation) inherently subject to variation and dispute.[46] It is therefore unremarkable that the Noahide laws are neither fixed in number nor invariable in content. They are no different from any other subject arising from Scriptural exegesis and traditional teaching, as indicated by Rava's somewhat matter-of-fact attribution of the existence of different lists to the teachings of different schools.

[43] The Bavli contains a baraita that corresponds to sections (a), (b), and (d), but lacks (c).

[44] Hebrew 'af implies that each tradent offers his teaching as an addition to, not a substitution for, any of the items in the previous list. Bockmuehl (2000, 160) notes the variability of the list throughout the talmudic period.

[45] In the Bavli sugya that expands on this tradition, the stam identifies circumcision and procreation as among the commandments given to the Noahides (b. San 59b), a position not maintained in other rabbinic texts.

[46] Novak (2011, 13) acknowledges that in the tannaitic period there was debate over the number and content of the Noahide laws, but evidently sees no tension between that fact and the claim that these laws are universal and rational.

The toseftan passage also belies the common characterizations of the Noahide laws as providing a perspective on "the common human element" in rabbinic texts (Morgenstern 2011, 48) and bridging the gap between peoples and religions. In fact, in the glosses in section (c) the Noahide laws are utilized precisely to *inscribe* rather than erase differences between Jew and non-Jew. In the case of idolatry and blasphemy, for example, the mode of punishment differs for Jews and non-Jews.[47] One might argue that positing different punishments for Jews and non-Jews who engage in idolatry and blasphemy is not necessarily inconsistent with the claim that reverence for God is "universal, an attitude written into human nature" (Novak 2011, 2), since a universally prohibited act may be punished in different ways by different communities. This is not, however, a watertight assertion. Arguably a prohibition is universal only if it is prohibited everywhere *to the same degree*. Since diverse punishments are associated in rabbinic law with diverse degrees of severity, the prescription of different punishments for the same crime when committed by different human groups implies different degrees of prohibition and mitigates the extent to which the prohibition is both invariable and universal.[48]

More troubling for those who wish to see the Noahide laws as establishing a fixed and invariable standard for all humankind is the fact that some of the Noahide laws posit not just different *punishments* for Jews and non-Jews, but substantively different *prohibitions*. This is certainly inconsistent with the idea of a universally valid norm,[49] for surely the definition of a universal norm is that it applies to all persons everywhere (an act prohibited for one person is prohibited for all persons in the same manner and to the same degree). And yet, in the case of illicit sexual relations, for example, the baraita tells us that Jews and non-Jews are judged in the courts of their own communities because different sexual acts are deemed illicit in the two communities (specifically, sexual relations with a betrothed woman are among the forbidden sexual relations for Jews but not non-Jews). Even more remarkable is the assertion that as regards bloodshed, theft, robbery, and the law of the captive woman, a different standard, which is to say a substantively different prohibition, applies to Jews and non-Jews. A Jew is not liable for murder, theft, and robbery when the victim is a non-Jew, though a non-Jew in the reverse situation is liable, and a beautiful war captive is permitted to a Jew but not to a non-Jew. The blatantly inequitable application of these basic ethical laws is the single most compelling evidence that the seven Noahide laws featured in talmudic texts are not understood to be invariable and of universal application, and did not originate as a rabbinic version of natural law.

[47] For a fascinating analysis of these disparate punishments and the diverse conceptions of law to which they point, see Steinmetz 2008, 33–34.

[48] Morgenstern (2011, 63) concludes that the interpretation of legal regulations leniently for one group and harshly for another group shows that "the Noahide law can only be called 'universal' to a limited degree."

[49] Pace Novak 2011, 54.

The invariable and universal application of the Noahide laws is belied by another tannaitic text. In its discussion of the prohibition of eating a limb torn from a living animal, Sifre Deut 76 (L. Finkelstein ed., 141–42) wonders why this Noahide prohibition had to be repeated in the Mosaic Law:

> "... and you must not consume the life with the flesh" (Deut 12:20)—this refers to the prohibition against eating a limb torn from a living animal.
>
> But isn't this an *a fortiori* argument [in which case no repetition of the law at Sinai was really necessary]? If the consumption of meat in milk, which is permitted to Noahides, is forbidden to Israelites then all the more so should a limb torn from a living animal, which is forbidden to Noahides, be forbidden to Israelites [making the prohibition in Deut 12:20 redundant].
>
> No, the rule of the beautiful captive woman and similar cases proves the contrary, for she is prohibited to Noahides but permitted to Israelites. So it is not surprising that the limb torn from a living animal, though certainly prohibited to Noahides, might be thought to be permitted to Israelites. That is why Scripture states, "... and you must not consume the life with the flesh" (Deut 12:20)—this refers to the prohibition against eating a limb torn from a living animal.

The three steps in this dialectical exchange are as follows: first Deuteronomy 12:20 is identified with the Noahide prohibition of eating a limb torn from a living animal. The objection is raised that the verse is redundant. Since this act is prohibited to Noahides, then by dint of simple logic it is prohibited to Israelites because it cannot be the case that Israelites would be permitted what is prohibited to a Noahide. The third and final step of the exchange refutes this objection by pointing to at least one other case in which something prohibited to Noahides is indeed permitted to Israelites: an Israelite may take a beautiful war captive as wife (a reference to Deut 21:10–14), which a Noahide may not. This case and others like it teach that it is an error to assume that the Noahide laws are universal norms applying to all humans for all time. The Mosaic Law can, and sometimes does, overturn a Noahide law. Since one of the defining features of natural law is that no law can cancel or contravene it, the ability of the Mosaic Law to contravene a Noahide law is further evidence that the rabbinic conception of Noahide law does not conform to prevailing Greco-Roman conceptions of natural law.[50] It is not the case that the Noahide laws form a kind of natural law basis incumbent on all persons, to which the specific

---

[50] In the Bavli (b. San 58b), the opposite view—that Israelites would not be permitted something prohibited to Noahides—is asserted by Rava, a fourth-generation amora. Moreover, Rava does not perceive Noahide law to function as a law grounded in human nature. Indeed, the case to which Rava's comment is attached is a case of "unnatural" sexual intercourse, which is said to be permitted to both Gentile and Jew! Rava is making a point about the cultural superiority of Jewish law, which would never be more lenient or of a lower ethical standard than non-Jewish law.

positive laws of individual peoples (such as the Mosaic Law of the Jews) are superadded.

Novak (2011, 36) himself acknowledges that the Noahide laws are not controlling for Jews after the revelation of the Mosaic Law:

> Before the Sinaitic covenant all people were bound by Noahide law. After revelation, however, Jews are bound by the 613 commandments whereas non-Jews continued to live under Noahide obligations. It would seem, then, that this law continues to be relevant for gentiles but only *historically* relevant for Jews.

The view that the Noahide laws were of temporary validity, for one part of humanity, undercuts the claim that they were conceived by the rabbis as an invariable and universal natural law.

(II) THE BAVLI—CONSTRUCTION AND CONTESTATION OF THE NORMS OF CREATION

The locus classicus for the talmudic discussion of the Noahide laws is b. San 56a–60a, an expanded discussion of the baraita in t. AZ 8(9):4 cited above. The overriding impression conveyed by this protracted sugya is that Noahide law does not express a common human element or bridge the gap between peoples and religions. On the contrary, the single most striking feature of the Bavli's discussion of the Noahide laws is its intensification of the baraita's rhetoric of *differentiation* between Jew and non-Jew.[51] Each law is taken up in sequence, and each law is shown to apply in very different ways to Jews and to non-Jews in punishment, procedure, or actual substance. Thus: the sugya expresses different views on what counts as blasphemy for a non-Jew as opposed to a Jew (uttering the Tetragrammaton vs. uttering divine epithets; 56a); culpability for idolatry as well as the severity of punishment is said to be different for Jews and non-Jews (56b); the laws of robbery and a beautiful captive woman do not apply equally to Jew and non-Jew in that a Jew is not liable for robbing a non-Jew, and a beautiful captive woman is permitted to a Jew but not permitted to a non-Jew (57a); judicial procedures governing capital cases for Jews and non-Jews are different (with a more lenient standard of proof applying to capital cases in which non-Jews were perpetrators; 57b); according to R. Meir, all illicit sexual relations for which Jews are punished with death are forbidden to non-Jews but not punished by death, while illicit sexual relations merely prohibited to Jews (and not punished by death) are permitted to non-Jews (57b); the incest laws for converts are altogether different from those applying to Jews

---

[51] For the claim that the concept of the Noahide laws was not intended to lead people to Judaism but instead to set boundaries, and that it did not connect Judaism with the Gentile world but differentiated them from one another, see Morgenstern 2011, 58–59 and 66. Morgenstern (42, 66) cites Berthelot (2004) on the difficulty of finding an idea of humanity or a basis for a humanistic system of ethics in ancient Jewish sources.

and non-Jews (58a); and a non-Jew is permitted to marry his own daughter (a union prohibited to Jews; 58b). In short, the sugya's exposition of the Noahide laws is steeped in a rhetoric that emphasizes the lack of commonality between Jews and non-Jews, and frustrates any attempt to assert that these laws were viewed in rabbinic literature as invariable and universal norms.

And yet, this portrait of Noahide law is contested by an alternative portrait of Noahide law. In an insightful analysis of this sugya, Devora Steinmetz (2008) argues that the Bavli reworks and systematizes earlier teachings about the Noahide laws, creating two distinct and alternative traditions that differ radically in content and conception. The first tradition is found in b. San 56b as the view of the anonymous sages. This tradition, cited above, reads Genesis 2:15 atomistically in order to show that all seven of the Noahide laws were given as commandments to the very first human: Adam was obligated by the commandment to establish courts of justice and by commandments against idolatry, blasphemy, murder, illicit sexual relations, theft, and even the consumption of a limb torn from a living animal (which in parallel traditions such as Gen Rab 16:16 is deferred to the time of Noah). This first tradition grounds the Noahide laws in divine legislation.

Subsequently, the fourth-generation Babylonian amora Rava comments on a baraita that contains a somewhat different list of Noahide laws and attributes it to a tanna of the school of Manasseh:

> But Rava answered thus: The author of this baraita is a tanna of the school of Manasseh, who omitted courts of law and blasphemy [from the list of Noahide precepts] and substituted castration and the mixed fibers [in plants, ploughing, etc.]. For a tanna of the school of Manasseh taught: The sons of Noah were given seven commandments: [the prohibition of] idolatry, illicit sexual relations, murder, robbery, a limb torn from a living animal, castration and mixed kinds. (b. San 56b)

This tanna's alternative list omits commandments regarding courts and blasphemy, and substitutes commandments concerning castration and mixed kinds. As Steinmetz points out (2008, 25), the construction of an alternative list of seven Noahide laws is unique to the Bavli. More important, the stam of the Bavli goes on to provide an *alternative derivation* for each item in this list: rather than grounding these laws in a divine command, the text associates each with verses from the Noah story that point to the re-creation of the world and what is required to sustain it (Steinmetz, 26–30). The prohibition against idolatry and illicit sexual relations is linked to Genesis 6:12, in which all flesh is slated for destruction because it has "destroyed its way" (*hishhit kol-basar et darko*). The term "way" (*derekh*) has connotations of habitus or nature. Thus, idolatry and illicit sexual relations are destructive perversions of the natural way or habit of living things. Murder, robbery, and the torn limb are connected with Genesis 9:6, 5, and 4, respectively, verses that attend the "new creation" following the

Flood and seek to prevent future destruction. Castration and mixed kinds are also associated with verses from the Noah story that echo the creation story in Genesis 1 (Steinmetz 2008, 27), suggesting that they are prohibited as actions that also destroy rather than sustain the created order. Steinmetz concludes that for the tanna of the school of Manasseh

> prohibited acts are those acts that run counter to the way the world was created. Such acts uncreate the world: they are destructive acts that bring destruction to the world, that undo the work of creation. (29)

Steinmetz goes on to argue that the view attributed to the tanna is similar to natural law in its classical form: the world is created and operates according to certain principles that are normative and derivable from observation of the world as it is (31).[52] According to the tanna's view, the primary distinction between Noahide law and Sinaitic Law is that for Sinaitic Law

> commandedness is an essential characteristic; the prohibited act is criminal in that it is a violation of a command. In noachide law, in contrast, commandedness is not the essential characteristic ... the criminality of behavior for a noachide has nothing to do with intent to violate a command; it has to do only with the nature of the act that the person has done. For a noachide, the act is criminal in itself, while for those commanded at Sinai, the act is only criminal to the extent that the person knowingly and willfully violates the command. (34)

Steinmetz has done a brilliant job of uncovering in this baraita an entirely unprecedented rabbinic "vision of noachide law as natural law" (36). One can, of course, quibble about the details: it's not clear that the rabbis conceive of the law as a rational order (*logos*), and their inclusion of "all flesh" suggests a non-Stoic extension of "natural law" to animals,[53] but on the key points, Steinmetz is correct in her identification of a discourse of Noahide law that bears a striking resemblance to some classical natural law discourse.

The question is this: what is the *function* of this alternative natural law discourse within this sugya? Steinmetz herself states that this alternative vision of the nature, content, and source of law is presented by the Bavli in order to cast into sharp relief the rabbinic conception of Sinaitic Law (36). Without

---

[52] Steinmetz further argues that the sages' view of Noahide law is also distinct from positive law, because despite the use of command terminology, the Noahide laws seem to emerge from the origin of human society and in that sense are not fully dependent on a process of legislation. However, Steinmetz concedes that the sages' view of Noahide law is closer to contemporary natural law theories and shares little with the classical conception of natural law. Since we are interested in the classical conception of natural law, I streamline Steinmetz's very interesting argument and focus on the view of the tanna, since its alternative vision of law most closely resembles classical conceptions of natural law. The interested reader is referred to the full discussion in Steinmetz 2008, 31–33.

[53] Though this move was made already by the Roman jurists (see G-R 9).

discounting that view—quite persuasive in its own right—I would add the following: the position of the tanna is not treated as an equal, and the sugya in which it appears is not genuinely dialogical, because the tanna's view is not a genuine alternative. The view is invoked and subjected to extensive critique and contestation, so much so that it is possible to read this sugya and almost miss its presence altogether—as, indeed, so many readers before Steinmetz have done.

First, the view of the sages, rather than that of the tanna, is rhetorically privileged in the sugya.[54] It opens the discussion so that when the tanna's view is introduced, the latter is forced to play defense. As Steinmetz herself notes, the stam's effort to derive the tanna's list of Noahide laws from verses surrounding the Flood story is countered every step of the way (28). This is not unusual in itself, as many sugyot feature dueling exegeses in which side A adduces verses as proofs for its claims, and side B states that the verses teach something different and therefore do not support A's claims. But in this case, the stam works to disable the verses from teaching *anything* at all. As Steinmetz writes,

> The Gemara does not need to suggest that the Sages derive alternative laws from these sources, because these sources, from the perspective of the Sages, are not legal sources. They are not formulated as commands, and the source of the first two laws is not even a verse in which God speaks to a human being. It is simply narrative, and law cannot be derived from narrative. Narrative . . . simply tells us what happened. It cannot tell us what to do. (29)

In other words, the stam refuses to even "play the game" it normally plays in a genuine halakhic dispute, suggesting that there is something not entirely legitimate about the tanna's view.

Second, some elements of the tanna's view are revised in the course of the sugya, to make them more consistent with the view of the sages according to which the Noahide laws were commanded. For Steinmetz, this is not a problem because commandedness is not always incompatible with a natural law view (32). She maintains that even the view of the sages is a kind of natural law view (though a contemporary rather than classical brand). That's because for the sages, even if Adam was commanded to obey these basic laws, the laws nonetheless originate with the inception of human society, and thus their legitimacy turns on their content in line with the principles of justice and morality necessary for human community (32). We will return to this question of commandedness, and whether it is incompatible with a natural law view, below. For now, let us grant Steinmetz's claim that commandedness is not incompatible with a natural law view; even so, attributing commandedness to the tanna's view

---

[54] I recognize that Steinmetz understands the sages' view to also be a kind of natural law, though more modern than classical, but I will address this point below.

shifts it *away from a clear version of classical natural law* toward the less clear version of the sages. Thus, when the Bavli rejects the tanna's explanation of the prohibition of crossbreeding and redescribes it as based in legislation, it is "converting" the tanna's more robust natural law view into a weaker version.

Similarly, the stam avoids any kind of moral reasoning based on principles in nature when dealing with the Noahide laws. On the contrary, the stam continues to present Scriptural exegesis to constitute the Noahide laws and their punishments. Whatever one might think about the genuine or artificial nature of these derivations, they cannot be dismissed only as window dressing. It is surely significant that the stam *chooses* to assert against the tanna that the Noahide laws that govern the generality of humankind are divinely revealed commandments rather than self-evident rational principles embedded and discoverable in nature. Indeed, the rabbis locate Scriptural support for the very law whose foundation in natural reason might be considered to be the most secure of all—murder.

> R. Awia the elder said to R. Papa: Let us say that a non-Jewish woman who committed murder must not be executed, since it is written, "*at the hand of every man [who committed murder]*" etc. implying, 'but not at the hand of woman'?
>
> He replied: Thus did Rab Judah say: "*Whosoever sheds a man's blood*" implies whosoever it be [even a woman].
>
> Let us say that a non-Jewish woman who committed adultery is not executed, since it is written, "*therefore shall a man forsake [his father and mother, and cleave to his wife]*" implying that a man [must cleave], but not a woman?
>
> He replied: Thus did Rab Judah say: The verse, "*And they shall be as one flesh*" reassimilated them to each other [making the law of fidelity applicable to both]. (b. San 57b)

In this first passage, the late Babylonian amora R. Awia (sixth generation) asks R. Papa (also sixth generation) whether a non-Jewish woman is subject to capital punishment for murder. Now, there is no greater candidate for the status of natural law than the prohibition of murder, widely hailed as universally wrong regardless of gender or ethnicity (and included in all rabbinic lists of the Noahide laws). Yet R. Awia is prompted to ask the question not because philosophical speculation has led him to question the universal applicability of this "natural law" but because of a Scriptural verse whose wording he exploits to *undermine* the universality of the prohibition of murder. Once the prohibition of murder has been "denaturalized," R. Papa restores its universality but on the basis of a second verse, not on the basis of natural law reasoning! In this remarkable passage, the universality of the prohibition against murder is shown to depend on revelation alone.

To return to the question of commandedness, Steinmetz argues that the commandedness of the Noahide laws, on the view of the sages, does not convert them into positivistic law along the lines of Sinai because the commandedness of the law does not negate "the importance of the content of the law as grounded in essential principles" (2008, 32). Perhaps, but the difficulty here is this: the commandedness of the law means not only that it was given at a point in time but also *that it can be taken away.* In other words, commandedness can be a marker of temporariness, and insofar as commandedness entails *temporariness,* it *is* directly incompatible with a natural law view. The representation of the Noahide laws as positivistic commands that can be both given *and* taken away from peoples is found also in the following well-known tannaitic midrash:

When the holy one, blessed be he, revealed himself to give the Torah to Israel, he revealed himself not only to Israel but to all the nations. He went first to the children of Esau and asked them, "Will you accept the Torah?" They replied, "What is written in it?" He said to them, *"You shall not murder"* (Ex 20:13). They replied that this is the very essence of these people and that their forefather was a murderer, as it is said, *"But the hands are the hands of Esau"* (Gen 27:22), and, *"By the sword you shall live"* (Gen 27:40).

He then went to the Ammonites and the Moabites and asked them, "Will you accept the Torah?" They replied, "What is written in it?" He said, *"You shall not commit adultery"* (Ex 20:13). They replied that adultery is their very essence, as it is said, *"Thus were both the daughters of Lot with child by their father"* (Gen. 19:36).

He went next to the Ishmaelites and asked them, "Will you accept the Torah?" They replied, "What is written in it?" He said, *"You shall not steal"* (Ex 20:13). They replied that theft is their very essence and that their forefather was a thief, as it is said, *"And he shall be a wild ass of a man"* (Gen 16:12).

And thus it was with every other nation—He asked them all, "Will you accept the Torah?," as it is said, *"All the kings of the earth will give you thanks, O Yahweh, for they have heard the words of your mouth"* (Ps 138:4).

One might think [from this verse] that they heard and accepted [His offer]; therefore Scripture states elsewhere, *"And I will execute vengeance in anger and fury upon the nations, because they did not hear"* (Mic 5:14). Not only did they not hear, but they were not even able to observe the seven commandments that the Noahides had accepted upon themselves, and they cast them off. When the holy one, blessed be he, saw that, He surrendered them to Israel. A parable: A man took his ass and his dog to the threshing floor and loaded the ass with a *letek* [of grain] and the dog with three *seah.* The ass went along [easily], but the dog began to pant, so the man took off a *seah* and put it on the ass, and so too with the second and the third *seah*. So also Israel accepted the Torah, with all of its explanations and details, as well as the seven commandments which the children of Noah had not been able to observe and had cast off. Therefore it is said (Deut 33:2) *"And he said: Yahweh came from Sinai, and rose from Seir unto them."* (Sifre Deut 343, L. Finkelstein ed., 396–97)

Here the Noahide laws are configured on the model of positive law in that they are not only promulgated; they are also annulled.[55] God offered his Torah to other nations before offering it to the Israelites, but the other nations refused. The laws to which the nations object are basic provisions of the Noahide laws, and common elements of any formulation of natural law: the prohibition of murder, certain sexual violations, and theft. These prohibitions are positivized— they are among the laws God seeks to give to humanity, but the three nations listed here choose to reject them and indeed all of God's laws. In response to the nations' failure to observe "even" the Noahide laws, God gives to Israel both the Torah and the seven Noahide laws that the other nations have chosen to throw off.

Novak (1998, 160–61) finds evidence of a natural law view in this text. According to Novak, the midrash teaches that Israel's acceptance of the Torah in history presupposes the acceptance of natural law as a requirement of human nature, and that human nature and its normative requirements are common to Israel and the other nations. Such an interpretation seems remote from both the tone and the content of the text. The midrash, which is at once apologetic and polemical, praises Israel for blindly accepting the entirety of God's law without seeking prior knowledge of its contents and without prior acceptance of natural law. The midrash contrasts this with the behavior of the nations who reject laws that are widely recognized by cultures everywhere to be wise and indispensable foundations for human society. In its (apologetic) effort to justify God's covenant with Israel rather than the other nations,[56] the midrash adopts a polemical rhetoric that serves not to establish the common humanity of Israel and other nations but precisely to differentiate them. The three nations described in the midrash operate at a submoral level, which has the effect of raising doubts about their very nature as humans. In other words, the midrash conceives of the existence of human beings who do *not* share in a common

---

[55] Bockmuehl (2000, 150n16) also notes that the Noahide laws are represented by the rabbis as positive law, as distinct from natural law in the Roman sense.

[56] The apologetic purpose of this midrash is made explicit in the parallel version that appears in MekhRY BaHodesh 5 (Horowitz ed., 221). The midrash introduces the story of the nations rejecting the proffered Torah as follows: "And for this reason the nations of the world were asked [if they would accept the Torah], so that they wouldn't have a pretext before the *Shekinah* and be able to say 'Had we been asked we would have accepted it.' Behold, they *were* asked but they didn't accept it." This introduction justifies God's covenant with Israel—only Israel accepted his law unconditionally, while others rejected it.

humanity and have in fact cast off the norms that are presumably indispensable to human society.[57]

The positivistic character of the law is underscored not only by the language of acceptance and nonacceptance (on the part of Israel and the nations) but also by the motif of giving *and taking* on the part of God, as suggested by the parable that concludes the midrash. The bestowal of the Noahide laws upon the nations and the Torah upon Israel are symbolized by the two burdens placed upon two animals. The parable suggests not merely that the nations rejected the Noahide law but that God *took it away from them*. In short, God not only *gives* these norms to humanity; he can also take them away with the result that the nations are *unable to observe them*, suggesting that they are not embedded in (human) nature or discoverable by human reason (indeed the nations object that it is their *nature* to do what natural law proponents would claim is counter to human nature!). It is difficult to reconcile this positivistic portrayal of the Noahide laws with a natural law position.

In b. San 56a–59b, the stam's staccato emphasis on the commandedness of the divine law overwhelms the alternative natural law view of the tanna of the school of Manasseh. Thus, we see in this sugya what we have seen so many times: the *conscious* articulation of an alternative point of view informed by natural law categories. This view is not accommodated—it is engulfed and obscured.

We close with a text that epitomizes the non–natural law view of Noahide law: it highlights both the inequitable application and the commanded—in the sense of temporary—nature of Noahide law. The passage, which expands upon the midrash about God removing the Noahide laws from the nations, appears in b. BQ 38a (see also b. AZ 2b–3a) and centers on Habakkuk 3:6, which may be read as follows: "he stood and shook the earth; he beheld and permitted [or released] the nations [vayyatter et hagoyim]." Three interpretations of this verse are presented:

> R. Abbahu said: Scripture says, "*he stood and shook the earth; he beheld and permitted the nations*"—he beheld the seven commandments which the Noahides had accepted. Since they did not uphold them, he rose up and permitted their property to Israel ...

[57] Novak admits (1998, 161) that the three nations in this midrash are depicted as operating on a submoral level, but he identifies their inability to accept natural law as *culturally* determined, rather than naturally determined, so that the midrash is rescued from the claim that these nations do not share in a common nature. Yet this interpretation is belied by the language of the nations themselves. The nations claim that murder, adultery, and theft are their very "essence" ('*etsem*—a term that may fairly be construed as "their nature"). Thus, the midrashic denigration of these three nations appears to turn on their nonhuman character, as seen by their casting off even the norms basic to all known human societies. For the appearance in rabbinic texts of the idea that non-Jews do not share the same human nature as Jews, see Noam 2009 and Rosen-Zvi and Ophir 2011. However, the former relies on an ambiguous phrase that appears only once in a single text, and the latter homogenizes texts of widely divergent character and content.

R. Mattena said: ... what did he behold? He saw the seven commandments that he commanded the Noahides, but they didn't fufill them. He
rose and exiled them from their land ...

R. Yosef said: ... what did he behold? He saw the seven commandments which the Noahides accepted upon themselves but didn't fulfill.
He rose and released them. Does this mean they benefit [because they
don't have to fulfill the law!]? If so, it's a case of a sinner benefitting from
his sin!

Mar the son of Ravana said: it means that even if they observe them
they receive no reward.

In b. BQ 38a, the midrash in which the nations reject the Torah appears in a
sugya attached to m. BQ 4:3. This mishnah states that if an Israelite's ox gores
a Canaanite's ox, the owner is exempt; by contrast, a Canaanite in the reverse
situation must pay full damages, whether the ox is a first-time gorer or a known
gorer. R. Abbahu's interpretation provides a narrative that justifies this inequitable law. The inequity, he declares, is divine punishment: when the Noahides
rejected the Torah, God handed over their property to Israel (meaning perhaps
that God established inequitable laws of compensation for damages that were
beneficial to Israel). The second interpretation of Habakkuk 3:6, offered by
R. Mattena, justifies the expulsion of the Canaanites from their land. These two
interpretations do not appear in the tannaitic versions of the midrash. They are
added here in order to adapt the midrash to its local context (the inequitable
law of m. BQ 4:3 that disadvantages Canaanites). The third interpretation, by
R. Yosef, is an expansion of the original midrash rather than an insertion intended to adapt the midrash to a new context. According to this interpretation,
the nations failed to uphold the Noahide laws that were *given* to them, and as a
result God released them from those laws altogether. In the ensuing dialectic
this assertion is moderated somewhat. It is not the case that the nations are
entirely exempt from the law (that would be a benefit to them!). Rather, they
are exempt from reward, even if they observe the laws. In a further exchange
(not cited here) the harshness of this statement is mitigated—they do receive
reward, but the reward they receive is less than the reward of those who are
commanded to obey the law.[58] All three responses address the inequitable
character of certain provisions of the law; rather than removing the inequity,
these rabbinic authorities adopt a narrative that can justify its existence or moderate its severity.[59]

[58] For an excellent analysis of this midrash as it appears in b. AZ 2b–3a, see Rubenstein 1999a, 212–
42. Rubenstein is alive to the polemical character of the text, its rhetoric of differentiation between Jew
and Gentile, its overall negative view of Gentiles, and its tensions regarding the future salvation of
Gentiles.

[59] For a discussion of tannaitic and amoraic negotiations of the anxiety raised by this and other inequitable laws, see Hayes 1997, 148–53. For a discussion of the effort to eliminate the double standard

The cumulative evidence provided by the sources examined in this chapter strongly suggests that the talmudic rabbis did not understand the Noahide laws in primarily natural law terms. Moreover, the Bavli's unprecedented construction and subsequent contestation of an alternative position that *does* represent Noahide law in natural law terms suggests that the rabbinic rejection of a natural law view of Noahide law was a self-aware one.

Steven Wilf (2008, 62) writes,

> Not only has the idea of the Noahide code as a repository for natural law *in potentia* failed to materialize, but it has also inhabited a conceptual hinterland in Jewish thought every bit as particular as Jewish law itself.

Morgenstern (2011, 65–66) concurs that despite later developments, in its rabbinic origin the notion of Noahide law did not function as a kind of natural law:

> Although the Noahide norms take on characteristics that according to the definition of Italian canon lawyer Silvio Ferrari, are proper for natural law in the Roman Catholic tradition ... namely, "universality, immutability, and obligatory character," the usage of this idea with the intention as a natural law cannot be found in the backbone of Jewish tradition.

CONCLUSION

Pre-Sinai norms, including the Noahide laws, are not represented in rabbinic literature as invariable laws of universal application embedded in nature and discoverable by human reason, or as objectively valid moral goods that obligate us. Certainly, some of these laws are understood to be logical and so self-evident as to be widely observed in human societies, but the dominant rabbinic conception of the norms guiding humans prior to Sinai is positivistic: these norms were given to Noahides and the patriarchs by God, just as the Mosaic Law was given to Israel by God. And yet, there is a crucial difference. The Noahide laws that obligate humankind can be taken away; the Sinaitic Law never will be—a brilliant inversion of Greco-Roman and early Christian discourses that assert the eternal character of the natural law and the temporary nature of positive law.

---

particularly in the post-talmudic period, see Novak 2011, 41–45. However, the primary impetus for such efforts has less to do with addressing the basic inequity in light of the common humanity of the non-Jew than it has to do with the fear that non-Jewish awareness of the inequitable law is likely to cause the non-Jew to curse and profane the name of Israel's god (see, e.g., b. BQ 113b; p. BM 2:5, 8c; Novak 1998, 79).

Writing the Next Chapters

This book has told the first part of a very large story that extends far beyond the chronological period explored here. The dueling conceptions of divine law whose confrontation in antiquity is charted here have continued to confront one another, and to inform and animate religious and secular conversations about law and about the nature of divinity, to this very day. It is my hope that specialists in Jewish, Christian, and Islamic divine law discourse in the medieval and modern periods will take up the categories and questions raised by this book and write the next chapters of this story. To that end, I offer some brief remarks on how the ancient debates surveyed here continued to resonate in Jewish, Christian, and even secular reflections on law.

Consider the following three quotations by Jewish thinkers:

> There is a group of human beings who consider it a grievous thing that causes should be given for any law; what would please them most is that the intellect would not find a meaning for the commandments and prohibitions ... they think that if those laws were useful in this existence and had been given to us for this or that reason, it would be as if they derived from the reflection and understanding of some intelligent being ... But ... the contrary is the case—the whole purpose [of the law] consisting in what is useful for us ... [so that] even all the statutes will show to all the nations that they have been given with wisdom and understanding.

> —Maimonides, *Guide of the Perplexed*, 3:31, trans. Pines 1963, 523–24

> The Torah does not recognize moral imperatives stemming from knowledge of natural reality or from awareness of man's duty to his fellow man. All it recognizes are Mitzvoth, divine imperatives ... A man can worship God only by committing himself to observance of the Mitzvoth, which are the expression of the divine will and not means for the satisfaction of his needs, not even of his spiritual needs.

> —Yeshayahu Leibowitz, *Judaism, Human Values and the Jewish State*, 1992, 18, 20

Not only the *halakhot*, but also the *hazaqot* (established presumptions) [our Sages of blessed memory] introduced are indestructible. You must not tamper, not only with the *halakhot*, but even with the *hazaqot*. For the *hazaqot* [the Sages] spoke of rest, not upon transient psychological behavioral patterns, but on permanent ontological principles rooted in the very depths of the metaphysical human personality, which is as changeless as the heavens above.

—Joseph Soloveitchik, "Surrendering to the Almighty," 1975 address

These three quotations, separated by eight centuries, are a study in contrasts. Yet, as different from one another as they are, they share a common denominator. *Each exemplifies a Jewish internalization of the basic dichotomy that underwrites Greco-Roman discourses of law: law is grounded in reason or in will.* The internalization of this Greco-Roman dichotomy began to become more explicit and unabashed after the end of the period surveyed in this book: in the medieval period. Within a few centuries of the close of the Talmud, the three biblical religions embraced the fundamental categories of classical thought and constructed theological systems informed by those categories. These three quotations represent three different attempts to make sense of the divine law of biblical tradition in light of that basic dichotomy.

For the twelfth-century Jewish philosopher and halakhist Maimonides, as for Philo, God's Law or Torah is grounded in divine reason. Maimonides mocks those who insult the deity by suggesting that he could be anything less than fully rational. To search for and demonstrate the reasons for the commandments is to glorify God. Maimonides took aim at the views of Islamic thinkers in his day, who understood divine law to be an expression of the divine will, and who viewed the effort to identify reasons (moral, social, political, intellectual) for divine commandments as anathema. He might just as well have taken aim at voices within the talmudic tradition that God revealed his Law in order to bring humans to obedience, and obedience may be more perfectly demonstrated in the absence of a rationale for one's actions.

Maimonides's rationalist defense of the commandments of the Torah is distant not only in time but in spirit from Yeshayahu Leibowitz's understanding of the nature and purpose of the commandments, as exemplified in the second quotation. For Leibowitz, as for Sifra Aḥare Mot 9:13, the rational character of the commandments is immaterial—all that matters is the divine imperative, which must be obeyed. According to Leibowitz, religion must not satisfy the needs, and put God in the service, of humans. It should impose obligations so that humans become the instruments of a divine purpose that transcends them.[1] To search for and demonstrate the reasons for the commandments, to

---

[1] Leibowitz, "Religious Praxis: The Meaning of Halakha," in Leibowitz 1992, 14.

ground the commandments in human needs, deprives them of their *religious* meaning as service to God (Leibowitz, 17).

Maimonides and Leibowitz emphasize opposite poles of the reason-will dichotomy in their construction of biblical divine law. The third quotation, from Joseph Soloveitchik, unites the two poles in a manner reminiscent of some Second Temple writings reviewed in chapter 3. 1 Enoch, Jubilees, and some sectarian texts bridged the gap between the biblical and classical conceptions of divine law by adopting an incipient legal realism according to which the elements of the revealed Torah are understood to conform to an objective, mind-independent reality or "truth." In contrast to the later talmudic tendency to deny, explicitly and self-consciously, an essential and comprehensive correspondence between divine law and various measures of "truth," these texts appeal to the immutable order of nature when determining the law. One of the most fascinating developments in the story of divine law in the West is the reemergence in the modern period of a desire to ascribe a mind-independent reality to the Torah of Israel. The ascription of ontological reality to Torah—down to elements of its rabbinic elaboration—may be seen in the Brisker school.[2] The address cited above exemplifies this tendency. Here, Joseph Soloveitchik engages in a realist conversion of an explicitly nominalist device. In the talmudic sources, legal presumptions are employed in the *absence* of certainty, when a conclusion about facts is needed but the facts are *unknown*. A presumption can always be set aside if the facts become known. But Soloveitchik forecloses that possibility by removing legal presumptions from the realm of uncertainty and inscribing them on "the heavenly tablets"—endowing them with the highest form of certainty and immutability. A rabbinic device traditionally understood to signal the unavailability of truth and certainty is thus reconceived in a manner strikingly consistent with Greco-Roman divine law discourse: the legal presumption takes on ontological and metaphysical reality (it is *true*), it is embedded in human nature, and it is as changeless and indestructible as heaven itself.

The internalization of the dichotomy that underwrites Greco-Roman discourses of law, and the debates they inspire, also informed Christian reflection on divine law, as may be seen from the following contrasting quotations:

Does law belong to reason?... [One might argue:] Law induces those subject to the law to act rightly. But inducing to act rightly belongs in the strict sense to the will ... Therefore, law belongs to the will rather than to reason ...

---

[2] For a detailed analysis of this tendency and its history, see Sinai and Golding forthcoming. Yair Lorberbaum's insistence on a widespread halakhic realism (2012) is an anachronistic retrojection of this post-talmudic development, and relies on a definition of realism as "reality" rather than "mind-independent reality." See pp. 195–98 and esp. 196n.

I answer that law is a rule and measure of acts that induces persons to act or refrain from acting ... And the rule and measure of human acts is reason, which is the primary source of human acts ... For it belongs to reason to order us to our end, which is the primary source regarding our prospective action ... And the source in any kind of thing is the measure and rule of that kind of thing ... And so we conclude that law belongs to reason.

—Thomas Aquinas, *Summa Theologica*, Question 90, Article 1

Scripture, however, represents man as one who is not only bound, wretched, captive, sick, and dead, but in addition to his other miseries is afflicted, through the agency of Satan his prince, with this misery of blindness, so that he believes himself to be free, happy, unfettered, able, well and alive ... Accordingly, it is Satan's work to prevent men from recognizing their plight and to keep them presuming that they can do everything they are told. But the work of Moses or a lawgiver is the opposite of this, namely to make man's plight plain to him by means of the Law and thus to break and confound him by self-knowledge, so as to prepare him for grace and send him to Christ that he may be saved.

—Martin Luther, *On the Bondage of the Will*, ed. Rupp and Watson
1969, 193

The first of these passages opens Thomas Aquinas's reflections on law in his magisterial *Summa Theologica*. The twelfth-century Christian theologian holds that law—all law—is first and foremost an ordination of reason with a moral purpose, despite the fact that it is promulgated by one who is entrusted with the care of the community (i.e., an authority-wielding entity). Aquinas identifies four distinct but interconnected types of law. The highest is eternal law—the plan of divine wisdom directing the actions and movements of all creation. Eternal law may be divided into natural law (from which human law derives) and divine Law. Natural law is the light of natural reason by which we recognize good and evil; it is the moral knowledge "written on the heart." Human law is the detailed application of natural law to the particular circumstances of human life. Divine Law is an expression of divine reason *promulgated by special revelation* (rather than natural reason) in order to direct human life, certainly and infallibly, to the end of ultimate perfection and eternal blessedness.

Aquinas's rational defense of *both* the divinely revealed Law and positive human law (grounded in natural law, a species of eternal law) may be contrasted with Martin Luther's assessment of the Law divinely revealed to Moses. Luther drew on certain strands of Pauline (and Augustinian) thought to assert that the divinely revealed legislation of the Hebrew Bible is not a species of the eternal wisdom that directs the movements and actions of all creation; it does not lead to ultimate perfection and eternal blessedness. According to Luther, the Law was given through Moses to expose human sinfulness, to convince us of our utter dependence on God's mercy and saving grace. As for human law, Luther, like Augustine, saw the civil laws of the state as restraining our sinful nature through coercive threats of punishment. Since law does not and cannot provide for our perfection or salvation, lawmaking should be left to magistrates, whose laws, even when informed by general moral principles found in the Bible, are no more than the expression of the human authority's will. In this way, the Reformation gave rise to a new civil order in which the regulation of society was left to these authorities. Luther wrote, "The basis of natural law is God, who has created this light, but the basis of positive law is the earthly authority" (Weimar Edition, *Tischreden* 3:3911, cited in Witte, 115).

In the modern period, the debate over the essential nature of law as grounded in reason or in will continues in a secular context. From Jeremy Bentham's separation of legal rules and morality, to John Austin's command theory of law and H.L.A. Hart's elaboration of law as rules, legal positivism entails an understanding of law as first and foremost an expression of will rather than reason. Law's primary claim to our fidelity lies not in its rational or moral content (though such content is not precluded) but in its issuance from a lawmaking authority according to a conventionally established or agreed-upon rule of recognition; its claim to our fidelity lies not in reason but in power. While modern natural law theories differ from classical and Christian natural law theory (they do not insist on either a rational natural order or a God-given set of moral principles written on the hearts of men), they are united against the positivists in asserting an essential connection between rule and principle, between law and moral reasoning. The legitimacy of law cannot be divorced from considerations of its conformity to foundational moral principles (such as justice and equity), universal rights (for example, basic human freedoms), or an inner coherence—criteria of content.

Unsettling these dichotomies is the school of historical jurisprudence that arose in the nineteenth century in opposition to both natural law theory and legal positivism. Historical jurisprudence, as represented in the work of German jurist Karl Friedrich von Savigny, locates the sources of law in the history of individual nations. According to Savigny, law is a people's living group memory; the primary source of law is not, therefore, morality or politics but history, not reason or will but tradition, not equity or legislation but custom and precedent.[3] Law is not a set of rules abstractly formulated and imposed upon a society. Law has deep roots in a people's habits and customs and is integrally connected with other social rules—especially moral and religious rules.[4] The

---

[3] Harold Berman (2006) provides a heavily Christianized account of the possibility of integrating these three elements, but non-Christian and secular accounts might also be imagined.

[4] For a discussion of the historical school's legacy for the study of law and religion, see Richardson and Westerholm 1991, 8–13.

historical school was eclipsed by other trends in the later twentieth century, but its basic insight concerning the rootedness of law in a particular society's experience of the world, and the stories it tells about itself, resurfaced in the work of Robert Cover, who argued that all societies have narratives that situate and give meaning to law—communal narratives that contextualize and nourish the behaviors regulated by law.

The focus on history is one way to manage or even overcome the dichotomy of reason and will in accounts of the law. Insisting on the interdependency of all three elements—reason, will, and history—in order to create a multidimensional model of the law would be another way to manage or overcome the dichotomy, and there may well be more. At the very least, understanding the discursive and conceptual roots of Western conversations about the law *and* Western conversations about the divine reminds us of the historical contingency of those conversations and invites us to weigh new options, to explore new possibilities.

———

Our survey of ancient perspectives on divine law has revealed unexpected continuities and discontinuities among our sources. To the extent that they sought to bridge the gap between biblical and classical conceptions of divine law, Philo and 1 Enoch were allied in a common project distinct from that of Paul. To the extent that they accepted and worked within the framework of the Greco-Roman dichotomy of divine and human law, Philo and Paul may be seen as continuous with one another but discontinuous with the rabbis. To the extent that they attributed to Mosaic Law the characteristic features of positive law as defined by Greco-Roman tradition, Paul and the rabbis spoke a common language against Philo, but to the extent that they viewed these features as vice or virtue, Paul and the rabbis were not only discontinuous with, but "antipodal" to, one another.

In one respect, however, rabbinic literature is discontinuous with the other ancient writings examined here: although the rabbinic construction of divine law is certainly contested and multidimensional, to the extent that the rabbis *considered and rejected* the Greco-Roman dichotomy according to which divine law is inherently universally rational, true, and unchanging, while human law is not, they stood alone. The rabbis' construction of Torah did not stem from systematic philosophical commitments, and in this respect the rabbis were like the Roman jurists, whose writings show a general if eclectic familiarity with theoretical accounts of the law but lack a serious engagement with these theories as they work at the jurist's trade. In full awareness of the fact that they were a scandal in the eyes of others, the rabbis breached conceptual boundaries by insisting that a law could be divine *and* divorced from truth, divine *and* not inherently rational, divine *and* subject to moral critique and modification. Seeing themselves as others saw them, the rabbis occasionally moderated this insistence and even accommodated the alternative view. And yet, the overall trend of talmudic literature is clear: the Torah is divine because it originates in the will of the god of Israel, and the attribution of divinity to the Torah does not confer upon it the qualities of universal rationality, truth, and stasis; on the contrary, Israel's god divorces law from truth, issues commands that sometimes lack intrinsic rationality, and modifies his Law in response to the needs and circumstances of his people—and these very features are *proof* rather than *disproof* of the Torah's divinity. For the rabbis, *that's* what's divine about divine Law.

BIBLIOGRAPHY

Primary Sources

Classical Writings

Aristotle. *Nicomachean Ethics*. Translated by David Ross. 1908. Rev. ed. New York: Oxford University Press, 2009.

Cicero. *On the Commonwealth and On the Laws*. Edited by James E. G. Zetzel. Cambridge Texts in the History of Political Thought. Cambridge: Cambridge University Press, 1999.

Diogenes Laertius. *The Lives and Opinions of Eminent Philosophers*. Translated by C. D. Yonge. London: G. Bell and Sons, 1915.

Gaius. *Gaius Institutiones or Institutes of Roman Law by Gaius*. Translated by Edward Poste. 4th ed. Rev. E. A. Whittuck, with an historical introduction by A.H.J. Greenidge. Oxford: Clarendon Press, 1904.

Herodotus. *Histories*. Translated by A. D. Godley. Loeb Classical Library 117. Cambridge, MA: Harvard University Press, 1920.

Justinian. *The Digest of Justinian*. Edited by Alan Watson. Philadelphia: University of Pennsylvania Press, 1998.

———. *The Institutes of Justinian*. Translated by J. B. Moyle. Oxford: Clarendon Press, 1913.

Lucretius. *De rerum natura*. Translated by W.H.D. Rouse. Revised by Martin Ferguson Smith. Loeb Classical Library 181. Cambridge, MA: Harvard University Press, 1992.

Ovid. *Metamorphoses*. Translated by Frank Justus Miller. Loeb Classical Library 42. Cambridge, MA: Harvard University Press, 1916. Reprint, 1984.

Plato. *The Collected Dialogues of Plato*. Edited by Edith Hamilton and Huntington Cairns. Bollingen Series LXXI. 1961. New impression edition. Princeton, NJ: Princeton University Press, 2005.

Biblical Texts

Hebrew Bible/Tanakh: Jewish Publication Society Translation.

New Testament: New Revised Standard Version.

Septuagint. *A New English Translation of the Septuagint (NETS)*. Edited by Albert Pietersma and Benjamin G. Wright. New York: Oxford University Press, 2007.

Second Temple and Hellenistic Jewish Sources

1 Enoch: A New Translation, Based on the Hermeneia Commentary. Edited by George W. E. Nickelsberg and James C. VanderKam. Minneapolis, MN: Fortress Press, 2004.

4 Maccabees. NETS.

Aristeas to Philocrates. Edited by Moses Hadas. Translated by H. St. J. Thackerey. Eugene, OR: Wipf and Stock Publishing, 2007.

The Book of Jubilees: A Critical Text. Edited and translated by James C. VanderKam. (Louvain: E. Peeters, 1989).

Dead Sea Scrolls. All translations are based on García Martínez Florentino, and Eibert J. C. Tigchelaar. *The Dead Sea Scrolls Study Edition.* 2 vols. Leiden: Brill, 1977.

Josephus. *Flavius Josephus: Translation and Commentary.* Edited by Steve Mason. Leiden: Brill, 2000–2008.

Philo. Translations taken from Loeb Classical Library vols. 226, 261, 289, 320, 341. Cambridge, MA: Harvard University Press.

Sirach—*NETS.*

Rabbinic Sources

Abot deRabbi Nathan. Edited by Solomon Schechter. New York: Feldheim, 1967.

Mekhilta de-Rabbi Ishmael. Edited by H. S. Horowitz and Israel Rabin. Jerusalem: Bamberger and Wahrman, 1960.

Mekhilta de-Rabbi Shimon ben Yohai. Edited by J. N. Epstein and Ezra Zion Melammed. Jerusalem: Meqitze Nirdamim, 1959.

Midrash Bereshit Rabba: Critical Edition with Notes and Commentary. Edited by Yehudah Theodor and Chanokh Albeck. 3 vols. Jerusalem: Wahrman, 1965 [1912–36].

Midrash Debarim Rabbah. Edited by Saul Lieberman. Jerusalem: Shalem, 1992.

Midrash Rabbah (Pentateuch and Five Scrolls; standard text based on the 1887 Vilna Romm edition). Jerusalem: Hotsa'at Sefer, 1969.

Midrash Shemot Rabbah, Chapters 1–14. Edited by Avigdor Shinan. Jerusalem: Dvir, 1984.

Midrasch Tannaim zum Deuteronomium. Edited by David Hoffman. Berlin: H. Itzkowski, 1908.

Midrash Tanḥuma. Edited by Solomon Buber. Vilna, 1883.

Midrash Wayyikra Rabba: A Critical Edition Based on Manuscripts and Genizah Fragments with Variants and Notes. Edited by Mordechai Margulies. 3rd printing. New York: Jewish Theological Seminary of America, 1993 [1953–60].

Pesiqta Rabbati. Edited by Meir Ish-Shalom. Vienna, 1880.

Pesiqta de Rav Kahana according to an Oxford Manuscript. Edited by Bernard Mandelbaum. 2 vols. 2nd edition. New York: Jewish Theological Seminary, 1987.

Sifra: Commentar zu Leviticus. Edited by I. H. Weiss. Vienna: Schlossberg, 1862.

Sifre Numbers. Edited by H. S. Horowitz. Jerusalem: Shalem, 1992 [1917].

Sifre on Deuteronomy. Edited by Louis Finkelstein. New York: Jewish Theological Seminary of America, 2001 [1939].

Sifre Zutta. Edited by H. S. Horowitz. Jerusalem: Shalem, 1992 [1917].

Synopse zum Talmud Yerushalmi. Edited by Peter Schäfer and Hans-Jürgen Becker. Tübingen: Mohr Siebeck, 1991–2001.

The Tosefta according to Codex Vienna. Edited by Saul Lieberman. 4 vols. 2nd edition. New York: Jewish Theological Seminary of America, 1992 [1955].

SECONDARY SOURCES

Adler, Yitzhak. 1989. *Iyyun beLomdut*. New York: Bet Sha'ar Press.

Albeck, Hanokh. 1952–58. *Shisha Sidre Mishnah*. Tel Aviv: Devir.

Alexander, Elizabeth. 2006. *Transmitting Mishnah: The Shaping Influence of Oral Tradition*. Cambridge: Cambridge University Press.

Alt, Albrecht. 1934. "Die Ursprünge des israelitischen Rechts." Reprinted in *Kleine Shriften*, 1:278–332. Munich: Beck, 1959.

Amichay, Aryeh. 2013. "Law and Society in the Dead Sea Scrolls." PhD diss., Princeton University.

Atkins, E. M. 2000. "Cicero." In *The Cambridge History of Greek and Roman Political Thought*, edited by Christopher Rowe and Malcolm Schofield, 477–516. Cambridge: Cambridge University Press.

Atlas, Samuel. 1978. *Netivim ba-Mishpat ha-Ivri*. New York: Sefer Harmon Press.

Barton, John. 1979. "Natural Law and Poetic Justice in the Old Testament." *Journal of Theological Studies*, n.s., 30:1–14.

Bartor, Assnat. 2007. "The Representation of Speech in the Casuistic Laws of the Pentateuch: The Phenomenon of Combined Discourse." *Journal of Biblical Literature* 126, no. 2:231–49.

———. 2010. *Reading Law as Narrative: A Study in the Casuistic Laws of the Pentateuch*. Atlanta, GA: Society of Biblical Literature.

Bauckmann, E. G. 1960. "Die Proverbien und die Sprüche des Jesus Sirach: Eine Untersuchung zum Strukturwandel der israelitischen Weisheitslehre." *Zeitschrift für die Alttestamentliche Wissenschaft* 72:33–63.

Baumgarten, J. M. 1977. *Studies in Qumran Law*. Studies in Judaism in Late Antiquity 24. Leiden: Brill.

Bazak, J. 2004. "The Element of Intention in the Performance of *Mitsvot* Compared to the Element of Intention in Current Criminal Law." In *The Jewish Law Association Studies 14: The Jerusalem 2002 Conference Volume*, edited by H. Gamoran, 9–15. Binghamton, NY: Global Academic Publishing.

Becker, Lawrence C., and Charlotte B. Becker, eds. 1992. *Encyclopedia of Ethics*. New York: Garland Publishing.

Beckwith, R. T. 1969–71. "The Modern Attempt to Reconcile the Qumran Calendar with the True Solar Year." *Revue de Qumran* 7:379–96.

Ben-Menahem, Hanina. 1987. "Is There Always One Uniquely Correct Answer to a Legal Question in the Talmud?" *Jewish Law Annual* 6:164–75.

Ben-Menahem, Hanina, Neil S. Hecht, and Shai Wosner, eds. 2005. *Controversy and Dialogue in the Jewish Tradition: A Reader*. New York: Routledge Press.

Benovitz, Moshe. 1998. *Kol Nidre: Studies in the Development of Rabbinic Votive Institutions*. Atlanta, GA: Scholars Press.

Berkowitz, Beth A. 2012. *Defining Jewish Difference: From Antiquity to the Present*. New York: Cambridge University Press.

Berman, Harold J. 2006. "An Ecumenical Christian Jurisprudence." In *The Teachings of Modern Christianity*, edited by John Witte, Jr., and Frank S. Alexander, 1:752–64. New York: Columbia University Press.

Berman, Saul. 1975. "Lifnim Mishurat Hadin." *Journal of Jewish Studies* 26:86–104.

———. 1977. "Lifnim Mishurat Hadin II." *Journal of Jewish Studies* 28:181–93.

Berner, Christoph. 2007. "The Four (or Seven) Archangels in the First Book of Enoch and Early Jewish Writings of the Second Temple Period." In *Angels: The Concept of Celestial Beings—Origins, Development and Reception*, edited by Friedrich V. Reiterer, Tobias Nicklas, and Karin Schöpflin, 395–411. Deuterocanonical and Cognate Literature Yearbook 2007. Berlin: Walter de Gruyter.

Berthelot, Katell. 2004. *L'"Humanité de l'autre homme" dans la pensée juive ancienne.* Leiden: Brill.

Bevan, Edwyn. 1923. "Hellenistic Popular Philosophy." In *The Hellenistic Age*, 79–107. Cambridge: Cambridge University Press.

Blenkinsopp, Joseph. 1995. *Wisdom and Law in the Old Testament: The Ordering of Life in Israel and Early Judaism.* New York: Oxford.

Bloch, Moses. 1970. *Sha'are torat ha-takanot.* Jerusalem: Makor.

Bockmuehl, Markus. 2000. *Jewish Law in Gentile Churches: Halakhah and the Beginning of Christian Public Ethics.* Edinburgh: T & T Clark.

Borkowski, Andrew. 1994. *Textbook on Roman Law.* London: Blackstone Press.

Bottéro, Jean. 1982. "Le 'Code' de Hammurapi." *Annali della Scuola normale superior di Pisa classe di lettere e filosofia* 12, no. 3:409–44.

———. 1992. *Mesopotamia: Writing, Reasoning and the Gods.* Chicago: University of Chicago Press.

Boyarin, Daniel. 1990. *Intertextuality and the Reading of Midrash.* Bloomington: Indiana University Press.

———. 1994. *A Radical Jew: Paul and the Politics of Identity.* Berkeley: University of California Press.

———. 1995. *Carnal Israel: Reading Sex in Talmudic Culture.* Berkeley: University of California Press.

———. 2004. *Border Lines: The Partition of Judaeo-Christianity.* Philadelphia: University of Pennsylvania Press.

Brague, Rémi. 2007. *The Law of God: The Philosophical History of an Idea.* Chicago: University of Chicago Press.

Brodsky, David. Forthcoming. "'Hirhur ke-ma'aseh damei' ('Thought Is Akin to Action'): The Importance of Thought in Zoroastrianism and the Development of a Babylonian Rabbinic Motif." In *Irano-Judaica* 7, edited by S. Shaked and A. Netzer. Jerusalem: Ben Zvi Institute.

Brown, Eric. 2009. "The Emergence of Natural Law and the Cosmopolis." In *The Cambridge Companion to Ancient Greek Political Thought*, edited by Stephen Salkever, 331–63. Cambridge: Cambridge University Press.

Centrone, Bruno. 2000. "Platonism and Pythagoreanism in the Early Empire." In *The Cambridge History of Greek and Roman Political Thought*, edited by Christopher Rowe and Malcolm Schofield, 559–84. Cambridge: Cambridge University Press.

Charlesworth, James, ed. 1983. *The Old Testament Pseudepigrapha*, vol. 1, *Apocalyptic Literature and Testaments.* New York: Doubleday.

Cohen, Boaz. 1966. *Jewish and Roman Law.* Vol. 1. New York: Jewish Theological Seminary of America.

Cohen, Shaye J. D. 1983. "Conversion to Judaism in Historical Perspectives: From Biblical Israel to Postbiblical Judaism." *Conservative Judaism* 36, no. 4:31–45.

———. 1984. "The Significance of Yavneh: Pharisees, Rabbis and the End of Sectarianism." *Hebrew Union College Annual* 55:27–53.

———. 1991. "Can Converts to Judaism say 'God of our Fathers'?" *Judaism* 40:419–28.

———. 2013. "Antipodal Texts: B. Eruvin 21b–22a and Mark 7:1–23 on the Tradition of the Elders and the Commandment of God." Preprint. Near Eastern Languages and Civilizations, Harvard University.

Collins, Adela Yarbro. 2007. *Mark: A Commentary*. Minneapolis, MN: Fortress Press.

Conzelmann, H. 1971. "The Mother of Wisdom." In *The Future of Our Religious Past: Essays in Honor of R. Bultmann*, edited by J. M. Robinson, 230–43. New York: Harper and Row.

Cover, Robert. 1983. "Nomos and Narrative." *Harvard Law Review* 97:4–68.

Crawford, M. H. 1996. *Roman Statutes*. Bulletin of the Institute of Classical Studies, Supplement 64. 2 vols., 555–723. London: University of London.

Daube, David. 1956. "Public Retort and Private Explanation." In *New Testament and Rabbinic Judaism*, 141–50. London: Athlone Press.

Davidson, Maxwell J. 1992. *Angels at Qumran: A Comparative Study of 1 Enoch 1–36, 72–108 and Sectarian Writings from Qumran*. Sheffield: Sheffield Academic Press.

Davidson, Maxwell J., and R. T. Beckwith. 1981. "The Earliest Enoch Literature and Its Calendar: Marks of Their Origin, Date and Motivation." *Revue de Qumran* 10:365–403.

Dor, Zvi Moshe. 1971. *Torat Erez Yisrael beBavel*. Tel Aviv: Devir.

Dulkin, Ryan. 2011. "The Rabbis Reading Eden: A Traditions-Historic Study of Exegetical Motifs in the Classical and Selected Post-classical Rabbinic Sources on Genesis 1–3." PhD diss., Jewish Theological Seminary.

Dunn, James. 1988. "The New Perspective on Paul: Paul and the Law." In *The New Perspective on Paul*. Tübingen: Mohr Siebeck. Reprint, 2005.

———. 1990. *Jesus, Paul and the Law: Studies in Mark and Galatians*. Louisville, KY: Westminster/John Knox.

Dworkin, Ronald. 1986. *Law's Empire*. Cambridge, MA.: Belknap Press of Harvard University Press.

Eilberg-Schwartz, Howard. 1986. *The Human Will in Judaism: The Mishnah's Philosophy of Intention*. Atlanta, GA: Scholars Press.

Elman, Yaakov. 1994. "Argument for the Sake of Heaven: The Mind of the Talmud: A Review Essay." *Jewish Quarterly Review* 84, nos. 2–3:261–82.

———. 1996. "Some Remarks on 4QMMT and the Rabbinic Tradition or When Is a Parallel Not a Parallel?" In *Reading 4QMMT: New Perspectives on Qumran Law and History*, edited by Moshe Bernstein and John Kampen, 105–24. SBL Symposium Series, no. 2. Atlanta, GA.: Scholars Press.

———. 2005. "World of the 'Saboraim': Cultural Aspects of Post-Redactional Additions to the Bavli." In *Creation and Composition: The Contribution of the Bavli Redactors (Stammaim) to the Aggada*, edited by J. L. Rubenstein, 383–415. Tübingen: Mohr Siebeck.

Elon, Menahem. 1994. *Jewish Law: History, Sources, Principles*. Philadelphia: Jewish Publication Society.

Falk, Ze'ev. 1980. *Legal Values and Judaism: Towards a Philosophy of Halakhah*. Jerusalem: Magnes Press.

Faur, José. 1986. *Golden Doves with Silver Dots: Semiotics and Textuality in Rabbinic Tradition*. Bloomington: Indiana University Press.

Finkelstein, J. J. 1961. "Ammi-Saduqa's Edict and the Babylonian 'Law Codes.'" *Journal of Cuneiform Studies* 15:91–104.

Finkelstein, Louis. 1942 and 1943. "The Meaning of the Word פרס in the Expressions בפרוס יפסח, בפרוס עצרת, פורס על שמע and בפרוס החג" *Jewish Quarterly Review* 32: 387–406 and 33:29–48.

———, ed. 1956. *Sifra or Torat Kohanim According to Codex Assemani 66 (Facsmile Edition)*. New York: Jewish Theological Seminary of America.

———, ed. 2001. *Sifre on Deuteronomy*. New York: Jewish Theological Seminary of America.

Fisch, Menahem. 1997. *Rational Rabbis: Science and Talmudic Culture*. Bloomington: Indiana University Press.

Fitzpatrick-McKinley, Anne. 1999. *The Transformation of Torah from Scribal Advice to Law*. Journal for the Study of the Old Testament, Supplement Series, 287. Sheffield: Sheffield Academic Press.

Fox, Marvin. 1990. *Interpreting Maimonides: Studies in Methodology, Metaphysics and Moral Philosophy*. Chicago: University of Chicago Press.

Fraade, Steven. 1986. "Ascetical Aspects of Ancient Judaism." In *Jewish Spirituality: From the Bible through the Middle Ages*, edited by Arthur Green, 258–88. New York: Crossroads Press.

———. 1991. *From Tradition to Commentary: Torah and Its Interpretation in the Midrash Sifre to Deuteronomy*. Albany: State University of New York.

———. 2004. "Moses and the Commandments: Can Hermeneutics, History, and Rhetoric Be Distinguished?" In *The Idea of Biblical Interpretation: Essays in Honor of James Kugel*, 399–422. Supplements to the Journal for the Study of Judaism 83. Leiden: Brill.

———. 2005. "Nomos and Narrative before *Nomos and Narrative*." *Yale Journal of Law and the Humanities* 17, no. 1 (Winter):81–96.

———. 2007. "Rabbinic Polysemy and Pluralism Revisited: Between Praxis and Thematization." *AJS Review* 31, no. 1:1–40.

———. 2014. "Response to Azzan Yadin-Israel on Rabbinic Polysemy: Do They 'Preach' What They Practice?" *AJS Review* 38, no. 2: 321–44.

Franklin, J. 2001. *The Science of Conjecture: Evidence and Probability before Pascal*. Baltimore: Johns Hopkins University Press.

Fredriksen, Paula. 1991. "Judaism, the Circumcision of the Gentiles, and Apocalyptic Hope: Another Look at Galatians 1 and 2." *Journal of Theological Studies* 42:532–64.

———. 2005. "Paul, Purity and the Ekklesia of the Gentiles." In *The Beginnings of Christianity: A Collection of Articles*, edited by Jack Pastor and Menachem Mor, 205–17. Jerusalem: Yad Ben-Zvi Press.

———. 2010. "Judaizing the Nations: The Ritual Demands of Paul's Gospel." *New Testament Studies* 56:232–52.

Friedman, Shamma. 1977. "A Critical Study of Yevamot X with a Methodological Introduction." In *Texts and Studies: Analecta Judaica I*, 275–441. New York: Jewish Theological Seminary of America [Hebrew].

Frost, Michael. 1992. "Greco-Roman Legal Analysis: The Topics of Invention." *St. John's Law Review* 66, no. 1:107–28.

Frymer-Kensky, Tikva. 2006. *Studies in Biblical and Feminist Criticism*. Philadelphia: Jewish Publication Society.

Fuller, Lon L. 1967. *Legal Fictions*. Stanford, CA: Stanford University Press.

Fuss, Abraham M. 1988. "Fact Skepticisim in Jewish Law." In *The Jewish Law Annual* 7, edited by Bernard S. Jackson, 125–38. Chur, NY: Harwood Academic Publishers.

Gagarin, Michael. 2008. *Writing Greek Law*. Cambridge: Cambridge University Press.

Garnsey, Peter. 2000. "Introduction: The Hellenistic and Roman Periods." In *The Cambridge History of Greek and Roman Political Thought*, edited by Christopher Rowe and Malcolm Schofield, 401–14. Cambridge: Cambridge University Press.

Gilat, Y. D. 1970. "A Rabbinical Court May Decree the Abrogation of a Law of the Torah." *Annual of Bar-Ilan University* VII–VIII:117–32 [Hebrew].

Gilbert, M. 1984. "Wisdom Literature." In *Jewish Writings of the Second Temple Period: Apocrypha, Pseudepigrapha, Qumran Sectarian Writings, Philo, Josephus*, edited by Michael E. Stone, 283–355. Compendium Rerum Iudicarum ad Novum Testmentum, sec. 2. Assen: Van Gorcum.

Gill, Christopher. 2000. "Stoic Writers of the Imperial Era." In *The Cambridge History of Greek and Roman Political Thought*, edited by Christopher Rowe and Malcolm Schofield, 597–615. Cambridge: Cambridge University Press.

Ginzberg, Louis. 1941–61. *A Commentary on the Palestinian Talmud*. Berakhot 2. New York: Jewish Theological Seminary of America.

Goldberg, A. 1963. *"Lehitpathut ha-Sugya ba-Talmud ha-Bavli."* In *Sefer ha-Yovel le-Rabbi Hanokh Albeck*, 101–13. Jeruslaem: Mossad ha-Rav Kook.

———. 2000. *"Letiv niv leshon haMishnah: Bittuyim shel Hiyyuv, sheyesh lahem gam Mashma'ut shel Niggud: Millat veken hamehabberet halakhah lehalakhah."* In *Qovets Ma'amarim bilshon Hazal*, pt. 2, edited by Moshe Bernstein, 172–85. Jerusalem.

Goldin, Judah. 1965. "Of Change and Adaptation in Judaism." *History of Religions* 4, no. 2:269–94.

Gordis, David. 1991. "Prozbul and Poseq." *Sevara* 2, no. 2:71–73.

Gray, V. J. 2000. "Xenophon and Isocrates." In *The Cambridge History of Greek and Roman Political Thought*, edited by Christopher Rowe and Malcolm Schofield, 142–54. Cambridge: Cambridge University Press.

Greenberg, Moshe. 1976. "Some Postulates of Biblical Criminal Law." Orig. in *Yehezkel Kaufmann Jubilee Volume*. Jerusalem: Magnes Press, 1960. Reprinted in *The Jewish Expression*, edited by Judah Goldin. New Haven, CT: Yale University Press.

———. 1983. *Ezekiel 1–20*. New York: Doubleday.

Griffin, Miriam. 2000. "Seneca and Pliny." In *The Cambridge History of Greek and Roman Political Thought*, edited by Christopher Rowe and Malcolm Schofield, 532–58. Cambridge: Cambridge University Press.

Gulak, Asher. 1933. "Peah Pereq 3 Mishnah 7 as Compared with the Edictum de Alterutro." *Tarbiz* 4:121–26 [Hebrew].

Hahm, David E. 2000. "Kings and Constitutions: Hellenistic Theories." In *The Cambridge History of Greek and Roman Political Thought*, edited by Christopher Rowe and Malcolm Schofield, 456–76. Cambridge: Cambridge University Press.

Hahn, S. W., and J. S. Bergsma. 2004. "What Laws Were 'Not Good'? A Canonical Approach to the Theological Problem of Ezekiel 20:25–26." *Journal of Biblical Literature* 123, no. 2:201–18.

Halberstam, Chaya. 2007. "The Art of Biblical Law." *Prooftexts* 27, no. 2:345–64.

———. 2010. *Law and Truth.* Bloomington: Indiana University Press, 2010.

———. 2014. "Justice without Judgment: Pure Procedural Justice and the Divine Courtroom in *Sifre Deuteronomy.*" In *The Divine Courtroom in Comparative Perspective,* edited by Ari Mermelstein and Shalom E. Holz, 49–68. Leiden: Brill.

Halbertal, Moshe. 1997. *People of the Book.* Cambridge, MA: Harvard University Press.

———. 1999. *Interpretative Revolutions in the Making.* Jerusalem: Magnes Press [Hebrew].

Halivni, David Weiss. 1986. *Midrash, Mishnah, and Gemara: The Jewish Predilection for Justified Law.* Cambridge, MA: Harvard University Press.

Handelman, Susan. 1982. *The Slayers of Moses: The Emergence of Rabbinic Interpretation in Modern Literary Theory.* Albany: State University of New York Press.

———. 1985. "Fragments of the Rock: Contemporary Literary Theory and the Study of Rabbinic Texts—A Response to David Stern." *Prooftexts* 5:75–95.

———. 1986. "'Everything Is in It': Rabbinic Interpretation and Modern Literary Theory." *Judaism* 35, no. 4:429–40.

Havlin, Shlomo Z. 1995. "*Hukkim uMishpatim*: In the Torah, Rabbinic Literature and Maimonides." *Bar-Ilan* 26–27:155–66.

Hayes, Christine. 1997. *Between the Babylonian and Palestinian Talmuds.* New York: Oxford University Press.

———. 1998a. "The Abrogation of Torah Law: Rabbinic Taqqanah and Praetorian Edict." In *The Talmud Yerushalmi and Graeco-Roman Culture,* edited by P. Schäfer, 643–74. Tübingen: J.C.B. Mohr.

———. 1998b. "Displaced Self-Perceptions: The Deployment of *Minim* and Romans in Bavli Sanhedrin 90b–91a." In *Religious and Ethnic Communities in Later Roman Palestine,* edited by Hayim Lapin, 249–89. Bethesda: University Press of Maryland.

———. 2000. "*Halakhah le-Moshe mi-Sinai* in Rabbinic Sources: A Methodological Case Study." In *The Synoptic Problem in Rabbinic Literature,* edited by Shaye J. D. Cohen, 61–119. Providence, RI: Brown University Press.

———. 2002. *Gentile Impurities and Jewish Identities: Intermarriage and Conversion from the Bible to the Talmud.* New York: Oxford University Press.

———. 2004. "Authority and Anxiety in the Talmuds: Legal Fictions." In *Jewish Religious Leadership: Images and Reality,* edited by Jack Wertheimer, 1:127–54. New York: Jewish Theological Seminary of America.

———. 2006. "Rabbinic Contestations of Authority." *Cardozo Law Review* 28, no. 1:123–41. *Text, Tradition, and Reason in Comparative Perspective,* edited by Suzanne Last Stone and Adam Seligmann. New York: Benjamin N. Cardozo School of Law.

———. 2008. "Legal Truth, Right Answers and Best Answers: Dworkin and the Rabbis." *Dine Yisrael: Studies in Halakhah and Jewish Law* 25:73–121.

———. 2010. "Theoretical Pluralism in the Talmud: A Response to Richard Hidary." *Dine Yisrael: Studies in Halakhah and Jewish Law* 25:257–307.

———. 2011. "Legal Realism and Sectarian Self-Fashioning in Jewish Antiquity," in *Sects and Sectarianism in Jewish History,* edited by Sacha Stern, 119–46. Leiden: Brill.

————. 2012. *Introduction to the Bible.* New Haven, CT: Yale University Press.

————. 2013. " 'In the West, they laughed at him': The Babylonian Talmud's Mocking Realists." *Journal of Law, Religion and State* 1, no. 2:137–67.

Hayward, Robert. 1996. "Heaven and Earth in Parallel: The Key Role of Angels in Ancient Judaism." In *Christ: The Sacramental Word,* edited by D. Brown and Ann Loades, 57–74. London: The Cromwell Press.

Heger, Paul. 2003. *The Pluralistic Halakhah: Legal Innovations in the Late Second Commonwealth and Rabbinic Periods.* Berlin: Walter de Gruyter.

Heinemann, Isaac. 2009. *The Reasons for the Commandments in Jewish Thought: From the Bible to the Renaissance.* Boston: Academic Studies Press. Translation by Leonard Levin of *Ta'amei haMitzvot baSifrut Yisrael,* 1966.

Heinemann, Joseph. 1971. "Profile of a Midrash: The Art of Composition in Leviticus Rabba." *Journal of the American Academy of Religion* 31:141–50.

Heszer, Catherine. 1997. *The Social Structure of the Rabbinic Movement in Roman Palestine.* Tübingen: Mohr Siebeck.

Hidary, Richard. 2009–10. "Right Answers Revisited: Monism and Pluralism in the Talmud." *Dine Israel* 26–27:229–55.

————. 2010a. *Dispute for the Sake of Heaven: Legal Pluralism in the Talmud.* Atlanta, GA: Society of Biblical Literature.

————. 2010b. "Rhetorical Criticism of the Talmud: Arguments from the Excluded Middle." Paper presented at 2010 Association for Jewish Studies conference.

————. Forthcoming. "Why Are There Lawyers in Heaven? Rabbinic Court Procedure in Halakha and Aggada." In *Purifying the Reptile: Greco-Roman Rhetoric and the Talmud.*

Higger, Michael. 1927. "Intention in Talmudic Law." PhD diss., Columbia University.

Horst, Friedrich. 1961. "Naturrecht und Altes Testament." Orig. in *EvT* 10 (1950/1): 253–73. Reprinted in *Gottes Recht: Gesammelte Studien zum Recht in Alten Testament,* edited by H. W. Wolff, 235–59. Munich: C. Kaiser.

Jackson, Bernard. 1987. "Secular Jurisprudence and the Philosophy of Jewish Law: A Commentary on Some Recent Literature." *Jewish Law Annual* 6:3–44.

————. 2011. "Judaism as a Religious Legal System." In *Religion, Law and Tradition: Comparative Studies in Religious Law,* edited by Andrew Huxley, 34–48. London: Routledge.

Jaffee, Martin S. 2001. *Torah in the Mouth: Writing and Oral Tradition in Palestinian Judaism.* New York: Oxford University Press.

Janowitz, Naomi. 1998. "Rabbis and Their Opponents: The Construction of the 'Min' in Rabbinic Anecdotes." *Journal of Early Christian Studies* 6:449–62.

Johnston, David. 2000. "The Jurists." In *The Cambridge History of Greek and Roman Political Thought,* edited by Christopher Rowe and Malcolm Schofield, 616–34. Cambridge: Cambridge University Press.

Jolowicz, H. F., and B. Nicholas. 1972. *Historical Introduction to the Study of Roman Law.* 3rd ed. Cambridge: Cambridge University Press.

Kalmin, Richard. 1994. "Christians and Heretics in Rabbinic Literature of Late Antiquity." *Harvard Theological Review* 87:155–69.

————. 1999. *The Sage in Jewish Society in Late Antiquity.* London: Routledge.

Katzoff, Ranon. 1980. "Sources of Law in Roman Egypt: The Role of the Prefect." *Aufstieg und Niedergang der römische Welt* II.13:807–44.

Kensky, Meira. 2010. *Trying Man, Trying God: The Divine Courtroom in Early Jewish and Christian Literature.* Tübingen: Mohr Siebeck.

Kiel, Yishai. 2013. "Cognizance of Sin and Penalty in the Babylonian Talmud and Pahlavi Literature: A Comparative Analysis." *Oqimta* 1:1–49.

———. 2014. "Penitential Theology in East Late Antiquity: Talmudic, Zoroastrian, and East Christian Reflections." *Journal for the Study of Judaism* 45:1–33.

King, Peter. 2011. "Peter Abelard." In *The Stanford Encyclopedia of Philosophy*, edited by Edward N. Zalta. http://plato.stanford.edu/archives/win2010/entries/abelard/.

Kirschenbaum, Aaron. 1991a. *Equity in Jewish Law: Beyond Equity. Halakhic Aspirationism in Jewish Civil Law.* Hoboken, NJ: Ktav.

———. 1991b. *Equity in Jewish Law: Halakhic Perspectives in Law. Formalism and Flexibility in Jewish Civil Law.* Hoboken, NJ: Ktav.

Klawans, Jonathan. 2000. *Impurity and Sin in Ancient Judaism.* New York: Oxford University Press.

Koester, Helmut. 1995. *History, Culture, and Religion of the Hellenistic Age*, vol. 1, *Introduction to the New Testament.* 2nd ed. New York: Walter de Gruyter & Co.

Kraemer, David. 1990. *The Mind of the Talmud: An Intellectual History of the Bavli.* New York: Oxford University Press.

———. 1991. "Prozbul and Rabbinic Power." *Sevara* 2, no. 2:66–70.

Kraus, F. R. 1960. "Ein zentrales Problem des altmesopotamischen Rechtes: Was ist der Codex Hammurabi?" In *Aspects du contact suméro-akkadien*, 9th Rencontre assyriologique international, Geneva, *Genava* 8:283–96.

Krauss, Samuel. 1964. *Griechische und Lateinische Lehnwörter im Talmud, Midrasch und Targum.* Hildesheim: Georg Olms.

Kronman, Anthony. 1983. *Max Weber.* Stanford, CA: Stanford University Press.

Kugel, James. 1983. "Two Introductions to Midrash." *Prooftexts* 3:131–55.

Labendz, Jenny. 2003. "Know What to Answer the Epicurean: A Diachronic Study of the Apikoros in Rabbinic Literature." *Hebrew Union College Annual* 74:175–214.

———. 2013. *Socratic Torah: Non-Jews in Rabbinic Intellectual Culture.* New York: Oxford University Press.

Lachs, Samuel Tobias. 1970. "Rabbi Abbahu and the Minim." *Jewish Quarterly Review*, n.s., 60:197–212.

Lafont, Sophie. 2006. "Ancient Near Eastern Laws: Continuity and Pluralism." In *Theory and Method in Biblical and Cuneiform Law: Revision, Interpolation and Development*, edited by Bernard M. Levinson, 91–118. Sheffield: Sheffield Phoenix Press. Reprint.

Laks, André. 2000. "The *Laws*." In *The Cambridge History of Greek and Roman Political Thought*, edited by Christopher Rowe and Malcolm Schofield, 258–92. Cambridge: Cambridge University Press.

Lamm, Norman, and Aaron Kirschenbaum. 1979. "Freedom and Constraint in the Jewish Judicial Process." *Cardozo Law Review* 1:99–133.

Landman, Leo. 1974. "'In Truth They Said': *be-emet amru.*" In *Joshua Finkel Festschrift*, edited by S. Honig and A. Stitson, 123–37. New York: Yeshiva University Press.

Lane, Melissa, 2013. "'Lifeless Writings or Living Script?' The Life of Law in Plato, Middle Platonism and Jewish Platonizers." *Cardozo Law Review* 34, no. 3:937–64.

Laporte, Jean. 1975. "Philo in the Tradition of Biblical Wisdom Literature." In *Aspects of Wisdom in Judaism and Early Christianity*, edited by Robert Wilken, 103–41. Notre Dame, IN: University of Notre Dame.

LeFebvre, Michael. 2006. *Collections, Codes and Torah: The Re-characterization of Israel's Written Law*. New York: T & T Clark.

Leibowitz, Yeshayahu. 1992. *Judaism, Human Values and the Jewish State*. Edited by Eliezer Goldman. Cambridge, MA: Harvard University Press.

Levenson, Jon. 1985. *Sinai and Zion: An Entry into the Jewish Bible*. New York: HarperCollins.

Levinson, Bernard M. 1992. "The Human Voice in Divine Revelation: The Problem of Authority in Biblical Law." In *Innovation in Religious Traditions: Essays in the Interpretation of Religious Change*, edited by Michael A. Williams, Collette Cox, and Martin S. Jaffe, 35–71. Berlin: de Gruyter.

———. 2002. *Deuteronomy and the Hermeneutics of Legal Innovation*. New York: Oxford University Press.

Levy, E. 1949. "Natural Law in Roman Thought." *Studia et documenta historiae et iuris* 15:1–23. Reprinted in E. Levy. *Gesammelte Schriften*, 1:1–19. Cologne: Böhlau Verlag, 1963.

Lichtenstein, Aharon. 1975. "Does Jewish Tradition Recognize an Ethic Independent of Halakha?" In *Modern Jewish Ethics*, edited by Marvin Fox, 62–88. Columbus: Ohio State University Press. Reprinted in *Contemporary Jewish Ethics*, edited by Menachem Kellner, 102–23. New York: Sanhedrin Press, 1978; and in Lichtenstein, *Leaves of Faith*, 2:33–56. Jersey City, NJ: Ktav Publishing House, 2004.

Lieberman, Saul. 1944. "Roman Legal Institutions in Early Rabbinics and in the Acta Martyrum." *Jewish Quarterly Review* 35:1–57.

———. 2002 [1955–88]. *Tosefta Ki-fshutah: A Comprehensive Commentary on the Tosefta*. 10 vols. 3rd printing. New York: Jewish Theological Seminary.

Lloyd-Jones, H., and N. G. Wilson, eds. 1990. *Sophoclis Fabulae*. Oxford Classical Texts. Oxford: Oxford University Press.

Long, A. A., and D. N. Sedley. 1987. *The Hellenistic Philosophers*. Vols. 1 and 2. Cambridge: Cambridge University Press.

Lorberbaum, Yair. 2011a. *Disempowered King: Monarchy in Classical Jewish Literature*. New York: Continuum.

———. 2011b. "Theories of Action." In *Inner Religion: The Phenomenology of the Inner Religious Life and Its Reflection in Jewish Sources from the Bible to Hasidism*, edited by Ron Margolin. Ramat Gan: Bar Ilan University [Hebrew].

———. 2012. "Halakhic Realism." *Shenaton Mishpat haIvri* 27:61–130 [Hebrew]. (Unless otherwise indicated, references are based on the English version accessed at http://law.huji.ac.il/upload/HalakhicRealism.pdf.)

Lull, David J. 1986. "The Law Was Our Pedagogue: A Study in Galatians 3:19–25." *Journal of Biblical Literature* 105:481–98.

Lutz, Mark J. 2012. *Divine Law and Political Philosophy in Plato's Laws*. DeKalb: Northern Illinois University Press.

Maccoby, Hyam. 1999. " 'Statutes that were not good' (Ezekiel 20:25–26): Traditional Interpretations." *Journal of Textual Reasoning* 8.

Maimonides, Moses. 1963. *Guide of the Perplexed*. Translated by Shlomo Pines. Chicago: University of Chicago Press.

Malul, Meir. 1990. *The Comparative Method in Ancient Near Eastern and Biblical Legal Studies*. Alter Orient und Alter Testament 227. Kevelaer: Butzon und Bercker.

Marböck, J. 1971. *Weisheit im Wandel: Untersuchungen zur Weisheitstheologie bei Ben Sira*. Bonner biblische Beiträge 37. Bonn: Hanstein.

Martens, John W. 2003. *One God, One Law: Philo of Alexandria on the Mosaic and Greco-Roman Law*. Ancient Mediterranean and Medieval Texts and Contexts, edited by Jacob Neusner and Robert Berchman. Studies in Philo of Alexandria and Mediterranean Antiquity, edited by Robert Berchman and Francesca Calabi, vol. 2. Boston: Brill Academic.

Metso, Sariano. 2006. "Creating Communal Halakhah." In *Studies in the Hebrew Bible, Qumran and the Septuagint Presented to Eugene Ulrich*, edited by Peter W. Flint et al., 279–301. Leiden: Brill.

Milgrom, J. 1978. "The Temple Scroll," *Biblical Archaeologist* 41, no. 3:105–20.

Moles, John. 2000. "The Cynics." In *The Cambridge History of Greek and Roman Political Thought*, edited by Christopher Rowe and Malcolm Schofield, 415–34. Cambridge: Cambridge University Press.

Morgenstern, Mattias. 2011. "The Quest for a Rabbinic Perception." In *The Quest for a Common Humanity: Human Dignity and Otherness in the Religious Traditions of the Mediterranean*, edited by Katell Berthelot and Matthias Morgenstern, 41–66. Leiden: Brill.

Moscovitz, Leib. 2003. "Legal Fictions in Rabbinic Law and Roman Law: Some Comparative Observations." In *Rabbinic Law in Its Roman and Near Eastern Context*, edited by Catherine Hezser, 105–32. Texts and Studies in Ancient Judaism. Tübingen: Mohr-Siebeck.

Naeh, Shlomo. 1997. "The Structure and Division of Torat Kohanim (A): Scrolls." *Tarbiz* 66, no. 4:483–515 [Hebrew].

———. 2000. "The Structure and the Division of Torat Kohanim (B): Parashot, Perakim, Halakhot." *Tarbiz* 69, no. 1:59–104 [Hebrew].

———. 2001. "Make Yourself Many Rooms: Another Look at the Utterances of the Sages about Controversy." In *Renewing Jewish Commitment: The Work and Thought of David Hartman*, edited by Avi Sagi and Zvi Zohar. Jerusalem: Shalom Hartman Institute and Hakkibutz Hameuchad [Hebrew].

Najman, Hindy 1999. *Seconding Sinai: The Development of Mosaic Discourse in Second Temple Judaism*. Supplements to the Journal for the Study of Judaism 53. Leiden: Brill.

———. 2003. "A Written Copy of the Law of Nature: An Unthinkable Paradox?" *Studia Philonica Annual* 15:55–63.

Nanos, Mark. 2009. "The Myth of the 'Law-Free' Paul Standing between Christians and Jews." *Studies in Christian-Jewish Relations* 4:1–21. http://ejournals.bc.edu/ojs/index.php/scjr/article/view/1511/1364.

Nel, P. J. 1982. *The Structure and Ethos of the Wisdom Admonitions in Proverbs*. Beiheft zur Zeitschrift für die alttestamentliche Wissenschaft 158. Berlin: de Gruyter.

Neusner, Jacob 1988. *Sifra: An Analytical Translation*. Vol. 1. Atlanta, GA: Scholars Press.

Nickelsburg, G.W.E. 1981. *Jewish Literature between the Bible and the Mishnah: A Historical and Literary Introduction*. London: SCM.

Niehoff, Maren. 2011. *Jewish Exegesis and Homeric Scholarship in Alexandria.* Cambridge: Cambridge University Press.

———, ed. 2012. *Homer and the Bible in the Eyes of Ancient Interpreters.* Leiden: Brill.

Noam, Vered. 2005. "Divorce in Qumran in Light of Early Halakhah." *Journal of Jewish Studies* 56:206–23.

———. 2006. "Traces of Sectarian Halakhah in the Rabbinic World." In *Rabbinic Perspectives: Rabbinic Literature and the Dead Sea Scrolls,* edited by Steven D. Fraade, Aharon Shemesh, and Ruth A. Clemens, 67–85. Leiden: Brill.

———. 2009. "Stringency in Qumran: A Reassessment." *Journal for the Study of Judaism* 40:342–55.

Novak, David. 1998. *Natural Law in Judaism.* Cambridge: Cambridge University Press.

———. 2011. *The Image of the Non-Jew in Judaism.* 2nd ed. Edited by Matthew Lagrone. Portland, OR: The Littman Library of Jewish Civilization.

Novick, Tzvi. 2008. "Law and Loss: Response to Catastrophe in Numbers 15." *Harvard Theological Review* 101:1–14.

———. 2009. " 'They Come against Them with the Power of the Torah': Rabbinic Reflections on Legal Fiction and Legal Agency." *Studies in Law, Politics, and Society* 50:1–17.

———. 2010. "Naming Normativity: The Early History of the Terms *Šurat ha-din* and *Lifnim miš-šurat ha-din.*" *Journal of Semitic Studies* 55:391–406.

Panken, Aaron. 2005. *The Rhetoric of Innovation: Self-Conscious Legal Change in Rabbinic Literature.* Lanham, MD: University Press of America.

Patrick, Dale. 1986. *Old Testament Law.* London: SCM Press.

Patterson, Dennis. 1996. *Law and Truth.* New York: Oxford University Press.

Patton, Corinne. 1996. " 'I Myself Gave Them Laws That Were Not Good': Ezekiel 20 and the Exodus Traditions." *Journal for the Study of the Old Testament* 21:73–90.

Paz, Yakir. 2009. "Prior to Sinai: The Patriarchs and the Mosaic Law in Rabbinic Literature in View of Second Temple and Christian Literature." MA thesis, Hebrew University of Jerusalem [Hebrew].

Penner, Terry. 2000. "Socrates." In *The Cambridge History of Greek and Roman Political Thought,* edited by Christopher Rowe and Malcolm Schofield, 164–89. Cambridge: Cambridge University Press.

Raaflaub, Kurt. 2000. "Poets, Lawgivers, and the Beginnings of Political Reflection in Archaic Greece." In *The Cambridge History of Greek and Roman Political Thought,* edited by Christopher Rowe and Malcolm Schofield, 23–59. Cambridge: Cambridge University Press.

Räisänen, Heikki. 1987. *Paul and the Law.* 2nd ed. Tübingen: Mohr Siebeck.

Rajak, Tessa. 2000. "Josephus." In *The Cambridge History of Greek and Roman Political Thought,* edited by Christopher Rowe and Malcolm Schofield, 585–96. Cambridge: Cambridge University Press.

Reinhartz, Adele. 1983. "The Meaning of *nomos* in Philo's *Exposition of the Law.*" *Sciences Religieuses/Studies in Religion* 15, no. 3:337–45.

Richardson, P., S. Westerholm, et al. 1991. *Law in Religious Communities in the Roman Period: The Dispute over "Torah" and "Nomos" in Post-biblical Judaism and Early Christianity.* Canadian Corporation for Studies in Religion. Waterloo, ON: Wilfred Laurier University Press.

Rodriguez-Pereyra, Gonzalo. 2011. "Nominalism in Metaphysics." In *The Stanford Encyclopedia of Philosophy*, edited by Edward N. Zalta. http://plato.stanford.edu/archives/fall2011/entries/nominalism-metaphysics/.

Rommen, Heinrich. 1936. *The Natural Law: A Study in Legal and Social History and Philosophy* [German]. Translated by Thomas R. Hanley. Introduction and bibliography by Russell Hittinger. Indianapolis: Liberty Fund, 1998.

Rosen, Mark D. 2013. "Beyond Interpretation: The 'Cultural Approach' to Understanding Extra-Formal Change in Religious and Constitutional Law." *Journal of Law, Religion, and State* 2, no. 2:200–233.

Rosen-Zvi, Ishay. 2011. *Demonic Desires: "Yetzer Hara" and the Problem of Evil in Late Antiquity*. Philadelphia: University of Pennsylvania Press.

———. 2012. "Midrash and Hermeneutic Reflexivity: *Kishmu'o* as a Test Case." In *Homer and the Bible in the Eyes of Ancient Interpreters*, edited by Maren Niehoff, 329–44. Leiden: Brill.

———. Forthcoming. "The Mishnaic Mental Revolution: A Reassessment." *Journal of Jewish Studies*.

Rosen-Zvi, Ishay, and Adi Ophir. 2011. "*Goy*: Toward a Genealogy." *Dine Israel* 28: 69–112.

Rosenthal, A. 1993. "The Oral Torah and Torah from Sinai." In *Meḥqerei Talmud II: Talmudic Studies Dedicated to the Memory of Prof. Eliezer S. Rosenthal*, 448–89. Jerusalem: Magnes. [Hebrew].

Rowe, Christopher. 2000. "The *Politics* and Other Dialogues." In *The Cambridge History of Greek and Roman Political Thought*, edited by Christopher Rowe and Malcolm Schofield, 233–57. Cambridge: Cambridge University Press.

Rubenstein, Jeffrey. 1999a. *Talmudic Stories: Narrative Art, Composition, and Culture*. Baltimore: Johns Hopkins University Press.

———. 1999b. "Nominalism and Realism in Qumranic and Rabbinic Law: A Reassessment." *Dead Sea Discoveries* 6, no. 2:157–83.

———. 2003a. *The Culture of the Babylonian Talmud*. Baltimore: Johns Hopkins University Press.

———. 2003b. "The Thematization of Dialectics in Bavli Aggada." *Journal of Jewish Studies* 54, no. 1:71–84.

Rupp, E. Gordon, and Philip S. Watson, eds. 1969. *Luther and Erasmus: Free Will and Salvation*. Louisville, KY: Westminster Press.

Sanders, E. P. 1990. "When Is a Law a Law? The Case of Jesus and Paul." In *Religion and Law: Biblical-Judaic and Islamic Perspectives*, edited by Edwin B. Firmage, Bernard G. Weiss, and John W. Welch, 139–58. Winona Lake, IN: Eisenbrauns.

———. 2001. *Paul: A Very Short Introduction*. Oxford: Oxford University Press.

Sandmel, Samuel. 1971. *Philo's Place in Judaism: A Study of Conceptions of Abraham in Jewish Literature*. New York: Ktav Publishing House.

Sarna, Nahum. 1966. *Understanding Genesis*. New York: Jewish Theological Seminary of America.

Scallen, Eileen A. 1995. "Classical Rhetoric, Practical Reasoning, and the Law of Evidence." *American University Law Review* 44:1717–1816.

Schäfer, Peter. 1978. "Das 'Dogma' von der mündlichen Torah im rabbinischen Judentum." In *Studien zur Geschichte und Theologie des rabbinischen Judentums*, 153–97. Leiden: Brill.

————. 1998. *Judeophobia: Attitudes towards the Jews in the Ancient World*. Cambridge, MA: Harvard University Press.

Schiffman, Lawrence. 2011. "Laws Pertaining to Forbidden Foods in the Dead Sea Scrolls." In *Halakhah in Light of Epigraphy*, edited by A. I. Baumgarten, H. Eshel, R. Katzoff, and S. Tzoref, 65–80. Journal of Ancient Judaism Supplements 3. Göttingen: Vandenhoeck & Ruprecht.

Schnabel, Eckhard J. 1985. *Law and Wisdom from Ben Sira to Paul: A Tradition Historical Enquiry into the Relation of Law, Wisdom, and Ethic*. Tübingen: J.C.B. Mohr (Paul Siebeck).

Schofield, Malcolm. 2000a. "Approaching the *Republic*." In *The Cambridge History of Greek and Roman Political Thought*, edited by Christopher Rowe and Malcolm Schofield, 190–232. Cambridge: Cambridge University Press.

————. 2000b. "Epicurean and Stoic Political Thought." In ibid., 435–56.

Schultz, Joseph P. 1975. "Two Views of the Patriarchs: Noahides and Pre-Sinai Israelites." In *Texts and Responses: Studies Presented to Nahum M. Glatzer on the Occasion of His Seventieth Birthday by His Students*, edited by Michael A. Fishbane and Paul R. Flohr, 43–59. Leiden: Brill.

Schüssler Fiorenza, Elisabeth. 1975. "Wisdom Mythology and the Christological Hymns of the New Testament." In *Aspects of Wisdom in Judaism and Early Christianity*, edited by Robert L. Wilken, 17–41. Notre Dame, IN: University of Notre Dame.

Schwartz, Daniel. 1992. "Law and Truth: On Qumran-Sadducean and Rabbinic Views of Law." In *Dead Sea Scrolls: Forty Years of Research*, edited by Deborah Dimant and Uriel Rappaport, 229–40. Leiden: Brill.

————. 2008. "On Pharisees and Sadducees in the Mishnah: From Composition Criticism to History." In *Judaistik und neutestamentliche Wissenschaft*, edited by Lutz Doering, Hans-Günther Waubke, and Florian Wilk, 133–145. Göttingen: Vandenhoeck & Ruprecht.

Shapira, Haim. 2010. "The Debate over Compromise and the Goals of the Judicial Process." *Dine Israel* 26–27:183–228.

Shemesh, Aharon. 2011. "The Laws of Incest in the Dead Sea Scrolls and the History of Halakhah." In *Halakhah in Light of Epigraphy*, edited by Albert I. Baumgarten, Hanan Eshel, Ranon Katzoff, and Shani Tzoref, 81–99. Göttingen: Vandenhoeck & Ruprecht.

————. 2013. " 'For the judgment is God's' (Deut. 1:17): Biblical and Communal Law in the Dead Sea Scrolls." In *Law and Religion in the Eastern Mediterranean: From Antiquity to Early Islam*, edited by Anselm C. Hagedorn and Reinhard G. Kratz, 347–62. Oxford: Oxford University Press.

Shiffman, Pinḥas. 1991. "Prozbul and Legal Fiction." *Sevara* 2, no. 2:63–65.

Shiner, Roger A. 1994. "Aristotle's Theory of Equity." *Loyola of Los Angeles Law Review* 27:1245–64.

Shremer, Adiel. 2001. "*Ha-Parshanut ha-Oqeret ve-ha-Aqira ha-Meforeshet*" ["Between Radical Interpretation and Explicit Rejection"]. In *Renewing Jewish Commitment: The Work and Thought of David Hartman*, edited by A. Sagi and Z. Zohar. Tel Aviv [Hebrew].

Sigal, Phillip. 2008. *The Halakhah of Jesus of Nazareth according to the Gospel of Matthew*. Leiden: Brill.

Silman, Y. 1984–85. "Halakhic Determinations of a Nominalistic and Realistic Nature: Legal and Philosophical Considerations." *Dine Israel* 12:249–66 [Hebrew].

Sinai, Yuval, and Martin Golding. Forthcoming. "Disagreements on Matters of Fact."

Soloveitchik, Joseph. 1975. "Surrendering to the Almighty." Address to the Rabbinical Council of America, November. Reprinted in the *Jewish Press*, October 16, 1998:32.

Spade, Paul Vincent, and Claude Panaccio. 2011. "William of Ockham." In *The Stanford Encyclopedia of Philosophy*, edited by Edward N. Zalta. http://plato.stanford.edu/archives/fall2011/entries/ockham/.

Sperber, Daniel. 1984. *A Dictionary of Greek and Latin Legal Terms in Rabbinic Literature*. Ramat Gan: Bar Ilan University Press.

Statman, Daniel. Forthcoming. "Natural Law and Judaism." In *The Jewish Legal Tradition*. New York: Yeshiva University Center for Jewish Law and Contemporary Civilization.

Steiner, Deborah Tarn. 1991. *The Tyrant's Writ: Myths and Images of Writing in Ancient Greece*. Princeton, NJ: Princeton University Press.

Steinmetz, Devora. 2005. "Justification by Deed: The Conclusion of 'Sanhedrin-Makkot' and Paul's Rejection of Law." *Hebrew Union College Annual* 76:133–87.

———. 2008. *Punishment and Freedom: The Rabbinic Construction of Criminal Law*. Philadelphia: University of Pennsylvania Press.

Stendahl, Krister. 1963. "The Apostle Paul and the Introspective Conscience of the West." *Harvard Theological Review* 56, no. 3:199–215.

Stern, David. 1985. "Moses-cide: Midrash and Contemporary Literary Criticism." *Prooftexts* 4:193–213.

———. 1996. "Midrash and Hermeneutics: Polysemy vs. Indeterminacy." In *Midrash and Theory: Ancient Jewish Exegesis and Contemporary Literary Studies*, 15–38. Evanston, IL: Northwestern University Press.

———. 2004. "Anthology and Polysemy in Classical Midrash." In *The Anthology of Jewish Literature*, edited by David Stern, 108–39. New York: Oxford University Press.

Stone, Suzanne Last. 1991. "Sinaitic and Noahide Law: Legal Pluralism in Jewish Law." *Cardozo Law Review* 12:1157–1214.

———. 1993. "In Pursuit of the Counter-text: The Turn to the Jewish Legal Model in Contemporary American Legal Theory." *Harvard Law Review* 106, no. 4:813–94.

Stowers, Stanley. 1994. *A Rereading of Romans: Justice, Jews and Gentiles*. New Haven, CT: Yale University Press.

Strack, H. L., and Gunter Stemberger. 1996. *Introduction to the Talmud and Midrash*. Minneapolis, MN: Fortress Press.

Strauch-Schick, Shana. 2011. "Intention in the Babylonian Talmud: An Intellectual History." PhD diss., Bernard Revel Graduate School, Yeshiva University.

Strich, Adam. 2007. "Paul, Palestinian Judaism, the Popular Philosophers, and the Law." Honors thesis, Harvard University.

Sussman, Yaakov. 2005. "The Oral Torah." In *Mehqerei Talmud III: Talmudic Studies Dedicated to the Memory of Professor Ephraim E. Urbach*, 209–394. Jerusalem: Magnes [Hebrew].

Taylor, C.C.W. 2000. "Democritus." In *The Cambridge History of Greek and Roman Political Thought*, edited by Christopher Rowe and Malcolm Schofield, 122–29. Cambridge: Cambridge University Press.

Thiessen, Matthew. 2011. *Contesting Conversion: Genealogy, Circumcision, and Identity in Ancient Judaism and Christianity*. New York: Oxford University Press.

Thomas, J.A.C. 1976. *Textbook of Roman Law*. Amsterdam: North Holland Publishing Company.

Urbach, E. E. 1975. *The Sages: Their Concepts and Beliefs*. Translated by Israel Abrahams. Jerusalem: Magnes Press.

van der Horst, P. W. 1978. *The Sentences of Pseudo-Phocylides*. Studia in Veteris Testamenti pseudepigrapha 4. Leiden: E. J. Brill.

Van Ruiten, Jacques. 2007. "Angels and Demons in the Book of Jubilees." In *Angels: The Concept of Celestial Beings—Origins, Development and Reception*, edited by Friedrich V. Reiterer, Tobias Nicklas, and Karin Schöpflin, 585–609. Deuterocanonical and Cognate Literature Yearbook 2007. Berlin: Walter de Gruyter.

Van Spanje, T. E. 1999. *Inconsistency in Paul? A Critique of the Work of Heikki Räisänen*. Tübingen: Mohr Siebeck.

Vriezen, T. C. 1958 [= 1970]. *An Outline of Old Testament Theology*. Oxford: Blackwell.

Walbank, F. W. 1984. "Monarchies and Monarchic Ideas." In *The Cambridge Ancient History*, vol. 7, edited by F. W. Walbank, A. E. Astin, M. W. Frederiksen, and R. M. Ogilvie, 62–100. Cambridge: Cambridge University Press.

Watson, Alan. 1974. *Law Making in the Later Roman Republic*. Oxford: Clarendon Press.

———. 1984. *Sources of Law, Legal Change, and Ambiguity*. Philadelphia: University of Pennsylvania Press.

———. 1991. *Roman Law and Comparative Law*. Athens: University of Georgia Press.

Watts, James. 1999. *Reading Law: The Rhetorical Shaping of the Pentateuch*. Sheffield: Sheffield Academic Press.

Weber, Max. 1967. *Ancient Judaism*. Translated by Hans H. Gerth and Don Martindale. New York: Free Press.

Weinfeld, Moshe. 2000. "Things Which Satan/the Nations/*Yetzer Hara* Criticize." In *Atarah leHayim*, edited by D. Boyarin et al., 105–11. Jerusalem: Magnes Press.

Weinrib, Ernest. 1989. "Law as Myth: Reflections on Plato's *Gorgias*." *Iowa Law Review* 74:787–806.

Weiss, Dov. 2011. "Confrontations with God in Late Rabbinic Literature." PhD diss., University of Chicago Divinity School.

Westbrook, Raymond. 1985. "Biblical and Cuneiform Law Codes," *Revue Biblique* 92, no. 2:247–64.

———. 1989 "Cuneiform Law Codes and the Origins of Legislation." *Zeitschrift für Assyriologie* 79:201–22.

———. 2006. "What Is the Covenant Code?" In *Theory and Method in Biblical and Cuneiform Law: Revision, Interpolation and Development*, edited by Bernard M. Levinson, 15–36. Sheffield: Sheffield Phoenix Press. Reprint.

Wilf, Steven. 2008. *The Law before the Law*. Plymouth, UK: Lexington Books.

Winton, Richard. 2000. "Herodotus, Thucydides and the Sophists." In *The Cambridge History of Greek and Roman Political Thought*, edited by Christopher Rowe and Malcolm Schofield, 89–121. Cambridge: Cambridge University Press.

Witte, John, ed. 2008. *Christianity and Law: An Introduction*. Cambridge: Cambridge University Press.

Wolfson, Harry Austryn. 1947. *Philo: Foundations of Religious Philosophy in Judaism, Christianity, and Islam*. Cambridge, MA: Harvard University Press.

Worrell, J. E. 1968. "Concepts of Wisdom in the Dead Sea Scrolls." PhD diss., Claremont Graduate School. University Microfilms 71–21, Ann Arbor, MI.

Yadin, Azzan. 2004. *Scripture as Logos: Rabbi Ishmael and the Origins of Midrash*. Philadelphia: University of Pennsylvania Press.

———. 2006. "Resistance to Midrash? Midrash and Halakhah in the Halakhic Midrashim." In *Current Trends in the Study of Midrash,* edited by Carol Bakhos, 35–58. Leiden: Brill.

Yadin-Israel, Azzan. 2014. "Rabbinic Polysemy: A Response to Steven Fraade." *AJS Review* 38, no. 1:129–42.

Zeitlin, Solomon. 1947. "Prosbol: A Study in Tannaitic Jurisprudence." *Jewish Quarterly Review* 37:341–62.

Zemer, Moshe. 1992. "Purifying *Mamzerim*." In *The Jewish Law Annual* 10, edited by Bernard S. Jackson, 99–113. Chur, NY: Harwood Academic Publishers.

Zuri, Jacob Samuel. 1939. "*HaHahshavah haHuqit baMishpat haIvri*." In *Sefer ha-Yovel leDr. B. M. Lewin*, edited by Y. L. Fishman, 174–95. Jerusalem: Mossad HaRav Kook.

INDEX OF PRIMARY SOURCES

GENERAL INDEX

Abelard, Peter, 196
Abraham: and Sodom and Gomorrah, 25–28, 38. *See also* patriarchs
Adam: and law, 331–32, 334, 336, 338–39, 342n19, 343n23, 352, 362, 364
Adler, Yitzhak, 213, 213n65
Albeck, Hanokh, 171
Albo, Joseph, 329
Alexander, Elizabeth, 32
Alt, Albrecht, 22n
Amichay, Aryeh, 105n21, 195n43, 197nn45, 46
Anaximander, 55
antinomianism, 75, 78, 154, 225n75, 351, 352n33
Antiphon's *Truth*, 74, 254n
Apocalypse of Baruch, 94, 127n49, 133n55, 353n35
Aquinas, Thomas, 374
Arad, Aviva, 157n35
Archytas, 67
Aristeas, Letter of, 94, 98, 105–10, 116, 120, 138, 169; on the rationality and truth of Torah, 105–8, 138, 246, 246n, 259, 267, 285–86
Aristophanes, 75
Aristotle, 13, 34, 66n12, 80, 86, 115n36, 155–56, 187n37, 311; on equity, 67–70, 311, 324–26; on *phronesis*, 67–70, 324–26; on rhetoric, 70, 325
aspirationalism: in Bible, 49, 52
Atkins, E. M., 80
Atlas, Samuel, 213, 213n65
Austin, John, 375
autonomy, 267–71

barishonah. See innovation
Barton, John, 28
Bartor, Assnat, 41n, 44n, 45
Bauckmann, E. G., 96n6
Baumgarten, J. M., 132n53
Bazak, J., 203n53
Beckwith, R. T., 98n8, 129n

Ben-Menahem, Hanina, 174n8, 175n10, 176n14
Benovitz, Moshe, 228n83
Bentham, Jeremy, 375
Bergsma, J. S., 50n
Berkowitz, Beth, 250n
Berman, Harold, 375n3
Berman, Saul, 177nn17,20, 178n20, 187n36
Berner, Christoph, 128
Berthelot, Katell, 361n51
Bevan, Edwyn, 88, 88n36
Blenkinsopp, Joseph, 29, 30n, 40–41, 44, 96n5, 126n48
Bloch, Moshe, 293n11
Bockmuehl, Markus, 25, 26–27, 28, 39, 94, 109, 112, 352n34, 354n37, 355n38, 358n44, 367n55
Borkowski, Andrew, 85, 85n33, 86n34
Bottéro, Jean, 32–33
Boyarin, Daniel, 134–35, 150n21, 151n23, 155n31, 160n38, 161n40, 162n42, 164, 174n8, 175nn9,10
Brague, Rémi, 2, 4, 42
Brodsky, David, 203n53
Brown, Eric, 54, 55, 56, 61, 62, 75n

calendar: in 1 Enoch 104; in Jubilees 104–5; at Qumran, 104–5; in rabbinic literature, 200–201, 236–37
Centrone, Bruno, 67, 79
Cicero, 70, 80, 81, 82, 85, 112, 325; on Roman law, 80; on Stoic divine law theory, 55n3, 56–58, 61, 355
circumcision, 143–46, 160–61
The Clouds, 75
Cohen, Boaz, 177n18, 355n38
Cohen, Shaye J. D., 7, 171n3, 174n8, 175n9, 215–16, 224, 229, 229n84
Collins, Adela Yarbro, 228nn82,83, 229, 229n84, 283n34
conversion: as legal nominalism, 214–18. *See also* identity, Jewish
Conzelmann, H., 126n48

Printed in the USA
CPSIA information can be obtained
at www.ICGtesting.com
JSHW021537291223
54565JS00003B/96